News from the
Land of Freedom

News from the Land of Freedom

German Immigrants Write Home

Edited by **Walter D. Kamphoefner,
Wolfgang Helbich,
and Ulrike Sommer**

Translated by **Susan Carter Vogel**

Cornell University Press *Ithaca and London*

Contents

II. WORKERS

III. DOMESTIC SERVANTS

APPENDIX

Preface

Immigration continues to be a subject of ambivalence for most Americans. The 1980s saw the passage of legislation granting amnesty to several million illegal aliens, but also the rise of the "English only" movement. While seven of ten Americans questioned in a recent *Newsweek* poll believed that immigrants improve the country, a slight majority also maintained that they take jobs away from Americans and that the nation admits too many Hispanics. Americans find it hard to oppose immigration on principle, since almost all are descendants of people who immigrated at some point; nearly half can trace some roots to Ellis Island alone. But often one encounters the view that earlier immigrants were somehow "better" than the present-day variety.

This collection deals with German immigrants, a group whose position in the nineteenth century was in several respects similar to that of Hispanics today. A diverse lot, they were by far the largest foreign language group at the time, and had considerable success in placing their mother tongue in the schools and other areas of public life. Historical analogies are never perfect, and parallels between contemporary and previous immigrations can be exaggerated. Nevertheless, it is reassuring to discover that even for a group such as the Germans, who were frequently touted as a model minority, acculturation was often a slow, painful, and incomplete process. Some immigrants gave up and returned home, and many more toyed with the idea. But separate cultural identities were not incompatible with full political loyalty to the adopted homeland.

The commonalities of the immigrant experience (shared also by de facto immigrants in present-day Germany) rather than any filiopietistic litany of "special contributions" by German-Americans initially attracted us. From the outset, our work was inspired by our interest in both American and German social history. It was part of a growing scholarly trend on both sides of the Atlantic during the last generation to focus on European mass-migration to the New World not only in isolated segments but as part of an entire social process extending from its source to its destination. As a pioneer of this new social history, Frank Thistlethwaite, put it in his 1960 essay, the "salt-water curtain" needed to be flung open.

Immigrant letters did and continue to do just that—they establish a connection, a bridge between the beginning and end points of a migration. Beyond that, they are uniquely valuable as documents of social history, showing what no immigration statistics, no consular reports, no theories of assimilation can convey: how individual immigrants came to know and appraise a new society, how they met the challenges and tensions of living between two cultures, and perhaps most important, how they felt about this process that called many of their old values into question. It is no accident that this edition consists almost exclusively of letters of "ordinary" immigrants. In previous collections, letters from the lower social classes have been all too rare, while excessive attention was given to members of the educated bourgeoisie who made up no more than 5 percent of total German immigration. This volume was thus also conceived as a contribution to the history of everyday life and "history from the bottom up."

Inspired by the material at our disposal, but also as a matter of principle, the editors set an ambitious goal: to present a work that would meet the highest scholarly standards of documentation and authenticity, that would make a solid contribution to research in social history, but that at the same time would provide to general readers with historical, political, or social interests an informative and even exciting piece of literature. For the editors, it is not only a civic obligation, but also a personal challenge and aspiration to be heard beyond the ivory tower and the narrow circle of colleagues—ideally even to see their scholarly findings applied in current decision making. Thus we have attempted to address, without watering down or "popularizing" in the negative sense of the term, this perennially fascinating subject with a book that is not just up-to-date with historical scholarship in its approach and methods but also readable and attractive.

This volume could not have come together without the existence of the Bochum Immigrant Letter Collection (or in its German acronym,

BABS), which as of this writing includes more than five thousand letters. A collection of this size and comprehensiveness would have been totally inconceivable without the generous financial support granted by the Volkswagen Foundation to the research project "Immigrant Letters as a Source on the Acculturation Process of German-Americans, 1820–1920" at Ruhr University-Bochum. The 1988 German edition on which this translation is based was one of the results of that project. Without Volkswagen financing of a large support staff during the various phases of collection and preparation, the three editors might nevertheless have been able to publish a much less ambitious volume—whose appearance in English could perhaps be expected around the year 2000. The book in its present form was possible only with the assistance of a great number of co-workers in the narrower and broader sense—those employed on the project and the many who helped purely out of interest in the subject. They are named individually in the Appendix, Contributors and Assistants. To all of them, and to the foundation that made this undertaking possible in the first place, we extend our sincerest thanks for their interest, their dedication, and their helpfulness, which often exceeded all expectations.

With the English translation we have incurred an additional round of indebtedness, above all to the National Endowment for the Humanities for a translation grant, and to the Fritz Thyssen Stiftung, which provided additional matching funds under this grant. Finally, the three members of the editorial team thank our translator, Susan Carter Vogel, for her dedication to excellence without regard to the time, effort, or financial reward involved. Although the translator is ultimately responsible for all matters of language, the editors take full responsibility for all matters of fact and content.

WALTER D. KAMPHOEFNER
College Station, Texas

WOLFGANG HELBICH, ULRIKE SOMMER
Bochum, Germany

Introduction

German Immigration to the United States

German immigration to the United States extends far back into colonial times: the celebrated thirteen families from Krefeld, who founded Germantown, Pennsylvania, in 1683, were not the first Germans to arrive but the first to come over as a group. In the course of the next hundred years at least one hundred thousand of their countrymen followed. When the first U.S. census was taken in 1790, about one-twelfth of the population in the United States was of German descent. By far the greatest concentration was in Pennsylvania, where as early as 1751 Benjamin Franklin expressed the fear that, instead of becoming Anglicized, the Germans were threatening to Germanize the Anglo-Americans. In Pennsylvania at the time Germans made up about 30 percent of the population; then came Maryland (over 10 percent), New Jersey (9 percent), and New York (8 percent)—all states that border on Pennsylvania.[1]

The American Revolution brought immigration to the colonies to an overall standstill, although this was partly offset by the influx of about five thousand mercenaries, mostly from Hesse, who during or after the war went over to the American side and stayed. The French Revolution and the Napoleonic Wars kept most potential emigrants of the next generation from putting their plans into effect. The restricted flow of new immigrants contributed considerably to the assimilation of the early German-Americans. Where the German language was not reinforced by

[1]Germans were very rare in New England and, apart from a few areas, also in the South (Conzen [1980], 406–10).

other ideological factors, as it was, for example, among the Mennonites and related sects in Pennsylvania, its use declined sharply in the early nineteenth century. Typical of many German-Americans of this period was an elderly Herr Klein in North Carolina, whose many great-grand-children bore his name in various spellings—Klein, Kline, and Cline—and in the translated versions of Small, Little, and Short.[2]

The Nineteenth Century

The famine of 1817 set off a new wave of emigration in Germany. It began in the region where emigration had been heaviest in the eighteenth century, the southwest, particularly the Palatinate, Württemberg, and Baden. Something new, however, was the increased share of Catholics, who had earlier tended to move eastward to Austria and Hungary instead. Until 1832 emigration was restricted for the most part to these areas of southwest Germany. Only after that time did it come to be a mass movement, spreading north and east to affect all of Germany, to varying degrees, by the mid-1850s.[3]

The predominance of southwest Germany—in terms of both its early start and the intensity of emigration—prompted contemporaries, such as Friedrich List, as well as later scholars to argue that mass emigration was caused by the custom of dividing up an inheritance among all the children and the resulting progressive splintering of peasant landholdings. This argument is not completely wrong, but it must be modified to a certain extent: equal division among heirs was neither a necessary nor a sufficient cause of high emigration rates. There were areas in northwest Germany which suffered population losses just as heavy as those in the southwest, despite the fact that estates in the northwest were passed on to a single heir. And there were also areas characterized by both partible inheritance and extreme splintering where emigration rates nevertheless remained low.

Until the middle of the nineteenth century, one of the most important factors promoting emigration was the decline of cottage industry in the face of mechanized, often foreign, competition. Hardest hit was hand-loom linen weaving, although in rural regions such as the Eifel protoin-dustrial charcoal-iron production succumbed to a similar fate. One of the main centers of linen weaving was the area around Osnabrück and northern Westphalia, which had among the highest rates of German emigration in the 1830s and 1840s, despite the prevailing system of

[2]Hammer (1943), 33, 95–99.
[3]Hippel (1984), 148–49, 175–80.

impartible inheritance. Splintered landholdings in the southwest, too, not only resulted from inheritance practices but were also tied to cottage industries in the Black Forest and viniculture along the Neckar. Emigration from the Osnabrück region was heavier in the 1840s, when a collapse in linen prices coincided with poor harvests, than it was in the 1850s. In southwest Germany, by contrast, the bountiful wine vintage in 1846 did much to offset losses in other sectors, but crop failures in the early 1850s, which coincided with the worst wine vintages in decades, drove emigration rates in Württemberg, Baden, and the Palatinate to record heights. Also, the centers of emigration in Württemberg shifted from the previous decade to areas most dependent on viniculture.[4]

German emigration can thus be explained better by local economic conditions than by the monocausal factor of inheritance systems. The areas with the lowest emigration rates in all of Germany, after all, were located in the Rhineland, a state with partible inheritance: they were the emerging industrial centers. The general influence of urbanization and particularly industrialization curbed population loss considerably, as can be seen in the cases of Saxony, Silesia, and the Berlin area.[5]

During the last third of the nineteenth century the region east of the Elbe became the most prominent source of emigration. Before the 1860s it had still been possible to support the growing population of the area by intensifying agriculture. But starting in that decade, East Elbian grain producers faced increasing competition on the world market, not least from the German and Scandinavian immigrants who had settled the fertile North American prairies. Economic problems were further compounded by legal and political difficulties: despite the highest rates of per-acre indebtedness in Germany, mobility remained low and large estates continued to be passed on undivided. The existing legal system thus reinforced the one-sided system of property ownership and social inequality.[6]

Although economic factors as a cause of emigration have thus far been emphasized, other factors, such as political motives, were not insignificant. Politics played a particularly important role in setting off waves of emigration after the revolution in 1848 and, although the earlier case is less well known, after 1830. The educated bourgeois elite who found refuge in the United States exerted an influence on the German-American press and politics which can hardly be overestimated.

Recent emigration research has correctly emphasized that this group made up only a small minority of German emigrants as a whole, but it

[4]Kamphoefner (1986a), 183–88.
[5]Kamphoefner (1987), 12–39.
[6]Puhle (1975), 41–47.

German Empire (1871)

Denmark

Gl

SHo

20

HH

8

Elbe

GO

HB

Ha

Sa

The
Netherlands

19

Hanover

Magdebu

1

We

Sa

15

17

Essen

FWA

10

HNa

Cologne

Rhine

GH

Belgium

Rp

11

7

3

5

Frankfurt

6

12

Luxembourg

16

GH

zu GO

Nuremberg

zu KB

13

4

14

France

Strasbourg

18

Danube

Stuttgart

Rhine

GB

KW

Munich

Switzerland

Sweden

Königsberg

Danzig

Op

Wp

⑨

Pm

Stettin

Weichsel

Oder

Po

Russian Empire

②

Berlin

Br

Posen

Elbe

Leipzig

SI

Dresden

Breslau

Oder

KS

Kingdoms

KB	Bavaria
to KB	Palatinate
KS	Saxony
KW	Württemberg

Grand Duchies

GB	Baden
GH	Hesse
GM	Mecklenburg
GO	Oldenburg
to GO	Birkenfeld

Principalities

| FWA | Waldeck |

Free Cities

| HB | Bremen |
| HH | Hamburg |

Prussian provinces

Br	Brandenburg
Ha	Hanover
HNa	Hesse-Nassau
Op	East Prussia
Pm	Pomerania
Po	Posen
Rp	Rhine Province
Sa	Saxony
SHo	Schleswig-Holstein
SI	Silesia
We	Westphalia
Wp	West Prussia

Numbers correspond to the numbering of letter
series in the table of contents and show places
of origin of letter-writers.

——————— National boundaries
——————— Boundaries between German states
------------- Boundaries between Prussian provinces

Cartography: S. Crass

should not be forgotten that ordinary emigrants had much in common with the more renowned "Dreißigers" and "Forty-eighters": if they did not hold an abstract concept of democracy they had at least a decided propensity for egalitarianism and the rejection of authoritarian government. Thus in 1846 a county official in Nassau expressed the opinion that all those who were thinking of emigrating were no longer fit for their homeland, since they had been infected with the dizzy spells of freedom and chimeric notions of government. A Hessian county magistrate similarly complained in 1857 that the greater freedom enjoyed by the serving classes in the United States made the locals rebellious. Moreover, the boundaries between economic and political grievances of the rural lower classes were often fluid, as can be seen in their excessively heavy tax burden, inability to pay for military draft substitutes, and in particular the disadvantages they accrued when common lands were divided.[7]

OCCUPATIONS AND WEALTH

Information about occupation and wealth clearly indicates that emigrants were recruited primarily from the lower and lower-middle classes.[8] It should be noted at the outset, however, that a precise occupational breakdown is impossible, due to the large number of emigrants who left without official permission and the widespread practice of combining artisan trades with farming (where only one of the two occupations could be listed). Designations in emigrant lists sometimes reflected life-cycle stage more than social origins: a young farmhand, like letter-writer Wilhelm Stille, could be a substantial farmer's son and have considerable means at his disposal. Female emigrants gave occupations, if at all, only if they were unmarried; most were simply listed as "maid" or "servant girl."

The occupations listed for male emigrants reflect the different agricultural structures in various parts of Germany. Between 1840 and 1855 in Baden, exactly half of the emigrants were employed in agriculture; only 27 percent were artisans. In nearby Württemberg, by contrast, artisans accounted for over half, farmers for only about one-third of emigrants. The explanation for these differences, however, is to be found not in the economic structure of two regions but rather in recording procedures. Many of the Württemberg artisans farmed on the side as well. At mid-century one-quarter to one-third of all heads of household were actively engaged in both agriculture and a trade at the same time. A comparison

---

[7]Kamphoefner (1987), 58–68; Struck (1980), 132–33.
[8]This section is based on Hippel (1984), 226–50; Marschalck (1973), 74–80; and Kamphoefner (1987), 40–52.

of the amount of money taken along by emigrants from Wüttemberg and the price of land at the time indicates that the farmers who left were "small" and "smallest" landholders and that the vintners were even worse off.

In northwest Germany, by contrast, the few peasant proprietors who emigrated were far wealthier than most of their fellow travelers. About two-thirds of those who left, however, were recruited from the rural lower class of farmhands, tenant farmers, and day laborers. Artisans, many of whom farmed on the side to supplement their incomes, fell somewhere in the middle, though from the information on funds taken along it is also evident that many artisans were hardly better off than farmhands or tenant farmers. In the southwest as well as in the northwest the artisan who emigrated had little in common with the proud master craftsman belonging to a guild, who owned his own workshop, employed numerous journeymen, and could look back on generations of tradition. Instead, he usually came from a background where trades were combined with agriculture.

In the rural area east of the Elbe, artisans and independent farmers were even less significant in the emigration. Between 1855 and 1875 at least two-thirds of all who left Mecklenburg were day laborers or farmhands. The share of artisans seldom rose above 10 percent. Industrial workers achieved a larger share in the late nineteenth century, particularly from areas like the Ruhr District, but even at the turn of the century the number of factory workers who emigrated from Saxony was far smaller that that of artisans and those employed in cottage industry. Overall, professionals had the lowest rates, seldom reaching more than 2 or 3 percent. The commercial sector, too, seldom accounted for more than 10 percent of male emigrants, and the fact that "merchants" were usually young and unmarried suggests that this occupational listing had more to do with future aspirations than with current status.

The modest economic circumstances of the great majority of emigrants are seen most clearly in the amounts of money they took along. As might be expected, exported assets were lowest in areas and times of highest emigration. For single men around mid-century, the median value (50 percent of those recorded above, 50 percent below) amounted to between 60 and 85 talers in the Osnabrück, Münster, and Württemberg regions. The corresponding figures for families were somewhat lower, between 50 and 75 talers per person. (The cost of passage was some 30 talers per adult.) Compared to daily wages, these were no small sums; compared to the high price of land in Germany, they were insignificant. Crossing the ocean to start a new life was not a viable alternative for the starving: emigration subsidies for the poor were granted on a large scale only in southwest Germany and only for a short time, between 1845 and 1855.[9] Yet if emigrants had heeded the advice of one emigration handbook, which discouraged families with less than one thousand talers from leaving, 95 percent would have stayed at home.

TYPES OF EMIGRATION

Although organized groups of emigrants occasionally made headlines, and their usually well-educated leaders left more written evidence behind than normal emigrants, most Germans who came to the United States in the nineteenth century traveled either with their families or alone. Before mid-century, however, there were several religious and secular emigration societies that deserve mention. The Gießen Society was founded by two friends and fellow students, Friedrich Münch and Paul Follenius, who decided to establish a model republic in the American West after the failure of the 1830 revolution. In 1834, some five hundred people sailed to the United States in two groups, but they were plagued by sickness and dissention: their common venture hardly survived the crossing. Upon arrival they divided up the funds and abandoned their plans for establishing a closed community, although a few families settled in Missouri near the two leaders. Two other societies of the time, from Solingen and Thuringia, suffered a similar fate.[10]

The largest society—the so-called Adelsverein headed up by a group of titled Germans who tried to settle Texas in the 1840s—suffered "the greatest catastrophe in the history of German emigration."[11] Over seven thousand people were transported to Texas between 1844 and 1846 before the society went bankrupt in 1847. The emigrants saw little evidence of the preparations agreed upon and the free land they had been promised, and many died on the arduous journey inland from the harbor at Galveston. After this, colonization societies were regarded with great skepticism—and with good reason.[12]

In general, religious minorities were overrepresented among emigrants. This was true especially for Jews but also, for example, for the Mennonites from Bavaria. In quantitative terms, however, the most important group of religious emigrants in the nineteenth century were the Old Lutherans in the 1830s and 1840s. In protest against the forced unification of the Lutheran and Reformed churches in Germany, three major groups sought freedom of religious expression in the United

[9]See the introduction to the Klinger series, Chapter 18.
[10]Kamphoefner (1987), 94–101.
[11]Auerbach (1985), 24.
[12]Jordan (1966), 40–48, 64.

States. One group of Lutherans from Silesia and Pomerania went to Buffalo and Milwaukee, a colony of Franconians settled in Michigan, and a community of Saxons was established in Missouri.[13]

The significance of these colonies should not be overestimated. Even in the peak year of 1843, no more than 1,600 Old Lutherans left Germany, comprising only one-tenth of emigration that year. Among the small number who left in 1834, only 3 percent were members of the Gießen or Solingen societies, and the Adelsverein accounted for only 6 percent of emigrants between 1844 and 1846. How few followers were subsequently attracted by these groups can be seen in the regional backgrounds of Germans living in these states. Despite the settlement founded by the Gießen Society from Hesse and the Old Lutherans from Saxony, Hessians and Saxons were both slightly underrepresented in Missouri in 1870. And despite the closed community of Old Lutherans near Frankenmuth, relatively few Bavarians were among the Germans living in Michigan. Only the high proportion of Nassau Germans in Texas shows evidence of the aftereffects of an emigration society on the state's population.[14]

Much more important for the course of German migration were families and individuals, perhaps accompanied by a few friends and neighbors but without common funds or a larger organizational framework. The dangers of such a venture were considerably reduced by chain migration. In the early twentieth century, when American officials asked German arrivals if they were immigrating to join relatives or friends, only 6 percent said no. Friends provided the initial contact for some 15 percent, almost four-fifths were awaited by relatives, and more than one-third traveled on prepaid tickets sent from the United States.[15] These percentages, of course, cannot be simply projected back onto the early nineteenth century, though the available figures for Scandinavians show little change between the 1880s and 1910.

Additional evidence of chain migration is also found in the development of informal colonies in the United States. In 1860, for example, without any organized colonization efforts, one-twelfth of all Germans from Brunswick lived in one single county in Missouri, accounting for one-quarter of all German-Americans there.[16] Of the letter-writers in this edition, the Blümner brothers emigrated in 1832 with a small emigration society, settling in an area extolled in a well-known guidebook written by Gottfried Duden (1829). When Wilhelm Stille moved to Ohio the following year, he was already planning to join personal friends.

[13]Barkai (1986), 202–19; Blendinger (1964), 431–87; Iwan 1 (1943); Owen (1947), 32–33, 39. On the Lutherans, see also the introduction to the Pritzlaff series, Chapter 9.
[14]Marschalck, 35–37, 56; Kamphoefner (1987), 73–77.
[15]Reports 3 (1911), 360–65.
[16]Kamphoefner (1987), 84–85, 57–58.

TIME TRENDS OF MIGRATION

In order to demonstrate the effects of "push" factors, promoting emigration in the country of origin, Figure 1 shows the waves of German emigration in relation to real wage development in Germany. For 1832 no economic reason for the onset of mass emigration is apparent; the political events of 1830–1832 and the publication of several emigration guidebooks probably played a more important role. The effects of economic forces are clearly evident in the 1840s, however, when crop failures and the potato blight sent food prices and emigration rates sky-high. Following a brief recovery in the late 1840s, buying power sank again in the 1850s, setting off another wave that culminated in 1854 in the highest migration rate in all of German as well as American history. But emigration was not exclusively determined by economic factors: in spite of the fact that real wages reached their all-time low in 1855, emigration sank by more than half that year, probably as a result of an upsurge of antiforeign activity in America.

From this point on, factors in the United States exerted a stronger influence. After 1857 the worsening economic situation led to a drop in immigration, and rates fell even lower during the Civil War. Only in 1866 did the annual number of German arrivals again surpass one hundred thousand. This wave, partly fed by the pent-up demand of the previous five years, continued until 1873.

In the last third of the nineteenth century, the migration curve largely reflected the rollercoaster ride of the American business cycle (see Figure 2). The Panic of 1873 and the depression that followed curbed immigration for five years; recovery after 1879 set off the last and, in terms of absolute numbers, largest wave of emigration in the early 1880s. Towards the end of the 1880s, the health of the American economy is not as directly reflected in the number of German emigrants, but the effects of the economic downswing after 1892 are clear. Then, at the turn of the century, a new trend emerged: despite improvement in the American economy, German immigration (in contrast to that of other nationalities) remained constant at a fairly low level. Rising real wages and a growing demand for industrial labor in Germany had finally made it unnecessary to leave. By World War I, manpower shortages had even led Germany to import labor, more than any other country but the United States. The end of German mass migration to the United States was thus the product of German economic development and not, as is frequently claimed, the closing of the American frontier in 1890.[17]

[17]Bade (1984b), 433–44.

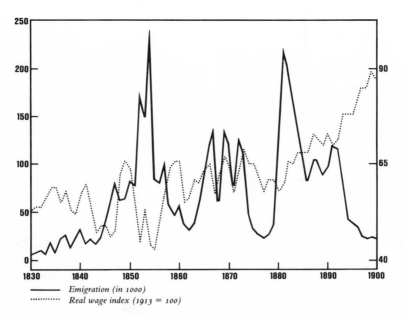

Figure 1. Time trends of German overseas emigration (in 1,000s) and real wages in Germany (1913 = 100). *Sources:* Marschalck (1973), 35–37; Göm-mel (1979), 27–29.

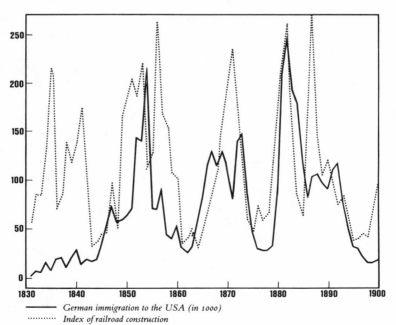

Figure 2. Time trends of German immigration to the United States (in 1,000s) and the American business cycle (index of railroad construction, % deviation from long-term trend). *Source:* Thomas (1973), 397, 402. For 1832, 1843, 1850, and 1868, Thomas's figures on immigration have been adjusted to represent full calendar years rather than the longer or shorter periods covered by the original U.S. statistics.

Settlement Patterns

Apart from the general push toward the West, the centers of German settlement remained fairly constant throughout the nineteenth century. As Figure 3 shows, Germans were concentrated in the cities of the Northeast between New York and Baltimore and above all in the urban and rural Middle West. Comparing the number of persons of German descent (immigrants and their children) with the number of persons of foreign descent as well as total state population in 1900 identifies a compact block of states in which the percentage of Germans lay above the national averages of both 10.5 percent of the total population and 30.7 percent of all immigrants and their American-born children. The "German belt" stretched from Ohio in the east to Nebraska in the west, from Missouri in the south to Wisconsin in the north. This region offered climactic conditions that were most nearly familiar to Central Europeans. Still, the continental climate with its extreme temperatures required considerable adaptation. Most of the United States lies far to the south of Germany: New Orleans is on the same latitude as Cairo, and Munich in the southernmost part of Germany lies north of Montreal. Although many Germans lived in states along the Canadian border from Michigan to the Dakotas, they were not as heavily concentrated as other immigrant groups, particularly Scandinavians. On the other hand, to the south and southwest of the German heartland was a group of states whose relatively small immigrant populations included a disproportionate number of Germans.

Surprising as it may seem at first, in view of the fact that the overwhelming majority of immigrants came from rural areas, German-Americans were more highly urbanized than either their former countrymen at home or their fellow American citizens. In 1850 only 8 percent of the total population but almost 30 percent of all German-Americans were living in the eight largest cities in the United States. Much like letter-writer John Bauer and his brother, however, many immigrants lived in the city only temporarily before moving to a small town or to a farm in the country. This pattern was more closely related to an immigrant's age than former occupation: the cities attracted single young men and women who earned relatively high wages, and since they usually boarded, their expenses were comparatively low. The size of this temporary urban population becomes clear toward the end of the nineteenth century, when Germans resisted the general American trend toward urbanization. Although they had the reputation of settling down in one place and not moving, between 1850 and 1860 they had the highest outmigration rates

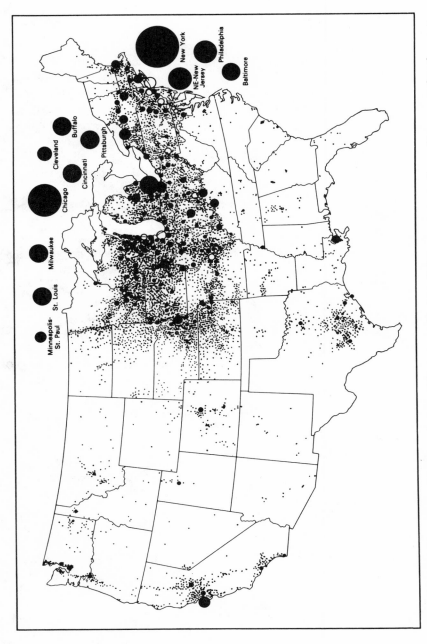

Figure 3. Distribution of German-born in the United States, 1890. Each small dot = 100 persons. *Source:* Hannemann (1936), map 5.

Map of Germany to same scale:

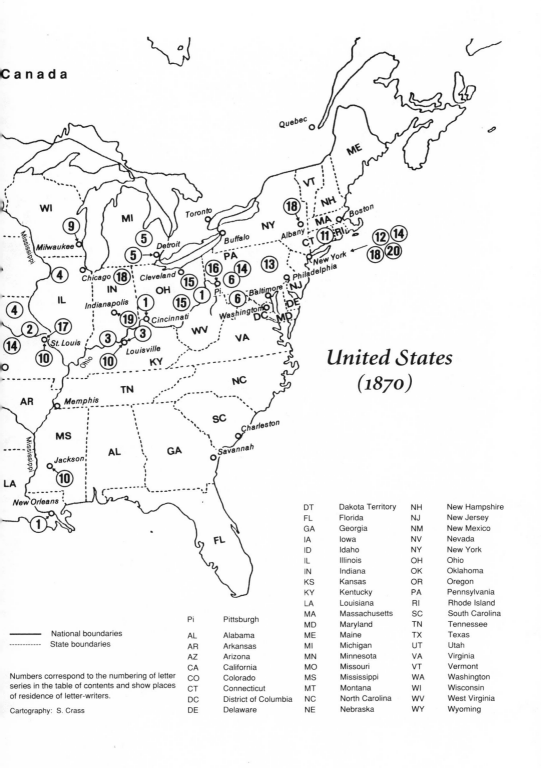

Canada

Quebec

ME

VT

NH

WI

MI

Toronto

NY

Albany

MA   Boston

⑨

⑤

Detroit

Buffalo

CT ⑪ RI   ⑫ ⑭

⑤

New York

⑱ ⑳

Milwaukee

PA

Philadelphia

④

Chicago ⑱ Cleveland ⑮ ⑯ ⑭ ⑬

IN

OH

Pi.

NJ

④

IL

Indianapolis ① ⑮ ① ⑥ Baltimore

DE

② ⑰

⑲

Cincinnati

⑥ Washington MD

⑭

⑩

③

Louisville

WV

DC

St. Louis

Ohio

⑩

VA

KY

United States
(1870)

NC

TN

AR

Memphis

SC

Charleston

MS

GA

Savannah

AL

Jackson

LA

⑩

New Orleans

FL

①

DT	Dakota Territory	NH	New Hampshire
FL	Florida	NJ	New Jersey
GA	Georgia	NM	New Mexico
IA	Iowa	NV	Nevada
ID	Idaho	NY	New York
IL	Illinois	OH	Ohio
IN	Indiana	OK	Oklahoma
KS	Kansas	OR	Oregon
KY	Kentucky	PA	Pennsylvania
LA	Louisiana	RI	Rhode Island
MA	Massachusetts	SC	South Carolina
MD	Maryland	TN	Tennessee
ME	Maine	TX	Texas
MI	Michigan	UT	Utah
MN	Minnesota	VA	Virginia
MO	Missouri	VT	Vermont
MS	Mississippi	WA	Washington
MT	Montana	WI	Wisconsin
NC	North Carolina	WV	West Virginia
NE	Nebraska	WY	Wyoming

Pi	Pittsburgh
AL	Alabama
AR	Arkansas
AZ	Arizona
CA	California
CO	Colorado
CT	Connecticut
DC	District of Columbia
DE	Delaware

——— National boundaries
----------- State boundaries

Numbers correspond to the numbering of letter
series in the table of contents and show places
of residence of letter-writers.

Cartography: S. Crass

from the city of Milwaukee; many were on their way to rural Wisconsin.[18]

For a hundred years after the first enumeration of immigrants in 1850, Wisconsin remained the state with the largest percentage of Germans; in 1900 over one-third of the population was made up of German immigrants and their children. In second and third place came Minnesota and Illinois, the only other states with more than 20 percent; then came in close succession Nebraska, Iowa, New York, and Ohio.[19] Of the cities, New York always had the largest German-American population. Around the turn of the century, more German immigrants lived there than in all but seven cities in Germany. Including the second generation, the 800,000 New Yorkers of German stock came second only to Berlin, and Chicago, with its 400,000 Germans, was the eighth-largest German city in the world. The cities with the highest percentage of Germans, however, were all in the Middle West. In relative terms Milwaukee always came first: according to the 1860 census, more than half of the heads of household and a good third of the city population were German-born. Cincinnati and St. Louis followed, both with over 30 percent. In 1910 Milwaukee still led the nation, but faster-growing cities like Buffalo, Detroit, and Chicago now had a higher percentage of Germans than Cincinnati or St. Louis.

In the neighborhoods, German predominance was often even more striking, although the impression of a "pure German" quarter might arise even where significant minorities of Americans and other nationalities were present. German-Americans lived in somewhat greater concentration than the British or the Irish, but they never reached the degree of segregation of subsequent southern and eastern European immigrant groups, much less that of twentieth-century blacks or Asians. Generally speaking, they were more highly segregated in the fast-growing cities in the Middle West than on the east coast. In the four wards of New York's Little Germany in 1855, for example, not even 30 percent of the population was German born; in the two leading wards of Buffalo, German immigrants made up 51 percent and 45 percent of the inhabitants. But since the census counted the native-born children of immigrants as Americans, the adult population is a more accurate reflection of ethnic influence. In the two Buffalo wards, the German share of the eligible voters rises to 68 percent and 60 percent, respectively. In 1860, Germans comprised 75 per cent of heads of household in the northwest quadrant of

---

[18]Kamphoefner (1983), 171–72. This article has three errors in its Figure 3: Kentucky, West Virginia, and South Carolina should have the same shading as Texas and Oklahoma (Kamphoefner [1987], 81–85).

[19]Hutchinson (1956), 36, 40, 49; Kamphoefner (1983), 171–72.

Milwaukee. A good third of the Germans in St. Louis lived in two wards on the south side of the city, where in 1858 they accounted for more than three-quarters of the voting population. Although such strong concentrations declined over time, as late as 1890 in Cincinnati's "Over the Rhine" district there were two wards where Germans (second generation included) dominated with 80 percent and 71 percent respectively.[20]

NATIVISM AND POLITICS

Anglo-American inhabitants, especially in the big cities, did not remain indifferent to the constant stream of foreign immigrants. This was particularly true for the cities with the highest concentration of newcomers. In 1857 a local Buffalo newspaper reported that the four predominantly German wards were "as little American as the duchy of Hesse Cassel." A comparison with the situation now suggests that such charges were not entirely groundless. Even Miami in 1980, leading the nation with a foreign-born figure of 37 percent, would hardly have stood out among American cities a century before. Despite the anxieties that Hispanics have aroused in contemporary America, the 1980 census showed 6.5 percent of the population was of "Hispanic heritage," a category that includes people of the third generation and beyond, whereas first- and second-generation Germans alone made up over 10 percent of the U.S. population at the turn of the century. Miami in 1980 pales by comparison with Milwaukee in 1860, with over one-third of all inhabitants and a majority of heads of households born in Germany alone.[21]

In the 1850s, the United States experienced the highest rate of immigration in its entire history, a flood that amounted to 10 percent of the existing population. During this decade, too, the Germans overtook the Irish to become the largest immigrant group. This was also the period when anti-immigrant sentiments, whether measured in terms of election results or incidents of violence, reached their peak.

As a political movement, nativism had existed since the 1830s; the driving force behind it was Protestant revivalism in the North. Nativism was primarily directed against the Irish, the first large group of Catholic immigrants, heavily concentrated in the cities in the Northeast and politi

[20]Conzen (1979); Conzen (1976), 126–36; Hershberg et al. (1981), 461–91. Calculations based on the 1855 New York State Census and 1858 St. Louis City Census, published in *Anzeiger des Westens,* October 20, 1985, and Dobbert (1980), 17.

[21]*Commercial Advertiser,* June 12, 1857, quoted in Yox (1983), 63; Ward (1971), 76–78; U.S. Bureau of the Census, *1980 Census of Population,* PC80–1-B11: 404–5; PC80–1-C1: 14–17; PC80–1-C11: 673; Conzen (1976), 14–16. Miami figures are for all of Dade County, which corresponds more closely than the city alone with the metropolitan area. In 1870 the average foreign-born percentage for American cities of over 25,000 inhabitants was 34 percent.

cally active. As early as the 1830s and 1840s, riots and numerous violent attacks against Catholic institutions occurred. As a political party, however, nativists acquired national significance only in 1854, when the collapse of the existing party system coincided with a particularly large influx of immigrants. Having grown out of lodges about which its members, sworn to secrecy, professed to "know nothing," the party was generally called the Know-Nothings. The main goals of the party were to deny immigrants the right to hold office entirely and to grant naturalization and voting rights only after 21 years of U.S. residence. At the time, any white could become a citizen after only five years, if he submitted a declaration of intent ("first papers") at least two years before, swore to uphold the Constitution, and forswore any allegiance to a foreign government. Until 1906 there was no need to prove any knowledge of English or the American political system. In some states, such as Wisconsin after 1846 and a dozen others by the 1880s, immigrants even received the right to vote along with their first papers, long before they were naturalized.[22]

Nativism was always closely connected to the temperance and prohibition movements, partly out of fear that immigrant votes could be bought with free rounds of beer or whiskey. A cartoon of the 1850s personified German beer and Irish whiskey as two rogues making off with a ballot box. In April 1855 the Chicago City Council, dominated by Know-Nothings, tried to raise the liquor license fees from fifty to three hundred dollars a year; a three-day city "civil war" was the result. Three companies of infantry and one of artillery were required to defend City Hall from the siege of the outraged alcohol supporters, the majority of whom were Germans. One German was killed and one policeman severely injured, but the license fees were reduced to one hundred dollars.[23]

At the height of Know-Nothing strength, election campaigns were fought in the literal sense of the word: in 1854 riots in St. Louis cost ten lives; in Baltimore that year ten people were killed and fifty injured. The election in Louisville was the bloodiest, leaving over twenty dead. But although in 1854 and 1855 the Know-Nothings managed to seize power in a few states and dozens of cities, the party proved to be a flash in the pan. Its violence repelled many voters, and it was just as divided on the slavery issue as its predecessor, the Whig party, had been.[24] Although most nativists later joined the Republican party, they were unable to determine party policy. The Republican presidential aspirant Abraham

[22]Udea (1980), 737–40.
[23]Transcript of letter by John Dieden, Chicago, May 18, 1858, BABS; Holli/Jones (1981), 34–35.
[24]Billington (1964), 417–25.

Lincoln even purchased a German newspaper in his hometown in 1859 to reach out to immigrants. The Republican platform on which he campaigned in 1860 included several planks cut to suit German voters; above all, existing naturalization laws were to remain unchanged.[25]

The wrenching effects of the Civil War did much to promote the integration of foreign immigrants, especially the Germans. It is often claimed that the latter voted unanimously for Lincoln in 1860, but they did not—traditional immigrant support for the Democrats was far too strong, and the Republicans in some areas were too anti-immigrant. But men who had dodged the draft back in Germany now signed up by the thousands to bear arms for their adopted nation. The most dedicated were the radical Forty-eighters and members of the ideologically related Turner movement.[26] At the start of the war, German volunteers earned distinction in the defense of the important Union arsenal in St. Louis. Six of the first seven volunteer regiments in Missouri were predominantly German, as well as three more out of the first twenty. Although such enthusiastic support was an extreme, on the whole Germans were overrepresented in the Union Army.[27]

ETHNICITY AND POLITICS

After the war, the Republicans tried to consolidate their hold on the German vote, not only with slogans such as "Vote like you shot" but also with deeds. German-language instruction was introduced in public elementary schools—often after years of struggle—in a wave that was anything but coincidence: St. Louis (1864), Chicago (1865), Buffalo (1866), Milwaukee (1867), Indianapolis (1869).[28]

General opinion has it that German-Americans as a group were too divided to ever form a political power block like the Irish. Compared to the latter, German religious, regional, and occupational diversity was just as conspicuous as their vacillating political loyalty. But it was by means of this very lack of firm partisan ties that the German-Americans managed to gain political support for their demands. This was particularly true on the local and state level, where the issues involved policy

[25]Thompson/Braun (1967), 132–37.
[26]The Turner movement, inspired by Friedrich Jahn and associated with the liberation movement fighting Napoleonic domination, sought to apply the principles of gymnastics and physical fitness to the cause of German unification and democratization. Carried to the United States in the wake of the 1848 revolution, it was closely associated with urban political radicals and freethinkers (Schem 11 [1874], 45–47).
[27]Lonn (1951), 669, 577–78.
[28]Troen (1975), 55–60; *Illinois Staatszeitung,* July 4, 1867; Gerber (1984), esp. 45; Schlossman (1983), esp. 164; Ellis (1954), esp. 135–37.

questions that were emotionally and politically explosive—the public schools and alcohol, for example.

In view of the reputation of the Irish as "born politicians," it is surprising that since 1820 more German immigrants (thirteen) than Irish Catholics (ten) have been elected mayor in the fourteen largest cities. The second generation, too, produced almost the same number of mayors from both groups, 28 to 32, although if Protestant and nonaffiliated Irish are included, their number rises to 43. And German ethnic candidates were no mere tokens; their political platforms also reflected German interests.[29]

When it came to laws regulating the teaching of German in the public schools, the Irish were often the most bitterly opposed, but usually with no effect. In questions regarding alcohol restrictions, German beer usually fared better than Irish whiskey. Where the Republicans were persuaded by Puritan fanatics to attempt prohibition, revenge on the part of the German voters was quick to follow. In Wisconsin, in reaction to tighter control of licensing in 1872 and 1873, the Republicans suffered their only defeat between 1855 and 1890. In the 1880s, prohibition in Iowa and tighter blue laws in Ohio led to a mass German exodus from the Republican party, resulting in victories for the Democrats in both states.[30]

The conflicts that developed in Illinois and Wisconsin in 1889 were even more bitter. In these two states, almost identical laws were passed, defining compulsory education more strictly and precisely, requiring that reading, writing, arithmetic, and history be taught in English, even in parochial schools, which were placed under closer supervision. These laws were seen as a frontal attack on all German parochial schools and served to unite German Catholics and Lutherans, normally hostile to one another, against a common enemy: the Republican party. These two groups of German-Americans were primarily responsible for the Democratic landslide in 1890, in which Wisconsin Republicans lost all state offices and all but one seat in Congress. When Illinois voted in 1892, the two groups helped elect a German immigrant, John Peter Altgeld, as governor—the first Democrat since the Civil War and the first immigrant ever to hold the post. The school laws in both states were quickly repealed.[31]

German-American Schools

Catholics and Lutherans attempted to maintain their own German-language schools for both cultural and religious reasons. Where public

[29]See Holli/Jones, which records all the mayors from 1820 to 1980.
[30]Troen, 68–70, 73, 76; Johnson (1967), 70; Jensen (1971), 92–122.
[31]Jensen, 123–48, 219–21.

schools were available at the start of mass immigration, they were often anti-Catholic or at least had strongly Anglo-Protestant overtones. Old Lutherans felt threatened by what they saw as the same ecumenism that had driven them away from Germany. Within the Catholic church, Germans were caught in a struggle with the dominant Irish. As soon as a parish or congregation had been established, therefore, members tried to start their own schools as quickly as possible. In 1869 the approximately 700 German Catholic parishes had more than 130,000 children enrolled in their parochial schools; by 1881 the number of German parishes had almost doubled, and the over 1,000 parishes provided schooling for 160,000 children. The most important group of Old Lutherans, the Missouri Synod, was already supporting schools for over 10,000 children in 1861, for a good 30,000 in 1872, and for over 50,000 in 1881; at the turn of the century almost 100,000 children were enrolled in more than 2,100 Lutheran schools. A third German-American denomination, the Evangelical, also maintained its own schools, but the number of students never exceeded twenty thousand. A comparison of the number of baptisms per year with parochial school attendance reveals that only one-third or at most one-half of Catholic and Lutheran children went to parochial schools. Interrelated with the rise of German-language parochial schools was the issue of German instruction in the public schools.[32]

Laws permitting the teaching of German in the public schools existed in Ohio and Pennsylvania before 1840. German as a subject or medium of instruction, however, became widespread only in the last third of the nineteenth century. In 1880 laws providing for foreign language instruction existed in New York, Wisconsin, Iowa, Minnesota, Indiana, Michigan, Colorado, Oregon, and elsewhere, as well as in the cities of Louisville, St. Louis, San Francisco, and Chicago. In homogeneous rural areas, local school board initiatives often introduced German into elementary schools even without legal authorization. In Gasconade County, the most heavily German in all Missouri, half of the public grade schools taught German.[33]

Around the turn of the century, an unofficial and incomplete survey conducted by the German-American Teachers Association revealed that over half a million children were being taught German in elementary school. The largest group, 42 percent, attended public schools, more than one-third Catholic, 16 percent Lutheran, and the other 7 percent were divided among Evangelical and other private institutions. The leading state was Ohio with some 100,000 students. According to a 1908

[32]Lenhart (1959), 312–15; *Statistical Yearbook* (1938), 150–73; *Statistik nach den Distrikts-Protokollen* (1890–99). There were at least two schoolchildren for every Catholic and Lutheran baptism, but not even one for every Evangelical.
[33]Kloss (1977), 75–94, 147–62; *Report* (1888), 14–15; see Schlossman.

report, a total of 66,000 children there took classes in German in the
public schools alone—almost 8 percent of the population at a time when
German immigrants and their children did not even amount to 13 percent
of the state population. This means that about half of the German children in Ohio were being taught their native language.[34]

Such instruction could either promote or hinder assimilation, depending on the way it was set up. In Cincinnati, Cleveland, Baltimore, and
Indianapolis, the school day was divided between German and English,
and the only English-speaking schoolmates of the German children were
those who also attended the classes in German. In St. Louis, Chicago,
and New York, by contrast, German was taught only one hour a day;
otherwise the children spent a normal school day together with the
Anglo-American pupils. By the turn of the century, those taking part in
German instruction included a growing proportion of non-German children. In 1900, of the approximately forty thousand pupils learning German in Chicago, only fifteen thousand were German-Americans, and of
the rest, half were composed of other immigrants and half of Anglo-
Americans. The situation in Indianapolis was similar: in 1916 less than 20
percent were German-Americans. Attendance in many of these programs had already peaked by the turn of the century.[35]

THE GERMAN-AMERICAN PRESS

German-language publications also played an ambivalent role: to a
certain extent, they exerted a conserving force since they promoted
language maintenance and the protection and defense of ethnic interests.
But by familiarizing immigrants with American ways, and in particular
the American political system, the foreign language press eventually
contributed to its own downfall.

Three German newspapers already existed in Pennsylvania during the
colonial era. A couple survived from the eighteenth century into the
twentieth; most came into existence during the period of mass immigration. The *New Yorker Staatszeitung,* founded in 1834, the St. Louis *Anzeiger des Westens* (1835), and the Cincinnati *Volksblatt* (1836) were the first
viable German papers in their respective cities; up until 1843 the only
German-language daily was in Cincinnati. The political refugees of 1848
brought a considerable influx of talent and energy into German-American journalism. Between 1848 and 1852 the number of German-language
newspapers published in the United States rose from seventy to almost
twice that number.[36]

[34]Viereck (1902), 659; Kloss, 161.
[35]Viereck, 645; Ellis, 359, 371; Schlossman, 169–76; Kloss, 91–93. For Chicago and Indianapolis it is unclear how the third generation was counted.
[36]Arndt/Olson (1965), 250–51, 454–55, 399–400, 587–88; Wittke (1957), 262–63.

In quantitative terms, German immigrants were astoundingly well supplied with publications in their native language, even in comparison with their former countrymen in Germany. With its four German dailies in 1850, New York was ahead of Berlin and Leipzig; in 1856 circulation amounted to one copy for every fifth German in New York. By 1872 the *New Yorker Staatszeitung,* circulation 55,000, called itself the largest German paper in the world. The 1876 centennial festivities in the United States were celebrated by 74 German-language dailies, with a combined circulation large enough to reach one-sixth of all German-Americans. Weekly papers were published by the millions—enough for more than every second immigrant.[37]

A county population of one thousand to two thousand Germans was all the "critical mass" needed to support a German-language weekly, as shown by evidence from Iowa, a typical state in the Middle West. In 1885, at the peak of the last great wave of immigration, two counties in Iowa were even able to support a German-language weekly with fewer than one thousand potential readers. Aside from one county dominated by the Amana colonists, known for their lack of interest in worldly affairs, at least one German-language paper was published in each of the sixteen counties where more than two thousand Germans were living.[38]

At the time, German publications accounted for almost 80 percent of the immigrant press in the United States. In 1894, when the number of German papers reached its peak of eight hundred (including 97 daily papers), two-thirds of all foreign-language publications in the country were still German. From this time on, however, the German-American press declined slowly but steadily. Between 1884 and 1910, even in a city like Milwaukee with its strong German contingent, daily newspaper circulation sank from a total of 92,000 to 50,000, a mere third of the English-language competition.[39]

WORLD WAR I

World War I resulted not in a radical break in ethnic ties and identity but rather in an acceleration of the decline which had begun by the turn of the century. Many German-Americans shared the view expressed by Carl

[37]Wittke (1957), 75–77, 207, 213–14.
[38]Two competing weeklies were launched in only two counties with more than six thousand potential readers, although one county, with a population of almost five thousand Germans, supported a daily paper. The approximately ten thousand Germans living in the Forty-eighter capital of Davenport and the surrounding county were the only ones who could choose between two local papers more than once a week. Of the 21 counties with one thousand to two thousand Germans, nine had a German-language weekly; in eight others none had ever been tried; and the other four counties had had a paper, at least temporarily, before 1885 (Iowa State Census) [1885], 273–89; Arndt/Olson, 130–57).
[39]Park (1922), 310–20; Wittke (1957), 201–5.

Schurz that love of one's old and new homelands was no more incompatible than love for one's wife and one's mother. However, this view holds true only as long as the two women get along with each other. Sympathy with Germany was clearly strong in many circles of German-Americans. But it is equally clear that, when the time came to choose between the two sides, loyalty to the United States had top priority for the overwhelming majority.[40]

Among the letter-writers in this edition, there is a surprising affinity between John Witten, the German nationalist, and Louis Dilger, the socialist: both emphatically condemned the American entry into the war. Those in the middle of the political spectrum were probably somewhat more restrained, but in almost all of the letters in the Bochum collection, sympathy for Germany in World War I is clearly evident. With regard to the attitudes of German-Americans in general, however, the picture created by these letters may well be skewed: we have no access to the feelings of all those who no longer corresponded with relatives and friends in Germany. And that must have been the great majority of the second generation, a group that as early as 1910 was twice as large as the group of actual immigrants. Very few of the letters in the Bochum collection, in any case, were written by anyone not born in Germany.[41]

In many circles of German-Americans, despite all their religious and social differences, enthusiasm for the old fatherland knew no bounds, especially at the start of the war. German rallies and assemblies enjoyed record attendance, and the superiority of German culture was loudly proclaimed. But enthusiasm began to wane—or people grew more cautious—as the probability of American involvement increased. In 1917 the president of the German Evangelical Synod of North America denounced the "spirit of lies and hypocrisy," emphasizing that "we do not want this English spirit," but the following year he described the young members of the Synod, now marching off to war, as filled with "much noble enthusiasm and unfeigned, completely natural patriotism for their Fatherland," i.e., America. The Chicago *Abendpost* also reported how German-American soldiers were doing irreproachable service in the U.S. Army.[42]

Still, when the United States finally entered the war, it was not only the agitators who had to pay for the excesses of German-American

---

[40]Detjen (1985), 23; Trefousse (1982), 180.

[41]Helbich (1985a), 185–87. The number of German immigrants had already peaked by the 1900 census, but the number of their children and the total of first- and second-generation German-Americans continued to rise until 1910. Between 1910 and 1920, these numbers also declined.

[42]Luebke (1974); Holli (1984); Detjen, 81–146; *Berichte* (1918); *Abendpost*, September 17, 1918.

chauvinism during the years of American neutrality. No German-American was beyond suspicion; speaking German was enough to call one's loyalty into question. Hysteria degenerated into all sorts of absurd campaigns to stamp out everything German. Bach and Beethoven were taken off concert programs, streets and stores were renamed, even sauerkraut was turned into "liberty cabbage." In Cincinnati, superpatriots debated whether to tear down the memorial to Friedrich Jahn, the founder of the Turner movement, but allowances were made for the fact that he had been dead for seventy years and that, given his democratic attitudes, he would probably have preferred the United States to the kaiser. Such differentiation, however, was rare among the superpatriots. This was most clearly demonstrated by the persecution of the German Mennonites, a group of pacifists (and largely immigrants from Russia) who had absolutely nothing in common with Prussian militarists except the German language.[43]

Intolerance—directed not only against Germans—continued almost unabated even after the end of the war. Prohibition would have been inconceivable without the demagogic excesses and convulsions produced by the war. The same is true of the immigration restriction laws passed in 1921 and 1924. Ironically, these hit other groups of immigrants much harder than the Germans, who received a relatively generous quota compared to southern and eastern Europeans.[44]

One major consequence of the war was the virtual disappearance of the German-language from public life and the schools. Not only were the last surviving German language programs in public elementary schools abolished, but cuts at the secondary level went even deeper. Before the war, German was by far the most important foreign language in the high school curriculum. The number of students learning French never reached 10 percent, but one out of four students took German. By 1922 nothing was left of this dominance: only 0.6 percent were enrolled in German classes. The German language has remained insignificant to this day. In 1968 enrollment reached a new high of 3.3 percent. In seven states it was against the law to teach German in the elementary schools, including parochial schools; a 1922 referendum in Oregon went so far as to abolish all private and parochial elementary schools in the state. In 1925 the Supreme Court declared both sets of laws unconstitutional, but by then their goals had largely been accomplished. By the end of the 1920s the German language had almost completely disappeared from Lutheran schools.[45]

[43]Luebke (1974), 225–93; Tolzmann (1983), 131.
[44]See Detjen; Bickelmann (1980), 37–39, 43–46, 162.
[45]Gilbert (1981), 262–63; Luebke (1974), 312–16.

The transition to English in the churches was closely connected with this development. Where Germans made up a minority in a predominantly English-speaking denomination, bilingualism had been common even before the war. The 584 Catholic parishes that had used German exclusively in 1906 were reduced to 206 in 1916, compared to the 1,684 parishes where a combination of English and German was used. In the majority of German Methodist congregations, the language shift began by 1917. Change was slower in the strictly German denominations: in 1905 the Evangelical Synod still held 90 percent of its services in German; in 1917, it was down to 71 percent. The next two years saw a loss of a further twelve points. In 1907 only 15 percent of the congregations in the Lutheran Missouri Synod used any English at all, and by 1917 it had reached only 20 percent. But within three years, the percentage of congregations still holding services exclusively in German had fallen to 23.[46]

The decline of the German press took a similar course. Between 1894 and 1910 the number of German newspapers fell from 800 to 554, although circulation size was less affected. The war news, in fact, sparked a brief increase in sales. But with the American declaration of war came the pressure of public opinion, censorship, translation requirements, and postal restrictions. The war cut the number of German-language publications by half and their circulation by three-quarters. In 1919 only twenty-six dailies were left; circulation was large enough for only every eighth immigrant or, including the second generation, every twenty-ninth German-American. Many papers that struggled to survive the 1920s then finally collapsed during the Depression.[47]

If any traces of German-American identity remained, they were only in voting patterns: at the national level the Democrats had to pay for President Woodrow Wilson's policies of war and peace. In congressional and gubernatorial elections, it depended on which party or person had been the biggest "Hun-baiter." If neither of the two major parties was acceptable, a large share of the German vote, even of conservative Lutherans and Catholics, went to Socialist and Farmer-Labor candidates. Except at the ballot box, however, German-Americans as an identifiable ethnic group had all but disappeared.[48]

---

[46]Dolan (1977), 80; Heidemann (1950), 50, 58, 74; *Statistical Yearbook* (1938); *Statistical Tables* (1919), 654; Tolzmann, 254–56.

[47]Luebke (1974), 241–43, 271; Yox, 413; Park, 310–20.

[48]Luebke (1974), 294–302, 324–29.

Immigrant Letters

LETTERS AS HISTORICAL DOCUMENTS

Between 1820 and 1914 some 250 to 300 million letters were sent from the United States to Germany.[1] For the years in which reliable figures are available, 1870–1909 in the German Empire (excluding Bavaria and Württemberg), the average volume amounts to two million letters a year in the 1870s, four million in the 1880s and 1890s, and a good seven million in the first decade of the twentieth century.

A comparison of these figures with the number of immigrants as well as the number of Germans living in the United States shows that the letter curve runs roughly parallel to the other two until about 1884; before 1890 some correlation can still be found, but then the curves diverge sharply: the number of potential letter-writers goes down, and the number of letters keeps going up.

---

[1]This figure is based on the "hard core" of 164 million letters sent from the United States to the area served by the Imperial Postal Service (not including Bavaria or Württemberg) between 1870 and 1908, documented by the annual publications *Statistik der Deutschen Postverwaltung* (1871–76) and *Statistik der Deutschen Reichs-Post* (1877–1913). For earlier years, sources are *Amts-Blatt der Norddeutschen Postverwaltung* (1869) and *Statistik der Postverwaltung des Norddeutschen Bundes. Jahr 1870*, n.d., GStA B, Rep. A 181, Nr. 2291. Added to this sum were estimates for Bavaria and Württemberg, the former based on a set of handwritten statistics for 1883 (Übersicht über die Post- und Telegraphen-Betriebsverhältnisse in Bayern für das Kalenderjahr 1883, Ba. StA M, ehem. Akten der Oberpostdirektion, Verz. 2, Sch. Nr. 203–5). The Württemberg estimate was based on its share of letters handled by the Imperial Postal Service. The figures for 1910–14 and 1820–69 are also estimates. The volume is known only for three years: 1.36 million in 1868 (*Amts-Blatt der Norddeutschen Postverwaltung*); 1.06 million in 1857 (Koch [1964], 21); and 0.71 million in 1854 (Koch, 21).

Although noticeable cuts in postage rates might explain such an increase in correspondence, these did not occur in 1884 or 1890 but a decade earlier, in the 1870s.[2] The only plausible explanation lies in the steady increase in the relative share of business as opposed to private correspondence. Here any estimate is risky indeed, since official statistics ignore this distinction. But the figure of 100 million private letters for the entire time period is probably not totally off the mark.[3]

Whether 280 million or 100 million, these numbers clearly illustrate two points. Just as immigration from Germany was a mass movement, letters written home were not mere isolated missives but amounted to a vast stream, a veritable flood of paper that poured into Germany.

Compared to this flood, the five thousand immigrant letters acquired over many years by the Bochum collection are hardly even worth mentioning: whether they represent 0.0018 percent of 280 million or 0.005 percent of 100 million makes no difference at this order of magnitude.[4] We editors feel that the twenty letter series printed here, however, are not only far from atypical but in fact representative of millions of similar letters.[5]

Emigrant letters served not only to tie together families separated by the Atlantic and as important documents of social history; they were also the decisive factor triggering emigration, whether for economic or other reasons. This fact was long overlooked by historians who focused primarily on emigration handbooks, newspapers, emigration agents, and propaganda brochures. Then, in 1929 and 1931, Theodore C. Blegen pointed out for Norway the importance of these reports—the accounts from relatives and acquaintances were the only trustworthy ones for the "common man."[6]

Officials on both sides of the Atlantic had been fully aware of this connection much earlier. The county magistrate in Trier reported in 1852 that the letters written by relatives and friends in America "hold out the prospect of a secure living and invite their relatives here to join them. Journeys of 10 to 12 hours are made to hear the contents of such letters, especially when written by persons known to be trustworthy, and par-

[2]Postage for a normal letter, weighing up to half an ounce from Germany to the United States cost (in marks) 1.66 in 1835; 1.30 in 1852; 0.40 in 1868; 0.25 in 1871. In dollars the cost was 0.30 in 1852; 0.15 in 1857; 0.07 in 1870; 0.06 in 1875. Until about 1860, therefore, the cost of sending a letter was not negligible to someone with a low income (Koch, 14–25; Hargest [1971], 16, 111, 199–224).

[3]This estimate, based on the sources in n. 1, above, as well as "Der Briefverkehr" (1880), is supported and documented in Helbich (1987).

[4]How these letters were obtained and what criteria were used in the collection have been reported elsewhere (Helbich [1985b], 208–9).

[5]See the section "The Sample," below.

[6]Blegen (1929), 7, 17; Blegen (1931), 196, 212–13.

ticularly young people tend to decide [to emigrate] on the basis of such news."[7] The U.S. Immigration Commission conducted an investigation in the first decade of the twentieth century, in particular of southern and southeastern Europeans, but its clear results also applied for the Germans: emigrants relied far more heavily on letters as a source of information than on anything else.[8]

Seen in this light, immigrant letters can also be regarded as a detailed direct or indirect answer to the question most frequently posed by those who stayed behind—whether they should follow. Thus we find the following in a letter written from Germany to a friend and fellow worker of one of our letter-writers: "Dear Peter, I also have to let you know that we were firmly intending to join you but then we heard bad news everywhere, from America, that everything is at a standstill and there are no chances of earning money. My wife and I, we still want to come to America, but you must write and tell me specifically if we should follow, how things are now."[9] This letter supports the view that immigrant letters are not untrustworthy sources that should be dismissed on the grounds of unreliability; on the contrary, although they must be examined critically, like any other type of source, they are historical documents that possess an unusually high degree of subjective truth value.[10]

A straight answer to the question whether those at home should follow was quite rare—and with good reason. Instead, a long list of arguments for and against emigration was usually included, along with a set of objective criteria to be used in making the decision, and letters often ended with a statement to the effect that every person has to decide for him- or herself. Immigrants may well have been overjoyed when their relatives came to join them, but the new arrivals were also a great burden until they found jobs and places to live. And the last thing one needed was to be reproached for having painted too rosy a picture of life in the United States.

These factors constrained letter-writers from yielding to the temptation of exaggerating their own success. Another deterrent was the fact that emigrants who did well were expected to send home money and presents. And a third can be seen in the brisk traffic back and forth between Germany and the United States: bluffs could be called all too easily.

---

[7]April 10, 1852, LHA KO, Best. 442, Nr. 6808, Bl. 53–54. Other similar official reports are in Mergen (n.d.), 9–10.

[8]*Reports of the Immigration Commission* 4 (1911), 56–57, 59–60.

[9]Written to Peter Büch (see the Klein series, Chapter 13) by his brother in Güchenbach, undated, probably in the spring of 1858 (BABS).

[10]Some letter-writers, of course, did boast and exaggerate; see the Heck series, Chapter 12.

Of course, a critical appraisal of letters as sources must also consider the letter-writer's personality, his or her relationship to the rest of the family and other close or more distant relatives and friends, and the level of education and social status. Most important, however, is an examination of the two-sided nature of communication itself, the relationship between writer and recipient as well as their common background of shared experience. It stands to reason that the more we know about the individual from other sources, the better the effects of these factors can be taken into account.[11]

One important feature of the great majority of the letters in this edition (and of letters in general) is that they are documents penned not by members of the middle and upper class who were skilled in writing but rather by the lower middle and lower classes, by people who would hardly ever have taken up the pen if they had stayed at home. Along with the need to bridge great distances, the average letter-writer was also motivated by the fact that he faced an exciting, possibly terrifying, but above all strange world. His or her observations, too, were made not from the frivolous distance of a tourist but by someone directly involved and affected, for better or worse.

The lower class in nineteenth-century Germany left behind regrettably few personal documents: emigrant letters constitute a considerable portion of them. In letters many of the hopes and fears, values and concerns of this group are revealed, especially in the way the United States is understood and described. With regard to images of American society and the adjustment process, their ignorance and naiveté may well have kept open many avenues of insight and emotion that necessarily remained closed to the educated, "well-trained" observer. Both perspectives are valuable; until now that of the lower class has been largely inaccessible. This volume, although primarily conceived in terms of the history of emigration and adaptation, is thus also a contribution to the history of the inarticulate, history from the bottom up, the history of everyday life.

THE CONTENTS OF THE LETTERS

The comprehensive apparatus of introductions and notes is intended to help the reader understand the letter texts, interpret their contents, and relate the fates of individual letter-writers to the overall historical context. We believe we have made the letters accessible, but they have been left to speak for themselves, directly to the reader. What is at issue here is

[11]See the section "Sources," below.

not the specific "message" of individual letters but a few general topics that play an important role in most of the letters. Our purpose is to prepare the reader, not present foredrawn conclusions.

In almost all the letters, considerable space is devoted to family and friends on both sides of the Atlantic. Particularly striking is the prominent role played by the "personal network" in the United States: neighbors, friends, people from the same hometown or the vicinity.

Employment, earnings (and especially in this connection the importance of speaking English), purchasing power, prices, and leisure time activities make up an important complex of topics that are frequently compared to past experience in Germany. Closely related, too, are the lovingly detailed descriptions of food, drink, and clothing, reflecting interests perhaps best explained in terms of the letter-writer's previous social position in Germany.

These subjects overshadow two others that are also worth mentioning: the Americans (frequently referred to as "the English") and the Germans in America (not personal acquaintances). American society is sometimes presented in a positive and at others in a negative light, highlighting aspects that struck continental Europeans as particularly remarkable. Politics, as a rule, appears only in the form of presidential elections and of wars—or as a result of experience with nativist hostility.

The many facets of German-American ethnic life, institutionalized in the big cities but also highly developed in rural areas, left but few traces in these letters. The German church plays a certain role, and the existence of a sense of German identity is clear, despite the tension among the various factions, denominations, and splinter groups. Loyalty conflicts between the old and the new homeland surface occasionally, even before World War I, and German-language newspapers are frequently mentioned. But that is about it.

Covering all these topics as well as a host of others, immigrant letters are a unique source of information about the stages, determining factors, and subjective experience of the adjustment process that all German immigrant groups who were contemporaries of our letter-writers (apart from small groups such as the Amish) have by now completed. It is basically the same for our letter-writers who immigrated one hundred fifty or one hundred years ago as it is today for almost all groups of minority immigrants: integration, assimilation, or in this particular case, Americanization.

From a number of different types of sources—statistics, church and school records, newspapers—we know quite a lot about the general course of German-American assimilation, its specific forms in particular cities and rural areas—in other words, about the process as it affected larger groups. Aside from diaries and—with considerable reservations—autobiographies, however, only letters can provide insight into the process of adaptation for the *individual,* its stages and their sequence, and the various levels at which changes occurred.[12] Above all, they reveal attitudes to change and emotional reactions: whether an individual tried to speed up the process of assimilation or slow it down.[13]

In short, the letters should provide a more detailed and personal view of the highly complex process at the beginning of which stood the German who had just set foot on American soil and whose final result was an American indistinguishable from the majority of his countrymen. Between beginning and end, there may have been several generations as well as the transitional phase "German-American."[14]

THE SAMPLE

How representative are the letter-writers in this edition for German immigrants as a whole? The question can be answered here only in terms of a very rough matrix of factors such as age, sex, marital status, religious affiliation, occupation, place of birth, and place of residence. On such a basis, the extent to which the largest and most important groups of German immigrants are represented is assessed here.

In terms of age at the time of emigration, the present sample reveals a strong concentration of young adults, higher than for German emigrants in general. The primary letter-writers, with one exception, were all between 16 and 33 years old when they left Germany. The only one who left for the United States accompanied by a spouse and children was Christian Kirst, aged 54. Three others married shortly before or after leaving. A good three-quarters of the letter-writers were unmarried when they arrived in their new homeland, but many had brothers or sisters who either preceded, followed, or accompanied them.[15]

It is difficult to make a precise assessment of the general level of education in Germany during the nineteenth century, but if the letter-

---

[12]In the fairly extensive, primarily American, literature, distinctions are usually made between cognitive, identificatory, social, and structural assimilation, although the concepts overlap (Esser [1980]; Gordon [1964] and [1978]; Abramson [1980]; Yinger [1981]).

[13]The optimal degree of assimilation, ranging from what are often referred to as Anglo-conformity (total adaptation), "melting-pot" (a mixture of both cultures), and "cultural pluralism" (cultural coexistence), has been a subject of debate since the early nineteenth century. On German-Americans in the nineteenth century, see Conzen (1985b); on the early twentieth century, see Adams (1984); and on the present, see Abramson.

[14]In view of the fact that the letters printed here were written almost exclusively by first-generation immigrants, they illuminate only the first part of this process. In many cases, however, this went quite far.

[15]Children under ten comprised a steady 10 percent of emigrants; only 5 percent were over fifty years old; more than half were married (Marschalck [1973], 72–75; see also Hippel [1984], 211–26).

writers deviate from the average, then they did so positively. It is highly probable that 10 percent of the sample had at least some secondary schooling and another 10 percent finished their studies at a Gymnasium (which qualified them for university admission). When the German Empire was established in 1871, Prussian students attending public schools above the elementary level accounted for only 5 percent of their age group, and only 2 percent at the most graduated. One illiterate out of twenty in this edition is a higher proportion than in German statistics; after 1877, the literacy rate of army recruits was above 98 percent.[16]

If the sample were to reflect the relative strength of the various religions in the German Empire as a whole, six or seven Catholics would need to be included, instead of the three Catholic letter-writers in this edition.[17] But Catholics were a relatively homogeneous group, whereas Protestants were more diverse. Representatives of the three major groups of German Protestants—Lutherans, Reformed, and Evangelical—as well as converts to Anglo-American denominations appear here. Apart from specific institutional affiliations, a wide range of attitudes toward religion are revealed—from zealous activism to indifference and free thinking.

In a random sample of twenty German emigrants, the chances of finding a Jew would be only one in four. The fact that there are no Jewish letter-writers in this volume, however, does not reflect an intentional omission on our part. Not one of the 250 letter series sent in by contributors to the Bochum collection was written by a member of the Jewish faith, and efforts to obtain comparable materials from American archives proved unsuccessful.

The regional backgrounds of the letter-writers can easily be checked against the 1870 U.S. Census, revealing several differences. Of German emigrants as a whole, 45 percent were Prussian—compared to 55 percent of the sample. Despite the high percentage of Prussians here, however, only two series written by East Elbian emigrants could be included, owing to a lack of material from this region in the Bochum collection. The state with the second-largest number of emigrants, Bavaria, is not represented at all, but this omission seemed justified by the fact that almost half of the Bavarian emigrants actually came from the Palatinate, which belonged to the Kingdom of Bavaria at the time. Since a substantial edition of letters from the Palatinate will be published in the near future, we decided to exclude writers from this region from the present volume.[18] Neighboring regions west of the Rhine are well represented. Baden-Württemberg, by contrast, is somewhat underrepre-

---

[16]Jarausch (1984), 72; Hohorst et al. (1975), 165–67, 24.

[17]Hohorst et al., 54.

[18]USC 1870.1, 338–39. The edition of letters written by emigrants from the Palatinate is being prepared by the Institut für Pfälzische Geschichte und Landeskunde, Kaiserslautern.

sented, whereas Hesse, with 20 percent, is clearly overrepresented. One series from Hanover and two from rural Westphalia cover northwestern Germany's due share, and the Hanseatic cities are adequately represented by one writer.

In Germany, the occupations of emigrants were not registered with sufficient precision or consistency to permit any conclusions about whether the letter-writers make up a representative sample. Better data are available on the American side. Using the figures from the 1870 census, we find our writers present a relatively typical occupational profile of German-Americans as a whole. The five full-time farmers included here correspond almost exactly to the 27 percent of German immigrants employed in agriculture. Farmhands accounted for one-quarter of this group in the census records, but such employment was often only a temporary stage in the life cycle of new arrivals, as in the case of letter-writer John Bauer.

Outside the agrarian sector, the most common occupational listing was laborer (not specified)—about one-tenth of the gainfully employed. William Buerkert and Christian Kirst belonged in this category all their lives, and others such as Matthias Dorgathen and John Pritzlaff temporarily. In the artisan sector, almost all of the statistically important German-American occupations appear. Listed in order of frequency are tailor Nicholas Heck, carpenter Franz Joseph Loewen, shoemaker Henry Miller, (a blacksmith is missing); butcher Engel Winkelmeier's husband, (cabinetmaker and mason are missing); baker Louis Dilger (temporarily), (cigarmaker is missing); and cooper Christian Lenz. In the industrial sector, mining is overrepresented by Dorgathen and Peter Klein, but they were included to represent returning immigrants and illiterates, respectively. In business and trade, the most important occupation, clerk, appears only as temporary employment; the same is true of work as a teamster. Dilger was a grocer for a while; other businessmen include Carl Blumner and Pritzlaff (he started his business after the letter series ended). Although many German-Americans worked in the saloon and restaurant business, this group is only indirectly represented: Wilhelmine Wiebusch's husband ran a saloon and later a hotel. Teachers, clergymen, doctors, politicians, and public officials comprised hardly 10 percent of German immigrants. Carl Blumner and Randolph Probstfield thus suffice to cover this group.[19]

Women, here represented by merely 20 percent of the primary correspondents, receive only half their due, according to their share in German

[19]USC 1870.1, 703–16. The 1870 census was the first to publish the occupations of members of each separate ethnic group, but not according to sex.

immigration, but more than their roughly 15 percent share of the entire Bochum letter collection. In 1880 about half of the women who were gainfully employed were domestic servants, compared to three-fourths in this edition, but the second most frequent source of female employment—the textile industry—appears at least on the side in the Heck and Loewen letters.[20]

In terms of the size and regional location of immigrant settlements, the letter-writers deviate only slightly from the overall distribution of Germans in the United States. Like half of all German-Americans at the turn of the century, half of the writers lived in the country or in small towns with a population of less than 25,000. Compared to the figures for 1870, however, rural areas are somewhat underrepresented in this edition. The eight largest cities also receive less than their share of 25 percent, while smaller cities are slightly overrepresented. Of the most important large cities, Chicago, Philadelphia, and Baltimore play only a marginal role, while New York and Louisville appear several times. The geographic regions with the most German-Americans, the Middle West and the central Atlantic seaboard, are also most frequent in the edition. Slightly overrepresented, however, are the more exotic places for Germans to settle, like New England, the Rockies, and the West Coast.[21]

Marriage patterns are a good indicator whether the letter-writers were more assimilated or less so than the average German immigrant. About 70 percent of our authors married other Germans. At the turn of the century, this was true for 72 percent of all German males, and the rate for females was somewhat higher. In keeping with national averages, only 4 percent of the letter-writers married members of other immigrant groups. The term "American" as used in the census includes many spouses who were in fact second-generation German-Americans: 12 percent of the spouses here fit this category, and another 12 percent were "true" Americans.[22]

The primary goal of this edition was not to achieve a representative sample in statistical terms, and the composition of the sample was only one of the selection criteria used. What has been achieved, however, is a group of individuals who were a fairly typical cross-section of German immigration as a whole.

[20]USC 1880.1, 756–59; Marschalck, 72.
[21]USC 1870.1, 338–39, 388–89; Ward (1971), 51–83.
[22]Kamphoefner (1984), 28.

This Edition

Texts not taken from emigrant letters but written by the editors take up a considerable amount of space in this volume: general introductions, chapter and series introductions, explanations in the text and in the notes. Their scope and purpose are explained elsewhere.[1] The purpose of this section is to introduce the sources, some of which are unfamiliar even to historians, on which these supplementary texts are based.

Parish registers[2] (German originals usually found in the parishes, copies often in regional church or state archives) are one basic and often the only source of information about the origin and family background of an emigrant letter-writer. Protestant records are usually more valuable to the historian than Catholic ones. Aside from the fact that Catholic records were often still kept in Latin, Protestant pastors usually noted, besides names and dates of demographic events, the occupations of persons involved.[3]

In some cases parish registers permit more than a simple reconstruction of family relationships and at least a vague impression of an emigrant's social background. Conscientious pastors often noted when a parishioner left (often with date and destination), so that the records can provide a comprehensive survey of migration out of a particular parish.[4]

[1] See the section "Introductions," below.
[2] Abbreviated as KB (from *Kirchenbücher*) in the notes.
[3] See also Ribbe/Henning (1975), 53–66.
[4] See also Struck (1980), 111.

A useful complement to the data and information contained in parish registers is *family tradition*—passed down in either written or oral form—concerning an emigrant's private and personal affairs that found no expression in official documents.

Contemporary collections of statistics, as well as state and county historical and geographical publications, exist for almost all of the German states. Similar to the census returns and county histories published in the United States in the late nineteenth and early twentieth centuries, these collections provide information about the population, economy, and social structure of the area where the letter-writer came from—and hence insight into any possible economic or social reasons for emigration. They also often contain more or less detailed descriptions of individual villages and towns, giving a good impression of the surroundings of an emigrant's home in Germany.

Another group of sources is related to the stages of the emigration itself. The most important of these are *emigration files, lists,* and *announcements.* By the first third of the nineteenth century, hardly any German state expressly prohibited emigration.[5] This did not mean, however, that anyone who wanted to could simply leave his or her homeland. On the contrary, potential emigrants were required—at least according to the letter of the law—to apply for official permission to leave. Each state had its own regulations and procedures, but they all amounted to the same thing: the applicants had to prove that they would be leaving no unpaid debts or needy dependents behind and that they had enough cash for the journey; in most states they had to present a certificate of nonobjection from the local authorities. Male applicants also had to prove they had served their time in the military or at least convince the officials that they were not leaving the country to avoid the draft.[6]

As a rule, applications were processed by town or county officials, and as a result the files are normally found in the district archives. Ideally the files include not only the emigrant's name, age, and place of origin but also occupation, financial situation as well as destination, and reasons for leaving. In actual fact, however, the files are seldom so complete, since the authorities were unable to keep up with the flood of applications without shortening and formalizing the entries. Thus, information about

---

[5]In the eighteenth century, however, this was usually the case. According to mercantilist economic principles, a large population was seen as a prerequisite for national prosperity, and attempts were therefore made to prevent subjects from leaving. In the early nineteenth century freedom of emigration began to be incorporated into the constitutions and laws of the German states. See the pertinent documents in Philippovich (1892); Schöberl (1982), 324–25; and Bretting (1985), 28. Until the end of the nineteenth century, however, the emigration files indicate that official attitudes toward emigration were negative.

[6]See the pertinent documents in Philippovich and Adams (1980).

occupation and available assets is often missing, the destination is usually
listed as a generalized "America" or "North America," and the reasons
for leaving, if given at all, are soberly bureaucratic: "to take up residence"
or "to make a better living."[7]

The information contained in the individual files was often collected
by the authorities in *emigration lists* or *registers*. In some states, laws also
required that an applicant's name be printed in the newspaper or government publications to give creditors a change to lodge any claims before
permission was granted.[8]

For several states or regions, the emigrant files, lists, and notices have
been analyzed and published by genealogists or historians.[9] Several archives, too, have started index files of emigrants—the most recent and
ambitious project of this kind is a computerized catalog of emigrants
from Hesse-Cassel in the Marburg State Archives.[10]

Even when all of these documents (files, lists, and notices) have survived, however, the chance of finding a specific letter-writer or an individual mentioned in a letter is at best fifty-fifty, because a large number of
emigrants—in some areas more than half—left Germany without even
having applied for official permission to leave.[11] For many, the administrative procedure was probably just too much trouble; uneasiness in
dealing with the authorities certainly played a role as well, along with a
general mistrust of government officials, to whom many emigrants did
not wish to reveal the particulars of their personal situation. Some, like
our letter-writer Christian Kirst, may well have had good reason to keep
creditors or tax collectors in the dark. And it is hardly surprising that
young men who had not yet been drafted were almost always clandestine
emigrants. Yet another factor promoted "illegal" emigration: once German citizenship was renounced, emigrants encountered great difficulties
if they decided to return to their old homes—a possibility that many
preferred to keep open.[12]

Nor were government officials as a rule terribly strict about enforcing
these regulations; the increasing number of emigrants made it hard
enough to keep up with the paperwork. Besides, it was virtually impossible to keep illegal emigrants from leaving, let along bring them back.
And many districts were pleased when the number of poor and unemployed began to decline, whether emigration was legal or not.[13]

[7]Adams (1980).
[8]As, for example, in Nassau and Waldeck; see Struck (1966), 18; and Thomas (1983), 7.
[9]A bibliography of published emigrant lists (up to and including 1975) is found in Smith/
Smith (1976), 207–32.
[10]Ehmer (1980), 155; Scherer (1980), 91; Struck (1980), 115–16, 131.
[11]See, for example, Hippel (1980), 199–200.
[12]Schöberl, 325.
[13]See, for example, Philippovich, 148, and Struck (1966), 11.

Passenger or *ship lists*[14] are available from only one of the European ports of emigration—Hamburg. In the others (Bremen, Rotterdam, Le Havre, Liverpool, and Plymouth) records either were not kept at all or have since been destroyed.[15]

Beginning around 1840, shipping agents in Hamburg were required to turn in passenger lists to the police for all ships bound for North America with more than 25 persons in steerage. In the early 1850s the requirement was extended to ships carrying emigrants to England, where they then embarked for America. Two different series of lists resulted: one of "direct" emigrants between 1850 and 1934 and one of "indirect" emigrants between 1854 and 1934.[16]

The lists include the name of each ship and its captain, date of departure, and port of destination, as well as the names of the passengers and information about their place of origin, occupation, marital status, age, and sex.[17] These entries, however, are by no means always reliable. Shipping agents simply wrote down what the passengers said, a practice that resulted in a wide range of spellings; and emigrants who had left without official permission often gave false information to avoid getting into trouble.[18] The lists are also difficult to use unless the exact year of emigration is known because they are only partially indexed by initial letter.

Much the same is true of the passenger arrival lists compiled in the ports on the other side of the Atlantic (New York, Baltimore, Philadelphia, Boston, New Orleans, and Galveston).[19] Finding aids that are based on passenger names exist for some time periods and for several ports, but the chance of locating the entry for a particular immigrant is in most cases good only when both port of arrival and year are already known. The information in the lists, too, is often highly unreliable since it was taken down by officials who knew as little German as the new arrivals knew English.[20]

The major source of information on the American side is the *U.S. Census,* conducted every ten years since 1790.[21] During the course of the nineteenth century, what had begun as a modest survey used to calculate

[14]Abbreviated in the notes as PL.

[15]Smith/Smith, 199–221.

[16]Filed in StA HH. These archives also include a list of emigrants who left the United States and returned to Germany between 1920 and 1935 (Richter [1980], 135). The U.S. Library of Congress, Manuscripts Division, also has microfilm copies of these records through 1873.

[17]Richter, 136.

[18]See the introduction to the Möller series, Chapter 6.

[19]Published in microfilm by U.S. NatA, Washington, D.C.

[20]Smith/Smith, 186–87. Glazier/Filby (1988) represents the most recent indexing project.

[21]Abbreviated in the notes as USC; the microfilm version by Research Publications, Inc. is used as the basis for citation.

the proportional distribution of direct taxes and seats in the House of Representatives grew into a large-scale collection of official data.[22] Urbanization, industrialization, and mass immigration presented new problems to planners and politicians, and the census seemed well suited to provide an "objective" statistical base for questions of economic and social policy. The scope of the survey and its results broadened accordingly. In 1790 the census forms (not yet standardized) had only included six categories of questions, and the results were published in a slim volume of only 57 pages. Sixty years later, six different forms were in use, more than 3,000 patronage employees worked to fill them out, the published results filled some 1,200 pages, and the total cost of the undertaking amounted to approximately 1.5 million dollars. Professional enumerators were first employed in 1880, and by 1890 special machines were being used to tabulate the results. These were published in 25 volumes, along with a compendium, a summary, and an atlas—altogether more than 26,000 pages.[23]

The claim that virtually everything of statistical value found its way into the census is certainly somewhat exaggerated, but the scope of areas covered over the years is almost overwhelming. A detailed discussion of all the various categories is impossible here, but the innovations most important for this edition deserve brief mention. The results of the 1850 census included the first data on the numerical strength of immigrant groups in each state and in the largest cities. The 1860 census, in addition, recorded the total number of foreign-born living in each county; and starting in 1870, the figures were broken down according to ethnic groups. From 1870 on, occupational statistics also began to distinguish, in increasingly differentiated form, between various ethnic groups.

The census not only provides aggregate data in the form of published results but also provides information at the individual level, based on the original forms used to prepare the published statistics. These returns are available for all except one decade through 1910 (the records of the 1890 census were destroyed in a fire).[24]

Until 1840 the *Manuscript Census*[25] included the name of the head of a household and general information about the other members. Starting in 1850 every person was listed by name, and more specific questions were asked about age (in 1900 also exact month and year of birth), sex, marital

---

[22]Holt (1929), 2.

[23]Ibid., 3–4, 15–17, 30; Wright (1900), 2–17, 39–50, 69–76.

[24]Originals in U.S. NatA; microfilms available in various regional branches of the U.S. NatA and other libraries and archives.

[25]Abbreviated in the notes as MC; entries include county; township (Twp.), ward (W), or enumeration district (e.d.); and family number (#).

status, relation to head of household, occupation (at first, however, asked only about males), country or state of birth, parents' country of birth (starting in 1880), year of immigration (in 1900 and 1910), property holdings (from 1850 to 1870), home ownership (in 1900), school attendance (after 1850), and a number of other categories (such as, for example, the ability to read and write).[26] When letter-writers can be found in the Manuscript Census—and this was almost invariably the case—our knowledge about their family situations, occupations, and financial circumstances, as well as other aspects of their lives, is much more detailed than what we know, on the German side, about the years prior to emigration.

If a letter-writer operated a farm, we can reconstruct even more. The original manuscripts of the *Agricultural Census*[27] (starting in 1850) include precise reports about the size of landholdings, whether a farm was owned or rented, land value, wages paid, implements, and livestock. They also contain detailed information about the types and yields of agricultural products.[28]

Immigrants who settled in larger towns can often be traced in the local *City Directories*.[29] Because new editions were usually published every year or two, the directories are a useful complement to the decennial census. The city directories listed, with varying degrees of completeness, males who were gainfully employed and female heads of households with name, occupation, private address, and occasionally additional information about employer or place of work. The directory also usually noted if the person in question was a boarder living in someone else's house.[30]

The city directories have the advantage of more precise occupational information than the census materials. One serious disadvantage, however, is that they do not include any indication of age or place of birth, making it difficult—if not impossible—to identify a particular individual if the name is common.

Although the directories were compiled by private companies (often as a more or less profitable sideline for printers or newspaper publishers) and had no official status, as a rule they are quite reliable. The publishers had a commercial interest in providing information that was as complete and accurate as possible; and, for people living in the city before the

[26]A complete list of the categories included in the census forms is found in Wright, 131–99.
[27]Abbreviated in the notes as MC A.
[28]Categories are in Wright, 233–304.
[29]Abbreviated in the notes as CD; the microfilm collection by Research Publications, Inc. was used in the preparation of this edition. A comprehensive bibliography of CDs up to 1860 is provided by Spear (1961).
[30]Knights (1969), 5–6.

advent of the telephone, being listed in the local directory was the only way to guarantee being found.[31]

County Histories are another type of useful source.[32] These were published commercially (often by companies specializing in this line) and contain histories of local county settlement and descriptions of the towns, economic structure, churches, newspapers, and the like. They also include biographical sketches of local notables. It was hardly necessary to have done great deeds to be included in the local county *Who's Who;* being a prosperous farmer was usually sufficient. These short biographies may occasionally portray an individual too positively, but since they were almost always based on interviews with the person in question, they are a valuable complement to the evidence contained in the letters.

A general overview of life in various German-American communities can be found in the local *German-language press;*[33] it was not without good reason that the historian Carl Wittke referred to the immigrant press as "the voice, the mirror and the most active catalyzer of the life of any immigrant community" in the United States.[34]

For many German immigrants, too, newspapers written in their own native language were the main source of information about current events in the United States and in Germany. News items reported in the German-language press are not only mentioned frequently in immigrant letters, they also prompted many immigrants to write another letter to friends or relatives back home.[35]

EARLIER EDITIONS

As early as the eighteenth century, a few scattered letters written by German emigrants were published. Larger numbers began to appear in the German press in the 1830s, partly because of their exotic curiosity or instructive informational value, but mostly either to encourage or to discourage others from emigrating, depending on the point of view of the publisher. The same is true of collections of letters published in book form. No fewer than four of these collections appeared on the market soon after the start of mass immigration: *Auszüge aus Briefen aus Nord-Amerika* (1833); Lange (1834); Martels (1834); Dellman (1835). A dozen more were published in the 1840s and 1850s.

During the next hundred years, the publication of letter collections

[31]Ibid., 4.
[32]A comprehensive bibliography is provided by Peterson (1963).
[33]A comprehensive annotated bibliography is provided by Arndt/Olson (1965).
[34]Wittke (1957), v.
[35]See, for example, the Berthold series, Chapter 10, letter of February 23, 1853.

declined considerably, but the genre did not die out completely. Two are particularly noteworthy: the remarkable and highly successful volume compiled by Johannes Gillhof (1917)[36] and the voluminous edition by Louis Frank (1911), which was also published in German in the United States. In recent years, an impressive number of letters have been published in periodicals, especially those of local historical interest.[37] Book publications, by contrast, have been relatively rare, and since they are often published privately, they are rather difficult to track down. Some are based on letters written by one emigrant (e.g., Bartolosch 1986) or by persons from one particular region, often defined quite narrowly, such as Lübbecke County in Westphalia (Kammeier 1985) or a section of the Odenwald in Hesse (Seidenfaden, 1987).[38] Only one substantial edition of letters written by members of one *family,* such as the one by Frank, has appeared in recent years.[39]

Almost all the letters published in Germany reflect either genealogical or regional historical interest (and financial support). An edition covering the entire country does not exist for Germany.

Since the 1950s national editions have appeared for emigrants from Sweden, Norway, Denmark, England and Scotland, Wales, Poland, the German- and the Italian-speaking parts of Switzerland.[40] It is surprising that the two countries that supplied the largest and second largest number of immigrants to the United States in the nineteenth century are missing from this list. A comprehensive edition of letters is being prepared for Ireland,[41] and the present volume is designed to close the gap for Germany (the territory as of 1871).

In national editions the experiences of particular individuals and families as well as the history of specific towns or regions understandably play a less prominent role. The focus of such a collection, although presented through the eyes of individual letter-writers, is an ethnic group's emigration/immigration experience as a whole and the general processes of adaptation to life in the new homeland, in this case, the United States.

[36]This was not, strictly speaking, an edition, but it was based on authentic letters written by emigrants from Mecklenburg between 1868 and World War I (Ensslen [1964], 139–40).

[37]One, Schwarzmeier (1978), deserves special mention as a model of historical method and annotation.

[38]These last three editions grew out of contact or cooperation with the Bochum project.

[39]Bruns (1988). This is not for lack of suitable material. The Bochum project alone is aware of half a dozen such series.

[40]Barton (1975); Blegen (1955); Hale (1984); Erickson (1972); Conway (1961); Kula (1973) and the English translation of Kula (1986); Schelbert/Rappolt (1977); Cheda (1981). The "classic" collection by Thomas/Znaniecki (1918) does not belong to this group: the letters included were mostly written in Poland.

[41]Miller (forthcoming). Herbert Brinks of Calvin College is directing a project involving Dutch letters. In addition, David Fitzpatrick in Dublin and Eric Richards in Canberra are working on Irish-Australian and British-Australian letters, respectively.

The fact that no comprehensive edition of German immigrant letters has appeared to date is not due to lack of interest in such phenomena. Two other factors are at least partly responsible for this lack.

One of them is historical. In West Germany social history (as opposed to political history) has taken much longer than in other Western countries to become accepted as a legitimate field of academic study. The subject of migration has suffered from particular disrepute, primarily because of earlier ideological interest in ethnic Germans abroad during the Third Reich. In terms of method, too, West German historians were slower to accept the "biographical approach," one based on the written or oral evidence (oral history) of contemporaries of no particular prominence.

Second, and of equal importance, is the fact that the work that lies behind such an edition—gathering materials (mostly from private individuals), deciphering and transcribing letter texts, checking transcripts against originals, archival and local research on both sides of the Atlantic—is extremely costly and time-consuming. It is almost impossible for an individual to accomplish, and an edition like the present one could not have been prepared without generous foundation grants.

It is therefore not surprising that only a few of the national editions mentioned above have been able to meet the criteria that the editors of this volume regard as essential for a solid contribution to immigrant studies. These include the exclusive use of previously unpublished letters, the availability of originals to ensure textual authenticity, the inclusion of entire letter series rather than unconnected communications, clear indications of any cuts made in the original texts, the identification of letter-writers and the tracing of their biographies on both sides of the Atlantic, as well as their placement in the economic and social context of their German and their American communities. It is also important that a large number of letter series be available to choose from, so that the selection may include texts that yield a maximum of information for the social historian yet are to some degree representative of German emigration as a whole.

Witold Kula's collection (Poland) meets these requirements to a certain extent; its deficiencies are largely caused by the nature of his material. Giorgio Cheda presents an edition of Italian-Swiss letters from California based on exemplary conceptual and linguistic methodology, and when his two-volume *Epistolario* is supplemented by a planned interpretive volume,[42] it should satisfy all our criteria. But only one work we regard as truly exemplary is actually available now: Charlotte Erickson's *Invis-*

[42]"Storia dell'Emigrazione"; a volume of illustrations will round out the project.

ible Immigrants (England and Scotland). Her book served as a model to the editors of this volume, although we naturally hoped to surpass it, and convinced us that a good edition of emigrant letters is both a feasible and a worthwhile undertaking.

EDITORIAL POLICY

Selection Criteria. The letters in this edition were selected from some five thousand letters in the Bochum collection, according to criteria that can be briefly summarized as follows: First, we decided that only entire series of letters should be included, that is, sequences of letters written by one person or members of one family over a period of several years. As a rule, a series offers a more comprehensive picture of people and living conditions than does an individual letter. Above all, though, a series provides evidence of the process of change in circumstances and attitudes as well as long-term developments such as an individual's adaptation to and integration into the society of his new home.

High priority was given to previously unpublished letter series for which the originals or copies were available to the editors. This policy contributes to the authenticity of the edition, in that "improvements" as well as outright forgeries could be excluded. More important, use of the originals enabled the editors to produce truly "letter perfect" transcriptions of the letters. The originals of three letter series (Heck, Pritzlaff, Witten) were not available; the series were nonetheless included, since their quality demanded inclusion, and the circumstances of their preservation seemed to warrant a high degree of authenticity and textual accuracy.

Among the letters meeting these requirements, two more general criteria were used in the selection process. First of all, the letters were to contain numerous and precise statements which are of use to the social historian reconstructing the migration and adaptation processes from the point of view of the immigrants themselves. Second, they ought to offer as much as possible to the general reader. For example, the personality of the letter-writer should come through, the story of his life and adventures should be clear, the letters should reveal the writer's impressions of the New World as well as the tensions between the familiar and the unusual aspects of her new environment, and they should be entertaining, perhaps even gripping.

Other criteria reflect the attempt to provide a representative sample of German immigrants as a whole. Socioeconomic class as well as geographic distribution—where individuals came from in Germany as well as where they settled in the United States—were taken into account.

With regard to the immigrants' occupations and levels of education, letters from the educated middle class were deliberately limited to reflect their relative numerical insignificance (although a much larger number of their letters have been preserved). This decision also reflects the fact that correspondence of intellectuals predominates in most published editions of German immigrant letters: there is a longstanding backlog of demand for letters written by the lower class, the common people.

Treatment of the Texts. The goal of the original German edition was an exact transcription of the letters. No attempts were made to correct the orthography, punctuation, dialect, grammar, or idiosyncrasies of the original, even when unusual forms were difficult to understand. If the texts had been modernized, the numerous clues to the author's use of dialect, educational background, and expressive ability—as well as the influence of English and "German-American"—contained in the original texts would have been lost.

The goal of the English translation, however, is necessarily rather different. Here, we have tried to maintain the impression of letter-writers with varying amounts of training. Some writers never set a period and thus write one continuous sentence; others, by contrast, write highly formal and impeccably correct letters. We did not attempt to reproduce antiquated forms, dialect expressions, or grammatical errors. Spelling also reflects modern norms, but with one major exception: the original spelling of personal and place names is retained. This adds a touch of "local color" to the texts without impeding comprehension, and over time, changes in spelling, for instance, from Wilhelm to William, can be an important—though indirect—source of evidence for Americanization. The basic goal of the translation, however, has been to achieve, in clear, idiomatic, and contemporary English, the same level of colloquialism or formality and the same degree of sophistication or simplicity of vocabulary as in the originals.

In view of the fact that the letters were treated with such great respect in the German edition, it may seem somewhat contradictory that the texts of the series were abridged by between 20 and 50 percent. The English edition, too, is based on the abridged versions. This intrusion on the integrity of the texts was deemed necessary for two reasons. Many letters contain long lists of prices and verbose comments about the weather, ritualized pious reflections, detailed descriptions of delays in mail delivery, instructions with regard to drafts of money, as well as endless lists of persons to whom the letter-writer wishes to send his or her best regards. Further, nearly every series in the edition contains numerous repetitions. All these things are important constituents of the

truly authentic immigrant letter, but they also make it much more te-
dious for the nonspecialist to read. Only some of the cuts, however, were
made for the sake of readability. The majority reflect decisions with
regard to space limitations. If all the letters in each series had been printed
in unabridged form, six or seven series would have had to be excluded
from a volume this size. The loss of several entire series seemed less
tolerable than careful abridgment, and the disadvantages of the cuts have
been reduced to a minimum by the use of a system that gives a fairly full
description of omissions.

In the interest of transparency (the reader should know exactly what is
missing) only cuts shorter than one line are marked by the conventional
three dots [. . .]. In the case of longer cuts, the square brackets contain
the number of lines cut (ca. 65 characters per line) and a brief summary of
the topics discussed or messages included in the omitted passage.[43]

Square brackets are used exclusively to mark the editors' comments,
including the summaries of omissions just described, as well as their
reconstructions of letters or words that are illegible or destroyed. An
added question mark indicates considerable doubt about the validity of
the solution, and dashes signal that the editors could not suggest any
plausible one. Thus, [----], for example, means that a word about four
letters long was illegible and that even intelligent guessing has led nowhere.

Words or phrases underlined in the letters are also underlined in the
translation. Italics have been used to mark words or phrases, German or
English, (other than personal and geographic place names) taken directly
from the original. Italics are thus used to indicate instances in which the
letter-writer uses an English word, provides explanations or translations
of English terms (often giving their German equivalent, which is also
italicized), or uses a word in German dialect for which the editors were
unable to find a standard German equivalent and hence could not translate. German handwriting used a different script than English, but some
Germans also used a second, "Latin" script similar to English handwriting for English or other foreign words, for proper names, and sometimes
for emphasis. While we distinguished between the two kinds of script in
the German edition, we did not do so here.

A few further notes on the presentation and translation of the text

---

[43]Some of the terms used are quite general. "Correspondence," for example, covers thanks
for letters received, comments on the writer's own letters, requests for letters, questions about
postage, delivery, and the time it takes for a letter to be delivered. "Family" covers a letter-
writer's remarks, news, and questions about his or her addressee's family in the United States or
Germany. "Details" refers to additional comments on the topic discussed before the beginning
of the omitted passage.

follow. Separate paragraphs in the original letters are usually indicated by separate paragraphs in both the German and English editions; but to save space, short lines frequently found at the beginning or end of a letter are occasionally combined, separated by a slash (/). This means that a new line was begun in the original. In the letters, German weights and measures as well as currency terms have been left in German but written out in standard orthography (and hence not italicized), even when abbreviated in the original texts. A table of weights, measures, and currency equivalents is included in the Appendix. German legal terms and administrative titles, many of which have no direct English equivalents and may be unfamiliar to the reader, have been translated into idiomatic English as consistently as possible. The translation of biblical passages cited in the letters is based on the Authorized King James Version. All dates have been changed to conform to U.S. norms (month, day, and year).

Explanatory Notes. Notes and editorial comments are given either in the letter texts (in square brackets) or in the footnotes. The former provide a brief explanation of terms, names, phrases, or expressions in foreign languages in which the original spelling is preserved and which the nonspecialist might find difficult to understand.[44] Footnotes are used to supply additional information about the letter-writer, family, friends, original home in Germany, or place of residence in the United States.[45]

In general there are no notes such as "the identity of X (or the meaning of Y) could not be established." When a name or unusual term receives no explanation, one can assume that the editors either were unable to provide clarification or decided that the word was too unimportant to warrant explanation, or else considered it to be self-explanatory.

Introductions. As well as this general introduction, the volume includes 23 introductions: one to each of the twenty letter series, and one to each occupational grouping, namely farmers, laborers, and domestic servants.[46]

The introductions to the letter series summarize the information avail-

---

[44]"Schigago," for example, receives no comment, but "Rebbe" or "Rewwe" is followed by the explanation [river].

[45]The archival materials used by the editors are indicated by abbreviations that reflect the original language, e.g., USC for United States Census, or ev. KB for *evangelisches Kirchenbuch* [Protestant parish register]. A list of these abbreviations and a glossary of foreign terms are included in the Appendix.

[46]This tripartite division—exclusively determined by occupation in the United States—is admittedly problematic, but it seemed more viable than other types of ordering principles that might have been used.

able about the personal, family, social, and economic background of the individual letter-writers—in Germany as well as in the United States.[47] The borderline between these introductions and the notes discussed above is permeable: data might be found both in the introduction and in the footnotes. In general, however, facts that add to the reader's understanding of particular passages in the letters are found in the footnotes, whereas the introduction includes information about the series as a whole. Series introductions summarize what the editor was able to find out about the letter-writer, his or her family and environment. In our opinion, this type of supplemental information is crucial to the full comprehension of the significance of these texts. Presented alone, these letters would remain truncated historical sources and documents of life in the past.

The introductions to the three major occupational groupings are designed to summarize common trends and problems and to enable the reader to place individual letter-writers in a larger socioeconomic context. Section introductions also serve to avoid repetition in the introductions to the letter series, permitting these to concentrate, instead, on the individuals themselves and local conditions on both sides of the Atlantic.

Division of Labor. All three editors share the responsibility for this volume, although the editing of each letter series, the introductions, and background research were divided. This division of joint labor may seem somewhat contradictory, and it deserves some explanation.

Decisions pertaining to the selection of the letter series and general editorial principles were made by the group as a whole. Research in archives on both sides of the Atlantic, however, was not restricted to one's "own" series. Research was conducted in the United States by Walter Kamphoefner, assisted by Cornelia Vogt (Bochum), and in Germany by Ulrike Sommer and Wolfgang Helbich.

Otherwise, work on the texts and introductions was done independently by one of the three editors. Despite the fact that the team remained in close contact, each member had the final say on his or her own texts. Drafts of the introductions, footnotes, and other material were read and

---

[47]Due to limitations in both time and financial resources the editors have had to restrict their archival work and travel to the cities, towns, and villages where the letter-writers lived (on both sides of the Atlantic) to those types of archives and locations that promised the greatest accessibility and hence efficient working conditions. The materials and possibilities available were utilized to their full extent; but the relative importance of the data had necessarily to be weighed against the time and expense necessary for their collection, and particularly time-consuming investigations could not be carried out. This was the case both for the background research to the introductions of the letter series and for all the other work on which this volume is based.

criticized by the other editors, but each decided which changes should be made. The product of this joint enterprise is a homogeneous edition, but each editor remains fully responsible for his or her own work.

Walter Kamphoefner edited the Stille-Krumme, Blumner, Bauer, Loewen, Probstfield, and Witten series; Wolfgang Helbich the Pritzlaff, Weitz, Klein, Buerkert, Dorgathen, Kirst, and Dilger series; Ulrike Sommer the Lenz, Miller, Berthold, Heck, Klinger, Winkelmeier, and Wiebusch series. Kamphoefner also authored the introductory essays "German Immigration to the United States," and "The Sample," as well as the Farmers Introduction. Helbich wrote the introductory sections "Letters as Historical Documents," "The Contents of the Letters," "Earlier Editions," and "Editorial Policy," as well as the Workers Introduction. Sommer contributed the essay "Sources" as well as the Domestic Servants Introduction.

For the English version, Wolfgang Helbich added notes on each letter-writer's original German orthography, grammar, and style. General translation policies were set by the editors together with the translator, Susan Vogel. They also decided on changes in annotation from the original German version to meet the needs of an English-speaking readership. The translator worked closely with the three editors, who checked the accuracy of the translation of their own original texts and their own letter series. Drafts were then submitted to at least one other editor for additional comments. Walter Kamphoefner, the chief editor of the English version, then worked through the entire manuscript, adding final corrections with an eye on textual consistency.

I. Farmers

Introduction

The popular image of German immigrants in the United States is dominated by two clichés: most Germans (or at least more than average) farmed for a living, and the majority settled on free government land. Although these notions can even be found in the historical literature on German immigration, both are incorrect. German immigrants were disproportionately rural in their origins, but compared to the U.S. national average, they remained underrepresented in the American agricultural sector throughout the nineteenth century and into the twentieth.[1] The Homestead Act, making free land available to settlers, came into effect in 1862, when the first large wave of German immigration had already passed. Nor should the effects of this law be overestimated for subsequent periods; the majority of new farms continued to be purchased with hard cash, though compared to prices in Germany it often seemed as if land could be bought for a song.

Federal government policy regarding the sale of its considerable holdings set the framework for the German settler's acquisition of land. A few basic policies, in particular the systematic rectangular survey, had been established shortly after the Revolution. Starting in the late eighteenth century, the price of land was gradually lowered, and minimum purchase requirements were reduced, making it easier to buy land. In 1832, when the first significant wave of German immigration began, land cost $1.25 an acre, and a minimum purchase of forty acres was required. Thus, for

[1]According to Marschalck (1973), 82–84, for example, the closing of the American frontier around 1895 played a significant role in the decline in German immigrants, but cf. Kamphoefner (1987), 32–33, 80–82.

only $50 in cash, a settler could buy enough land for a viable farm. Policy was further liberalized in the pre–Civil War period. In 1841 right of preemption was granted to "squatters" who had settled extralegally on unsurveyed government land, and the 1854 Graduation Act gradually lowered the price of Federal land that had been on the market for ten years without being sold.[2]

So the stage was set for the free distribution of land to settlers by the Homestead Act. As soon as it became feasible with the exodus of Southern Democrats from Congress in the Civil War, the Republicans enacted this program, to attract the immigrant vote, among other reasons. The law of 1862 promised settlers 160 acres of government land if they built a house and lived on the land for five years—for only a filing fee of about ten dollars.

Other factors, however, limited the effects of this law for the poorer sectors of the population, especially in the cities. Aside from the cost of the land, establishing a farm required a considerable amount of money. A sum of $500 was probably the minimum required at the outset. Most of the available Homestead land was located on the prairies west of the Mississippi, and this caused additional problems. Wood for buildings and fuel was scarce. Although clearing land was difficult, it could be done on one's own and at no great expense. Breaking the black, sticky virgin prairie soil matted with grass roots, however, required a special plow and at least three teams of oxen or horses, which an ordinary farmer seldom owned. This "prairie breaking" alone incurred expenses of about $3 an acre, more than twice the standard government price of land.[3]

In addition, the Federal government also used its landholdings for economic and sociopolitical purposes that collided with the policy of promoting the agricultural middle class. Top priority was accorded to subsidizing the transcontinental railroad, and construction was advancing rapidly in the 1860s. A considerable amount of land was also granted by law to individual states and school districts, the proceeds of which were used to finance elementary schools and universities. The railroad companies alone received government land grants amounting to an area larger than the state of Texas. They were also permitted to choose their allotments first, before the rest was released for public purchase. The farmer came last in line: after the railroad companies, after the education system, and not infrequently after the speculators and frauds. It is hardly surprising, therefore, that during the last third of the nineteenth century, more farmers bought land from the railroad companies for four dollars an acre than received free land under the terms of the Homestead Act.

[2]Johnson (1976), 42–45, 61–64; Gates (1960), 51–80.
[3]Bogue (1963), 70–71; Gates, 179–88.

Whether on government or railroad land, a tremendous number of new farms were established in the post–Civil War period. In the 1870s alone, the number increased by some 50 percent. Regional and geographic preferences, however, prevented the Germans from taking as much advantage of land offers as some other immigrant groups. Their regional distribution and occupational profile were closely related. According to the 1870 census, the first to record the occupations of individual ethnic groups, Germans filled only 80 percent of their "quota" in agricultural occupations (compared to their share of the total work force). These patterns showed little change before the turn of the century, although a slight upward trend can be noted.[4]

A comparison with other ethnic groups, however, indicates that low German representation in the agrarian sector was not solely the product of high land prices. Although more Germans owned land than Irish, let alone members of the "new" immigrant groups like the Italians or East European Jews, they were clearly surpassed by the Norwegians, Danes, Swiss, and Dutch, and equaled by the Swedes and Bohemians or Czechs. Since the majority of these groups arrived in the United States after the Germans and hardly had more means at their disposal, these contrasts can be attributed to previous occupational experience and in particular geoclimatic preferences. The Scandinavians, for example, were apparently far more willing to accept the climatic extremes of Minnesota and the Dakotas in exchange for free farm land provided by the Homestead Act. Russian-Germans, too, having been acclimatized by several generations on the steppes, differed from other Germans in this regard.[5]

The expansion of the railroad network improved the possibilities for commercial agricultural production, exploited by Anglo-Americans and immigrants alike. Earlier, farmers on or near navigable rivers, like letter-writer Wilhelm Stille, profited from their convenient location. In the late nineteenth century, however, the railroads permitted increasing regional agricultural specialization. German settlement was concentrated in two economic areas: the Corn Belt, a wide band extending from Ohio to Missouri and Iowa dominated by corn and hogs; and, to an even greater extent, the Dairy Belt, a zone to the north extending across Wisconsin, Michigan, and upstate New York, particularly in the hinterlands of major urban areas. Wheat farming continued to shift westward into the prairies of Kansas and the Dakotas, an area too dry for corn and less attractive to the Germans. West of the one hundredth meridian, irrigation

---

[4]Hutchinson (1956), 79–82, 99–101, 122–24, 172–75, 220–21. It is unlikely that earlier German immigrants were more heavily engaged in agriculture. The 1850 and 1860 censuses show heavier German concentration in the larger cities (see Kamphoefner [1987], 80–82).
[5]Hutchinson, 34–46.

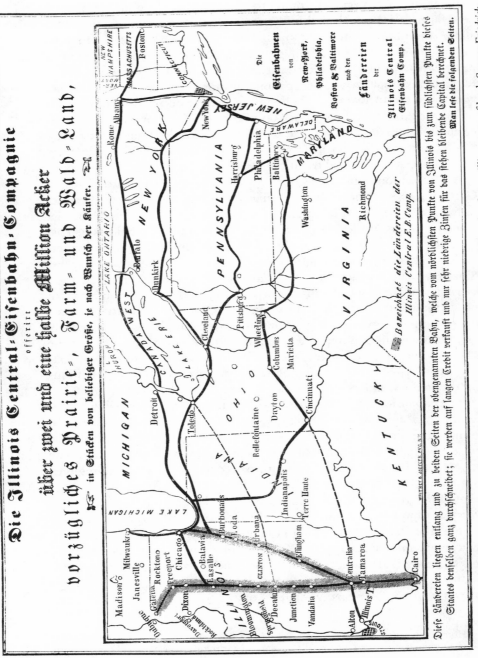

Figure 4. Advertisement in an immigration newspaper by the Illinois Central Railroad for sale of 2.5 million acres of land. *Source: Friedrich Gerhards: Wöchentlicher Unentgeltlicher Wegweiser*, August 6, 1855 (Hs. StA MR, Best. 122, Nr. 842).

was required for everything except cattle raising, and young animals were still driven to the Corn Belt for fattening. This specialization, although it made farms more efficient, also rendered them more prone to crisis.

Toward the end of the nineteenth century, farmers in the United States increasingly became victims of their own productivity. More about the agrarian protest movement of the 1890s can be found in the Probstfield series, Chapter 7. Suffice it to note here that crisis and protest were most intense in areas of agrarian monoculture—wheat on the western prairies or cotton in the South—whereas farmers in the Corn Belt, who were more diversified and had several alternative crops, were neither as hard-hit nor as radically politicized.[6]

Regardless of the similarities or differences to German landscape and climate, immigrant farmers were confronted by a sharp contrast in the cost of the two most important production factors. Land in the United States was incomparably cheaper, but labor was considerably more expensive than in Germany. This difference led almost automatically to larger average farm size and more widespread use of farm machinery.

The social structure of rural America differed from rural Germany above all in its much lower percentage of part-time and dwarf operations, an almost complete lack of a class of (white) farm laborers and a higher proportion of farmers who worked their own land. In all three German agricultural censuses, conducted in 1882, 1895, and 1907, farms under five acres, which were mostly part-time operations, accounted for about 58 percent of all farms. Farm size in the United States changed little in the late nineteenth century: from 1880 to 1910 the average size ranged from 134 to 147 acres, and only 9 percent of all farms in 1890 were smaller than twenty acres. Excluding farms in the South, figures not distorted by the effects of slavery and more applicable to the immigrants emerge. Although toward the end of the nineteenth century farm tenancy began to increase in the North as well as in the South, in 1880 less than one-fifth of all Northern farms were affected. As a result of the agricultural crisis, by 1900 tenancy rates surpassed one-quarter. At the turn of the century, however, 63 percent of all farms in the North were owner-operated without any rented land, compared to only 41 percent in Germany around 1895.[7]

Despite the larger size of operations, American farms always tended to

---

[6]Puhle (1975), 269; Bogue, 239–40. On the agrarian political movement see Puhle, 126–46; Shannon (1961), 291–328.

[7]The German figure increases to 54 percent if farms under five acres are excluded (*Historical Statistics* 1 [1975], 465; *Statistik des Deutschen Reichs* 112 [1898], 17*–18*; Grünberg [1922], 137–42).

rely more exclusively on family labor than those in Germany. According to the 1870 census, the average farmer paid $115 in cash or goods for labor, roughly the wages for one farmhand for about eight months. Around 1900, aside from the owner, there were four hands for every five farms, but two of them were family members. Nonfamily hands accounted for only one-quarter of agricultural labor; in Germany, by contrast, they were almost half. German (and also German-American) women were found working in the barns and fields much more frequently than their American counterparts.[8]

One of the most important questions for an American farmer, according to agricultural historian Allan Bogue, was "how to farm sitting down." It is much easier, however, to date the invention of a particular machine than to find out when it came into widespread use. The cultivation of wheat, by far the most important small grain in the United States, may serve as an example. Wheat was the first and most intensely mechanized crop. As early as 1834, Cyrus McCormick patented his first reaper, which initially did not even rake the bundles, much less bind them. The machines came into more widespread use only after 1848, when McCormick began mass production in Chicago near the heart of the grain-growing region. Innovations of this kind first took hold on larger farms, particularly in areas of specialized production. The number of McCormick's machines that were sold in only eleven highly productive counties in Illinois, for example, accounted for one-quarter of his total sales. On the eve of the Civil War, a day's work of ten to twelve acres could be accomplished by the reaper, now of the self-raking variety, which formed the bundles but still left them to be tied by hand. Lack of farm labor during the war then led to an increased demand for reapers: more were sold between 1861 and 1865 than in all the previous 25 years. The most important subsequent invention was the self-binding reaper. After it was perfected around 1880, there was little change in the wheat fields of the Middle West until the combine was introduced in the 1930s. It is significant that the number of wheat cradles peaked as late as 1880 but then rapidly declined.[9]

[8]USC A 1880.1, ix, 11; Shannon, 364; *Historical Statistics* 1:468; Grünberg, 167. Of all persons employed in the agrarian sector in Germany, the proportion of nonfamily farm laborers was 48 percent in 1882 and 45 percent in 1895. In 1907 it was only 34 percent, but this was because the number of female family members who worked on farms had almost tripled, reflecting more a change in definition than in behavior. Of persons employed in agriculture on a full-time basis in 1895, two-thirds were male, in 1907 only 52 percent. American statisticians apparently used a more restricted definition of female employment than did the Germans, but even in the 1910 census, which included a more thorough survey of women than usual, only 13 percent of farm workers were female. According to the census, German-American women were even somewhat underrepresented in farm labor, compared to other ethnic groups, but evidence to the contrary is provided by contemporaries, e.g., Rothe (1885), 190–92, and Bogue, 237.

[9]Puhle, 148; Bogue, chap. 8; Gates, 166, 186–88; Shannon, 126, 134–35; Rogin (1931), 69–119; USC M 1900.1, 351.

Other machines followed a similar pattern of development. The two-bottom riding plow existed as early as the 1860s, but its production accounted for only 5 percent of total plows in 1890 and 14 percent in 1900. But in 1880 it already accounted for almost 13 percent of production at the John Deere plant in Illinois, indicating that it was used more frequently in the Middle West than in the South or Northeast. Letter-writer Randolph Probstfield used such implements in the 1870s, a sign of his progressive attitude toward technology.[10] One operation—harvesting corn—remained largely unaffected by mechanization throughout the nineteenth century. There was no great need to innovate, since corn did not need to be harvested as quickly as wheat and could be left standing in the fields for two or three months without significant loss.[11]

In Germany bundles of grain were stored in barns before being threshed in the off-season, but in the hot, dry prairie summers, by contrast, wheat could be threshed straight from the fields after the grain had been cut and left to dry in shocks for several weeks. In the extremely dry climate west of the Rocky Mountains, farmers like letter-writer John Witten used a "header," which cut off the grain heads and loaded them directly onto wagons; they were then driven to be threshed immediately. Threshing machines, too, were constantly being improved. Before the Civil War, small machines powered by two horses on a treadmill were most commonly used. Larger machines driven by eight- to ten-horse circular "power sweeps" began to appear after 1850 in the main wheat areas on the prairies and came into general use during the 1860s. During the course of the 1870s, horsepower was gradually replaced by steam.

The spread of steam-powered threshing machines dramatically illustrates the differing pace of mechanization in the United States and Germany. In the United States as early as 1880, the main centers of wheat cultivation had converted to steam and less than one-fifth of the entire wheat harvest was still being threshed by horsepower. According to the German agricultural survey in 1882, by contrast, only 20 percent of farms that used threshing machines at all powered them with steam. In the following 25 years, too, the increase was only modest: in 1907 only one-third of all threshers were powered by steam. Of the farms between 50 and 250 acres, about one-quarter were using steam, and even on the estates with more than 250 acres, the figure was only two-thirds. Despite the fact that German farmers were under less time pressure to finish their threshing, the contrast is striking.[12]

The difference in extent of mechanization between the two countries

---

[10]Broehl (1984), 201–2, 212–16; USC M 1900.1, 351.

[11]Shannon, 136–37; Gates, 170.

[12]Rogin, 182–91; Bogue, 157–59; Rogin, 175–76; USC M 1900.1, 351; Grünberg, 140–42. See also the comparison of harvesting and threshing techniques in Franz et al. (1969), 306–27.

Figure 5. Wheat harvest with header on the farm of John Witten's son Henry, Douglas County, Washington, 1915.

can be observed for other types of machines as well. In the United States in 1861 more mowing machines were produced than were in use in Germany in 1882. German surveys include information about the number of farms that used threshing machines, mowing machines, grain drills, or any kind of steam power. Even when farms under five acres are excluded, the proportion of farms using machines is quite small: one-sixth in 1882, a good third in 1895, finally more than half in 1907, when the list of machines enumerated was expanded to eleven.[13] There is some evidence that American influence may have played a role in this increase. The effect, direct or indirect, that German immigrants had on this development is difficult to assess. But at any rate, the advantage of mechanization is one of the standard refrains of letters written by immigrant farmers.[14]

Immigrant farmers were confronted not only with new machinery but also with unfamiliar crops and methods of cultivation. In terms of acreage in Germany in 1895, rye was in the lead with fifteen million acres, followed by oats with ten, potatoes with seven and a half, and only then wheat with five, just slightly ahead of barley. The 125,000 acres of corn did not even amount to one half the acreage devoted to vineyards. In the United States around 1880, by contrast, corn overshadowed all other grain crops, with nearly double the acreage and four times the yield of wheat. Only half as much oats as wheat was grown, barley accounted for only 6 percent of the acreage of wheat, and rye even less. Potatoes were not as important to the daily diet as in Germany, and other root crops were so insignificant that they were not even listed in the agricultural census. Immigrants had little to do with the important staple crops like cotton and tobacco, as these were almost exclusively grown in the South.[15]

---

[13]Grünberg, 136–42; *Statistik des Deutschen Reichs* 5 (1885), 6; 112 (1898), 35*–37*; 211 (1913), part 2, 76–77. The figures for Germany do not indicate the exact number of machines in use, but instead the number of farms that used a given kind of machine in the past year. One machine, therefore, might have been used on several farms or several machines on one. The 1907 survey also included milk separators, potato planters and diggers, cultivators, and feed mills.

[14]In the 1890s the farm machinery industry in the United States experienced a boom in exports; total value increased five-fold during the decade to reach $16 million. A large part of this increase was due to the German market; in 1891 Germany was only the fourth largest customer, but by 1900 it challenged France for first place. Mowing machines and reaper-binders accounted for 86 percent of the agricultural machines imported by Germany—just the types of machines that were rapidly coming into widespread use. According to the 1882 survey, not even 20,000 farms had mowing machines for hay or grain, in 1895 about 35,000, but in 1907 the number had jumped to over 300,000. In terms of prices at the time, imports in the 1890s amounted to at least 150,000 mowers or 60,000 reaper-binders. Around 1910 about 50,000 foreign reapers per year were being imported into Germany (Haushofer [1972], 225–26; USC M 1900.1, 355). The figures above are based on an estimated price of $40 for a mower and $125 for a reaper-binder (see Broehl, 237; Shannon, 140; Franz, 307).

[15]*Statistik des Deutschen Reichs* 112:26; *Historical Statistics* 1:512–14.

Several recent studies in the United States have investigated the effects of the "cultural baggage" an immigrant brought to his agricultural practices in the New World. They conclude that Germans and other immigrants adapted with remarkable speed to geographic and climatic conditions. Both in Texas and Missouri, information in the agricultural census on an individual level indicates that Germans got used to corn very early and almost without exception, both in the field and on the table. In 1861 an immigrant in Missouri wrote in his first letter home, "Corn, that is Turkish wheat, . . . that's the most important thing in America, man and beast live from it." Although the Germans did not depend as exclusively on corn as their Anglo-American neighbors, they planted their other fields with wheat and only rarely with the old familiar rye. In their use of farm machinery, too, they hardly lagged behind the Anglo-Americans. The claim frequently made that German farmers were more productive, however, can hardly be substantiated.[16]

The effects of the German immigrants' "cultural baggage" are most clearly revealed in the Germans' attitude toward land. Land ownership was much more important to people who had known the problems of population pressure and land shortages than it was to those who viewed America's land reserves as vast and unlimited. As early as 1850 a higher percentage of Germans than Americans were landowners in both Missouri and Texas. Not only those who could exchange small, expensive plots in Germany for large and cheap pieces of real estate became landowners in the United States, but even immigrants from the rural lower class were able to achieve this status. The difference between peasant proprietors and their previous tenants was no longer based on whether one owned land at all, but merely on the size of landholdings. Land acquisition was also closely related to the German reputation for geographic persistence, compared to the "restless" Americans. Immigrant ambitions also extended to the following generation, and matters of inheritance were often settled when the owner was still alive, lest the farm be divided up according to U.S. inheritance laws. It is striking how many letter-writers in this edition helped their children to get started in farming by providing them with land. In this way German settlements in rural areas consolidated and expanded, while American neighbors gradually sold out and moved on. This cultural heritage has persisted to the present. In contrast to their lower representation in the nineteenth century, German-Americans comprised the largest ethnic group engaged in agriculture in the 1980 census. Of an American farm population of 5.6 million, one million claimed to be of "pure" and a further million of

---

[16]Kamphoefner (1987), 125–32; Jordan (1966); quote from Kamphoefner (1982), 196–98; Bogue, 211–13, 237–38.

"mixed" German descent, altogether more than one-third of all American farmers.[17]

Rapid economic adaptation, however, does not imply full social integration of German immigrants in Anglo-American society. This may sound paradoxical at first, since the network of German-American institutions that developed in the cities—the whole array of German clubs, for example—was unavailable in rural areas. Immigrant farmers living on their own, like letter-writer John Bauer, may well have experienced more pressure to assimilate than their urban counterparts, but when a "critical mass" was reached, rural immigrant settlements could largely shut themselves off from the rest of American society. The number of immigrant grandchildren who continued to speak German was two to five times higher in the country than in the big cities. The fact that these areas were sparsely populated certainly came into play: American farms seemed lonely and isolated even to immigrants used to the scattered farmsteads of northwest Germany, let alone those accustomed to the agricultural villages in the southwest.

The fate of German settlements depended to a great extent on whether immigrants were able to establish their own church congregations. Institutional life in rural areas was often restricted to the church and the local school (often church-affiliated). In fact, the role of the church in general, as the focal point of a rural community, can hardly be overemphasized. One study of settlement patterns in the Middle West has shown that German settlements in townships with their own congregations grew and flourished, while those without churches tended to decline. In all the letters written by farmers in this edition, except by freethinker Probstfield, the role of the church is clearly evident. Particularly striking in Franz Joseph Loewen's letters is his active participation in the small rural church and then his passive membership in the large urban congregation. If any living traces of German immigration can still be found in the United States today, they are in rural enclaves and above all in church congregations, some of which did not abandon the use of German until after World War II.[18]

[17]Conzen (1985a); Gerlach (1976), 37–38; Kamphoefner (1987), 173.
[18]Jordan, 104–6; Johnson (1951); Kamphoefner (1984), 30–32; Kamphoefner (1987), 170–200.

1

The Stille and Krumme Family

When Wilhelm Stille left his family farm in Lengerich in the Prussian Province of Westphalia in 1833, emigration from northwestern Germany had just begun. But the wave of emigrants swelled rapidly and soon carried other members of his family along: in 1836 his nephew, the following year his sister Wilhelmine and her fiancé Wilhelm Krumme from the neighboring village of Lienen, and ten years later a distant relative, Ernst Stille. All in all, at least eleven Stilles and twelve Krummes left these villages before 1871.[1] And they were by no means the only emigrants from this and other towns in the county of Tecklenburg. The entire area, which includes the neighboring districts of Osnabrück and Minden, shows the highest rate of emigration in Germany during the 1830s and 1840s. Throughout this period, about one percent of the population of the Osnabrück region left every year. The official figures in Tecklenburg are somewhat below this, but only because many people, such as Wilhelm Stille, emigrated illegally.[2] This was quite easy to do, since Lengerich and Lienen were located on the border. The officials in Hanover shed few tears over the recruits who escaped the Prussians, and the shippers of Bremen passed up no business opportunities on that account.

The demographic development of this region was strongly marked by waves of migration. Tecklenburg, which had been the most rapidly

[1]Schumann (1974), 11; Hunsche (n.d.), 147–48.
[2]Kamphoefner (1987), 12–16; Hunsche (1983), 145. Accordingly, more than one-seventh of the population of Lienen emigrated in the first ten years.

growing county in the Münsterland in the period following the Napoleonic Wars, experienced a downturn around 1834; stagnation was followed by a loss of population which continued for several decades. Between 1843 and 1858 the number of inhabitants declined by 6 percent, and in Lengerich as much as 10 percent. The population of Lienen and its two neighboring villages, Ladbergen and Westerkappeln, was lower at the founding of the German empire in 1871 than at the end of the Napoleonic era. It was not until 1927 that the population of Lienen regained the level it had attained in 1813.[3]

This loss of population can be traced above all to the decline in cottage linen production. Seasonal work in Holland, where the eldest Stille brother had settled in 1820, also became less profitable. The people who suffered most from this development belonged to the rural lower class, the so-called *Heuerleute* [tenant farmers], who depended most heavily on sources of income outside farming. They owned neither house nor land and had to rent a cottage and a few acres of land from a peasant farmer or *Kolon.* Combining migrant work in Holland, the production of home-grown flax, and occasional work for the owner of the large farmstead, the tenant farmers attempted to keep their heads above water. As the population increased, survival became increasingly difficult. The situation grew even more critical when the common lands belonging to the villages were divided up in the 1820s (without taking the tenant farmers into account), when conditions for the seasonal workers in Holland began to deteriorate in the 1830s, and with the decline of the cottage linen industry in the 1840s as a result of industrialization. The only route of escape from this predicament was thus to go abroad. Large farmsteads were bequeathed to one heir undivided (in Tecklenburg usually to the youngest son), but this, too, offered no protection against the pressures of a growing population.[4]

Wilhelm and Wilhelmina Stille's father did own a full farmstead, but they were not his heirs. They could have stayed on the family farm only as unmarried hands, as did several of their other siblings. Learning a skilled trade and working in the village might also have been an alternative, at least theoretically, but the decline in the linen industry meant that opportunities here were also few and far between. In their village, thus, there was no viable alternative to the life of a tenant farmer. Marriages such as the one between the farmer's daughter, Wilhemina, and the tenant farmer's son, Wilhelm Krumme, were not regarded as appropriate and

[3]Reekers/Schulz (1952), 45–50; Hunsche (1983), 145.

[4]Johann Rudolph Stille, born in 1785, married a Dutch woman from a neighboring village on May 30, 1820, in Meppel, Holland. Further entries in the ev. KB Meppel suggest he settled there permanently (Gladen [1970], 27–71, 139–49; Kamphoefner [1987], 40–51).

acceptable, a fact that no doubt influenced their decision to emigrate as well. Family members who left the farmstead did receive a considerable lump-sum settlement from the heirs, but it was easier to begin a new life with this money in America than it was at home. Farm owners emigrated only very rarely, their children more often. The more typical emigrants from Tecklenburg and other areas in northwest Germany were tenant farmers or their children, like Ernst Stille, who left in 1846, and Wilhelm Krumme, as well as the majority of their other friends mentioned in the letters.[5]

Although the phenomena of chain migration and strong cohesion within groups from the same part of the country can be found everywhere in the new world, these tendencies are especially evident in the Stille/Krumme correspondence, and among the emigrants from Tecklenburg in general. The towns of Ladbergen and Westerkappeln could claim daughter villages in rural Ohio and Missouri, respectively, and these also attracted many countrymen from the neighboring towns of Lengerich and Lienen as well. But immigrants from Tecklenburg also maintained "outposts" in all of the larger cities along the major traffic routes—New Orleans, Baltimore, Wheeling, Louisville, and above all St. Louis and Cincinnati.[6] No other series of letters contains so many references to relatives, friends, and acquaintances. The extent to which accommodations, jobs, and even marriage partners were arranged by this network of countrymen is truly striking. Both Ernst Stille and Wilhelm Krumme (after the death of Wilhelmina Stille) found marriage partners from Tecklenburg. Wilhelm Stille's choice of a Swiss girl, however, was influenced by his location: in Monroe County, Ohio, where Stille settled, there were almost as many immigrants from Switzerland as from Germany, and in Switzerland Township where he lived, even more.

His brother-in-law Wilhelm Krumme remained on the other side of the Ohio River near Wheeling, Virginia (after 1863 West Virginia). German settlers there made up about one-seventh of the population in 1860, but it was 1880 before they were able to support a daily German-language newspaper, although there had been a short-lived weekly publication as early as 1850. The nearby village of Triadelphia could count only a few Germans among its two hundred inhabitants, but in 1850 three other families from Lienen lived in Krumme's immediate neighborhood. Cincinnati, where Wilhelm Krumme found his second wife and where Ernst

[5]Background information on the case of the Stille family is provided by Schumann (1979); tax assessments are given by Leesch (1974), 296; for a discussion of the occupations of emigrants see Kamphoefner (1987), 40–51.
[6]Fleischhauer (1970), 23–34; Kamphoefner (1987), 73–78, 85–99.

Stille settled, was an important transshipment center on the Ohio River. Of all the cities in America, Cincinnati was second only to Milwaukee in terms of its percentage of German inhabitants. In 1850 almost 30 percent of the population had been born in Germany, many of them in the northwestern region. Naturally, the German population affected the cultural life of the city. The German-language weekly that was founded in 1836 had become a daily newspaper as early as 1838. By 1860 there were three daily papers for the 45,000 German immigrants, as well as one Catholic and several Protestant weeklies and one Jewish publication.[7]

At the time of Stille's arrival, Wheeling, with its five thousand residents, was about the same size as the parishes of Ladbergen or Lienen, including outlying farms, but the latter then suffered subsequent losses, whereas Wheeling tripled in size in the following thirty years—yet fell behind other comparable American cities. Cincinnati's growth was much more dynamic, particularly between 1830 and 1850, when its population more than quadrupled, reaching 115,000 by mid-century.

What practical experience did the Stilles and Krummes bring along to help them adapt to this strange and rapidly changing environment? Unless they had served in the army, it is doubtful that they were familiar with any German cities larger than Münster or Osnabrück, both of which were about 25 miles away and had populations under twenty thousand. Although he was already 32 when he emigrated, Wilhelm Stille had clearly spent a long time, and perhaps all of his life, on the family farm. In the list of emigrants, the 28-year-old Wilhelm Krumme is referred to as a smith, but there is no evidence that he ever worked this trade in America. Ernst Stille was just a farmhand, emigrated at the age of 24, and had hardly more than the money for his crossing. He came from a family that had to "slave away terribly" and could hardly even pay for the postage for their letters.[8] The handwriting in these letters, too, hardly suggests that the writers were particularly sophisticated. A keen business acumen, however, is as evident as the bad spelling and traces of local dialect.

Wilhelm Stille, for example, undertook a speculative business trip on a flatboat, shipping a load of agricultural products 1,500 miles down the Ohio and Mississippi rivers to New Orleans. And after Wilhelm

[7]In 1860 6 percent of the population of Monroe Co., Ohio, were Germans and 4 percent Swiss; MC 1850: Ohio Co., Va.; USC 1850.1, 399; Arndt/Olson (1965), 433–59, 645–46.

[8]Osnabrück had a population of only eleven thousand in 1833; Münster reached twenty thousand only in 1843. Wilhelm mentions more than once that his "sweat" had contributed to the assets of the farm. Details on Krumme are given in Müller (1964–66), #422, as well as in the corresponding files in StA MS; #3094 may be the Ernst Stille mentioned here.

Krumme had bought his own farm, he rented it out so as not to pass up the high wages being paid for work on public construction projects. When buying his land, he considered not only the fertility of the soil but also its convenient access to markets. Ernst Stille worked in subtropical New Orleans in the winter and in Cincinnati in the summer, and he saved on his travel costs by working on the river boat that plied between the two cities. All of this had less to do with the previous experience of these people than with the fact that they were now living in an environment in which they could, and in fact had to, develop their gifts and talents. As soon as she arrived, Wilhelmine Stille noted that her brother Wilhelm, who had emigrated four years earlier "is so much smarter than he was in Germany." Of course the new start was easier for people who emigrated with money or were supported by their relatives at home. The case of Wilhelm Stille gives one the impression that his appetite grew with the eating. After he had bought land, he needed a house; after the house, a barn; after the barn, farm machinery. The money he took along amounted to almost 300 talers; during the next 25 years he received again as much from home. The tenant farmer's son Krumme was worse off; Kolon Stille had to pitch in to outfit him with sturdy shoes for the journey. But his fiancée Wilhelmina was endowed with over 300 talers worth of money and goods (some of which was paid after her death) which Krumme then inherited.[9] Ernst Stille and many of the other emigrants from Tecklenburg who appear in the letters had to make do with far less.

Though in this series we have to deal with five different writers, their characterization need not be overly long or complicated, since four of them write quite similarly. Wilhelm Stille shows the results of undoubtedly good schooling. His spelling is acceptable, his punctuation good, his sentences clear and well constructed.

His sister Wilhelmina has very similar writing, though she seems to have less practice than her brother. Wilhelm Krumme, by contrast, appears slightly superior to Wilhelm Stille, for in addition to good mechanics, he expresses himself more precisely. Caroline Krumme's writing is not too different, either, though she combines a fine vocabulary with utter disdain for punctuation. All of the above reveal a certain influence of Low German, both in spelling and in syntax.

Outstanding for this group of Krummes and Stilles is Ernst Stille, whose writing is so accomplished that one is tempted to assume that he received the equivalent of a good grammar school education.

[9]Not all of the money transfers are mentioned in the letters, but the heir to the farmstead, Eberhard Stille, kept records of them all (see Schumann [1979]).

Wilhelm Stille

[Spring 1834]

Dear parents, brothers and sisters,

If I can still call you that, and you are all still alive, I want to let you know that I am as healthy as I've almost never been before, I'd like to hope it's the same with you and I'm not in the position to tell any of my relatives to come here except Rudolph,[10] if he were here, he'd do all right. He could learn cabinetmaking and earn ½ dollar from the first day on, also learn to read and write English and also good clothes, but then he'd have to stay till he's 21, by that time he'd be earning money and after that he could earn one dollar and even 1½ dollars a day, but young boys like that have to have someone give bond so they don't run away toward the end, now he could do well with my boss's brother, I told him about it already, he said it was a shame I didn't bring him along, he wanted to give him a job right now. If he wants to risk it and come here, write me a letter and he can best come here when the families whom Wittenbrok[11] wrote to come over, and he must also bring at least 15 talers with him across the ocean otherwise he can't get to here, travel in this country costs quite a lot, and Heinrich[12] hasn't got enough money to come here and buy anything, if you can't bring 1,200 talers you have a tough time, but then it can all work out, but even someone like that still has to work, there's no other way. I haven't made a lot up to now, here at the mill I only made 5 dollars the first month, after that 6½ dollars with free board and washing, after that I went to the distillery and get 10 dollars a month, but that'll be over soon. He [his boss] wants to rent out the distillery and maybe sell the mill. My boss is a joiner and his brother is a carpenter, now they both want me to work for them, I don't know yet if I'll do that, and the mill isn't sold yet and the distillery isn't rented yet, and if I can get work in a distillery that's the best, that's a good *Profesjon,* if you know what you're doing you can earn 300 talers a year. That's better than working at the whetstone, where what you earn in the summer you use up again in the winter. Here there are enough people running around who've been here 6, 7, 8 years and still don't have 5 talers to their name, what they earn in the summer they spend in the winter, but that won't happen to me, I left with 44 pistoles and when I come back to you I think I'll bring 100 pistoles back, then you'd have something to rely on, and whether I will

[10]He is probably referring to his nephew Rudolph Stille, born in 1815 (hereafter designated by b.), the illegitimate son of his sister Marie Elisabeth. Rudolph did, in fact, emigrate (illegally) in 1836 (Müller [1964–66], #4611).

[11]Probably Ernst Heinrich Wittenbrock (b. 1789), *Kolon* from Lienen, who emigrated in 1833 with his wife and seven children between the ages four and nineteen (Müller [1964–66], #6304; see also Hunsche [1983], 251).

[12]Probably his brother Heinrich Stille (b. 1789).

come again I don't know myself, and if I'd learned a trade like Buddmeier I'd never want to see Germany again, all winter long he made 1 taler 1 silbergroschen a day and what'll happen to those who don't know a trade I can't imagine, for they can't save enough to start a farm. [. . .] The Americans want to see a lot of work done in a day, and anyone who thinks he can get by easy shouldn't come here. The Americans are strong and quick, they can do more in one day than the Germans, but they don't want to work every day. Here around me some 80 families have settled, and almost all of them have a hard time keeping themselves clothed and having enough to live on, that's why it's best if Heinrich doesn't come here and tries to get married there, and if he or Teljohan wants to buy something I'd say they should buy something small and not get into debt, then they'll be ruined fast even if they don't think so at first and Rudolph he can still come in two years' time and in that time I can write you more than today. And if I can't earn 10 dollars a month here with board then maybe I'll go to Neuorliens toward winter, to South America, that's another 2,100 miles farther than where I am today, that's where you can earn the most money and here the least, but I came here together with Wittenbrok and other Germans looking for a good chance to buy something. Rider Schilling Schmitte and Delbrüge from Lienen they stayed in Baltemore, they may earn more than I do, and Stapenhorst wrote and told me what they had written they also wanted to come here but they all didn't have enough money to come here, when I was in Baltemore I went to see Pastor Stapenhorst's widow's son,[13] he said Sporleder wasn't there any more, where he was and where he is now he didn't know. [9 ll.: had written him, no answer] Now don't any of you worry about me, if I can't stay here any longer then I can go back again as easily as I came here. So enjoy your work and the time won't seem so long. Also please watch out for dear mother that she doesn't do any work that's hard and anytime she doesn't have any money one of you should give her one taler, that will help out for a long time and won't hurt you much, don't any of you drink liquor, it's a very bad thing. [4 ll.: closing; signature]

When you write to me again then take the letter to Otten so it can be put in Wittenbrok's letter. And write and tell me about everything and as soon as you can and don't gossip about this letter, and copy out the other letter and send it to sexton Plage in Ibbenbüren [3 ll.: instructions] for I had to swear to the sexton and many other people that they would hear from me.

[13]Florenz Stapenhorst, son of a pastor's widow, emigrated from Lengerich as one of the first in 1832. Conrad W. Stapenhorst, perhaps a relative, traveled with Stille in 1833 (Müller [1964–66], #6, #63; and Schumann [1979]).

And write a note to the stage drivers in Osnabrük, tell them that I wrote and that even if they were my own brothers then I couldn't tell them they should come here or stay there, some like it here and some don't, and tell them I'm grateful that they helped me get to Bremen and put the letter in Benat's house and address it to the stage drivers Brune or Wolf. [9 ll.: advice on emigration: bad for beekeepers, good for wooden shoemakers]

And if you get a letter from the postmistress you can read it and then put it in the next letter you write me. I wrote her a nice letter. And you should tell all the Drieses that I wrote that bread grows on trees here.

Write and tell me when I was born, and you should take out more fire insurance on your house.

Pauhetten Peint [Powhatan Point, Ohio], February 16th
[1836; see below]

Dear parents, brothers and sisters,

[8 ll.: was sick for two months, now recovered] And up until New Year's I was at the steam mill, where I had my first job, but now I work for a merchant, ¼ hour from my old boss, there I get 10 dollars a month again, plus board and washing, and that's all grand, and I don't have to work much, we don't have any land besides a small garden behind the house, but two horses to ride that I have to take care of and watch out for a bit at the *Pathaus,* and enjoy a contented life such as I never had in Germany. Dear parents, someone wanted to know if we have German churches here, there are enough here, and it's a great pleasure for us to hear the gospel preached as well as in Germany, but I wouldn't tell any family to come here just because of that, except young people, for it's hard to travel as a family and it costs quite a lot, and when you first come to this country you don't know the language and face an uphill climb, that's why many people take a long time to get over their trip. But when they've been here for a while and get a feel for freedom, and see the good crops growing here and all without manure, and that the land is so easy to work, then they think differently, then they feel sorry for their friends who are still in Germany, and spending all day from early morning to late evening working to pay their taxes, and having to eat such bad food, not even meat every day, and here even three times a day, and all sorts of dishes that I can't write about very well. You also wrote me that our brother-in-law bought part of the Shulte place but if someone comes over here with so much money he'll do much better, that I can write to my countrymen in good conscience. Families that come over here and want to buy land should bring all kinds of tools along but no axes, they're

not even worth picking up compared to the American ones. If you have clothes bring them along but if you bring the money for them it's almost as good, I don't see any difference in the prices, except for linen, that's almost three times as expensive here, a family would be wise to bring along a piece of linen and of flannel along with their own clothes. One thing I'll tell you, I talked to a friend of mine who's been here over a year already, he told me the people over there say what an awful country this is, people don't even have any milk to put in their coffee, that's true and that's because they drink coffee here without milk because the cows don't come home all the time, and the cows suckle their calves, like over there sheep suckle the lambs, and when the cows have calves they don't come home then they stay in the woods, and the women are too lazy to go and get them if they don't have a horse and saddle, there's nothing they'd rather do than ride around a bit and go to the stores and buy all kinds of things that's their favorite pastime, and to sleep late in the morning, then the husband has to make the fire, and the men here are like this, what they earn one day they have to drink up the next. [6 ll.: details about food] But I'll tell you the most unpleasant thing as far as I know that's when you don't know the language and you're not with your friends and the Americans want to talk to the Germans. [35 ll.: instructions about the trip to Bremen, equipment and behavior at sea; wages; closing]
I remain your / true son / Wi Stille 1836
[2 ll.: address]

Pauhatten Peint, October 18th [1837; see below]
Dear parents, brothers and sisters,

Divine Providence and love of you leads me to send news of us to you; and my news is that I am now quite well, have little work and am still earning well, my wage has improved I get 12½ talers a month, and free board and washing. Besides I can write that Wilhelmina and Wilhelm Krumme arrived in good spirits, they came to me to the Kaptin on August 19th[14] and are both quite healthy, they're both working at a German tavern not 10 paces from my house. Wilhelmina gets 1 taler a week and Wilhelm Krumme gets 9 talers a month. But I must tell you the sad news about Rudolph[15] that is sure to hurt you. He was overcome by an illness which is not easy to cure. He had dysentery, and at the end dysentery with blood and it caused him great pain and anguish, although

[14]Wilhelmina Stille and Wilhelm Krumme left Lengerich on May 23, 1837 (see Schumann). Müller (1964–66), #422, lists Krumme as a blacksmith. "Kaptin" is Captina Creek, which flows into the Ohio at Powhatan Point.
[15]See n. 10 above.

he had a good doctor who came twice a day and at the end even at night, he couldn't help him though, now I am forced to write you the sad news that he has gone to his death. [5 ll.: condolences] And with the funeral everything was very proper, a large number of Germans and also many English were at the funeral, and he was buried in the German graveyard and the pastor gave an excellent speech about him, the pastor thought so highly of him, he went to church twice almost every Sunday and got to know the preacher as soon as he came to Pittsburch. He went straight from the Kaptien to Pittsburch to learn a trade, since he got chilled so quickly and was so sickly people said he should learn to be a glassmaker, that's an easy *Propheffesjon,* in a warm room in the winter and not in the sun in the summer, and all so easy, he signed up for three years. [12 ll.: details about wages; he was soon ahead of the other apprentices] I can't write anymore this time.

I remain / your devoted son / W Stille / 1837.
[10 ll.: greetings, address]

Howe got smallpox on the ship and was taken to the hospital in Baltemore and died there.

Wilhelmina Stille

[probably October 1837]

Dearly beloved parents, brothers and sisters,

[11 ll.: health, about Rudolph's death] I like it very much here, I have an easy job and peace of mind and the fact that Wilhelm is so nearby makes me very happy, he eats three times a day at our house and the other two clerks too, and that Wilhelm is so much smarter here than he was in Germany I wouldn't have believed it, but I think it's because he has so little work that is easy and he goes all around and talks with all the clever people about all kinds of business and so on, the people are all so good to me, one person says to me come to my house for a week and another one says the same thing, so I don't know where to go, one time we went riding after church, me and the two Wilhelms and one of the clerks and we rode to his parents' and there we were treated like at a wedding, but the one thing that weighs heavy on our hearts is that we think about our dear mother so often and it makes us so sad that she had to suffer so much because of us and still has so much to fret about and suffer what with our bad father that she still has no rest day or night, but dear brother Friderich and Eeberadth and Schallote please do what you can for our dear mother, let her eat and drink whatever she wants to, the dear Lord will repay you many times over, and dear mother, thank you a thousand times for the good things you did for me, but don't grieve for me, I'm much better off here than with you, that's because you can live in peace over here and the people aren't so false. And Friederich, we thank you for the address, dear sister Elisabeth don't grieve for your son that he died, he's sure to be much better off now than anyone with even the best place in America.

And as for your coming here it's no good, there are people who have three thousand talers and are sorry that they came here, the trip cost so much that I didn't believe it myself, the Americans aren't ashamed to overcharge the Germans, dear sister Schallothe,[16] I can't say you should come here, because you're too old to be a servant and buying land isn't like what everyone says, now one other thing for you, dear brother Eeberadt, please send me a woollen coat, blue or brown but a nice one like the rich folks in Lengerich wear, give my best to Heinerich Jäger, and his wife can sew the coat for me, she knows best how it should be, and I must tell you that everyone should bring silver and gold along and not get a draft for it for people get cheated with drafts, and then I want to tell you something about the trip we were on the water for 52 days, it's not very pleasant and it's far worse for those with children. [6 ll.: details] We wanted to buy some land but we don't have enough money, one third has to be paid at once, if you would be so kind as to send me 100 talers more I would be very pleased. Now I hope that you do as I ask, you mustn't think we don't like it in service, that we want to be our own masters, we still want to work for two years to earn the rest. [3 ll.: greetings] So write me as soon as you can what's happened at home and who else wants to go to America. [4 ll.: wages, as in Wilhelm's of October 18, 1837; signature]

Wilhemina Stille Krumme

[Winter 1838–39]

Dearly beloved mother, brothers and sisters,

[4 ll.: received first letter, but not second] The third one we received on August 24th and read that our father was dead[17] which upset us because we didn't expect his departure but one must be content for he had quite a long life, I have to tell you that Krumme left his first boss in April, and went to Adolp Oberhelman, he gave him 15 talers a month and now he's given him 2 miles of rocks to pound[18] now he's got it, since he's working he earns a lot and that's how he wanted to have it, for work is a real pleasure for him. Here now he had to go into boarding with someone

---

[16]It is unclear which of the four Stille sisters was named Charlotte; none was so baptized. Elisabeth's three sisters were 43, 36, and 32 years old.

[17]Their father died on January 13, 1838, at the age of 81.

[18]Stille worked on the National Road, which led from the east coast through Triadelphia to Wheeling.

else, that came to 2 talers every week and then he had to pay 2 gute groschen for each piece of washing and here everything has to be washed every week, so Oberhelman told him to get married, for he wouldn't lose anything on it. 2 talers would easily do for food for the two of us. And also because his work clothes were all torn and the Americans don't want to mend the old clothes of the Germans, so we got married on August 10th, Oberhelman drove with his nice wagon to pick up our German pastor named Langforst, born in Unnau, that's four hours away and we ate and drank at his house, from there we drove to Alxander which is 1 hour from there, there he married us and the text we had was Psalm 2 verse 11. Serve the Lord with fear, and rejoice with trembling, and when we came back we had another meal and a good time then he took him home again and all for free, but we gave the pastor 2 talers. [3 ll.: food prices, higher because of the drought] So we want to tell you that we've bought 80 acres of land and our brother has too, they are next to one another but his is so much better it cost 400 talers and ours 300 talers, we paid 200 talers of it since we didn't have any more, but our brother paid for all of his, we were supposed to pay it all too, but we begged so much that they gave us time until July 4th, if we don't pay, it will be sold again. So we're asking you, dear mother and brothers in the name of the Lord, send me the rest of my money, add up everything I've already gotten, even if it isn't much I'll be happy. Buy me a coat first and have it made for me because it costs too much here, dear mother and brothers, please don't fail me because we have nowhere else to turn. The new start cost us a lot, we had to buy feathers for the beds, a pound costs 16 gute groschen, and we bought a cow [. . .] and then all the other things that you have to have, send it with Friederich Krumme since we think he is coming to stay with us, you wanted to know how big the city is where we live, there are two storekeepers who trade in carpenter's tools, all sorts of things, cloth and dry goods, hardware, plows, shovels, axe and all sorts of pots and pans, flour and a little of every kind of *Merdesien* [merchandise]. A steam mill, a tavern and also a few more houses they're all in a row along the water, that's called the *Rewe* [river] that's where the steamboats come and load everything in and out and when people want to get on or off the steamboat they have to go there, the place is 22 miles from Welingen [Wheeling] and Piethsborg is another 45 miles beyond Welingen. I also want to tell you that my brother Wilhelm left his boss last fall and went down the river on a boat that was loaded with all kinds of goods, flour, potatoes, string beans, cabbage, onions, apples, half of it was his and two others had a quarter of it each. The city is called Neuoliens which is 15 hundred miles away it's in South America there they can't grow such things but none of them made much with it because last year there was too much of everything. And when he got back he started to work on his land, he's built himself a house and has already cleared 3 acres of farmland. [10 ll.: his plans to marry a Swiss girl didn't work out] We live 3 hours away from Welingen right on the road and are very happy for I have a happy marriage and live in peace. Peace nourishes, discord consumes. The Otthermans want to stay here this winter[19] because the water is so low they can't go any farther inland. I must also let you know that old Witthenbrock is dead and the eldest daughter is married.[20] [16 ll.: correspondence, greetings from W. Krumme] Friederich Krumme has to pay for half of the postage.

[about 1839]

Dearly beloved mother, brothers and sisters,

[6 ll.: received letter, is happy and healthy] My brother Wilhelm is also quite well, he is eleven German hours away from us, he's working in a distillery and earns 18 talers a month in the clear, I think he'll be getting married next fall if it's God's will, for he's built a nice house on his place and cleared 15 acres and he can plant a lot there. We live near Oberhelmann's, three hours from Weelingen, Wilhelm still works for Oberhelmann for he is a good man. Everything here costs a lot. [5 ll.: prices] Wilhelm took the letters to my brother himself he told him he couldn't write this time for it was Saturday when Wilhelm was there and on Sunday he had to be a godfather for a child three hours away from there, the Germans all have their children baptized but the Americans don't know anything about that, if it's a boy the father gives it the name, and if a girl, then the mother, there are such strange beliefs here, when people are grown up the pastor puts them completely under water then they believe they are all clean, they can never sin again, and some think that once they've had communion they can't do anything evil. [7 ll.: financial affairs; greetings; closing]

You three have to pay for the postage together.

Dear mother please send me some thread. [30 ll: from *Wilhelm Krumme*, probably at the same time as the previous letter: mostly about financial affairs; also signed by Wilhelmina]

[probably Fall 1839]

Dearly beloved mother, brothers and sisters,

[4 ll.: correspondence] We also want to let you know that I gave birth on July 13th to a beautiful baby boy who amazes everyone. His name is

---

[19]Johann W. Ottermann (b. 1811) emigrated with his sister and widowed mother in 1838. He later settled in Missouri (see Müller [1964–66], #564; Kamphoefner [1982], 188).

[20]Wittenbrock was about fifty years old when he died; his daughter Catharina Elisabeth was twenty at the time. See n. 11 above.

Johannes. [6 ll.: named after the neighbor's boy who fetched the doctor] The baby was born before the doctor came. They don't have midwives here everyone has a doctor, for the first 2 weeks I was very weak but afterwards quite healthy. I also want to tell you that my brother Wilhelm got married on July 4th which is a holiday here to Chatharina Kreps,[21] born in Zweitzerland, her father lives near his place, further we want to tell you that we have sold for 500 talers the 80 acres we bought and have bought another 120 acres where 25 to 30 acres have been cleared, but we still owe 100 talers on it which we have to pay by July 4th; you wrote us that you wanted to send us some more money, we talked about it with Wilhelm, he said that's too little, he figured out he should get another 300 talers besides what he's already gotten, he figured it for the work he did, but we don't want to tell you what you have to do, do what you think is fair according to your conscience, when we add it all up it comes to 137 talers that we've already received, you can add it all up yourselves when you write again let me know how little Friedericka[22] is doing for she means a lot to me, I dream about her so often and call out her name. Dear sister Schallotha if you can't marry well over there and would like to, I think it would be better for you to come over here with Friederich Krumme, if you all agree and our dear mother and brothers there are satisfied with it, if you bring all your money then you can buy something here and then you'll be much better off than over there. For my life I wouldn't want to live in Germany again since I live here so happily and in such contentment as a person could wish but you have to follow your own mind, if you don't really want to then it's better that you stay there. [. . .] [39 ll.: from *Wilhelm Krumme:* financial affairs]

Wilhelm Stille

Traiedelphia December 25th, 1840

Dear mother, brothers and sisters,
    [14 ll.: suffers from arthritis]
    2. I want to tell you what happened 2 years ago this fall, then I went to South America to see what it was like there and I also wanted to earn something trading since many have made a fortune there doing that, but that year all the speculators lost money, but not me because I was lucky enough to have so many different kinds of foodstuffs. [8 ll.: details] But because of all the different things listed above I still earned 80 talers, but I can only say 40 talers since I was gone for 4 months, and I didn't like the

[21] According to MC 1850 Catharina Kreps was 23 years old at that time.
[22] Presumably the illegitimate daughter of Wilhelmina's sister Maria Sophia, born on March 23, 1831.

area since they have to buy all their food and there are too many sicknesses.

3. I want to tell you that I didn't have any land yet, and I felt weak and
tired of making the crooked straight for other people and wasn't all that
content, and then I thought I'd risk buying myself some land and then get
married, so I'd finally have a home for myself before I turn gray, and I did
both. The land I bought is quite good, but my wife is much better. She is
25½ years old, pretty, easygoing, friendly, hard-working and virtuous,
and we live in such pleasant harmony that I can't even tell you how happy
and content. She came with her family 1 year ago from Switzerland, and
my father-in-law lives 3 miles away from us that is one German hour,
right on the Ohio River, his place is worth 2,000 talers and he has money
besides, and there are 9 children, she is the oldest and did the most work,
and he promised her the most, and what she received you can read as
follows, an old bed, that was the long and short of it, and I had a
wedding. On July 4th, 1839, and a young son on March 26th, 1840. All
very fine.

4. I was supposed to write whether it would be good for Ernst to
come here or not, I and Wilmena and Krumme think he should come
here, if he can't get work right off then he can come to me I'll give him
work for one year or 2 years, the first year I'll give him 50 talers if I can't
give it to him right away then I'll give him interest on it and my wife will
also mend his clothes.

5. The rumor is out that my sister Eliesabeth is uncertain if she should
come here or not, but we strongly advise stay there stay there. They
know what they have and don't know what they can get again.

6. You wanted to know how such poor families here get along, they
rent a room or a chamber and then they work for a daily wage in the rain,
snow and cold wind and when such people are lucky, in 4 to 6 years they
can maybe earn enough to buy a 40 acre piece of bush, then they have to
work 5 years more before they get anything done and that is hard work, a
weak man can't get through it. [7 ll.: 7. brother Friedrich's health; 8.
thanks for money sent—was desperately needed]

9. I read the settlement contract and as far as I'm concerned it's done in
quite a brotherly manner but you don't need to be alarmed, you can still
get a paunch with it, as big as Obermeier in Alstiegen near Ibbenbüren [7
ll.: details]

10. If Friederich Krumme comes over here please send me as much
money as you can since I really need it since I have 160 talers debts, which
you maybe don't believe but it's the sad truth, [6 ll.: was sick for three
months] And my land cost me 385 talers, my house 118 talers! My house
is all made of wood with English windows and I have a *Flohr* made of

pine upstairs and down, [. . .] and I had 10 acres of land cleared, that cost me 70 talers, 7 talers an acre and when it was done I gave the people a tip of 1 taler. [6 ll.: gave them beer and bread at the end, they were needy] And 4 months after my wedding I wanted to move in, the house was there all right, but nothing inside. Then I went to Wehlingen [Wheeling] and bought another 95½ talers worth of things an iron cook stove 26 talers, a copper kettle to please my wife 6 talers, 6 chairs etc. If I listed everything it would take too many words.

11. Then with God's help we moved in and worked hard and all the livestock we had that was [- - - - -] a cat up to July 1st then I bought a cow for 18 talers and also a calf and 2 oxen for 44 talers and a plow that's good with the roots for 5 talers.

12. And what do you think of my 12th verse I built a double barn which cost me 250 talers besides my neighbors' help for which they only take food and drink. [45 ll.: still more to build; details; 13. prices for his produce; 14. correspondence; 15. trust in God, his wife stands by him, they're hard-working; health matters] And just as I have no doubts about God's help, so also I have faith that you will send me something with Ernst and Krumme to pay off the 160 debt mentioned earlier, for which I have to pay 10 talers per 100 interest.

16. Finally I ask all of you together to take as good care of our dear old mother as you can and be so kind as to send me a few seeds from the big curly cabbage and a few sweet pea seeds. And also a bit of thread.

No 17. At the very end I have the privilege to give you all my best [4 ll.: questions about their well-being; closing]

Wilhelmina Krumme

[probably early 1841 or 1842]
Dearest beloved mother, brothers and sisters,

We want to let you know that Schoppenhorst and Sophia Krummen arrived and stopped by on October 24th, and they are well and brought everything for us, so we heard that you are well which makes us very happy and that we have a new sister-in-law[23] which is just as we would wish. [10 ll.: congratulations; thanks for cloth; all are well] These are bad times now, there's not much work and if you work the pay is not good, that's because we're getting a new *Presedenten,* here there's a new one every 4 or 8 years, if he's good then he stays for 8 years otherwise only 4 years, with the changeover it's always a little bad, we've lost our best

[23]Sophia, Wilhelm's sister who was born in 1816, emigrated without official permission (Hunsche [1983], 147). Wilhelmina's brother Eberhard Stille was married on December 11, 1840.

payer, namely Adolp Oberhelman, he went down the *Rewe* to buy land since there wasn't any more work on the roads which hurts us too, in terms of money we're not any richer now but we have more in the household, that is we bought ourselves namely a nice cow and we've raised our own heifer and a horse and a foal that's 2 years old and a cart to haul wood and stones, and a bedstead and a table, the cow we bought cheap for 13 talers, the people went down the *Rewe* and couldn't take it along. [25 ll.: further details, have rented out land; advice to Ernst, in case he comes; thanks for money and thread; closing; signature; greetings from Wilhelm Krumme]

[probably early 1842]

Dear mother, brothers and sisters,

[40 ll.: correspondence; religious admonitions and reflections; all are well, but chances to make money are poor] Brother Wilhelm is still in good health but his wife is poorly, she gave birth to a baby boy on July 22nd, and the first one died three months ago which grieved him very much, otherwise he had a good year all of his crops turned out well. He is pleased that you want to send him the money. [7 ll.: details; Wilhelm's child is ill] I also want you to know that we're still living on the same place where we've always been, we've rented out our land for 2 years, since for one year we couldn't rent it out so well, since it gets better every year, but when the 2 years are up we'll go and live there ourselves, God willing. [12 ll.: closing; signature; advice to Ernst; greetings]

Traidelphia, May 30th, 1842

[10 ll. by *Wilhelm Stille:* all are healthy; asks for money]

[*Wilhelm Krumme* continues:]

Dear mother, brothers-in-law and sisters-in-law
parents, brothers and sisters,

The reason I must write you a sad letter, which I cannot conceal from you, is that my dear and your dear Willemina fell sick on February 14th. [16 ll.: details] And the Lord God who called her into this life and gave her to me took her away on April 21st at midnight when she passed away in my arms, and she died of consumption and dropsy. [5 ll.: details] The time had come for her to leave these earthly tabernacles for the merciful God had prepared her a better home. [15 ll.: religious reflections] At first I sometimes wished that if it were God's will then all three of us should lie in one coffin, but it was not God's will, but I still miss her all the time. [2 ll.: God's will] For I can tell you that it was almost 6 years ago since we swore our love to one another and since that time it never grew cold until this moment. Even if I can no longer see her with my eyes, my thoughts are always with her, and I will never forget her, since we never had quarrels, instead we lived in peace and harmony as a married couple should, believe you me. [15 ll.: religious thoughts; 3-year-old son and he are in good health]

I also want to tell you the circumstances of the burial, that here in this country many people are buried like animals, but I had the preacher to the house since he is my neighbor and a good preacher at that, but he is English: the text you can find in Job 19, verses 25 to 27. Dear Eberhardt, my brother Wilhelm wants to have his proper baptism certificate, please get it and send it when you write again but please write again soon, here I have to stop
I am and remain your brother-in-law Wilhelm Krumme.

[probably early 1843]
Dear brother-in-law Wilhelm Schulte,

You mustn't mind my calling you this, since the times have brought it about that I have to call you this, for love did not allow the two of us to do anything else, so we got married on December 29th, and on that day we stopped by Ernst Bierbaum in Cincineti where we had a small party with your brother Ernst and Friederike and the Schröers from Ladbergen[24] who were all agreeable. And I hope that none of you has any objections, that means all of you, for I hope she will have a good life with me that means peace and quiet and food and drink if the Good Lord grants me health. [4 ll.: closing, greetings, signature]

[*Karolina Schulte Krumme* continues:]

Dear parents, brothers and sisters,

I also want to write a few words about my change, namely that I left maidenhood, and entered matrimony on December 29th I think you will all be quite content, like Ernst and Friederike were, since I am also happier than I ever was in Germany and ever could have been. [12 ll.: hope, greetings; signature]
[10 ll.: from *Wilhelm Krumme* to his brother-in-law Eberhard: correspondence; advice on emigration; address]
[36 ll.: undated fragment from *Wilhelm Krumme,* perhaps written at the

[24]Ernst Bierbaum left Lengerich without official permission in 1836; Christine Elisabeth Schroer emigrated from Ladbergen with her younger brother in 1840 (Müller [1964–66], #4333, #755). Ernst H. W. Schulte (b. 1807) and his sister Karoline (b. 1814) seem to have left Lengerich without official permission. Ernst Schulte appears for the first time in CD Cincinnati 1843 as an unmarried clerk in H. Sieburn's coffeehouse and grocery.

same time as the previous letter; weather, correspondence; address; asks
about relatives; greetings; signature]

                                    Traidelpfia, January 27th, 184[3]
Dearly beloved mother, brothers-in-law and sisters-in-law,
    I'm writing to let you know that I and my little Johan, with God's help
and succor, have been quite well; but the two of us have had a hard time,
first I had to send little Johan away to strangers for almost seven months
and that cost me 4 talers a month, and the whole time I lived by myself,
cooked and baked for myself, I can tell you that was a tough year for me.
[6 ll.: but God knows what is best] My earnings have been very low
[. . .] I've been set back almost 200 talers; the people are quite good here
but they don't do anything for free. [3 ll.: hopes it will be better now]
And in November I went down the *Reewe* 400 miles to Cincineti to visit
my countrymen I met up with a lot from our area but I was there for three
weeks to get to know people and then I sought and found my heart's
desire, if you ask what was that then I have to answer that it was Caroline
Schulte, we got married on December 27th [*sic*], I hope none of you has
anything against it, for I can tell you she's very good for me and my little
Johan, that is the greatest joy that I have and it will certainly be for you
too, for love is the best, it makes you happy. [5 ll.: wishes peace and quiet
for himself] The times are very bad for the people have no money but
thank God enough food and drink for everything turned out well, here I
must stop, I am and remain your brother-in-law Wilhelm Krumme.
    Now I must turn to my dear parents, brothers and sisters,
[15 ll.: asks about family in Germany and sister in St. Louis] Finally, dear
father, you wanted an answer from me about my brother Rudolph if I
think it would be good for him to come here. I don't want to write much
about that this time, for things are bad here now and people have no
money but we're all waiting for better times but they're a long time in
coming. The farmers don't want to pay more than 5 talers a month and
the factories are closed, they're all waiting for better times, that's why I
don't know what I should write you have to decide for yourself if you
really want to come, then come. [5 ll.: greetings, closing, signature]
[41 ll.: probably January 23, 1843, from *Wilhelm Stille:* primarily about
money matters]

Wilhelm Stille
                        Manroh Counti Pauhatten Peint Ohio.
                                [probably January 1, 1844]
Dear m., b., and s., I received your letter of April 4th, 1843, and in grief I

read it so often that I almost know it by heart, and that Eberhardt's loss[25] was so great, that I can well believe since our brother-in-law W. Krumme acted like he wasn't the same man anymore and when my eldest son died I didn't know what to do and that was far less of a sorrow. [3 ll.: religious consolations] We are all well, and I hope the same for you, we have plenty to eat, but I still have debts of 55 talers and I have to borrow more since I'd like to have a windmill,[26] it takes me forever when I have to winnow 80 to 100 *Bussel* [bushel] in the basket, then I have to build a new house, but for that I want to take 5 years, and if my house had a cellar and it was ⅓ bigger then I wouldn't think of building but it's very hot here and very cold, you can't be without a cellar here. [13 ll.: received a draft for $101.50] Dear brother Eberhardt I have been wondering for a long time if I might dare to ask you to pay off the people with cattle, hay, rye and money so I can keep the 49 talers since you manage to get along better than I do, put yourself in my position, way too much work and a hired hand costs <u>a lot</u> here. Up until now I couldn't keep out of the heat and the cold what with all the work. If you don't do it you'll still be my <u>dear brother Eberhardt</u>. I will keep the money until I get an answer from you even if Brinkman comes, another thing Eberhardt if I heard that you were sowing the seeds of hate, ranting and raving, it would sound to me as if there's a great gulf fixed between us. [. . .] Here I must close and remain your brother Wilhelm and ask that none of you drink a lot of brandy, and write back faster this time and not a little, since I would like to hear about each and every one.

I almost forgot one thing, on July 10th my wife gave birth to a daughter. Now I'll stop writing since my arm is starting to hurt.

Dear Eberhardt you mustn't take it amiss that you have to get the money together also from Brünsttrup.

[29 ll.: January 11, 1844, *Wilhelm Krumme* continues on the same page: New Year's wishes; consolation for Eberhard; hymn verses; closing, signature]

[postmark: July 14, 1846]

Dear mother, brothers and sisters, I am happy that I am in America.

[5 ll.: correspondence; health] You wanted to know how much land and how much grain I harvested, and all in German measures, that I will tell you so you can clearly understand. 1st I bought 100 scheffelsaat of bush where there are lots of different kinds of trees. [17 ll.: details; maple sugar production]

---

[25]Eberhard Stille's wife died on March 14, 1843, at the age of 42.
[26]This refers to a grain-cleaning machine.

2nd I'll tell you what crops and how much I received in 1844. 190 to 200 scheffels [bushels] wheat. 180 scheffels oats, 120 scheffels potatoes, 80 scheffels corn, and a few odds and ends that aren't listed here. I also want to let you know that people here have started to grow buckwheat, that gives a good yield. [12 ll.: one harvests one hundred times the amount of seed; 3rd Rudolph Brinkman visited him] 4th I'll tell you about the kind of land and about fertilizing, the land here is so different that there's nothing like it, and also not flat, on the hills, except on the Ohio River. The soil seems to me to be a light *Kleh* [clay] when it rains a lot it's soon too wet to plow and when the weather is dry it becomes hard and packed, and you have to fertilize here too, if you want to have it like over there. When a piece of land isn't any good anymore then clover is planted and cut one time and then you let the clover grow again to 1 to 1½ feet and then plow it under, then you can count on it to be good enough for 3 to 4 years, wheat and oats here are also cut at 1 to 1½ feet above the ground, that's just like half fertilized, 5th I'll tell you what kind and how many animals I have, 2 milk cows, 2 beef cows, 2 plow oxen, 2 young oxen and a saddle horse, which doesn't do much other work, but the people who live a long way from the Ohio River they have a lot of livestock, they make money on them, and the people near the river stick to crops. I don't have any meadow. [3 ll.: details] 6 I can tell you that this year nothing grew very well, but I would be ashamed to complain since every week I read in the newspapers about Holland, Engeland, Rußland etc. [10 ll.: harvest] I can be content, I have no debts and am well set with wagons, plows etc. and my taxes hardly come to 5 dollars. Why shouldn't I be content, and thank the Gracious Father. We have 2 children, my Johannes is 4½ years old and my Maria 2½. And my wife is expecting again and everybody healthy as I proved earlier, and we have enough to live well. But we've had to work pretty hard up to now what with the *Klahren* [clearing] and building. [9 ll.: almost finished now; details about location]

[*Wilhelm Krumme* continues:]

Dear brothers-in-law and sisters-in-law

[21 ll.: pious reflections on the death of his mother-in-law on June 2, 1845; illness, recovery of his son Johann] I thank the Lord for that, he turned 7 years old on the 13th of this month, he now goes to the English school every day which costs 8 talers a year, he can already read pretty well, and I hope he'll take a shine to learning so he won't have to do any heavy work, since he is weak in stature just like his dear mother Wilhelmina but big for his age, I and Caroline have been quite healthy, thank God, and two children have also been born in the time since we married, namely a daughter whose name is Wilhelmina and the youngest is a boy his name is Wilhelm Theodor and both are quite well, and we're still living at the same place where we used to live on the road, and I would like to sell the land that I have, I've already sold 40 acres for 275 talers and still have as much as Wilhelm but I want to sell that too since we don't like the area, there are too many hills and it's not a good place to bring up children, that is for them to learn something. As soon as we sell we want to buy something else where the land isn't so high and where the market is a bit better, since where Wilhelm lives the market is bad and the land is poor, so they must work hard and still can't make much. Here it's not like over there, here you can buy land anytime, if you just have the money. [7 ll.: a good year, prices, wages]

But there is one thing to fear, that we'll have war, and it's already heating up and it's just like it was in the year of 1833 with Holland and Brabant and France that's the case here now, with us and Tecksas and Mäckziko, we elected a different president last year and he took over Täcksas and the two are fighting each other[27] and now we have to fight a war, they've already had two battles and it went very well for us we lost about 60 men and Mäckziko 15,100. I hope that if they don't get any help they'll give up soon. [6 ll.: congratulations on the remarriage of Eberhard on July 25, 1845] And finally, dear Eberhardt, a few words to you.

Please be so good and write me how things stand between us and what you intend to do with what you decide we should have. You know we are all mortal men so that we never know how long we'll still be here, so please be so good and write it, and don't take it hard. [14 ll.: greetings, asks about emigration plans of brothers and sisters; closing, signature; address]

Ernst Stille

Cincinäti, May 20th [postmark 1847]

Dearest friends and relatives,

I can't neglect sending a short letter from a foreign country to you in the Fatherland. We all arrived here in America hale and hearty as we were when we left you, we went from Bremen to Neuorlians in 2 months. [21 ll.: sea voyage] It was November 2nd at 4 o'clock in the afternoon when we landed after a safe trip[28] we went right into town and met a few

[27]The Republic of Texas, independent since 1836, was annexed by the United States in 1845. The border conflicts with Mexico which arose in consequence prompted the Americans to declare war on May 12, 1846.

[28]Ernst Stille, aged 24, made the crossing on the ship *Alesto* with 167 other passengers; many came from the county of Tecklenburg (NOPL, Roll 25). He cannot be otherwise identified with any certainty. It is also unclear whether Eberhard Stille was his real uncle or if the term is used figuratively.

friends: Homann who used to rent from Erpenbeck, W. Tostrik and many from Lienen. The first thing one of them said was: what on earth are you doing here, why didn't you stay with the Stilles. This was not a pleasant thing to hear but it didn't scare me because I already knew about that in Germany. When we went back to the ship in the evening where we had a place to stay for one more night, Wilhelmiene Henschen came with her husband Johan Munders because they'd heard that a ship had arrived from Germany and wanted to see if any friends were on it and were not a little pleased when they saw F. and Wilhelm Henschen. J. Munders lives from his teamster trade, he has 8 mules and since he needed 2 stableboys he took his two brothers-in-law on as drivers and gave them 12 dollars a month. He kept B. Brinkmann on as a servant for 5 dollars a month, and I worked for three weeks as a day laborer and earned ½ dollar and board, my work was loading dirt. [2 ll.: details] When this job was over I hired myself out to another carter and my wage was 15 dollars a month, my work was hauling cotton with 2 mules, here good luck seemed to come easily. [8 ll.: but then he had an accident] Then I needed the care of a doctor but I didn't want to pay the costs, since doctors and druggists in Neuorliens skin you alive so I had myself put in the hospital where all the service and medical care is free, since that's what the 3 talers sickpay are used for that every passenger has to pay. When I could get along on my own again and could walk pretty well [3 ll.: but still unfit for work] having to pay ½ dollar for board annoyed me and I set off to a trip to visit Uncle Wilhelm. The trip from Neuorliens to Cincinäti took 12 days and cost 2½ talers. I stayed there 2 days and visited all the friends I could find, then I got back on the steamboat to Uncle Wilhelm's, this trip took 4 days and cost 1½ talers. Wilhelm was still living with his wife and children, happy and healthy, and I stayed with him for 14 days I also wanted to go to see W. Krumme but because of the hard frost the steamboats couldn't run and so I didn't get that far, but I hear that he is well off, also little Johannes is quite healthy. [. . .] On the first of February I left Wilhelm and traveled back to Cincinäti when I got here there was little work and wage in the city since it was the worst time of the whole year that there is, but I was lucky enough to get a job with Fr. Lutterbeck from Ladbergen[29] I didn't earn more than 6 talers a month and my job was hauling bricks. At the beginning of April all the brick-makers started to work again, many Germans work this trade and earn a good wage and I set to work at this too and earn 1 dollar a day, of that I have to pay 7 dollars a month for board and washing, I work for Kuk from Brochterbeck, I have my board with Ernst Fiegenbaum from

[29]Friedrich Lutterbeck (42) (hereafter used to designate age), farmhand from Ladbergen, emigrated to Ohio in 1837 (Müller [1964–66], #503).

Ladbergen who works with me.[30] Every brickmaker has 2 horses and 6 men each one has a different job we make 8,500 a day and it's hard work but when we start at 4 o'clock in the morning we can be finished by 3 o'clock, if I can stay healthy I will keep working here since if you're healthy and can stand the work, it pays the best. [. . .] Now some of you might like to know how conditions are in general for the German immigrants here but I can't write too very much about that since it's so varied here. The only people who are really happy here are those who were used to hard work in Germany and with toil and great pains could hardly even earn their daily bread, when people like that come here, even if they don't have any money, they can manage, they rent a room and the husband goes to work, earns his dollar a day and so he can live well and happily with a wife and children. But a lot of people come over here who were well off in Germany but were enticed to leave their fatherland by boastful and imprudent letters from their friends or children and thought they could become rich in America, this deceives a lot of people, since what can they do here, if they stay in the city they can only earn their bread at hard and unaccustomed labor, if they want to live in the country and don't have enough money to buy a piece of land that is cleared and has a house then they have to settle in the wild bush and have to work very hard to clear the trees out of the way so they can sow and plant, but people who are healthy, strong and hard-working do pretty well. Here in Cincinäti I know a lot of people who have made it by working hard, like Ernst Lots for example he does very well he also owns a brickyard[31] and earns good money, I know a lot of other people who lead happy and carefree lives, R. Saatkamp who used to rent from Drees[32] and F. Katkamp are also here and are doing quite well. F. K. works with me and earns 30 dollars a month. He sends along his best regards to you and that he is healthy and he's doing well, he says I have to work here like in Germany but things are better for my wife and children, and that's what it's like for everyone I've met here, the women have nothing to do except cook the food and keep things clean, that's all the servant girls have to do too, but the men have to eat their bread in the sweat of their brow, although you don't have to work from dawn to dusk, a good worker can do his day's work in 10 hours, earn one dollar and live well on that with a wife and children, and have such good food and drink like the best

[30]There is an Ernst Fiedenbaum listed in the CD Cincinnati 1849–50 as a laborer at the address of a brickyard.

[31]Among the 56 brickyard operators in the business directory of 1848–49 there was one Ernest Leots [sic].

[32]Rudolph Saatkamp emigrated in 1845 as a 28-year-old tenant farmer from Ringel, Lengerich, with his wife, whose maiden name was Drees, and three children (Müller [1964–66], #1914).

burgher in Lengerich. [14 ll.: advice for those who want to emigrate; greetings; address; closing]

Cincinäti, July 10th, 1848

Dearly beloved friends and relatives,

[73 ll.: repetition of the letter of May 20, 1847, presumed lost, up to his job in the brickyard] On Oct. 10th last fall work ended and since I once again had no way to make money I went back down the *Rewwe* to Neuorleans, not as a passenger but as a worker, on the trip I earned ½ dollar a day and board, from N. I went 43 miles farther downstream and got work in a sugar house [refinery] and earned 20 dollars a month and board, I worked there 4 months, and afterwards went up the *Rewwe* again, this trip I was third cook on a steamboat, and earned a half dollar daily again. At the beginning of April I came back here and the next day I started working for Ernst Lots in the brickyard, since I promised him before I left that I'd be back around April 1st since he'd start up again and work for him this summer. I now earn 31 dollars a month that's about the best you can do here, since this job only suits those who like to work hard and also have a firm and healthy body, for the day's work is a lot we make 8,500 a day and when you work you can never be in the shade, instead you always stand in the bright sun, it's also not the custom that you spend the whole day at it. [24 ll.: working processes in the brickyard] The bricks are sold for 3½ dollars per 1,000, they are about 50 such brickyards where in each one 8,500 are made every day all summer long, and they are all used here in the city, so you can imagine how fast this city is building up and expanding, if this would stop then thousands of men would soon be without work, you can see that when in the winter no one can work at this trade because of the snow and ice, then there's a huge number of idle people, the main work in the winter is with fat livestock, this is brought in from the country in large herds, on the outer edge of the city there are large buildings where about 1000 a day are slaughtered and cleaned, then they're brought into the city where they are cut up and salted and put in barrels that's how they're sent from here to other countries, this is a pretty hard and dirty job, that's why most people would rather do nothing for ¼ year than do this, but if you want to put up with this you can earn 1 to 1½ dollars a day. I also want to let you know that I got married on the 4th of May of this year, to Heinriette Dickmans, the daughter of one of Dieckman's tenants in Leeden, she is 20 years old, left on the same day from Bremerhafen as we went on board but she went via Baltemor, I didn't know her before, neither in Germany nor here, but I got to know her this spring through her uncle Rudolph

Espel from Lienen, a good friend of mine who also works for Ernst Lots, who is his son-in-law,[33] I live with her in peace and harmony since she doesn't lack for virtues and peacefulness, she was just poor since she suffered a long time last winter from dropsy and what she had earned before she had to spend on doctors and druggists, but I had earned so much that we could buy all the household implements that you normally need here and nice ones too, since they cost less here than in Germany. [4 ll.: prices] The whole marriage cost me a bit more than 100 dollars, housing costs me 2½ dollars a month. Firewood ½ or ¾ dollar, food is cheap here, and it is not as expensive for me with my wife as before, since I took my board with someone else and had to pay 7 dollars a month, and now I can have more what I want, for there is certainly no burgher in Lengerich who eats or drinks better than I, here it's nothing special if you have ham and roasts 3 times a day, since that's normal, I also drink more beer than water on hot summer days, and every now and then a bottle of wine, for anyone can do that here and still save enough money if he's healthy and wants to work, there are also enough people here who have been here for a long time and seldom have more than 5 dollars to their name and in the spring owe 10 to 20 dollars, these are mostly people who came here young and stay unmarried for a long time, they get to know all kinds of spendthrifts, are often in boardinghouses with 20 to 30 such fellows, and they all go from one tavern to the next and play cards to pass the time and only work when they are forced to because of lack of money, the much more fortunate are those who come here with a wife and children, and with no money, they keep up their German thriftiness and diligence the best and therefore make progress like for example R. Saatkamp, Fried. Katkamp, I would guess that Saatkamp has more than 100 dollars in cash and I know a lot of people like that, F. Katkamp also lived well here at first, worked hard and earned a lot of money, but he died about 6 weeks ago. [7 ll.: drank himself to death; left behind a wife and five children, but two sons earn $12 a month at the brickyard] And the boys according to the law here have to work for the parents until 21, and the girls until 18. My plan is if I stay in good health for the next couple of years to buy a piece of land and live there, since from my childhood I've been used to farming, I'd rather do that than stay in the city all my life, you can't start very well unless you have 300 dollars, you

[33]Leeden borders on Lengerich, but it lies on the other side of the crest of the Teutoburg Forest. Heinriette Dieckmann probably emigrated illegally, as well as one Eberhard Dieckmann from Leeden who emigrated in 1846. Rudolph Espel, a 37-year-old widower and day laborer, had emigrated in 1837 (Müller [1964–66], #5021, #4092–93; Hunsche [1983], 68). In MC 1850: Cincinnati, Ohio, W. 8, #2454, Espel is listed as a member of Ernst Lots's household, and Lots (more correctly Lotz) is listed as a brickmaker with $1,000 worth of real estate. According to the tax lists, Lotz was almost certainly from the tenant farmer class (Leesch, 292–302).

can still buy 80 acres of wild land for 100 dollars, if you then build a house and barn that takes 50 dollars a horse or 2 oxen takes almost 50 dollars a few cows and pigs and farm implements 50 dollars, then you have to live for a year before you can harvest then it takes another 3 to 4 years before you earn any money. I hope you will be so kind as to let my other relatives read this letter and read it to your tenants, since they all will want to know how I am and I can't write to everyone I promised to write to.

With best regards to you all, your friend Ernst Stille

Cincinäti, July 20th, 1848

Dearest mother,

[4 ll.: had not yet written] I didn't want to write you a letter so you wouldn't have to pay anything. I have been quite well up to this moment and have always earned good money, now that is 31 dollars a month. [3 ll.: has married] I am sending you 5 talers Prussian money with this messenger, and I hope that you receive it in good health. You may think I could have sent you more money, that's also true, but since I haven't heard anything from you since I left, I didn't think it was wise to send a lot, and I also have something else in mind, that is, my dearest wish is to have you here with me, to do my filial duty and to take care of you in your old age, this is also the dearest wish of my wife, she too will receive you with joy, and I am sure that you could live in peace with her and have good days even in your old age. [34 ll.: recommendations for the trip over, travel costs; address; closing; signature]

[probably July 20, 1848]

Dear Uncle Eberhard,

[16 ll.: asks him to advance his mother the travel costs] If all of this comes to naught, then I will have to send the money next summer this means that she will have to come a year later and has to slave away terribly there, or even go knocking at someone else's door, but she could be very useful here, if she were here this winter or next spring around the beginning of April, I would take in 10 to 12 boarders, which I'd have a good chance to do next summer, I could earn a lot doing that, and then she'd have brought in the money for the trip. [5 ll.: would have sent the money already if he were sure she was coming] If my niece Friederike wants to come over here, that would be a good idea, since it's not hard to imagine what will become of her in Germany, it will be hard for her to marry a good farmer, and if things turn out badly she'll have to slave

away all her life with hard work and often trouble and strife, without ever getting anywhere.[34] Things here aren't quite like the way many young girls think they are, namely that rich gentlemen are waiting for them and coaches fetch them, but if Friederike comes over here and works as a servant, her job will be cooking, washing and mending, that's not too much, and then if she later marries a man who doesn't have any more than I do she can still have a good and pleasant life, since I know that no farmer's wife in Ringel lives such a happy and carefree life as my wife. [2 ll.: only takes care of the house] If she does want to come, it would be best if she leaves next spring, as soon as ships leave from there to Neuorleans. [11 ll.: advice on emigration] B. Brinkmans was a good girl and faithful, and I know her intentions were honest, up until she got to her brothers' house, they forced her almost with violence to renounce me completely before their own eyes and they told me never to come to the house again. I then kept my distance, and she also didn't agree to do anything her brothers wanted, I don't know what she really thought about it. Last winter when I was gone she joined the Methodist church, and so I knew there was no hope. She's still working as a servant and she's been offered nothing better, I'm sure she regrets it already.[35] [. . .]
[21 ll: no date, but written shortly after the previous letter: encourages niece to emigrate; greetings; instructions about money]

Wilhelm Stille

December 20th, [1848]
Schwitzerland Taunschipp Manroh
Caunti in Ohio in Amerika

Dear brothers and sisters, I am so happy to be in America and I and my wife and the three children are all quite well. [11 ll.: harvest, Ernst's visit]

Dear ones, I read that Krumme and I should think hard about Ernst's position, about coming over here, that wouldn't be so dumb, if they could come with some other people to Cindsinäti or Wehlingen, and we know that Ernst has to work every day for his daily bread, so do we, but we make more progress. When you write again write about the *Rewelutsiohn* [revolution] too, and if you get a chance to send me 3 pipes I would like that. [11 ll.: began growing wine grapes; closing; signature; his brother Friedrich should write]

[34]Probably because she was an illegitimate child; see n. 22 above.
[35]B. Brinkmann was on the same ship as Ernst and remained at first in New Orleans. The Methodist Church was originally English, but as early as 1835 it sent out the first German missionary, William Nast from Cincinnati. In 1870 there were half as many Methodists as Catholics among the German clergy in Ohio (Arndt/Olson, 426–27, 450).

[*Wilhelm Krumme* continues:]

Traidel[phia], Dec. 24th, 1848

Dear brothers-in-law and sisters-in-law,

I must tell you a bit about our situation, I am still working on the road where I've been working for 10 years already, I have plenty of work and we're getting ahead, but it's hard work, I now have three horses, two to work and one three-year-old that can't work yet, I want to sell one in the spring and I want to stay at my old job for one more year if we stay healthy, and if you want to send Ernst's sons over here to us then do it. I will take as good care of them as I can, for I have a better chance to get them work than brother Wilhelm, if they come it would be best if they leave in the spring then they could already earn something in the summer since the summer is the best time to make money I have one man who works for me according to your money he earns 1 taler 8 gute groschen a day.

You wrote me that I should write to you how much money we have received, to tell you the truth I can't say, I believe it was 80 or 90 talers that father gave us to take along, and afterward 50 talers and the cloth for the coat, that's all I know now I'll leave it up to you to do what you think is right. I greet you all and remain your brother-in-law / Wilhelm Krumme. [8 ll.: inquiries about power of attorney, greetings]

Wilhelm Stille

Schwitzerland Taunschib Manroh Caunthi Ohio

January 1st, 1850

Dear brothers and sisters, now it's been over a year since I wrote to you and still haven't received an answer, I don't know what the problem is. [. . .] I was sick for a long time, so bad I didn't know where I was heading, to be crippled or die. [86 ll.: had severe rheumatism in his hip, the doctor burned it twice with a hot iron; is somewhat recovered but still remains frail; doctor bills; since he was unemployed for almost one year, high costs for day laborers; wife and children were also ill]

Now dear b. and s.: it should not surprise you that what with this affliction I would <u>really really</u> like the rest of my inheritance, follow your conscience and send it to me. [. . .]

Dear brother Friederich, if you can also send me a small sum, after this affliction I'd take it gladly, since you don't have a family, if it doesn't work out then you're still my dear brother. But it certainly would help a little bit to patch up the holes. [13 ll.: wishes to hear soon; Ernst's visit; money matters; closing]

Wilhelm Krumme

Traidelphia, March 21st, 1850

Dear brothers-in-law and sisters-in-law,

I want to let you know that we are all still healthy, thank God, and we hope you are too, further we want to let you know that we want to move to Cincinneti since my job here is over and I think that we'll buy land again if we can get a good buy that will be the safest thing since our children are growing thank God,[36] first Jahn will be 11 this spring and he's growing very fast and has a good time since he doesn't have to do anything so far, he goes to school every day and he's a good pupil, that is in the English language since he can handle books fairly well but he doesn't know much German. But if the Dear Lord grants us health, I want him to learn German since I want him to go to a good school so he won't need to work so hard like a common day laborer. [15 ll.: confirms Stille's letter; closing; signature; address]

Caroline Schulte Krumme

[ca. 1858]

Dear brother-in-law and sister-in-law,

I feel the need to write you a few lines about the money you are thinking of sending I see clearly from your letter that you are afraid I will use up the money since I have to hear all the time that it's for Johann's benefit, as far as I am concerned you don't need to send anything, don't think that we've counted on it or are counting on it that's far from the truth, then we'd have been cheated a long time ago. We have to get way more than 200 Prussian talers together by next fall and we can do it too if we stay healthy and the Dear Lord doesn't send us a total crop failure, then we'll rely on working with our own hands and not on such money. [3 ll.: difficult year, but they'll make it] And what we have then we have earned with our own hands and not inherited. You should also know that Johan is in Cincinnäti at my brother's and he's doing well he took along his mother's gold ring and also Wilhelm's watch from Germany and the linen that was still left I will keep for him till he needs it also her clothes I never wore since I had enough clothes myself even though I didn't have any money, yes dear brother-in-law I know that I have a sinful soul and only a short time to live that's why I will take care not to soil my soul with a few worldly goods that are not mine and Wilhelm has enough

---

[36]The MC 1850: Triadelphia, Ohio Co., Va. (now W. Va.), #263, lists William and Carolina Cromey [sic] with their children John (11), Willimina (6), William T. (5), and Louisa (2).

right as the father to ask for it while he is still in good health, after all they left Germany 20 years ago and your sister would have been 50 already and Johan will be of age in 2 years and then he can demand it now you can figure out how much use Wilhelm would have out of it and remember she was his wife and not his servant and sickly as long as they were married. [6 ll.: exchange rate; asks for a fair hearing] I also want to ask you when you see my sister please tell her about our letter and if she still has even a little spark of love she'll put a note in with your letter and give her my best. [8 ll.: greetings, closing]

[*Wilhelm Krumme* continues:]

Eberhardt, be so kind and tell my sister that I wanted to write to her but this letter will be too heavy she should be so kind as to write to me I'll gladly pay for the letter.
I've forgotten my brother-in-law's name / Wm Krumme

[10 ll.: February 1, 1858, by *Wilhelm Stille:* instructions about filling out a draft]

[*Wilhelm Krumme* continues:]

February 1st, 1858

Dear brother-in-law and sisters-in-law,
[16 ll.: they are well, are visiting Wilhelm Stille; harvest; wine growing] Now I want you to know that since last fall Johannes has been with Ernst Schulte in Cincinnati in his *Stohr*[37] and he likes it very much, he goes to school every evening and every day to the store, now he has to learn and that's what he does since he has a good head for learning. [10 ll.: inquiries about neighbors; will send tree seeds]
Your brother-in-law, Wm Krumme,

[12 ll.: September 1, 1858: receipt from *W. Krumme* to Eberhard Stille for 162 talers; all claims are thereby settled]

Wilhelm Stille
[probably written at the same time as Wilhelm Krumme's receipt]
[9 ll.: confirms he received the full share of inheritance]
Dear b and sisters and brothers-in-law and sisters-in-law
Tell the school masters that they should teach the children when

---

[37]Ernst took over the store from his previous employer ca. 1845 (see n. 24 above). In the 1850s he appears fairly regularly in the Cincinnati CDs as a grocer, in 1859 even as wholesaler. In the MC 1860: Cincinnati W. 3, #1516, he is listed as owning no real estate but having $6,000 in assets.

someone emigrates something important, if they want to write a letter
the state and Caunti [county] must be written in full and right, whole
inheritances have been lost because of that. [9 ll.: details] Here I will close
and drink a glass of wine since I'm writing this while making wine. W.
Stille

[probably May 1859]

Dear sister-in-law

[12 ll.: religious condolences on the death of Eberhard Stille on October 14, 1858] Dear sister-in-law, please write again soon about all of my
brothers and sisters, also how many are in America and where they are,
maybe I can visit them, also what your children are called by name, ditto
something about your neighbors especially about Erpenbek, Kätter from
Latbergen told me a bit, but not much since he was a preacher—he also
died ½ hour from here, a changed man, his name will live on a long time.
Forgive me dear sister-in-law that I want you to write so much, but
you'll forgive me, if it's too much for you take on a scribe for the day,
another thing, have the school inspector read this letter so the children
learn to write Latin, since Latin script is good almost all over the world.
Dear sister-in-law, love me as I love you. Wilhelm Stille.
my address reads M. W. Stille Pauhatten Point
Balmount Counte Ohio / Amereka

[*Wilhelm Krumme* continues:]

Traidelphia

Dear sister-in-law and children

[11 ll.: correspondence; they are well] I haven't seen Johan, Wilhelm-
ena's son, for 2½ years since he is in Cincinneti which is 400 miles away
from us, but he is quite healthy, thank God, and is doing well, he earns 30
talers a month but has to pay for his own board, he is with people who
have tobacco shops and they push pretty hard, Johan writes that they
have 100 to 120 men working there, and he is a clerk there. [10 ll.:
harvest; inquiries about Eberhard's successor; greetings] Fare thee well
and forget me not
Your brother-in-law William Krumme.

It is unknown whether Ernst Stille ever realized his dream of having
his own farm, if he followed the river to the West or the South, or if he
perhaps succumbed to an epidemic such as cholera.

Wilhelm Stille spent the rest of his life on his farm in Switzerland
Township. After the middle of the century his economic situation hardly

changed at all. The value of his property had increased in the 1850s from 900 to 1,600 dollars, but the amount of land under cultivation had only increased by five acres to forty acres. Until 1880 his estate remained basically the same. At the age of 78, he still farmed 25 acres of land, helped only by his eldest son, who was "insane" and could neither read nor write. His son Theodor lived in the same area, and at the age of 29 he already owned a farm of eighty acres, half of which was cultivated, worth $2,500. It was no doubt bought with the help of his father. In the second generation, too, the feeling of ethnic solidarity continued to be strong; Theodor's wife was born in Ohio of German parents.[38]

At the start, Wilhelm Krumme's chances of success did not appear as good as those of his brother-in-law Wilhelm Stille. Krumme emigrated four years later, received much less financial support from Germany and pounded rocks on road-building projects, whereas Stille worked in a mill and in a store. But Krumme and Stille worked themselves into farming, with obvious success. In the 1860 census Krumme's farm was valued 400 dollars higher than Stille's. He could afford to send all three of his children, ranging in age from twelve to sixteen, to school. After 1860 Krumme was no longer to be found in Triadelphia.[39]

For his son Johann, Krumme had wished for something better "I want him to go to a good school so he won't need to work so hard like a common day laborer" (March 21, 1850). Johann's ability to speak English must have been very good indeed, since his employers in the tobacco wholesale business were two American businessmen. Until about 1862 he remained a clerk or salesman with the same company; in 1863 he appears as a foreman. He had married at about the same time and was then listed with a home address instead of as a boarder. In 1866 he appeared for the first time as an agent, 1869 as a traveling agent with his own office address. Evidently this remained his profession and the Cincinnati area remained his home; in 1880 he is listed in the census as a traveling salesman. That he was well assimilated is also seen in the fact that his wife Melissa was an American whose parents had been born in the United States. The third generation, Johann Krumme's children, were probably fully Americanized. In 1900 one son was a milk merchant in Cincinnati; his wife and son had the distinctly Anglo-American names of Phoebe and Howard. And although the head of the family was named William Krumme, he had little in common with his grandfather Wilhelm Krumme.[40]

[38]MC 1850: Switzerland Twp., Monroe Co., Ohio, #60; 1860: #149; 1870: #117; 1880: e.d. 134, #132, #194; also the local MC A 1850, 1860, 1880.

[39]MC 1850: Triadelphia, Ohio Co., Va. (W.Va.), #263; 1860: #365.

[40]Cincinnati CDs for 1859–79; MC 1880: Cincinnati, Ohio, W. 3, e.d. 109, #177; MC 1900: Cincinnati, Ohio, W. 1, e.d. 4, #119.

2

August and Carl Blümner (Charles Blumner)

The annual number of German emigrants to America exceeded ten thousand for the first time in 1832. As before, the majority came from southwest Germany, even though a few areas in northwest Germany began to be affected during this period. From the region east of the Elbe, however, there were only a few hundred emigrants at the most, among them the two brothers August and Carl Blümner from Friesack in Brandenburg, about forty miles west of Berlin.

As was often the case with the trailblazers of emigration from a particular area, the Blümners stood out in many ways from the great mass of other emigrants. Both of their grandfathers, as well as their father, had been leaseholders and managers of royal estates; their elder sister Johanna (nicknamed Hannchen) had married the owner of a noble estate, Fritz Bismark (referred to as "Brother Fritz" in the letters).[1] There is hardly any doubt that the brothers received their secondary education at a Gymnasium, and there is good reason to assume that one or both also attended a university. At the time they left, August and Carl were already 29 and 27 years old, respectively. August had recently married Sophia Oesterley, the daughter of a university counsel at Göttingen, and their youngest brother later studied law in Berlin.[2] In this they were quite

[1]Information about the family was primarily provided by the contributor. The father of the emigrants, Daniel Blümner, died between 1812 and 1824.

[2]Carl served in the military as a one-year volunteer, which suggests he received a high school education. According to the ev. KB Göttingen (Albani parish) Sophia Dorothea Ernestine Oesterley was born on April 1, 1811; see also Martels (1834), 168–69. Her father, Georg Heinrich Oesterley (1774–1847), was a judge, assistant professor from 1804 to 1821, and then university counsel until he died (Frensdorff [1887b]).

typical politically motivated emigrants of the of the early thirties, mostly members of the well-educated intelligentsia. This was the period of a thwarted uprising in Hesse, the persecution of "demagogues," and general ideological suspicion in the German universities. According to family tradition, the brothers "emigrated to America, full of liberal ideas, to seek their fortune."[3] The Blümners, inspired by the book written by Gottfried Duden, founded a small society in order to settle the Missouri valley, forty miles west of St. Louis, the area that had been praised so highly by Duden.[4]

The Blümners are the only letter-writers included in this edition—and among the very few in the entire Bochum letter collection—who show the definite influence of emigration propaganda. They also belong to the small minority of emigrants who settled in groups. Group migration was more typically motivated by religious beliefs, but secular groups were not unusual in the early thirties. In 1834 two other groups, the Solingen and the more famous Gießen societies, chose as their destination Warren County, Missouri, the subject of Duden's glowing reports. The fact that a strong concentration of Germans developed here, however, is due more to the emigration of peasant farmers which began at the same time. In 1850 almost as many Germans as Americans were living in the county, and in 1860 they predominated. A pastor reported in 1836 that in the area ten miles around the Blümners there were at least 150 German families and relatively few Americans.[5]

Duden's writings also attracted Baron von Martels and his three sons from Osnabrück, who became acquainted with the Blümners' group in Baltimore harbor and traveled with them to Missouri. They are often mentioned in the Blümners' letters; the published letters written by the young Heinrich von Martels, together with the reports by Friedrich Münch and others of the Gießen Society, are the principal sources of information about the "Berlin Society," as the Blümners' enterprise was called.

The group sailed from Hamburg, arrived in Baltimore on September 10, 1832, and after traveling some 1,100 miles on land and river, finally arrived at their destination on October 28. Within a month the society had bought "a very nice farm with a stone house, liquor distillery, mill

---

[3]Letter of June 7, 1904, from Paul Blümner, the emigrants' nephew, to his nephew Hugo Blümner (BABS).

[4]Martels, 9, 49, 175; Duden (1829). The Swiss emigration society in St. Gall published two special editions of Duden's book in 1832 and 1835; see also the recent, annotated English translation (1980).

[5]August Blümner bought 125 acres of land in 1833 from Louis Eversmann, Gottfried Duden's traveling companion, and sold it again the following year to Friedrich Münch, the organizer of the Gießen Society (Warren Co., Mo., Deed Records, Book A, 59, 180–81). On the emigration into this area and for citations of translated primary documents, see Kamphoefner (1987), 86–105, and Büttner 1 (1844), 190.

and the entire harvest" for $1,600. According to Friedrich Münch they maintained "for a time a common (communistic) economy," but by the time Heinrich von Martels's book appeared in the spring of 1834 the society "had decided it would be best to disband, and all members now lived on separate properties."[6]

According to Martels, the society consisted of "14 persons, all relatives and friends." Cofounder of the society, along with the Blümners, was Friedrich Rathje from Stade. He, as well as Friederich Morsey from Hanover, was the son-in-law of Wilhelm von Bock, a well-educated and wealthy landowner from Mecklenburg who was the financial and perhaps the intellectual godfather of the enterprise.[7] He seems to have been—and here all of his contemporaries agree—something of an amiable eccentric. He built many castles in the air, the most elegant being a town, made up of 168 building lots (1980 population was 100), which he named "Dutzow" after his hometown in Mecklenburg.[8]

Bock, with his "unlimited hospitality," formed the center of an active social life with singing, music, and dance accompanied by a pianoforte, which attracted curious Americans from fifteen miles around. The festive mood of the early days is reflected in Martels's letters: "New Year's Eve was celebrated in Herr Rathje's and Blümner's house, and the last bottle of Rhine wine was drunk to the health of Germany and its lovely ladies. . . . The next morning the new year was greeted with song from the crest of a hill, the view of which dominates the entire region. — A wonderful effect was created by 'Herr Gott dich loben wir' sung by 12 strong male voices."[9] But disillusionment came soon enough.

Emigrants of this type were often called "Latin farmers," in allusion to the fact that they often knew more about Latin than about farming. Once the money they had brought along was used up, they usually had quite a struggle and "some ended up very sadly," according to a contemporary who reported that the members of the Berlin society "either left no, or a few of them very unpopular, traces." In fact, by the 1850 census only one member of the society could still be found in Warren County.[10] The

[6]Martels, 9, 49, 175; Münch (1870), 197–202, 230–35, 201–2.

[7]Martels, 175. On August 30, 1833, F. W. Bock and Friedrich Rathje bought out the property of "Rathje and Company," ca. 250 acres, for $2,000. The contract was signed by Friedrich Rathje, August Walcke, Carl and August Blümner, and Edward and Julius Hutawa (Warren Co., Mo., Deed Records, Book A, 61–62; BPL, Quarterly Abstracts, Roll 2, 118; list of German settlers in Duden [1980], 312–13). According to the applications for citizenship and BPL, the Blümners, Hutawas, Rathje, and Walcke all crossed on the same ship. Bock arrived in Missouri in July 1833 (Warren Co., Mo., Circuit Court Records, Book A, January 10, 1834, and February 17, 1834).

[8]Büttner 1:188–90; Göbel (1877), 7–8.

[9]Göbel, 8; Martels, 53–54. Translated, the hymn title is "The Lord My God Be Praised."

[10]Göbel, 7; a good summary of sources is provided by Ravenswaay (1977), 31–37. In 1850 Friedrich Morsey was a surveyor in Warren County, and he later became a lawyer, politician, and colonel in the Union cavalry during the Civil War.

"unpopular traces" probably refer to the Martels, who were held in no higher esteem by other contemporary writers than by August Blümner.

Aside from his problems with debt, which were not necessarily his own fault, August gives the impression of a competent, progressive farmer. When he took out a mortgage in 1838, he owned over 220 acres of land as well as the following inventory:

> Two horses four mares, one two year old young filley two colts four cows, one heifer four calves 10 Sheep, 60 head of hogs more or less being said Blumners Stock. One ox cart one wheat fan, & one iron tooth harrow four plows with all other farming utincels. all his household and kitchen furniture with three Bureaus one cupboard with all its contents one sideboard, two Clocks, two pocket watches, two dozen Silver Spoons, two dozen knives and forks, four bedsteads and furniture and all his table linen. One large brass Kettle, one thousand feet of plank about two hundred german and English Books. One mans saddle and two womens saddles & bridles about forty bushels of wheat and Rye, 20 acres of growing corn three stacks of timothy hay one of Clover. One Clothespress, & including the whole of said Blumners property of every description & now in his possession.

The fact that Blümner was appointed to be an estate administrator in 1841 is further proof that he had gained the trust of his American neighbors. This can also be seen in his second marriage, after his 21-year-old wife Sophia died in childbirth in September 1833. Before the end of the year he married Mathilda McLean, the sister of a prominent doctor, who had moved from Kentucky to Missouri as the child of pioneers.[11]

His brother Carl seems to have had none of this good luck. Perhaps von Martels's remarks about the society applied to him: "The young gentlemen are no longer satisfied with celibacy." Among immigrants, there was almost always an overabundance of men, and for the well-educated there was even less chance of finding a socially appropriate mate. But it was not so much disappointment in finding a partner as his poor economic prospects in Missouri that led Carl Blümner to leave the underdeveloped settlement. Instead of retreating to the city like many bourgeois emigrants, however, he struck out into the still wilder West.[12] As Carl himself claimed, pure spirit of adventure led him to join a trading

[11]Warren County, Mo., Deed Records, Book B, 274 (for inventory); Martels, 168–69. On December 20, 1833, Angus Blimmer [sic] and Matilda McLean were married by a justice of the peace (Woodruff [1969]; on the family see History of Franklin . . . Missouri [1888b], 781–82).

[12]Martels, 169. Among the other "Berliners," one Hutawa brother became a lithographer in St. Louis; one of his creations is the letterhead reproduced in Figure 24 (see the Berthold series, Chapter 10). Rathje's widow married someone named Krüger and moved to Louisville, Kentucky (Münch [1870], 202).

company in the spring of 1836 and to travel by covered wagon across a thousand miles of prairie and mountains to Santa Fe. Although it was the capital of the Mexican province of New Mexico, Santa Fe had only three thousand inhabitants. The trade route, opened some fifteen years earlier, was no longer as dangerous as it had been at the start because American and Mexican troops accompanied the caravan to protect it from Indians. But by 1836 the opportunities that came with the initial years of the Santa Fe trade, when capital investments could be multiplied tenfold, were already a thing of the past. At the time of Blümner's trip the Texans were fighting for their independence from Mexico. Their struggle led to increased tension between Mexicans and Americans in Santa Fe and the surrounding area, until in 1846, during the Mexican War, the United States annexed the entire Southwest, including California.[13] To hold one's own in such an unstable economic and political climate was a challenge that more than quenched Carl Blümner's thirst for adventure.

The Blümner brothers are probably the most highly educated letter-writers in this edition. It is therefore no surprise that they do not struggle with the language; instead, they command it like a musical instrument used to express all shades of feeling. It is also reasonable to assume that, unlike other emigrants, they had been writing family letters long before they left for America.

This characterization is true of both August and Carl, although the latter's language is somewhat livelier and more colorful. But both of them, as could be expected from people of their educational background, always keep their native German apart from their new languages. There is no recognizable invasion of English or Spanish, and even a word like "farmer," when used, is dutifully translated into German.

Carl Blümner

Warren County, March 24th, 1836

[26 ll.: is waiting for letters; will send letter with an acquaintance who is returning] But I want to write to you, dear mother, one more time before my departure.—

"Before his departure?!"—I hear you repeat with astonishment; but so it is, my good mother; don't be shocked or amazed; it is so; I am just about to embark upon an important trip in a few weeks, in early April. You may think, dear mother, I have traveled enough; from Germany to here; but so it is with man; fate sometimes knocks us about in the world. I

[13]Billington (1956), 23–40, 125–33, 178–87.

myself used to believe that having found a home here in a far corner of this endless North America; that I would put down my walking stick, saying "This far and no further!"—But—I am picking it up anew, will try it again; ever onward in the good wide world; God's dear sun shines everywhere; His hand guides us everywhere!!—Who actually knows in which harbor of rest my ship will land!—Well! Anyhow!—This journey now, my beloved mother, or rather the reasons that have led me to take this journey, I will relate to you. The journey itself is actually a trading venture to a distant Spanish province, Mexico; southwest of here. For several years now a caravan or *Compagnie* of traders have gone from here to a province of Mexico, that is to Santa Fee; in order to sell or trade necessary wares and goods to the Spanish who live there; since the Spanish cannot obtain their goods from any other, or at least from any more secure or nearby source as from here, this journey is very profitable for those trading with Santa Fee. This wagon train leaves here every year in the month of April and returns in October or November. Up until now no one has made the journey but Americans; last year however a German went along for the first time; a Swiss fellow by the name of Sutter; now, after his return, several Germans are joining him, since he is a clever man of good character, one you can believe and trust; also because we have known him for a long time.[14] The reasons that led me, dear mother, to join the caravan are two very simple ones, to earn money and—to make the journey! In the situation in which I have been living here up to now, I couldn't earn anything; the place isn't right for it yet; there isn't enough of a market; the population is too sparse; in short it is still too early here to be able to earn much money; especially for people who don't have the means to get help, to buy a slave or rent one (by the way, the price of a Negro is now between 700 and 1,000 dollars and the yearly rent 90 to 100 dollars).[15] Then, it is also a main requirement for a *farmer,* or for anyone who works here, —he must be married, otherwise nothing works out. I am not, I have no wife, and will probably never be so lucky here!! For these reasons, on the one hand, and on the other hand just for the sake of the journey itself, I have decided to become a kind of merchant; but this kind of business is very different from what one usually thinks of in terms of a merchant. I think the spirit of speculation

[14]This was the same Johann Sutter who owned the ranch where gold was discovered in California in 1848 (see Chapter 13, n. 9). Under Sutter's leadership, Dr. Edward Simon from Hamburg, Herr Kaiser, and Herr Künzel traveled from Warren County, with others "who had no real pleasure in the backwoods life of the time," after they had bought goods on credit in St. Louis. They were able to sell their goods, but they then invested the profit in mules and wild horses, which turned out to be a "complete failure" (see Münch [1872], 2–3).

[15]Some of the educated Germans in this settlement bought slaves, but according to the MC 1840: Warren Co., Mo., p. 158, August Blümner did not own any.

alone would never have attracted me to this venture, had it not been necessarily coupled with the interesting trip. The distance from here to Santa fee is about 1,800 English miles;[16] / 4½ English miles is one German. / For more than half of our journey we will be in uninhabited areas, where only the Indians who still live there occasionally come to the caravan to trade or barter. At the Spanish border the caravan is met by a detachment of the Spanish cavalry and accompanied to the gates of the capital, Santa fee. So, my dear mother, I have told you the essentials of my venture; I hope to write more in my last letter from here; this letter must leave tomorrow morning.—

I have rented out my *farm* here to one of our friends, to Walcke;[17] since I couldn't sell it at a good price before my departure; I have taken out a loan on it, and have made August my legal agent during my absence. You will receive August's letters earlier; he sent them off earlier. And so now, my beloved mother, I will begin this journey in God's Name; there will be quite a number of us, as a precaution against possible danger; the caravan had 150 to 160 men last year; in this year probably even more, there are 16 of us Germans; all are well acquainted, among them older experienced men; as well as two doctors. Two days ago I obtained my horse for the journey from August; we traded; I gave him a very beautiful horse and he gave me a good, solid horse and 20 dollars besides! — Well! — My beloved mother! Perhaps, if I am lucky, I can perhaps make enough to venture a trip to Germany; then I would be happy enough with my fate; then my deepest wish would be fulfilled! Farewell, dearest mother! Farewell, dearest sister and brother Fritz! Farewell, my loved ones! Give my best to mother Bismark; Angers; both of the dear brothers; Peters, Voigts, etc.
Farewell! / Your true son forever / Carl Blüm.

Santa Fee, April 3rd, 1838
A long time has transpired, my most dearly beloved mother, since you have had word from me; a long time! Do not be angry with me, dearest mother! Do not be angry with me, dearest sister and brothers! It was because of the conditions under which I have been living during this time, that I did not write to you! I wrote two letters in the 2 years which I have lived in this country; one was lost, as I know for certain; I know nothing as yet about the other; the first was lost through the death of a

[16]On today's highways, more like one thousand miles.

[17]According to his citizenship application, August Walcke was a Swedish citizen, but had lived from 1820 until his emigration in 1832 in Mecklenburg (see Warren County, Mo., Circuit Court Records, 18).

German, one of my friends, who was robbed and killed by the Indians on his return from here to the United States; I had given him my letter to you. But I will report that in greater detail. You know, dearest mother, from my last letters from Missoury, that I had joined a *Compagnie* of a small German trading company going to Mexico; we thought we could do good business; but our expectations were dashed, conditions in this country had worsened so much that all trading ventures for the most part failed; the reason for this change is the Indians; they rob the Spaniards incessantly, the most significant part of their wealth consists of livestock; the Indians steal horses, mules, thousands of sheep, and kill the Spaniards wherever they can. In a period of 2 to 3 years they have stolen over 2 million sheep from this one district of Santa Fee. — In short, our enterprise failed; all the others of our *Comp.* returned to Missoury; I couldn't bring myself to go back like that to the United States; I couldn't do it, I didn't want to return poor after having made this long, dangerous journey, I did not want to return without money; I remained! My poor friend with my letter to you, my dear ones, went back; but he met his death on the vast plains, full of prowling Indians. He, his name is Sanders, and 2 others, a Frenchman and a Spaniard, were killed. My decision here was quickly made; I was without money; I went to the gold mines, in the hopes of digging up a treasure there; I worked hard, with one other German who stayed on; we found gold, but too little to fulfill our expectations, and after 3 to 4 weeks the illness of my comrade forced us to give up this arduous business and return to Santa Fee. Here I started a small store and a wine tavern, since some Americans, who knew me, gave me everything I needed on *Credit!* In this business I made some money, after some time I added a *Billard* and did good business. The other German left Santa Fee soon after our return from the gold mines, and went with a *Compagnie* of Americans back to the United States. I myself made some money on this, but in the revolution that broke out here in Santa Fee in August of the year 1837 I lost about $300, which I had in part lent and in part sold on credit to the most prominent man in the city, the most important official in Santa Fee. The revolution was bloody! The people, upset by long repression and bad government, rose up as a mass and marched against Santa Fee! The Governor marched against them; lost the battle; escaped with the other important men of the town; was captured, and killed in an atrocious and bloody manner! The Governor, Don Alvino Perez, was killed and his head cut off of his body; Don Santiago Abreow, his tongue was cut out; he was one of the most powerful and most hated; his two brothers, Don Jesus Maria Alarid, the Secretary to the Governor and several others more were killed. They

carried the mutilated corpses right past my door to the churchyard![18] Things quieted down after a few weeks; I then went with an American to Chihuahua, an important town perhaps 12 to 1,400 miles south of here; my expectations were not fulfilled in Chihuahua; I therefore went back after 5 to 6 months to Santa Fee, since an American, who had gone back to the United States by sea, had left me his entire and not insignificant business in Santa Fee. I am now living from these enterprises just mentioned, and earn not insignificantly. How long I will stay in these circumstances or in this country is somewhat uncertain; I intend to be here one more year; and after that is over to return to the United States by way of Mexico, the capital of this country, by way of Old Mexico, Vera Cruz, and Neu Orleans. Then, my dearest mother, my beloved brothers and sisters, then, when my wish comes true; then I will hurry back to your midst! If I could only keep up pace with my longing for you, oh! nothing would keep me back, I would hurry without stopping back to you! But it is not possible! [5 ll.: correspondence] I can only send a letter from here once a year with the *Comp.* returning to the United States. [16 ll.: correspondence; greetings]—We shall meet again!! farewell!
Your true son forever and ever,
Your true brother forever Carl Blümner
[2 ll.: correspondence]

August Blümner
        [fragment on the last page of Carl's letter of April 3, 1838]
2) If I had said what I just said aloud in Germany, they would have shut me up in no time—I know that; for over there, alas, common sense and free speech lie in shackles. But enough of this, it is not exactly your favorite subject. Instead I invite you to come over here, should you want to obtain a clear notion of genuine public life, freedom of the people and sense of being a nation, you'll agree that I am right. I have never regretted that I came here, and never! never! again shall I bow my head under the yoke of despotism and folly. Come on over, steamships now sail reg-

---

[18]In a passage in his letter of March 18, 1841, not included here, he repeats the story and adds: "We, the foreigners here, were also prepared during this time for a heated battle, since we had been informed by spies that the revolutionaries would plunder all the shops and houses of foreigners when they entered Santa Fe. At that time there were about 200 foreigners here, mostly Americans; since the revolution broke out just at the time that the caravan from Missoury arrived here. The shops of the Americans here are all in a row in the street at the market place; here we all gathered together, waiting for an attack. We had at least 5 to 600 rifles loaded and were prepared for a heated battle. Horses and mules were saddled and standing in the courts and stalls, so that if we were outnumbered, we could retreat if necessary. But everything went quietly."

ularly from New York and Baltimore to London and Liverpol, and you can get there from Hamburg every week. When can I come to see you? only the gods know and oh! my longing to have you in my arms, my loved ones, knows no bounds.—It's all the fault of von Martels, all this trouble, lost time, lost money. I must renew my efforts to improve the lot of my family and myself. I had saved enough to pay the costs of the crossing, without my family having to suffer any want, but now that is all gone to blazes. Ferdinand Osterly[19] presses me more and more urgently, he himself has debts to pay off. He wrote me a long and very friendly and warm and truly brotherly letter. If you, my dears, could help me in this matter, I would be eternally grateful to you. If Martels runs me to the ground, I'll sing the new song about the boozing scissors-grinder—and start all over again; if I then *muve* a few hundred miles farther away from you; that doesn't matter in the least. And God will help; he who does not forsake Him, will not be forsaken by Him, and he who helps himself, will be helped by Him. [10 ll.: considers whether he should turn to a friend of the family] —The court case about the inheritance is still not settled. Ferdinand is doing his utmost but the wheels of justice are just as slow in Hanover as they are in Prussia. F. O. wrote me further: as soon as the money is paid out to him, he wants to make it over to you, dear mother and Bismark, unless I give other instructions. I will write to him that he should send it to you to pay off my debt to mother and Bismark, or whoever advances me now the amount that I owe F. O. I am sending a money order made out to you, dear mother, from here to F. O. He, for his part, will send you a receipt after receiving the money. It is bitter and painful for me to burden you somewhat with this, but F. O. reassures me in that the payment of the inheritance is certain, but it may take a long time.—

August 7th. I no longer know what interrupted me. — Now the end of my litany! — The Martels!!!

Carl Blümner

Santa Fé, March 18th, 1841

My dear Hannchen, my dear beloved sister,

My hand pauses involuntarily as I am writing the date above! 1841! I ask myself "Is it possible that 10 years have already slipped by since I said my last farewell to my beloved sister?!" [15 ll.: reflections on hopes, expectations, and life; longing for home] But, my sister, whether my life

[19]The brother of August's first wife Sophia (died in 1833 [hereafter designated by d.]).

is short or long, I will see you again! The dark ruler of our fates will not refuse to grant this wish, when he sees how heartfelt and sincere it is!—

It has now been 5 years that I have had no word from any one of you! Everything that I have heard about you during this time was in August's letters. Whether a single one of my letters from here ever reached you, I still don't know. And these letters from August I can only receive once a year, because of the lay of the land, namely with the caravan from Missoury which arrives here in the summer. With the same caravan, we sometimes receive newspapers from the United States; and then with what emotion I read that this or that steamship has gone from England to Neu York in the unbelievably short time of 12 to 14 days. In my mind I see myself transported to Neu York! I go on *bord* the mighty ship! Fly across the enormous ocean in 8 to 10 days! Land in Liverpool! In 2 or 3 days I'm in Hamburg! From there—But halt! I am traveling too fast! You laugh at me, dear Hannchen! You laugh at my somewhat overly "swift fantasy"!!—

Here in this country, I have been in so many different positions, my dear sister! In 5 years, since I left August and Missoury and have been staying here, in these 5 years I have been through a lot and I have been in various situations and positions. I've had good luck and bad luck! Seen good times and bad times! Have been rich and poor; poor and rich! [10 ll.: his numerous activities] I am at present the manager of one of the American trading companies here. I have no lack of positions of this kind, and I have never had a lack of them, since I became well known here and mastered the English and Spanish languages. Neu Mexico, where I am staying, is a province of the *Republik* of Mexico; it is very mountainous, on all sides, in all directions it is surrounded and crossed by ranges of higher or lower mountains; in the valleys, formed by the latter, which are usually very large and extensive, with larger or smaller rivers flowing through them, the settlements of the Mexicans are found. The land is rich in gold and silver to the highest degree, above all in gold. One can really say that in almost every mountain more or less gold or silver can be found! [107 ll.: largely a repetition of the description of occupation and revolution as in April 3, 1838; agriculture, mineral resources, climate of Mexico; appearance of population, their passion for gambling and dancing; their love of cockfights and bullfights] The entire Mexican nation is strictly Catholic; no other religion may be practiced within the borders of the *Republik*. When a foreigner, a non-Catholic, wants to marry a Mexican girl, he must follow the laws of the Church here and be baptized. If such a poor devil dies, a nonmember of the "only true church," a *"heretik"*—here, if he hasn't been baptized before his death, he is denied the cemetery or any kind of "consecrated ground" and he is buried far away, without any, without the least religious *Ceremonie!* Here, in Santa F. for example our last resting place is on a high hill, far away from the church and churchyard! Oh! Mankind! As if it made the slightest difference, <u>where</u> the housing remains after the "spirit" has escaped from the mysterious machine! — When! — When will "papist rule" stop trying to keep the people in spiritual ignorance and darkness?! [20 ll.: Indian attacks, largely repetitions]—You ask, dear sister, why I have lived so long in this country?! Circumstances and situations; business deals and wishing and hoping to earn next year <u>that</u> which was lost in the year before; or perhaps even more. All this, dear sister, has kept me here from one month to the next, from one year to the next. But—I think this should be the last one! [6 ll.: reflections on life] Oh! My dear sister! How I still feel now, how deeply and strongly I have loved you and still love you! It seems as if fate has kept me from enjoying the pleasures of all those more tender feelings and happier states of this life! If this should be the case, if I should be destined to wander through this life, alone, with no companion, to the end of same, be it sooner or later,—Oh, then I will unite all the love and devotion of a brother, all the emotions which lie slumbering deeply, in eternal love of my sister! Then I will not have to share with anyone! All the feelings in this self-sacrificing and devoted breast are then for her! — How quickly, how unbelievably quickly, my dear Hannchen, these years have passed for me! How much may have changed in your circle! [29 ll.: correspondence, greetings] I am sending this letter to August, because it is safer and quicker. — Farewell, my beloved Hannchen, farewell! Farewell, dear Fritz! Farewell! My dear beloved / mother, Farewell! Your eternally devoted brother / Carl Blümner.

August Blümner

[attached to *C. Blümner*'s of March 18, 1841, but written on June 7, 1841] [6 ll.: received Carl's letter on June 5, 1841] This is the most extensive letter that Carl has written in at least 5 years. I doubt that you received his first letters, which he refers to in this one, they must travel a vast distance, thousands of miles, and there a letter is exposed to more hard luck than even a man is. When Carl sent off his letter, he couldn't have received my last letter, but now he certainly has it in his hands, I wrote him <u>a lot</u> about you. I am expecting him for certain this fall, you can imagine how much I am looking forward to it. Whether he will become a farmer again, he doesn't even know himself, I myself think he's too spoiled for that, anyhow the situation here is such that you're one thing today and something else the next, today a farmer, tomorrow a merchant, today a *Doctor,* tomorrow a lawyer, today a wine and beer saloonkeeper, tomorrow a preacher, etc. I hope though that Carl, whatever he ends up doing, will keep on living with me.

[19 ll.: correspondence] Dear sister, the calculation you made for me of the money we received from our dear mother is completely in order, not for the world would I want our mother to suffer privation because of me, or even to be in tight circumstances in her old age. With the next post I will write to F. Osterley, I think he will listen to reason and wait, if he doesn't want to wait, he'll just have to! At least he cannot force mother, and to take me to court here would be too much trouble, even though he could. If he writes to you again, write him briefly that he should turn to me if he doesn't want to wait. The amount that I am obligated to pay him is—as it stands in my IOU to mother [from] 1838: 762 talers *p.C.* [Prussian courant]. If I don't get more than 262 talers from my Sophie's inheritance, then that can be taken from the 762 talers, leaving me only 500 talers in debt to F. O., for this I will pay him 4 and *not* 10 *pr.* Ct. interest. So don't worry, and refer him to me, I don't know how he comes up with his figures: or else he is figuring: interest on compound interest! — It doesn't work like that, just tell him to write to me and he'll see that I also learned some arithmetic. From a prominent family from Göttingen, who settled in St. Louis two years ago and who were acquainted with the old great aunt of Sophie's who left 1,000 talers to her, I heard that the entire estate was large enough to pay out all the old woman's bequests in full. Now, even if I could I wouldn't pay F. O. before he sends me the court certificates; if he sends them to you, go over them with a lawyer to make sure they are in order. F. O. is a lawyer himself and very smart and cunning.[20] Now von Martels: it is *not* the court costs that I am demanding from county magistrate v. M., no, it is the interest on the capital sum of 1,200 dollars, which was at 15 *pr. Ct.* from 1834 to 1839 and now amounts to over 900 dollars, which I had to pay out of my own pocket, [and] for the most part have paid off. That is what has set me back so much. The old v. Martels, the father, is also in my debt like his two sons here, he still has 1,300 talers in Hanoverian Cr. in the hands of county magistrate v. Martels, so I should think I have every right to demand it, and if the fellow doesn't pay, he's as much of a scoundrel as his brothers here, then I'd do what I've threatened. I don't care about the Most Honorable Sir County Magistrate v. Martels, if he

[20]Heinrich Ludwig Ferdinand Oesterley (1802–1858), the brother of Blümner's first wife, Sophia, was "assistant professor" of law from 1826 to 1848, became city counsel in 1831, and was mayor of Göttingen from 1853 to 1858 (Frensdorff [1887a], 512; Selle [1930]).

pays I will be much obliged and that's that! His father here owed me the money just as much as his two brothers, his brothers ran away in secret, the old man is dead, but he has 1,300 talers in Germany, in the County Magistrate's hands! And he isn't bound to pay his father's debts with his father's money? — I bet the lawyer Lochius would be able to contrive a demand that would stand up in court even if it were based on an even shakier argument. Charles v Martels was shot by Indians on October 8th last year in Texas, as Gustaw v. M. wrote me last week. He even had the gall to write to me from Texas. He and his brother had bought 800 horses and mules for the Texas *Guverment,* which is presently fighting another war with Mexico. While they were driving the animals, they were attacked by Indians, his brother Carl was killed and the 800 horses and mules were stolen from them. I am however strongly inclined to regard this as sheer fantasy.[21]

I am so pleased that your dear Marie is better, may the all-merciful Father keep your dear children safe, as well as mine. Yes, Hannchen, it is also my greatest happiness when my lively children jump and dance around me. You should see my little iron-jaw, Charles, he's only 14 months old now, a strong, robust boy who can already knock Johanna and Leana down to the ground. I assure you Mathilde is right proud of the boy. Your words and those of mother, when I read them to Mathilde, they brought her to tears! She can't write herself, that is in German. [6 ll.: it wouldn't be the same in English] Mathilde understands almost everything, I mean in German, she can also speak fairly well, but she doesn't dare to write it; my children though should learn it. — But what weighs so heavily on your heart, dear sister, I have noticed sad and melancholy remarks in several of your letters. [6 ll.: declares his affection] I have thought up great plans for my Charles: when he's grown up and is ready for university studies I want to bring him to brother Wilhelm in Berlin; isn't that thinking ahead? One really ought not to make such long-range plans; I certainly thought I would be with you last Christmas. Then Mathilde was laid up sick for a long long time and my journey is foiled again. It's possible to find the time for such a journey, the distance is nothing anymore, since steamboats and railways run from here, 3 miles

[21]Most of the details of the financial entanglements of the von Martels family can no longer be unraveled. According to a mortgage deed of 1838, August signed bond for Charles von Martels for the sum of $1,500 and was held accountable for it. The head of the family, Baron Ludwig von Martels, had sold his estate to the Imperial Knight Baron von Landsberg Velen for 75,000 talers. Of that sum, 10,000 was paid immediately, the rest in three-year payments of 5,000 talers. The two sons Charles and Gustav each received 1,000 or 1,500 shortly after their emigration, as an advance on their share of the estate, the rest of which was paid in yearly installments of 100 talers (Warren County, Mo., Deed Records, Book B, 274; Ns. StA OS, Rep. 950 Pap., Nr. 121, 142, 145). Von Martel's violent death is corroborated by Münch (1870), 202.

from my house to just as close to yours;—but the confounded money!!! I would really like to go for a year or two to the Mexican gold mines that brother Charles writes about, to get myself a few mule-loads of gold. Just now my two girls came bouncing up and both wanted to write to their Grandmother and Aunt and to Marie and Eliese, and they don't know any letters; I told them they should learn to write first, now they can't do anything but a scrawl that looks like owl or crow's-feet, Johanna said though that she knew quite well what she wanted to write and even if it looked like nothing but *Türky*-feet— / *türky* is what wild *Puter* are called here / you'd still sure be able to understand it! When I asked her why she thought so, she answered: why? because I love them all so much, and they love me too!—

I hope to have a good harvest this year; although I had a lot of trouble getting the corn to come up, because the moles in the ground ate up all the grains of seed. My wheat is growing very well, as is my timothy grass and clover. Last year I tried barley for the first time, I sowed 14 *Buschel* and harvested 176. [14 ll.: experiments with Chinese oats] —Everyone here complains about hard times and it is true that times here are now miserably poor, as for example, I usually sell one hundred pounds of smoked pork for 7-8–9 and 10 dollars now I've been offered 3¼ dollars. [4 ll.: prices] And all farm products are down so much, but at the same time the wages for skilled labor and day labor are as high as before, as are the prices of all factory and colonial goods. If things stay like this I'll become a preacher or a doctor or both at the same time. Skilled trades are always the best here.

My occupations, of which I already had enough on my farm, have been increased on the other hand by an *Administration* that was given me by the *County Court* last month. Last year one of my neighbors named Wenz was murdered in a shocking manner in his own house. The murderers still haven't been found. The *Court* appointed me guardian of the only son of the murder victim, and administrator of the estate. The boy has a very good farm and 1200 dollars in cash.[22] A lawsuit is pending against his father; which as the guardian I am required to go through with. *Nolens volens.*

The sun is sinking and I still have to bring my letter to my friend Rasmuss who lives 9 miles from me, I fear I will not get to finishing my letter to Voch, but I will as soon as possible; give him my warmest regards! I can't tell you how much I have come to like and respect the

---

[22]According to MC 1840, Blümner's household included a man between the ages of twenty and thirty, who was engaged in farming, as well as two women between the ages of fifteen and twenty. It is possible that one or more of the victim's children lived there with him.

man, and God knows, if all the nobility was made up of such genuinely noble men like Voch, I'd like to be one myself. He told me once that I had an awful vicious tongue when it came to preachers, princes and nobles: I admitted it for the first two but not for the last. I respect a nobleman when he really is what he is supposed to be, when he walks this world and acts with true nobility of soul or spirit. I believe I know Voch better than you and respect him very highly and everywhere he became known during his brief stay here, with Germans and Americans, he won the love and respect of everyone, and even each and everyone. [12 ll.: further details] —Give everyone my warmest regards! [18 ll.: family; greetings] Hanchen you should make an alphabetical list of the greetings so you don't forget any! Dear sweet mother, sister and brothers farewell! You will hear from us again soon! Yours forever / A B

Independence, Jackson County. Missouri.

April 23rd, 1849

Have you not, my dearly, so warmly, so deeply loved souls, received even one of my nine letters? Is there no one left alive who remembers the loving ones here—so far away? For 3 years we have heard nothing from you. Oh mother mother! what are you doing? And you, sister and you my brothers? With a bleeding heart I have left my wife and children behind, am now over 300 miles away from them, and I still have 800 ahead of me; I would cross the savannahs and prairies with a lighter heart if I had news from you, but like this! — I have been here for 6 days and will move on next week, with the first caravan to Santa Fé. A Mexican caravan from there arrived here the day before yesterday and brought me a letter from Brother Charles, he is well off and is living happily with his Feliciana. If you haven't received any of my letters, then you don't know that he is married to a Mexican girl, named Feliciana Alaryda Cluintana; an acquaintance of mine, and a friend of Brother Charles, Doctor Waldow, who was in Santa Fé for a long time and now lives here in Independence, told me: the Cluintanas are one of the best and most highly respected families in New Mexico, and Feliciana is the *hübschste / pretty /* and most beautiful girl he had ever seen, with a sharp mind, and he is convinced that they will live happily together. And our good brother certainly deserves this good fortune. How highly he is regarded there and how sound his unshakable honesty and sincerity is can be proven by the following: during the entire war he was in Neu Mexico, and both the German and the American *Voluntears,* who had saved something on the campaigns, gave it to Charles to keep for them, and he was elected Treasurer and head Customs Officer by our *Gouverment,* and he still has these posts today. May God grant that these lines reach you, and I call on you by all that is sacred to you and me—"Answer!"—

I am sure you have read in the public papers about the immense gold mines that have been discovered in California in the last 1½ years, namely on the Sacramento River and the small tributaries, where gold sand stretches along the banks—and many miles into the interior, and can be washed clean easily and without much work. Fact is: that people in one day have washed from 30 to 300 dollars and even 500 dollars of gold sand. Now there's a genuine mass migration from the United States to there. Here there are no rooms available, all the boardinghouses are full, more than 10,000 people are lying around the town in tents with their wagons, mules, horses and oxen. The whole thing looks like a big army camp, and not a minute goes by when you don't hear rifle and pistol shots. The grass on the prairies is still too short for traveling. It is as lively here now as in the big cities on the coast. Independence has perhaps between 2 and 300 houses, 3 miles from the Missouri River, on the edge of the boundless savannahs and prairies, thousands of miles away from the Atlantic Ocean, and thousands away from the Pacific Ocean; —and yet here you hear people speaking English, Spanish, German, French, Polish, Italian and many different Indian languages. All are going to the far west over the Cordilleras Mountains, to dig for gold. I have met people here who are 60 to 65 years old. Many have their families with them; some will never see their old homes again; several have died here of cholera, two have been shot, one by accident, the other in a duel. There are also double-dealers among the emigrants and pickpockets and the like rascals, almost no one walks around without a pistol and a dagger.

April 28th [7 ll.: impressions of the prairies; departure of the caravan delayed] Charles writes he wants to return with me together with his wife in the fall, but will go back to Santa Fé next spring. What I will do is still uncertain. [5 ll.: wishes a rapid reply]
Address your next letter:
Mr. Charles Blümner
Treasurer of the Territory
of New Mexico Santa Fé.
Care of Mr. S. Kaufmann, Independence
Jackson County. Miss. [Mo.] U.S. of North America.

Carl Blümner
                    Santa Fé, New Mexico, October 31, 1852.
My dearest, my eternally beloved mother,
    [14 ll.: professes his undying filial love]

Your reproach, my dear mother, is justified; years have passed without my writing to you; I don't want to try to excuse myself, only to the extent that I knew for certain that August had sent you all my news, which I sent to him for you, until he left for California. From that point on, since August's departure for California, why haven't I written since then, you ask, my dearest mother?! Yes, mother, for this time I have an excuse! I wish to God I didn't have one! — I have received all of your letters, that is, I have received 3 letters since August left for California; the first one from July 1849, the second one from March 1850 and the third and last one from September 1850. All were letters of sorrow! One blow after another! I knew nothing of the death of our beloved sister! Nothing of the death of our brother Wilhelm! Oh, mother, how can I describe my grief as I received your first letter which reported the death of Hannchen! And right afterwards Wilhelm! And then— Oh my dear mother, I too must bear sad tidings; my letter too must bear sad news! Mother! Mother! Brother August is no more! He followed soon after sister Hannchen and brother Wilhelm, in the month of July, 1850.

[7 ll.: couldn't and can't write because of his grief] I am so alone here, in this part of the world, since Brother August has left me. Hope and wait! We shall meet again in the Hereafter!— —

August came here, to Santa Fé, in the spring of 1849; but he only stayed with me for a few months, and went from here to California, thinking and hoping to make a fortune more quickly there. He arrived safely in California; went to the gold mines and wrote his last letter to me from the gold mines in Mariposa, in California, in the winter of 1849. Then I didn't hear anything from him for a long time, until I finally received a letter the following year from his brother-in-law, who informed me that he had died in August 1850 in the gold mines on the Yuba River, in California. He fell ill with abdominal ailments, and he passed away, calm and composed, after about a month. A German, who worked with him, wrote that he was buried decently. Peace be to his ashes in a foreign land, in an unknown place! His spirit will hover about us in love! — His wife and children are well, according to the last news from Missouri, but I haven't had a letter from them in some months. His brother-in-law is a wealthy and generous man; with no family, and he is sure to take on the children like a father.[23] And for me it will be a sacred duty to care lovingly for the children of my brother. August left nothing behind; no one found out if he had anything in California, nor will it ever be known. I myself helped him out as much as I could; I gave him, at

[23]His brother-in-law, the doctor Elijah McLean, had real estate valued at $24,000 and was in fact well-to-do. He was not, however, without a family of his own; he had a wife and a six-year-old daughter. The former died in 1855, the latter before 1860.

various times up to his departure for California, about 12 to 1300 dollars, that is about 1,500 to 1,600 Prussian talers.[24] I long to see his wife and children, but I don't know when my affairs will permit me to go to Missouri.

I myself, my dear mother, have almost always been well, in this country, since 1836; the climate here is one of the nicest, at least the healthiest, on earth. You know from August's letter that I've been married for about 4 years; my wife is a Mexican, the youngest daughter of a good but poor family; she is named Felisiana Quintana y Alarid. She is short on money, but she has a good heart and a noble character. She is pretty and about 26 years old.[25] She presented me with a daughter as first-born child, whom we baptized Carlota, (Charlotte). The little one grew to be a pretty, intelligent child until she was just 1 year old; then— she died! Oh, mother, I can never and will never forget my little Charlotte! She was my soul! My second is a boy; named Carlos, (Karl or Charles) and is about 15 months old; a beautiful, lively and intelligent boy; may God preserve him for me. My business here has almost always been as a merchant; about a year ago I gave up my trading company and am mostly employed in the service of the government. Since the United States of North America took possession of this country, as a result of the war, as you all should know, since the year 1846, I have always had one or the other government post; *Treasurer (Schatzmeister), Collector (Erster Steuereinnehmer), Vice Secretair* (the second post next to the *Gouverneur*), which I took over during the absence of the *Secretair*. The last two posts I only had for a certain time; the first one though, *Treasurer,* I have had since 1846 and I still have; my yearly salary is 500 dollars, about 700 Prussian talers. I have had both good and bad luck, my dear mother, as is usually the case, especially as a merchant; I have lost about 7,000 to 8,000 talers here since my arrival in this country.

---

[24]In 1838 August had to take out a loan of about $1,400 to cover the bond for $1,500 which he had signed for Charles von Martels. To do this, he had to take out a mortgage on his entire property as well as livestock, farm machinery, and household effects, with 10 percent annual interest. By 1843 he had paid off the mortgage, but he then took out another mortgage (without livestock and household effects). This served as the security for a bond of $6,000 which he had to sign on behalf of a German neighbor in order to serve as estate administrator. In 1844 he had to take out another mortgage on the farm to cover three IOUs totaling $642 which he had signed in the previous year. In April 1847 he took out a third mortgage on the farm. The three obligations from 1843, 1844, and 1847 were taken care of in 1848 when he sold his three-hundred-acre farm to a man named Henry Brus for $1,350 (Warren County, Mo., Deed Records, Book B, 274; Book D, 116, 289; Book E, 47, 185, 190).

[25]Blümner reduces their age difference somewhat. Less than two years earlier, in December 1850, he reported in the census that his wife was twenty, and in June 1860 he recorded her as 29. This corresponds more or less with the statement of her son, who thought he remembered that his mother died in January 1886 at the age of fifty-eight. Accordingly she must have been only eighteen and Carl over forty when they married in 1848.

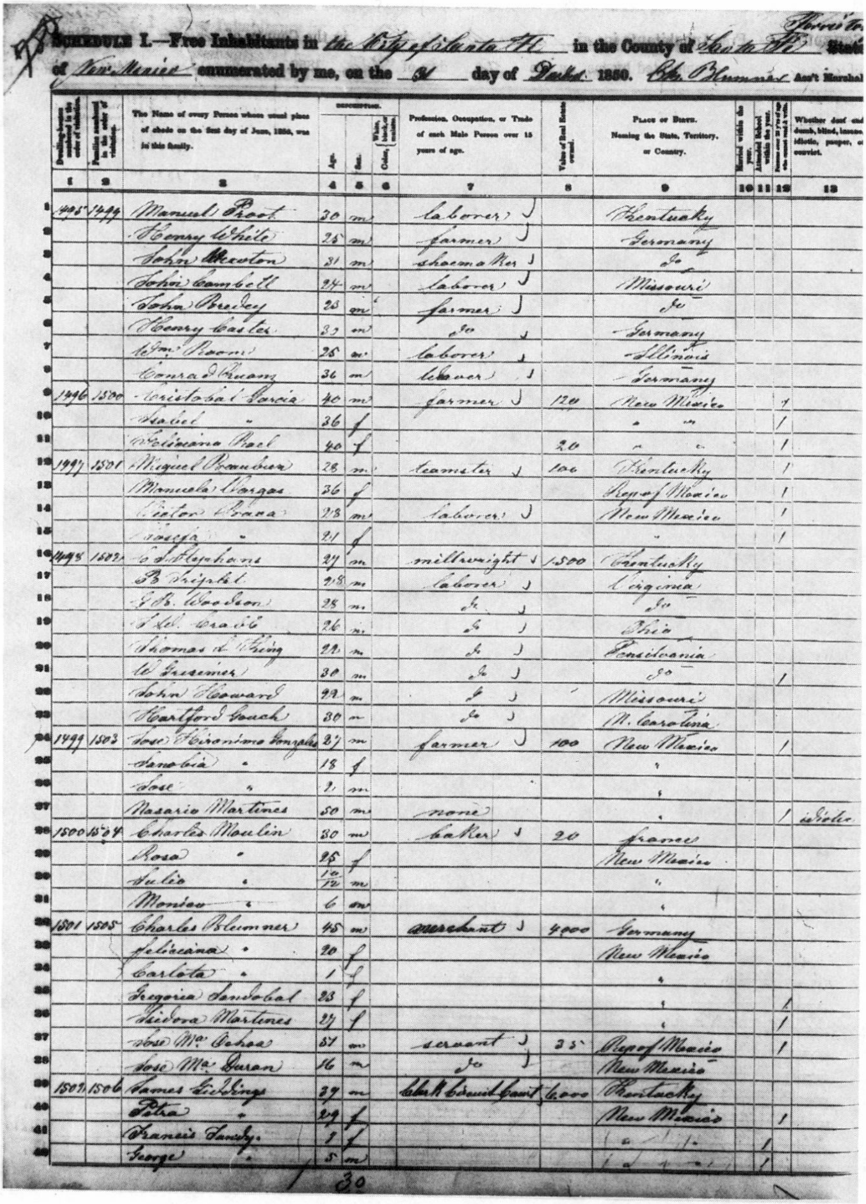

SCHEDULE I.—Free Inhabitants in *the City of Santa Fé* in the County of *Santa Fé* State of *New Mexico* enumerated by me, on the *21* day of *October* 1850. *Chs. Blumner* Ass't Marshal

Dwelling-houses numbered in the order of visitation	Families numbered in the order of visitation	The Name of every Person whose usual place of abode on the first day of June, 1850, was in this family.	Age	Sex	Color	Profession, Occupation, or Trade of each Male Person over 15 years of age.	Value of Real Estate owned	Place of Birth, Naming the State, Territory, or Country.	Married within the year	Attended School within the year	Persons over 20 years of age who cannot read and write	Whether deaf and dumb, blind, insane, idiotic, pauper, or convict
1495	1499	Manuel Prost	30	m		laborer		Kentucky				
		Henry White	25	m		farmer		Germany				
		John Newton	31	m		shoemaker		do				
		John Campbell	24	m		laborer		Missouri				
		John Bradley	23	m		farmer		do				
		Henry Castor	32	m		do		Germany				
		Wm Room	25	m		laborer		Illinois				
		Conrad Ruan	36	m		laborer		Germany				
1496	1500	Cristobal Garcia	40	m		farmer	120	New Mexico		1		
		Isabel	36	f				do		1		
		Feliciana Real	40	f			20	do		1		
1497	1501	Miguel Brambica	28	m		teamster	100	Kentucky		1		
		Manuela Vargas	36	f				Rep of Mexico		1		
		Victor Graca	23	m		laborer		New Mexico		1		
		Josefa	21	f						1		
1498	1502	O S Stephens	27	m		millwright	1500	Kentucky				
		P B Prigtel	28	m		laborer		Virginia				
		J B Woodson	25	m		do		do				
		J H Davis	26	m		do		Ohio				
		Thomas L King	24	m		do		Pennsylvania				
		W Grasmer	30	m		do		do		1		
		John Howard	43	m		do		Missouri				
		Hartford Leach	30	m		do		N. Carolina				
1499	1503	Jose Hieronimo Gonzales	27	m		farmer	100	New Mexico		1		
		Senobia	18	f				do				
		Jose	2	m				do				
		Nasario Martinez	50	m		none		do		1		idiotic
1500	1504	Charles Moulin	30	m		baker	20	France				
		Rosa	25	f				New Mexico				
		Julia	10/12	m				do				
		Moran	6	m				do				
1501	1505	Charles Blumner	45	m		merchant	4000	Germany				
		Feliciana	20	f				New Mexico				
		Carlota	1	f				do				
		Gregoria Sandobal	23	f				do		1		
		Teodora Martinez	27	f				do		1		
		Jose Ma Ochoa	57	m		servant	35	Rep of Mexico				
		Jose Ma Duran	16	m		do		New Mexico				
1502	1506	James Giddings	37	m		Clerk Board Comr	6000	Kentucky				
		Petra	24	f				New Mexico		1		
		Francis Tandy	1	f				do		1		
		George	5	m				do		1		

30

Figure 6. 1850 Census entry for Charles Blumner (#1505) in his own hand as census taker. *Source:* U.S. NatA.

[12 ll.: wishes for news; correspondence] —Tell Rudolph he should write me a detailed letter about the political situation in Prussia and in Germany in general; you can well imagine that I would like to know how things are in Germany, after the unrest and revolutions there. Rudolph should also send news of the situation in the rest of Europe; his reports as an eyewitness are certainly more accurate than those in the newspapers here. [16 ll.: wishes for letters; greetings] Feliciana sends you, dear mother, her filial love and devotion, and all of you a dear and sisterly kiss, and kneeling I lay my little Charles in your arms, dear mother, that you may give him your blessing!
Farewell! / Forever / Your true son
and your true brother and uncle. / [6 ll.: address]

Santa Fé, New Mexico, / February 1, 1854
My beloved mother,
    [31 ll.: correspondence; reflections on life; would like to visit relatives in Germany, which is impossible because of his official position; family is well] I haven't had a letter from August's family for quite a while; but according to the last letter they were all fine. [15 ll.: family in Germany] Oh, my dearest mother, I am often, often in your midst! I see you often in my mind's eye, and I shed many a tear, and send my prayers to the Lord for your well-being, for the well-being of all of my loved ones there.
    I often feel so alone here, when I give myself over too much to memories, and especially since brother August is no more, and I must seek an antidote in the circle of my family, and distraction in serious preoccupation and active work in my post.
    [4 ll.: cannot write to all the relatives individually] I received from brother Wilhelm, I don't know how long ago, the first, and—the last letter!
    I often fear, my dear mother, from what is in the European newspapers, that it is quite possible that a general European war could break out, and that, in that case, the evening of your life could be troubled, and your quiet family circle disturbed. May Heaven grant that the threatening clouds pass over you quietly; but should it be written in the book of fate that the storm that has been pent up so long should break, that the peoples of Europe should throw off the old, decayed fetters, which in our times have long been unfitting and degrading, and which can only be held together with great effort by the bayonets of the princes, if it should come, in short, in Germany, in Europe, to a war of the people, to a war of mankind, as I would call it, against the absolute power of a few persons,

called princes, who <u>against</u> the will of the people and only through fear, violence, bayonet, swing the scepter of despotism over the trembling peoples, if it should come <u>to this</u>, Oh! Then may Heaven grant that rapid destruction fall on these crowned heads, so that only the <u>guilty</u> must suffer, and the people, mankind, may safely, rapidly, and victoriously emerge from this holy battle!
[11 ll.: greetings, closing; signature]

Santa Fé, New Mexico, / May 15, 1857
My dear and most beloved mother,
[5 ll.: excuses] The main reason for my so lengthy silence is my present duty as *Marshal* of the United States in New Mexico. My duties are so extensive that I must travel 8 to 9 months a year and am only home for 3 months.[26]

With the greatest joy I have seen in brother Bismark's letter that you are alive and well, my good mother, and we, my wife and my little son and I ask the Lord to keep you for us for many years to come.

I cannot tell when I can come to see you; as long as I keep my present post it is not possible. My position here as *Marshal* carries great responsibility; I had to put up 20 thousand dollars security for the honest and exact administration and payment of the public funds of which I am in charge. Every year I receive about 15 to 20 thousand dollars from the government in Washington which I then pay out again here annually, for the various expenses of the various courts in New Mexico.
[35 ll: August's family are doing well; package from Germany was lost; family, acquaintances, greetings, signature]

Santa Fé, New Mexico, / December 28, 1858
My most beloved mother,
[20 ll.: correspondence; wishes; well-being; family] I only have one child now, my dear mother; Charles is now a little over 6 years old; a

---

[26]In areas such as the Territory of New Mexico, the U.S. marshal held the highest police power; in fact, however, his duties were primarily administrative. The actual police functions were normally carried out by deputy marshals, who were usually county sheriffs at the same time. U.S. marshals were responsible for the administration of the federal courts in the territory, including the summoning and payment of the jurors. The court was not located in one particular place; judges and officials rode the circuit of all the important towns of the future states of New Mexico and Arizona. Within a period of eight weeks in the spring of 1854 Blümner covered one thousand miles on horseback in carrying out his court duties; he repeated the same circuit in the fall. Marshals played an important role as intermediaries between the Spanish and American population. Appointment to such a post indicates good connections to the leading circles (Ball [1978], 23–32).

good, innocent, intelligent child; with a good heart and an open mind. He's been going to school here for about one year, where he is learning English and Spanish; in time I will teach him German myself. At the first opportunity, when a good painter is here, I will send you portraits of all three of us.

Since my last letter to you, a change in my occupation has occurred. I have recently *resignirt* [resigned] from my post as *Marshal* of the United States; for a number of reasons; because, first of all, I was almost always on the road, and I had to leave my family behind in Santa Fé, and, secondly, because my salary was too insignificant in comparison to such duties, extensive and arduous. After I gave up this *Marshals* business, the *Gouverneur* of New Mexico appointed me *Treasurer* of New Mexico, the post I now hold. My salary is 500 dollars a year, somewhat more than 600 Prussian talers. A *Treasurer* is what we know in Germany as a *Schatzmeister*. I receive all the taxes in the country, and pay the money out again, following court orders from the *Gouvernement*.

[7 ll.: has started doing business on the side] —In my last letter I wrote you about brother August's family; according to the latest news they are all well; mother, daughters and sons. The eldest daughter, Judith, is married, as I wrote earlier, to a Mr. Ogletree, a *farmer (Landmann)* in Missouri; the youngest daughter, Elisabeth, lives with her mother, as well as the youngest son, Rudolph; the eldest son, Charles, is a *farmer.* [9 ll.: inquiries; greetings]
Carl Blümner.
Brother Bismark, your true brother. Marie and Elise, your true uncle Carl.
[2 ll.: greetings, address]

Santa Fé, New Mexico, August 1, 1860
My most beloved mother,
[10 ll.: correspondence; possible loss of letters because of Indian attacks] With deep sorrow, my dearest mother, I read the part of your letter where you reported the great loss of Brother Bismark; and about Brother Rudolph as well. It hurts me deeply to think of my beloved family thrown from a state of happiness and contentment into one of want and grief! [6 ll.: consolation] I was very pleased to read in your letter that you want to leave the rest of your assets to my dear nieces Marie and Elise, and that you believe that I will not lay claim to it for myself. Believe me, my good mother, I never counted on expecting even the least amount, when such sad circumstances have afflicted your family. If it is in my power, I myself will do my utmost to improve the lot of poor Marie and

Elise. I have deep and sincere sympathy for brother Fritz; I believe, my
dear, good brother, that your intentions were the best and most noble;
you wanted to improve the lot of your dear children; you wanted to
make their future more pleasant and secure; you risked the game of
hazard! The die was cast! You lost![27] — What earthly goods you have lost
for your children, dear brother, you should replace with your fatherly
love; with true, fatherly wisdom and succor in the hour of need, tribula-
tion and distress! — Our life here, my dear Marie and my dear Elise, is
inconstant and subject to change, like everything in this world, on our
earthly journey through life. The great *philosophie* of life, my dear nieces,
is to regard our life here not as the ultimate purpose of our "being," but
rather as preparation, virtually a school, for the great unknown "Hereafter."

Have you not read the great French author, Alexander Dumas? He
writes in his wonderful book, *Monte Cristo,* "The entire *philosophie* of life
is contained in these three words: *"Wait and hope!"* (*Warte und hoffe!*) [9 ll.:
family]

I started up a merchant business about 1½ years ago here in Santa Fé;
and I pursued it 1½ years; the times, prices and all other business conditions became so poor that I sold the rest of my business and am satisfied
not to have won or lost anything. Now I have no particular business but
my post as *Treasurer* of New Mexico; and I am willing to wait until the
circumstances are better before I start any merchant business again. [8 ll.:
August's family, as before, greetings]

Write soon to your eternally devoted son / Carl Blümner.
[6 ll.: greetings]

August Blümner still appears with his wife and children in the 1850
census of Washington, Missouri, a small town on the Missouri River
across from Warren County, although he had already left for the West a
year before and was perhaps already dead. It is uncertain how much was
left over from the sale of his farm in 1848 after the debts were paid off;
at any rate he is not listed as owning any real estate. Carl's assumption
that August's widow would not suffer want, however, was correct. In
1860 her brother, with assets amounting to $90,000, was probably the
wealthiest of the twelve thousand county inhabitants. A mere 25 houses
away from her brother lived the propertyless Mathilda Blümner and her

[27]Fritz Bismark lost his estate by gambling and moved with his two daughters and his
mother-in-law, the widow Blümner, into an apartment in the neighboring town Hohenofen,
where the latter lived until her death in 1867.

youngest son in the house of her daughter Elizabeth, who had married a widowed clergyman some years earlier. The other two children were no longer to be found in the area. Perhaps they had already moved two hundred miles west to Kansas City, Missouri, where the family lived at the turn of the century. Interestingly, both of August's daughters married Americans, even though they grew up in a strong enclave of German immigrants.[28]

Carl Blümner's advancement is also recorded in the census records, indeed in his own hand, since in 1850 as well as 1860 he served as the official enumerator for Santa Fe. Both times he gave his occupation as merchant. During the course of the decade his real estate holdings had doubled in value, reaching $8,000. In 1860 moveable assets of $10,000 were also recorded. Ten years later, at the age of 64, Carl was perhaps retired; in any case his occupation is listed only as "former U.S. Treasurer." His real estate had risen to $12,000, although his total assets had declined somewhat. Not even ten houses away lived the former governor and the treasurer; in 1860 the governor also lived in Blümner's neighborhood.[29]

Blümner was one of the very few Germans who dared to go to such an exotic area. As late as 1850, after the American annexation, there were only 229 Germans in the entire Territory of New Mexico, which at that time extended all the way to the California border; ten years later, the number had only reached 569. Many of these had come with the American army, which in 1870 continued to employ more than one-third of the Germans working in New Mexico. Though Blümner was one of the first, he was by no means the only or even the richest German merchant in Santa Fe. But his position as treasurer of the Territory of New Mexico was remarkable. In 1870, 24 years after his appointment, there were 85 German merchants working in New Mexico but still no more than nine persons employed as government officials and employees.[30] Carl Blümner died in 1876 at the age of 73 and was buried by his Freemason brethren in their cemetery. Later his remains were transferred to a national cemetery, presumably in recognition of his services to the government.

Only one of Carl's children lived to adulthood: his son Carl. German relatives established contact with him in 1904. He replied in English with

[28]MC 1850: Franklin Co., Mo., #1638; 1860, (town of Washington): #572, #596. The households were numbered in the order they were registered, and it can be assumed that they were in the immediate neighborhood. See the letter of March 9, 1905, from Carl Blümner (Jr.) in Santa Fe to H. Blümner, in Berlin (BABS).
[29]MC 1850: Santa Fe, N.M., #1505; 1860: #329; 1870: #468.
[30]USC 1850.1, 118; USC 1860.1, 621; USC 1870.8, 749; see Jaehn (1986), 319–27.

Figure 7. Charles Blumner at age 68, ca. 1873.

the request not to write again in German, because he could not understand this language. His father had always spoken English or Spanish
with him. He also excused himself for his (genuinely) poor English, since
he usually spoke and wrote Spanish. He reported that he was about 54
years old, had married a Mexican girl in 1881, and that they had had
eleven children, only four of whom had survived childhood. He wrote
on the stationery of the insurance salesman Paul Wunschmann, a German, for whom he had worked for eighteen years. But he was apparently
not a white-collar employee. As he wrote himself: "I am not in good
circumstances. I will tell you the true, I am poor." The census of 1900 lists
him as a "laborer." It also neglects to mention—inadvertently or deliberately—that his father was a German.[31] Although he was born an American citizen, this Spanish-speaking Carl Blümner had become a de facto
member of an ethnic minority that experienced more discrimination than
his immigrant father ever had.

[31]Letters from Carl Blümner, Santa Fe, of October 30, 1904, November 26, 1904, December
10, 1904, March 9, 1905, June 12, 1905, September 16, 1905, February 15, 1906 (BABS); MC
1900: Santa Fe, N.M., e.d. 127, #695.

3

Christian Lenz

The 24-year-old Christian Lenz apparently emigrated to America in the first half of 1848 when the revolution in Germany still showed promise of success, and this fact alone indicates that he did not belong to the group of emigrants who were affected by the "dizzy spells of freedom" or "revolution fever."[1] His letters not only confirm this suspicion but also give the impression that economic or family pressures did not lead this conservative to turn his back on his homeland; instead, he left out of fear of political unrest.[2] Lenz thus seems to represent the (probably not so small) minority of German emigrants who, in the words of the American historian Mack Walker, "took radical action in order to conserve." These emigrants found America attractive not for reasons of freedom, equality, and progress; rather, they sought a chance to lead a life that was traditional, quiet, and orderly, and in Germany this seemed increasingly impossible.[3]

Christian Lenz came from a poor family; the son of a cowherd and the fifth of eight children was born in 1823 and presumably raised in Laubuseschbach, a village in Runkel Township, Nassau.[4] One of his letters

[1] *Über die Auswanderung* [On emigration] (1853), 9. See also Struck (1966), 81, and Struck (1978a), 101.
[2] See Struck's assessment (1978b), 1; on events in Nassau in 1848 see Spielmann (1899).
[3] Walker (1964), 69.
[4] Ev. KB Blessenbach. His siblings were Susanna Catharina (b. 1812), Johann Georg (b. 1814), Elisabetha Margaretha (b. 1815), Georg Wilhelm (b. 1818), Christiana (b. 1825), and Catherine Rosine (b. 1827). Around 1840 Laubuseschbach, between the Lahn and Weil rivers and far away from any large town, had a population of 792, most of whom were farmers and artisans. A copper and lead mine had closed in the 1820s (Demian [1823], 250–51; Vogel [1843], 790–91).

implies that he later lived with his elder brother Wilhelm, first in Gräveneck (Weilburg Township) and then in Freiendiez (Diez Township).[5] Wilhelm's wife only grudgingly tolerated his presence, however, and at her insistence, Christian finally had to find another place to live. His relationship to his brother does not seem to have suffered any permanent damage, since they continued to correspond for several decades, but the quarrels with his sister-in-law and what was probably a rather bleak existence as a boarder in a family of strangers must have made it easier for him to decide to leave.

The young man's occupation in the years before his emigration is unknown. We know that his brother was a miner and even became a foreman;[6] and it seems at first glance reasonable to assume that Christian worked in one of the small mines in the Lahn-Dill region. On the other hand, the mining industry in Nassau experienced rapid expansion in the period from 1830 to 1860, offering passable employment possibilities.[7] One would also expect that if Lenz had had any experience in mining, he would have sought employment in a related profession in the United States, rather than learning an entirely new trade. It is therefore much more likely that he had earned his living as a day laborer or as a farmhand and that his economic prospects were severely limited. He does not seem to have learned any trade, and there were hardly any other employment possibilities in Nassau, a predominantly agricultural region.[8]

Since Christian's first letter or letters from the United States have not been preserved, it is impossible to reconstruct the exact date of his departure from Germany or the stations of his journey.[9] Chance, or perhaps design, led him to southern Indiana (probably in the summer or fall of 1848), where he first found lodgings and employment with a wealthy countryman, Philipp Zollmann, born in Mensfelden (Limburg Township).[10] As we know from the first letters that have been handed

[5]Gräveneck was ca. six miles away from Laubuseschbach on the Lahn river; its population in 1840 was 322, and it had one lime kiln (Demian, 354; Vogel, 801). Freiendiez was ca. eighteen miles away from Laubuseschbach, near Limburg on the Aar River; its population in 1840 was 638, and it had two iron-ore mines (Demian, 199–200; Vogel, 761).

[6]As can be seen from the addresses on Lenz's letters.

[7]Jacobi (1913), 124–58; Lerner (1965), 32–33; Schüler (1980), 138–39.

[8]More than half of the ca. 400,000 inhabitants of Nassau in 1842 lived exclusively from agriculture, and another quarter lived partially from farming, though rather poorly. Mining and the artisan trades were the only other sources of employment worth mentioning (Lerner, 57; Schüler, 133–39).

[9]In MC 1900: Louisville, Kentucky, e.d. 24, #90, Lenz gave 1848 as the year of his emigration. According to the letter of August 19, he must have left in the summer of 1848 at the latest. There is no emigration petition in the pertinent files (Hs. HStA WI). In 1848 only 358 persons officially left the Duchy of Nassau to go to the United States (Struck [1966], 127).

[10]MC 1850: Harrison Co., Ind., Franklin Twp., #773, #778; see also the letter of August 19, 1849. In the emigration files, Hs. HStA WI (Nr. 232, 105), Johann Philipp Zollmann from Mensfelden is listed as having left Nassau in 1842 with the remarkable sum of 10,000 guilders.

down, within three months Lenz had learned the cooper's trade from one of Zollmann's sons, and met his future wife, 21-year-old Susanna Bley, stepsister of his "master."[11]

After his marriage Lenz seems to have considered returning to Germany; a letter from his brother—which in all probability contained news of the latest flare-up of the revolution in Germany—prompted him to give up these plans. Instead he began setting up an independent livelihood. In Lanesville,[12] not far from Zollmann's farm, he rented a house with a few acres of land and bought tools and wood in order to work on his own account as a cooper.[13]

In the beginning Lenz had no reason to regret this decision. On the contrary, one receives the impression that he had come a step closer to fulfilling his expectations and goals when he wrote that one could live in America in peace and without fear of war (which to Lenz was also a synonym for "revolution"); when he reported with unmistakable pride to his brother about his property; but also when he said that in the United States he had become a true Christian for the first time.

Lenz did not, however, cherish high hopes for his future. From the very beginning his letters are marked by a lack of illusion that borders on fatalism—the product of his deeply traditional and religious world view. He was convinced that true well-being could be expected only in the hereafter; earthly existence, by contrast, was merely a time of trial, a God-given and ultimately inescapable fate to be borne without protest and mastered to the best of one's ability.

In the tone of a sober report and without a hint of disappointment or bitterness, Christian thus informed his brother in May of 1855 that economic conditions had forced him to give up his home and business in Lanesville and move with his family to Louisville, Kentucky.[14] As he

---

Despite the fact that his age does not agree with the census information, it seems safe to assume that this was Christian's subsequent employer.

[11]Lenz probably learned from the twenty-year-old Friedrich (also born in Germany), who still lived in his father's house in 1850 and two decades later had become one of the most prosperous farmers in the township (MC 1870: Harrison Co., Ind., Franklin Twp., #14). As Lenz reports, Susanna was a daughter from the first marriage of Zollmann's American wife. According to the census she was born in Indiana and was not named Susanna but Sarah (MC 1860: Harrison Co., Ind., Franklin Twp., 1850, #773; 1860: #855; see the NatA pension record of Christian Lenz in NatA).

[12]Harrison County's population in 1850 was 15,286; in 1880, 20,274, of which 778 were born in Germany. Lanesville, which today is part of the metropolitan area of Louisville, had only 157 inhabitants in 1870, and 280 in 1880. According to the original census manuscripts, these included a large number of Germans (USC 1850.1, 780; USC 1880.1, 105 and 505; MC 1850, 1860, 1870, 1880).

[13]In 1850 there were 3,700 coopers in Indiana, the fifth most frequent occupation (USC 1850.1, 784). Barrels were used to store and transport almost all types of foodstuffs (not just beer).

[14]The population in 1850 was 43,194; in 1880, 123,758, of which 13,500, or 11 percent, were born in Germany. In the 1870s there were several German newspapers, fifteen German parishes,

writes in his letter, he had found a job there despite the unfavorable economic situation, but he had had to make do with a "poor wage," and to make matters worse, his wife and children fell ill shortly after their arrival.

Lenz's readiness to accept circumstances that were less than happy, however, was also put to a further, and possibly more difficult, test. Just as he had overcome his economic difficulties and family misfortunes, he was confronted by political unrest and violence, though only a short time earlier he had been so confident that he was safe from such a threat.

The unstable economic situation, prone to crisis since the beginning of the 1850s, helped fan the flames of anti-immigration sentiment in the Anglo-American population. This was true above all in the large cities, where glaring social problems arose in the wake of the massive influx of immigrants.[15] Louisville, too, was no exception. In addition, the political activities of a small group of German "Forty-eighters" in the town had caused a stir. In 1855 Karl Heinzen, a former publisher of the Louisville *Herold des Westens* and a radical democrat, wrote and distributed, together with a handful of like-minded German immigrants, a manifesto containing twelve points. This document, according to the hardly modest claims of its authors, was supposed to mark the beginning of a reform alliance between liberal Germans and progressive Americans. It attained dubious notoriety as the "Louisville Platform." The platform not only propagated "freedom, prosperity and education for all," but also abolition of slavery, political and social equality for blacks and women, protection of the working classes from capitalists, exclusion of religious display from public life, repeal of all temperance laws, and measures in favor of immigrants as well as fundamental legal and election reform. The culmination of this radical platform for a truly democratic America, however, was the demand for the abolition not only of the Senate but also of the office of President, the "King in a dressing gown," who seemed to embody a dangerous compromise with the monarchical traditions of Europe.[16]

It is hardly surprising that the Anglo-American public received these extreme proposals not only without enthusiasm but with indignation,[17] and the manifesto served to aggravate further the situation in Louisville, which had already been tense. The consequences of the platform were soon to become apparent.

---

and a large number of German lodges and societies (USC 1850.2, 365; USC 1880.1, 538–39; Schem 6 [1872], 631–39).

[15]Billington (1964), 322–45; see the section "Nativism and Politics" in the Introduction.

[16]Dobert (1967), 173–76; Wittke (1945), 94–95; Wittke (1952), 163–65.

[17]The authors of the Louisville Platform did not receive positive responses from their countrymen, or even from many "Forty-eighters."

During the local elections the following spring, militant nativists (as Lenz reports to his brother) tried to prevent the Germans and Irish from voting, and incidents of violence occurred.[18] But nativism was not restricted to such relatively mild outbreaks of xenophobia. On August 6, 1855, election day for the state of Kentucky, pent-up emotions exploded in a much more violent way. During the course of the day the situation in the city began to resemble a civil war, as Anglo-Americans and immigrants fought hefty battles in the streets, houses and shops were plundered and destroyed, 22 persons were killed, and hundreds more were wounded.[19]

The effects of this "Bloody Monday"—which ultimately served to discredit the nativist movement despite its sizeable victory at the polls— were felt for a long time. Many Germans fled the city, a state of emergency was in effect for several days, and only gradually did a certain degree of normality return to the lives of Louisville residents. Immigration was to remain stagnant for many years to come.[20]

That Christian Lenz was deeply shocked and upset by the events of August is evident in his letter of October 1855. The manner in which this otherwise taciturn and reserved man describes the riots to his brother leaves no doubt about his horror and dismay. His indignation at the displays of intolerance and violence were apparently stronger than his usually rather disapproving and critical attitude toward the majority of his countrymen, whose way of life he regarded as undisciplined and impious. At the same time the events seem to have given him cause to doubt the soundness of his original decision to emigrate. His graphic and proverbial observation that bread, potatoes, and salt at home are better than meat three times a day in a foreign country seems to be something like a self-reproach. Did he not try, in leaving Germany, to interfere with God's holy plans, and could this now be the punishment for his presumption?

During the years to come, Lenz seems to have become all the more intensively engaged in church and religious affairs. We can safely assume that while he was living in Indiana he had already joined the German Reformed Church,[21] which—with its strict doctrines, scriptural orientation, rejection of outward display, emphasis on the laity, and high de-

[18]Kennedy (1964), 21.
[19]Billington (1964), 421; Kennedy, 22–23; Schem 6:638; Wittke (1952), 187–88.
[20]Schem 6:638; Stierlin (1873), 164–74.
[21]At the time that Lenz settled in Harrison County there were not yet any German Reformed parishes, but there was one in neighboring Floyd County. Lanesville is situated on the border between the two counties (USC 1850.1, 799–806).

mands in terms of its members' piety and devout lifestyle—probably met his religious expectations better than the other Protestant churches.[22]

According to his letter of June 1858, he held several offices in the German Reformed (Zion) parish in Louisville and attended church services at least four times a week.[23] It seems, however, that despite all of these activities he continued to be somewhat isolated. His reports remain strangely impersonal, and there are hardly any hints of contacts or relationships with other members of the congregation beyond what was necessary.

After four or five years in Louisville, Lenz decided to move back to Lanesville with his family,[24] and although he had repeatedly complained to his brother about his poor wages and loss of income through illness, he must have saved enough money during his years in the city to buy a small farm. According to the agricultural census lists of 1870 and 1880, he farmed about twenty acres of land, owned another twenty acres of cleared woodlands, and by 1880 had acquired another twenty acres of woods—considerably more than most of the farmers in his native Nassau but not very much by American standards: with a listed value of $400, his farm was one of the smallest in Lanesville.[25] Aside from his work on the farm, Lenz also continued to work as a cooper, but even with this combination of farming and skilled trade he was hardly able to make ends meet. In 1869 he still had debts to pay on his property, and he had a large family to support.

Between 1848 and 1868 Lenz's wife gave birth to eleven children (three of whom died in childhood).[26] This large number of offspring was less an indication of a happy marriage than an expression of traditional economic mentality. Children could start working for the family at an early age and thus help save the cost of expensive labor, and they were also expected to care for their parents in their old age.[27] That Lenz clearly

[22]Corwin et al. (1902), 52–143, and Schem 9 (1873), 284–85. The German Reformed Church should thus be considered one of the "pietistic" religious bodies, in which rule-governed behavior and individual piety were of central importance. Ritual, on the other hand, played only a secondary role (Jensen [1971], 63–68; Kleppner [1970], 71–91).

[23]Established in 1854; in the early 1870s it had ca. one thousand members (Schem 6:635).

[24]At the end of 1859 the family was living in Lanesville; their daughter Sarah was born there in November.

[25]MC A 1870 and 1880: Harrison Co., Ind. The largest farm (the owner of which was born in Germany) was valued at $7,000, the average farm value lay between $1,000 and $2,000. In the Duchy of Nassau the average holdings were slightly more than five acres (Vogel, 450–51).

[26]Heinrich (b. 1848–49), Friedrich (b. 1855), Elisabeth (b. 1857), Sarah (b. 1859), Philipp (b. 1862), Ludwig (b. 1864), Christian (b. 1866), Maria (b. 1868); Wilhelm, Johanette, and (another) Christian died before 1865 (MC 1860, 1870, and 1880; see also details in the letters).

[27]See Conzen (1984), 375–77.

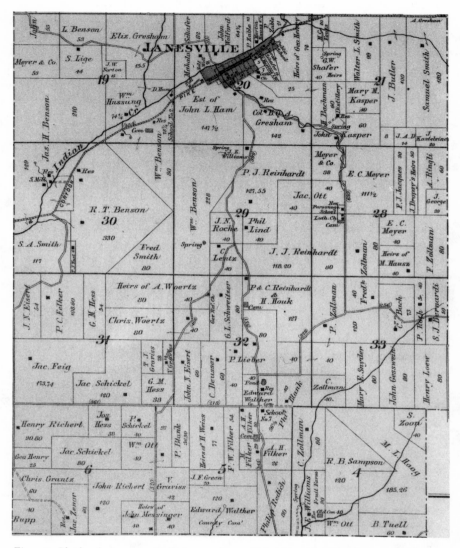

Figure 8. Plat book showing the forty-acre farm of "C. Lentz" at the bottom of Section 29. *Source: Atlas of Harrison County* (1882); photo courtesy of Indiana Historical Society Library (negative no. C4672).

expected his children to do both is evidenced not only by the fact that a fourteen-year-old school-age son is listed in the census as a "farm laborer" (on his parents' farm)[28] but also by a series of remarks in his letters—in particular his indignant comments about his two eldest sons, who turned their backs on the family and, to his great consternation, did not even send home any money.

Lenz's hopes of living a peaceful and quiet life after he returned to the country were also dashed. In the last year of the Civil War, the 41-year-old was called to arms. The Union government had begun to draft soldiers at the beginning of the previous year in order to fill the gaps in what had been up to that time a volunteer army.[29] Christian's economic situation would hardly have allowed him to pay for a substitute, which his more prosperous contemporaries often did, and his sense of duty was also probably too strong. In mid-October, therefore, he was inducted in Jeffersonville, Indiana, and shortly afterward he was transferred to an Indiana infantry regiment that was stationed in Tennessee.[30] Soon thereafter he fought under the command of General George H. Thomas in Franklin and Nashville; both of these battles (Union victories) contributed to the fact that the following summer the "rebels" finally lost the war.[31] Shortly after the Confederates capitulated, Lenz was able to return home, and he arrived in July 1865 "fairly healthy, but still more or less unfit for work," on top of the fact that his nine months in the army had occasioned a serious loss of income.

Christian's letters about his time in the army hardly give the impression that he (like many Germans) identified with the "fight against slavery" and the Union cause. His reports focus on the hardships that the poorly supplied soldiers, living primarily on what they could plunder, had to endure; the path of destruction and violence that the Union Army cut on its march through the South; those who were killed, wounded, widowed, or orphaned by the war. But it is significant that he makes no mention of the causes of the conflict.

It is all the more surprising, therefore, when five years later he shows such vehemently nationalistic interest in the Franco-Prussian War, urging

[28]MC 1880: Harrison Co., Ind., e.d. 93, #44.
[29]Under the Conscription Law of March 1863 all men between the ages of 20 and 45 were eligible for the draft. Whoever could pay $300 for a substitute, however, could avoid being drafted (Nevins 2 [1960], 463–66).
[30]U.S. NatA: Muster Rolls, 9th Regiment, Indiana Infantry. For a report of the actions seen by this regiment see Dyer 3 (1959), 1121. The muster roll provides some incidental information about Lenz's physical appearance: he was 5'4" tall, and he had blue eyes and fair hair.
[31]See Kaufmann (1911), 436–37; McPherson (1982), 465–70; Nevins 4 (1971), 173–88.

the Germans on to victory against the "haughty Napoleon"—signs of a late-blooming nationalism.[32]

The passage of time left its mark on Christian Lenz in another connection. Despite his fundamental opposition to modernization, by the end of the 1870s at the latest he had no choice but to use time-saving machines at least in the cooper's shop if he wanted to stay competitive. He never came to like these technological triumphs of the industrial age; rather, he regarded them as the cause of overproduction, declining prices, lower wages and unemployment: in short, an enemy to adequate subsistence.

Lenz was already 62 years old when he was finally able to put long-cherished plans into action and make a new start. He sold the farm in Lanesville and moved about thirty miles farther west to Leavenworth, Indiana, a small town on the Ohio River.[33] Here he probably hoped to spend the last years of his life in quiet comfort, but this was not to be. The area did not appeal to the family, old age and illness gave Lenz no end of trouble, and life in Leavenworth became an episode that lasted only one year. In the early months of 1886 he finally gave up farming and moved with his wife and three youngest children back to Louisville.

Lenz's fairly random spelling, punctuation that is limited to (rare) periods, plus the considerable impact of Hessian dialect present some difficulties for the reader but generally allow him to get his messages across. There is little change over the 39 years between the first and the last letters. Even though his wife was not German, almost no English turns of phrase influence his German, although the spelling of unfamiliar words becomes slightly more bizarre. But at no time can he hide the fact that his educational opportunities were severely limited.

Christian Lenz

Lensville, August 1[7], 1849

Dear brother I have received your letter of May 19th and see from it that you are all well again and that things in Germany are very bad again. Dear brother I also have to let you know that I am now a cooper, I signed on for 8 months with a man named Zollmann born in Mensfelten the one in the state of Intiana, his son is a cooper. For the 8 months he promised me and Christian Köpller from Nauheim, who came to Amirka 3 weeks

[32]On the stance of German-Americans with regard to the Franco-Prussian War and the newly established Reich, see Trefousse (1985) and Wittke (1952), 345–66.

[33]Leavenworth is in Crawford County, and its population in 1880 was 716. In the same year the entire county had a population of twelve thousand, of which only 85 were German (USC 1880.1, 150–505).

before me, for the 8 months 30 talers or in German money 75 guilders, with board and washing, then when I had learned for 3 months I married his daughter. On January 31 I entered matrimony, my wife though is from the first husband, she couldn't speak any German but now she can get on well in German. After I had worked for 6 months I got a fever and was sick for 3 months. Thank God I had a wife, for if I had been in boarding I don't think I would still be alive, but my wife did her best for me, she spent the whole day next to my bed and waited on me. [4 ll.: effects of the fever]

Dear brother now I have rented myself a house and 4 to 5 acres of land for 20 guilders a year. And I have bought my own tools now since I work for myself, I have wood now too. Dear brother I have 5 pigs, many chickens, a dog, that is my livestock. I've had the house since August 1st. Dear brother you wrote me in your letter of Nov. 19th 1848 which I received on Feb. 16th that I should come back to you, but since I was already a husband you can easily imagine how hard it was for me, because I wasn't sure that my wife wanted to go with me, but when I explained it to her she was content to go to my Fatherland, since she would like to see you all and the sooner the better. When I received the 2nd letter of May 19, 1849, I was badly shocked since my wife had been looking forward to going very much. But we had to put it off for a while. Dear brother you write that my sister wanted to come to me if she had had the money, if I hadn't been sick I would have sent it to her, but you know if you don't earn anything for 3 months, doctor and druggist cost me a lot of money and tools, livestock and everything I need in the house. That all costs a lot in this country. But I don't only wish to have my sister alone, but all of you living with me, for here you can live in peace, here there's no fear of war, but what the sword is for you is here the *Korlra* [cholera]. Every country has its plague in these times. Here the sickness was so common that in the big cities half the people have been buried. Many houses have died out completely.[34]

Dear brother you write that in Germany religion has fallen off, here too in part but not for everyone, in Germany I also believed I was a good Christian, but I was lacking a lot. Here we have a pastor who knows the way to Heaven and shows us the right way, and I've had to learn a lot. May the Lord help me further. I also used to pray in my Fatherland when I had the time [. . .] but dear brother here I pray to my God and to your God, to my Father and to your Father with all my heart and fall on my

[34]Cholera epidemics caused by unhealthy living conditions repeatedly decimated the population of American cities up to the end of the nineteenth century. In 1849 the epidemic was particularly widespread. The only "antidotes" known were "flight, fasting and prayer" (Smith [1911], 25).

knees 2 times a day and when I sit at table I don't forget the Lord Jesus Christ. Dear brother and all who read this letter, I tell you Eternity is everything, think about what God said to Abram follow me and be godly. And about Jesus suffering on the Mount of Olives for our sins, don't forget the Crucified One, go and read the Scriptures, I am also following the path of reading the Scriptures, here we have nothing but sorrow, there Eternal Peace, but we must read the Scriptures here, there's no time for it there. Imagine what Hell is like and then you will strive to go to Heaven and not to go to Hell with the sinners. Read the Prophet Isaiah, Chap. 2, Verse 18.[35] [11 ll.: says he will write again soon and asks for an immediate reply; name of his wife; greetings; address]

Lensville, January 29th, 1852

Dear brother,

[2 ll.: thanks for his brother's letter] Now your question whether I long for Germany. 1st, that is in God's hand. 2nd and if it were in my power I wouldn't long for Germany in these times for there is no peace in Germany. I read the newspaper every week and see there is no peace yet. [8 ll.: consoles his brother with their meeting again in the hereafter; reports the arrival of an acquaintance and thanks for a present; Wilhelm should lend his sister the money to emigrate] Whether it will be good for my sister to be in Amerika I don't know, God knows, He who knows everything. 5th you write that I should help her, but I can't now, I have lots to buy now.

I bought myself a horse that cost 100 guilders, now I still don't have a wagon or a plow or any seed and no harness for the horse and all the other things I need, so if she wants to wait till the fall I can help her, I can't do it any earlier.

Dear brother you write that our sister wants to marry a Catholic fellow and that you don't want this and she won't obey you. She will shame herself in front of God and man if she takes up such a life, if I were there she certainly wouldn't do it. This is what I write to you dear sister Christiana, if you want to stay my sister forget this completely and think on God, He will help you to find your proper home. Dear brother you think that our brother-in-law would do well in Am [America], that is true, he would soon make a fortune, I want to teach Wilho and Gristian[36] the cooper trade and they should learn for one year and want to give each one 100 guilders, board, washing, and pocket money, too and a servant

---

[35]"And the idols he shall utterly abolish."
[36]These are presumably his brother's sons.

girl gets 2 guilders 30 kreuzers to 4 guilders a week and doesn't have to work in the fields. Dear brother my wife can't write German. [3 ll.: cold spell and its effects on farming] Now I want to tell you what I own, one horse, 2 cows, one 2-year-old heifer, one calf, 2 pigs, 45 to 50 chickens, 9 geese, 2 dogs, 2 guinea hens and wife and child one farmhand and a lot more which I can't write about.

[8 ll.: food prices, greetings for friends and relatives] / I remain your / true brother and brother-in-law
Christian Lenz. / Susanna Lenz
I guided my wife's hand.

Louisville, May 29th, 1855
Dear brother,
[3 ll.: thanks him for his letter] Soon after your letter barrels went down so that I couldn't work anymore, since the wood cost me more money than I got for the barrels, so I sold everything and moved to Louisville where I found work but for a poor wage so that I have nothing to spare. When we had been in Louisville for a few weeks my wife got sick, she was sick for 2 weeks then she went into labor which also didn't go well, but the Lord helped us in our need and gave us a son. He was born on March 20th this year and on March 25th he was baptized, Friderich Schmidt from Freiendiez is his godfather, he lives near me. And after many weeks my wife got well, and all the children got sick. [5 ll.: details] Yes these are sad times in America, the Americans are rising up against the Germans with a strong hand.

They don't want to let them vote and everywhere they want to beat and force them back, in the last election in Louisville they didn't let any Germans through and beat them back, destroyed German houses, shot and beat them up, and its the same all over America, and you can't easily imagine what its like in America, soon a war will break out. Do you think I should send someone travel money so his blood can flow because of maybe a bullet or *Colra* which is also already breaking out in all the cities? And we also had famine, in the winter here in Louisville the poor people are given food everyday, up to 4000, unemployment is still here, many have no work and everything costs a lot. [9 ll.: examples of prices; he is not able to pay his debts in Germany; greetings to friends and relatives] And I greet you in tears, your only brother. Fare thee well.
Christian Lenz
Till we meet in Heaven. Amen
[3 ll.: will send two newspapers along; address]

Luisville, October 22nd, 1855

Dear brother, since I have waited so long for your letter but I don't hear or see one so I will write again. [8 ll.: again about the birth of his son Friedrich; family is suffering from a fever epidemic] You write about the children if I want to have them come or not, I already wrote you in the last letter that the Germans are unwanted in America, but from last February till now it's cost a lot of blood, on August 6th there was an election in Louisville where they had it in for the Germans and those from Aierland [Ireland], they wanted to cast their votes like always but they got beaten and pushed around, then there was a real fight with much bloodshed, the Americans got shot at from all the houses where many were staying inside, they got fed up with this and set fire to the houses, destroyed many dwellings, murdering, burning and robbing what they could get, they hanged, burned, cut off people's heads, shot. In short many people lost their lives in these days, Germans and Americans, many women and children that they wouldn't let out of the houses burned to death. Dear brother I watched how they ran through the streets like the screaming seven[37] to see human blood. Since that time many Germans have fled and have moved away, one this way and the other that way. Now dear brother should anyone else move to America, no—stay where you were born that is your home, if I were still in Germany I wouldn't look at America, even if there's nothing besides bread and potatoes and salt that is still better than meat three times a day in a foreign country. [10 ll.: new address; greetings from one of his brother's friends; inflation; examples of prices] The cooper trade is good, many other *Proffionen* [professions] are at a standstill. I didn't earn much this summer because I was sick all the time, I have made a lot of money in the last weeks when I could work the whole week I earned 22 guilders, but now the last 3 weeks I haven't earned anything, I had fever again, we have a mutual aid society in our church which I am in too, a sick man gets 7½ guilders a week that's a great thing, every craftsman pays 38 kreuzers a month. [5 ll.: greetings and good wishes]
Your true brother
Christian Lenz
I am sending you this printed newspaper so you can read something yourself.

Dear brother I wanted to stop writing but I want to tell you something. Your wife sends her love but I don't believe she really means it.

---

[37]This is a possible reference to the Apocalypse, in which the imminent end of the world is depicted in the form of symbolic images and visions. Here, in connection with disasters and afflictions, the number seven plays a central role (Michl [1957], 693–94). See also Lenz's references to the impending Final Judgment in the letter of July 15, 1886.

Dear brother you know as well as I do that she didn't like me already in Gräfenek and even less in Freiendiez, and you also know that I had to leave your house and go into boarding with another family. I think about it now and then and wonder what I did to grieve her. I have shed many a tear over this, and I know that I didn't always do the right thing, so I beg her forgiveness and send heartfelt greetings to you Elisabeth.
[6 ll.: asks about sister Christiana; further greetings] / Christian Lenz

Louisville, June 21st, 1858

Dear brother,

[7 ll: thanks for a letter from his brother; regrets that sister Christiana is ill; words of religious comfort] You write me that I don't write much about American conditions. Yes, that is true, but I don't want to write much about it since you wouldn't like many things. It is certainly no Germany, the laws are tough enough but there's too much godlessness and most of all among the Germans who live like animals who don't want to work and scoff at God and His justice, if you see someone lying on the street who is drunk then it's a German, the courts have nothing to do but deal with Germans or with the Ailanter [Irish], it's the Ailand which belongs to Eneland, they and the Germans are equally hung up on cheating and boozing, otherwise business is better again, I earn 9 talers a week as a cooper, I've worked already 2½ years for a master craftsman and have the best work, but it's also cost me much money in the 3½ years as long as I've been in Louisville, with sickness in my family, but since the winter I've been pretty well. And I plan to send the money to Eschbach[38] by the fall, it's not lost, I'd have sent it a long time ago but it was impossible. Tell Schmidt I'll send it as soon as I can. Dear brother we have nothing to do with the war, it is far away from us,[39] America is as big as all Germany, but if you want to volunteer you can go, but only unmarried.

You ask me if we have schools and churches, I thought I'd written to you about it a long time ago, I belong to the Reformed Church in Louisville where the true Word of God is preached, but where there are strict rules too. No man addicted to drink or any other vice is admitted, if you live sinfully and don't give it up after 3 warnings you get thrown out. We have four days of school a week in our church where our preacher is also the teacher, on Sundays we have 2 hours of school in the afternoon where I've been the teacher for 3 years already. We have services Sunday

[38]Presumably a reference to money that Lenz had borrowed to pay for his trip to America.
[39]Possibly the "Mormon War" of 1858 (Smith [1975], 65–68; Henretta et al. [1987], 384).

morning and evening; Tuesdays and Thursdays we have prayers, we have a mutual aid society in our church where I've been the secretary for 2 years, my salary is low, I get 3 talers a year, where I write the minutes, we meet every month. We also have a mission which I'm also secretary of. I don't want to write you any more about it this time. [25 ll.: visit of one of his brother's friends and a countryman who wants to return to Germany to get his family; asks about sister and sister-in-law; greetings; says he'll send a photograph of the whole family; good wishes]

Lensville, July 28th, 1865

Dear brother,

[7 ll.: thanks for a letter from his niece and a draft for 20 dollars] I thank you with all my heart for sending me the money at this time when I need it so badly, I am thank God back at home again but everything is in a mess, business is bad, everything is pretty much at a standstill. The barrels which usually bring a high price this time of year you can't even sell now, I don't know if it'll get better this year but it doesn't look like it, I was a soldier for 9 months, saw many things, was in 3 battles, in the first battle the rebels lost 37 hundred dead not counting the prisoners and there were 700. In the second and third, that was on December 15th and 16th, 1864, out of 75 thousand rebels not more than 30 thousand came out of it, the others were killed or taken prisoner. In the first battle we had 700 dead, in the second and third almost 2 thousand dead and wounded. Dear brother those were hard days for us, the last two days we had to take their stronghold by storm, the enemy had over 100 cannons aimed at us and thousands of guns and we still had to take it, they fell to the left and to the right of me, but the Lord brought me through safely and brought me back to my family.[40] I'm fairly healthy again but still more or less unfit for work, in the 9 months all we did was march, cook and wash when we could and when we couldn't do that sometimes we ate it raw when we had something, but sometimes we went hungry and with ragged clothing, and almost half the army was barefoot once and that was in the winter. Many people fell sick from hunger and cold, and many thousands died from these sicknesses. That was a hard war for America, it cost 3 times a hundred and 50 thousand men that are listed dead[41] and

[40]In the battle of Franklin, Tennessee (November 30, 1864), the Confederates lost six thousand out of a total of twenty thousand men: 1,750 dead, 3,800 wounded, 702 missing. In Nashville, Tennessee (December 15 and 16, 1864), 8,600 out of 23,000 were taken prisoner and the Rebel army practically ceased to exist. Union casualties were more limited: 189 dead, 1,033 wounded, and 1,104 missing in Franklin; 387 dead, 2562 wounded, and 112 missing in Nashville. See Nevins 4:176, 187–88; a description of the battle is given on pp. 183–87.

[41]The casualties were in fact even higher; more than 600,000 people died in the Civil War (McPherson [1982], 488).

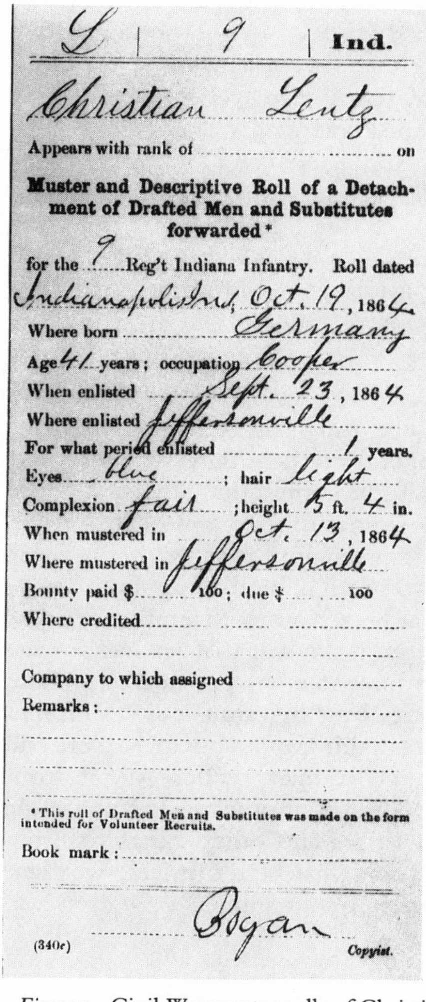

L | 9 | **Ind.**

Christian Lentz

Appears with rank of .... on

Muster and Descriptive Roll of a Detachment of Drafted Men and Substitutes forwarded *

for the *9* Reg't Indiana Infantry. Roll dated

Indianapolis Ind, Oct. 19, 186*4*

Where born .... *Germany*

Age *41* years; occupation *Cooper*

When enlisted .... *Sept. 23,* 186*4*

Where enlisted *Jeffersonville*

For what period enlisted .... *1* years.

Eyes ... *blue* ...; hair *light*

Complexion *fair* ; height *5* ft. *4* in.

When mustered in *Oct. 13,* 186*4*

Where mustered in *Jeffersonville*

Bounty paid $ *100* ; due $ *100*

Where credited ....

Company to which assigned ....

Remarks: ....

* This roll of Drafted Men and Substitutes was made on the form intended for Volunteer Recruits.

Book mark: ....

(340c)   *Bryan*   Copyist.

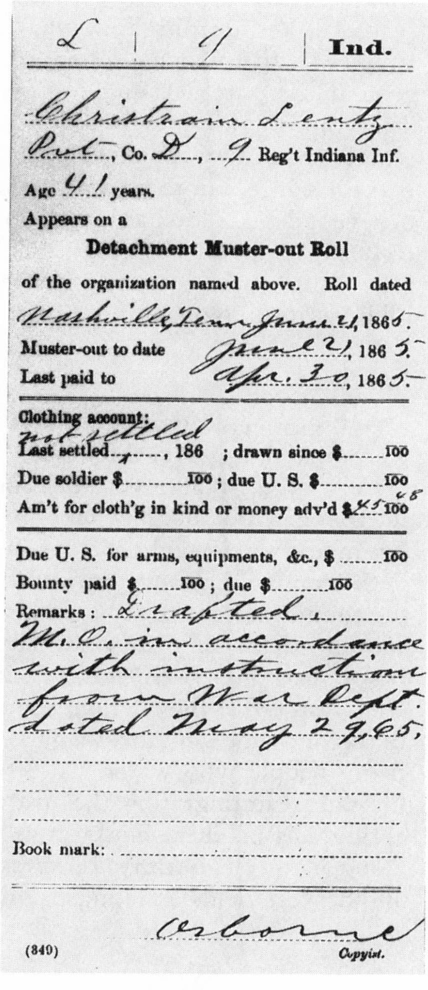

L | 9 | **Ind.**

Christian Lentz

Pvt., Co. *D*, *9* Reg't Indiana Inf.

Age *41* years.

Appears on a

Detachment Muster-out Roll

of the organization named above. Roll dated

Nashville Tenn. June 21, 186*5.*

Muster-out to date *June 21,* 186*5*

Last paid to *Apr. 30,* 186*5.*

Clothing account: *not settled*

Last settled ...., 186 ; drawn since $ 100

Due soldier $ ...... 100 ; due U. S. $ 100

Am't for cloth'g in kind or money adv'd $ *45.68* 100

Due U. S. for arms, equipments, &c., $ 100

Bounty paid $ ...... 100 ; due $ 100

Remarks : *Drafted. ... in accordance with instruction from War Dept. ... May 29, 65.*

Book mark: ....

(340)   *Osborne*   Copyist.

Figure 9. Civil War muster rolls of Christian Lenz. *Source:* U.S. NatA.

many of those who are still alive now who also suffered from it will also die. There are many widows and orphans at a time like this, they've already built many orphanages and they're still building more to take care of the children who have no father and whose mothers can't feed them. There is misery upon misery, the Lord keep and protect us and you from such evil. Yes, dear brother, we marched for days without seeing hardly any houses that weren't destroyed, even whole towns were razed to the ground, these are all things that I saw with my own eyes, I can't describe it to you in writing, and the army corps I was with wasn't even everywhere, we only went through the beginning Temsü [Tennessee], Alabama, George, but there were 11 *Stäht* [states] that left the Union and I believe it doesn't look any better there, I'll stop for now and if you want to know about anything else write me, I'll answer as best I can. [3 ll.: wishes his brother a speedy recovery; greetings] / Christian Lenz. I'll be writing to our brother-in-law soon.

Lanesville, March 6th, 1867

Dear brother I received your letter of Sept. 2nd, 66 in good time and from it I see that things over there are no longer the same as they used to be, but there's nothing that can be done about it, the hardest thing that hits you is the soldier's life, that they take anyone who is fit and up until 40 you can live in fear when war breaks out, here it's even until 49 when there's a war in the country, then everyone has to go when he's called up, but outside the country no one has to go when war breaks out with another King or country, that's only the volunteers, also in the war that we had for the first 3 years only volunteers went, but since so many people died and the war wasn't over they drafted three times[42] the first time it didn't hit me, the second time it hit me, then there was a third round but there were still many people who weren't affected. [35 ll.: many young people from Nassau are immigrating; the brother of his neighbor wants to come in the spring, his brother should give him letters and other things to bring along; family is healthy; business is somewhat better; prices, weather, and harvest yields; greetings; signature; more greetings]

Lenesville, January 7th, 1868

Dear brother,

[3 ll.: thanks for his brother's letter] You write that your son Wilh. is getting married soon but that you don't like it that Wilhelm is in love with the girl and the girl is in love with your Wilhelm, then for God's

---

[42]See n. 29, above.

sake let them get married. It's not right when parents want to force their children on someone they don't love, then they don't have a peaceful marriage only quarrels, and it's the parents' fault. You also had your freedom in this, I know that our parents never would have forced us on anyone we didn't love. I think you were perhaps also somewhat at fault with your daughter, for girls don't have any great fondness for a man who has an open leg[43] but does have money, if I am wrong, please forgive me, I immediately thought that was the case when you wrote me that your daughter had married, your Wilhelm wouldn't do well here since he hasn't worked for a long time, and he can't be a foreman here because he can't speak the language, blacksmiths do much better here, since smiths earn a lot of money here, for school teachers it's also better here than over there in Germany, in the big cities the teachers are well paid, from 30 to 50 dollars a month[44] if he knows German and English he gets even more. He can learn English soon if he has a good head, here there's German and English schools and also ones where both are used, food here is also very expensive, there's been no full harvest for two years. I can't write much about Carl Wihl since we live 10 to 12 away from each another, when I saw him the last time 3 years ago he told me that he no longer lives with his wife rather they both live on their own, the big boy is with him, the other children with his wife. I don't know for sure who's to blame, him or her, he said it was his wife's fault, but I've heard it was his fault, he beat his wife for every little thing, and that's not done here, here a wife must be treated like a wife and not like a scrub rag like I saw in Germany so often that a man can do what he wants to with his wife. He who likes to beat his wife had better stay in Germany, it doesn't work here, or soon he'll not have a wife anymore, that's what happened to Carl Wihl. [15 ll.: news of the death of a mutual acquaintance, who had been a boarder with the Lenz family] You write that it puzzles you that here one fellow stays poor and another gets rich, but I think you've seen it enough in Germany, if you can lie and cheat and take advantage of everyone you get richer faster than if you're fair and square, it is true that lazy Germans get rich, I know many who have a lot but they have drinking houses and there're others who keep houses that are even worse and get enough money the wrong way, but you wouldn't expect me to earn money like that for it only gets burned up. Look, in these 20 years I've seen a lot and also seen it happen that the old people were rich but their children are now very poor

[43]Originally *flus am Bein,* which can mean that he had thrombosis. It is more likely, however, that he suffered from rheumatism or gout (Ribbe/Henning [1975], 283).

[44]In the mid-nineteenth century in Nassau an elementary schoolteacher received an annual salary of 100 to 150 guilders (ca. $40 to $60), on which it was difficult to feed a family (Spielmann, 120).

that's because of their wrong-doings. If you were to walk through the streets of Louisville, in some streets you'd see nothing but taverns and it's the Germans who have almost all the drinking houses and I tell you they're all Hell-holes, the men sit there and guzzle away and their wives and children don't have any bread and no clothes on their backs. I've known quite a few who came here rich and spent it all on drink and in the end put a bullet through their head and left their wife and children behind in misery and who's to blame? Everyone who has a saloon, or do you think there's a blessing in it? I don't believe it. You also mustn't believe everything that's written here, some write that they're rich here but it's not always true. [10 ll.: report about an emigrant who enticed his brother to America with tales of his unbelievable wealth but who remains poor]

As far as women are concerned, it's like in Germany, the rich women don't have to work, particularly in the towns, but things are different in the country, as for me, I have 40 morgens of land, but I still have debts on it. If I hadn't become a soldier I'd have been better off than I am now, but I'm quite content. My oldest son isn't with me he works in a trading house 40 hours from here, the first year he gets 150 talers, food and laundry. The second son goes to school, the oldest girl is 10 years old and goes to school too, the two of them cost me 1 taler a month for schooling[45] the others are still too little. I still have 7, 3 are dead. All the best to your brother from all of us, your brother

Christian Lenz

Lenesville, April 13, 69

Dear brother,

[9 ll.: thanks his brother for his letter and recommends a remedy for his illness] You write if I couldn't come back to Germany again, there's still no chance of that now. In the first place I still have debts on my land my oldest son has also become foolhardy, he's no use. He hasn't been home in 1 and ½ years, and he doesn't send any money either, if I'd have known that I wouldn't have let him go away, if I'd kept him here I'd be better off than I am now. [4 ll.: ages of the other children] You can figure it out for yourself whether I can leave them or not. When my children are all grown and I am out of debt I would like to see you all again, God willing, as soon as I can sell my land I will do it and move again because we aren't doing very well here, the land in this area isn't the best but otherwise it's healthy and there's good water here, which it isn't everywhere in Amerika. I don't know what I should write about your children, a young man

---

[45]From this we can assume that the children attended a private (probably parochial) school. Attendance of public schools was free.

can come here without a trade and be lucky but if he doesn't like it he can always go back to Germany again, there are already quite a few who've gone back. Some like it here, some don't. Servant girls do pretty well here, when they work in the city they earn 2 to 3 talers a week and the work isn't so hard. I will do as much as I can for them that they get a job with good people, in the city it's not by the year but by the week. If a girl doesn't like it, she leaves, for there's always a shortage of servant girls. Do what you think is best for them, if the children don't want to come it's better for them to stay in Germany, if they do want to come then it's much better, since if they don't like it, it's no one's fault.

As for Carl Will, I can't write the best about him. He left his wife for a long time but now he's back with his wife. He now lives in Louisville and is a carpenter, builds houses out of wood. I heard he built himself a big house but had to sell it again because he was so much in debt. The saloon is his ruin. He drinks too much, that's what I recently heard about him. I haven't seen him for three years now and his wife for 10 years. He is and always was a rolling stone. [8 ll.: about a portrait the brother had sent; greetings] The Lord be with you all, your loving brother / Christian Lenz

Lensville, Sept. 26th, 70

Dear brother and sister-in-law,

[4 ll.: complains about the lack of mail from Germany] And I still want to know how things are with you and how many of your children are in the war or don't you and my sister have any children in the war. Be so good and write me now and tell me if yours are all alive and well and what else is new. I and mine are all hale and hearty, my oldest son we haven't seen for 3 years, nor gotten anything from him. He didn't turn out well, he spends all his money, but I don't know how. He writes every now and then and that's all. [14 ll.: ages of the other children; harvest yields; weather] Here in Amirüka all you hear is what comes from Germany, namely the war, the Germans are all enthusiastic about Germany, thousands of talers were collected and sent to Germany for widows and orphans and cripples or the wounded. But it's the same for France by the French, they also send to France but the majority is for Germany. Many a prayer is sent from the pulpits here by the preachers and other people up to God, that God may give victory to Germany for we believe that Germany is in the right. The proud French have put them down for a long time already, and God grants the proud no victory, the proud he abandons, that's what God did to the haughty Nabolion and delivered him to the Germans, if Germany wins that will also be a victory for all Germans wherever they are in the whole world, we know that here in Amirika. Here too there are many Frenchmen who think they're better than the Germans but now they've shrunk a little, they see that the German Müchel [Michel][46] doesn't have to put up with everything. [3 ll.: best wishes, greetings] / Christian Lenz

[28 ll.: letter of January 10, 1871, from Lanesville, in which Christian reports the death of his eldest son. Working for the railroad, the son had lost an arm; two months later he died of complications resulting from the injury.]

Lenesville, May 17th, 1872

Dear brother,

[21 ll.: complains that his brother doesn't write; the state of his health—and that of his wife—leaves much to be desired; ages of the children; prices; potato-bug blight] This fall there's an election again for many officials, president, and up to now I've also had a post for the fourth year, namely keeping the road in good order. Every man from 21 to 50 years old has to work on the road; there are 45 men in my *Distrük* [district] that I have to ask to come. I have to go from house to house since each one lives on 40 or 60 to 200 morgens of land, and each one has to come or else pay. Every day that I go around or work on the road I get 1 D. and 50 cents. The road is mowed twice a year in the spring and in the fall and every man has to work for 4 days. What we still need is paid for with money, so I take along 8 or 10 men who are paid, I don't have to work but I have to be there from 8 to 12 in the morning and from 1 to 5 o'clock. That's a day's work here. I'm still an elder in the Reformed church, but here it's not such an easy job like in Germany, for we keep order here, everything that is godless is not allowed, there's a lot to fight against. I'll send you the church regulations, then you can read for yourself, it wouldn't hurt you to have a look at the Reformed Church. [9 ll.: asks about his brother's health; greetings; signature]

Lenesville, March 8th, 75

Dear brother,

[14 ll.: makes excuses for his long silence; health; poor harvest; bad weather; high prices and continuing potato-bug plague] Otherwise times are bad here, there's almost no work to do, hope it will be better in the

---

[46]A symbolic figure for the German nation, roughly equivalent to Uncle Sam.

spring. I would like to sell my land but there's no one who wants to buy land. If I could sell I would move again to where land is much better land than here, I have 80 apple trees, many peach trees but we haven't had any fruit for 2 years. I have a horse that cost me 65 talers, is 7 years old, 3 cows, 4 pigs, 50 chickens. I sold and got rid of the geese and ducks because I couldn't get any corn. [14 ll.: farm prices; ages of each member of the family; asks for reply soon; greetings; signature; asks about the children of his sister Christiana]

Lenesville, March 22nd, 1876

Dear brother and relatives,

[15 ll.: standard introduction; lists the children with ages and mentions the upcoming confirmation of one son and one daughter] Things are pretty bad here, everything's at a standstill, no work to do, with earnings it's now much worse than it ever was in Germany, all the trades are shut down. Where there's work the money is poor, food is also very cheap which is good at least. [3 ll.: examples of prices] But there's no money among the poor people. Where there's money there's piles of it, there's not even any hope until the election is over. This year is another election year, then it's altogether a bad year. [9 ll.: weather and effects on the harvest; news about German friends] I can't write you anything about Carl Will, I haven't seen him for a long time. He and his wife lived apart for quite a few years but I hear they're back together again. He loves his liquor and beer too much. I don't like to have much to do with people like that, when I saw him the last time he drank too much, too, that was 10 years ago. When I go to Louisville the next time I'll look him up again. [3 ll.: standard closing; greetings]
Christian Lenz

[13 ll.: letter from Lanesville of April 24, 1876, in which Christian reports the death of his eighteen-year-old daughter Elisabeth, who contracted neuritis.]

Lenesville, September 24, 78

Dear brother,

[4 ll.: thanks for his brother's letter; words of sympathy for the death of a grandchild] It hurts when your children die, but those who die young have overcome, we should be glad for them. 5 of our children have died. [3 ll.: list with ages] In the South a terrible sickness has broken out, many thousands of people are dying of this sickness, it's yellow fever, here too almost all business is at a standstill, there's no trade, it's all been abandoned, and everything is very cheap, too, almost for nothing. [3 ll.: examples]

You want to know what they believe here. There's no lack of churches and schools. Near here there are 3 churches, Catholic, Lutheran and Reformed, for there are still good and evil people here like everywhere, I think it's much the same in Gräfenek, do the Grävenekers still drink as much brandy as in earlier years,[47] Carl Wihl came to visit me not too long ago, but he looked like nothing but liquor. He said you should write and tell him what happened to his mines. He lives 4 or 5 hours away from me, I believe he's doing badly. None of his children live with him, he and his wife just live alone. My children all live here except the oldest Fridrich. He works as a hand for a farmer in the country, gets 16 dollars a month, the others I need myself on my land. I can't say we're doing badly, we've always had enough to eat, but there's never much left, something always gets in my way. This spring my horse died it cost me 65 dollars, I had to buy another one right away for 30 dollars, it's old. My wife is also not in the best of health and I have what I think our father had, for more than two years I've had stomach pains, not all the time but every 2 or 3 weeks I am in great pain.[48] We send you all the best.
Your loving brother Ch. Lenz

[14 ll.: letter from Lanesville of October 6, 1879, in which Christian complains that his brother doesn't write and reports about the harvest.]

Lenesville, Sept. 20th, 1880
Dear brother and sister-in-law,

[3 ll.: standard introduction] This year '80 hit us hard again. I was sick for 7 weeks then Ludwig had a hernia, had to be operated on, two doctors had him lying on the table for over 3 hours before everything was all right, then the doctor came 12 or 13 more times before he was well again. I don't know yet what that will cost, 30 or 40 dollars at least, Ludwig is 16 years old by now. Then our horse died, it cost 30 dollars, that is the

[47]On this subject, the following comment by his contemporary, Vogel, 437: "Many of the time-honored and hence genuine traditional pastimes of the townsfolk and farmers have been destroyed by the spirit emanating from the French Revolution. Daily visits to the tavern and drinking of brandy, on the other hand, have taken over in some places and markedly contribute to impoverishment."
[48]According to a physician's statement in his pension records (NatA), Lenz suffered from a rupture and a "fatty tumor on abdomen."

second horse in two years, the other one cost 65 dollars, that's 95 dollars in two years. Otherwise things are better than they have been for years, business is booming and the harvest was good. [16 ll.: harvest yields, weather, and prices; news about the children] I work as a cooper when I have the time, none of my sons want to learn a trade they all want to farm which is almost the best. Because of all the invented machines, *Fäktri* [factories] workers are in bad shape, the wages are too low they make too much of everything. In the time I can make 3 barrels out of wood by hand I can make 8 or 9 with the machine. It's the same for the shoemaker, carpenter and almost all the trades. I've been fighting my stomach pains now for 3 to 4 years, warm greetings to you, your wife and children, my sister and children. Your brother, Christian Lenz

Lenesville, October 8th, 1883

Dear brother and relatives,

I received your letter of August 29th and see from it that our sister Susanna has died, but I didn't know that she was 71 years old. I always thought she was only 7 years older than me and you were 5 years older.[49] On October 31st I'll be 60 years old and thus we are the only two brothers left on this side of the grave. It won't be much longer before the bell tolls for us, may God in His Mercy prepare us for the Heavenly Kingdom, for the sake of Jesus Christ, Amen. [12 ll.: still suffers from stomach pain; children's ages and places of residence] We've always had enough to live on and we still do but we have to work hard, never have anything left over because of all the many misfortunes which have afflicted us in our time. [7 ll.: harvest is not too good; prices low] Otherwise in terms of trade, all the *machinri* wrecks everything, too much is being made, everything is cheap, wages are pushed down, won't be getting any better, more and more keep getting invented, not much work is done by hand anymore, the *machün* does everything. I'll give you one example: when the land is plowed it's planted by machine, the machine does the cutting, the machine does the binding, the machine does the threshing, it's ground in the mill by *Stüm* [steam] and is made into bread at the bakery with steam and baked without much being done by hand and all of this with only a few people and it's like this in almost all the trades. I used to make 2 to 3 barrels a day with my hands now I make 10 to 12 a day and everything is finished, it only needs to be put together, it's like that in almost all the trades. I must close. We send you all our best wishes. Your brother / Christian Lenz

[49]See n. 4, above.

[presumably Leavenworth, Ind.] May 11, <u>1885</u>

Dear brother and relatives,

I received your letter of Nov. 14th but I couldn't write to you, I was right in the middle of selling my land and I didn't know where I should move to. Then this spring I moved and in this place 30 miles away I've rented this place for one year, but I won't stay here longer, we don't like it here. The land here is pretty well situated, but somewhat too wet you can't grow wheat here, it freezes in the winter. [7 ll.: health problems; news about the children] The last 3 are still with us to do the work, I and my wife can hardly work anymore. [5 ll.: cold spell and its effects on farming]

Otherwise trade is going pretty well, but this winter it was bad for all the trades, I hope soon to get a pension from my life as a soldier, I've been promised one but I don't know yet how much I'll get.[50] I'll write you about that the next time when I know more. [6 ll.: greetings; the consolation of reunion in the hereafter; signature]

[18 ll.: letter from Louisville of March 22, 1886: Christian reports that he has sold his land in Leavenworth and has been living in Louisville since March 12; news about the children and ages of the parents; he receives a pension of 4 dollars; business is bad]

Louisville, July 15, 1886

Dear brother,

I've been sending you some newspapers, did you get them? Every week I send you 2. If you still want them I'll be happy to send them to you, then you can read the news about what is happening here and what Amirkia is like. I really can't write it like that, you can read it yourself. As for me I'm in pretty good health but I can't work any more. I had a bad fall, I also have a growth under the ribs. No doctor has been able to tell me what it is, it's 5 inches long and 3 inches across, sometimes I'm in pain, sometimes not. My son Ludwig and my daughter Sara are living with us and I get 4 talers a month pension, so we can make do. My youngest daughter got married last week to a young man named August Makel, he's a baker. We have 2 married and 4 unmarried children. This year is a pretty good one, everything turned out well, wheat, corn, potatoes, hay, all did well. Still the workers are in bad shape, many people are out of work half the time. There's too much on hand. Louis-

---

[50]See Lenz's applications in the pension file (NatA).

ville is a big city but it's been quite quiet up until now, there aren't so many godless people here like in the other big cities, and the Germans are the most godless, they are the worst of all, they want to get rid of all discipline so they can lead their godless lives, we've been working hard to oppose this, when godlessness is the greatest the Final Judgment is near. Almighty God is still alive. [5 ll.: requests an answer soon; greetings; signature]

Louisville, Sept. 15, <u>88</u>

Dear brother,

I received your letter of January 27th on Feb. 14th and see from it that you and your wife are still walking this earth, I and my wife are still here too, but we've gotten old, for I've been 64 since October 31 (87), my wife is 60 and what can we still do. Since last summer I have had a job at night as a watchman in a large clothing store, from 7 in the evening till 7 in the morning. I get 6 dollars a week, don't have to do any work, have to sleep during the day. [3 ll.: poor harvest, high prices] I have to pay 7 dollars and 50 cents a month rent for 2 rooms, coal and wood are very expensive here, everything has to come a long way. Louisville is a very big town, some 5 hours long and 1½ hours wide. I haven't seen my eldest son for 7 years, he's far away. He's 32 years old and still single, has not had good luck. Last year the house burned down where he was boarding, he got out with only the clothes on his body on Feb. 14th, 87. He broke an arm and in October he broke his shoulder again.

Now he writes though that he is well again, the second boy is still in Lanesville on the farm. His mother is there for a visit. They're expecting their 5th child, she'll stay there 5 to 6 weeks. 3 children are still with us and are unmarried. Both of the boys were sick all winter, one is now well again the other is still doing poorly. The other daughter is married here in Louisville, has a little girl 3 months old. [4 ll.: news about German friends] You must send your letters to Christian Lenz No. 608. / 7, *Sübte Straße* [Seventh Street]. Warmest greetings from all of us to you and wife and children. Your brother / Christian Lenz

With this letter, the series breaks off; we can assume that the death of his 80-year-old brother put an end to the correspondence. Christian Lenz lived another thirteen years in Louisville with his wife, daughter Sara, and youngest son Christian.[51] Up until 1896 he is listed in the city

[51] MC 1900: Louisville; CD Louisville 1887–1900.

directories as a watchman—an indication that even in his early seventies and despite his poor state of health he was unable to enjoy a comfortable retirement.[52] Economic prosperity was denied him all his life, although it was certainly not for lack of effort. Not only were the uncertainties of fate responsible, which Christian himself always blamed for his modest circumstances, but his own limited ability and unwillingness to adjust to new developments played a role.

Lenz also seems to have been unable to provide his children—who presumably had a rather hard time with their sanctimonious father—with a good start in life. All of the sons remained unskilled laborers. Although Ludwig and Christian worked at various jobs,[53] Philipp, the second oldest, lived with his wife and ten children as a day laborer in Lanesville. The 1900 census notes that he could not even read and write, nor could his eldest son, nineteen-year-old Philipp Jr., also only a day laborer.[54]

[52]CD Louisville 1889–1896. Lenz died on March 16, 1901, at the age of 77 (NatA, pension records).

[53]Ludwig is listed as a "laborer," "driver," and "teamster"; Christian as "laborer," "watchman," and "painter" (MC 1900: Louisville; CD Louisville 1887–1901).

[54]MC 1900: Harrison Co., Ind., e.d. 75, #38.

4

Johann Bauer (John Bauer)

In the year 1854, when Johann Bauer set out for America, emigration from western Germany reached its peak. Hardest hit, aside from the nearby Palatinate, was the region of north Baden around the village where Bauer was born, Heidelsheim near Bruchsal. In 1854 the number of officially recorded emigrants alone amounted to 1 percent of the population of the county of Bruchsal; the year before it had been even higher. Between 1852 and 1855 the county lost more than 4 percent of its population, above the average for Baden. All of Germany was afflicted by crop failures and rising food prices; the county of Bruchsal, in particular, was affected by poor yields from the wine harvests of 1850, 1851, and 1854, which reached a low equaled by only one other year in the nineteenth century. It is thus hardly surprising that almost two-thirds of the emigrants from the county of Bruchsal had been employed in agriculture.[1]

In terms of his family background, the 26-year-old Johann Bauer also belonged to this group. He himself, however, should be counted among the 15 percent of emigrants who were not engaged in farming, wine-growing, or artisan trades. There is some indication that he had worked for a merchant for some time. At one point he sends greetings to his old *"Prinzipal"* Lindner in Bretten, most likely referring to the merchant Georg Andreas Lindner, born in 1803, who was married to the daughter

[1]*Beiträge zur Statistik des Großherzogtums Baden* 5 (1857), 16–17. On the wine harvest see *Württembergisches Jahrbuch* (1890), 55–57.

of the mayor of Bretten.[2] On his arrival in New York, Johann seems to have looked for a similar position, but he soon had to realize that his previous job experience was of little use. Although he obviously had a broader horizon than the average peasant's son, there is no firm evidence that he went beyond elementary school. Perhaps he was self-taught; he was in any case an avid reader.

Johann also differed from the mass of other emigrants in that he was not impoverished.[3] He was able to make the crossing not in steerage but as a cabin passenger, and in America he occasionally received money from home. His brother Georg, two years younger, already lived in New York State, a fact that certainly facilitated his decision to emigrate; more important, however, were poor economic prospects and above all disagreements with his stepfather, which show through repeatedly in his letters.[4]

Johann's independence—perhaps even obstinacy—soon came to light in America. Not only his brother but also numerous friends lived near New York and Philadelphia, but he stayed on the east coast for only a few months before setting out for Chicago. There he remained only a few days before taking a job with a farmer. This time Georg followed his brother Johann, or John.

John Bauer exemplifies the type of immigrant who sought to adapt completely to the American way of life. When his employer (evidently American) moved from Illinois to Missouri the next year, Bauer went along too. Here he obviously found what he had been looking for; he lived within a radius of ten miles for the rest of his life. Germans were only a tiny minority in this area. Sand Hill Township, where John was living in 1860, counted only sixteen immigrants in 1870, and all of Adair County listed only 116 Germans, a mere 1 percent of the population. After his brother's death, John makes almost no further mention of

²Bretten was the neighboring township, population 3,500, eight miles from Heidelsheim. Johann Bauer's father was a baker by trade, but he was presumably a fruit or crop grower on the side; his stepfather was a full-time farmer. On Lindner see Brettener Standesbücher, GLA KA, Abt. 390, Nr. 541, 542. Bauer is also listed as a merchant from Bretten traveling in the second cabin on the *General Jacobi* in NYPL, Roll 138, May 3, 1854.

³By contrast, 89 persons emigrated from Bruchsal in 1854 with financial support from the village (Härdle [1960], 140–43).

⁴The children of Johann Georg (1803–1840) and Katharina Bauer, née Scheder (1809–1883), were the following: Johann (1828–1904), the letter-writer; Johann Georg (1830–1864), who emigrated to America before 1854 (hereafter, the underlined name of a pair of names indicates the one the individual used); Andreas (b. 1832); Catharina (b. 1834), whose husband was Heinrich Zimmermann, addressee of the later letters; Margaretha (1835–1838); and Carl (1838–1886), a farmer in Heidelsheim. In 1841, just one year after the death of Johann's natural father, his mother Katharina married for the second time. There were two children from this marriage to farmer Andreas Manz (1803–1876): Friedrich (b. 1841), who later emigrated to America, and Johann Heinrich (b. 1846), who died in infancy.

contacts with Germans; in 1880 he was one of only seven Germans in his township. In Kirksville, the county seat, and for fifty miles around, there was never a German newspaper, and the first Lutheran church was not founded until 1922. John's choice of a place to live thus determined the conditions under which he could find a wife or join a church congregation.[5]

Bauer married sometime around 1862. The letter in which he "introduced" his American wife to his family has not survived; she is seldom mentioned in the remaining correspondence and never referred to by name. If they had not had any children, one would hardly know that John Bauer was even married. It is certainly somewhat hazardous to draw any conclusions from his silence, but John's marriage does not seem to have been one of kindred souls, to say the least. Perhaps intellectual differences played a role: according to the 1870 census his wife could neither read nor write. Immigrants could not always be choosers. His brother Georg's wife was much younger than he, besides that an orphan, and at most seventeen years old when they were married.[6]

In terms of politics and religion, too, Bauer was largely Americanized. His early and strong sympathy for the Republican party was probably due to the influence of his mostly northern neighbors. At such an early date such political views among German-Americans were usually restricted to the "Forty-eighters" and educated elite. He had been baptized a Lutheran in Baden, but he joined a Methodist congregation in America. In both form and style the zealous revivalist movement was the exact opposite of the cool rigor and austerity of German Lutheranism. Bauer's understanding of religion did not manifest itself in agonizing self-examination, however, but in a boost of self-confidence. It was in any case fully compatible with capitalistic thinking.

John Bauer quickly grasped the American principle that the price of land depends primarily on the density of settlement, and this above all prompted him to ask for financial help from home. Even taking into account the 140 dollars he received during the 1860s, he made rapid headway. As a farmhand working for his brother Georg in 1860, he reported assets of only 180 dollars. Ten years later he owned a farm worth $3,000 and another $1,000 worth of moveable assets. In the 1870s he was able to double his land, so that in 1880 he was farming some 125 acres. By

[5]USC 1870.1 and 1880.1; Arndt/Olson (1965); Sueflow (1954), 67, 183.
[6]John Bauer was married to Sarah Ann Stout on May 11, 1862, by a justice of the peace (Marriage Records of Adair County, Mo., Book 1, p. 133, Missouri State Archives). Sarah Bauer's illiteracy is confirmed by the fact that she signed with her mark in Record of Deeds, Adair County, Mo., Book O, p. 280 (on the Bauers' literacy see MC 1870: Adair County, Mo., Twp. 63, R. 14, #75; on Sarah's age see MC 1860: Scotland County, Mo., Sand Hill Twp., #912).

American standards, Bauer's wealth was considerable, but not unheard of; in Germany it must have seemed fantastic. Among the 35,000 people living in the county of Bruchsal when he left, there was only one man who could outbid Bauer's stock of six horses, and only two who owned more than his twenty cows.[7]

For someone who may have gone no further than elementary school, Bauer's spelling and syntax are truly remarkable. There are virtually no grammatical errors, and only rare instances where he deviates from conventional German spelling. Living as he did in an almost totally English-speaking environment, it is perhaps not surprising to see increasing English influence in his sentence structure, choice of verbs and prepositions, and use of idioms.

The clearly discernible difference between Bauer's manner of writing and that of truly educated letter-writers like the Blümner brothers is in the field of vocabulary. Apart from religion and occasionally politics, Bauer confines his remarks to rather down-to-earth matters, and he rarely ventures into abstract ideas. His writing is clear and to the point, but hardly sophisticated.

Johann Bauer

New York, May 11, 1854

Dear parents & brothers and sisters,

So now I have arrived safely in New York and considering the many sleepless nights you have probably had since I left you, I will use my first free day to inform you of my safe arrival. It was on March 11th when I boarded the steamboat in Mannheim with many other emigrants and the moon lit up the Rhine so splendidly as I said farewell again to you and all those whose friendship & esteem I enjoy. This was the moment in which the period of my life up to now passed before my eyes and when I gratefully remembered all of those who stood by my side with their teachings & their good example. That night between 11 & 12 o'clock (of M. 11) we finally came to an inn in Cöln [Cologne], a real thieves' den, where we had to stay until Monday the 13th, because on that day an extra

---

[7]Although he does not list it in the 1860 census, Bauer had made his first land purchase of ca. 280 acres for $350 on October 24, 1855. On February 2, 1857, he sold eighty acres to his brother George, but he lived on one quarter section of his original purchase his entire married life (Record of Deeds, Adair County, Mo.; *Atlas of Adair County* [1876], 85; *Standard Atlas of Adair County* [1885], 5; *Plat Book* [1911], 6; MC A 1860: Scotland County, Mo.; MC A 1870, 1880: Adair County, Mo., Clay Twp.; *Beiträge zur Statistik des Großherzogtums Baden* 6 [1858], 92–93).

train went from Cöln to Bremen. We boarded the train in the morning of the 13th M. & arrived toward evening in Münden [Minden], where our passports were examined & at 12 o'clock at night we came to Bremen, hungry & tired, but to an inn which was much worse still, so we left the next day & were lucky enough to come upon a decent innkeeper. [15 ll.: itinerary, stay in Bremen] At midday on the 18th the ship finally sailed. When we departed from Bremen the crowd of emigrants was so large that the price of passage rose to 106–108 guilders for a poor berth & 120 guilders for a better one, but since I already had a ticket I could go for 96 guilders & had nothing to regret in this regard. On the ship there were 263 persons, about 100 with better berths which comprised 2 parts & since I was on the ship early I could pick out the best spot, namely in the cabin which was set up for 18 persons; I also had my own place to sleep, whereas in the other parts sometimes 3 & 4 had to sleep together. It is no small matter to live in a dark room with ca. 160 to 200 people for 40 to 50 days, therefore I advise everyone not to worry about a few guilders and to go in the cabin. The difference amounts to 12–15 guilders.

[55 ll.: voyage] In the morning of May 2nd we saw land in the distance, by midday woods, & in the evening at 5 o'clock already green fields along with houses, yes, when we were across from New Y. about 8 and the lights of the large palaces in the harbor shone towards us it was a lovely sight. I've already been to visit Herr Kreuzer & Frank. They want to do their utmost to find me a place in a business. On May 5th, 6th & 7th I visited Gg.[8] who was very glad to see me. He's done very well & wants to stay for 1 more year because he gets more pay now. He speaks English well & it is quite possible that I'll go live with him, since his boss is an American & I could then soon speak English, too. I slept in his house & ate there. The journey there is made on a large river with mountains running along both sides where there are the most beautiful houses & farmen.

My brief stay in this city makes it impossible for me to write more about conditions in America & you must therefore make do with my description of the journey; I haven't been to Philad. yet. I gave the letter for Catth. Maier to Diefens, because she is far away from here; 2 hours as I was told.

In the letter which Father tore up, G. had written that I should bring Carl along, because it is best when people come here at that age.[9] He would already have found a job, for he could get 10 places to my one. He

---

[8]John's brother Georg lived in Albany, New York; he is probably the George Bauer, farmer, age twenty-two, who arrived from Bremen on the *Gesine* June 7, 1853 (NYPL, Roll 126).
[9]His brother Carl Bauer was sixteen years old at the time. John was already ten years older.

shouldn't start a trade if he wants to go to America, since he'd have to
here again anyway & one has to see what one will do later.
[7 ll.: closing; signature, greetings]

Princeton [Illinois] June 10, 1855

Dear parents & brothers and sisters,

Your letter from Novb. last year was properly delivered to me by W.
Fink in Philadelphia & it is with particular pleasure that I see from it that
you are all healthy & well. I already wrote to you in my last letter that I
am happy in America, but in spite of this fact you are still concerned &
worried about me, which I regret very much & therefore ask you to stop,
for even if I were doing poorly, it would not improve my condition by a
hair's breadth. In your future letters please refrain from such comments &
write instead that you got together in Oberaker or Bretten or somewhere
else & drank to my health; this will give me more pleasure than the
contents of your last letter. [6 ll.: elaboration] From my last letter you
will have learned that I intended to go to St. Louis or Cincinatty, but
careful consideration led me to set out in another direction. Various
friends in Philadelphia entreated me not to make such a long journey at
the beginning of winter, because this often causes many difficulties, but I
was determined not to waste the money that I had in Ph., waiting for
good luck, but to go towards my fate, whatever it might bring.

I haven't had to regret this decision. On October 26 I left Ph & on the
27th I arrived in New York from whence I traveled to Albany by steamboat & on the 28th visited Georg, and talked things over with him &
went on by steam to Buffalo, Detroit & Chigago, all beautiful, thriving
towns. [7 ll.: weather; journey] When I arrived in Chigago, which is 1200
miles from New York, I thought you've come far enough, put my things
in safety, & while my traveling companions sought to enjoy themselves
with drinking & gaming in the taverns, I immediately started looking for
employment, which they laughed about & said one ought to allow
oneself a bit of rest. I was lucky enough to find employment right that
afternoon, & although the conditions were not brilliant, I accepted,
because I had nothing better in sight for the moment & I was concerned
about the approaching winter. After I had been in this job for 4 days I met
a *farmer* & since he offered me much better conditions I left Chigago &
went another 110 miles farther inland. I stayed the entire winter with this
farmer & in my entire life I've never gone sledding so much as here. You
have probably often thought how will our Johann spend the winter; oh, I
spent it much better than you could imagine. In Germany they still have
the impression that there are no happy hours here, but this is mere

foolishness. The people here know how to make life just as pleasant as in beautiful Germany. An old musician from upper Baden always came to our house, a lively fellow, just like the old fiddler Hör in the *Judengasse* [Jews Alley]. He played us many a nice piece, so that our feet were itching to dance, and many times dancing even broke out. I've never had a more delightful New Year's Eve than here.

I am presently located in an area which 21 years ago was still fully in the hands of the Indians or savages.[10] Only a few years ago you wouldn't have found a single *farm* here. Then, 4 or 5 years ago the land was put up for sale for 1¼ dollars per acre, which in your money is 2.45 guilders, and now it is no longer to be had for under 10 to 15 dollars, or 25 to 40 guilders in your money. An American dollar is 2.30 guilders. You can see from this that it takes quite a bit of money at the start here, because almost all of the uncultivated land is in the hands of speculators & before I start out by filling the purse of such speculators I'd rather go 1000 miles farther inland. It doesn't matter to me, because in 6 to 8 years things there will be just like here. A journey of 1000 miles is of no more consequence here than when you go to Carlsruhe.[11] From the above description you can see how thriving the conditions are here, & that with a bit of hard work & stamina it is easier to get ahead than in Germany. I know people here who 4 or 5 years ago didn't even have 25 dollars to their name & now 2 to 3000 dollars. You mustn't think of America as a wilderness or nothing but shrubs & bushes & mountains. Sometimes you find areas 30 to 50 miles long & wide nothing but the most lovely fruitful hilly prairies or plains; with sufficient water but not always enough wood. [3 ll.: how the prairies developed] Since the month of March I've been working somewhere else. I was again very lucky in this, since I am with an American family who treat me very nice & friendly. We have a lot of fun, for American girls always come to the house & they always ask me if I wouldn't rather have an American wife than a German one. My present employer recently sold his land & bought himself land in Missouri. He'll be moving there in the fall & always says I should go with him, because I could still get good land there for a cheap price. My next letter will therefore be from the State of Missouri. My plan to start something here this year could not be carried out, because I didn't want to take the risk on my own.

You will be particularly pleased to learn that brother G. arrived here two weeks ago. He is hale & hearty & boarded in our house for 2 days &

[10]Illinois was largely ceded by the Indians in 1816 and 1819, but one area, which lay a few miles north of Princeton, remained in Indian possession until 1834 (see Johnson [1976], 123).
[11]Today Karlsruhe, the capital of Baden, only about fifteen miles from Heidelsheim.

was lucky enough to find work right away. We live about 12 minutes from each other, get together every Sunday, sometimes during the week as well. We consider ourselves very very lucky, but above all our dearest wish is to start next spring if we have good luck & stay healthy. 4 weeks ago I went to a Protestant church for the first time. It is very hard to learn enough English in one year to be able to understand the pastor. The sermon that I heard had to do with the immortality of the soul & was so beautiful that I could write down the whole sermon for you. Things here are very religious, although in the towns quite a few crimes are committed like in Germany. You can reassure Johannes Durst's family and tell them that I myself put the letter into their son's hands, & every time I visited him I entreated him to write to his parents. If he hasn't done it yet, it's not my fault. [3 ll.: has delivered another letter] No one has heard anything for a long time from Andreas. [11 ll.: health; greetings; closing, signature; postage; address] [16 ll.: written by Georg Bauer]

Sand Hill / Nov. 30th, 1856

Dear brother-in-law,

[3 ll.: thanks for letter] I have already thought a thousand times what a joy it would be to see you again, only circumstances have never yet permitted it. In fact I believe that if I were to live again for a short time in Germany, I would long for America again. I can well imagine how it would be. At first I would be surrounded by friends who would interrogate me about absolutely everything, and as soon as that was over and I would be seen again as something old, you would go about your business again, then I would sit around, and since I would under no circumstances be able to decide to start anything, I would set out again for America, which would only cause you sorrow and distress once again. America has advantages (at least for me) that you don't have in Germany.

Under the given circumstances I have always preferred to stay unmarried. I've always thought that as a bachelor I can go where I want and I always manage to pull myself through, but it will soon be time to change my mind. There is no lack of opportunities *to find a match,* as the Americans say. One major reason that I am still unmarried, too, is that I still wish to see my old homeland again. If I should decide to make the journey I would write ahead of time, so you can slaughter a fat sow and serve me a good blood sausage when I visit, and hopefully you will see to it that there's a good pitcher full of wine. Don't be anxious to get rich too quickly and don't sacrifice your health to your selfishness; but I don't mean by that that you should miss out on a good bargain if you can make about 1000 guilders profit. The presidential election which had the country in such a terrible uproar went off quietly on November 4th. The Democrats carried the day and elected James Buchanan as *President*.

I belong to the Republican Party, which wanted to elect John C. Fremont but didn't have the good fortune to carry it through. *I do not care*, says the American, the majority must rule. [. . .]

I must close now. Warmest greetings to you, Catherina, *and* all the friends who ask about me.

Your brother-in-law / John Bauer

Sand Hill September 2, 1857. / Scotland County Mo.
Dear mother,

[23 ll.: started a business, had to give it up again due to illness]

I had planned to visit you during the course of this year, but I don't know if this will be the case, I've planned to visit you 3 times already & each time difficulties got in my way, so that it almost seems that it is not supposed to be. One time, just as I was thinking about you, it was like someone said to me, He that loveth his father or mother more than me is not worthy of me. What do you say to that, Mother? During my illness I have found friends whom I will honor as long as I live, yes, I have found a father & a mother, and how can I leave the people whose love was so great as to pray for me. Who knows whether I would be alive today, if these prayers had not been sent to Heaven, and would it not be cold and heartless toward Georg to leave this country now? Do not be discouraged and sad, dear Mother, for I can assure you that we will meet again in that land where there will be no more disappointment, no more death, and no more separation. George can reassure you of that. [4 ll.: reward for devotion in the hereafter] I often think about father's cursing & swearing & whether he still has the same evil habits. Oh, if he could only come here once & see & hear what a true Christian should do to enjoy an inner peace which the world cannot give. [5 ll.: religious exhortations] George was very godless for a time, cursing & swearing, but he has changed completely now. On August 24th he was so filled with the love of Our Savior that he did nothing but shout *Glory* for about a quarter of an hour, that means *Ehre* in German and *Preis zu Gott;* His Spirit seems to be out of this world. You can see such examples openly here. [5 ll.: has had the same experience himself] You can go ahead and call America a wilderness, but I like it more every day, in terms of religion Germany can't be compared to America.

I myself, since I was surrounded for a long time by people who didn't care about religion, was so taken with this world that I became indifferent in this respect. But everything is different now. Dear parents, live for the next world and do not let yourselves be taken prisoner by the cares of this world, for what shall it profit a man if he shall gain the whole world and lose his own soul?

George was married on August 24th to a girl named Sarah Caldwell, she is an orphan and was adopted by a good family.[12] She is not rich, true, but she is of excellent character, very religious, thrifty, hard-working and amicable. I couldn't wish a better person for myself. [7 ll.: would like to come to Germany; harvest; conclusion is missing]

Sand Hill Scotland County / Missouri
Sunday morning, May 20th, 1860

Dear parents & brothers and sisters,

[22 ll.: enjoying the Sunday quiet; thinking about Germany] With regret I see from your letter that the power of attorney is still not correct. [11 ll.: details] I intend to write to the Consul of Baden before I make out the power of attorney, & then it will finally be correct. [3 ll.: weather] America is now made up of 33 states, some of which are smaller & some bigger than the Kingdoms of Würtemberg or Bavaria and that is why the climate in such a large country is so different. [23 ll.: weather; harvest; prices; hard times] You can get some idea how rare money must be here when I tell you that you can't get any money here for less than 25 to 30 percent per year and even then you have to have very good friends. At the root of this scarcity of money are the many worthless banks, which often go broke & this is partly due to a frenzy of speculation; you can't say that it's real poverty, & it is often attributed to the fact that many, yes even most people, are trying to get more land than their means permit, but the American doesn't care, he must speculate and win or lose. [4 ll.: this can change quickly, like many things in America] In political life there is much excitement at the moment, which will increase every day until the 1st Monday of the month of November, when the great question will be decided by the election. Since this is the year a new *President* will be elected, all the signs indicate that this will be one of the hottest election campaigns there ever was in the United States. When I speak of a hot campaign, however, you mustn't imagine that there are soldiers everywhere and that anyone who speaks out is grabbed by the hair or the coat. [3 ll.: comparison to elections in Heidelsheim] I will also be taking part in this campaign & this for the first time, since the American laws require that every immigrant must have been in the country for 5 years before he is allowed to vote.

[12]This is corroborated in Dodge (n.d.), 5; in MC 1860: Scotland Co., Mo., George is listed as 29 and Sarah as nineteen years old.

There will probably be 4 candidates for *President* in the running. One Republican, one Democrat from the northern states, one Democrat from the southern states, and the 4th will be from the *Wigpartie* with which the *Knownothings* or in German *die Feinde der Ausländer* [the enemies of foreigners] are connected. The latter party has the principle that foreigners should hold no offices and have to be in the country for 21 years before they are allowed to vote; they won't elect a President all that quickly since the true American believes in the idea that all men are created equal before God, with the same rights. I will naturally vote for their candidate, that is against the (*Knownothing*)—A while ago I read in the newspaper that there will probably be a great war in Europe, between the Pope and France or Austria and France, I don't know which, perhaps it wasn't so serious; I thought, by the way, that if I were in danger of being stuck as a soldier in Germany, I'd rather be in America, even if it is not the best just now. [4 ll.: closing; greetings] / Johan
[16 ll. to brother-in-law, Karl, and his sister: he misses the local wine, otherwise things are fine; they should come, if dissatisfied in Germany; greetings; signature: John]

John Bauer / Kirksville / Adair County, Mo.
Sunday, February *the 19th*, 1865
Dear parents, friends & brothers and sisters,

Deeply moved in spirit, I finally take up my pen to interrupt our long mutual silence. [9 ll.: correspondence] When I last wrote to you, I wrote in great agitation, for we feared the worst from the Rebels, but the worst didn't happen, & thank God we are living here again in safety & more or less in peace, although the war continues without interruption. [10 ll.: bad year; drought; illness; bad harvest] But we suffer no lack of food, the wool from our sheep is enough to keep us clothed since the war; & having food & raiment let us be therewith content, says the Scripture. We have had very good years here & these will come again when it is time, & it may please God to give them again.

In my family last summer there was great sorrow, caused by the unexpected painful loss of my beloved & promising child George Whashington. This dear child, after his recovery, had begun to blossom like a rose in the fall of 1863, his mind had developed unusually quickly & he had such a good-natured & obedient spirit like I have seldom seen, & had thus filled us with the best of hopes, but then came the Angel of Death & suddenly snatched him from our midst. He died within two days from cramps & whooping cough in the 2nd week of the month of August. But we do not grieve as do those who have no hope. [5 ll.: religious reflec-

tions] I never put all my hope, or too much hope, in this dear child, but I had often thought that when I reach old age that he might be a help to me in some ways, because otherwise I have no one here, but now this hope is gone & I must try to make my way through this vale of sorrow as best I can. But besides this sad news, I have another piece of sad news for you, one which may cause you even more grief. [4 ll.: like Jesus and Lazarus] Our son & brother George sleeps or rather is no longer of this world. He died on June 22nd in the army hospital in Memphis, Tennesse, patiently & devoted to God & without doubt he has gone to join those who have washed their clothes in the blood of Jesus. His letters were always a great comfort & it put my mind to rest that in the army, where such horrible godlessness reigns, he had always sought to serve God & to be prepared when the Lord called him. [29 ll.: religious consolation; Georg's wife and two children are well taken care of, receive a war pension, among other things] It is indescribable, the woe and misery that this disastrous war has caused. [5 ll.: examples] This abominable war has cost more than 2 million lives & it's not over yet. Since my last letter, the government has taken various strong fortresses from the Rebels & given them a bloody 2-day battle where they lost more than 100 cannons in all. There is talk here & there of peace talks but no one has much trust in that & there is fear that it will have to be fought out to the bitter end. All foodstuffs, clothing & just about everything you see is now very expensive here. Many items cost 5 & 6 times what they did before the war. [3 ll.: prices] It has now been one year since I heard anything from you & I ask you please to write soon how you are & whether you are all still alive. Oh, how much can change within a year. I also would like to know how Karl & brother-in-law Zimmerman are & all of our friends who still remember me.
[10 ll.: religious consolation; closing; signature; correspondence; he is sending turnip seeds]
[in the same envelope:]

                                                                March 13th, 1865
Dear parents, friends & brothers and sisters,
    [8 ll.: correspondence] There are people here who were worth millions of dollars before the war and are now beggars; indeed, there are cases where these people, who spent their whole lives in wealth & luxury, now gratefully receive food and clothing from the hand of the government; and their only wish was to destroy this very government. The capital Washington was recently illuminated on order of the President, following the great battle victories against the Rebels. [12 ll: war almost over; cost, destruction] A certain author said recently that the 30-Year's War in

Germany was nothing compared to this war here which hasn't even been going on for 4 years. In the state of Missouri we are looking forward to a better future; *Sclavery* (or trade in human beings) has ceased forever. [10 ll.: weather; correspondence]

There are men like Prof. Schenkel here, too, but I know what I believe in. Men like that are wolves in sheep's clothing, & our Lord Jesus told us that they would come.[13] [23 ll.: false doctrines disappear, as did Voltaire's hostility toward religion in the face of death; closing; greetings; signature]

Willmothville,[14] February 2nd, 1867 / Adair County, Mo.
Dear parents, friends & brothers and sisters,
[30 ll.: excuses for delayed answer; well-being; harvest]

When I first started to make my home on this great prairie, conditions were such that it would have caused great expense to build myself a good house & since I didn't have the means to carry out such a project, I decided to build myself a small temporary house, intending to build a better one as soon as my circumstances would allow. The time has now come & I already have part of the building materials at the sawmill & unless something unfortunate happens I may be able to spend the next winter in my new warm house. Several of my old friends may have done well in the old homeland, I prefer to live here, and even if my progress to prosperity is slow & connected with great effort, I can still assure you that every year I have come a step forward. In the beginning it is very hard & difficult here & these difficulties have been overcome. [6 ll.: earthly hopes and eternity] George's wife has married again, & you don't need to worry about his children. [6 ll.: details] Since the end of the war everything in Missouri has experienced an enormous boom. The immigration from the older states & also from Germany is very large & thank God it is clear that people are beginning to be concerned about religion again; I, too, have had two new Christian, amicable neighbors since last fall, and I only wish that even more would follow. [5 ll.: rail connection for Kirksville; United States still agitated despite peace]

Our hypocritical president, who during the time of war wrapped himself in the resplendent robes of a true friend of the Fatherland, has finally taken them off and has appeared in his true light for what he is, a

---

[13]Georg Daniel Schenkel (1813–1885), appointed professor of theology in Heidelberg in 1851, denied all miracles except those of healing, which he explained in psychological terms (Holzmann [1890], 82–89).

[14]The various addresses in Adair County reflect the opening of new post offices in the area. After his marriage Bauer apparently never moved.

friend of those who tried to destroy the government with sword in hand. [10 ll.: fight between President Johnson and Congress about the treatment of the defeated Southerners] It is hard for them to give up their rights as American citizens, but this must happen, everything must be made new, otherwise all the blood was shed for naught and the fruits of victory lost and it would not be long before people were again sold like animals.

Much better a second war. The men who were in the army prophesy that if they have to unsheathe their swords again, they will revenge themselves terribly. May God give to all of our leading statesmen wisdom & forgiving hearts.

One still hears about many murders, mostly arising from old hatred or private revenge. In our area though it is quite peaceful, & business is normal. The reason is that we are 10 Union men to every Rebel, but where the Rebels have the upper hand, there it is the opposite and the Union men must be somewhat more careful.

I was very pleased to see from our cousin Stoll's letter that in the war between Prussia & Austria lovely Baden received a somewhat milder treatment than some other provinces and still has its independence. That was more than I in fact expected, for I feared that Baden would receive the first blow from its powerful overlord, as a result of the old Prussian hatred of everything that bears the name *Revolution*; [8 ll.: examples] Prussia has been made bold by its success & I sorely fear you can sing, *Wer weis wie nah mein Ende* [Who knows how near my end may be].[15] While I hate Austria as the enemy of all religious & political progress, I have no *Simpathy* for Prussia; a Prussian hates everything that does not bear his name.

On the whole I much prefer my new homeland to Germany; for if we have an unjust President, we can elect another one after 4 years, and for certain crimes we can even bring him to court during his period of office, which may still happen with the current one.[16] [13 ll.: letter is also for his cousin Stoll; greetings; signature]

My oldest girl, who will be 3 years old in April, insisted that her mother include a small lock of her hair; she dearly wishes to see her grandmother.

[15]Title of a well-known German Protestant hymn, authored by Countess Amilie Juliane.

[16]Vice President Andrew Johnson, "our hypocritical President," succeeded to the presidency after the assassination of Abraham Lincoln. As a Union supporter from the South, he was much more favorably disposed toward the South than his predecessor, which brought him into increasing conflict with the Republican majority in Congress. As Bauer suspected, on February 24, 1868, Congress initiated impeachment proceedings against Johnson; in the Senate, however, the prosecution failed to achieve the necessary two-thirds majority to convict him (McPherson [1982], 513–20, 530–33).

<u>Willmothville, February 9th, 1868 / Adair Co Mo.</u>

Dear parents,

Your letter of the 8th of December, including a draft of 80 dollars, reached me safely about 10 days ago. [8 ll.: is relieved and grateful; had been somewhat dejected about having to ask for it] Since it always seems to me that you think Johann is doing poorly, he writes for money and others send money. This prompts me to explain the situation better to you. I still remember well the conversation in H. [Heidelsheim]. Wilh. Fink, he's doing well, he has a tavern, and also about other people & when I arrived in Philadelphia I looked all around to find his tavern. I finally found Mr. Fink, who even cheated me out of 7 dollars, & it turned out that he had rented a boarding house together with a wretched bar.[17] However, they often do well, there is more money in the towns than in the country, but if they don't do well, it doesn't matter at all, they go bankrupt & since they have no property except their liquor glasses no one can take anything away from them; then they go somewhere else & in a short time they're as well respected as all the liquor dealers are here. I might have been able to do as well in one of the many large towns as this fellow, but I thought differently & acted differently. With the frequent & often sudden changes in circumstances there is always a danger of losing what you've acquired with great trouble & effort; *for* the merchant as well as other tradesmen. Under these circumstances, I preferred to invest the means I had at my disposal in land, which is always good here. I thought in times of confusion, land remains a refuge & with some effort & work I can always feed myself & my family, & when the time comes when the area is more *angesettled* [settled], the land will be more valuable, & I am therefore more secure than in any other business. I also speculated correctly, for the area is being built up very quickly since the end of the war, & the railroad to our young & blossoming county seat Kirksvill is so far along that we expect the first train by the 1st of July or August.[18] This is a big boost to our area & gives us the chance to sell our products at the railroad, whereas we used to have to go great distances, before the railroad was built.

[17]Wilhelm Fink's financial situation was somewhat better than Bauer may have thought. He presumably emigrated in 1850, and he appears regularly as a hotel keeper in CD Philadelphia. According to the MC 1860: Philadelphia, Pa., W. 14, #1425, Fink was thirty years old; he owned no real estate, but he claimed moveable assets of $9,000. Half of his 24 hotel guests were Americans, the others were mostly Germans, primarily craftsmen by trade, as well as a few merchants. Fink died in 1864 (two obituaries by German lodges for their member William Fink).

[18]During the 1860s, the county seat Kirksville, ca. twelve miles from where Bauer lived, was able to more than double its population (from 658 to 1,471). In the following decade, the population rose to over 2,300 (USC 1860.1, 1870.1, 1880.1).

With great effort I have managed to get to the point where I will have
45 acres of cropland in the spring, which will yield a rich harvest, if we
have a good year. My land is owned clear, my livestock, & everything I
have & what I received also pays off my newly built house, which we
moved into on December 13. [2 ll.: not yet quite finished, due to an early
cold spell] But we live a lot more comfortably than in our log cabin. We
are expecting money to become very tight in America; if this happens
now, it won't hurt me very much. [23 ll.: he is well; dryness; weather]

I was very surprised to learn from your letter that my brother Friedrich
has also set off for America; that leaves you with no help at all when you
need it most. I would very much like to see him, but it's hard to say
where the best place is, because some make good where others don't; if
he should find his way here, however, & I can help him, I would be very
glad to. Many Germans prefer to stay in the towns, I enjoy the quiet life
in the country. In Germany, Sunday was usually the hardest work day,
here I look forward to this holy day with pleasure, very often even with
gratitude, when on Saturday evening, after a week of labor and toil, the
sun disappears amid glowing colors behind the hill a mile away from
here. As you requested, I include a receipt for the sum that you sent me.
[3 ll.: parents desire a power of attorney] In November 1860 I received
from you: one draft of 61 dollars and 64 cents; on January 25, 1868, one
draft of 80 dollars.[19]

[. . .] This fall we have to elect a President again. The excitement is
starting already. [. . .] Each party praises its own men & scorns the
others; when you read the newspapers, you would think they were all
angels; may God grant that we elect a better man than our traitorous
President Johnson. [10 ll.: closing; greetings; signature; weather; all are
well]

Willmothville, April 11th, 1868 / Adair Co Mo.
Dear parents, friends & brothers and sisters,

[22 ll.: correspondence; had chest pains; weather; farming; planted
fruit trees; wrote to his brother Friedrich, who had already returned to
Germany] I don't feel in the least hurt that he didn't visit me, although I
had dearly wished it; on the contrary, I can't help smiling that he got so
terribly homesick & left America in such a hurry, bitterly disappointed
that it's not possible to make a fortune here in one year. America only has
a few great advantages that you don't have in Germany, the greatest is
that you can be more independent than there, that you can start something today, & if you're not happy or satisfied you can start something

---

[19]A letter by Georg Bauer of April 10, 1859 (BABS), suggests that the Bauer children owned
land that they sold to their stepfather.

else tomorrow & without making a stir. That is the main thing that makes America so dear to people, the freedom of movement, in many other things Germany is almost as good. If Friedrich had come to see me, I could have given him some useful advice. [9 ll: is in an awkward position with regard to his neighbors, whom he had informed about the visit; he will not invite him again]

[12 ll: it is now April 24; correspondence; weather; garden] Our area has been gaining population very quickly since we have the railroad & there's much building going on, also many schoolhouses are being built, which is very necessary; I don't like the American school system, by the way. The Americans think there's nothing in the world better than the schools here, which is a great self-deception. There are even many people here who cannot read a word, and when they have to write their names they make a + like for example

$$(\text{Carl} \quad \overset{\text{his}}{\underset{\text{sign}}{+}} \quad \text{Bauer})$$

also in religious things it's getting much better; that is more efforts are being made to reduce godlessness & vice. But it is here like in Germany; many aspire only to wealth & luxury & the gratification of their desires; they don't consider how quickly they can be called away from this evil world to appear before the Last Judge. [. . .]

[5 ll.: new President] It is not true that the wages of the workers have risen since he took office; one would hardly notice a change in the government if the newspapers didn't tell us the news. I don't know what prompted Brother Friedrich's friend to write this. [8 ll.: religious reflections on fifteen years in the United States] Finally, I prophesy to you that Friedrich will come back to America. America, with all its adversities, has a power of attraction like no other country, because here you can take up whatever you want. It is a great mistake to think, like Friedrich does, that you don't have ask anyone for anything, he can be convinced of this later. [12 ll.: asks for flower seeds; greetings; signature]

Willmothville, December 12th, 1868 / Adair Co Mo.
Dear parents, friends & brothers and sisters,
[16 ll.: thanks for letters; has heard nothing from his brother Friedrich] The behavior of my brother F strikes me as very strange. I am very sorry that he did not like my letter, but I can't do anything about it. As far as I know, I wrote him a friendly letter; that I didn't advise him firmly one way or the other is also true; but I only said with some emphasis that I would be very happy to see him here & if I didn't exactly say he should

come here, it's because I thought if he comes here & he doesn't like it, he could blame me and say, You should not have written. I dealt much the same way with George. [10 ll.: correspondence; weather] If I had your good stalls & barn I could face winter without fear, but they don't have them here yet, for you can only make improvements bit by bit. Imagine, a carpenter gets 1½ to 2 dollars a day, some who do fine cabinet work in the towns get 3 dollars a day, that is 7.30 guilders in your money. I am very happy that I now have a small, good house & I thank you again for the help I received. I could have fought my way through alone, but your help has made it much easier. If I stay healthy for a few years & suffer no misfortunes, then I want to build myself a small barn, but not before I have the means. A barn that is not very large will cost me about 4 to 500 dollars, without most of the materials, which I must provide.

[8 ll.: no winter lull like in Germany, therefore he is sometimes homesick; his strength is failing] I haven't worked one hour less, with the thought that I would some day get such and such an amount from you; so I can only advise you to take it somewhat easier & not toil away to your final hour, as far as you are able to. [3 ll.: should still enjoy their property for a long time] If some more comes from you I will accept it gratefully & try to invest it wisely, to improve my new homestead, which I would be hard put to leave, unless misfortune should force me to, or too good of an offer. There are people here who are always moving around. They buy themselves a piece of land, live & work like animals and when they don't get rich in a few years, then they curse about the area, sell everything for a trifle, go somewhere else & do even worse, & sometimes come back again & would often be happy just to have their land back again; they often move 5 to 6 times like this before they come to their senses & learn that riches don't fall into everyone's laps. [7 ll.: power of attorney; money transfer] This time we have elected the famous General Grand. I also voted for him; may God grant him the wisdom & understanding & moderation & strength to govern this troubled country for the best. I can't help saying that I feel proud at the thought of being an American citizen; it makes me forget almost all of the unpleasant things in America. It is a wonderful feeling to realize that you can replace a hateful government with another one, but on the other hand there are many things in Germany that they don't have here. This general was a leather merchant in Illinois at the start of the war, joined the volunteers, moved up to become a general & in the end he was appointed Commander in Chief of the whole American Army & now the next elected President; just imagine such an ascent for a simple citizen.[20]

[20]U. S. Grant (1822–1885) was, in fact, a leather merchant at the outbreak of the war, but he had graduated from West Point, participated in the Mexican War as a captain, and served a total of eleven years in the U.S. Army (DAB 4:492–501).

George's children are hale & hearty, as last I heard. [8 ll.: religious exhortations; greetings, signature; has received a letter from his brother Fritz after all]

Willmothville, August 18th, 1869 / Adair County, Mo.
Dear parents, friends & brothers and sisters,
[59 ll.: state of health; trust in God; harvest of varying quality around America; number of settlers increasing; paid $18.25 for school construction] Of course I would rather pay this sum than live in a neighborhood where the schools are poor.

As soon as this is finished, they will probably build a new church which will naturally cost more than the schoolhouse. It's not compulsory, for many rich men don't give a cent for it, although they are often blessed by Providence with everything; there are also people here who never go to church & think more about a fine horse than a fine church. I do not want to take a back seat here, and if God gives me life & means I intend to contribute my share. You don't need to do this in Germany, but here the government does nothing at all; it is the same with the railroads.[21] Here don't let me forget to mention that the great Pacific railroad is now open, that goes from New York to Californien, the largest railroad in the world and 3,313 miles long, the same railroad where Brother Friedrich was. [14 ll.: inquiries; health; greetings, signature; request for flower seeds]

Willmothville, January 9th, 1870 / Adair Co Mo.
Dear parents & brothers and sisters,
[26 ll.: correspondence; thanks for God's blessing; harvest better than expected; daughters are well]
I am thinking of enlarging my farm, so that I can rent out part of my land; I have to work as much as I am able, not as much as I want to; the strength of my youth will never return & I often worry what would happen to my children if Providence should take me from their midst. [14 ll.: religious reflections, wants to live a life more pleasing to God] Our only succor is in Jesus, our Savior. We received the small present (gold dollar) as well as the flower seeds & I thank you very much for both; when I have the good fortune to see & smell flowers in my garden, I will feel just like I am back in Germany; there aren't very many flowers here; but the area is being improved every year & is being built up very quickly since we got the railroad; from my place I can see about 10 to 15 houses, which

21In fact they received considerable subsidies; see the Introduction to Part I.

has lessened the look of wilderness the area had a few years ago. Speaking in general, the Americans don't care much about natural beauty, they only want to get rich. Some have lived here for 10 to 20 years & have never eaten an apple & some even end their lives without having had one, just because they don't take the trouble to plant & prune the trees; many don't want to do anything that doesn't pay off immediately & with trees you have to be patient until they bloom & bear fruit.

[6 ll.: photographs] I must also tell you that a son was born to us on July 16th, we've named him Carl Friederich. Dear mother, I doubt very much if it will ever be possible for me to visit you, because I have no one to take my place. [10 ll.: requests flower seeds; longing for spring; religious wishes for the New Year; weather; greetings] / John Bauer

Willmothville, April 24th, 1870 / Adair Co Mo.
Dear parents, & brothers and sisters,
[9 ll.: quiet Sunday] Oh how differently I greet the sweet day of rest here in comparison to the time when I was in Heidelberg, where the boozing & bustling & noise-making went on into the night. Just a few steps from my window my young peach trees stand in full bloom & in the full glory of nature. What a change! A few weeks ago everything still dead & no sign of life & now everything breaking forth with renewed strength & beauty.

As I promised, I am enclosing the receipt for the draft which you sent me. Since I didn't ask you for any help I was very pleased at first, because I thought that although so far away you were showing so much love for me, but I was deeply hurt that Father was so reluctant & even fears that I have more than you yourselves. I believe I wrote to you earlier that it is my wish that you enjoy the property you have acquired for many years to come. [8 ll.: Georg's children are well; thanks for flower seeds] Putting in the garden is taking a long time this year, for my wife just started working in the house today for the first time this year, she hasn't been able to do this since March 5th. She suffers from rheumatism or an ailment of the joints, a chronic & painful disease; more painful than dangerous. Otherwise, all are quite hale & hearty.

[14 ll.: farm work; weather; fruit; religious reflections on the death of his cousin Manz] I fear that you will worry unnecessarily about my wife's illness; man must have a cross to bear like the flowers & fruits need rain, else he will care so much for the world that he will neither seek nor strive for a better life.
[20 ll.: Cousin Manz; weather; daughter Catharina is starting school; fruit; closing, greetings; signature]

<u>Willmothville, September</u> 25th, 1870 / <u>Adair Co Mo.</u>
Dear parents, friends & brothers and sisters,

Since the time I learned that war had broken out between France &
Prussia I have been waiting with the greatest anxiety & longing for a
letter from you. [6 ll.: fears the mail service has been interrupted; but has
received letters:] from cousin Stoll, Mr. Scheuer & from you, mother.
Although I extend my warmest thanks to the two gentlemen for the
kindness with which they informed me of the situation in Germany, it
will surprise you not a little when I tell you that I am familiar with the
entire situation from my newspapers. I subscribe to one political, & one
very good religious paper, along with a *County* paper, a weekly, only
much more interesting & almost as good as a Carlsruhe newspaper.
Several times I have read telegraph news from Carlsruhe; it usually takes
4 to 5 days to hear what has happened over there, and if I could make the
trip to Germany via telegraph then I would quickly decide to pay you a
visit. [. . .]

In order to convince you of what I read in my newspapers a few days
ago, I want to give you some particulars: Strassburg Sept. 8th via London 10th The siege of Strassburg continues in full force, the Prussians are
making the most formidable efforts to win the town. [4 ll.: details] 40,000
troops from Baden are ready to march in as soon as there is an opening.
Germans who have the misfortune to be taken prisoner are beheaded &
their heads stuck on a stake. [2 ll.: details] All of this I already read in my
newspaper on Sept. 13th. The great battles of Sedan, Woerth Gravelotte,
etc. are all well-known to me. I already read on Sept. 6th that the
Emperor Napoleon had surrendered to the King of Prussia.[22] You can
thus see that we in America know about things too, even though we are
far away from the scene of battle. At first I feared that the French would
cross the Rhine & consume all that you have gained by the sweat of your
brow, as used to be the case. Since I read about the great victories I am
much reassured. [. . .] The *Simpathy* of the majority of the American
people is with Prussia; but a few Catholics around me can hardly hide
their bitter hatred that Protestant Prussia has been victorious so far. [7 ll.:
fears heavy fighting over Paris] You have thousands of reasons, & all
Germany has too—to thank Divine Providence that [2 ll.: family spared]
German soil is not soaked with blood, like the soil of France. I can only
wish that Germany may come out of this war victorious & glorious, that
it may become more united & strong. [32 ll.: wish that religious piety
also increases; family is well; drought; closing; greetings, signature]

[22]Napoleon III surrendered at Sedan on September 2, 1870.

Willmothsville, March 1st, 1871. / Adair Co Mo.
Dear parents & brothers and sisters,

[45 ll.: correspondence; religious reflections; illness, recovery of his daughter; rumors about the end of the war] Germany should pray every day, Forgive us our debts as we forgive our debtors & Vengeance is mine, I will repay, says the Scripture. [5 ll.: fears German arrogance] May God grant that Germany be humbled in spirit & give the glory to Him alone who is worthy of it & has wondrously led & protected it. Germany requires, and very urgently, a thorough reformation. Your beer & taverns, your stores & butcher shops should be closed on Sundays. Sunday exists in Germany in name only, & if this abuse is not corrected, I have little doubt that God will afflict you severely in His time. There are often bitter complaints here that the Germans, with few exceptions & especially in the big cities, profane the day of rest so much & seek nothing but pleasure, taverns & theaters.

[29 ll.: weather; power of attorney; money would be welcome; memories of his youth; closing, greetings] / Johann Bauer.

Willmothville, November 14th, 1871. / Adair Co Mo.
Dear mother,

[8 ll.: thanks for letter and gift of money for the children; health] I didn't tell you everything in my letter about my poor health because I feared you would be upset without it being any help to me. [12 ll.: unable to work from June to August] This illness came just at the time when there's the most to do; as a result I only got half a crop of corn, but I had good hay, oats & rye; Providence has never forsaken me yet. In these circumstances I thought even if my situation is somewhat difficult, when the draft comes from Germany I will get some help, then I found what you sent me & perhaps should have kept for yourself. In my heart I feel no hatred for father; if he fears he needs it himself, let him keep it. [2 ll: the same]

He thinks Johann has received enough help; many others live there & can expect nothing. [6 ll.: will get over it] You say there is hope that you can convince him this winter to part with something more, I don't share this hope, although I don't deny that one dollar is worth more to me now than 2 or 3 later, because my situation always improves, with God's blessing. But I don't want to complain any more. All things work together for good to them that love God, with this I shall also be reassured. You write that Carl bought himself a house for 3,800 guilders. — isn't this too great an undertaking for him? But he ought to know best.

[35 ll.: fruit is growing well; great fire in Chicago; greetings] John Bauer

I did put stamps on the letter to mother, as I always do. The stamps must have fallen off. [. . .]

Willmothville, Nov. 3rd, 1872 / Adair Co Mo.

Dear parents,

[20 ll.: thanks for draft of $150; good harvest; bad prices] I haven't gotten into grain yet, because experience has taught me that the high wages, the cutting & threshing machines that you have to have to get the grain in dry, eat up all the profits. [16 ll.: harvest; settlement increasing rapidly] If this huge country is ever settled completely, the influence it will exert in politics & religion can hardly be imagined. There is hardly any country or island today where no American missionaries are to be found; yes I wouldn't even be surprised if you would hear American missionaries all through Germany. It is a shame that we get so many of the Jesuits & barefoot monks you've driven out. They are viewed by the Protestants with great anguish & suspicion & indignation. If the great & world-famous Minister von Bismark had locked them up for life on bread & water, we would have thought much more highly of him.[23]

[28 ll.: harvest; 1872 presidential election] Cousin Shütz writes me to my great amazement that the daily wage over there is now very high & a day laborer gets about 1.00 guilder a day & bread & wine, unheard of here. Here, you eat your breakfast & work till noon & from noon till evening without a bite of bread. Our newspapers tell us that the emigration from Germany is extraordinary & that the Imperial German government has taken steps to prevent emigration. Many of the emigrants improve their lot here & many worsen it as I know from experience. It takes some years until one gets to know the situation in America reasonably well.—

It seems I have, thank God, been delivered of the constant discomfort which I have had to fight for many years. [18 ll.: treatment; riding accident; correspondence; family is well] The President has issued a proclamation that the 27th of November should be a day of Thanksgiving & says if any nation in the world has a reason to thank God for the blessings it has received, it is the American nation; I say the same & add that if any person has a reason to thank God, then it is I. Finally, many warm greetings to you from your son & brother Johann.

[23]As a result of the so-called *Kulturkampf* [government anti-Catholic measures], including the dissolution of the Jesuit order in July 1872, many German priests and members of the order fled to America (Holborn 3 [1969], 262–63).

Willmothville, Feb. 27th, 1873 / <u>Adair Co Mo.</u>
Dear parents & brothers and sisters,

[30 ll.: correspondence; gratitude; God's goodness and mercy; flower seeds; weather] It causes me great pain that my brother Carl shows such indifference toward his aged mother; if he were here in this foreign land separated from all his friends, he would change his behavior. With regard to father's behavior I am not surprised, his heart is set on this world. [9 ll.: money would be welcome, but not absolutely necessary]

You write that this & that causes you grief, but you can't imagine what I have had to endure in this country in terms of money & deceit & pretense. Many can cope with injustice better than I; they speak their mind in anger & then it is all over. This is not the case with me, it all goes to my heart & gnaws away for days & often weeks. [11 ll.: children talk about their grandmother; George's children are fine] My children are named Catharina, who will be 9 years old next April 12th, my younger daughter is named Mary Elisabeth and was born on May 22nd, 1866, and will be 7 years old on her next birthday.

[34 ll.: much work to do, son is too young, hired hands too expensive; religious hopes; greetings] John Bauer.

Willmothville, <u>September 15th, 1873</u> / <u>Adair Co Mo.</u>
Dear parents and brothers and sisters,

[50 ll.: correspondence; has suffered no discomfort in a long time; weather; harvest; dry spell]

This area where I live is making rapid strides forward in everything that has to do with civilization.

This fall we are also going to build a new church, the name of the religious society is *Methodisten* which I also belong to. [12 ll.: in provisional quarters up to now; building should unite and strengthen the weak parish, make a good impression] My voluntary contribution is 75 dollars, 185 guilders in German money.[24] This is a large sum, aside from the many expenses which I have to meet, but everything depends on God's blessing. [. . .]

In Germany you don't have to do this, but here the people have to do everything. If people don't build any schoolhouses & churches themselves the government doesn't do anything. Thus we now have in Kirksville, our county seat, a small college with 500 to 600 students, the building cost about 150,000 dollars. The State of Missouri pays 50,000, the people have to pay the rest; everything is voted on & of course the majority rules. [5 ll: children]

[24]Bauer was one of the approximately ten founding members of the Bethel Methodist Episcopal Church, which was built in 1874 (*History of Adair . . . Missouri* [1888a], 104).

The newest thing here now is a society which has been formed and is spreading through all the states under the name of *Granger,* or to give you a better idea, a brotherhood of *Farmer* or *Landwirthe.* The reason is this: for many years already in all the trades, societies or unions have been formed for the purpose of forcing through their demands. [3 ll.: e.g., merchants, blacksmiths] The railroad companies, who know that we have to sell our grain & cannot send it any other way than by railroad, make shameless calculations, & in many cases *Transportation* costs half of what we receive. It's like this everywhere; the price of everything we need & have to buy is high & the price of what we sell is low. The aim of the farmers' union is to work against this to help each other, in times of need or misfortune or, when everything is too cheap, to provide an advance until prices are better. It is a very good cause. If you want to become a member, it costs 5 dollars which go into the society funds. I haven't joined yet. Everything costs money here; they all just want money. Finally I want to tell you that I have been called for jury duty on the 1st of October, for the first time since I came to this country.
[5 ll: asks for a quick reply; greetings, signature]

Willmothville, Jan. 5th, 1874 / Adair Co Mo.
Dear parents & brothers and sisters,
[49 ll.: correspondence; loss of time due to six days of jury duty, five days of work on the church, still brought in harvest; religious reflections; family is well; children; promises photographs; weather] You ask if I belong to the union & must mean the great new union of American farmers.

I hadn't joined up to now because everything costs too much here & because I didn't know all about it; however I was asked several times to join & thus I finally agreed; the membership fee is 5 dollars. It is somewhat difficult to become a member because if there are 3 votes against admitting someone, he cannot become a member ever or anywhere. [3 ll.: hopeless if one has a bad reputation; did not force himself on them] Did you all have a good Christmas celebration? — Here it is not like in Germany; but we had a joyful time among ourselves; my wife baked different kinds of cake, we had buried very good apples for Christmas which tasted very good & even if we didn't have anything special. [2 ll: are content with little] From what I read in your letters everything over there is very expensive, so expensive & different from how things used to be that I would scarcely believe it, if I weren't convinced it were true. You write that all is quiet with respect to dividing things up. That I can well believe & it will stay quiet, too, as long as father is alive & thank God I can feed my family with my own healthy hands, even if father doesn't divide things up. How painful it must be to come to the end of life & leave everything your heart is set on behind, with no hope of a better life on the other side of the grave.

[4 ll.: winter chores] I have 25 head (young & old) of cattle to take care of, 25 head of hogs, several sheep & 3 horses & what with all that & even with the greatest thriftiness there's not much left at the end of the year. To give you a better idea I'll list a few things for you. This year I paid 37 dollars in taxes; about 60 dollars as a contribution towards the church & when it is finished this year I will probably have to pay another 25 to 30 dollars; 8 dollars for the preacher & then it is expected that you give some more for missions, Sunday schools & the like. Those who only care about getting rich don't have to do this. For mowing during the harvest, hay-making, threshing & help only in times of greatest need I spent no less than 40 to 50 dollars. Everything is excessively high & it is almost impossible to stay out of debt, especially if one is unfortunate & often sick; that is the reason that the *Farmer* has finally woken up from his sleep, about which I hope to write more later. [8 ll.: flower seeds; asks for turnip seeds; greetings, closing; best wishes for the New Year] / John Bauer.

Floyd's Creek P.O. June 13th, 74 / Adair Co Mo.

Dear parents & brothers and sisters,

[37 ll.: correspondence; health; children all go to school; weather; harvest; livestock] I hired a farmhand this spring because I had so much to do & cannot work as much as I used to, but then we had bad weather & for about 3 weeks we couldn't do anything, but since the weather has gotten better we have done almost everything I had hoped to do. A farmhand gets 16 to 20 dollars a month here; I pay 16. You can also get cheaper ones, but you can't trust them. [19 ll.: harvest prospects]

No one knows much or anything at all about the great misery that you spoke of; on the other hand it is true that there is great misery & unemployment in the towns. Here they all want to play the gentleman & pass through this world in pleasure & whatever their hearts desire. Young boys, as soon as they are dry behind the ears, become dissatisfied with life on the farm when they hear about the cities, from pleasures & getting rich fast. [11 ll: immigrants, too; then bitter disappointment] The Americans are too proud to believe that in many ways there is as much poverty and misery as in other countries. [34 ll.: disasters, flooding of the Mississippi; Methodist bishop visiting Germany; wishes relatives could hear him; asks for vegetable seeds; greetings; signature; thanks for photograph]

Floyd's Creek, Dec. 4th, 1875. / Adair Co Mo.

Dear mother,

If pure indifference had kept me from answering your last letter, I would indeed be ashamed of myself, but this is not the case. [71 ll.: much work; flooding; is sending pictures; weather; thanks for God's goodness and mercy; harvest; church consecration, gave $10] Our area is being settled very quickly & it won't be many years before we run out of pasture for the livestock & every farmer will have to feed his stock like in Germany; but I am pleased to see this & at least the area doesn't look as wild as it did about 12 to 15 years ago. [7 ll.: pain in his foot; death of one cousin; letter from another] He thought much like I do, that worldliness & unbelief are getting the upper hand. Our American preachers take the position that the world is getting better every day & Christendom is marching forward every day & faster than ever before. [13 ll.: American revivalists] Our good newspapers often have news about Germany. Thus this summer we read about a duel between two young students in Heidelberg; / H. von Menkel and H. Herrschel from Frankfurt a/M./ that the latter lost his life & since the town's greatest source of income is the boisterous noble students, they didn't dare to bring the murderer to trial. Duelling is strictly forbidden here, yet it does happen sometimes, but only in secret. I have read everything about Heidelberg with the greatest interest & my thoughts fly instantly over the beautiful hills of this unforgettable town, where I used to go walking in silence, far removed from the world.

[6 ll.: asks for letter soon; New Year's greetings; closing, signature]

Floyd's Creek, May 21st, 1876. / Adair Co Mo.

Dear mother, friends & brothers and sisters,

[19 ll.: correspondence; planting delayed by rainy weather] I am still able to do some plowing, thank God, & so I can help out because I can sometimes go to work with 2 plows. I intend to plant about 35 to 40 acres of corn & will hardly be finished by the 10th of June. This will surprise you, but everything grows very fast here. [11 ll.: harvest; flooding in Germany]

I also read here in the newspaper that the business situation in Germany is not very good & they suspect it is caused by the surplus of money from the war. [29 ll.: details; religious reflections; 48th birthday; growing settlement] On the 4th of July, 1876 of this year the 100 years of independence of the United States will be celebrated in the town of Philadelphia. The many preparations have already been made to receive the guests who will come from all nations to visit this town, especially since

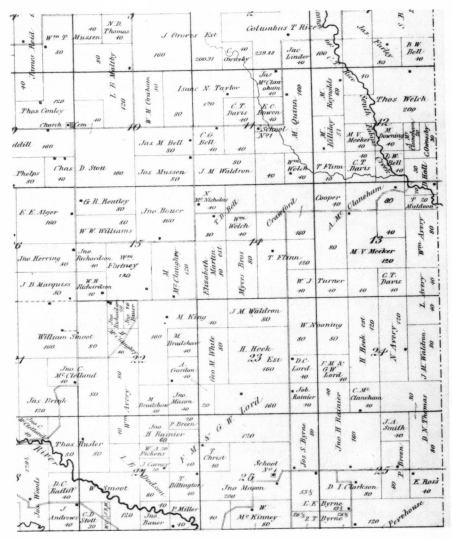

Figure 10. Plat book showing John Bauer's 160-acre farm in Section 15, surrounded by Anglo-Americans. *Source: Atlas of Adair County* (1876), 85; photo courtesy of the Library of Congress.

there is an art exhibition connected with it. This festivity is already the
talk of the town everywhere & will be celebrated throughout the whole
country by high & low, rich & poor, in the crowded city as well as on the
quiet lonely farm, even in the wilderness wherever there is a settlement,
some kind of celebration will take place. We too, here on our quiet farm
will all get together & celebrate the holiday, no doubt with some fried
chicken & other good things & since we've asked for a good, enthusiastic
speech about freedom, we will enjoy ourselves here as much as we can.
[18 ll.: population growth of the United States; settlement of the area;
weather] I am very pleased that you have such a pleasant friend as our
cousin Stoll nearby & I was somewhat surprised when I read the news,
since I always think of our cousin as a young man: a teacher in Heidelsheim & in the same room perhaps where I sat in my school days with our
teacher, Bühler; [. . .] how vividly I can still recall my classroom, even
though my memory isn't as good as it used to be, with the map & the
blackboard & a pretzel on examination day. [15 ll.: correspondence;
memories of his confirmation; health; closing; greetings; signature]

<u>Floyd's Creek, Feb. 1st, 1877.</u> / <u>Adair Co Mo.</u>
Dear mother,
   [2 ll.: correspondence] The news that our father passed away came
unexpectedly, for I thought, now that brother Friedrich is at home, you
would move upstairs & he would take over.[25] The news of his death
would not have been so painful in itself, if you could have told me that he
was as willing to depart as our father Bauer. [3 ll.: religious reflections]
From what you write I assume that he struggled with his soul until the
end. But didn't you all pray? and didn't you try to find a pastor to pray
for him in his anguish? [. . .] I have often & for many years prayed for
our departed father, that God's Spirit may wake him from the sleep of sin
& lead him to the path of Eternal Life. [7 ll.: religious reflections, prayer]
   When you wrote to me in an earlier letter that father had started to read
the Bible, I was full of hope & felt that God might hear my prayer. Father
probably never thought that I prayed for him like I pray for all of you. [12
ll.: religious reflections] You write that there will now be a settlement. I
for my part have never worked a day less in the hopes of ever receiving
anything from you. [17 ll.: concerned about health and the children;
sledding accident; weather] Our situation as a nation is very agitated at
present & the worst is unemployment, lack of confidence, & serious lack
of money. This misery started before the presidential election which

[25]His stepfather died on December 6, 1876, at the age of 73.

always brings hard times, due to the great mistrust of the capitalists who pull back their millions because no one can say which side will win. Our presidential election is still not decided to this day & God only knows how it will be decided. The fight is now in *Congress* & each side is trying to win. Each state has as many votes as it has *Congressmänner* [congress-men] & the campaign was so heated that one candidate only had one more vote than the other. Both sides accuse the other of fraud. In the slave states, the blacks were forced under threat of their lives to vote like the ones who have the upper hand wanted them to & many were shot & hanged.[26] It is shameful, even heart-rending, the atrocities committed during this election.

[23 ll.: disasters; no need to worry about Georg's children; closing, greetings, signature]

Floyd's Creek, Feb. 8th, 1880 / Adair Co Mo.

Dear mother, friends & brothers and sisters,

[36 ll.: was not able to answer letter; religious reflections; economic upswing] One doesn't go to the doctor because of minor ailments here because it costs so terribly much, & because of the problems one often encounters here one learns to be half a doctor & we usually keep some home remedies for emergencies, for if you live 12 miles away from town, you can't go to the druggist's like in Germany and having some medicine for sudden attacks is often of the greatest importance. We usually have some doctors in the country, & if they come, the nearest one to us costs 3 dollars for one visit; a week of illness costs 20 to 25 dollars.

[33 ll.: harvest; religious reflections] My fat hogs brought 205 dollars, in all I will take in 456 *or* 475 dollars from livestock and everything, but the costs are also very high. My farmhand costs me 13 dollars, 117 dollars for 9 months.

George's children have promised to send pictures of themselves & as soon as I receive them I will send them. Don't worry about the settle-ment. [5 ll.: aphorisms] His invisible Hand will guide me. Warmest greetings to you all. John Bauer / [2 ll.: correspondence]

Floyd's Creek, Dec. 12th, 1880 / Adair Co Mo.

Dear mother & brothers and sisters,

[26] At the end of February 1877, shortly before the new President was due to be inaugurated, the contested election was decided by congressional committee in favor of the Republican candidate, Rutherford B. Hayes. In the South the Republicans may well have lost a quarter of a million votes to violence and the intimidation of black voters (McPherson, 598–604).

[19 ll.: correspondence; riding accident; his brother Friedrich's complaints unwarranted: wrote to him as soon as he could but they only go to the post office on Saturdays] He helped me through the harvest & when he left I asked him what I owed him and he said nothing. I thought he had come more for a visit & so I let it rest, but a few days later when I went to town the German barber, where he had gotten a shave, told me that he had been very angry & had said he would never write to me. The reason was that he thought I had swindled him out of his work. Instead of saying to his brother: you can give me what you think is fair, he chose to rant about me to a perfect stranger. It is possible that I made a mistake. [5 ll.: can't be changed] I treated him as nicely as I could but he is peculiar. My wife & daughters would have happily done his washing but instead he preferred to go to the well to wash. He had hardly gotten here when he started talking about leaving. He didn't like the quiet comfortable family life; he wants to be where you can have something to drink & entertainment. We invited him to come along to church with us, he didn't want to do that either. Before his departure, under the influence of beer, I heard his creed which amounts to Let us eat and drink today, for tomorrow we die. [4 ll.: details] With all his possessions he is unhappy and dissatisfied & I doubt that he will find what he is looking for, even if he wanders through all the states. I will give my opinion & that is there is no help for him but the Savior of the world. [9 ll.: religious reflections; weather; greetings]

<u>Floyd's Creek, January 12th, 1884.</u> / <u>Adair Co Mo.</u>
Dear sister & niece,
[9 ll.: correspondence] The news of the death of our mother & grandmother did not grieve or surprise me too much, for in the last letter that she wrote she clearly said her end could come any day & so it was, then my last letter must have arrived a few days before she passed away.[27] I hope that she has come to that peace that is promised to all of us when we stay true to our faith to the very end. [6 ll.: reflections on blessed death]
Dear sister, I have often thought about you since your husband passed away, how you are getting along in this unfriendly world. Mother wrote to me that you have a son who is a great help & that was at least a comfort, but I know that over there they all must become soldiers, I have often feared that you can't count on him too much. I am very glad to learn that he is still at home.
[20 ll.: fears war with France; is in good health but somewhat weak; children are well]

[27]She died on March 15, 1883, at the age of 74.

On Sundays when we don't have church I usually read the Bible, my good religious paper or a good book. For 10 years I've had to have a hand, but my eldest boy will be 15 years old in July & we want to try *farmen* without help this year.

[15 ll.: tornadoes; fruit growing] Here in the country no one knows anything about drinking wine, we made some sweet cider once but not more than we usually drank ourselves. [. . .] Most of what you see here to drink is liquor & that causes more evil than beer does in Germany & will soon be legally forbidden.

[21 ll.: his brother Friedrich's obstinacy delays division of the inheritance; religious exhortations; greetings] / John Bauer [. . .]

Sperry, June 17th 1888. / Adair Co Mo.

Dear sister & friends,

[10 ll.: correspondence; money transfer]

It is no longer so easy to write for on May 22nd I reached my 60th year. I can't work any more and my 2 sons, 14 & 18 years old do the work & that is a great blessing from God, otherwise I would have to sell my estate. I also had 2 daughters but the eldest was called to Eternity & passed away peacefully on March 22, 1886. [8 ll.: religious reflections, death of friends of his youth] You write that Fried. is in St. Louis; he could get here by train in 8 to 10 hours, but I don't expect to ever see him again, for he took his leave in anger.[28] What will happen to his property God only knows. He will come to no good here in a strange country, working for strangers & leaving his property in the hands of strangers. [4 ll.: wants to enjoy life, forgets his mortality] Like father, like son. He is a Manz through and through. He doesn't believe in anything sacred, if I'm not sorely mistaken.

[17 ll.: harvest; thanks for the grace of God; hopes for peace with France] You write that you don't see much of Karl's family; I'm very sorry to hear that. I hope that you do not carry enmity against one another in your hearts & would have liked to have heard from them. [. . .]

If you ever go to Bretten don't forget to go to see my old *Prinzipal* Herr Lindner & tell him I often think about them & ask if they are all still alive & don't forget to write me about it.

[28] A letter written by his stepbrother Friedrich Manz in St. Louis on October 22, 1889 (BABS), indicates how serious the quarrel between the brothers really was. He had been ill since the spring, had just gotten out of the hospital and was already in debt for twenty dollars. But instead of turning to his brother John for help, he wrote to his sister in Germany and asked for 200 marks. Bauer's prognosis regarding his brother was not entirely off base: the 1900 census still lists Manz as an unmarried musician living in a boardinghouse not far from his 1889 address (MC 1900: St. Louis, e.d. 67, #34).

[23 ll.: storms; religious reflections; signature; has read that the German Kaiser is dead]

[80 ll.: February 10, 1891, to his sister and friends: correspondence; pictures; state of health; weather; trust in God and thanks for good harvest; riding accident of his son; reflections on the death of his cousin, daughter, friends; greetings, signature; sends and asks for photographs]

John Bauer appears in the 1900 Census as a 72-year-old; only his wife was living with him in the house. Although he was listed as the owner of a debt-free farm, he had probably retired. His youngest son, William, who had been married for three years, lived next door and is listed as renting a farm, which he had probably taken over from his parents. In 1904 John Bauer died at the age of 75. A few months before his death, he suffered the loss of his son William who had not even reached the age of thirty. John Bauer, his wife, and three of their children are buried in Bethel Cemetery, not far from the farm where he spent the last 42 years of his life.[29]

[29]MC 1900: Adair Co., Mo., e.d. 6, #196–97; *Cemeteries* (1981), 23–24.

5

Franz Joseph Löwen (Franz Joseph Loewen)

When nineteen-year-old Franz Joseph Löwen left his home village of Alf on the Moselle in 1857, secretly crossed the Belgian border, and embarked from Antwerp for New York, the impending threat of being drafted into the army was perhaps the immediate but by no means the most important reason for emigrating. His decision to leave was no doubt made easier by the fact that his brother Peter and sister Katharina had already settled with their families near Detroit, Michigan, in 1855. That his brother had to advance him the passage money points to the bleak economic situation in the Moselle and Eifel regions. Both wine-growing and the small-scale iron industry were experiencing a serious crisis; in the 1850s the region had the highest emigration rate in all of Prussia. As the son of a "poor nailmaker" and without training in any skilled trade, Franz judged his prospects at home in Alf, a village with a population of about 1,200, to be very poor. His dissatisfaction with his situation also resulted in family conflicts, which are hinted at in the letters and which even his pious protestations cannot obscure.[1]

Franz Löwen's destination of Detroit is located on the river that connects Lake Erie and Lake Huron. Due to its location astride shipping

---

[1] Peter Löwen appears for the last time in the kath. KB Alf in January 1854, his sister Katharina only up to July 1850. Peter Löwen's family, and perhaps Katharina's as well, emigrated in 1855. The time of Peter Löwen's arrival in Wyandotte can be narrowed down by the birth of one child in New York in 1855 and of the next in Michigan in 1858 (MC 1870: Detroit, Mich., W. 6, #375; letter from Gertrud Löwen, Peter Löwen's daughter, March 10, 1874 [BABS]; Bödicker [1874], iv–vii; Graafen [1961], 22–52).

---

routes, Detroit first developed as a trading town, and it was only after Löwen's time that the city achieved its leading position in the automobile and steel industries. From 1860 to 1890—the times covered by Löwen's letters—the population of Detroit rose by 450 percent to over 200,000. This growth was primarily due to immigration, especially of Germans, who comprised at least one-third and in 1890 as much as 43 percent of the foreign population. Many of the "Americans" were the children of immigrants, too. In 1880 only 19 percent of all heads of households were native whites of native parentage; 27 percent had been born in Germany. As late as 1900, 15 percent of the Germans in Detroit could speak no English, nor did they really need to. Two daily newspapers, published by the two major political parties, were available in their native language, along with four weeklies of various hues, ranging from socialist to Catholic. Although only one-third of the Germans were Catholic (like the Löwens), they overtook the Irish as the largest Catholic group in the 1880s, remaining dominant until they were surpassed by the Poles at the turn of the century. Löwen hardly mentions religious life in the city, but he belonged to a German parish: there were three to choose from even as early as 1875, and one church was located on the street where he lived.[2]

The letters contain little information about Löwen's work in the city, but some things can be reconstructed from other sources. At first he worked with his brother, who remained an unskilled laborer all his life. In the course of the following three years, however, he moved on. In 1860 he wrote from Portage Lake (presumably the town of this name in the copper district on the upper peninsula of Michigan, about 250 miles from Detroit) and reported that he had been working for a year with the man who delivered the letter. His sister wrote in March 1861 from Wyandotte, near Detroit, that Brother Franz lived too far away to visit her. Later letters indicate that Franz moved to Detroit in 1862, but he first appears in the 1864–65 city directory as a carpenter working for the Michigan Central Railroad. In the 1867–68 directory he is again listed, this time as a cabinetmaker on St. Antoine Street. After 1869 he is always listed as a carpenter, and in 1870 he moved to the house next door to his brother Peter's, in a German neighborhood, where he lived for the next seven years.[3]

[2]Information from Zunz (1982), 35, 104–7, 186; Arndt/Olson (1965), 211–14; CD Detroit 1875; letter from Old St. Marys parish, Detroit, August 10, 1990.
[3]Franz could not be found in Portage Township, Houghton County, Michigan, nor anywhere else in the indexed MC 1860, but in an area experiencing such rapid growth, where many people lived as boarders or in barracks, there were many gaps in the records. His sister Katharina also mentions "Lake Superior" in her letters, and appears with her family in MC 1860: Marquette Co., Mich., Negaunee Twp., #382, about sixty miles away. The other information is taken from the CD Detroit 1862–1890.

Neither the city directories nor census data indicate when Franz went into business for himself. It is only certain that he learned his trade first in America and, before moving to a farm in 1877, he called himself a builder and contractor, and employed at least one laborer. In 1870, with real estate worth $2,000, his assets had already surpassed those of his brother by $400—despite his later arrival in the United States. Detroit's rapid growth guaranteed expansion of the construction industry, and the Germans knew how to turn this to their advantage. Although in 1880 there were almost twice as many gainfully employed Americans as Germans, the two groups were almost the same size in the building trades.[4]

It was nothing unusual for a successful German skilled craftsman like Löwen to leave the town and become a farmer. The reason he gave was a downturn in the contracting business, but the family conflict between his wife and his sister-in-law next door may well have played a role, too. Löwen was not totally unprepared to be a farmer since his father, although a nailmaker, had also been engaged in wine growing and agriculture. Rising land prices in the latter part of the nineteenth century made it increasingly difficult to purchase a farm. Although land bought from the Federal government cost only $1.25 per acre, Löwen had to pay $20 per acre for a farm bought privately, with only half of the land cleared and without any buildings. The 1880 agricultural census lists him with only about thirty improved acres, producing a total yield of $450.[5] What prompted him to return to the city in 1883 is unknown.[6] Nevertheless, he seems to have suffered no financial losses. In 1888 Löwen wrote that he had a house with fifteen rooms and enough money to visit Germany, only his family held him back from making the trip.

There are several writers in this edition who are significantly more—or less—articulate than their years of formal education would lead one to expect. The discrepancy is probably greatest with Franz Löwen, who does not write flawless, intellectual German like the Blümners, but gets his messages across very effectively, with a fairly large vocabulary, rather good spelling and punctuation, and clear sentence structure.

This becomes even more striking in contrast to the letter of his sister Katharina, who probably attended primary school as briefly and as irregularly as Franz (that is, for three or four years during the winter months) and writes accordingly.

[4]MC 1870: Detroit, Mich., W. 6, #336, #375. According to MC and CD, his brother Peter was a teamster. In his marriage certificate in Germany he was listed as a nailmaker (from Standesamt Zell/Mosel, February 18, 1986 [BABS]).
[5]MC A 1880: Saginaw Co., Mich., Maple Grove Twp., see also MC 1880: e.d. 290, #142.
[6]Frank Loewen, carpenter, first reappears in CD Detroit in 1886, but in 1884 and 1885 the carpenter Joseph Loewen is listed at the same address—both presumably the letter-writer Franz Joseph.

There are only a few traces of his regional dialect, and even after thirty years in America his German, remarkable as ever, is virtually free from English influence.

Franz Joseph Löwen

Wiandotte, July 29th [presumably 1857]

Beloved parents and brothers and sisters,

After a long and difficult journey I've finally had the good fortune to reach the town of Wiandott. I met with many a dark hour on this journey, because it was not well arranged the way we set it up. [58 ll.: route to Antwerp; since his trunk did not arrive in time, he had to make the forty-five-day ocean voyage without any additional provisions and "depend on the mercy of good people"] So it was that we landed safely in Newiork on Saturday, June 20th. Having already forgotten all my suffering, I got off the ship, and since no trains or steamboats run on Sundays I went to find a boardinghouse, where I could stay until the next Monday. On the Monday I went by steamboat to Albani, then took the train to Bufalo, then again by steamboat to Wiandott. And so it was Friday when I got off there. Then I asked the first person I saw if he knew J. P. Loewen.

He did and he led me to his house and just then Peter was looking out of the window, Now Peter, said this fellow, I've brought you a countryman. So, that's fine, he said, and didn't move a muscle. Don't you know your own brother, for this here is your brother. Yes, he said, I know my brother, but that isn't him. Then we sat together for a half an hour and talked to each other, how many brothers and sisters I had and what all their names were, and when I had answered many things, he still wanted to bet 1000 talers to 5 groschen that it wasn't me. In the meantime, little Franz came running in and I recognized him on the spot. Then I said, look Peter, there is my godson. Then he jumped up and cried, it is him after all, and he came up to me and gave me his hand with tears in his eyes. Then as much beer as they always drink here and so we drank ourselves quite full, and so I was there and am there, and will stay there until I don't like it any more, then perhaps I'll move on. The next week I went to work with my brother Peter, and I'd been working for 1 month when your letter reached us. Here I work from 7 o'clock in the morning until 6 o'clock in the evening, and then I get 1 taler 20 silbergroschen. If I work from 4 in the morning until 9 in the evening, which is often the case now, I get 2½ Prussian talers. Since I don't want one of my brothers and sisters to have to do anything for me for nothing I give our Peter 12 silbergroschen a day for food and laundry. I like it very much here and if it works out that you can come in the fall, next year at this time we ought to have our own house here. I was thinking about it and think that if the wine is good this year, you may well be able to do it. I'll send you the money gladly, for when you are here you won't need to live with such worries as in Germany. 45 talers will be coming. I had planned to send you 100 talers by the fall, by then I thought you'd have come over, but if things keep on like this, you won't need to come so late. From Newiork it costs another 45 talers, I'll send you that too. But if it doesn't work out like you think then let either Heinrich or Margret come now, for you know it's hard to hold on to money. You can't just sweep it up over here, either, it all has to be earned. [conclusion missing]

                                        Portage Lacke, October 7th, 1860
Dear parents and brothers and sisters,
    [8 ll.: correspondence] On October 1st a man named Kasper Klasen from Bausendorf[7] left this place where I am now living to visit his old home and his birthplace. He wants to cross the ocean by steamboat to speed up his trip as much as possible. After safely ending his voyage, he will come to Alf and visit you and give you a letter along with my portrait. And you can expect him any day after you get this letter. I wrote various things in the letter, and if you ask him, Kasper Klasen will tell you everything you want to know, since he knows me and he also knows the place where the two of us have been working for one year, and pretty much all the conditions in America. When he gives you my portrait, you will see me in my Sunday clothes. [8 ll.: details]

Dear Sister Margaretha,
    [11 ll.: has not forgotten brothers and sisters; left reluctantly] Thus did I leave my brothers and sisters, in the hopes of finding a better place for myself as well as for the others, since I am still unmarried I can move easily from one place to another and I get along the best with the English language. You may have thought I may have left because of the quarrels or to attain more freedom. On no, you are mistaken. I left Germany, knowing full well what I was doing, what kind of a journey I was undertaking, knowing full well and having thought about what I was leaving behind. My only goal was the well-being of our whole family; and this has continued to guide me up to this very minute. I also didn't go to America just to make my living, I also wanted to see something, experience something, or learn something that may be of greater use to me. I am also reasonable and experienced enough to know what I ought

[7]Fifteen miles southwest of Alf.

to do in order to get on as a decent person in this world, to know what is right and what is wrong. I can look any man square in the eye, I can go back to any place where I've been and be received with joy, I am liked everywhere for being so hard-working and well-behaved. They all like having to do with me, working with me, and are pleased if I can just be around them. When I go to visit my friends in another house every now and again, they always say, why haven't you visited us for such a long time. So don't worry, you can rest assured that you won't hear anything bad about me. I have always done what I could for my brother and sister here, and if they have written you that I haven't done so, I have a good right to be angry at them. I have already written to my sister twice that she should move back to her house in Wiandotte. If she takes Helena with her, it would be just as easy as it would be for me to be with her. And you shouldn't judge things without knowing what they're all about. America is not Germany; here you have to go where you can earn money, since people who have no money here are almost worse off than in Germany. You also write me that I should come back to you, which I would also like to do, but the mere thought of the Prussian authorities arouses my anger, how would that work if I, used to the free life in America, was a Prussian soldier, ordered around by everyone. It would certainly be the greatest misery for me. For I wouldn't put up with it. The lot of every man has been cast, and whatever shall be, shall be. The Lord is our guide, and no hair falls out of your head without its being the Lord's will.
[11 ll.: wishes, greetings, signature; exhortations to brothers Heinrich and August to honor their mother and father]

Dear father and mother,
    [7 ll.: protests his love] It is only from a far distance that I have truly realized your love and worth; oh how I regret having insulted you often, having treated you badly, but you will forgive your son, who begs your forgiveness from afar, for what wrongs he did to you unknowingly. Do not weep about fate that has separated us, for it was God's will, and I love you all the more. And God who has separated us will also unite us once again. Do not grieve for me, for he who trusts in God shall not perish. [12 ll.: further declarations of devotion; greetings] / your most devoted son / Franz Joseph[8]

[8]Chronologically follows: *Katharina Löwen*

Weindotte, March 21, 1861
Dear parents and brothers and sisters,
    After waiting a long time I have reached my goal of writing a few lines to you. I didn't want to write before I could send you our portrait. It was a lot of trouble, last winter I saved the money from my sewing for the portrait and the little thing that Helena has hanging around her neck, it looks like a watch, it has my and my husband's portrait inside as an eternal remembrance. The

Wyandotte, January 17th, 1862

Dearest parents and brothers and sisters,

[18 ll.: New Year's wishes; declares his devotion and hopes to see them again, at least in the hereafter]

Thus, dear brothers and sisters, I would like to address a few lines of my letter to you, to warn you about treating our parents badly, be as good to them as possible and treat them like you will later want to have treated them, for this I say as a true brother, later you will regret the slightest wrong that you did them. And remember, a man reaps what he has sown.

If I say again that I can't come over to see you, don't take offense, for, although I would give everything to be able to see you again, I have the feeling when I think about everything else, that it would be like going to my death. So be content, for fate would have it so, also do not worry or grieve for me, for I will always know how to support myself decently and honestly. [9 ll.: his brother Peter's wife had a baby, was unwell]

As far as my sister Katharina is concerned, she is still in the same terrible condition and we will soon have to give up hope that a doctor here can cure her; for we have tried almost everything that was possible

---

two portraits cost me 5 dollars and the postage cost 2 dollars. I also had a 4 dollar gold piece saved for you but I had to give it to the doctor last fall. I can't depend on my husband's earnings, when he's worked for two weeks then he wants to rest for two weeks. Dear parents, at Lük Subirgen [Lake Superior?] I earned a lot of money sewing but here I'm happy just to save enough for postage. Dear parents, at Läk Siebirgen my husband earned good money, if he had held on to it but the barkeepers got most of it and I, poor creature, had all the trouble. He plagues me to death, he's never even taken consideration of the fact that I am sick, but I suffer everything with great patience, I think God will repay me, for here I have no comfort. My brother Franz is too far from me here, I have sent him your letters, he will certainly be pleased when he hears that you received his portrait. Dear parents, in October we came back to Waindott since at Läk Sibirgen it was too cold for me, I couldn't stand it anymore because of the pain of all that water. On November 22nd the doctor drew off all the water and it was 36 pounds of water, then I was so weak I couldn't stand up anymore, I lay in bed for 8 days, but otherwise not a single day, but I am heavy again, I always drink juniper tea, it helps you pass water. Dear parents my blood doesn't run to water, it has affected my liver. It is a stomach dropsy. Dear parents, I thank God that I have my girl, she is as helpful as a girl of 20, she does everything for me, washes and cleans. She is my only comfort. [Her daughter Helena was born in 1849 and was thus twelve years old at this time.]

Dear Brother Heinrich, I am sending you a chain made out of my hair as a present. It cost me 2 Prussian talers to have it made. Therefore I ask you to help our old parents as much as you can, you don't know how much it hurts when one can't be there and you, dear Sister Margaretha, I'm sure you are doing your duty.

Dear Brother August and sister-in-law, do what you can for our parents, God will repay you and Sister Helena and brother-in-law should come over here, they'd have it better than over there.

I must close my letter with many heartfelt greetings and remain until death your true loving daughter, sister, and sister-in-law / Katharina Löwen

[3 ll.: greetings] No one knows about this letter, otherwise I would have been kept from writing again. / with tears I close

[51 ll.: undated letter by Katharina to her sister Margaretha, similar to that of March 21, 1861, in content and time period covered]

here but with no success. There are only a few in this world with a character like hers, for she has suffered so much that the doctors wonder how she can stand it; but she is never downhearted, always cheerful and happy, and still does her housework and still sews for other people, she can't be idle. Every few months she has to have the water drawn off because it keeps on collecting. She would like to come to see you by the spring to try a cure with the doctors over there, but we will let you know more about that later.

As far as work is concerned, it isn't as bad as all that here yet, although many factories have stopped work like they did a few years ago. But you can still earn money, we chop cord wood, which is what people normally do here in the winter. Many people think the work doesn't pay well enough and so they prefer to do nothing. I can earn 6 to 7 shillings a day at it. Food is very cheap. [3 ll.: examples] But coffee and tea have gone up to twice what they were since they've put a higher tax on it to pay for the costs of the war.

As far as the war is concerned, they don't talk about it and fear it as much here as in Europe. They say that England wanted to start a war with the United States too, but it is probably not so serious, and the English will take some time to think it over, for there are already over six hundred thousand volunteers in the field, and if England wanted to start something, then they would get together an army of a million within a very short time if they had to.[9] I read the newspapers all the time and am quite well informed about how things stand, and I think the European newspapers know how to lie as well as the American. [6 ll.: closing, signature, greetings]

Detroit, March 4th, 1868

Dear brothers and sisters,

We received your letter and since you asked for a quick answer I have undertaken to send you the desired reply. But since I was unable to make much sense out of your letter, I have decided this time not to beat around the bush, and in your next letter I request that you first answer, briefly and without a lot of unnecessary words, the questions which I will ask you here.

Now, the first one is

Did the case that you wrote to us about come to court? and how did it come out?

[9]A crisis in Anglo-American relations, the so-called Trent Affair of November 8, 1861, developed when an American warship stopped an English mail-steamer and took two Confederate diplomats prisoner. Although public sentiment on both sides clamored for war, a compromise was reached (McPherson [1982], 202, 219–21). Löwen, not yet an American citizen, was exempt from the draft.

2. When are the 40 talers to be paid to each child, or under what conditions are they to be paid, and what security do the other children have that the 40 talers will be paid out properly?

3. Can you sell the aforementioned share of the inheritance without a power of attorney from us; and without the aforementioned money having been paid?

4. How do you want to arrange things in case you stay in Germany or in case you come to America?

5. What do you require of us, in the latter case?

In your letter you write again about coming to America, but you don't seem to be too serious about it, you don't even dare to cross the high mountains, and the love of your brothers and sisters will not exactly push you either. You are unable to make sacrifices for this, I had to sacrifice a great deal to leave mother and father and to carry my young and inexperienced life out into the wide world, it was so hard I can't even describe it, but I thought we would see each other again, and the thought alone was enough to carry me over the mountains and water. One word to you, Sister Margaretha. You write you would go along if someone came to pick you up. You didn't think about the fact that I have a wife and children, and not even the greatest happiness on earth could convince me to leave them. God alone has set us our goal, and this we will achieve. No sparrow even falls off the roof except it be His will. My words here are in vain, since it is God alone who guides. Often, when I attend the solemn mass here I sometimes think, Oh, if only my sister Margaretha could once see this church. Her terrible prejudices against America would disappear, she would be amazed and cry out, No, I never thought I would find such faith and such devotion in America. [5 ll.: she is heartily welcome, but it is impossible to come get her] You shall live under my roof and eat at my table as long as you want to. Now a word to you, Brother Heinrich:

You want to know if you can start in with your trade right away here. There's no lack of opportunities for such a trade here; but I think it will be soon enough to get you a job after you get here, for I think you are not in such a great hurry and it will probably take longer for you to prepare yourself than it will for you to travel. But don't take offense, and in your next letter I want to hear something more definite about it. The price of a shave is as follows, ten faces for one dollar

four faces including the head wool, one dollar, but you wouldn't earn much on me, since I let everything grow and it wouldn't surprise me if you came and saw me and looked at me like I was a wild American.

Now I also have to mention that my wife's brother from Neuerburg may also come to America. In case you come, write first to Neuerburg and find out if he wants to come along. His name is Peter Tholl, and address the letter to Ignatz Neis, baker in Neuerburg, Bittburg County.[10] I. Neis is my brother-in-law, and I also wrote to him a short while ago.

I would also be very pleased if you could bring along one or the other of my nieces and nephews, for their lot would in any case be a better one here. When I hear from you, I will write more about it. [5 ll.: would like to have a portrait of his parents]

Business is also slow here now and there is general unemployment in the country, and food is very expensive which makes things worse. But, they think it will change soon. I also didn't have work for two months this winter, but now I am quite busy, and in 4 weeks I have made up for the losses. We are all quite healthy and I hope this letter reaches you in good health. As I see from the newspapers there is a general famine in Europe and the reports from some areas are truly dreadful. [10 ll.: closing; address]

                                        Maple Grove, May 20th, 1877
Dear brothers and sisters,
    [7 ll.: hasn't written for a long time, but has often thought of them]
    As you can see from the heading, I am no longer in Detroit, but I have left the town in which I lived for 15 years with wife and children and all my belongings. Years ago I started toying with the idea of going into farming, if the dear Lord allowed me to earn the means to buy a farm.

And since last year business went so badly and there were no prospects of improvement in sight, I decided to put my plan into action and so last August I bought 77 acres of land for our homestead, and on October 25th last year we moved and arrived hale and hearty in our new homestead where, God willing, we will spend the rest of our lives.

Our *Landgut,* or *Farm,* as they call it here, is 105 miles away from Detroit. I paid 2000 dollars for it, but only 30 acres are in cultivation, the rest is American virgin forest. But the woods are being cleared more and more every year, and it looks wonderfully picturesque to see, between the high trees, the beautiful wheat, oat, corn and potato fields growing so lushly.

You may think I'm sitting all alone in the middle of the woods, but that is not true. I live on a cross-roads and all four corners are inhabited, and then almost every 10 minutes there's another farm. The following example should give you an idea of how they turn the woods into fruitful fields here: my neighbor on the other side came here 13 years ago and hardly a

---

[10]Neuerburg is in the Eifel region, about thirty miles away from Alf.

tree had been cut down. He bought 240 morgens of land for which he paid 2 dollars an acre. Last fall he planted 40 bushels of wheat and the same for the other grains (1 bushel is 1 Simmer) and 1 acre is a bit less than 1 morgen) now land here costs from 15 to 40 dollars an acre, depending on if it's woodland or cultivated.

[6 ll.: planting] Since I only bought the bare land, it cost me a lot of money for food for the family and to buy livestock for the first year, for that is all very expensive. I have bought 1 team of horses, 2 cows, 2 hogs, chickens and the like, I ought to have more cattle, however, but I am out of cash because since we have been here I have spent another 800 dollars, but the harvest is not so far off. [5 ll.: prospects good]

We are all hale and hearty. [6 ll.: wishes that a son will become a priest]

Brother Peter and his family are still in Detroit. The last letter I received from him was not very encouraging, for earnings are poor and there's a lot of smallpox in the neighborhood where he lives and where I lived, too. One laborer who worked for me still last summer and was in and out of our house every day has already died of it. Out here in the country such diseases are unheard of, the climate is very healthy here.

[6 ll.: has received portrait of his sister, would like others] I often think that my brothers and sisters would have done better to have emigrated to America, but they might not have liked it here, for there are also people here who, like the Jews of old, still murmur against God and this free, fruitful land even when their fleshpots are full. Europe would have almost starved to death several times already, if America hadn't opened her full granaries for them. What would I have been able to achieve in Alf, the wild, unruly, poor son of a nailmaker. In Germany there is nothing but oppressors of humanity and slaves.

[17 ll.: has received portraits of his parents and had photographs made of them for 20 dollars]

Since the war between Russia and Turkey has been going on for so many weeks and will most probably entangle all of Europe, Germany may experience hard times again, for, if the dear Lord begins his *Kultur-Kampf*, then what was written may come to pass = The Lord shall strike through kings in the day of his wrath, He shall wound the heads over many countries.[11]

For a long time the newspapers have had nothing good to report any more from Germany, thus I would like to hear from you. I wish with all

[11]The Russians went to war against the Turks in April 1877, but Bismarck maintained a course of firm neutrality. The Prussian attack on the Catholic Church, called the *Kulturkampf* (literally, "struggle for civilization"), began in 1873 with the so-called May Laws, giving the state power to examine and veto appointments of candidates for the priesthood and otherwise interfering with church administration. As a result, by 1877 almost one-third of all Catholic parishes were without priests (Holborn 3 [1969], 238–39, 261–72).

my heart that you are well, but even more do I hope that you all remain true to the holy Catholic Church, and stand firm in the fight against Her enemies. [22 ll.: closing, signature, address; greetings from his wife Elisabeth]

Maple Grove, January 1, 79

Dearest brother-in-law, brothers and sisters,

[13 ll.: New Year's greetings] We are a scattered generation, for we were unworthy to live together. Instead of loving one another, we would have perhaps hated one another, that is why it is better this way. But in one thing we could still be united and closely tied together, namely in faith and in love for the Holy Catholic Church. How things look here, I don't want to judge, since who does not hope that the dear Lord in his inconceivable love and mercy may lead even the farthest strayed sheep back to Him. How things look over there, that you know better than I. Many unbelievers have crept even into your area, I read it in the newspapers and hear and see it from the younger immigrants, but how poor and miserable is he who who forsakes the dear Lord. No drop of comfort and hope flows in his poor, suffering heart, and if life itself is already weary and heavy laden, who does not dread spending his last hour without God.

[17 ll.: are well; now seven children, another one expected] Our eldest daughter Katharina turned 12 last September, she is almost as tall as her mother and helps her mother faithfully with her work. I don't want her to have her first Communion yet this coming Easter since I want to have her properly prepared first.

Our son Johann Peter is 10 years old, feeds the horses for me, harnesses and unharnesses them, drives them when harrowing and he wants with all his heart to start plowing, but his will is greater than his strength. He does the sexton's duties at church, rings the bells for Angelus three times a day and serves as an altar boy. How happy we would be if we could see one of our children become a priest, not for the sake of our own honor, but to make the dear Lord a perfect gift in return. But who knows.

Our four oldest children go to school regularly, the others make even more of a racket in the house, since there is deep snow outside and our house is almost too small for so many. If all goes well I will start on a new house this year. The harvest this year was a good one all over the country. [4 ll.: details] I'm up from 2 to 5 head of cattle and now they multiply quickly, and I have the best hogs in the county. I slaughtered 3, each weighing 225 pounds, for our own use, but that isn't enough for the whole year. Here there's more grease on top of the dishwater than there is on top of the soup in Germany, but still not everyone likes it here, for he who is not satisfied with but a little at the start will never get very far. [12 ll.: seeds; prices; closing]

[*Elisabetha Löwen* continues:]

Dear brother-in-law and sisters-in-law,

[17 ll.: New Year's greetings; complains about the lack of priests; wants to send pictures] As far as the family here is concerned, we had a letter a while ago from our niece Helena Löffler[12] it seems that she is bringing up her children properly in religion after all. Her oldest boy serves at Holy Mass, that is still a sign that she hasn't totally forgotten the dear Lord. Brother-in-law Peter in Detroit is still quite hale and sends his best regards. I do not wish to write anything about his wife Gertrud for she does not deserve to bear the name Löewen. I herewith close my letter in the hope that it reaches you in good health. Many greetings to you all from your true sister-in-law
Elisabetha Loewen

Franz Joseph Loewen

Maple Grove, January 25, 80

Dear brothers and sisters, brother-in-law and sisters-in-law,

[27 ll.: general reflections on "fleeting time," the condition of man and the "turmoil and tribulations of human life"; New Year's wishes]

The newspapers continue to bring sad news from Germany and from the rest of Europe in general. [3 ll.: details] The *Cultur Kampf* is not over yet and it won't be over soon unless a new war is on the way. Bismarck is only negotiating with the Pope for the sake of appearances so that in case there is a war he will still have a chance to make peace with the Catholics, since then he'd need them to fight. If therefore today or tomorrow the German government were to make peace with Rome and repeal the unreasonable May Laws, every mother's son in Germany can prepare for the outbreak of a dreadful war, and then, Oh woe is Germany. For I fear the German Reich will see the end of its days. Although I have been in America for 23 years I still like to think now and then about the dear homeland where my cradle stood and where I spent a happy childhood, despite many a hardship. I am happy when I linger in thought among my dear brothers and sisters and relatives and the friends of my youth, as well as at the graves of my blessed parents, sister and relatives and then a quiet ache creeps into my heart, and how true the old saying becomes—be it ever so lovely in a foreign land, it never will be home—but then all at

[12]Name changed by the editors, at the request of the contributor.

once all the troub es and hardships that a poor though honest laborer must endure pass before my eyes, and then I thank the dear Lord a thousand times tuat I escaped that land that can't even feed its own people. Yes, I thank all who scorned the poor son of a nailmaker, since only because of the miserable treatment I received in Germany could I decide to leave my homeland.

America was blessed with another bountiful harvest this year and although many million bushels of grain have been shipped to Europe, there are still immense reserves of grain in the warehouses, hoarded by the speculators who push the prices way up to the disadvantage of the buyer. There is really very little surplus left in the hands of the farmer. [8 ll.: good wheat harvest] In general we are pleased with our situation now, and we have not regretted giving up our trade and the life in the city, for it is really not easy to manage to feed and clothe a family of eight children decently in a large city, where things are often expensive. What I had worked so hard to achieve, I no longer wanted to risk unnecessarily, since a contractor can sometimes earn a lot of money, but he can also lose all of what he has earned for years, as has happened to many of my fellow contractors. [27 ll.: farming; weather; children] I visited my brother Peter in Detroit before Christmas. They are all well, their oldest daughter will be married soon. His oldest son Franz was here to visit at New Year's. He stayed with us for a week. He already has two wonderful children. [9 ll.: niece Löffler and her family] Awaiting a speedy reply we send you all the warmest regards
Elisabetha Löewen

Franz Joseph Loewen

Layton Corner, February 24, 81
Dearest brother-in-law, sister-in-law, and brothers and sisters,
[23 ll.: excuses; well-being; good harvest] America wouldn't know what to do with all its food if it didn't find a willing customer in ever-starving Europe, and that is why it is understandable that so many are tired of Europe, tie up their bundles and set off for the shores of America, and thus last year's immigration exceeded that of all the previous years and all signs point to the fact that immigration hasn't even reached its peak yet.

[6 ll.: still lots of room in the United States] As far as our own home is concerned, it gets bigger and more beautiful from year to year, when we came here 4 years ago we met 27 German Catholic families, now we are 70, and each supports himself and his family from his own land. No one is his master's servant, and after a day's hard work and toil there is a good table set for all.

[10 ll.: weather] Last year we harvested 200 bushels of wheat, 80 oats,

80 potatoes, 400 corn and many other products. We also tried planting sugar cane [i.e., sorghum] and it turned out well. It can be made into an excellent syrup for the household. We now have 12 head of cattle, 3 cows came fresh this month and in March we'll get two more. All we need now is sheep and I will buy some in the fall.[13]

[10 ll.: children] I have built us a new house, God willing, it will be finished by June so we can move in. The old house was the only thing that we didn't like here, for first of all it was too small, and secondly we were used to having a better place to live.

I can't tell you anything about Brother Peter this time since I haven't heard anything from him myself for a long time, in general he's not much of a writer. The last I heard from him was that their oldest daughter was going to marry a Protestant.[14] His son Franz was here for a visit. He is a skillful, hard-working fellow and he is our favorite of the whole family. Mrs. Loewen caused us a lot of trouble and we are glad to be out of range of her tongue. Brother Peter is dear to us and there's never been even a bit of trouble between us, but to keep the peace in his house he couldn't have much to do with us. [25 ll.: about his niece Helena Löffler; greetings] Writing a letter to each and every one of you is really not necessary, and therefore this is for you all. I'm addressing this in particular to my sister because that's the surest way, in my opinion, of getting a prompt reply. [7 ll.: greetings, signature]

Layton Corners, Saginaw Co. Michigan [presumably 1883]
Beloved brothers and sisters, brother-in-law, sister-in-law and children,
[19 ll.: correspondence; addition to the family; good harvest]
There were only poor buildings on the land when I bought it and I am forced to keep putting up new buildings. I have built a spacious house to live in and this spring, God willing, I will put up a new barn 36 by 50 feet and 18 feet high. I have almost all the materials on hand. Up to now I've lost a lot of grain and hay because I didn't have the necessary shelter for it. I've also lost valuable livestock because of it. Making an American wilderness into a fruitful place and a wonderful garden takes a tremendous amount of hard work, patience and stamina, and often privation too, and the pioneers who go on ahead first to settle the uninhabited woods and prairies of America seldom reap the rewards of their work.

[13]This information is roughly confirmed by the MC A 1880. Loewen had 32 acres of land under cultivation; since 1877 land clearance and improvements had increased the value of his farm from $2,000 to $2,500. His livestock comprised a team of horses, two milk cows, four more head of cattle, and four hogs (MC A 1880: Saginaw Co., Mich., Maple Grove Twp.).

[14]When Loewen's nephew John married the daughter of Irish immigrants in 1884, the match was not considered scandalous or at least elicited no comment in the letters (MC 1900: Detroit, e.d. 113, #140).

Brother Heinrich asked in his last letter how the land here is worked. Nothing here is dug by hand like over there, everything is plowed and harrowed with horses or oxen. Potatoes, corn and such are done with a 2–3 or 5-shovel so-called cultivator pulled by a horse to get out the weeds, they are hilled up by a shovel plow. For every kind of work in the field there are machines but it often takes a long time before you can buy them because they are very expensive and a new farm that is only partly in cultivation often doesn't yield more than what one needs for one's own use. Then little by little, as his income increases, a farmer buys the machines he needs. In general all the farm machines here are very light and elegant but very strong. And you will find it hard to believe that I cut 22 acres of grain and meadow alone, and by hand.

But the strength of my younger years has passed somewhat and so for the last season I bought myself a reaper for the price of 120 dollars. I can reap 5 to 8 acres of grain a day, then I also have a 10 foot wide hay rake so that I can rake up all the hay and leftover grain with a horse. Now I only need a mowing machine for grass which costs 80 dollars, then later perhaps a sowing machine. But for now I am happy not to have to do the hardest work by hand any more. [9 ll.: advice and pious admonitions to nephew]

Last May our son Peter and daughter Anna attended their first Holy Communion. For the celebration I had entreated brother Peter to visit us. He did comply with my request and came, but I couldn't keep him here for longer than two days. He had no rest at my house. A sweetheart or something must have pulled him away. I gave him all of your letters to read, also the exemplary letter of your worthy priest. He read them and didn't say a single word to me, and I didn't want to ask him since I didn't think he would leave us so quickly. But, the next day I had to take him to the train station. When I gave him my hand to say goodbye, he wept like a child, and if he hadn't been ashamed to embrace me in front of so many strangers I am sure he would have. He loves his brothers and sisters and if any one of you came to America he would certainly prove it. Much of what I know must be covered with the cloak of Christian charity. Do the same yourselves, the Dear Lord sets everything right. A number of weeks ago I got a letter from Brother Peter's youngest daughter saying that brother Peter has married a young widow with three children under 12. We for our part wish him well in his new union. Brother Peter's eldest son and daughter, both with their families, came here for a long visit last summer.

Now I must answer the esteemed letter of your Reverend Father and I ask you to tell him what little I can say as well as you can. When I bought this piece of land more than 6 years ago, there were 26 German-speaking Catholic families here. They had a small chapel where every 1–2 or 3 months a priest came from far away to celebrate mass before going back to his own parish since there are still very few priests here. For 25 English miles all around the little flock was hemmed in by Protestants of various types. The Catholic children together with those of other faiths thus attended the dangerous state schools that we also have to pay taxes for here. Thus the first thing was to start a Catholic school. With the approval of the priest and after I and two others had been made elders in the church by the Reverend Bishop, we set up a school in the small chapel and called a Catholic teacher. In the beginning all went well, but the Evil Foe looked on the young seed with envy and malice and sowed discord among its own members. Since I was devoted to the Catholic school with heart and soul we had to make great sacrifices and endure much abuse, but every year we managed to secure the means to run the Catholic school for at least 6 or 7 months. But last year, after the children had had their first Holy Communion, the priest who usually visited us every month failed to appear and for 6 months we had no priest at all in our midst. In the meantime the Catholic families had increased to 70, but the more that came the worse it grew, and the Catholic cause seemed to degenerate into a kind of Old Catholicism.[15] Fearing the worst, I wrote to the Reverend Bishop and the dear Lord sent us a zealous priest by way of the Reverend Bishop. The priest travels 40 English miles but only once a month. The Reverend Father is our guest when he is here, and it is a day of rejoicing when he comes. The parish is again at one and the school is again in operation. We already have 40 thousand feet of lumber to build a worthy house for the Lord in Heaven. The Protestants fear the cross and willingly sell out and Catholics take their places. It will cost us every cent we can raise to bring this work to completion.

Dear sister, I learned from the newspapers that times are very bad over there and all over Germany, couldn't you turn your back on this land of hunger and come over here? Where so many are living there must be a livelihood for yet another. When I stand on our doorstep and look up at the sky I see the same stars as from our doorstep in Germany. The only difference is that the house in Germany did not belong to us. Dear sister, write soon and I will also send you a quick reply.

He who hopes for better times in Germany will be sadly disappointed. The Germans are bold blasphemers and the government a slave driver to

[15]Old Catholicism was a religious movement that developed out of rejection of ultramontanism and the proclamation of papal infallibility (1870). Two characteristic features were stronger lay participation and the use of the vernacular in the liturgy. The parish in Maple Grove was founded in 1875, but it only received a resident priest in 1883. By 1892 it included over one hundred families, all but three of which were German, and a school with two teachers and 104 pupils (Müller [1882], 185; Enzlberger [1892], 129).

Figure 11. "We already have 40 thousand feet of lumber to build a worthy house for the Lord in Heaven. . . . It will cost us every cent we can raise to bring this work to completion." Catholic church in Maple Grove, begun 1883. *Source:* St. Michael Church of Maple Grove.

its people. The best thing is to get away. The good must suffer along with the evil. The great plagues that are afflicting Germany must be punishments sent by God, since they can no longer be taken for things that are completely natural. Now I will close, for this paper is too short for me to even try to write down all my feelings and thoughts. If I could only talk with you for one day, I know you would gladly follow me to the shores of America, but only God alone knows what is best for each one of us. [4 ll: His will be done; greetings]
Your brother, brother-in-law and uncle / Franz Joseph Loewen.

Detroit, Apr. 29th, 1888
Dearest Nephew Heinrich,
   Since you have given us the pleasure of a letter for a second time, this time I want to send you a special answer. You can see from this letter that your uncle Franz is still alive and that I am fond of good boys. It is right that you are endeavoring to learn a trade since a good craftsman can always find a living in any country.[16] Therefore spare no effort to learn everything thoroughly and practically. And since your parents may have to tighten their belts during your years of training, as a good son you will not forget this later when you are earning money yourself. It was a great disadvantage to me that I never had the chance to learn a trade in my youth. When you are old you can still learn something decent but it is harder and it can make your hair turn grey like it did mine. The trade you have chosen is no good for America since here everything is made by machine, but in Germany and in particular in your local area it could be quite good. So just learn what you best see fit, since I don't know anything about conditions in Germany anymore. If you are hard-working and learn well, I will send you a present sometime.
   Our eldest son Peter is now 19 years old and a first class worker. He can do all the carpentry work according to plans so that I already let him build entire houses.[17] See what an advantage it is when you start to learn a trade early. What I learned with hard work and much effort he can learn almost at a glance. Although our children all speak German and learn to read and write German at school, they are more familiar with English since it is, after all, the language of the country. Ask your cousin Peter to write you. Cousin Franz is 14 years old and a hard-working boy. He is learning to operate the machines used to work all the materials needed for construction. It is one of the best paid businesses here in America since all

[16]His nephew Heinrich Reitz (b. 1872) was an apprentice locksmith and later became a journeyman (information supplied by the contributor).
[17]In the 1888 CD Detroit, Peter Loewen was listed a carpenter, still living with his parents.

America is almost nothing but one big machine shop. Our Franz already makes 4 dollars a week.[18]

Uncle Peter's eldest son, Cousin Franz, is an excellent machinist in the building trade, about the best in the city. He actually earns 2¾ dollars *per* day.[19] [10 ll.: about his other children; promises to send photos]

Now dear Heinrich be a good fellow and heed the commandments of the Catholic Church and so I commend you to the protection of God and Our Dear Mother Mary. Your Uncle Franz.

Dear sister and brother-in-law,

This time you must excuse me for not writing very much, but my wife is not doing very well. It should soon be better when the dozen has been filled. She is due in May, may the dear Lord grant that all goes well. We can certainly feed another one and there's enough space in our house, since it has 15 beautiful rooms, some even elegantly furnished.

[5 ll.: all is going well] Brother Peter has a job with the city and earns 2½ dollars *per* day.[20] Everyone in the family is well, as far as I know.

Before June a man from Hetzhof[21] will be going over for an inheritance matter. He has already done a lot of work for me and he promised he would stop by to visit you, then he can tell you a lot about us.

My purse is certainly large enough to make the trip to see you, but I can't bring myself to leave my wife and children. If the dear Lord grants us long life we may well be able to see each other again. So I send you my warmest greetings and remain forever yours. Franz Joseph Loewen / [6 ll.: address]

2 weeks ago Alouis Behrens was accused of a shameful crime against a 6-year-old child, found guilty and sentenced to 15 years in the penitentiary.

Franz Loewen actually did visit his old home again in 1891, when he went to see the exhibition of the Holy Garment in Trier.[22] On his return

[18]Starting in the 1888 CD Detroit, Frank X. Loewen is listed as a machine hand.
[19]Frank Loewen, born in 1853, appears regularly in the CD as a machinist employed by an American company, and also as a machinist and the owner of a house free of debt, in the MC 1900: Detroit, e.d. 29, #271.
[20]Until 1883 Peter Loewen regularly appears in the CDs as a teamster, in 1884 with a new address and a meat market, in 1885 as a contractor with another new address, and in 1886 and 1887 simply as a laborer living at yet another address, which he kept at least until 1889. In 1888 and 1889 he is then listed as a foreman.
[21]Village near Alf.
[22]The Holy Garment, supposedly the robe of Jesus woven without seam from top to bottom, was a relic in the possession of the Diocese of Trier and was exhibited for the public in 1891 for

he took along his nephew Joseph to America. In the 1900 census, Franz Loewen is still listed as a contractor and the owner of a house free of debt; his wife had died, but three of his children still lived at home. Ten years later he was no longer listed, but the influence of the German Catholic on the next generation still shows through clearly. His son John P. Loewen was also a carpenter and an independent contractor; his wife was of German descent at least on her father's side. In eighteen years of marriage they had nine children, and some of their names, such as Norbert, Urban, and Hilda, show evidence of both their German and their Catholic heritage.[23]

---

the first time since 1844. During the 45-day exhibition almost two million pilgrims visited Trier, including a large number from America; more than three thousand came via Antwerp and Rotterdam alone (Kempel [1891], 1–2, 101–3).

[23]MC 1900: Detroit, e.d. 52, #107; 1910: e.d. 197, #53.

6

Heinrich Möller (Henry Miller)

Heinrich Möller, the fourth son of the peasant Johannes Möller and his wife Katharina,[1] was born on September 25, 1846, in the Hessian township of Marköbel (Hanau County). Not much is known about the economic situation of his parents, but there are many indications that it was fairly modest. Although the county of Hanau is located in the most productive agricultural region of Hesse, for centuries the farmland had traditionally been divided equally among heirs. This caused a progressive splintering of holdings and meant that most farms were quite small—the average peasant had only about eight acres to cultivate.[2] Johannes Möller's farm was apparently also part of this "dwarf economy," and even in good years profits were hardly sufficient to support a family. These small farms, too, were often heavily mortgaged, and peasant landholders usually had to depend on income from a nonagricultural occupation on the side.[3] Probably for this reason all three sons learned a skilled trade, besides working on their parents' farm. Since Johannes Möller's holdings

[1]The marriage produced seven children, but two died in 1843 (probably of diphtheria); only Peter Heinrich (b. 1845), Heinrich (the letter-writer), Heinrich Jacob (b. 1848), Anna Margaretha (b. 1855), and Katharina (b. 1858) reached adulthood (Ev. KB Marköbel). Marköbel's population in 1865 was 1,093 (255 families, 164 houses) (Hs. StA MR, Best. 16, Rep. II, Kl. 1, Nr. 1).
[2]Heßler 2 (1907), 736; Hildebrandt (1853), 30, 98; Mayer-Edenhauser (1942), 54.
[3]The Möller family moved several times within the community of Marköbel (as indicated by birth registrations of the children in the KB), and this alone points to their poor economic situation. Probably in the 1870s Johannes acquired the mill in Marköbel, but its annual profits (according to the list of property taxes paid between 1880 and 1881) remained considerably below the village average.

203

were so small that they could not be further divided, the Möllers hoped that training as artisans would later enable the sons to support themselves. Because of increasing competition among rural tradesmen, however, such training did not always guarantee economic security.[4]

In comparison with his two brothers (his elder brother Peter became a carpenter, and his younger brother Jacob was a blacksmith), Heinrich Möller's prospects were undoubtedly the poorest. He became a shoemaker, a trade which, like tailoring, faced tremendous competition since it required neither a special workshop nor expensive tools—only a certain degree of manual dexterity. In Marköbel alone, with a population of slightly over one thousand there were nine shoemakers in 1825,[5] and it is safe to assume that forty years later there were even more. Supply, however, was not in harmony with demand: in rural areas there was no need for elegant footwear, just for simple sturdy shoes, and the standard shoes that could be bought at the marketplace were just as sturdy as expensive handmade ones. Most village shoemakers earned what they could from making simple shoes and repairs, hardly managing—just like their numerous colleagues in the towns—to eke out a scanty living.[6]

Poor economic prospects most likely prompted Heinrich Möller's decision to emigrate to America—as many people from Marköbel had before him. A few individuals had left in the 1820s and 1830s, many more in the 1840s, and even more during the years of economic crisis after 1850.[7] In the following decade the overall number of emigrants sank at first, as a result of economic recovery in Germany and the Civil War in the United States. In the mid-1860s, when Heinrich Möller left Marköbel, however, the number rose again significantly. This new wave of emigrants came primarily from the northern and eastern German states, but a considerable number, like Möller, continued to leave the states in the southwest.[8]

Aside from economic motives, however, Möller's impending military service may also have prompted his decision to leave. This was at any rate the most likely reason why he neglected to secure official permission to leave (as the law required).[9] Shortly after his departure, however, his

---

[4]The Hessian guild regulations (in force until 1867) permitted only certain trades in rural areas. Because of the enormous growth in population (570,000 in 1816; 700,000 in 1850) and lack of economic alternatives, most skilled trades in the villages were overrun and scarcely provided sufficient income (Assion [1983], 96; Bovensiepen [1909], 17–39; Vanja [1978], 43–44).

[5]For comparison: also nine tailors, four blacksmiths, one carpenter (Bott [n.d.], 97).

[6]On the position of shoemakers in the nineteenth century, see Rumpf (1907); Schmoller (1870), 257–317.

[7]Hs. StA MR, Best. 180 Hanau, Nr. 159; see also Bott, 98; on emigration from Hesse during this period see Auerbach (1985).

[8]Marschalck (1973), 42–44; Mönckmeier (1912), 54, 78–79.

[9]Young men eligible for military service in Hesse were not prohibited from emigrating, but the authorities tried to prevent short-term absences from the state, a means of escaping the draft, and examined the petitions of young men very carefully (Auerbach, 20–21).

father made up for this omission; the mayor of Marköbel, a family relative, seems to have helped in obtaining the official release.[10]

Supplied with only a small amount of money, Heinrich set off on his journey in late September or early October 1865, only a few days after his twentieth birthday. In Hamburg he boarded the steamship *Teutonia*, together with a few other Hessian countrymen. In the passenger lists he gave "A. Möller, laborer" as his name and occupation and "Braunsch-weig" as his home—probably because he did not have the papers to document his official permission to leave.[11]

His destination in the United States, Cumberland, Maryland, had been arranged ahead of time. Cumberland was the home of the Lottig family, which had left Marköbel at the beginning of the 1850s. Conrad Lottig, who had achieved certain prosperity as a "beer-saloon keeper," had also apparently offered to help Heinrich get started.[12] When the young man finally arrived in Cumberland in early November, penniless and having been through many adventures, Lottig kept his promise, gave Möller a place to stay, and found him a job within a few days. Lottig's motives in providing this help, however, were apparently not entirely selfless. Möller had to pay four and a half of the five dollars he earned for food and lodging (and on top of this the money that Lottig had lent him to cover his debts).

Möller stayed in Cumberland until 1869, about four years. During the first two and a half years, he worked for three different shoemakers, at least two of whom were also German. His wages of five to six dollars a week were poor, but not unusual or surprising. Since the early 1860s, small shoemaking enterprises had been in decline, faced with increasing competition from an expanding shoe industry. Until the middle of the century, shoes had had to be imported from Europe (often from Germany), but the 1850s saw the introduction of new machines and mass production, with which traditional artisans who still made shoes by hand could hardly compete.[13]

This was probably the reason why Heinrich Möller took the opportunity in 1868 to get a better paying job as a mason. He had also learned to read and write English by this time, and he was no longer restricted to

---

[10]The emigration application, submitted by Johannes Möller, is in the Hessian archives StA MR (Best. 180 Hanau, 4584, Bd. 10, Nr. 34) along with the report of the village council attesting to the fact that Heinrich had a good reputation, owned no property, and owed no taxes to the state.

[11]StA HH, Auswanderungsamt I, VIII A 2 (HPL).

[12]In the Hanau County emigration lists for the years 1822–1872 (Hs. StA MR, Best. 180 Hanau, Nr. 159), only Johannes and Georg Lottig are listed, both of whom left in 1851, but not Conrad. According to the Marköbel parish records (ev. KB), the Lottigs (also spelled Lottich) were stocking weavers. Conrad appears in the 1870 census as a "beer-saloon keeper" with assets of $2,000 (MC 1870: Allegany Co., Md., Cumberland, #172).

[13]Heckscher (1895); Nübling 3 (1895), 231–34.

working for a German–American employer. The construction business in Cumberland must have been expanding at this time since the Baltimore and Ohio Railroad Company had recently built several rolling mills, and the town, previously a mere trading and transshipment center for the nearby Great Coal Basin, was experiencing a phase of brief prosperity. The population rose from 7,300 in 1860 to 11,300 in 1873, but the proportion of immigrants remained relatively low.[14]

Although Möller was able to make a living (but hardly a decent one), his attitude toward the American environment remained quite negative for the first few years. It first became more positive when he married Maria Christina Ursula Bauer, a teacher's daughter from Baden about his own age. Pointing out that chances of earning money were better in the United States, he even urged his younger brother Jacob to emigrate.[15]

After the birth of their daughter Anna in the summer of 1869, the Möllers left Cumberland and moved to nearby Somerset County, a rural area on the border of Pennsylvania. In 1870 there were only a handful of Germans and Irish living in the area, and in the following decades their numbers remained comparatively low.[16] In the country conditions were obviously somewhat better than in Cumberland, and Heinrich returned to his old occupation, working first as a journeyman in a shoemaker's shop. Shortly after the move, however, his wife died unexpectedly, and since he felt unable to take care of his two-year-old daughter alone, he felt compelled to remarry quickly. Elisabeth Deist,[17] also from Hesse and two years his senior, became his new wife. His second marriage, although, in contrast to his first, motivated more by practical considerations than by romantic love, improved his material circumstances considerably. Thanks to the financial support of his father-in-law, Möller was able to move into his own house in Meyers Mile (in Somerset County) shortly after the wedding. Despite a few setbacks and the fact that eight more children[18] were born over the next fifteen years, his economic situation improved every year. By 1879 he could call a second

[14]Lowdermilk (1878), 425–28. Of the 8,000 people living in Cumberland in 1870, about 1,500 were immigrants; in the entire county 7.5 percent were German and about 6 percent were Irish (USC 1870.1, 163, 358).
[15]Jacob, however, remained in Germany; after returning from the Franco-Prussian War, he married and moved to Eichen (now Nidderau), Hanau County (information provided by the contributor).
[16]MC 1870: Somerset Co., Pa., Summit Twp., #233. Of the 18,190 people living in the county, only fifteen were German and eighteen Irish (USC 1870.1, 358).
[17]Born January 3, 1844, in Herlefeld, the daughter of the farmer Hermann Deitz and his wife Elisabeth (Ev. KB Herlefeld). According to Heinrich Möller, she had emigrated with her parents, brothers, and sisters in 1857.
[18]Katharina (b. 1872), Allen Francis (b. 1873), John Freeman (b. 1876), Peter Jacob (b. 1877), Friedrich Wilhelm (b. 1879), Heinrich H. (b. 1881), Elisabeth (b. 1883), Karl F. (b. 1887). See MC 1880: Westmoreland Co., Pa., e.d. 105, #198; MC 1900: Somerset Co., Pa., e.d. 187, #435.

house in Scottsdale[19] his own, later he bought a third one in Meyersdale.[20] A letter written in 1893 indicates that he not only was free of debt but also had built up considerable savings.

Several times during the 1870s and early 1880s Möller had to work outside his trade for short periods of time because he could not earn enough money, but he always returned to his shoemaker's lasts. Then in 1885 he finally went into business for himself. With a partner (probably an American), he ran a shop that sold men's boots, shoes, hats, caps, and furnishing goods. He also owned a small farm on the side, primarily to meet the needs of his own family. His way of life was thus much the same as it might have been in Germany, if conditions there had been better.

The modest prosperity the Möllers achieved over the years was the result more of hard work and thriftiness than of good fortune. And although a certain amount of pride in his achievements comes through in Möller's letters, he continued to regard himself as a "humble fellow," and there is no evidence that this should be interpreted as false modesty. This also helps explain Möller's hurt and bitter reaction on receiving only part of his share of the family inheritance from his older brother Peter in 1901—more than twenty years after the death of his father.[21] Two decades earlier, when his financial situation was less secure, he had urgently needed the money. His brother, however, had probably been similarly strapped for funds, since paying out inheritance shares to younger siblings was a financial strain that could be difficult for a small business to bear. Peter's delay in sending Heinrich his share of the money, although on shaky moral grounds, was perhaps understandable; after all, his brother had left the family at a very young age. The dispute over the inheritance, however, seems to have led to a break in relations between the two brothers: Heinrich's letter of 1901 was apparently the last one written to Germany.[22]

Census documents reveal that in 1910 Möller—now 64 but still running his own business—was still living in his house in Meyersdale with his wife and their youngest daughter Elisabeth, now 27.[23]

The letters that Heinrich Möller wrote between 1865 and 1901 to his parents, brothers, and sisters in Marköbel contain precise and matter-of-fact reports about his material circumstances and occasional remarks about the general economic situation in the United States. The corre-

[19]This Westmoreland Co., Pa., town's population in 1880 was ca. 1,300; only about 2 percent of the people living in the county were German (USC 1880.1, 318, 526).
[20]In Somerset Co.; its population in 1880 was ca. 1,500 (USC 1880.1, 317).
[21]After the death of his father, Peter Möller had taken over the mill in Marköbel; see n. 3 above.
[22]His brother lived until 1913; their mother died in 1902 (Ev. KB Marköbel).
[23]MC 1910: Somerset Co., Pa., e.d. 146, #154.

spondence provides detailed documentation of the results of his efforts to improve his economic situation, down to the amount of sauerkraut he had—"a whole barrel full," as we learn from his letter of 1886—and the stately 214¼ pounds he himself weighed the same year.

The letters contain little information, however, about his professional life. There is no mention of the technological advances that confronted traditional artisans in the wake of the rapid industrialization process that took place during the second half of the nineteenth century. It is therefore highly probable that Möller was not seriously affected by these changes and that in the country he had found a "niche" where he could continue to work in the traditional way.

Other aspects of life in the United States, too, otherwise discussed frequently (and often at great length) in immigrant letters find no echo at all in Möller's. He is silent when it comes to topics such as the advantages and disadvantages of American society, the structure of American politics or the Constitution; and he makes no mention of the role or self-identity of his own ethnic group. These subjects and questions were apparently unimportant to Heinrich Möller. Only once does he report that his sons did not have to serve in the army, something which he clearly felt was an advantage of life in the United States. Otherwise, he seems to have actually believed what he often remarked in his laconic style, that almost everything in America was just like it was in Germany.

Bizarre spelling and heavy intrusions of Hessian dialect are the most conspicuous features of Möller's writing. Minor peculiarities include the use of the period but no other punctuation, frequent beginning of a sentence without capitalization, and a generally unconventional, somewhat breathless sentence structure.

Möller's vocabulary is rather limited, and his mostly rather undifferentiated statements may be due to his general difficulty in expressing himself combined with his use of clichés. Although three years after his immigration, in 1868, he claims he prefers English to German, his writing remains immune to English influence until the mid-eighties; only then do English idioms and sentence structure slowly make their appearance in his letters.

Heinrich Möller

[Cumberland, Md., probably written just
after his arrival on November 2, 1865]

Dear parents, b[rother] and siblings,
    May God bless you and Jesus keep you.

I pick up my pen to write to you. I have arrived safe in America at Conrad Lottig's. Now I will write you about my journey. From Mark-öbel to Friedberg[24] you know about, in Friedberg I paid 54 [kreuzers?]. When we arrived in Hamburg 12 o'clock in the evening, I signed up and had to pay 65 talers. Then I had to stay there until 3 o'clock on Saturday, 2 talers for food, 1 taler for a blanket and even more so I only had 2 talers left. So you can imagine what I felt like, but God was by my side, He helped me. We were on the water for 18 days, from October 7 to October 26th. When I got to Newjork a shoemaker who was with me on the ship took me along to an inn, then I wrote to Lottig for money. Then he sent me 15 dollars. I was in Newjork for 4 days, had to pay 4 dollars. He sent the money to a barkeeper that he knew and asked him to arrange things at the train station and he did so. Then I went as far as Harrisburg, that cost 5½ dollars, there I had to buy another ticket to Cumberland, but my money would only get me as far as Baltima. There was a young man in Harrisburg, I asked him to give me enough money so I could get to Baltimor, told him what the situation was, that I wanted to go to such and such a place and didn't have enough money any more. Then he took me along to a café since it was 3 o'clock in the morning and told them in English they should give me a cup of coffee. He paid for my trunk, bought the ticket, gave me 20 cents, so that made 75 cents or ¾ of a dollar, since 100 cents is one dollar. When I got to Baltimor there were no friends and no one I knew, I stood there all alone like I was lost. Then, all of a sudden I remembered Ernzt Traudmann,[25] I sought him out. I searched for 3 hours before I found him. I told him that I didn't have any money and wanted to go to Lottig's in Cumberland, then I had to stay the night and until the next evening 8 o'clock with him then I asked them to send a telegram for 10 more dollars, but the money didn't come the same evening. Then Traudmann bought me the ticket, that cost another 4½ dollars, it cost 1 dollar to bring my trunk from the train station to Traudmann's and from Traudmann's back to the other train station another 2½ dollars, that makes 7 dollars, and on November 2 at 5 thirty in the morning I got to Conrad Lottig's.

Then he right away called his wife Anderes and his three boys they were very happy, he had already gotten me a job, on Monday I start work.

My traveling companions were David Schenberg and his brother and Kal Stahl from Burg-Gräfenroth [Gräfenrode] and Schan Eikel and his bride from Lindheim and the Hanau girls and another fellow from

[24]About twenty miles northwest of Marköbel.
[25]Not listed in the Hanau county emigrant files. A shoemaker named Florentz Traudmann, however, is listed in CD Baltimore 1864.

Hanau.[26] I wasn't too thrilled about the trip since I was sick more than I was well, there were strong head winds, the ship rolled so much that the waves crashed over the deck and I got scared sometimes, but I put my trust in God and thought about the words, Whither shall I go from thy presence. [6 ll.: etc.]

Now dear parents I hope to see you again after I've been in America for a few years since it is sad to have to part, for as the proverb says parting makes many a heart grow sad. [12 ll.: asks for quick answer and gives his regards to friends and relatives] / Heinrich Möller
[2 ll.: greetings from C. Lottig]

[Cumberland, Md., probably in early 1866]
Dear parents, brother, and siblings,
[3 ll.: expresses his thanks for a letter from Marköbel] Now I will tell you what it was like on the ship. In the morning there was coffee and white bread, for lunch soup and different kinds of meat, bread, sometimes potatoes, plums, and dumplings. We made potato salad from the potatoes, I and David, you could have as much vinegar, pepper and salt as you wanted. We had to go to get our own food like this, one after the other. There were 12 men together, there were 4 beds, in each bed there were 3 men. They went to get the food 2 by 2. In the evening there was tea. My bed was like this, in Hamburg David and I bought 2 sacks of straw and covers. So I had 1 sack of straw and 2 covers, that was like a bed. Dear parents, brother, and brothers and sisters, the ocean crossings aren't as easy as one thinks, but I had a pretty good trip, thank God. Eieser from Ortenberg[27] put it the wrong way, but it was just like he said it would be. When I read the letter again I saw that I've been granted my official release and I am very pleased about this, especially about my cousin the mayor who helped me in every way.

I thank you a thousand times for this. When I got to Lottig's I had a job right away, no money but rather 25 talers or 62 guilders, that I paid off all but 14 as long as I was with Hoffmann. For 5 weeks the boss had no work for me and I went to Lottig's again for 3 days again then he went with me to another shoemaker, then I worked a while again for Hoffmann, that was his name. There I earned 8 talers 20 guilders a week, then when he didn't have much work to do anymore I was supposed to work for my board, but I didn't want to do that either so I went to Lottig's again for 4

---

[26]There is no David Schenberg in the HPL, but a "D. Schönthal" is listed as an 18-year-old laborer from Braunschweig right under Möller's name. "Schan Eikel and his wife" probably refers to Jean Eickel (30) from Lindheim, about five miles north of Marköbel, and Agnes Wolf (32) from Romsthal, thirty miles east in Schlüchtern County. The two Hanau girls were probably Johanna (18) and Marie (20) Germershausen.

[27]Ortenberg is about twenty miles northeast of Marköbel.

weeks, since the work was very bad there, I thought it better to work for my board than to run up 4½ dollars of debts a week, since when I eat at Lottig's I have to pay 4½ dollars. Dear parents, brothers and sisters, I don't like being in America very much, since I don't like the English language. In America everything is just the same as it is in Germany. The people and the animals are the same. But everything is very expensive, 1 pair of boots costs 20–25 guilders, 1 pair of women's shoes costs 10–12 guilders, 1 pair of trousers 40 guilders, 1 vest 20 guilders. 60 guilders for a jacket that is a lot of money and everything you see is expensive. When I have enough money to come back to Germany again and as much as it cost to get here and enough that I can please my parents with a small gift I will come back to Germany, for there is no place like Germany. [11 ll.: closing; signature; greetings and request for various addresses]

Cumberland, January 30, 1867

Dear parents, brothers and sisters,

[5 ll.: is concerned about whether his two previous letters and a photograph ever arrived] If I could be with you for just one hour or 1 day, I could tell you much about how I am doing and what I have been through. I am still in very good health, I am still with Mr. Lottig and eat there. Dear parents and brothers and sisters I wish I were with you again, then I'd never go to America again, since it is not like what some have written, they only write about what they earn but not about what things cost, for everything here is too expensive.

Dear parents and brothers and sisters, in many ways it is very different than you think. Work is slower this winter than it's been for a long time. Because of the war everything's become so expensive you can hardly buy anything. You can well imagine it, since I have to pay 20 dollars a month and one has to work very hard if one wants to come out even. Dear parents I think though it will get better by the summer. I liked it here a lot better at the start than I do now. [6 ll: closing]

Heinrich Möller

[2 ll.: date, address; greetings from German friends]

Cumberland, February 28th, 1868

Dear parents and brothers and sisters,

[3 ll: thanks for a letter] I am, thank God, still well and happy. I may be a poor shoemaker but it's no shame to be poor. I'm still working as a shoemaker, I am now working for my 3rd boss, but I didn't stay long with the first 2, but on March 1 I'll have been with the 3rd for 2 years and I will stay with him since I have it good there. His name is Wilhelm

Armbrüster. Dear parents, times in America are very bad, there is no work, I only earn a very small wage. I earn 5 to 6 dollars a week and pay 4 dollars for food *beseitz* [besides] my washing and by the time I pay to keep my clothes in order the money's all gone. [9 ll.: reports about his correspondence with friends and relatives in Germany] Mr. Lottig is not doing so poorly, but his beer-saloon, that's not doing well, but Georg and Katharina don't like it at all, Lottig's brother-in-law Heinrich Kohl is doing very well.[28] I don't have much news to write about, since in America everything is just like in Germany except for one thing, the English language is in America but that doesn't bother me any more, since now I like speaking English more than German. I can read English a bit and write, too. Dear parents, I hope to get better work this summer, since a factory is being built and a new railroad will be built and then there'll be more work for the merchants. [2 ll.: asks for various addresses] And when you write to me, don't forget the street and the house number for the cities are very big in America. And the farmers don't live like in Germany, here one lives at the Obertohr, another at the Untertor, another in hirzbach, another in aber Walt [Oberwalt], another half-way to berheim [Bergheim] or Rüthighem [Rüdigheim] and so forth, depending on where they own land.[29] [3 ll.: cost of postage] Dear brother, you also write that Jakob says there is a shoemaker in Cumberland from Diebach.[30] I don't know of one except my boss. Dear brother, there is more than one Cumberland in America. Where I am is Cumberland, Mariland and there is a Cumberland in Penselvenien.[31] Dear parents, I will close now / my letter in hope / I remain your son

    Heinrich <u>Möller</u>
    Henry Moeller
[39 ll: hopes to see them again; greetings; quotes several lines of lyrics of the songs "*Seele was betrübst du dich*" (Oh, my soul, how you are saddened) and "*Sehnsucht nach der Heimat*" (Longing for the Homeland)]

                           Cumberland. Md., July 12, 1868

Dear parents,
    [6 ll.: thanks for a letter] I am still quite healthy and happy, although I have to work very hard. I'm no longer working at the shoemaker's but as

---

    [28]Georg and Katharina Lottig were probably the children of Johannes Lottig, stocking weaver, who emigrated to the United States in 1851. Heinrich Kohl, although not from Marköbel, probably came from Hanau and must have arrived in the United States in the 1850s. (Hs. StA MR, Best. 180 Hanau, Nr. 159; ev. KB Marköbel).
    [29]He describes settlement in the Cumberland area by comparing it to Marköbel and nearby villages.
    [30]Village four miles east of Marköbel.
    [31]At this time there were in the United States eight more towns named Cumberland (Schem 2 [1869], 484).

a mason. I earn 1 dollar 50 cents or 1½ dollars every day. [26 ll.: financial affairs of a relative; mail delivery in the United States]

I am very glad that you sent me the address[32] and I wrote right away and if they write me that things are better where they are, I'll go there as fast as I can since I don't like Cumberland. Dear parents, I don't know of any other news to write you until the next time, then I will send you a picture of me and my betrothed, because in America they get married earlier than in Germany. And I think it's high time for me too, since I'm getting older every day.[33]

I will close now my letter in / hope I remain / your son / Henry Miller [8 ll.: greetings; asks about friends; has met someone from Marköbel]

Cumberland Md, January 24th, 1869

P.[Peter] H.[Heinrich] Moller

Dear father, mother, brother, sisters and sister-in-law,

[5 ll.: thanks for letters from Marköbel; he and his wife are in good health]

Dear Peter, you write that you are in the army again which we are not at all happy about, since many people say you will have to stay in the army for 3 years which wouldn't be very good for you or for our parents, for I see from the last letter that you had a lot of bad luck before you got married,[34] which wasn't true for me, on the other hand it was to be expected, but I hope it's not true. [7 ll.: asks about his brother Jakob and sister Katharina] I'm still hoping to see my brother Jakob in America, since if he knows his trade well he can have a better life in America than in Germany, since it's no big matter to go to America especially if one goes to stay with a brother, for I am well-known in Cumberland, and I can get him work, even if he has to stay with me for the first few weeks. And if you don't like it, you can go back to Germany again, I would help you there too. Dear Jakob, you should come over here, all you need is one good suit of clothes and enough to cross the ocean. Dear Brother Jakob, when you come you should go from Bremen to Balltimor, because once you're in Baltimor it's not far to here, and I'll gladly pay for whatever it costs you. Sure, you won't like it all that much at first, I didn't have a better time of it either because of the English language, but now it doesn't make any difference if an English person or a German speaks to me, I like to speak English better than German, and you, dear Jakob, will also learn it quickly, for my wife already knows a lot and has only been in America

[32]Probably the address of the Bär family, who had also emigrated to the United States. In the next letter, Möller reports that he had gotten in touch with the family.
[33]At this time, Möller was not yet 22!
[34]His brother was married the previous November (Ev. KB Marköbel).

for 1 year. [10 ll.: news about another man from Marköbel living in Cumberland]

Dear parents, I have already gotten 2 letters from my friends the Bäers[35] and if I had wanted to go there, they said they would help me. They'd already told me the easiest way to get there and I wanted to go, but since I got married I'm staying where I am. [8 ll.: his godfather hasn't answered his letter; he now has no contact with the Lottigs] One other thing, in case of emergency, if you want to write to my father-in-law I will send you the address.

To the Honorable Senior Teacher Ludwig Bauer / in / Gutach Dorf. / Wolfach = Waldshut / Kinzigthal Seekreis / Krosherzochthum Baden, Hoping for a quick answer we remain
sincerely and faithfully,
Heinrich Möeller / and / Maria Cristina Moeller [. . .]

Meiers Mill [Pa.], Dec. 15, 1870

Dear father-in-law,

Out of love for my Maria Cristina Ursula Möller, née Bauer and to [----] you, I must inform you how things stand here. I am very sorry to send such sad news. I, Heinrich Möller, and my Maria lived in wedlock only 2 years 2 months and 4 days, my Maria gave me one daughter and we were expecting the 2nd. We were happy and hoping for a son but Maria fell down the stairs and probably hurt herself, a short time later she lost her baby, it took about 3 weeks. When I came home from work Saturday evening she was not at home, I went to our neighbor's and collected her and the child and we spent a happy time together until Sunday. She didn't feel well at all, had to lie down, she kept losing more and more blood. I sent someone to get the doctor but all our efforts were to no avail, she cried out for help but no one could help her and then she died Sunday night at ½ past 9 on December 4th.

Before she died she prayed to God that He should be with her and her child, those were her last words! She was buried on Tuesday, December 6, on her birthday.

Her age was 23 years, less 2 days.

Peace be to her ashes.

Dear father-in-law, I do not hesitate to tell you how I feel for you know how it is when one loses something dear to the heart, so dear you can't buy it for all the world.

[8 ll.: closing; signature; address]

---

[35]Johannes Bär emigrated from Marköbel in 1855, the children of Jacob Bär in 1859 (Hs. StA MR, Best. 180 Hanau, Nr. 159).

Meiers Mill, May 27, 1871

Dear parents, brothers, sisters and sister-in-law,

I take up my pen to write to you again with joy, not with the joy I used to have but with the joy of being able to write this letter in my own house. You will also be pleased, yes, dear parents, I have bought myself a piece of land, it cost two hundred and thirty-five dollars. And I have built myself a house, it cost about 600 dollars. I haven't paid it all off yet but I am working day and night and I earn 10–13 dollars every week and so I'll be able to pay it off soon, and if I want to sell it it is worth 1,000 dollars. [2 ll.: health]

Dear parents! If God grants me life we will meet again before 2 years have passed, for then I will come to Germany to get you, then you will be near me and live in the land of Goshen like Joseph said. I have not received your answer to my last letter, we've been living in our new house since the first of May. [9 ll.: in his next letter he will enclose a photograph of his daughter; closing]

your son / Henry Miller

[5 ll.: address]

Meyer-Mill, July 30, 1871

Henry Miller / *Shoemaker* / Scott Dale

Dear parents, brothers, sisters and sister-in-law,

[3 ll.: thanks for letters] Dear parents, I will now write about what you asked me to, that is about my second wife. When my first wife died I was all alone except for my little Anna. She was only about 18 months old and so I needed to get married again. One of my friends told me he knew a good match for me. One evening he came to see me and said I should come along with him, when I got to his house there was a girl there, he introduced me to her and said that she was the one he had told me about. So, to make a long story short, we got as far as getting engaged. Then, when I took her home the doors were all locked, so I said to her, if you are willing to keep your promise, you can come home with me now, and so she came with me and by the next evening we were already married. Dear parents, that's how quickly you can get a wife in America.

Dear parents, now about how I got my house. The boss where I work had a lot for sale he said if I gave him $235 I could have it. Then, when I went home for lunch I told my wife that if I only had 235 dollars I could have a house soon. Then she said that if I would take care of the house then she would get hold of the money. I then went back to my boss and told him that I wanted to buy the lot, if he would settle for 135 dollars for the first payment and the other 100 dollars in a year's time. And he said I could pay like that. On April 1st my father-in-law came and paid the first 135 dollars, the rest is due in a year. Dear parents, then I went to a carpenter and asked him if he could build me a house and he said as fast as I could get the wood. So I ordered the wood and in about 4 weeks' time I had a house.

It is 24 feet long, 20 feet wide and 16 feet high, that is from the foundation to the roof, it has 15 windows. The cellar is 5 feet high. I have one living room, 1 bedroom and 1 kitchen. The kitchen though is as big as the living room, and four rooms on the second floor, and there are 12 doors in the whole house.

Dear parents, the lot is 60 feet wide, 100 long, the whole lot is a garden, except for where the house and the barn are. My father-in-law built the barn, it is not very big, 12 foot square. There's room for 3 cows. I only have 1 and a small calf, but my father-in-law said he wants to give me another one. I have 2 head of hogs, 4 old and 10 young chickens. Dear parents, I am doing very well now, thank God, we are also getting along quite well together, it wasn't so easy in the beginning but now everything is fine.

Henry Miller

Scottdale, July 17, 1879

Dear parents, brothers and sister-in-law,[36]

[10 ll.: complains that he has not received an answer to his letters; his family is well] Times are still bad, last winter I worked for a butcher for 3⅓ months, I got 30 dollars a month there but now I have my own shoemaker's shop. I own a house in Scottdale and also have a house in Meiers Mill.

My brother-in-law lives there. Dear parents, I have been thinking of visiting you for almost 14 years now, but I can't get enough money together now. I already have 6 children now, 3 *Madgen* (*girl*) and 3 *buben* (*Boy*) and with the wife and myself we're a family of 8, that costs quite a lot since everything is expensive. Last winter I slaughtered my hogs, they weighed 476 [lbs.] but the meat was all gone a long time ago since in America you eat meat three times a day. I don't want to write any more this time since everything over here is just like over there. If you want to know anything in particular, though, write and ask me about it in your

[36]His two sisters, Anna Margaretha and Katharina, both died on December 21, 1877—probably of diphtheria, which caused a number of deaths in Marköbel that year (Ev. KB Marköbel; the register of deaths includes references to medical orders for early burial—issued for Heinrich Möller's sisters as well). Möller seems to have been aware of their death since they are no longer included in his salutation. The fact that he does not mention their deaths, however, indicates that one or more earlier letters may have been lost.

next letter, and then I'll tell you about it, and I hope that you write back soon. [3 ll.: good wishes]
Heinrich Miller
[13 ll.: greetings; list of all the names of members of the family]

Scottdale, June 21, 1880

Dearly beloved parents,

I have received your letter and learned from it that your end is near, or perhaps by the time this letter reaches you, it will already be too late,[37] I hope not since my greatest desire is to see you once again, dear father, I have had no peace of mind for years now, I always think about coming back to Germany again but times have been so bad. This year looks better but it is not as good as you think, in the last 6 years I have lost over 5 hundred dollars in my business. My workshop has been broken into 3 times, which amounted to over 80 dollars. If I had all of that money I would come to see you straight away, but I haven't given up all hope of seeing you again. If it is not God's will, we'll have to accept it and hope to meet if not in this world then in the next, where all suffering comes to an end!

Dear mother, father writes that you are still in good health which I am very glad to hear. If you were here with us you wouldn't have to work any more. Here in America the women are better off than the men, a woman only has to do her housework, no woman has to work in the fields.
[13 ll.: closing; signature; address; greetings]

Scott dale, January 3rd, 1881

Dear mother, brother and sisters-in-law,

[7 ll.: words of sympathy about his father's death] We are all still well and have enough to eat and drink. On December 13 I slaughtered 3 hogs, one weighed 195 [lbs.] the other 215 [lbs.] and the third 247 [lbs.] I didn't fatten them up myself, though, I bought them for 44 dollars. We are doing quite well, I have one cow, she had a calf in November, she gives 7 [lbs.] of butter a week, I bought her in March for 32½ dollars.

Dear Peter,

In the letter you asked about my name being spelled Miller. In the English language, you spell Möller with an i, and not ö, or if you spell it

[37]This was the case: his father, Johannes Möller, died on June 25, 1880, at the age of 66 (Ev. KB Marköbel).

Moeller, the o is not pronounced but the e, and the e is an i in the English language, that's why I spell Möller with an i, not with an ö, I think you'll understand why now,
Read this according to the commas, so that you understand it correctly.
[4 ll.: his daughter Käthe encloses a short note in English and German]

Meyersdale, Pa., April 18, 1885.

Dear brother,
    [8 ll.: regrets that he has received no mail in 2 years] It has almost been 20 years since I left you but I still long to hear from you. [7 ll: asks about his mother and his brother Jakob; his family is well] I weigh 201 [lbs.], my wife is not so heavy, 115 [lbs.]. I am sending you my picture.
    Times are bad now, there are many people here who can hardly make a living. Thank God I have my own house and I have also bought more land, 10 morgens, last summer I lost a cow, 2 years ago I bought 2 horses and a wagon and worked as a teamster, I couldn't get by on shoemaking, but that didn't pay well either, so I sold it again and went back to shoemaking.
Henry Miller

Meyersdale, Feb. 18, 1886

Dear mother, brothers and sister-in-law
    [14 ll.: salutations; wants to send a dollar to his mother for her birthday] Even though I'm still not rich, I always have enough to eat, I slaughtered 3 head of hogs and a cow, one hog weighed 280 [lbs.], 240 [lbs.], 180. I have more potatoes than I need and a whole barrel full of sauerkraut and so you can see that I don't go hungry. I now weigh 214 [lbs.] and my wife 104. I am 39 years old and my wife is 42. She also comes from Herlefeld, 6 hours from Kassel. She came to America as a 13-year-old girl. Dear mother, she can't write German very well, otherwise she would write to you, my children also can't write German very well, and mine is almost as bad, too, since I sometimes go for a whole year without writing any German. [2 ll.: asks for an address]
    Times are now very bad in America, there are thousands of workers without jobs.
    And if I could sell my house I would move another 12 hundred miles. There you can buy 160 morgens of land for only 15 dollars, but there's a good side and a bad side to things there too.
    I will close now and hope that you get the dollar, it's as much as 4 marks, it isn't much but it comes from the heart / Henry Miller
[8 ll.: address; his son John adds a line]

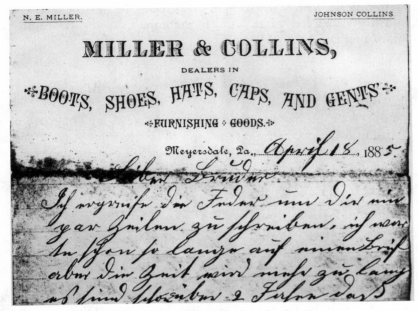

Figure 12. Letter of April 18, 1885, on business letterhead.

Meyersdale, July 15, 1893

Dear mother, brothers and sisters-in-law,

[4 ll.: standard salutations] In my last letter I said that I wanted to send Mother a dollar for her birthday and maybe bring the next one myself. But I didn't do either one. You always want to do more than you ever get around to doing. Now I want to send you the dollar, dear mother, I had 2600 marks in the bank and I thought I would come to see you but my house was very small and my wife wanted me to make it bigger so now I have built an extension and that cost 1,800 marks and I didn't want to spend all the rest of what I have in the bank on a trip since times are very bad, but if the Lord grants us good health we may meet again next summer. [3 ll.: birth of a grandson; weather]

October 6, 1893

Dear mother, I am going to send the letter I wrote on July 15 to you now. We are now living in our house, we have 7 rooms 3 downstairs and 4 upstairs. Times are very bad now but I am thrifty and so are my wife and sons. They like to work and on payday they bring their money home to us. We don't have any debts like so many other poor people, we pay as we go and still manage to have a dollar in our pockets. So, when you get this letter please write back straight away, don't be like me, and take 3 months to write a letter like I did. In the hope that you will fulfill my request / I remain your / H e i n r i c h

Meyersdale, June 4, 1894

Dear Brother,

[16 ll.: asks if his last letter arrived; health; weather] Times are now very bad in America, there are thousands of laborers out of work and all over there are many who have walked off the job because they want to pay them lower wages.[38]

[9 ll.: asks about friends and news of the Lottigs; asks for addresses] / I will close now / in the hope / of an answer soon / your brother / Henry [6 ll.: greetings; friend from Marköbel should write to him]

Meyersdale, Jan. 30th, 2 o'clock, 1895

Dear mother, brothers, and sister-in-law,

[8 ll.: thanks for letters from Marköbel; standard salutations] Dear mother, I am sending you another dollar, not because I think you are in need but just to do something nice for you. Dear brother, it has been almost 30 years since I left Germany, it is a very long time. I doubt that anyone would recognize me any more if I should happen to stop by, you shouldn't be startled if a humble fellow comes to ask for room and board for a month or something like that. [9 ll.: asks about friends and relatives; weather] In America my sons don't have to be soldiers, in America they have very few soldiers.

Dear brother, you write that I shouldn't take offense when you write down what mother says

Oh no, never

[2 ll.: hopes for an answer soon]

Your Son and *Broter* Henry Miller

[22 ll.: letter from Meyersdale of April 2, 1897, with news about the family: his son John got married, his son Peter was involved in an accident, one daughter came for a visit, and another grandson was born]

---

[38] In May 1894 the employees of the Pullman Company in Chicago went on strike because of wage cuts. Workers in the iron and coal industries joined in the strike, which quickly spread to other states, until about 750,000 workers were on strike throughout the country. The strike was brought to a violent end with the help of U.S. Army troops, without worker demands having been met.

Figure 13. Mill in Marköbel inherited by Heinrich Möller's brother Peter (early twentieth century).

Meyersdale, July 7, 1897

Dear mother, brothers, *and* sisters-in-law,

[2 ll.: thanks for letters] We are also still in good health, my wife was sick for three days, that is I bought medicine for tapeworms again and then she got sick and it still didn't go away and she said the next medicine I buy I should take myself, she doesn't want any more. [3 ll.: his son John has a daughter] On the 4th of July, my wife and I went for a drive in the *Cuntry (aufs Land)* and we had a fine time, of course we have our own horse and *Bugey (Bugey* is a *Kutsche).* [3 ll.: weather; closing] / Heinrich Möller / Henry Miller

[9 ll.: list of children, grandchildren, and great-grandchildren; address]

Meyersdale, Pa., July 21, 1901

Peter Möller,

You write that my last letter was very polite, don't you know what you shout in the woods echoes back. Why weren't you man enough to

give me my share of father's money when you gave Jakob his and as much as you gave him. Father gave you the mill so you could support mother, wasn't that enough. You kept my share for 20 years and then you dealt with me like a Jew. Between 500 and 700 marks, when you gave Jakob 1000 marks. 20 years ago I needed it very badly but I had to wait until you decided to pay me that little bit. You would never have heard about it from me, I counted it as lost, I was astonished when my Heinrich came back from the post office and gave me 2 letters, saying that my ship had come in, the 2 *Mony order* or *Geldschein* were made out to Somerset, 20 miles from Meyersdale, but I received it at the bank in Meyersdale, and so I thank you for that amount. We are all still well, my family keeps getting smaller, my children will all be married soon. [10 ll.: lists them, their spouses and their children]
I now have 3 houses, 2 of them I rent out

for 1 I get	6 dollars
and for the other	7½ a month
	13½

Henry gives me 20 dollars a month and I still earn a bit with shoemaking. I have 1 horse and 1 cow and have 2½ morgens of land. On one part I have potatoes and oats and on the other I have potatoes and corn. I have 1 plow and harrow, one *Bugee*. The enclosed picture shows you what a *Bugee* is.
[5 ll: visited his daughter Anna for her son's funeral]
Henry Miller

7

Michael Probstfeld (Randolph M. Probstfield)

The correspondence between R. M. Probstfield and his nephew Paul Sauerborn is quite unusual in that the two hardly knew one another. Sauerborn was born in 1854, two years after his uncle had left for America; he had probably met his uncle, however, as a six-year-old boy, when Probstfield visited his family in Kalt near Koblenz in the Prussian Rhine province. Their extensive correspondence grew more out of the shared intellectual and political interests of two educated men than out of emotional or family ties.

It would hardly be an exaggeration to characterize Probstfield's relationship with his parents as traumatic. The letters provide only a few hints about the cause of the breach (it was certainly more than the fact that Sauerborn's mother had been forced to marry against her will); but its consequences are clearly evident. Fifty years later Probstfield still referred to his parents almost without exception as "your grandparents." Another reason for his emigration might have been that his parents' farm was economically viable only if it could remain undivided. The family, however, was not without means; they owned ninety acres of land, and their grandson Sauerborn was able to study architecture. Probstfield, too, had probably completed secondary school in preparation for university studies in theology. But despite or perhaps because of this experience, he began to develop liberal attitudes at an early age. Although not an atheist, he clearly rejected institutionalized religion. It is also inconceivable that Probstfield would have remained unaffected by the spirit of

1848. For a man with his talents, his ambition, and not least his ideals, Germany had grown much too small.[1]

The first surviving Probstfield letter dates from 24 years after his arrival in America, the second one a decade later, but since he carefully kept a journal and participated in public life, many details of his early life in America can be reconstructed. He came to the United States in 1852 at the age of twenty, but he was not the first to emigrate from the area near his home or in his family. An aunt from a nearby village had emigrated with her husband and children in 1847 and was apparently his first contact in America. As long as he lived, Probstfield continued to write to her daughter, and he spent his first winter working as a lumberjack near his aunt's home on the border between Wisconsin and Michigan.

But he soon struck out on his own. By the following May he was living three hundred miles farther west in Minnesota, which did not become a state until 1858 and counted only 150 Germans in its 1850 population of 6,000. Probstfield was a true pioneer: he traveled one hundred miles in a dugout canoe in 1858, an indication of the primitive living conditions as well as of a certain thirst for adventure. In the 1850s he frequently changed jobs and addresses in the St. Paul area.[2] In March 1859 Probstfield reached the settlement on the western border of Minnesota, only 150 miles from Canada, where he spent the rest of his life. At the time, it was hardly more than a trading post for trappers on the Red River of the North. Buffalo still roamed the prairie, hunted by the Sioux Indians. In 1859 the first steamboat appeared, but twenty years later Probstfield could still hear the howl of the wolves.[3]

Although Probstfield already owned real estate worth $300 and was

---

[1]The primary sources of information about Probstfield's family background and early years in Germany are the family chronicle compiled by Paul Sauerborn's daughters, Drache (1970), which relies heavily on Probstfield's journals, and material provided by descendants in Minnesota, including a fictionalized account of his life between 1853 and 1872, Hack (1977), written by a granddaughter.

The claim that Probstfield attended university (Drache, 20) is probably false, but the family chronicle mentions that he attended a Gymnasium (or a Latin school) in Trier. According to the BistA TR (letter of May 8, 1987), Probstfield's name cannot be found in any record of students who attended the seminary or received scholarships. In a biographical sketch written for *The Legislative Manual* (1891), Senator Probstfield mentions having attended "common schools and private grammar schools," a description more appropriate for a Gymnasium.

According to the Sauerborn family chronicle, Probstfield was "involved in antigovernment activities" in 1848. A letter written by his brother in Kalt (May 8, 1858, BABS) reports that when Probstfield sent his family some issues of the *Minnesota Democrat,* they were suspected of propagating forbidden periodicals.

[2]Emigration details in Standesamtregister, town of Münstermaifeld; Probstfield filed for emigration papers on March 26, 1852, and reports in his biographical sketch that he arrived in America on May 5, 1853. Interview with Probstfield in a special edition of the *Moorhead Independent,* January 5, 1900 (USC 1850.1, 116).

[3]Drache, 6–7, 24–27, 88.

designated a farmer in the 1860 census, even ten years later he hardly had a serious start in agriculture. In the fall of 1860 he made a visit back to Germany; the occasion was his father's death on December 13, 1859. Early the next spring he returned with three of his brothers and two cousins. They had enough money to travel by steamship and to buy five draft oxen, ten cows, and fifty head of young stock in eastern Minnesota, which they then drove to the settlement. In the late summer Michael Probstfield traveled down to Notre Dame, Indiana, married Catherine Sidonia Goodman on September 10, and took an 18-day, 255-mile "honeymoon trip" from St. Paul back to the settlement by ox-drawn covered wagon. Their daughter Mary was the first white child born in the county (June 1862); their oldest son became the first to die there (August 1864). When Mary was only two months old, the family had to flee before an Indian uprising; it took one and a half years for the situation to return to normal. Two of the younger Probstfield brothers volunteered for the Union Army, and both died of disease in October 1863 in St. Louis.[4]

In 1864 Probstfield returned with his family to the Georgetown settlement on the Red River, where he worked until 1869 as postmaster, hotel manager, and agent for the Hudson Bay Company. As these occupations indicate, he must have been regarded as completely Americanized even then. Immigrants like Probstfield—young, single, and well-educated—generally had an easy time fitting into the new society. It is also possible that he had learned English before he emigrated. He changed the "*feld*" in his last name to "field" as early as 1860. When he changed his first name to Randolph, however, is unknown; he seems to have assumed this name about the time of his marriage. The little that we know about his wife also fits in with this picture of rapid assimilation. She was born in Ohio; her parents had both immigrated from Alsace in their youth. Her father, a prosperous farmer, had anglicized his name from *Gutmann* to Goodman. Mrs. Probstfield could speak German but the family spoke and wrote English at home. Even their milk cows had English names.[5]

[4]MC 1860: Breckenridge Co., Minn., #97; kath. KB Münstermaifeld. According to HPL, five Probstfields from Kalt sailed March 31, 1861 on the steamship *Bavaria* to New York; but Michael Probstfield does not seem to have been among them (Drache, 20; *History of Clay . . . Minnesota* [1918], 60–61; *Minnesota* [1890]). During the Sioux uprising, a member of the same party characterized Probstfield as "about the best man we had" and reported that the two of them shared most of the scouting duties. According to him, old age or cowardice left only 24 reliable men out of a group of 45 (Samuel Bruce to James [Bruce], Ft. Garry, September 19, 1862, Bruce Papers, Manitoba Provincial Archives).

[5]Catherine Goodman probably met her husband in 1856 when her family spent a month in St. Paul. Information provided by June Dobervich and Evelyn Gesell, Probstfield's granddaughters; see also Hack, 20–38, 57–58, 85–93. According to MC 1860: St. Joseph Co., Ind., Greene Twp., #1031, and South Bend town, #133, Catherine's father was a farmer with landholdings worth $5,000. The twenty-year-old Catherine was listed both in her father's household in rural

As a farmer, Probstfield had a positive attitude toward innovation, but things took their time in the early days of the border settlement. The entire county had a population of only 79 in 1860; in the wake of the Indian uprising, the number had sunk to 30 when Probstfield took the state census in 1865, and had recovered only to 92 by 1870. Probstfield was now one of only four farmers listed in the agricultural census; he had not yet begun to grow any grain, but he owned a farm worth $1,400, to which he had moved the previous year. The following decade brought much progress, and the 1880 census recorded Probstfield near the peak of his prosperity. At that time he cultivated 200 acres with five horses and four draft oxen; in addition he owned almost 275 acres of woods and prairie, with a total value of $10,000. Like most of the farmers in this region, wheat was his chief product, and Probstfield's almost 125 acres of wheat provided harvest yields about 20 percent above the county average. His farm, however, was also more highly diversified than most; with an advantageous location on the river only three miles from the town of Moorhead, he earned $400 from the sale of firewood and another $400 from vegetables and fruit.[6] Thus he was able to weather the agricultural crisis around 1890, caused by poor harvests and rock-bottom prices, but not without terrible sacrifices.

In 1880, when his eldest daughter was seventeen and his eldest son fourteen, two farmhands still lived in the Probstfield household, but they were the last to be listed before the census of 1910, even though hired help remained indispensable at harvest time. But it was above all the relentless efforts of all members of the family—not only the father and sons but also, following the European pattern, the mother and daughters—which brought the farm to prosperity in good times and kept it above water in bad. In the summer of 1875 Probstfield cut his barley with a scythe while his wife bound the sheaves, despite her pregnancy, which ended in a miscarriage. When she was only sixteen, his daughter Mary plowed with a team of four horses or a double yoke of oxen. She may have borne the greatest responsibility since she was the oldest. But there are also records of the younger girls plowing and of the whole family turning out to weed crops or pick wild berries for town markets. Probstfield was no easier on himself, either. One time, it is reported, he drove a load of grain to the mill in the evening, discovered the line was too long, and walked the entire 25 miles home and then back to the mill the next day, just to save the price of a night's lodging, and this at the age of 55.[7]

St. Joseph County and as a domestic in the household of a well-to-do Irish druggist in the town of South Bend (Drache, 20, 81, 236).

⁶Drache, 82; USC 1860.1 and 1870.1; MC A 1870 and 1880; MC Minn. 1865.

⁷MC 1880: Clay Co., Minn., Oakport Twp., #10; 1900: #57; 1910: #145; MC Minn. 1885, 1895, and 1905; Drache, 62–65, 96, 179–80, 195, 245.

The children do not seem to have felt exploited. They identified themselves fully with the family enterprise: four of them remained unmarried, and the others married at an average age of thirty. The good relationship between the parents and their children was not one-sided: Probstfield was a devoted and even indulgent father. Parents and children attended dances in the town together, and the sons and daughters gave parties at home for the young people of the area—which often lasted until three or four o'clock in the morning. Above all Probstfield was determined to give his children the best education he could afford. In the 1870s he taught them himself for at least three winters; later he served on the local school board. In 1880 he paid 126 dollars to subscribe to the *Encyclopedia Britannica*. The family also took out a loan to buy a harmonium for 130 dollars but were forced by hard times to sell it to a local church. One of Probstfield's greatest disappointments was that his financial setbacks kept him from providing his younger children the quality of education he felt they deserved.[8]

The agricultural crisis around 1890 also spurred Probstfield into active involvement in politics, leading to his election to the Minnesota State Senate as a candidate for the Farmers Alliance. Although an immigrant in politics, he was not an ethnic politician in the classic American sense. Immigrants did comprise some 40 percent of the population of his county and about half the voters, but only 10 percent of these were German. Scandinavians, particularly Norwegians, were the dominant group.[9] In fact, the Farmers Alliance in its origins had much in common with the Scandinavian agricultural cooperative movement; it soon developed into a political party that seemed quite radical in the American context.

The main goal of the Alliance was to improve the conditions under which grain was marketed and transported. The prairie farmers were victims of a depressed world market for wheat and the geoclimatic fact that their land was ill suited to grow anything else. In 1890 and 1900 Minnesota led the nation in wheat production with 10 to 12 percent of the national total. The situation was exacerbated by the fact that farmers often had to depend on local monopolies in order to get their crops to market. The railroads exploited their advantage to the fullest, charging higher prices per unit in the west to recoup the losses from the cutthroat competition they faced in the east. A large part of the Alliance platform on which Probstfield was elected was thus devoted to the improvement of grain storage and marketing conditions. At the top of the list was the demand for state regulation and eventually nationalization of the rail-

---

[8]Marriage dates included in a family tree provided by contributor (Drache, 132, 209, 216–18, 222–25, 296–303).

[9]Ibid., 209; information from the 1895 Minnesota State Census in *Legislative Manual* (1899), 546–47.

roads. With slogans like "Capital vs. Labor," the Alliance pronounced its solidarity with industrial workers and called for the union of all producing classes, a kind of Farmer-Labor party, as its successor called itself in the 1920s and 1930s. Among other things, the platform of 1890 called for the abolition of child labor, the introduction of mining and factory inspectors, strike arbitration, and "equal pay for equal work, irrespective of sex"; the platform of 1892 went even further.[10]

The success of the Alliance and the Populist party that it spawned remained limited. In the American electoral system, without proportional representation, third parties seldom receive enough votes to win; their goals are often achieved, however, when the major parties imitate them. In Minnesota the Populists joined forces in 1890 with the Democrats and were able to elect the speaker and control the organization of the legislature, but they were hardly able to enact much of their own legislative program. The Republicans, usually the party of big business, countered in the 1892 gubernatorial election with a Scandinavian pro–Alliance candidate and even included a mild plan for railroad regulation in their platform. In the 1896 presidential election, the joint candidate of the Democrats and Populists was defeated both in Minnesota and nationwide. The same coalition won back the office of governor in 1898, but by then the Minnesota legislature was firmly in Republican hands.[11] All in all, the farmers achieved little from their political activism.

Some historians have pointed to "the provincial insularity, the evidences of xenophobia and anti–Semitism, the feverish visions of conspiracy and cataclysm" that allegedly characterized the Populist movement.[12] One line taken from Probstfield's letters might fit this picture: "Great is our civilization under the Jew Rothschild's bank and financial system." His basic attitude, however, was quite different: convinced that something in his world was wrong, he made a sober and determined attempt to get to the bottom of it. He had no great illusions of his chances of success, as a letter written to one of his confederates in 1892 indicates: "I know we cannot reform the state, much less the United States or the world but, we can at least contribute our small efforts to keep the ball rolling, to accelerate it, or to keep it from standing still altogether."[13]

Probstfield writes like an educated German, one who emigrated a generation earlier, has used his mother tongue only rarely since, and has

[10]USC A 1900.2, 90–91; party platforms in *Legislative Manual* (1891), 486–89, (1893), 372–73. On the Populists and the Farmers Alliance in general see Hicks (1931) and Tindall (1966).

[11]Hicks, 148–52, 185, 258–63, 394–95.

[12]Tindall, x.

[13]Letter (written in English), December 15, 1892, to Charles W. Brandborg in Brandborg Family Papers, State Historical Society of Minnesota.

adopted English as his normal medium of communication. With this background, it is amazing how clear, articulate, flexible, and to the point his German still is. There is no doubt that he still masters the language, not vice versa.

Yet his German has a clearly alien or at least strange touch. This is caused not by occasional lapses or vagaries in spelling but by a heavy intrusion of English vocabulary, syntax, and idioms. He uses, for example, a Germanized (and plausible, but wrong) form of "interest" (on capital), having forgotten the German equivalent (*Zinsen*), which he later remembers and uses. Or he puts a German prefix on an English verb and gives it a German ending for good measure.

In many of these cases, he must have been aware of the language mixture. He almost certainly was not aware of it in the far more numerous cases when he used the wrong preposition (the one corresponding to English usage) or a Germanized version of an English syntactical structure, like the present participle: perfectly comprehensible, but entirely unidiomatic in German.

Much of this shows through in his handwriting. Although he uses the old German script, except for English or Latin words, he somehow manages to give his pages and words the "round" look of Latin and especially Anglo-Saxon handwriting rather than the sharp, angular look of German. It can hardly be a surprise that the handwriting of his English-language letters is as American as it could possibly be.

Randolph M. Probstfield
                    Oakport Farm / Clay Co. Minn. / January 7th, 1876
My dear nephew Paul,

I received your most welcome letter of November 19th on December 28th and was not only pleasantly surprised but also astonished to hear from you again at all, until I read the explanation that you really had answered my letter but I didn't receive it. I had interpreted it somewhat differently. In my letter I remarked that I hoped you wouldn't become a lazy priest, but rather a useful member of humanity, and I thought—since I received no answer—you really did become a priest and were so hurt by my remark that you did not want to write again to such a godless uncle. And thus you see that I was not expecting any answer. I am now all the more pleased to hear that you want to devote yourself to a useful profession. Permit me to make several remarks about the subjects that you will probably devote yourself to. When one is young, one is tempted to follow one's own taste, but despite everything often still apt to decide things wrongly, that is not so much wrongly as impractically.

Figure 14. House of the Probstfeld family in Kalt, built in 1853; sketch by Paul Sauerborn in 1880.

Figure 15. House of R. M. Probstfield near Moorhead, Minnesota, built in 1868; photo from 1884.

Architecture was my favorite and is not unrelated to painting. Painting was my taste, the priesthood, your grandparents' taste, that was my curse. If I had promised to be a priest and kept my word, today I would be (judging from all probabilities) a fattened-up, high-living hypocrite in the so-called vineyard of the Lord, and not a *Farmer* or *Bauer* earning his bread by the sweat of his brow.

And since I prize self-respect more highly than wealth, luxury etc. I am well satisfied with the exchange and today I wouldn't trade places with a wealthy hypocrite if I could, although being a farmer was not my choice, but I didn't have the schooling to become anything else here, without having to study again and where would the money for that come from? [. . .]

From a practical point of view, pharmacy, chemistry or a straight *Doctor Medicinis* would be the best or the most advantageous, more profitable as long as a *Doctor* is not a bungler, if an architect is a bungler, then he's bad off anyway, and I believe that good doctors are more scarce than good architects. Much depends on where your own interests lead you. [3 ll.: details] — You may like architecture best, but you could still be a passable *Doctor,* though you'd be a better architect, and the same applies the other way round. [. . .]

But good advice is a dime a dozen and you do not really need my good advice since you have men closer to hand who are in a better position to give you good advice than I am. Besides, I know and understand so little of Germany nowadays, conditions and needs there etc. that I shouldn't even presume to give you advice. If you were interested in coming to America, I might be able to help you in this way.

Since I do not know how many years you have been at Gymnasium, I can hardly know how far along you are, even if you never had to repeat a year. I also do not know whether there are eight or 6 grades in Coblenz. In Trier there were 8. [. . .]

I hope we will correspond occasionally before you are finished with Gymnasium.

Indeed, the work in the fields which the poets praise so highly is not done by the poets themselves, or rather, I do not want to deny that there can be poets among farmers, but they do not sing of farming work, and when every now and then someone does, he belongs to the category—I don't want the grapes, they are sour. — All the poetry in the world has never led anyone to work in the fields and it never will. We are only what chance, necessity and compulsion make of us and the fact there are a few exceptions to the rule does not refute the rule itself.

I am very sorry to hear that your family situation has not improved. I must admit that I can well imagine that you would all prefer to turn your backs on your home than to stay there. You are less to be pitied than your poor mother, who has seen little pleasure in her life, and the only pleasure that she can still expect is to see her children happy. Your sister Theresia has written me much about the situation at home.

I haven't heard from Uncle Paul for 13 years and also do not know where he is.

The winter here has been very mild so far, but we also had 30 below zero Fahrenheit once, between 27 and 28 degrees Reaumer. What we call a mild winter here is a harsh winter over there.

We are all quite well except for your aunt, she has been ill since Nov. 12th, the last 2 or three days she's been getting better.

I hold classes now every day for 6 of my children, 4 hours every day and I think they are making better progress than in a regular school. [8 ll.: cannot afford $25 for the requested photographs; greetings; signature]

Maybe you can get hold of the letter I wrote to your sister, it contains some things missing in this one. [10 ll.: inquiries about friends; apologizes for spelling mistakes; address]

[3 ll: address]

Oak Port Farm / February 26th, 1886

My dear Paul,

I received your completely unexpected letter of January 10 on February 20th after it had been sent God knows where all. [25 ll.: address, location of the farm] I received a letter from your sister Therese dated Dec. 20, 1883 which arrived in January 1884—but I never answered it. For in the first half of January I received a financial blow—which stunned me. I do not know if I wrote to you about it or not, but since I know that I have written you a letter since then I am convinced that I wrote to you about it. First I signed security (*Bond*) for a man as treasurer of the town of Moorhead and then I endorsed promissory notes for him for a sum of 3000 dollars. The man had a splendid business as a butcher, but then he collapsed on January 4, 1884. Before he had signed over property to me—9 acres of land on the edge of Moorhead with a nominal value of 1000 dollars and a building plot with a brick house, worth about (at that time) 6000 dollars. The house was mortgaged for 3000 which I thus also had to assume. In addition the *Interessen* on the debts had gone up to 500 dollars. [10 ll.: details] The whole fiasco cost me 7603 dollars. [5 ll.: interest and additional costs amount to $975 a year] On the other hand, as long as the property is rented, it brings in $780 annually. But since many houses and business properties in Moorhead are standing empty since the times here are terribly bad here as a result of the low crop prices, I can resign myself to having empty buildings too. As long as the grain prices stay like they are now I can't even think about paying off any of the debts, and if my *Credit* here weren't so extraordinarily good they would have hauled me off a long time ago. But since I pay my *Interessen* punctually, by making sacrifices of all kinds, no one bothers me. [8 ll.: grain prices] I haven't seen such bad times in America since 1858. Money seems to have just blown away. In the eastern states it is supposed to be just as bad and money goes begging for 2 percent a year.

[7 ll.: received no answer to letters written to three relatives] Then I wrote to Joh. N. Loehr—thinking he might still be in Zell on the Mosel, to find out if the whole region I had written to had disappeared from the face of the earth, also with no result. I wrote among others to my sister Marian, that I had given up my planned trip to Germany, and that, if I were to make the trip, I would most probably not come home, whether the letter annoyed her so much that she did not write back or something else, I do not know, I didn't get an answer from her, either. [17 ll.: since then he is obviously being punished with silence] So you see, Paul, even though I am already old (53 years old) and as white as a white horse, I can still be provoked to bite, since my teeth are as good as they were when I was 25. [. . .] My hearing isn't the best and I've needed glasses to read and write for about 6 or 7 years.

You asked me once if I had been told what happened to the relatives at the Heidger Mill.[14] No. I have never heard anything at all about them. [12 ll.: inquiries about friends] — One thing I'm sure of, that we live better here than the farmers in Germany who have three times as much money as I do, unless a great change in their way of life has occurred since I left. Anyone who isn't <u>able</u> to eat meat 21 times a week if he wants to is in bad shape. But wine and <u>spirits</u> we don't drink here that is too expensive in bad times like these now. [11 ll.: many of his hogs have died of disease] We only have two cows left, one I slaughtered. Our cows stay in the barn all year round, since I don't own any more prairie land, it's all plow land, and in the woods they do too much damage to the young trees. I have broken 185 more acres of land near Georgetown, but that is *verrentet* [rented out]. If I can pay for it, next summer I will have 100 more broken—that costs 400 dollars.[15] I have not forgotten that I offered to give Anna the money for her son's training, that was when I could—now I can't, and that is one of the reasons, or <u>the</u> only reason that the photographs haven't come. Now comes tax-paying time. I'll be driving into town shortly to pay my taxes—part of them, we are shipping 400 bushels of barley now for 50 cts per bushel. My taxes amount to 400

[14]The Heidger Mühle, a few miles from Kalt, was the farm that belonged to his mother's family.
[15]See the Introduction to Part I, n. 3.

dollars this year. [13 ll.: details; harvest; bad times] If it goes on like this for another three years, the whole country would be depopulated since there would be no farmers left, and if the farmers go bankrupt here and have to quit then everything will collapse, when the farmers prosper, all business prospers. Farmers like me can hold out the longest since we do all of our work ourselves except for harvesting and threshing. In addition I also do some gardening on the side, and when the vegetable prices are so low that I do better by keeping the horses hitched to the plow, then I let all the hogs into the garden and let them eat up what can't be sold. [8 ll.: details]

[13 ll.: weather; grain prices] I can't understand how the farmers in Germany pull through since our prices compete with theirs. I know that in England the wheat farmers are all going bankrupt, one after another, and that from year to year fewer acres are sown.

We are all quite hale and as hearty as the present times permit—we just vegetate—live on—in the same old rut. My sons, instead of sending them to advanced school like I started and intended to continue doing, now have to stay at home patiently and work. But the dissatisfaction that ruled our home we don't let in here. They know exactly how things stand, as well as I myself, and at the same time they know that I do my very best for all. Their needs at home are modest, clothing and tobacco— no one drinks—just I. They aren't temperance types. They hate the temperance people as much as the boozers. We are all living at home. Five boys and 6 girls. The eldest is 23 years old, the youngest 3 years. [15 ll.: inquiries about Paul's siblings, mother, other relatives] I don't want to have anything more to do with Mathes—self-interest is a thief. The sum of 60 dollars that I received for Brother Justus from the Hudsons Bay Co. I had to pay for twice. The first time in depreciated paper money, with which I was paid by the agent of the Hudsons Bay Co. The last time we settled it was deducted again in gold. Your mother and Zentner had nothing to do with the settlement and bear none of the blame. The matter is so insignificant that I wouldn't demand repayment even if I could get it immediately.[16] [6 ll.: details]

I have now written so much yet said perhaps so little and have perhaps forgotten what I should have said most, that I should perhaps now consider closing. [7 ll.: weather; closing]

Moorhead Minn., Dec. 13, 1890

My dear Paul,

[30 ll.: greetings; correspondence; he was working as a secretary of a mutual hail insurance company and was busy for two months with

[16]Probstfeld's brother Mathes was the heir to the farm; Justus died in 1863.

damage claims after a storm] Now I have not yet written you that I was nominated on July 22 by a newly formed party called the Farmers Alliance as *Senator* for the state senate—(for the State of Minnesota) and that as a result I had to join in the campaign. Since I didn't have the money to campaign by traveling, however, I was forced to carry it out by *Correspondence;* —since my eyes are not very useful even with glasses and my hand can no longer guide a pen like 30 years ago you can probably imagine what it meant for an old fool to write twenty to 25 and sometimes 30 letters daily—and nightly for 4 long weeks—until election day November 4th. My *Opponent* is a rich banker and the election cost him between $8,000 and $10,000—he tried to bribe his way into the senate (he got into the last session by such means). He started already on September 15th, was on the road every day and had helpers by the masses paid in hard cash. The senate district includes about 130 [sq.] German miles.

I only traveled around the area near my home on October 27th, 28th, 29th, 30th, came home October 31st, stayed home until Nov. 3rd and then went 27 miles (9 hours) and back again in one day around my home *County* (Clay) and the next day was the election.

All the stops along the railroad have saloons where people drink every day and where I expected to get beaten badly. My sons and daughters (my wife too) had their hearts so set on my expected victory that they were sitting on pins and needles in fear and expectation. When I came home on October 31st some people asked me—How's it going? Do you even have half a chance? etc. I told everyone that my election was certain, as far as anything in politics can be judged with any certainty ahead of time, but that my majority wouldn't amount to over 100 to 150 and could not surpass 200. Since at the saloons everyone was boozing it up a lot at my opponent's expense I knew how to figure out the results ahead of time and conceded ⅔ of the votes in Breckenridge, Moorhead Barnesville, Glyndon, Hawley and Detroit to my opponent. These places all lie along the railroad with telegraph connections. When the results from these places came in, you should have seen how disheartened my family was and what long faces they had—all were beside themselves. I said that all the news tallied with my estimates, that Hawly where I had conceded ⅔ only gave him ⅖ and so I had 40 votes more than I had expected—that they should just be patient until the news came in from the farmers' polling places—that was where my votes would come from. Nothing helped. They didn't believe me. Now all of this probably doesn't interest you much—I will just mention that I was elected with 350 more votes than I had estimated. Out of 5,100 votes I got over 2,800.[17] The cam-

[17] According to the official figures in *The Legislative Manual* (1891), Probstfield beat his Republican opponent by 2,812 to 2,308 votes.

paign costs amounted to about 95 dollars, 20 dollars of which you can count for postage—so only 75 dollars of travel costs and printing of ballots. The ballots alone cost 12½ dollars.

I have been elected for 4 years—the senate is in session from January to April, 90 days in 1891 and 1893.

The job is not worth any money—usually they are filled with money bags who make their money from cheating the populace. The pay is only $5 per day and many can't even make do with that—but I, my dear fellow, will just have to make do. [15 ll.: mail; is overwhelmed with correspondence]

My second daughter Cornelia (Nelly) got married on March 25th to a man named Charles B. Gesell and lives in La Crosse, Wisconsin, they have cigars, confections etc. My eldest son Alexander has been working since March 15th in East Grand Forks Minnesota as a bookkeeper and *Collector* in a brewery. Two daughters Amelia and Dora go to the *Normal* school in Moorhead. The eldest daughter Mary is learning dressmaking (ladies' dresses) in Moorhead. The third daughter Susanna Theresia lives at home and helps her mother. The second son Justus is here at home and oversees the farm work and <u>works</u> too. One son, the third, left on the 9th of this month to go to an *Academy* in Sauk Centre, 120 English miles from here in the direction of StPaul. He wanted to go to a polytechnic institute, since he wants to be trained as a machinist and electrical *Engineer,* but he couldn't find out where; so he is taking 13 weeks of private lessons at the *Academy* to improve his education since he neglected his schooling and also because of lack of money and opportunity. He was a machinist on a steam thresher and saved his money to pay for more training. If he had learned German I would almost be tempted to see if it wasn't possible to send him to the technical school in Zürich, Switzerland, but first he would have to spend a considerable amount of time learning German.

Times here are not the best, the harvest poor, prices low, only potatoes are high. [4 ll.: examples] Clothing and everything a farmer has to buy are very high by comparison. That is why the people have had their fill of electing rich big shots as legislators. [14 ll.: is in a hurry; correspondence; greetings, signature]

Dec. 14th

[18 ll.: had visitors all day Sunday: couldn't write] So, you were so little shy of Protestant <u>flesh</u> after all—I think it wasn't just your mother alone. Didn't love play a large part? I have little *Respect* for love which is abandoned for the sake of religion rather than let run its course. You shouldn't see this as a reproach—most marriages in the world, that I have seen, were marriages of *Convenienz,* for the sake of status or money—or because a girl simply has to have some man, or a boy a woman to mend, wash, cook for him etc.—and then finally the brute-marriages, to satisfy brutish lust. Ugh! At my age I am still too idealistic to make any further remarks about the disgusting common misuse of marriage. To this day I am still proud of myself that the dog-love, which attacks more or less every healthy young person, did not plague me much, and that I kept a tight rein on such passions. I believe I can ascribe much of my present vigor to this fact.

If I get out of my financial mess before I'm very old, you should not be surprised if I shake hands with you and yours some day! The last four years have been awful. [10 ll.: details] Our American national financial economy is just ideal for that, but the people are waking up, and soon if the ruling parties don't take quick and radical countermeasures you shouldn't be surprised to hear about bloody uprisings over here. But let's hope for the best, the worst comes by itself.

No, my children only know a little, or I guess I have to say speak almost no German, but they do understand some of everyday conversation. My oldest girl speaks enough to more or less get by, but understands more. Now almost all of them realize how foolish they were. They could just as well have learned German along with English, but they thought it was too hard to learn. The fact is, English is much easier—I call it Low German. The Low German–speaking Danes, Norwegians and Swedes learn it much easier than a South German. For the French it is very difficult.

I have strayed somewhat from my topic—my age is showing—yes and that I have to write German. — Don't you understand any English? It is often taught now in Germany, since your Kaiser's family has become so intertwined with the English Royal Family!

What I wanted to say was that instead of land—farmland—rising in value, it is falling. And why shouldn't it. If a man has say 2500 dollars invested in horses and machinery and cultivates 320 acres of land—which are supposed to be worth 3500 dollars without any buildings—so that's 7000 dollars, and slaves away with his whole family for a whole year to eke out a wretched existence—and ends up with debts and ragged clothing, worn out machinery, leaking roofs, old horses, broken window panes, run-down land and ruined *Credit*—how can the value of land increase? Thousands of acres have already returned to their original state, which 1, 2, 3, 4, and five years ago were good fields. The owners—many of whom I know—came here with 5000–8000–15000 dollars and some toiled away for 3 to 10 years and—today they are day laborers.

It's not quite that bad with us, we have saved, worked and worked some more, and if it weren't for our woods we would also be *Caput*, I also earn a few dollars that other farmers don't earn—buy nothing on *Credit* anymore—and we make old clothes into new ones as long as possible—or make one dress out of two—or a smaller one out of a bigger one, etc.

We have to get through this, even if it takes the skin off our backs. I have that reputation anyway—what Probstfield sets his mind on doing must be done, even if he dies in the process! It seems to me that I can see some daylight—but it will be so long so long until the sun is shining again—but some time after the longest night, comes the longest day.

Now, my dears, it is already late, 11 o'clock and my eyes are beginning to give out. [10 ll.: greetings; address]

St. Paul, February 20, 1891[18]

My dearest Paul and Mrs.,

I received your very welcome letter of January 3rd on the 24th, it went to Moorhead first and was forwarded from Moorhead to me here since I left my *Farm* already on December 28th and came to StPaul since on the 30th we had a big farmers meeting that lasted 5 days and was attended by 560 *Representanten* from all over the state. [9 ll.: salary as Senator barely covers costs] There are so many opportunities to waste money—theater, *Concerts,* saloons, *Museums* etc. etc. that it's not enough for many, especially for those who have never been here much. You can well imagine that the younger members—or many of them, go through every folly of the world as it is, and many a silly old ass too, since the human animal in general does not vary that much (whether here or in Europe). [7 ll.: at the hotel, noise from the streetcars keeps him awake] I am quite sick of the whole business here and would like to retire to the quiet of the countryside. But must stay.

[8 ll.: March 4, 1891, high cost of living; letter interrupted]
Sunday, March 8th [9 ll.: writing is tiring]

So you have gotten married? And already have a little one! Now that is a good boy! When the right two souls find their way to each other, it's fine—otherwise misery! I hope the two of you did things right—first got to know each other quite well, then got properly engaged and finally decently married, with a firm resolve, come what may, to be man and wife to each other in every sense of the word. I don't think much of the *Sacrement* business and the secular *hocus pocus*—or rather nothing at all—but it's a necessary evil in this world as long as there are people who need it in order to be satisfied. As long as people need shoes there will be shoemakers. [. . .]

Now don't be offended, I am what I am and can't change, nor perhaps

[18]Written on personalized letterhead from the state senate.

do I even want to be anything but—a man with a free-thinking independent spirit.

I just looked at the picture of your wife and the little one—it could be entitled Motherly Bliss!

Now, if you really liked the picture of our whole family and if I can get another one when I go home, I will bother you with it. Since I received your letter, or rather one day before, I and my wife became grandparents. Daughter <u>Nelly</u> who is married and lives in La Crosse Wisconsin had a little baby girl on January 23. [4 ll.: details] The poor thing suffered terribly from homesickness—something like that would never in my life have occurred to me—I had homesickness at home to get away. Of course one reason for that is the way I was treated, and the way I treat my children is a <u>stark</u> contrast.

I don't want to make any further comment about the unpleasant family situation in your old home except that I am very glad for you that you and your dear wife are so far away from the whole mess. I only feel sorry for your mother—she never had or saw any <u>good</u> times. When I think back on the 47 years I still boil with rage—But let the dead rest!

Since you wrote so much to me about your high prices I must do the same to you. [15 ll.: prices]

If *economic* political conditions were what they ought to be according to concepts of social philosophy, there would be an abundance of everything here and everyone would be rich. But we have more millionaires and more poor people than any country in the world—in the big cities. But that's enough now about this mess.

May I flatter myself that in the year 1893 you might be able to attend the Columbian Exhibition in Chicago? The government ought to give you special leave and pay your travel costs to come here as a teacher so you can take in what there is to take in here. I cannot presume to assert that the Germans could learn anything from American architects or vice versa since I am not in a position to have an expert opinion on this, but in my humble opinion there is no doubt that both could profit from an exchange. If I had known two years ago what I know now, I would have spared no effort and persuasion to convince you to come at least for a study tour of Chicago, StPaul and Minneapolis; since here even a bungler can get the miserable wage your professorship pays if times are good for building, without having any of the expert knowledge that you have to have to keep your position. But one thing is in your favor—because the salary is miserable—the job is not precarious—Your income, small as it is, comes in whether it rains or shines.

It cannot cost that much—to make the trip, but you might not be able to get away from your dear family for so long.

You wanted to know what a *Normal* school is. It is a school which takes the place of the *Lehrer seminar* in Germany and provides practical training of schoolteachers for the country. Minnesota has 4 of them and I returned to Moorhead on February 24 from a tour as member of the *Committé* to inspect the normal schools in the state. [6 ll.: details]

My dear fellow I must suddenly close, my eyes are about <u>worn out</u>. [11 ll.: cannot write any more; closing]

Moorhead Minn. U.S.A., January 1, 1892

My dear Paul,

[29 ll.: New Year's; time to make resolutions about keeping up correspondence; wonders why Paul hasn't written] Soon I'll also be sending you the picture you asked for. [10 ll.: details; weather]

I just cannot understand why we are getting so little for our grain this year here—from 25 to 30 cents—or one mark to 1 mark 20 pfennigs less than last year *per* bushel of 60 pounds for wheat. From that you would have to conclude that the wheat in Europe should also be cheaper than last year. But is this the case? It is well known that there is a great trade conspiracy against the producers that can lead to a great open rebellion soon. The political ferment is at its peak. I doubt that another revolution on the scale of the French one in 1789 can happen again, since everyone has voting rights, and as soon as the opposing elements can unite the whole wretched business will stop, but up until now special interests have kept the opposition groups from getting together. I would really like to have a weekly paper which reports the actual prices of *Farm* products. A newspaper from a German port city, Hamburg, Bremen or Lübeck would be the best. Inland prices are probably higher than at a port.

What is the price of wheat—the market price that the farmers receive *per* 60 [lbs.]. [8 ll.: conversion of weights and measures]

In my current position as state senator I, old fool that I am, have to try again to scrape off my rust, which at my age, turning sixty, is not exactly very easy to do. — But I don't need to worry as long as there are so many in the Senate who have never known or learned what I have forgotten.

If you want, I will send you a German weekly paper from StPaul—the owner, Carl Lienau is also in the state senate, but we are not political friends.[19] He represents the interests of the money men, bankers, wholesale traders, lawyers, in general the classes that have the others by the

---

[19]According to CD St. Paul 1893, Lienau was the president and managing editor of the *Volkszeitung*. Originally he was a Democrat. The paper favored the Democratic party from 1877 to 1882 and later became independent (Arndt/Olson [1965], 229–31).

throat. I represent those who are being choked—and have to fight with the disadvantage that at the moment the means of defense are in the hands of the rich.

History seems to repeat itself endlessly. The present trends are like those of ancient Rome. The more luxury there is, the more poverty, the middle class is gradually disappearing. [29 ll.: then who will defend the republic?; wheat prices; sale of wood]

I forgot to ask earlier what the duty is now on wheat imports into Germany. I believe it was one cent a pound—but I hear it's been cut 40 percent, is this true?

[6 ll.: after midnight, still has several letters to write] After I have written a long letter in German it takes me a long time to write, my hands and fingers are all cramped since it is a tremendous effort for me. I write about 12 to 15 letters in German every year—mostly to a cousin Mrs. Shugart in Marinette Wisconsin, née Eggener, from Münstermayfeld, the daughter of your grandfather Probstfeld's sister, who came to America about the year 1843. I wrote her a letter just today, too. [. . .]

So, how are my dear ones doing—and what does little Pauline say? Wait, I believe there is another little one—I'm right, but the name escapes me. — I would very much like to write something—in a serious vein—about the business of the Holy Garment. I received a letter from Kalt from Frau Fuhrmann—half of it was Holy Garment.[20] But I don't want to offend the feelings of my dear niece Frau Saurborn. It wouldn't do any good anyway—so why bother? [6 ll.: wishes, greetings, signature]

Moorhead Minn. May 17th, 1892[21]

[34 ll.: ill for three weeks, then away on a trip; work in the fields delayed]

The newspapers come regularly as you send them, but I can't get the prices and measures into my thick old skull, despite your explanation. As I understand it one kilogram is a bit more than 2 pounds, — or 100 kilo about 202½ [lbs.][22] — is that right? [. . .] How many bushels are in 1000 kilograms? Or 1000 kilograms are how many bushels? I learned all of that in my youth, also the metric system, but since back when I was in Germany and the whole time I've been here it's never been in practical use, I haven't the foggiest idea about all of this, although I believe that it is so far the best and most convenient system for quick calculations and easy comprehensibility—once understood—and I hope that it will become the system for the whole world. [. . .]

[20]See Chapter 5, n. 22.

[21]Written on Minnesota State Senate stationery.

[22]Incorrectly converted; instead of 202.5 it should be 220.5. Since he underestimates the German measure, he overestimates the price and thus the profit margin.

[14 ll.: amount of wheat planted drastically reduced, but wheat prices still remain low] Today 69 cents for 1 *bushel* N<u>o</u> 1 *Northern* or 2 marks 72 pfennigs, or as I figure it 89.67 marks *per* 1000 kilograms. We farmers cannot figure out where the fraud is. We know the transport costs but the cost of what is stolen, that will remain a secret of the American-European *Combination*.[23]

[11 ll.: has his wheat in storage, thus no money at the moment to send newspaper] You may stop sending newspapers, except for one or two *per* week, since during the summer I don't have nearly enough time to read all the German papers along with the English ones. From June 1 to the first of October I have my hands full as Secretary of our hail insurance which I founded in 1887 (Mutual Insurance)—All in all more demands are being made on me in my old age than I can do justice to, so in the face of what must seem to you to be negligence on my part I ask you mercifully to forgive me. You have certainly not been forgotten intentionally, believe me, for I am only too happy to hear from you now and then.

Have just enjoyed a glass of beer, which what with all this pouring rain gives me time and the <u>strength</u> to keep on scribbling—hope you can read it.

I just *überlaas* (or *laß* [read over] I don't know the *Conjugation* any more)[24] your letter of February 28, and don't want to mention anything about family matters, it is not easy to interfere the right way in things one perhaps only half understands or interprets correctly. Just one thing I want to mention. That is—if a brother or a sister—when there are as many as there were of us and of you—were to receive the full value from the others for the home place or the old house, it would really ruin the buyer financially with such small property as each would get. [30 ll.: argued when his inheritance was divided in favor of small settlements, but the heir to the farm, his brother Matthias, only repaid him with ingratitude] — I am very glad that I am out of that family feud. With my wife's inheritance it was ten times worse. [16 ll.: details, cheated out of $600] — If I knew that my own children would be guilty of committing a similar crime after my death my grey hair would turn red with anger and vexation.

I am reading along and find that you also once wished to go abroad but did not do so because of mother's tears, since your grandmother's tears softened you up. This does all honor to your heart, but, my dear Paul, if everybody felt that way—where would the world's progress have come

---

[23]By using incorrect formulas to convert kilos and marks, Probstfeld underestimates the costs of his grain in German measures and German currency by 16 percent; this covers at least a part of the "fraud." Exchange rates are taken from Pick/Sedillot (1971), 110, 323.

[24]Ironically, both of these are wrong. The correct form is *überlas*.

from? [7 ll: philosophizes] Neither you nor I can foretell whether you would have been happier or unhappier, dead or alive, if you had emigrated, but I believe that with your training and the thrifty and industrious nature you were either born with or have acquired yourself, emigration to a new country—whether Africa, America or Australia, would have gotten you further in terms of money and status than in Germany where the competition is so extraordinary. Now one must take comfort in the old proverb about muddling through. Every profession has its pleasures, and each one has its own hard lot. Enjoy that which you are granted, *gladly* do without what you have not. This is very convenient for Church and State. For sluggards and Philistines, but without the least hint of progress. [78 ll.: philosophizes; family quarrel thirty years earlier—did not take revenge; extreme climate; family; greetings]

Moorhead Minn. November 22nd, 1892[25]

My dear Paul,
[19 ll.: correspondence; thanks for newspapers; market reports prove farmers have been swindled] And this is the reason for the deep roots of our political movement. That it also tends toward socialism cannot be denied. The farmer's nature is not attracted to socialism or to any extreme position—he is too stupid to think far enough ahead, but in the last 10 years an enormous change has taken place. The thirst for knowledge is now on the rise. It is impossible to discuss the whole movement here in one letter. [20 ll.: promises to send newspapers about the Chicago Exhibition; can't afford to visit Germany with his family]

The harvest this year was much worse than in 1891, in all the states of the U.A. [United States] and yet the prices are only ¾ of what they were in 1891—perhaps it is because of an excellent harvest in Europe. How is it? Even though wheat is cheap—flour is high. [2 ll.: prices]

There are still people, however, going without bread who are too poor to buy it. They shout "overproduction" at the farmer when he complains about prices, the breadless shout back "underconsumption!" No comment needed. But it does seem strange to me that when the granaries burst from overloading, when heaps of stored clothing are being eaten up by moths, —there are so many hungry and naked even here in America. There's a screw loose somewhere—no doubt about it. But who is the mechanic who knows which one? And if he knew it—who would believe him? And if one were to be believed, would those who are living in the lap of luxury under present conditions help bring about any change?

[25]Written on stationery of his son, E. H. Probstfield (Figure 16).

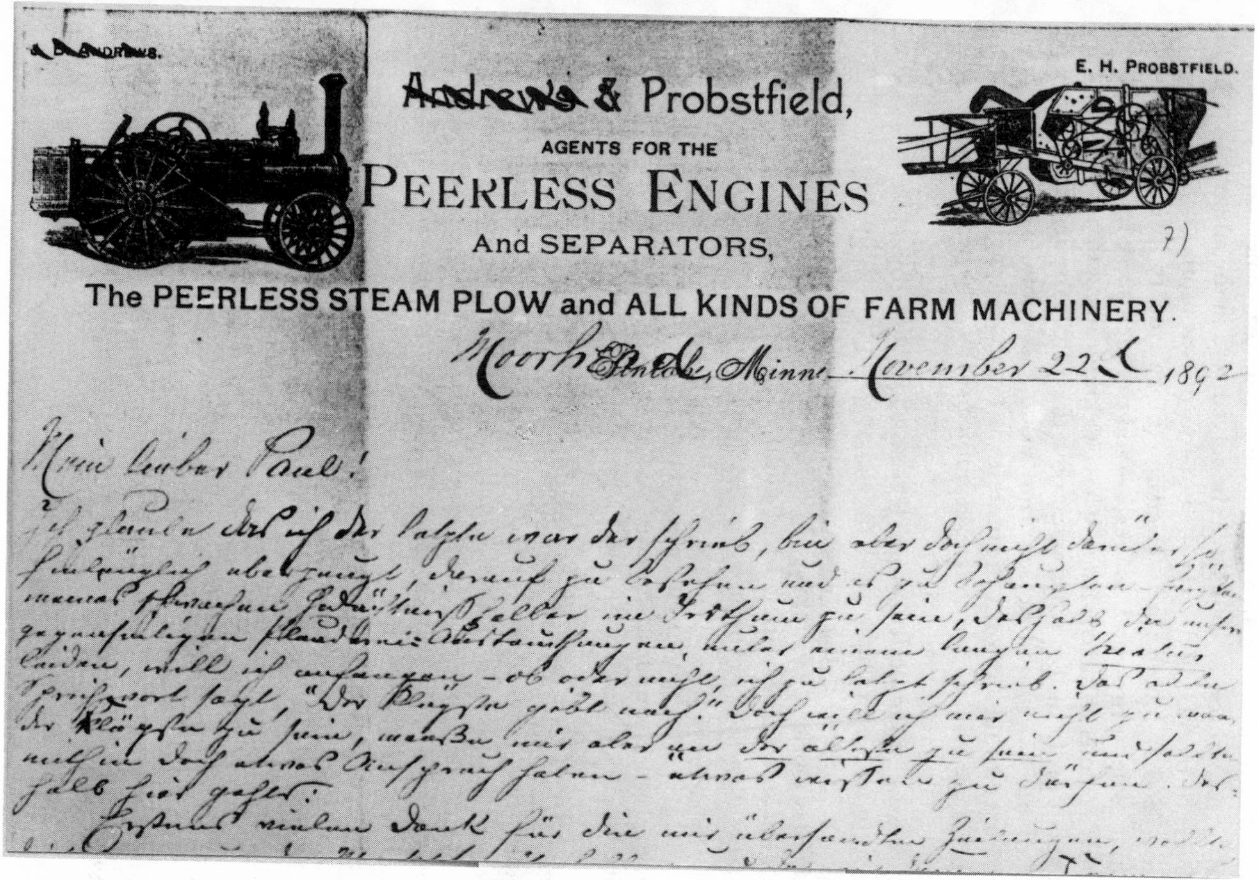
A. D. ANDREWS. E. H. PROBSTFIELD.

~~Andrews~~ & Probstfield,

AGENTS FOR THE

PEERLESS ENGINES

And SEPARATORS,

The PEERLESS STEAM PLOW and ALL KINDS OF FARM MACHINERY.

Moorhead, Minne. November 22 1892

Mein lieber Paul!

Figure 16. Letter of November 22, 1892, on letterhead of E. H. Probstfield, farm machinery agent.

unless they could then live in even _more_ luxury. The social welfare question is loathsome—will _never_ be solved, and in the attempt to solve it, rivers of blood will flow in the not-too-distant future.

Nov. 26th— [44 ll.: was interrupted; armaments race in Europe; weather, sale of firewood, wages] —You can well see why—since you are half a farmer as far as what you have to know about things—to figure out about _profit_ or _loss_ when you know the factors, wages, food prices, cost of machinery and horses, land value and debts on it, taxes and perhaps taxes in the form of interest on borrowed capital, which can never be gotten here for under $7/100$ but is usually $10/100$ here _per_ year, and then the _Net_ profit realized on the products.

According to my calculations, it costs $7 _per acre_ of wheat—to get the wheat to market. [8 ll.: with all the steps in the process, but not counting taxes or interest] If the average yield was 11⅕ bushels and if we take yesterday's price of 54 cents per bushel (for the best wheat) the average state income [in Minnesota] for wheat is $6.04⁴/10 or a straight loss of 95⁶/10 cents _per acre_. Here in our _County_ there are more farmers who had yields of less than 10 bushels _per acre_ than there are who had more. [3 ll.: details] The average on our whole farm is 15½ bushels on 193 acres of wheat. [17 ll.: similar calculation for barley]

In the cotton states it is supposed to be even worse. I can't resist telling a small anecdote—a true one. [144 ll.: Friedrich, a hard-working young German, bought a farm for $2000 in cash, took out a mortgage for implements. After six years of bad harvests, the farm was auctioned off at the courthouse door. His Irish farmhand, who had always been faithfully paid, took out a mortgage and bought the farm and then gave Friedrich a job as a farmhand. Six years later Friedrich then got his land back—the same way he had lost it.]

Please excuse this little _story_—it describes the plight of the farmers much better than page-long _essay's_.

Now we are all hale, hearty and happy enough, but we still cannot pay off any of our mortgages. I held on to the entire wheat crop of 1891 until the spring and summer, lost money on it. I'm now holding on to the 1892 crop—and—may win or lose— You have to keep calm, whether you fall on your face, whether profit is your fair grace, the world keeps on spinning, couldn't care less about your winning. All will be fine when life comes to its conclusion—but perhaps it is only the merest illusion! [5 ll.: closing, greetings, signature]

St. Paul, Minn. February 10th, 1893
[20 ll.: letters; family; senate is in session again; trip to visit his daughter] I think within the next 10 days the entire legislature is going to

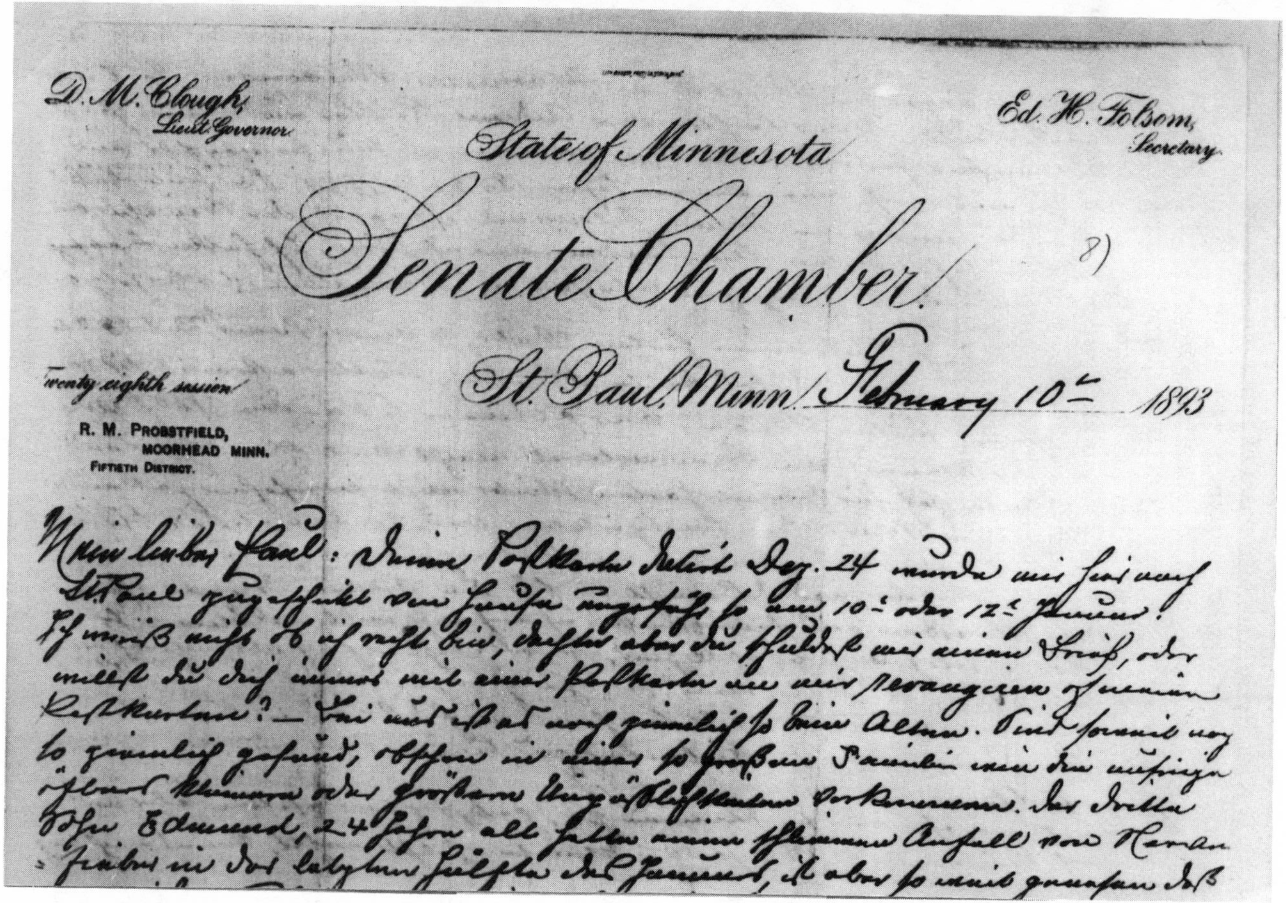
D. M. Clough,
Lieut. Governor

Ed. H. Folsom,
Secretary

State of Minnesota

Senate Chamber.

8)

twenty eighth session

R. M. Probstfield,
Moorhead Minn.
Fiftieth District.

St. Paul, Minn. February 10th 1893

Figure 17. Letter of February 10, 1893, on Probstfield's personal letterhead as state senator.

Chicago to dedicate—so to speak—the Minnesota state exhibition buildings. It is a totally superfluous waste of time, but there aren't enough
members opposed to it to prevent it. Minnesota has appropriated
$150,000 (750,000 marks) for the exhibition—which I call an unforgiv-
able waste. I agreed to $50,000 (250,000 marks) and voted against the
large sum, which went through with a slim majority.

[25 ll.: cousin has died; family situation; weather; weights and measures; belated New Year's greetings] I am still getting along as slowly as
my age permits. I still think, though, that I am more vigorous in my old
age than most people my age. It's nothing for me to walk 5 to 10 miles *per*
day, I could still walk from Kalt to Koblenz and back in a day, which must
be about 22 miles—crossing the Mosel at Dieblich and then turning
down at the Karthause. But I have a terrible time digging potatoes,
chopping wood and picking up and carrying sacks, even though I still
want to help. On the Red River we have from 2½ to 4 feet of snow,
haven't had so much since 1862. We are expecting high water in the
spring.

[12 ll.: no one writes anymore; closing; promises to send photograph]

Moorhead Minn., June 22nd, 1893[26]
My dear Paul: I received your valued and welcome letter of the 6th of this
month. [32 ll.: has sent relatives free books about the units from Minnesota that fought in the Civil War, which include the names of his
deceased brothers]

I received your letter of April 19 on May 10th, just at the time when
we starting planting after the most terrible winter "with regard to the
weather" that I have ever seen in my life. Since my 3 oldest sons are all
gone and since the farming business is such that I can't pay any hired
hands, at the age of 61 I have started following the horses in the fields
again. [4 ll.: prices, harvest prospects poor again] And so that we don't
get any further into debt than we already are I will have to limber up my
old bones again. [16 ll.: the three eldest sons are employed elsewhere]
None of them ever wants to have a *Farm*. The two young ones, Walter
turned 16 last March and Arthur will be 14 next July, help as much as they
can, but when it comes to haying and harvesting I have to hire some
people and can expect to pay 1.50 to 2 dollars *per* day with board. I still
can, when it <u>has</u> to be, walk behind the horses all day long, but I can't do
the hard work any more. I can still pick up and carry 1, 2, 3 sacks of wheat
(120 [lbs.]) but then my wind runs out. Your aunt, even though she is 7
years younger than me, isn't any better. No wonder, always working

[26]This and the previous letter were written on personalized letterhead from the state senate.

hard, even today, and having brought up 11 children and given birth to 13! Farming conditions here are wretched. [8 ll.: no improvement in sight]

You asked me for a collection of *"Columbian Exposition"* stamps, but nothing has been done about it yet, but one of my girls is going to put a collection together, I can't since I don't even know where my own head is at times. [8 ll.: intellectual effort even harder than physical work] —I would never dream of going to the *Columbian Exhibition*. I wouldn't be able to stand the noise even if my "cash" finances permitted. I can easily go without! It only makes me mad that I couldn't go if I wanted! Only the louts who skin the farmers can go, the ones who get skinned have to stay at home.[27]

Enclosed is a plan with all the names and ages of everyone in the family picture. [5 ll.: details]

I have neither the time nor the patience to come up with a lengthy response to your description of agricultural conditions in Germany, but it does seem to me as if the United States is in about the same situation as in Italy during the ancient Roman Empire at the time of the Grachi, with the one difference that the outward symptoms are different, due to the fact that education levels and the transportation situation have changed as a result of great inventions. I fear that Germany will also be up against hard times in the immediate future in terms of politics. Of course I have only an imperfect grasp of your present social conditions, but it seems to me that the Emperor's drive to carry out his plans for the army even without the approval of the Parliament is very dangerous, if it were only Prussia alone it might be all right, but it seems dangerous to me that he is isolating himself from the rest of Germany, and if bayonets have to keep the other German states in line, what will come of "united"? Germany in case of a hostile attack by the Russians or the French—or both together? Prey to the Russian bear and the French *Turko* spirit!

I shouldn't get too upset about Germany, since every day here we too are faced with questions which cause grave doubt as to their proper solution. The question of social welfare is "the question"—not only here but for all the so-called civilized peoples all over the world. [10 ll.: must close and get to work; signature]

Moorhead Minn. January 20, 1894[28]

My dear Paul,

I received your message of sorrow, dated Oct. 30 on Nov. 11th. [16 ll.:

[27]Probstfeld won a special award at the exhibition for his Saskatchewan wheat yield of 36 bushels per acre. The certificate is in the possession of his granddaughters, June Dobervich and Evelyn Gesell, of Fargo, North Dakota.
[28]Written on personalized letterhead from the state senate.

Paul Sauerborn's mother died in poverty, after relatives had taken possession of her assets]

Dear Paul, you can't know everything, I, too, was only 12 years only
when your mother married—but old enough to know how things stood,
and that your grandparents committed a genuine crime—in my eyes—
against your mother. I still remember the situation exactly—that she
would have been thrown out of her parents' home forever if she had
refused to marry. I can still vividly remember the bitter quarrels and the
many tears your mother shed before she agreed to sacrifice herself—all
for nothing but Mammon. I can't say a word against your father, we were
always good friends—he and I, and he always preferred me to my other
brothers. But he also should have had enough understanding to have
refused that sacrifice. My hair still stands up on end when I think back on
the day the wedding was celebrated in Kalt. Paul wanted to shoot himself,
and the cook, from Polch, an old woman and one of our relatives risked
her own life to take the gun out of his hand. I also turned into a lion and as
a 12-year-old boy, slung thundering oaths at my father and mother,
accused them of pimping and selling body and soul, I expected to be
beaten terribly for this and when I was threatened—I shouted in their
faces that I would be willing to be ripped into shreds if I could only undo
what had been done and make sure it stayed that way. [3 ll.: details] I was
not punished for my outbreak of rage. But your grandparents were
punished by—pangs of conscience, and your grandmother often cried
about this parental cruelty. Enough of this scene. [6 ll.: Paul's mother was
always his favorite sister]

Dear Paul, if I am not blind as a father, if my prejudices don't mislead
me, then a comparison of my children to many others makes me endlessly happy. Up to now I have not had any trouble with them. The
daughter who is married, married the man who asked for her hand, he
wasn't my choice, I never would have chosen him, but I couldn't get
your mother's fate out of my mind. None of my children will be "forced
onto or apart from" anyone. The only freedom I permit myself with
regard to marriage—if I am asked—is to speak my sincere opinion and
judgment about it, without threat, dis- or persuasion. And if all my
children are able to spend such happy years in marriage as I have spent
with my wife, I will be heartily pleased and satisfied with them.

Am I now the only one still alive or am I not? [8 ll.: brothers and sisters
all died young; his friend Loehr no longer writes]

The financial conditions here are now worse than even the oldest man
alive remembers—that is the general consensus. There is hardly any
money left in circulation. The unemployment, poverty and hunger are
great, and if that is <u>not</u> proof that the financial system is wrong—

granaries, meat storehouses, clothing stores are full to bursting—and thousands of people—without bread, skimpily covered with rags and— no work. Fear in the cities has grown so intense that people vie with one another to feed soup to the hungry. Great is our civilization under the Jew Rothschild's bank and financial system—which also rules all of Europe. In fear and trembling, everyone expects to face bloody uprisings. [11 ll.: livestock prices]

It would take a book to describe conditions here to you. From the newspapers you can't tell much, especially the papers from the larger cities, like the *Volkszeitung*. You have seen how a man named Albert Wolf, one of the most distinguished Germans in StPaul—for many years editor of the *Volkszeitung*[29] and a close friend of mine, committed suicide last October by throwing himself under the wheels of a locomotive, he was dead on the spot. It was out of poverty and in order to protect his wife from want that he took this desperate step, so she could have the $5000 in life insurance. Now bank after bank is going bankrupt, business firms, factories, fire and life insurance companies, all in all every kind of business without exception. The farmer disappears from the stage of life most silently of all; no bankruptcy trials there, no settling with creditors for 25, 30, or 50 percent. Just the mortgage and that is cancelled just like blowing out a candle, then just as silently with his family he falls into the city to enlarge the army of the proletariat. I always thought things would erupt first in Europe, but now I think that we could be facing it here even sooner! [17 ll.: prices] It is pitiful!

There is much talk about electing me again to the new legislature next November, but I don't know yet whether I want to campaign or not. The way politics are conducted here or anywhere else makes me sick.

If I have not covered everything you wanted to know, you will have to refresh my memory in your next letter. It is getting too dark now. I can't write by lamplight. [12 ll.: health; greetings; signature]

Moorhead, Minn. June 8, 1895

My dear Paul,

[8 ll.: letter delayed] I found your letter very interesting, especially because of the descriptions of your excursions to various places. I have, of course, only seen little of Germany, although I was in Hamburg for a week on my trip back to Germany in September 1860 and again for some

---

[29]Wolff (b. 1825) studied theology in Göttingen, took part in the Dresden uprising in 1849 and was sentenced to ten years in prison. Pardoned in 1852, he came to St. Paul, Minnesota, and worked for the *Volkszeitung,* which he edited from 1877 to 1895. He was also a Minnesota state legislator and immigration commissioner (Zucker [1967b], 355–56; Arndt/Olson, 231).

days on my return trip to America. [6 ll.: details] Here in America I traveled quite a bit before my marriage, since then, however, only in Minnesota, Wisconsin and Dakota. Many years ago I planned to come back to Germany again, but after I suffered the unfortunate loss of $8000 in January 1884 and the bad times since, I have been forced to give up this idea and at the moment there is also no chance that I could reconsider this plan, even though it doesn't cost as much now as it did 10 or 12 years ago. One time I could have gotten a free ticket (9 years ago) home and back here, with no strings attached. I knew that I would be expected, while in Europe, to speak well of Minnesota and Dakota, to encourage people to immigrate to here so that the railroad companies could sell their land to the immigrants. I did not accept the ticket because I lacked the means to cover adequately the additional traveling costs. This money, too, I could have gotten, *circa* 300 dollars, if I had acted as an official agent. But I won't serve as anybody's shoeshine boy.

Even today my heart still grows heavy when I let an overview of my family's suffering under the past circumstances of the last 11 years parade through my memory. They did not, of course, suffer from hunger, we were not that poor, but a thousand privations, and what makes me the most bitter yet today, the inability to enjoy what I would consider sufficient higher education. You mustn't think, though, that they only had common schooling in an ordinary village school like there were in my youth in Germany. Only the three youngest are wanting. One son, Walter, 18 years old, one, Arthur, 15 years, and one daughter, Josephine, 12 years.

My affairs are now in somewhat better order. We still owe $2035— roughly 8000 marks; but in order to get even this far I sold 320 acres of land for a ridiculously low price, since I couldn't stand my wife's anguish any longer. Since then she has been calmer and more content. We have here where we live *circa* 470 acres, 240 of farmland and 230 of woods and meadows or hay fields which are still mortgaged for 835 dollars. [9 ll.: bad times] I cannot adequately describe the economic situation here in a letter, and if you think you are reading the truth about current conditions in the StPaul *Volkszeitung* then you are terribly mistaken. The American press is a hireling of the stinking rich, and many a poor devil of an *Editor* thinks exactly the opposite of what he writes, and the *Editor* of the *Volkszeitung* is stinking rich and a *Corruptionist*. I know that he bribed two Senators in the 1893 session in order to get a bill passed that put money into his own pocket. I foiled several of his plans in the senate and even though we were on friendly terms for almost 40 years this turned him into a bitter enemy. He knows well that I am on the side of honesty and is now trying to get back in with me, even if I let him, I have lost all respect for him like for every giver or receiver of bribes.

As soon as I can, I will send you another newspaper from Milwaukee Wis. and cancel this <u>profiteer</u> paper.

Since last fall I have been having a hard battle off and on with gout, just like your grandfather Probstfeld. It often took the pleasure out of life. The doctors recommended I take an ocean voyage!! Ocean voyage! — Prescribe to a millionaire for his illness—poverty—and it would be easier to get the medicine for him than a voyage for me.

[19 ll.: health; hardly any mail from Germany] My brother's widow who lives in Verona Missouri wrote me recently. She wrote me before my brother died, I should please write a letter to her so she could read it to her husband, that it seemed there was something between us and that he could not die in peace before I forgave him. My letter arrived and was read aloud to him, and she wrote me that even though he could not speak and also seemed as if he had completely lost his mind, he quieted down and died, if I remember correctly, 10 or 12 days later. I do not know the woman, I've never seen her, nor do I know her family who used to live in Wisconsin. Her father died in Wis. at the end of June 1894. They seem to be of modest circumstances, she seems satisfied with her designated fate in this world.

[8 ll.: family; greetings; signature]

I wish you could read English, I would write more often. My hand is so cramped that I must stop, but I wasn't even nearly finished.

Moorhead, Minn. Jan. 17, 1898 / U.S. America

My dear Paul

[97 ll.: correspondence; nominated by the Populists against his will in 1894 and 1896; beaten by 11 and 35 votes, most probably by election fraud; will take part in next campaign but not as a candidate]

The agricultural conditions have still not improved, if anything worsened since my last letters. [14 ll.: details]

Currency exchange rates and weights you know. 4 marks is almost exactly one dollar. Our pounds are the same as your old pounds.

1 bushel wheat 60 [lbs.] here in Moorhead from 76 to 78 cts. [46 ll.: farm and food prices]

Walking plow; iron plowshare 14 inch	[$] 12.00
[5 ll.: more prices]	
Potato planting machine	——————— 65.00
Potato digging "	80 to 120.00
Mowing machine	from 38.00 to 55.00
Self-binding reaper	100.00 to 135.00

This will give more or less of an overview. That you usually buy our

American machines, sewing machines, and others included for less than we pay here is a well-known fact here, a natural intention of protective tariffs. But where does the farmer's protection come from? [12 ll.: protective tariffs just hinder their exports] This is a question that is inexhaustible but which has more than just two sides to it, and the more sides, the more the populace can be led around by the nose. [27 ll.: details and sociopolitical reflections; Sauerborn's children]

I can well believe that you will like it better in Barmen than in Buxtehude or Nienburg, but it must be a noisy place what with all the factories; perhaps you'll like it better, I certainly wouldn't.[30] I was always happier in the country than in a city, if that hadn't been the case, I wouldn't have become a *Farmer,* and either be in much better financial circumstances or, as they say in Berlin, "*gar nisch*" [nothing at all]. Civil public servants who can be transferred from one place to another and can't expect anything else, and even if every transfer means financial betterment, can only understand the full value and full sense of what the word *Heim* [home] really means only in the indirect and weakened sense of "*Heimath*" [homeland]. But he who feels at home no matter where he is, whether by choice or by accident or necessity, is perhaps the happiest of all, or at least of a more philosophical bent.

[20 ll.: has given up all hopes of a trip to Europe or a visit from Paul; has not answered letters from relatives because writing German is too strenuous] I don't even write one letter *per* year on the average, except when I write to Germany and when I want to read a German newspaper now and then it seems to me that the language has changed considerably in the last 45 years. And when I read a newspaper that is spelled in German-American, in completely Germanized English, I toss it to the side right away. It seems to me to be the product of a bungler, although I may be wrong. What do you think of garbled drivel like this: *Zwei Gambler und ein Saloonkeeper geriethen in Streit, sie waren boosy und wurden durch den Constabler in den Calabooce gebracht"* [Two gamblers and a saloonkeeper got into a fight, they were boozy and were put in the calaboose by the constable]. It's enough to make you want to faint.

[13 ll.: health; family] Yesterday morning a young man asked me for the hand of my third daughter, Susie—26 years old. He has a butcher's shop in Moorhead. My oldest daughter Maria and my oldest son Alexander are still unmarried and living at home. My second son is in West Superior Wisconsin and was married on Dec. 23rd, was here with his wife from Dec. 24th to Dec. 30th for a visit. Dora is a schoolteacher in

[30]After studying and completing his doctorate in Berlin and Hanover, Sauerborn moved to Nienburg on the Weser in 1890, to Buxtehude in 1894, and after 1897 taught at the Royal School of Architecture in Barmen (Sauerborn family chronicle).

Sheldon North Dakota. Millie, also a teacher, is at home without a job at the moment. Walter 20 years old and Arthur 18 years and Josephine 14 years live at home, all in good health and I may truly say, well-behaved. Edmund is in Moorhead and Fargo in the business of selling threshing machines.

Getting dark, I'm tired. Don't be angry. I will write again, will hope to be better about it. Warmest greetings from all of us to you and your dear family

Your R. M. Probstfield

Moorhead Minn. / January 17, 1900
1 o'clock in the morning

My dear Paul,

Today it has been two years since I last wrote to you. [29 ll.: has heard nothing since then; death of his wife on December 18, three weeks after she had a stroke]

What was particularly unfortunate for us is the fact that she died in StPaul. I and five children were at home, on the farm, 246 miles away. [. . .] One daughter is lying and was lying at that time in the hospital in St. Paul, hopelessly ill with a cancerous tumor in the *intestines (kleinern Därmen)*, and that was why my wife was in StPaul to be with her. [16. ll.: details; funeral]

I will not bother you here with the pain and the thoughts that fill me. Today it's been 30 days since she died, but my nerves are so shaken that I can hardly sleep any more.

On top of it the fact that my poor daughter is lying in the hospital, hopelessly ill—she may have one month to live and any day now may be her last. [14 ll.: since she still hopes she will get well, he feels forced to lie to her about her illness and the death of her mother] My domestic bliss is over and my life's purpose has become a mockery now.

The cost of all this is also terrible. If I had the money it wouldn't hurt me, but we are being plunged deeply into debt again and even though we know it won't spare the poor child even one minute of her pain. The doctors have already received 450 dollars and since January 1 the bills keep coming in. [3 ll.: details] All together $54 every week. I would be happy to keep on paying for a year, though, if it could only help my daughter. [. . .]

My health is very good for my age if it only weren't for my present nervousness. Maybe it would get better if I could just forget.

All of the others are healthy, but they are all taking their loss very much to heart, and what for? We certainly have no more right to be better treated by fate than anybody else. We all have to die at our appointed time, why be so unreasonable? Weakness! I once thought that as a philosopher I was a successful Stoic. I am like a small weak child. *Theory* is one thing, but fact, *Factum,* is another.

It almost makes me a bit angry that I have scribbled so much down here, since it is so uncertain whether you will ever receive or see it. You must excuse the poor writing since this is only the second German letter I've attempted in the last 1½ years and I don't get enough practice.

With the best wishes for you and your dear wife and children / I remain your only / still living Uncle
R. M. Probstfield

Moorhead, Minn. June 26, 1900
My dear Paul,

I received your <u>reminder</u> card without date at the beginning of this month and although I must confess to negligence, it was not for this reason alone that I have been silent for so long.

My nervous system is so destroyed that it is impossible for me to write when anyone else is around, especially if it has to be in German. [11 ll.: details]

I take comfort in my work, if not comfort then distraction, which takes my mind off my bitter loss. [9 ll. reflections on the pain of his wife's death]

My daughter Dora (Dorothea) died on March 26th and up until the last quarter hour she never let on that she thought she would have to die. Her sister Emilia stayed in StPaul until Dora died, her brother Edmund was also with her the last five weeks. [24 ll.: details]

I could not attend the funeral. My heart was broken since I had not yet recovered from my first loss, but despite everything I was glad that she was delivered from her terrible suffering for all time. [5 ll.: health]

We were almost out of debt last fall but this disaster that has hit us has plunged us again into deep debt, over 2200 dollars (about 8800 marks) and on top of it we have a very hard year ahead of us. We have no crops. On the 1st of May everything was still fine, under normal circumstances we could have expected to harvest 4000 bushels of wheat. Today we don't even expect to get back the seed grain. [7 ll.: drought] The horses must be kept for work next year, but what can we feed them. I am still, despite everything, better off than many others since we have a piece of land that we usually don't mow, it is wet and I didn't want to have it drained just because I can always mow it any year when it has to be <u>good enough</u> for us—coarse hay but better than none. It yields about twenty tons (at 2000 [lbs.]). We need 75 tons if we don't have any straw like this year. [31 ll.: weather, harvest prospects; speculators on bankrupt farms are getting rich off the poverty of others] I know several men who started off with a couple thousand dollars and were millionaires in 10 to 15 years. Although they were despised at the beginning—the money brought them *Respect* and esteem in the end—at least on the surface! Next generation, society has forgotten how they made their money.

I thank you very much for your last kind letter. I do not want to talk here about the situation of your family, your parents and your brothers and sisters as well as mine at home when I was still young—In my parents' house it wasn't quite as bad as in yours but not much better either. [7 ll.: thoughts about Paul's mother's marriage] The pity that I had for your mother then and afterwards still brings me to tears. What I learned and saw in my early youth is still much more vivid and clear in my memory than facts from 10 years ago. I would very much like to forget the evil along with the good, if only I could.

During the last 10 years I have often thought of coming back again to Europe but all present prospects of doing this are hopeless. If my health continues to be as good as the last 4 years, and if I get back out of debt, the farm will be sold so everyone can have his share, and then I might actually come; I can't promise myself much pleasure from seeing my relatives since so few that I knew or knew me are still alive. You are the only one with whom I still have direct contact and I can't help thinking about you and your family 20 times when I think back on Germany for every one time that I think about anyone else. Therese always used to write me nice long letters, I wrote the last one—she suddenly stopped. Anna never wrote me and since she had such great misfortune I couldn't expect her to. Sorrow and distress kill the desire to write. [5 ll.: relatives]

I would like to promise you that I will not allow our correspondence to falter like in the past—"the spirit is willing but the flesh is weak." But my will to improve is most sincere. It is getting dark, my hand is cramping. Give my best and warmest regards to my little great-nieces. Paula isn't so little any more, must be almost eleven years old. Also warmest greetings and best wishes to your dear wife and in hopes of seeing you after all— when we are older—I remain most sincerely with the best wishes for you and your dear family as ever / your R. M. Probstfield / [. . .]

The flesh was indeed weak. Despite his good intentions, this was the last letter Probstfield wrote to his nephew, or at least the last letter that has survived. After the turn of the century, rising grain prices gradually improved the farmers' plight. In Clay County, too, perhaps following

JUSTUS SUSIE DORA EDMUND NELLIE MILLIE

WALTER MARY RANDOLPH JOSIE CATHARINE ARTHUR ANDY

Figure 18. Probstfield family portrait, ca. 1891. *Source:* June Dobervich and Evelyn Gesell.

Probstfield's example, increased potato growing brought diversification. Wheat growing declined by 40 percent between 1900 and 1910; at the same time potato production rose by 500 percent and potatoes replaced wheat as the most important crop. It must have been a proud moment for Probstfield when the Minnesota State Horticultural Society presented him with a lifetime honorary membership in 1909.[31]

A few glimpses of the last years of Probstfield's life are provided by census materials. In 1900, shortly after the death of their mother, six children were still living at home, but in 1905 and 1910 only the eldest son and the two youngest daughters, still unmarried, remained. Although in 1910 his son was already 44, the 77-year-old R. M. Probstfield remained head of the household; at any rate the farm was still listed in his name. The 1910 census also lists him as owner of the farm, but this time, in contrast to 1900, finally free of debt. Randolph M. Probstfield died on September 11th, 1911, at the age of 78.[32]

In 1987 his farm, with its white wooden buildings only a stone's throw from the Red River, although uninhabited and somewhat in need of repair, still looked quite stately. The heirs have applied to have the house officially designated a historic monument. In Moorhead, today a town of thirty thousand, Probstfield is honored as one of the three original pioneers who settled the area. A school has been named after him and bears his name in large letters on the outside of the building, while an imposing portrait hangs above the staircase.

[31]Robinson (1915), 260–67; Drache, 99, 216–18.
[32]MC 1900 and 1910: Clay Co., Minn.; MC Minn. 1905; Drache, 331.

8

Johann Witten (John Witten)

The newlyweds Johann and Rebecka Witten left Selsingen near Bremervörde in the fall of 1882 as part of the last and—in terms of absolute
numbers—largest surge of German emigration, which in the first half of
the 1880s carried almost one million people to the United States. At this
time, East Elbian Prussia had become the region with the highest rate of
emigration, but it also had much in common with Witten's home in
northern Hanover. Both were predominantly rural and agricultural,
without any significant local industry that might have provided alternative employment opportunities. In both cases, too, the possibilities for
intensification of agriculture, either by planting new root crops or by
draining and cultivating the marshes, had largely been exhausted by
1865. Class tensions were no doubt of greater significance on the great
estates east of the Elbe, but they existed in northwest Germany as well.
Landholdings were also relatively large—Witten's father owned about
three hundred acres—and were passed on undivided to one heir. Farmers'
sons like Johann Witten, who did not have the good fortune to be the
firstborn, could only stay in farming if they were willing to forfeit a
considerable amount of social status.[1]

In terms of their occupation and social background, the Wittens were
quite typical of the emigrants from their region. Half of the gainfully
employed emigrants were, like Johann Witten, farmhands or agricultural
laborers. Like Rebecka Witten, another 21 percent were servants and day

[1]Extracts from ev. KB Selsingen; further information provided by contributor.

laborers. Farm owners comprised a mere 3 percent of emigrants, but the predominantly rural structure of the local economy is shown by the rather low percentage of artisans and industrial workers, only 16 percent.[2]

The fact that the Wittens were expecting a child when they married may well have been one reason for leaving.[3] The jobs they had held up to that time were practicable only for unmarried workers. Johann Witten's only chance of staying in farming, therefore, was to move down the social ladder to become a dependent *"Kötter,"* or tenant farmer, like his wife's father had been before him. Theoretically, too, he could have found a job in industry, perhaps in the Ruhr District, but this might have caused even more severe culture shock than the move to America. His brother Lütje, for example, became an industrial laborer and appears to have remained uprooted for the rest of his life.

The Wittens' way to America was paved by Johann's brother-in-law Angelus Viebrock, who had emigrated ten years earlier and was living on a rented farm in Illinois. The Wittens spent their first winter there and perhaps worked for one season on the Viebrock farm. The prairies of Illinois are some of the richest farmland in America, but by 1880 they were already densely settled and land prices were correspondingly high.[4] So Witten looked to the West. The first letter that has survived came from Reynolds, Jefferson County, Nebraska, five hundred miles west of his brother-in-law in Illinois. As he wrote, he had no personal contacts there, but the surroundings were familiar since three-fifths of the adults in his township were Germans.[5] But after a few years of living there as a renter, Witten decided that this also was not the best way to become a land-owner. So he risked yet another move, almost as daring as crossing the ocean, a trip of 1,600 miles to Douglas County in central Washington. Railroads were available for most of the trip, but the last stretch of 85 miles was made by covered wagon with two other German families. It was certainly not an easy trip, especially for his wife, in her eighth month of pregnancy, and with two children aged two and five. Like the trans-

[2]Witten is listed on November 6, 1882, among the passengers of the *Elbe* as a bricklayer, suggesting that he did briefly try city life, but the fact that he was traveling steerage and sharing just one trunk with his wife indicates his limited means (NYPL, Roll 458; *Preußische Statistik* 26 [1874], 302–3); the statistics are based on the entire district of Stade in the years 1867–1871, but they probably remained much the same for the following ten to fifteen years. Emigrants with other destinations are also included in these figures, but 85 percent went to the United States.

[3]The Wittens were married on October 5, 1882, and emigrated October 24. According to information provided by descendants, their first son was born on February 20, 1883, in Benson, Illinois; this is confirmed by MC 1900: Douglas Co., Wash., e.d. 11, #218, and 1910: e.d. 49, #55.

[4]Angelus Viebrock lived seven miles from Benson, Illinois (see MC 1900: Woodford Co., Ill., e.d. 133, #263, according to which he immigrated in 1873 and married in 1882). In 1880 Illinois led the nation in both corn and wheat production (see Shannon [1961], 163).

[5]Luebke (1969), 88–89, 190–92.

atlantic crossing, the arrival in Douglas County was softened by personal contacts: Klaus Viebrock, one of Rebecka's nephews, awaited their arrival.[6]

When he arrived in Douglas County, still undeveloped and connected to the railroad only in 1909, Johann Witten finally found what he had been looking for: fertile land that could be had for practically nothing, 160 acres of government land for only a small recording fee.[7] After that, nothing could stop him. As a result of a gap in the correspondence from 1889 to 1903, we unfortunately know little about how Witten managed to achieve his economic success, especially considering the severe agrarian depression in the 1890s which also affected population growth in Douglas County. For a while he owned threshing machines, which he used not only on his own farm but also doing custom work for other farmers. No matter how he managed it, in the 1900 census he is listed as the owner of a farm, free of debt, which according to the letter of 1903 was a good one thousand acres in size. In Germany, even the owner of a large farm could hope to establish only one of his children on a farm. Without having inherited a farm himself, however, Witten was able to provide farms for all of his eight children. Six of their farms were listed in the 1932 atlas of Douglas County; the smallest was a bit larger than Witten's parents' three-hundred-acre farm in Germany. All together the six children owned more than 2,500 acres or four sections.[8]

In terms of methods and the mechanization of his farming enterprise, Witten was obviously completely Americanized. The social environment in which he lived, however, looked quite different. Although German immigrants and their children accounted for only 7 percent of the population of Douglas County, more than half of Witten's immediate neighbors were German, and some of them came from similar regions and had followed similar paths of migration. Already one year after his arrival, the "critical mass" was reached to permit the founding of a Lutheran congregation (with Witten's enthusiastic support). German was the primary language spoken in the Witten home; his daughter still wrote

[6]Klaus Viebrock emigrated in 1884 and lived near Witten in 1900 (MC 1900: Douglas Co., Wash., e.d. 11, #188).

[7]Witten bought 160 acres for $1.25 an acre under the preemption law in February 1891 and an adjacent 160 for the same price at the same time. Beginning in fall 1892 he homesteaded another adjoining quarter section that he obtained for only $7.50 in filing fees, despite a legal challenge by the Northern Pacific Railway. He made his home on this last plot for the rest of his life (Cash Entry File and Land Entry File, National Archives Branch, Suitland, Md.; Ogle [1915]; *Waterville Empire Press* [Wash.], fifty-year jubilee edition, March 2, 1939, 17, 28; reminiscences of Witten's daughter Margaret Mittelstaedt, February 15, 1978, BABS).

[8]Shannon, 53. The population of Douglas County grew only 56 percent in the 1890s; in the following decade, however, it increased by 87 percent (MC 1900: Douglas Co., Wash.; *Metsker's Atlas* [1932], 21–22).

to him in German in 1923. All of his children, too, married Germans or German-Americans.[9]

Despite being well off and embedded in an ethnic community, Johann Witten does not give the impression that he was particularly happy. It is impossible to determine how much this can be attributed to the early death of his wife, since letters are missing from the time when he had achieved economic prosperity and his wife was still alive. But a fundamental pessimism can be seen even in his earlier letters. No matter how progressive Witten may have been as a farmer, he did not feel at home in the modern world. His melancholy cannot, however, be equated with homesickness—after all, Germany at the turn of the century seemed just as foreign to him. All of this was further exacerbated by World War I. Although he was in complete sympathy with Germany and decidedly opposed to America's entering the war, he kept informed from all sides and estimated the German chances of success much more soberly than most Germans at home or in the United States.

It seems that Witten was hardly interested in American politics or the democratic system at all, except as it affected relations with Germany. A certain similarity between his worldview and National-Socialist ideology cannot be overlooked: the "stab in the back" myth, his extreme nationalism, authoritarian tendencies, irrational hatred of socialism but also of plutocrats (there are, however, no signs of anti-Semitism). All of this might be considered cultural baggage; after all, there was widespread rejection of the democratic Weimar Republic in the area he came from in Germany.[10] But Witten was not as reactionary as many of those who stayed behind: he was a German, not a Hanoverian nationalist. He was not an enthusiastic supporter of the Guelph party, which wanted to repeal the Prussian annexation of Hanover in 1866 and restore the old dynasty. He was realistic enough and too well informed about world politics to deny the advantages of Prussian economic policy and its role in the rise of modern Germany. Johann Witten embodied a strange combination of the modern and the reactionary, of cosmopolitan and provincial.

The originals of Witten's letters were lost during World War II; the typescript was probably made in his hometown in the 1940s. Since the spelling, punctuation, grammar, and sentence structure are impeccable throughout, it is safe to assume that the copyist improved on the origi-

---

[9]The 1900 census shows not only Viebrock but nearly a dozen German and German-American families with Illinois connections in Witten's immediate neighborhood of Douglas precinct, and several more in 1910 (MC 1900: Douglas Co., Wash., e.d. 11, #166–218, and 1910: e.d. 49, #46–104; letter of Margaret Mittelstaedt, July 9, 1923, copy in BABS).

[10]Bohmbach (1982).

nal—though no one can say how much. There probably was not very much improvement, since the phrases sound very elaborate, even a little pompous, and it is hard to imagine that such dignified German could be accompanied by faulty spelling or missing commas. Still, his German is also frequently lively and colorful, most of which comes through in the translation.

Perhaps because of his contempt for fellow immigrants who neglect their native German, he unfailingly avoids obvious Anglicisms, let alone English terms. But in his later letters, English interference is clear: more and more, although the words remain perfect German, the prepositions and turns of phrase reveal that much of the time if Witten does not speak, he at least reads and writes English, not German.

Johann Witten

Reynolds, 6/10/1885

Dear brother,[11]

Since we shook hands in parting in Oberochtenhausen, no news has reached me. I think I wrote you a letter more than a year ago now and have not received any answer. Thus I will send you a second letter today. We are all hale and hearty. Last month we had a baby son. He only lived for 2 hours though and received emergency baptism from the midwife. Rebecka recovered quite quickly. Little Hinrich is quite healthy and happy and I hope the same is also true of you. Dear brother and sister-in-law, how are you doing otherwise? Do you have your decent living, or do you also have to be thrifty? Thrift is everything, that I know, and we have to be thrifty here as well. But it is still different from over there, since I only have a small family and that's not all, here one leads a different kind of life because bread and meat aren't so expensive here and there's no lack of luxuries at meal times. At the start I had very bad luck because my first crops were totally ruined by hail. That set me back a long way, but you mustn't lose heart. This year the crops look especially good. I have 10 acres of rye, 6 of wheat, 8 of oats and 50 of corn. I did all that with 2 horses. That's what you call work. And if no damage occurs, I'll have a rich harvest. In your country no one would be able to work so much land, but here there's no other work involved. Here there's no moor clearing and manure hauling, you also don't need to harrow the land. There isn't any quitch grass here, but just as much of other weeds, if not more.

I don't know anyone here from Selsingen or the area, but very many Germans, enough Low Germans too. There are already a lot of churches

---

[11]All letters were written to Witten's brother Christoph.

here, 3 right near where I live: one Lutheran, one Unified, and one Reformed. Everyone sticks to his own belief. There are many sects here that I had never heard of before.

The market prices are very low this year, the farther inland you go, the cheaper the prices. [9 ll.: closing; greetings; signature; address]

Tell Brother Lütje, if he still wants to come here, he should come soon.

Gladstone, 12/8/1887

Dear brother,

[4 ll.: Christmas greetings; all are healthy] I can't think of the time and day when I last had word from you. As long as I have been in this country I have not been in want for my daily bread, but you need more than that and the school of life teaches us something new every day. The last two harvests were not especially good, it was very dry here in the summer, not much feed grew for the livestock either and as a result they are very cheap. But it is still different from in Germany, the animals find almost all their own feed in the winter. Last summer I was in Dakota and visited my relative John Brandt from Sadersdorf.[12] He is doing very well, his brothers and sister are also there. I wanted to see what the land was like there. It is not very good, there are stones in the ground and that makes for hard work, you can't keep the plow sharp. We are going to leave here in the spring, I don't know yet where our home will be. I am going to go far away, where land is still cheap. Up until now I have only rented it. I don't want to do that any more, I want to have my own land. I have to sell most of the things that I have. I have 26 head of cattle, they'll bring quite a bit of money. We had 9 milk cows this summer. From May 1st until now we have made almost 90 dollars from butter, I've also made good money from my fat hogs. You have to save your money here just as much as over there and you have to work too, only there's more plowing here and that is tiring. Whoever wants to come over here should come on over, and whoever doesn't want to should stay away. I like it here very much. Up until now I've had nothing to complain about. My two boys are healthy and strong, especially the youngest, whose photograph I am enclosing today. It was taken on his first birthday, it was April 15th this year. [10 ll.: address; closing; signature]

Douglas, Douglas County, Washington, 9/22/1889

Dear Brother Christoph,

[17 ll: news of the death of their father; reflections on the finite nature of life]

---

[12]Sadersdorf is seven miles from Selsingen. Witten's mother's maiden name was Brandt.

As far as my family is concerned, we are quite well, my three children are always in good spirits. Hinrich, Johann and Anna are their names. As you have probably already heard from the others, we have moved to a completely new area because I wanted to own my own land. Land is plentiful here, you can get it for almost nothing, but it takes a lot of work to get this land into cultivation. There is no lack of labor and hardship here, like in every other country, and some people who left with their pockets empty have quite a struggle. The soil here is very rich and fertile, after many years we now have a nice German settlement, we'll also be getting a German Lutheran church and school. The congregation has been founded already and tomorrow we will discuss the building of the church. I have been elected as one of the elders. Dear brother, lots of Germans back home think, Oh, if only I were in America, there I could live better than here. That is certainly true, but if you are lazy here, you don't get any further here than in Germany. If you work here like it is fitting and proper, and save in the German manner, you need have no worries here about a living. But you can't get rich here as quickly as the good German back home always imagines. [26 ll.: making a decent living; church construction; description of the area; closing]

Douglas, Washington, 10/24/1903

My dear brother,

Today I feel compelled to write a letter to you. As far as we are concerned we are all quite well, except my wife, as you well know, is already lying in her grave, it's been 13 months now. Not much in particular has changed, things continue to take their normal course. Anna takes care of the house and the little ones, so that I am quite content.[13] The other children are also reliable about doing their chores, I can't complain about that. Why I am filled with particular solemnity today is this. You know it, you were present. 21 years ago today, at about the same time of day, we solemnly took leave of one another. That day is still fresh in my mind, I will never forget you and all the others. At that time we were a couple, fresh and newly joined to one another. For 20 years we walked together, saw and experienced many things, lived through hard and good times. Since a year ago I've been alone again and sometimes I even like being alone. Eight lively children give me all the distraction that I could wish. 4 boys and 4 girls. [4 ll.: his four-year-old son has dislocated his arm] In other things I am doing quite well. Everything is pretty well set up, I only need a better, bigger house, there is no lack of funds for this,

---

[13]Anna was born in 1888 and was thus only fourteen years old when her mother died.

but Anna is still too weak to be able to cope with a bunch of strangers all the time. I now own 1050 acres. 180 acres are in winter wheat again. There will be 500 acres to cut before the next harvest. The machine for that I own myself, it cuts 30 acres a day and is pulled by 6 horses. The grain is not bundled, it only cuts off the heads. The machine puts the loads into the wagon that drives along the side, which has an attachment 6 feet long and 8 feet wide.[14] Plowing is also on a bigger scale. I harness 6 horses to every plow, which has 2–3 14-inch shares. You can easily plow 5–6 acres with it.

We couldn't do that 15 years ago. For sowing you also use machines, mine is 12 feet wide, takes 4 horses to pull it. You can sow 25 acres a day with it. I don't have threshing machines anymore, there's only a small profit in that. The harvest this year was not very plentiful, wheat made 18–25 bushels per acre. [4 ll.: harvest, prices] I now have about 50 head of cattle, 22 horses.

So, dear brother, that is a short report about what I call my own. 21 years ago today I did not have much, but a good, hard-working, thrifty wife. She did very much, very much to help, even in her grave we must thank her. The cause of her death was consumption. She suffered for 1½ years, then on 9/25/1902 at 3 o'clock in the afternoon she passed away.[15] God has been a help up until now and will faithfully continue. I have good cause to look back on things today. Thank God for everything.
John Witten

Douglas, 2/18/1904
My dear brother and family,

I received your letter of January 21st, everything got here safely. We were overjoyed to get the pictures. [5 ll.: about the pictures] In the picture I see the clothing has changed a great deal, Mother Anna is also wearing different clothes. Is the local dress of the town of Selsingen disappearing, or what is happening? [5 ll: asks about young German relatives] The teachers in this country are hired by the month, usually for 3 months. If there is then general satisfaction, they stay for a whole year. Usually the school year is based on 9 months, there is no school in the summer. The monthly wage is 50 dollars in the country. It is not a very attractive profession, usually done by young girls, even men don't keep on after the age of 30. At this age they all start doing something else. You reported about Brother Angelus passing away. I am sorry there is bereavement in

[14]Such a machine is pictured in Figure 5, above.
[15]Rebecka Viebrock was born in 1858 and thus died at the age of 42.

the family, but we all go the same way sometime. Who can tell whether one of us will follow soon, or whether it will still take a while. But I think his children are all grown up. Things would be different if something should happen to me, may God forbid. There would be no danger for the older ones, but little Angelus would miss me very much. Hinrich and Johann have turned into fine young men, healthy in body and spirit. Anna, too, has turned out just as well, she will be 16 in April, has grown up into a lovely young woman, is nimble and quick with her housework. She still goes to school.

When your letter arrived here the evening of February 9th, everyone was overjoyed at first about the nice pictures. But when Hinrich got to the part in your letter, about who would be the first and the last of us 5, he wept quietly for a long time. The death of his mother, too, was a very hard blow for him. My children love me and I love them too. I have no reason to complain about them. They are all churchgoers. In terms of church matters here things are quite slack at times. Most of our Germans are East Frisians, pretty terrible people when it comes to religion not only in this country but also in Germany. But the worst one is a fellow from Harms' congregation in Lüneburg. The whole thing is a real nuisance. I have been elected head elder three times.

[20 ll.: asks about relatives and friends; weather; farming] You write about the great boom in Germany. What are the day wages for laborers and farmhands? Is the flail still being used for threshing, or are there more machines? I don't even have one scythe, just machines. [20 ll.: friend from Illinois has died; state of health; greetings]
John Witten
We'll just let the Russians and the Japanese go ahead and fight it out, right?[16]

Douglas, Washington, 1/1/1906
Dear Brother Christoph,
[5 ll.: asks about relatives] I haven't had a letter from Lütje for years now.[17] I heard then from you or H. Heins that he moved to Altenburg. I'm very sorry about his situation. I received your letter in the course of last winter. It does me so much good to get news from the old homeland. [9 ll.: how he is doing] The winter weather hasn't been too bad yet, up until Christmas we only had a little bit of snow. But now the sledding is good, which we needed badly. For there are still some loads of grain to

[16]The Russo-Japanese War had begun ten days earlier, on February 8, 1904.
[17]Probably Witten's brother Lütje.

haul. The harvest was very good. Wheat made up to 40 bushels. My boys, Heinrich and Johann hauled off 65 loads before winter started. That means 4 horses pulling the wagon, that's the only way you haul grain here. Dear brother, we've been reading in the papers about the lack of meat in Germany. I can well imagine how things are in the poor man's kitchen. I wish we could exchange things somewhat from there to here and from here to there. [4 ll.: prices] Many cattle breeders are selling their cattle because it's not worth it. I think differently. After cheap prices come better ones, you just have to wait until it gets better. The price of horses, on the other hand, is very high, you can hardly buy an ordinary animal for under 200 dollars. Grain prices are fairly good, but the transportation by railroad was blocked and every delay hurts the market. This crop will bring me a net profit of about 300 dollars. Almost all the work we do ourselves.[18] We only need help for the big harvest, about 3 men for 30 days. The daily wage for this harvest was 2½ to 3 dollars per day and laborer. Even at a wage like that they weren't too plentiful. We kept on threshing until the late fall, when the snow came and everyone just managed to get the threshing finished. The price of land is really going up fast, land is being sold for 30 dollars an acre without any buildings on it. But may God bless my brother Christoph and his wife in the coming year and my best wishes to you all. Please write about how your children are doing. In your last letter you didn't mention a single one of them. My children always say: the Germans are pretty negligent about sending pictures and writing. So write again soon, since in the summer one gets even worse about it, other things are more important. Give my best to my friends and relatives and a Happy New Year to you all, God willing. Johan Witten.

Douglas, 2/5/1907

Dear brother and wife,

[9 ll.: health; mediocre harvest] Up until Christmas we had good weather, then it turned cold and we had quite a lot of snow. It is very hard on the cattle, since they aren't in the barn, you only put calves and milk cows in the barn. [5 ll.: agricultural prices; catastrophes] You have probably heard about Sankt Franzisko, the earthquake caused terrible damage there. It should be considered God's punishment. It is after all the most godless city in our country. The great wealth in the area is probably why it is so godless. In your letter of March 17, 1906 you write that times are

---

[18]There were no hands or servants listed in Witten's household either in the 1900 or the 1910 census.

good for you there. I wish my friends and my Fatherland everything good and fine. The people in the country may be doing well, but the man in the city is suffering. The clouds of war which were threatening Germany have all disappeared and everything looks bright. Germany may have mastered the situation, but it doesn't enjoy the sympathy of the other countries. Germany's might and greatness is a thorn in the flesh for many others, particularly England and France. And our English America also distrusts Germany.[19]

[2 ll.: friends] When you write again, don't forget to tell me about the deaths of any of my acquaintances, I am very interested in reading about such things. You write that I should come to visit you again. I would very much like to do this, but put yourself in my shoes. It is just not possible yet. My family would be like a flock without its shepherd. The three oldest ones would get into all kinds of mischief and the three smaller ones wouldn't get enough attention. It is especially hard to keep children under control in this country. The influence of the English is worthless, English-American children lead a life without restraint. But as I live and God wills, I will visit my Germany again. But the circumstances must first be fitting. I certainly do not lack the means. [4 ll.: friends do not write much] I can't complain about my children. They all have obedient and thrifty characters. Anna has become a prudent housekeeper. She is almost 19 years old. And when she has learned everything, she will leave me. The next one is Maria, she turned 14 on January 30th. She is clever too and has grown into a sturdy girl. But it's all just a poor substitute for her mother. Remarrying wouldn't help the family either. They would only scatter and go away and that would hit me hard. So I will have to carry my burden alone. When the children get married they will be more entertaining for me. Until then they won't understand the wants of older people.

> Yes, there away so far
> high above every star
> there is my Fatherland.

There are no prospects yet of my sons getting married. The girl, on the contrary, has had many offers. But I can't let her go yet, if I did it would rip a terrible hole in the family. She is like the mother in the house. You can well imagine how desirable my Anna is.

The net profit from my harvest this year is almost 4000 dollars. [8 ll.: greetings]
John Witten.

---

[19]John Witten could be referring to the First Moroccan Crisis.

I almost forgot to write that we moved into our new house on November 6th, 1906. It is one of the best in the area, has 8 nice sunny rooms and cost 1700 dollars, not counting the work we did.

Douglas, 2/3/1908

Dear brother and wife,

[8 ll.: is feeling his age somewhat] I feel sorry for Lütje, that he makes life so difficult for himself, when he could have it better. I am totally different in this. Wherever I sit myself down, that's where I stay, as long as it's passable. I've been fortunate, I have found a true home. I wouldn't trade places with the best farmer in the Selsinger Börde. But there is a lot that glitters that isn't gold here, too. The greatest good a man can have is contentment. Yes, praise be to God that I have also been blessed with this. I have never run and chased after good fortune. And even though I have lived a fairly quiet life, it has been a burden sometimes. When my wife Rebecka died 5 years ago, my youngest son was 3 years old, and the youngest girl 5 years old. All of this is behind me now. There is still enough work, and you all know we carry these scars to the grave. Now the oldest children are coming into the marriageable years. One woman told me once: yes, the marriageable years are the worst of all. That is how it seems to me now. Again and again the German youth suffers temptation from the English. Many are nothing but heathens. Our German Lutheran religion gets pushed aside then. Anyone who wants to keep his children under control, like I try to, has to watch out very carefully. Many parents wish they were not in this country, just because of the mixed population. Among the English people, divorces are common. When life starts to be difficult, they just go their separate ways. Up until now all of my children are still at home, except for my second son who is visiting his mother's brother. He lives very far away from here in the state of Illinois. When we start working the fields in the spring, he'll come back. It costs 120 dollars on the train. [8 ll.: weather and harvest] The market prices for grain are not bad at the moment. In October and November 1907 there was a financial panic here. At that time you couldn't get any money at all. Now things are better again. But business as a whole is very cautious. Those who like to speculate are taking advantage of it now. [14 ll.: will visit Germany later; greetings; signature; notes about American weights and measures]

Douglas, 12/9/1909

Dear Brother Christoph,

[11 ll.: greetings, prices] Workers are hard to get and very uppity. Our little town of Douglas got a railroad connection. That changes every-thing completely. A tremendous amount of wheat is shipped from here. I wish you could be here to watch. I had ten thousand six hundred bushels. Oats were also good and cost 30 dollars a ton (20 hundredweight). Potatoes were only average.

[6 ll.: acquaintances] I'll have to give up my eldest daughter soon. It is certainly not what I want to do, but I won't be able to keep her back. The young man in question is also of German background, his parents immi-grated from Pomerania. But they trample all over the German language. People like that are never any good. My brother-in-law Angelus Vie-brock hasn't made it to owning his own property yet. He's still a renter, could easily have had his own home by now.[20] [6 ll.: weather; corre-spondence] I would like to give up the whole business, could also afford to, but it seems like it isn't yet time to quit. I don't do any plowing any more, the boys are better at it. But nothing seems to get done without my supervision. Sometimes it seems to me that my lot in this world has been a hard one. A joy shared is a double joy and a sorrow shared is half the sorrow. This saying doesn't much apply to me. I have to bear my joys and sorrows alone. Happy is the man who is not early made a widower in his best years. May God keep you in the coming year.
All the best / John Witten

Douglas, 1/26/1910

Dear brother and wife,

[8 ll.: extolls Hanover] May God's hand watch over you always, Hanover, my dear Fatherland. I was very pleased, too, with your report about church affairs. All in all, I am quite well-informed about the situation in the Church. But I am not as close to things at home as all that. The Free Church is the only one that can protect the people from un-belief, if the established Protestant Church begins to falter and give way to unbelief. That is the end of religious unity, even if Free Churches spring up. It spawns the growth of sectarianism, we have enough of that in this country. Little towns like Zeven often have 6–7 churches and none of them are very lively. The small groups end up unable to attract newcomers and lukewarm Christianity sets in. Most people are com-pletely lost to the Church, their children grow up without any religion at all. This makes it also hard for those who want their children to have religious instruction. The churches here are completely separate from the

[20]According to the MC 1900 and 1910, Woodford Co., Ill., e.d. 137, #163, Viebrock was a renter.

state and have to be supported by their own members. Except that churches and parsonages are tax-free. The public schools are supported by each district and cost a fortune. [3 ll.: details] I am also on the board of the Evangelical school and have been head elder of the German Lutheran church for many years. I've often had small positions like this without pay and often enough without even any thanks. I will treasure the newspaper you sent me, I'll also show it to all the people from Hanover here, and there are a lot of them here. [10 ll.: would like to have a local paper; is sending photographs of the family] We are all there, except for Mother. Her picture is hung in black in a golden frame on the wall and looks down on her flock with a smile.

May God keep you all / John Witten

Douglas, 12/2/1910

Dear Brother Christoph and wife,

I received your letter with the enclosed newspaper. [13 ll.: 55th birthday, still in good health, is thinking about retiring] Anna was married on November 2nd. At first it peeved me to no end. But now it looks like everything will turn out for the best. I haven't given her any share of the inheritance yet, first I'll wait and see how the two of them get along. There is no doubt about her being an excellent housewife. All summer long she acted like she was deaf and blind. I hope that in time she'll see the error of her ways, otherwise she'll only get a small share of my estate. I am in a position to give each child quite a bit of help, but I will give more to the other boys and girls than to one who goes against my wishes. He is also a fellow countryman. His parents come from Pomerania, are too easygoing and jolly by nature. That's why I was always opposed. Otherwise they aren't exactly poor people. Maria will have to take over running the household, that will be a little rough at the start.

[5 ll.: missed seeing a friend who came to visit] The harvest this year was light again, like last year. The market prices, too, are not high. 3 years ago my net profit was 8000 dollars. These are really slack times. Money is kind of short. When there's no market for wheat nothing works like it should. [9 ll.: prices; Christmas and New Year's greetings] Your faithful / John Witten

Douglas, 2/23/1912

Dear brother and family,

[22 ll.: fire damage, weather, prices] I only have 15 head of cattle. We had to sell the rest, because the new settlers here have taken up all the summer pasture land. There is no more government land left that is any good, except what has to be irrigated. Then even desert land is valuable, so that it is worth from 2–3 thousand dollars an acre (160 rods or 1⅓ morgens). By the way, our country is suffering greatly from the so-called *Trustgesellschaft* [trusts]. It is an agreement between the larger trading companies. They have their own prices for buying and selling. Whatever they want. None pays more than the other and none sells for less than the other. The President and his advisers are against it, but quite powerless, or don't want to have things any different. For most of these men also own part of one of these companies or have invested capital in the factories. If these men were to break up the *Trust,* they'd be hurting themselves. There's no honest government here like there is in Germany. That's what John Wilshusen wrote me, too. He said Germany has honest government officials and good laws too. Cheating and fraud have free rein in America. If someone makes a big haul then they say he was a *smart (kluger)* man. Also in terms of religion things are very slack. Well over half the English-speakers don't go to church. Have never even heard of religion. And many Germans are the same. You can tell from the new immigrants that they don't care much about the church, since they don't join congregations like they used to. One older man, who had been in this country for more than 30 years, went back to visit his old homeland. But with a heavy heart he cried out then: Oh, my dear Germany, how far you have fallen since I have been gone. I think it is the fault of the Social Democrats, along with the negligence of the state. In this country it is also the same, socialists stir up the people, disturbances of the peace and bombings are frequent. All who belong to this group are against the church and opposed to orderly government.

I have received and read your two newspapers carefully and suspect that you are a true Guelph. It is something high and holy, that the Hanoverian people are still so faithful to their royalty. But I think that the Guelph party is pleased when state policies are unfortunate and mistaken. It should not be like this. The article about the bankruptcy of Bismark's policies is a virulent smear. The province of Hanover has certainly blossomed under Prussian rule. Prospects for all but the high nobles were poor. This article says the Germans are more disliked abroad than any other nation. I think the Germans have taken over world trade and it is easy to understand that this has created some friction. The large growth in population makes it necessary to find new trade markets abroad. That calls for standing bravely at the front. Otherwise you will be pushed back. The Germans' Reich came about through Bismark's fearless advance. He laid the foundations, his successors are extending it further. I certainly regret the fall of the Cumberlands, because they were the ancestral rulers. I think you still have enough princes and rulers. All of these lords are only a burden to the people. They lead such extravagant lives. What does it profit the people who work, if they can hardly come up with the necessary taxes. The author of the article also sympathizes with the English. What England is and what it intends to do, however, has become public enough this summer. The Germans should have no mercy, no sympathy for their neighbors on the other side of the Channel. That is spoken like a true German. The old arch-enemy Frenchman is more to be trusted than one who is up to all manner of intrigues.

[15 ll.: information about photograph of his daughters] Hinrich now has a job as a grain salesman and earns 75 dollars a month. Earlier he had a job in a lumberyard. Anna and her husband are doing very well, they live 1 hour from here. They have bought some land there. But I have promised, or rather had to promise to help them out. They still have a lot of debts on their land. If it is too hard for them, I'll have to take it over and set them up as renters. [16 ll.: visited an acquaintance in Oregon; climate there] If I were to give up the business, what should I do then? Move into the city, like so many parents do? But I would be eaten up with loneliness, I am scared of that. Time will bring an answer, I think. The young and the old seldom live together in one house here. Young and old are sharply divided here. Enough for now. All my best and warmest greetings. May God continue to keep you. I wish you a Happy Easter.
John Witten.

Douglas, 2/2/1913

My dear brother and family,
[23 ll.: correspondence; weather; train accident]
The harvest was good, we harvested in abundance, about 14000 bushels of wheat (840 hundredweight) and about 4000 bushels (240 hundredweight) of oats.[21] [2 ll.: prices] You probably know that my eldest son got married last summer, I sent you the marriage announcement in the summer. He has now bought a place not far from me. The place cost 13760 dollars. He still has quite a lot of debts. But I think he'll manage. 200 acres of it are planted with winter wheat. If it makes it through the winter, he'll be fine. My daughter Anna and her husband (whom I was so afraid of) are doing very well. My first disappointment has turned into contentment. I will send a picture of her little son. I am also enclosing a card with a picture of me and my house. Next to me is Angelus and the 2

[21] Witten underestimated his crops in German measurements by a factor of ten, an indication of how different the scale of operations was. At sixty pounds per bushel of wheat, it was in fact 8,400 hundredweight of wheat; at 32 per bushel of oats, 2,400.

Figure 19. John Witten and family with their old house (ca. 1903).

Figure 20. John Witten and family with their new house (1912).

girls on the right are Margaretha and Maria. On the left is an outsider. Her parents come from the region on the lower Elbe near Horneburg.[22] Her name is Emma Prange. She is engaged to my second son. [4 ll.: promises more photographs] Dear friends, you are probably living in fear because of the threatening danger of war. When this letter reaches you, a decision will certainly have been made. For as one reads, everything is very tense.[23] The Paris fortune-teller said that Prussia would stop being a Great Power in the year 1913 (but who's to believe that). [9 ll: news from his sister, friends; greetings]
Your brother John Witten.

Douglas, 12/3/1914

Dear Brother Christoph and family,

Since I have not had a letter from you in a long time, I will try to write a few words to you. I wrote to you in the beginning of September and haven't had an answer yet. In my letter to you, I sent along an article from an English newspaper that presented the German soldiers as a rough gang. If the letter was opened it was certainly destroyed. One reads every day here about the victories or losses of the armies. All of us Germans are pleased that they are winning and that they will stay the victors in the future. If not, Germany's future looks dim. The plans of the Allies are terrible: surrender of Alsace-Lorraine. 2. Double compensation for Belgium. 3. cession of the Kaiser Wilhelm Canal [Kiel Canal] to England and surrender of the navy. 4. Reparations of 25 billion. Well, we hope that it will turn out differently. What is printed here in the English press is unbelievable. E.g. that the Kaiser has gone insane. The Crown Prince has been reported dead several times already and last week the Russians captured 50000 Germans at Lotz, along with the Kaiser's coach with his coat in it. I haven't heard anything more about it, so it's another dirty lie. Our English people know they are being entertained with lies. We Germans have more of the real truth. On the English side it was kept quiet that they lost one of their best ships along with another one off the Irish coast. It was kept secret for 10 days. The great majority of our people sympathize with England and even a few German-born wish the downfall of our Fatherland. How blind these people are. Lütje sends me a paper from Bremervörde.[24] It gives the losses from the community of Selsingen. Otherwise it is one month too late. All the events of the war are

---

[22]Horneburg is located near Stade, about fifteen miles away from Selsingen.
[23]This probably refers to international tensions in the aftermath of the Balkan War from September to December 1912.
[24]Most likely Witten's brother Lütje.

already in the papers here 3 days later. They are read with great excitement. But what hardship they are bound up with. It will be a costly
victory with much blood and human lives. The vanquished will be
completely devastated for many years to come. We wish and hope that
our brothers are victorious and that England's hypocrisy will be re-
venged by God's hand. The German papers are all of the firm opinion
that German victory is certain. But there is much to be done and when
will it end. Germany dare not rest until the English naval power is
broken, without this peace is only a cease-fire. The tension between the
nations will remain and all the blood will have flowed for naught.

[5 ll.: all healthy; Christmas greetings] You probably heard that I was
on my way to Germany. But the war thwarted my joy. I left here on
Sunday, August 2nd, then found out on the trip that war had been
declared and that all shipping was blocked. After I spent one month with
brother-in-law Angelus, I went home again. [9 ll.: patriotic reflections on
being German] Now, give the soldiers the treatment every human being
deserves and not like it used to be, that the soldier was at the mercy of
his superior's whims. One thinks of clumsy, uneducated sergeants and
young irresponsible lieutenants. Discipline is necessary, but one must be
treated decently both on and off duty. The military profession is there for
the protection of the country and not for brutal treatment by superiors.
In America they laugh about it, that the German soldier has to put up
with such treatment.[25] [11 ll.: harvest, markets]

Greetings and best wishes for the New Year and the glorious advent of
long-sought peace / your brother John Witten.

Douglas, 12/5/1915
My dear brother and family,

It has been quite a long time since I had a letter from you or anyone
else. I am sorry that things are the way they are. I wish you all good
health and contentment despite the sufferings and misery of the war. It
hurts my soul when I think of all the suffering and woe of my dear ones.
From what you read, things are looking good for the Germans, but the
end of this huge struggle is not yet in sight. It will still cost many a
sacrifice, both of money and of blood. I feel ashamed that I cannot take
part in the misery and suffering of our people. For I feel that those who
cannot suffer alongside cannot join in the joy afterwards. But we Germans in this country don't want that to be our fault. It is painful that our
President Wilson has put his services at the disposal of the English side.

[25]Witten served his three years of military duty in a guard regiment in Berlin.

Warnings and requests are addressed to him every day, to put a stop to these arms dealings. But the poor man, you know, is under pressure from the big capitalists. All the money that England pays for war materials is blood money. These deliveries only prolong the war and who knows how long the German nation can keep firm in its belief in fighting to the end and conquering its enemies completely. But believe you me, it will not all turn out like I and you wish. Germany may win on the land and take over part of other countries besides Belgium. But what can be taken from England, as long as it has its fleet? [5 ll.: English fleet is invincible] If it were possible for Germany to regain control of the Suez Canal and cause trouble for England in India, that might be a death blow to the enemy. But wait and see. Now you mustn't think that I don't wish for the downfall of the enemy, I do, as long as Germany has enemies. But they will still be enemies after peace has been agreed on. The majority of our people is against the arms dealings. But the English newspapers poison our people with all sorts of lies. The real truth is kept from our country. Our government policy is under English pressure and influence. Hopefully our president will yet learn of England's perfidy. But till then he helps England and thereby sends more soldiers to their deaths.

Otherwise we are fine and I wish it were the same with you. [4 ll.: effects of the war in Germany] I get the Bremervörde paper. But if I didn't know any more about the war than what it reports, I wouldn't know much. I read the English papers and the better German ones. Thus you can see things from both sides. At first the English papers wrote about all sorts of atrocities by German soldiers. That's all stopped now. Instead the discipline of the Germans is now praised and the wonderful organization of Germany. It is a model for the whole world. And hopefully it will be even more so after the war. May my dear Germany be spared an ignominious peace. That is my greatest wish.

Now, my dear brother, I would like to tell you something else. After the harvest I went with my children to the Sanfranzisko world exhibition.[26] [15 ll.: details; met friends there] Californien is a beautiful place, the climate is particularly nice. There is no winter there. The roses bloom in December and January just like in May. But I don't like the people. It is partly made up of descendents of Spaniards, Italians and Greeks. The exposition was wonderful, but there were no German exhibitors. I only saw the twin trademark of Henkel from Solingen, and a few valuable objects from the royal porcelain factory Berlin Wilhemstr. [7 ll.: greetings, Christmas wishes] from your faithful brother / John Witten. Have just crossed the threshold of my 60th year.
(Dec. 2nd 1855–Dec. 2nd 1915)

[26]The San Francisco exhibition was officially called the Panama-Pacific International Exposition.

Douglas, 9/11/1919

My dear brother,

Since the postal service is running again now, I will write a few words. We are all still alive and are fine. I wish that you too were doing so well. But it is not so. I got a letter from sister Metta. She writes that it hit her hard [two sons killed]. It is certainly regrettable, but it turned out like this, not like it looked at first. It has been a hard, very hard blow for you all. First the war years and then on top of that the reparations. It may be peace, but not a true one. Things still look very bad in America too, strikes everywhere, new ones almost every day. Wages are very high— 5–7 dollars a day in the country and in the cities 8–10 for eight hours' work. Everything you buy is very high in price and getting higher all the time. Will it ever end? The crash will have to come sometime. Labor and capital will have to have a showdown with each other, which will cause bad times, probably an overthrow of the government. And then, what kind of government. Just so it's not socialist, the world has enough of those, they are also the ones who broke Germany's back. It was the enemy inside the country. And what became of this country afterwards? Out with this victory. If Germany wants to become what it once was again, then rally round a prince again! No matter what it costs. It can't get any worse than it is now. It is very uncertain whether our country will join the League of Nations. I hope not. If not, it will be to Germany's advantage. [7 ll.: details] Most of our soldiers are back home again. They all speak well of the Germans, even if they were their enemies. They detest the French and the English. My sons didn't serve. Hinrich and Johann have their own *Farm*. Willi was exempt because I couldn't do without him. Angelus is unfit for service because his arm is part lame. So you see, that I was not directly involved. Only my daughter Margareta was more affected. She was practically engaged to a man who was involved in heavy fighting and got as far as Koblenz. There he died of influenza and was buried there. How did we fare during this time? I have nothing to complain about, no one bothered me. In many places the Germans had a hard time, churches and schools were closed down. But now everything is fine again. I have often had bitter quarrels.

The harvest of 1918 was very light here. [4 ll.: prices] So you see that our income stayed very low. But our expenses are enormously high and many a young beginner will not be able to pay his debts. All of that is the result of the war. But the money men have it made. New millionaires are shooting up out of the ground like mushrooms. [9 ll.: harvest; will send each of his three brothers and sisters $100]
Your brother John Witten.

[14 ll.: letter of September 14, 1919: has sent check for 2,260 marks]

Douglas, 9/18/1920

My dear and beloved Brother Christoph,

[12 ll.: correspondence; state of health, pain in one knee] Now I have given up the whole business, have sold everything, but not the land, to Willi and the son-in-law who married my daughter Margarete on Christmas day and lives here with me in the house. Willi is still unmarried, will soon be the next one. The other girl, the youngest, has just gotten married. Her husband is a machinist. For a while he was earning 15 dollars, is also a German. So I have no more girls to give away. [14 ll.: Socialist "stab in the back"; Germany's future] You don't hear one word about the war here anymore. It is as if our country is ashamed of what our gullible dumb president did. The presidential primaries were held on the 14th of this month. The Republicans won almost everywhere and one hopes that the Democratic dirt will be swept out again. For they are the ones who plunged our country into war. [10 ll.: correspondence; harvest] It is all the rage here in this country, that older people who can afford it spend the winter in the South. I am also thinking about making a trip in the winter to get away from the snow and the cold. Now that I am not burdened by business anymore, I can perhaps afford to. When it is snowing and blowing here, the flowers in southern California are blooming. John Schoshusen and his wife have written several times that I should come to visit them. They also want my Willi to meet their daughter. Their son is a professor and the daughter is a teacher at the high school. By the way, it is the custom here that parents have nothing to say about their children's marriages!

[6 ll.: childhood memories, correspondence] You write I should visit you sometime when everything is back in order. But when will that be. I think not until this government is overthrown again. And where will we be then? The people long for the good old days. And after many humiliating years of democracy, it can only achieve this as one people. As long as everyone is screaming for war, there can be no prosperity. If suddenly the Kaiser were to turn up again, he would be greeted warmly by the majority of the people. It is like this today; no defense, no honor. Then other countries would become your friends and saviors. We read all the time about how the other powers are afraid to ally themselves with Germany. The Poles must be crushed because they try to protect France with all their might. Let's hope that these two do not carry out their plans. For then the day will come for my dear Germany, which now lies crushed on the ground. We often read that Germany has 15 million people too many, which it cannot support. When all the connections with other countries are established then the danger is over. Foreign countries have all the raw materials and you have the technical utilization for them.

Everything else will get better and adjust to the circumstances. In November is the new presidential election here and it looks like Wilson and with him the rotten gang, his friends, his politicians, will have to leave his high office in shame. A better man will follow him, who will free our country from the yoke of the English. President Wilson was a willing tool of the English. With the departure of the current president, the League of Nations will also come to an end. But the financial princes rule America, everything is done according to their wishes, and the presidential candidates are nominated according to their wishes. The people go to the polls and vote, but the one to vote for is decided by the money party. The German vote will make itself especially felt in the coming election, so that it will be said: the Germans made the difference at the election.[27]

And now, dear brother, enough for this time. I thank you from the bottom of my heart for all your faithful words. May you be granted many more years to come! And if I should ever set foot upon German soil again, my joy would be so great that I am afraid. A reunion after so many years could break my heart, especially under these conditions. No one would recognize me, just as I would not recognize you. I, so dashing as a young man, have grown grey, but I have not lost any hair. Thus I will close with the most beautiful saying known to any language: May God bless you.

Your faithful brother Johann

Please forgive me if I don't write again right away, so many letters are arriving from other parts of Germany and from Africa.

[64 ll: letter of February 2, 1921: weather; family; harvest; money gifts; correspondence; childhood memories; complains about terms of peace; greetings and good wishes; signature]

[26 ll: letter of July 8, 1921: greetings and check for 700 marks; enclosed letter and check for 2,200 marks from nephew in Missouri]

Douglas, 2/20/1922

Dear brother and family,

I received your letter of 12/6/1921 quite a while ago, also a letter from sister Metta written at that time. I am certainly not in want of letters. But

[27]Witten's prediction was correct; the Democrats were defeated by the Republicans by a landslide of more than 60 percent of the votes. It also seems that German-Americans in particular turned their backs on the Democrats (see Luebke [1974], 322–28).

most of them are so short. It is very important to me to understand the feelings of the people. I certainly know there is suffering beyond all measure there. I would like to help everyone, but we have to call a halt to that here. We are not suffering from lack of bread and clothing like you, here we are suffering from lack of money. It is often quite a feat for us to pay for our running expenses. Wheat is below cost price. We suffer a loss on every bushel of wheat that we have to sell. [11 ll.: prices] Every day I wait for better news, but it has not improved yet. The world situation is regrettable and what are conditions like now. In Russia a famine has begun, such as the world has never seen. You write about a free Hanover, free from Berlin. I was also sent two articles. Our local paper says that the enemies have stirred up and promoted this idea, since a united Germany is not what its enemies want. And the socialist, the man of the hour, doesn't care much about the future and the glorious past. This is trampled on and destroyed. Dear brother, by chance I got to know a young man, Hinrich Grimme is his name, from Hanstedt.[28] I asked him to stop by and say hello in Eitze, I also gave him some pictures to take along. He ought to be there now. If you have the chance to talk to him I would be more than pleased. He too was forced to serve in our army, but he didn't get to the front. [10 ll.: the flu is raging; friends] On September 18 my youngest set himself up on his own, has a nice, pretty wife, her parents are from the Rhineland. And to give them something of their own I had to dig deep into my pocket. I bought him 400 acres at 80 dollars an acre. Half of it had to be paid right away. And then all the other equipment for 280 dollars. I thought I was finished with everything. And now, when I am old, I have to go into debt yet again. In such scarce times, you feel it is longer than otherwise.

Your brother John Witten.

Written on 2/26/1922

I might add and you will also see the difference in the date, I also went through a brief bout of the flu. Thought I would wait to send the letter so I could let you know I had died. But thank God I am still alive and am now well on the way to recovery. In the course of the week several old people have died. The young have been spared this time. Since one hears moaning and complaining beyond all measure now, I will therefore ask, how often can you eat for one dollar? We can only eat twice, that is in the town, and only a simple meal. Despite the fact that everything that belongs in a meal is so very cheap. [9 ll.: consumer prices] There is no more beer and liquor in the whole country, unless it is smuggled in, and then a bottle of wine costs 12 dollars. Whoever gets caught with liquor in

---

[28]Hanstedt is about six miles from Selsingen.

Figure 21. Passport photo of John Witten, taken shortly before his voyage to Germany in 1923.

the house is severely punished. A marriage license costs 5 dollars. After 3 weeks one can file for divorce. That happens all the time. There aren't many illegitimate children here. They are murdered before they are born. Families with a lot of children are laughed at. So, dear brother, enough for now. God bless you! Stay in good health. I am certain you will forgive me for not enclosing any money in this letter. When everything is open in the spring, I will not forget you, nor sister Metta and Lütje.
[9 ll.: weather, drought] / John Witten.

[21 ll: letter of June 15, 1922: correspondence; is sending $10, complains about high taxes and low prices; greetings]

Douglas, 10/3/1922

Dear brother Christoph and family,

I will fulfill your wish that I write back right away. Can say, nothing new in particular has happened here. We are all quite well, hope you are too. The bundle with the newspapers and picture arrived here safely yesterday evening. It was a particular pleasure to see your picture. It was like I was looking at our dear father once again. You look healthy and kind, as fitting for a grandfather, like a man who has gathered much experience. A pity that the last three of us are not together. Fate has thus determined it. [6 ll.: more about photograph; newspaper clippings] I have not yet heard anything from H. Grimm in Hanstedt, I don't know where he is.

Maybe he is footloose. I only had a few days to get to know him. Fall weather has set in. The winter crops are now being planted. It was very dry, so that the wheat we sowed couldn't sprout very well. Now it is cool and dark. The mountain peaks sparkle in the setting sun.
God bless you and keep you. / John Witten.

Johann Witten died on August 3, 1923, at the age of 67, at the end of a voyage to Germany. He had already waved to his relatives as his ship was docking in Cuxhaven. On his way to his cabin, probably to collect his luggage, he died of heart failure. He was buried in the family plot in the Selsingen cemetery, next to his parents and other relatives.[29]

[29]Obituary in the *Douglas County Spokesman Review*, August 23, 1923, which incorrectly stated that Witten was 72; further information from contributor.

II. Workers

Introduction

In the German Empire of 1875 almost half of the gainfully employed worked in the agricultural sector, 30 percent as artisans and industrial workers, and 21 percent in trade and services.[1] In the United States in 1870 the employment figures in similar categories were 47, 22, and 31 percent respectively. For German immigrants in the United States, however, the distribution looked quite different: 27, 37, and 36 percent.[2] In 1900, half of all German-born immigrants were living in towns with more than 25,000 inhabitants, while in Germany even some ten years later, only 41 percent of the population lived in towns larger than ten thousand.[3] Among German immigrants living in the United States, more highly urbanized than Americans as a whole or Germans back home, the proportion of laborers was also correspondingly higher.

Chicago, recently the subject of intensive studies in social and ethnic history, had a population of 29,963 in 1850, including 4,757 German immigrants. In 1900 the respective figures were 1.7 million and 171,000. In 1850, some 84.1 percent of the Germans could be considered members of the working class (1900: 71.6 percent). A clear majority were artisans and skilled laborers; only a minority could be classified as unskilled laborers.[4]

[1]"Workers" are understood here as persons working for wages outside the agricultural sector, in factories, cottage industries, mines, or on building sites.

[2]Kocka (1983), 65; Hutchinson (1956), 79.

[3]For the Irish, Italians, and Poles this figure was 60 percent, but the national average was 25 percent. Twenty-one percent of native-born Americans lived in cities with a population of more than 25,000.

[4]Keil (1983a), 21, 23.

As an ethnic group, German immigrants were lucky not to have to start out at the bottom of the occupational pyramid. In 1850, when the Germans and the Irish provided the two largest contingents of immigrants, 46 percent of the Germans in St. Louis, for example, were artisans and skilled laborers, compared to only 19 percent of the Irish. With unskilled laborers, the proportions were reversed: 37 to 56 percent. Even thirty years later, despite some leveling out, the Germans (39 percent skilled, 36 percent unskilled) still had a clear advantage over the Irish (28 percent: 42 percent). With more recently arrived ethnic groups, the differences were even more pronounced. The analysis of a representative sample of German and Polish heads of household who immigrated between 1878 and 1893 shows that in 1900, 20 percent of the Germans in Chicago were white-collar, 44 percent skilled, and 34 percent unskilled laborers. The corresponding figures for the Poles were 3, 33, and 62 percent.[5]

National statistics do not permit such a threefold division, but they do include one employment category that can clearly be assigned to unskilled labor: "laborers (not specified)." Here, the figures are parallel to those of Chicago: in 1880, 9.6 percent of gainfully employed Americans belonged to this group of the socioeconomically disadvantaged. The British were in a slightly better position with only 6.7 percent. Scandinavians and Canadians had a rate of 14 percent, and the Irish brought up the rear with 22.9 percent. Seen in this light, the position of the Germans, with 11 percent, was quite respectable.[6]

The concentration of Germans in particular trades or branches[7] can easily be explained: many immigrants had learned trades at home and were able to put these skills to use in the United States. What is not so easy to explain, however, is the advantageous socioeconomic position of urban Germans compared to other ethnic groups. National statistics comparing immigrant occupations before and after arrival in the United States exist only for the years 1899 to 1910, but according to these figures, some 30 percent of Germans were artisans and skilled laborers. The German position was weak compared to that of the British, almost half of whom fell into this category, but very strong compared to immigrants from southern Italy (15 percent), Ireland (13 percent), and especially Poland (6 percent). The U.S. Immigration Commission regarded

[5]Faires (1983), 39, 41; Keil (1984b), 397.
[6]In 1890 the German and Irish rates had improved to 9.7 percent and 17.8 percent (first and second generation). The highest rates were found among the most recent immigrants: Hungarians and Italians with ca. 33 percent (USC 1880.1, 744–45; USC 1890.2, 502–3).
[7]In 1880 some 28 percent of the 134,000 tailors in the United States, 38 percent of the 40,000 bakers, and 61 percent of the more than 16,000 brewers were German-born (USC 1880.1, 746–47; Hutchinson, 102–3; USC 1880.1, 748–51).

previous employment in industrial production as favorable for advancement and rapid integration; their surveys and estimates produced figures
that correspond to the proportion of skilled labor mentioned above.[8]

The general tendency toward a higher proportion of skilled labor also
characterized earlier generations of German immigrants. Of the Germans
who emigrated via Hamburg between 1846 and 1852, an annual average
of 60 percent were "artisans and tradesmen." Similarly, artisans represented a good 40 percent of emigrants from Hesse (1845–1847) and
Brunswick (1853–1856). Almost 57 percent of emigrants from Württemberg at a somewhat later time (1857–1871) had formerly worked in a
trade or industry. Artisans, under the pressure of both "overcrowding"
in their trades and competition from factories at home and abroad, fell on
increasingly hard times and sought their salvation across the Atlantic.[9] A
large share of Germans living in American towns had thus been well
prepared at home to take advantage of new opportunities in industry.

Were German workers better off in America than they were before
migrating? There are only complicated answers to this simple question.
Available statistics are meager and ambiguous, it is difficult to compare
what an individual did before and after arriving in the United States, and
other factors must also be considered: purchasing power and market-
basket of goods, working hours, unemployment, opportunities for saving, social services, agricultural self-sufficiency, and, last but not least,
the "quality of life."

One set of statistics on wages in Germany, well-documented and well-
suited to our purposes, comes from the town of Braunschweig (1840–
1877). According to this study, the weekly wages of an unskilled laborer
in 1860 amounted to only $1.79, compared to $3.42 in 1875. Unskilled
workers in a Pittsburgh nail factory, by contrast, were paid $5.01 in 1860
($6.39 in 1875).[10] Although in 1875 unskilled workers in the iron and
steel industries on the East Coast generally earned as much as or slightly
more than in Pittsburgh, wages in the Middle West were considerably
higher: $8.10 in Indiana, and around $9.75 in Illinois and Missouri.

Skilled workers in America were even better off in terms of wages.
In 1860 in Braunschweig, skilled workers and journeymen earned the

[8]*Reports* (1911), 1:100–101; 23:95–97. Comparative statistics on immigrant literacy rates
("cannot read, cannot write"; over fourteen years old) compiled between 1899 and 1910 also
confirm—in general if not in detail—other information about the level of modernization in the
various European countries. Scandinavian immigrants had the lowest rate of illiteracy (0.4
percent); of the larger contingents, the English (1.0 percent) headed the list, followed by the
Irish (2.6 percent). The Germans (5.2 percent) appear somewhat backward, but still far ahead of
the Poles (35.4 percent) and the Southern Italians (53.9 percent) (Ibid., 1:99).
[9]Mönckmeier (1912), 154; Marschalck (1973), 77; Mönckmeier, 158, 156, 159–66, 164.
[10]Schildt (1986), 383; USC 1880.2, 231.

equivalent of $2.64 a week (1875, $4.18), but in the same year their colleagues in the Pittsburgh nail factory were taking home $8.25 (machinist) or $6.75 (carpenter)—$13.80 in 1875 (both). Miners in the Ruhr District earned $0.42 per shift in 1860 (1880, $0.58; 1900, $1.00), but average wages for a miner in Pennsylvania amounted to $1.16 in 1860 ($2.07 in 1880 and $2.00 in 1900).[11]

This differential in nominal wages impressed contemporaries and is certainly worth noting. It cannot be used, however, as an index of improvement in an immigrant's standard of living. The results of a recent comparative study of real wages in England and the United States, despite the later time period covered (1899–1913), can also be applied to Germany, at least to demonstrate general trends: the span between the highest and lowest nominal wages was much greater in the United States. The real wages for unskilled workers in America were only slightly higher at best, but those of skilled workers and artisans were 50 to 100 percent higher than in England.[12]

In his classic and frequently quoted 1906 essay "Why Is There No Socialism in the United States?" the economist Werner Sombart drew a comparison between nominal wages and cost of living in the United States and the German Empire for the year 1900. Although his statistics are scanty and less differentiated than Peter Shergold's, they do confirm two trends: higher wages in America (except in the South; about 100–200 percent higher than in Germany, depending on the region) and, clearly evident from the numerical data though all but ignored by the author, a much larger span between highest and lowest wages in the United States. Sombart's generalizations are largely confirmed by the results of a study by the U.S. Bureau of Labor of hourly wages paid in 1903 in twelve categories of wageworkers (skilled and unskilled) in the United States and in three European industrial nations. According to this study, wages in the United States were 2.1 (unskilled laborer) to 4.0 (plumber) times higher than in Germany.[13]

The results of the studies of 1906 and 1982 show greater consistency when two further facts are taken into account: wages in England were considerably higher than in Germany, and one author was working with nominal wages, the other with real wages.[14] Unskilled workers, there-

[11]USC 1880.2, 533; Tenfelde (1977), 292–97, 603; *History of Wages* (1934), 330–32.

[12]Shergold (1982) compared the living standard of workers in Birmingham and Sheffield to those in Pittsburgh, Pennsylvania (see esp. pp. 224–26).

[13]Instead of the original text by Sombart (Tübingen, 1906), the English version containing a critical review of the statistical material used was our source (Sombart [1976], 74, 67–68; *Reports* 4:55).

[14]See Sombart, 63–74; Shergold, 29–63; Bowley (1900), 81–123; Tenfelde, 602–3; *Reports* 4:55. According to the information in the latter study, British wages in twelve categories of wage-dependent occupations in 1903 were 1.2 to 1.8 times higher than in Germany.

fore, could not expect any spectacular jump in earnings, but artisans and skilled workers certainly could[15]—if they found the right job, stayed in good health, and managed to stay on the job.

In both studies, however, insufficient attention is paid to the drastic effects of unemployment on income. From the Civil War to World War I, unemployment was endemic to the American economy—not only in times of economic crisis. At the lowest point of a recession, unemployment levels might surpass 15 percent, the unemployment frequency (percentage of workers out of work for more than thirty days a year) well over 30 percent and lasting an average of more than four months. But even during times of peak prosperity, the rate did not fall below 6 percent. The relatively normal years of 1890 and 1900 saw an unemployment frequency of 21 and 27 percent of industrial labor and unemployment periods of 3.4 and 3.6 months respectively. These numbers conceal the fact that the situation varied considerably from one occupation to the next. In Massachusetts in 1900, for example, brewers experienced frequencies of 7 percent lasting an average of 4.7 months, workers in shoe factories 55.6 percent and 3.3 months. This pattern held true for five decades: not only did unemployment result from downturns in the business cycle, it was normal for American industry, which was accustomed to the ready availability of a "reserve army" and fighting hard to preserve it by preventing immigration restrictions. Safe in the knowledge that enough labor would be available to permit expansion during periods of economic boom, companies could raise or lower production, keeping market risks to a minimum (in extreme cases, only filling orders already on hand). This may well have been an advantage for the employer; for workers, it often led to material losses and the psychological insecurity of not being able to count on a steady income. In 1900 only one third of all gainfully employed males were working in occupations with annual unemployment rates of under 10 percent; for the majority, unemployment was a constant threat, even in good times.[16]

Native-born Americans were no more immune to unemployment than any other ethnic group, and differences in levels of unemployment between Americans and immigrants were not drastic, but ethnic patterns are nevertheless clear.[17] In the year 1900 in Chicago, in the ten occupa-

[15]Depending on the industrial demand for a particular occupation: joiners and mechanics had a much higher income than tailors or shoemakers. It is also worth noting that increasing industrialization and the spread of machines in the last third of the nineteenth century led to a decline in the importance of skilled trades. The majority of German artisans and skilled workers accordingly suffered from falling wages and growing "alienation" from their work (see Jentz [1983]).

[16]Keyssar (1986), 52, 59, 300–305, 341, 318, 314, 69, 74–75, 61, 68.

[17]Germans living in the industrial state of Massachusetts enjoyed an extremely favorable position. In 1885 they were the group with the lowest incidence of unemployment (20 percent),

tions most prone to unemployment (with 40 percent or more experiencing at least one month-long period of unemployment per year), 21 percent of all Germans were employed, but 11 percent of all Americans; the British took a middle position with 15 percent. The percentage of all other ethnic groups in insecure jobs was considerably higher: 25 percent of the Irish and Scandinavians and over 40 percent of the Poles and Italians.

The position of the Germans in the United States as a whole (also in 1900) was much better than in Chicago. Only 13.9 percent worked in the ten occupations with unemployment frequencies of over 40 percent, just a fraction more than those born in America (13.7 percent). The Irish and British drew even at 18 percent, whereas one-third of the Poles and 42 percent of the Irish were subject to the strong fluctuations in these occupations.[18]

Unemployment in Germany, by contrast, remained relatively low, at least after 1871. Until World War I, the average rate was under 3 percent, and the higher figures in years of economic recession (e.g., 1892, 6.3 percent) were countered by other annual rates that were extremely low (1887, 0.2 percent).[19]

The effects of unemployment do seem to have been incorporated into one study of income in the United States and Europe. At least the results deviate sharply from those previously mentioned, although the sources are no less reliable, and the nature of the survey supports this assumption. In 1889 and 1890 the U.S. Commission of Labor collected information about 8,544 families of workers employed in nine industries (steel, coal, cotton, glass, etc.) in twenty-four American states and five European countries (Belgium, France, Germany, Great Britain, Switzerland). Using these data, family budgets were calculated for each country for heads of households divided into several age groups. Between the ages of 20 and 29, the average worker (usually the sole breadwinner) earned $344 (expenditures were $324, savings, $20) in Europe, as opposed to $557 in

even ahead of the Americans (26 percent) and far better off than the French Canadians, who topped the list (43.2 percent), and the Irish (40.6 percent). In 1900 only 24.2 percent of the Germans in Massachusetts were employed in occupations with unemployment rates of more than 20 percent, as opposed to 40 percent of the Irish and Scandinavians and 59 percent of the Italians. In view of the low percentage of German immigrants in the state (1.8 percent of the population), their privileged position cannot be assumed for the rest of the country. But the general tendency remains much the same, both for the United States as a whole and for large cities with a high percentage of German-Americans (ibid., 77–87, 337).

[18]Nationwide, close to 4.5 million people belonged in this category. The highly seasonal building trades, with six occupations (and with carpenters comprising more than half of the persons employed) accounted for 26 percent. Another 15 percent were glassworkers, fishermen, and miners, but 59 percent belonged to one category: laborers (not specified), i.e., unskilled labor. Calculations were based on Keyssar's method using data in USC 1900.18, 516–23, 64–77.

[19]Niess (1979), 26–32, 232–34; Schäfer (1981), 324–25, 328–29, 337–40.

America (expenditures were \$520, savings, \$37). For all age groups taken as a whole, American family income was 1.45 times higher than European income.[20]

Sombart came to the conclusion that workers in America lived in housing that was more spacious and comfortably furnished and consumed almost three times more meat and flour, four times more sugar and vegetables, and six times more fruit than their German counterparts. Workers in the United States ate like members of the prosperous German middle class; only potato and milk consumption were higher in Germany (almost twice the amount). American workers, and even more so their wives and daughters, were also much better dressed than those in Germany. According to Sombart's investigation, the considerably larger sums earned in America were not invested in savings but used to raise the standard of living—in terms of housing, food, and clothing—to levels unheard of in Germany.[21]

A recent critical investigation of the situation in New York City in 1882 has produced results not greatly at odds with this image of life in America. Based on a questionnaire devised by the socialist New Yorker Volkszeitung in 1882, the main items in the working-class budget corroborate Sombart's results: respondents spent just under 50 percent of their income on food and about 20 percent on housing. The study also confirms that German workers consumed only one-fifth to one-third as much meat as German-Americans and that butter—a real luxury in Germany—was taken for granted in the United States. That most of the people who filled out the questionnaire were nonetheless dissatisfied was probably due to the fact that they were not comparing themselves to laborers in Germany but to better-paid skilled workers in America.[22]

In terms of working hours, just under 60 percent of the companies and factories surveyed in the 1880 census had a ten-hour workday; in two-thirds of the rest, hours were longer. This was not much compared to Germany. In 1903 only unskilled laborers, working 56 hours a week, had comparable working hours. All other groups in Germany usually worked four to six hours more per week than in the United States.[23]

The economic situation of workers in the United States was also strongly influenced by the ups and downs of the economy as a whole, which influenced the level of both unemployment and wages.[24]

[20]Haines (1979), 336–37.
[21]Sombart, 75–105.
[22]Schneider (1983).
[23]USC 1880.2, xxviii; Reports 4:55.
[24]Thus, the average wage per shift earned by a Pennsylvania miner (like letter-writer Peter Klein) could fall to \$0.90 in 1858, reach \$2.58 in 1864, and fall again to \$1.75 in 1865. In 1869 it went up to \$3.44, the all-time high in the nineteenth century. In 1874 wages were back down to

But no arithmetic based on hourly wages, marketbaskets, rent, working hours, unemployment, and business cycles can provide an adequate description of the life of German laborers in the United States. To the extent that it was necessary and desired, they did adapt to their new environment; but in the larger cities (and to a lesser extent also in smaller towns) they held on to so many traditions that they constituted a group in their own right, creating or maintaining a German working-class culture, not only different from the American way of life or that of other ethnic groups but also distinct from the German–American subculture as a whole. On the one hand, there were many attempts to work together with workers of other nationalities on social and political issues. On the other hand, German working-class culture experienced considerable pressure from two sources—the demand for cultural assimilation to American society and the call for solidarity with the entire ethnic group's efforts to preserve its German identity.

It is not possible here to present the many facets of German working-class culture in the United States,[25] but this important aspect of German working-class life in the United States can be briefly characterized. Its most important organ—its link to politics and the unions, to the German labor movement, to Germany and to American society, as well as its medium for communication between leaders and rank and file, educational device and ideological directive, organizational aid for local associations, source of identity, and much more besides—was the labor press. Newspapers also provided readers with culture in the narrower sense by printing working-class literature and poetry, announcing and reviewing theater productions and festivals. In 1903 there were four German-language dailies considered labor or socialist papers: the *New Yorker Volkszeitung*, the Philadelphia *Tageblatt*, the *Chicagoer Arbeiterzeitung*, and the Cincinnati *Arbeiter-Zeitung*. Nine more weeklies were published in these cities and in Milwaukee, St. Louis, Buffalo, Detroit, San Francisco, and Sheboygan, Wisconsin. Even though total circulation may have been limited and financial worries ever present, the subscribers to these publications represented the hard core of the German labor movement in American cities. It seems that around 1900, one out of five laborers in the Chicago area bought or subscribed to a socialist paper.[26] Even if one copy

---

$1.71. For the last quarter of the century, the highest wage was $2.85 (1875), the lowest $1.41 (1884). A weaver in a woolen mill in Connecticut (like letter-writer Martin Weitz) earned an average of $0.48 a day in 1858 (twelve-hour day) and as much as $1.60 in 1865 (eleven-hour day) (*History of Wages* [1934], 330–31, 415–17). These wages, however, should be seen against the background of the overall deflationary tendency in the last third of the century, i.e., increasing real wages with unchanging nominal wages.

[25]It is documented and analyzed in Keil/Jentz (1988); see esp. pp. 221–23.

[26]List of the socialist press in the United States in the anniversary edition of the *New Yorker Volkszeitung*, February 2, 1903, in Hoerder (1985), 73. It is assumed that ca. 53 percent of

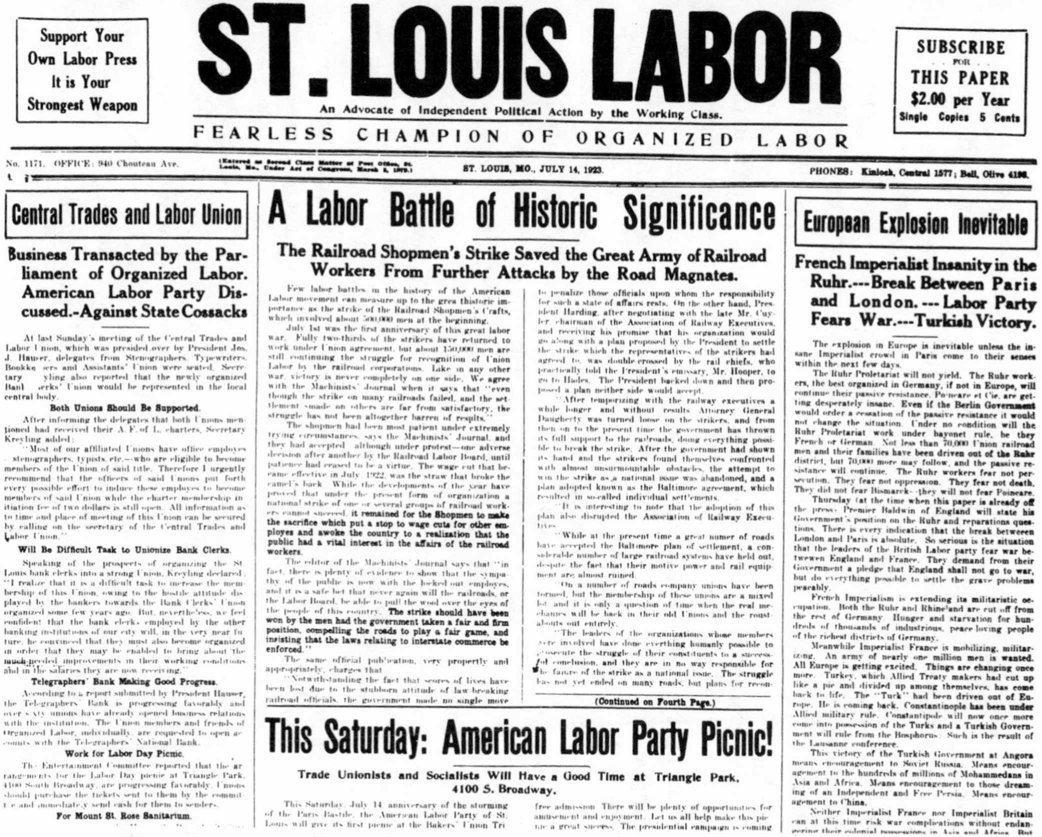

Support Your Own Labor Press It is Your Strongest Weapon

ST. LOUIS LABOR

An Advocate of Independent Political Action by the Working Class.

FEARLESS CHAMPION OF ORGANIZED LABOR

SUBSCRIBE FOR THIS PAPER $2.00 per Year Single Copies 5 Cents

No. 1171. OFFICE: 940 Chouteau Ave. (Entered as Second Class Matter at Post Office, St. Louis, Mo., Under Act of Congress, March 3, 1879.) ST. LOUIS, MO., JULY 14, 1923. PHONES: Kinloch, Central 1577; Bell, Olive 4198.

Central Trades and Labor Union

Business Transacted by the Parliament of Organized Labor. American Labor Party Discussed.-Against State Cossacks

At last Sunday's meeting of the Central Trades and Labor Union, which was presided over by President Jos. J. Hauser, delegates from Stenographers, Typewriters, Bookke ers and Assistants' Union were seated. Secretary yling also reported that the newly organized Ban erks' Union would be represented in the local central body.

Both Unions Should Be Supported.

After informing the delegates that both Unions mentioned had received their A. F. of L. charters, Secretary Kreyling added:

"Most of our affiliated Unions have office employes stenographers, typists, etc.—who are eligible to become members of the Union of said title. Therefore I urgently recommend that the officers of said Unions put forth every possible effort to induce these employes to become members of said Union while the charter membership initiation fee of two dollars is still open. All information as to time and place of meeting of this Union can be secured by calling on the secretary of the Central Trades and Labor Union."

Will Be Difficult Task to Unionize Bank Clerks.

Speaking of the prospects of organizing the St. Louis bank clerks into a strong Union, Kreyling declared: "I realize that it is a difficult task to increase the membership of this Union, owing to the hostile attitude displayed by the bankers towards the Bank Clerks' Union organized some few years ago. But, nevertheless, we feel confident that the bank clerks employed by the other banking institutions of our city will, in the very near future, be convinced that they must also become organized in order that they may be enabled to bring about the much-needed improvements in their working conditions and in the salaries they are now receiving."

Telegraphers' Bank Making Good Progress.

According to a report submitted by President Hauser, the Telegraphers' Bank is progressing favorably and over sixty unions have already opened business relations with the institution. The Union members and friends of Organized Labor, individually, are requested to open accounts with the Telegraphers' National Bank.

Work for Labor Day Picnic.

The Entertainment Committee reported that the arrangements for the Labor Day picnic at Triangle Park, 4100 South Broadway, are progressing favorably. Unions should purchase the tickets sent to them by the committee and immediately send cash for them to senders.

For Mount St. Rose Sanitarium.

A Labor Battle of Historic Significance

The Railroad Shopmen's Strike Saved the Great Army of Railroad Workers From Further Attacks by the Road Magnates.

Few labor battles in the history of the American Labor movement can measure up to the grea thistoric importance as the strike of the Railroad Shopmen's Crafts, which involved about 500,000 men at the beginning.

July 1st was the first anniversary of this great labor war. Fully two-thirds of the strikers have returned to work under Union agreement, but about 150,000 men are still continuing the struggle for recognition of Union Labor by the railroad corporations. Like in any other war, victory is never completely on one side. We agree with the Machinists' Journal when it says that "even though the strike on many railroads failed, and the settlement smade on others are far from satisfactory, the struggle has not been altogether barren of resplts."

The shopmen had been most patient under extremely trying circumstances, says the Machinists' Journal, and they had accepted although under protest—one adverse decision after another by the Railroad Labor Board, until patience had ceased to be a virtue. The wage cut that became effective in July, 1922, was the straw that broke the camel's back. While the developments of the year have proved that under the present form of organization a national strike of one or several groups of railroad workers cannot succeed, **it remained for the Shopmen to make the sacrifice which put a stop to wage cuts for other employes and awoke the country to a realization that the public had a vital interest in the affairs of the railroad workers.**

The editor of the Machinists' Journal says that "in fact, there is plenty of evidence to show that the sympathy of the public is now with the locked out employes, and it is a safe bet that never again will the railroads, or the Labor Board, be able to pull the wool over the eyes of the people of this country. **The strike should have been won by the men had the government taken a fair and firm position, compelling the roads to play a fair game, and insisting that the laws relating to interstate commerce be enforced.**"

The same official publication, very propertly and appropriately, charges that

"Notwithstanding the fact that scores of lives have been lost due to the stubborn attitude of law-breaking railroad officials, the government made no single move to penalize those officials upon whom the responsibility for such a state of affairs rests. On the other hand, President Harding, after negotiating with the late Mr. Cuyler, chairman of the Association of Railway Executives, and receiving his promise that his organization would go along with a plan proposed by the President to settle the strike which the representatives of the strikers had agreed to, was double-crossed by the rail chiefs, who practically told the President's emissary, Mr. Hooper, to go to Hades. The President backed down and then proposed a plan neither side would accept.

"After temporizing with the railway executives a while longer and without results Attorney General Daugherty was turned loose on the strikers, and from then on to the present time the government has thrown its full support to the railroads, doing everything possible to break the strike. After the government had shown its hand and the strikers found themselves confronted with almost unsurmountable obstacles, the attempt to win the strike as a national issue was abandoned, and a plan adopted known as the Baltimore agreement, which resulted in so-called individual settlements.

"It is interesting to note that the adoption of this plan also disrupted the Association of Railway Executives.

"While at the present time a great numer of roads have accepted the Baltimore plan of settlement, a considerable number of large railroad systems have held out, despite the fact that their motive power and rail equipment are almost ruined.

"On a number of roads company unions have been formed, but the membership of these unions are a mixed lot and it is only a question of time when the real mechanics will be back in their old Unions and the roustabouts out entirely.

"The leaders of the organizations whose members were involved have done everthing humanly possible to prosecute the struggle of their constituents to a successful conclusion, and they are in no way responsible for the failure of the strike as a national issue. The struggle has not yet ended on many roads, but plans for recon-

(Continued on Fourth Page.)

This Saturday: American Labor Party Picnic!

Trade Unionists and Socialists Will Have a Good Time at Triangle Park, 4100 S. Broadway.

This Saturday, July 14, anniversary of the storming of the Paris Bastile, the American Labor Party of St. Louis will give its first picnic at the Bakers' Union Tri free admission. There will be plenty of opportunities for amusement and enjoyment. Let us all help make this picnic a great success. The presidential campaign is coming

European Explosion Inevitable

French Imperialist Insanity in the Ruhr.---Break Between Paris and London.---Labor Party Fears War.---Turkish Victory.

The explosion in Europe is inevitable unless the insane Imperialist crowd in Paris come to their senses within the next few days.

The Ruhr Proletariat will not yield. The Ruhr workers, the best organized in Germany, if not in Europe, will continue their passive resistance. Poincare et Cie. are getting desperately insane. Even if the Berlin Government would order a cessation of the passive resistance it would not change the situation. Under no condition will the Ruhr Proletariat work under bayonet rule, be they French or German. Not less than 70,000 Union railroad men and their families have been driven out of the Ruhr district, but 70,000 more may follow, and the passive resistance will continue. The Ruhr workers fear not persecution. They fear not oppression. They fear not death. They did not fear Bismarck--they will not fear Poincare.

Thursday (at the time when this paper is already off the press) Premier Baldwin of England will state his Government's position on the Ruhr and reparations questions. There is every indication that the break betweeen London and Paris is absolute. So serious is the situation that the leaders of the British Labor party fear war betwewen England and France. They demand from their Government a pledge that England shall not go to war, but do everything possible to settle the grave problems peaceably.

French Imperialism is extending its militaristic occupation. Both the Ruhr and Rhineland are cut off from the rest of Germany. Hunger and starvation for hundreds of thousands of industrious, peace loving people of the richest districts of Germany.

Meanwhile Imperialist France is mobilizing, militarizing. An army of nearly one million men is wanted. All Europe is getting excited. Things are changing once more. Turkey, which Allied Treaty makers had cut up like a pie and divided up among themselves, has come back to life. The "Turk" had been driven out of Europe. He is coming back. Constantinople has been under Allied military rule. Constantipole will now once more come into possession of the Turks and a Turkish Government will rule from the Bosphorus. Such is the result of the Lausanne conference.

This victory of the Turkish Government at Angora means encouragement to Soviet Russia. Means encouragement to the hundreds of millions of Mohammedans in Asia and Africa. Means encouragement to those dreaming of an Independent and Free Persia. Means encouragement to China.

Neither Imperialist France nor Imperialist Britain can at this time risk war complications without endangering their colonial possessions in Asia and Africa. But

Figure 22. Headlines from *St. Louis Labor,* July 14, 1923, reflect a pressing domestic labor issue, international concerns affecting the paper's largely German constituency, and social functions of the labor party in the ethnic community. The railroad strike mentioned in the headline figures prominently in the Dilger series. Photo courtesy of State Historical Society of Missouri, Columbia.

passed through several hands, the fact remains that the majority of members of the working class preferred middle-class publications, some one hundred thousand copies of which were sold around 1900 in the Chicago area, as opposed to only fifteen thousand of the *Chicagoer Arbeiterzeitung* (in 1895).

Nevertheless, German labor played a significant role in the founding of socialist parties in the United States and for many years accounted for a disproportionate share of their members. One might even speculate that the strong German influence at least partly explains the miserable failure of the socialist movement in the United States, despite 140 years of grave social injustice and capitalistic exploitation. Rigid devotion to principles, constant ideological quarrels, and last but not least the conviction of party leaders (often simultaneously editors) that only they could point the way to salvation often led to isolation and sectarianism. Even if in one of the bastions of German socialism, Chicago, the Socialist Labor party was able to capture twelve thousand votes in the spring of 1879, six months later in the fall, its share had slipped back to five thousand.[27] Since this five thousand included a considerable number of votes cast by members of other nationalities living in the city of half a million, and since some 35,000 Germans were registered, it is clear that in terms of voting behavior—and in stark contrast to the growth of socialism in the German Empire—only a small minority of the working class stuck with the socialists through thick and thin.

It is safe to assume that active socialists in Chicago, like most union members, belonged to the group of skilled laborers in trades and industry which accounted for half of all German laborers in the 1880s. The degree of unionization in a number of industries was remarkable. In 1886, 59 percent of German metalworkers were organized, giving them a majority of 60 percent of union members, even though they accounted for only 20 percent of the workers in the industry. Among cabinetmakers and carpenters, bakers, butchers, and brewers, a significant majority of union members were Germans; 80 percent of the German masons were unionized, 84 percent of the bakers, and almost 99 percent (600 out of 608) of the brickmakers. In 1886 only 23 percent of Chicago's laborers were German, but they accounted for 31 percent of local organized labor.

German-Americans were gainfully employed (1880: USC 1880.1, 870; 1890: USC 1890.2, 650–51) and that in 1900 a good two-thirds were still members of the working class (Keil [1983a], 23). Thus, 70,000 of the 200,000 Germans living in the Chicago area, and 140,000 of the ca. 400,000 in greater New York City, were working class.

[27]*Chicago Freie Presse, Abendpost,* and *Illinois Staatszeitung;* Arndt/Olson (1965), 56, 70, 74, 58. In New York City, the situation for middle-class publications was even more favorable (Arndt/Olson, e.g., 370, 389, 406; Kiesewetter [1985], 203).

Germans were not only heavily overrepresented, they made up the largest group, even outnumbering native Americans (22 percent).[28]

Mass immigration and the presence of numerous ethnic groups exerted a strong influence on the development of the American labor movement, but it was the Germans in particular who played a large role, even if often on the losing side, in pushing American unions in the pragmatic direction that came to characterize the American Federation of Labor (AFL). At the same time that German union members and organizers contributed to the growth of the labor movement, the 1880s saw the development of the basic principles of the AFL which were to remain dominant for the next hundred years: the rejection of "ultimate goals. . . . we are opposed to theorists" and the strict limitation of union activity to improving material conditions for workers without attempting to change the political or social system as a whole. This position emerged partly as a reaction to socialist objectives supported primarily by German immigrants, who argued the need to combine concrete union activity with the struggle for social reform and social revolution.[29]

Although the primary rationale for union organization was economic, unions also provided opportunities for socializing and met the need for identification, just like the rich variety of clubs and associations. In most of such groups, one nationality predominated among the members. If only a few Germans lived in one place, there might be only one singing club and one *Turnverein*. But the larger the German community grew, the more numerous and more varied the clubs became—based on regional background, religious affiliation, and social class. Among the more than two hundred singing clubs in Chicago at the turn of the century, there was plenty of room for more than one *Arbeiter-Gesangverein, Arbeiter-Männerchor,* and *Arbeiter-Sängerbund,* just as the *Arbeiter-Turnverein* and *Arbeiter-Sportverein*[30] were separate from their middle-class counterparts and had their own political program and activities. Apart from the aspects of working-class culture mentioned above (theater, literature, etc.), less well-organized and even spontaneous forms of social contact also deserve mention, such as going on a picnic or gathering in a beer garden in the summer or meeting in one of the numerous German saloons any time of year.

At a time when no system of social security, health insurance, or welfare existed, the lodge was of central importance—a mutual aid fund or association, either organized by religious orders or secular groups

[28]Keil (1983a), 23; Keil (1983b), 164, 162–63.
[29]Quote from Adolph Strasser in Brody (1980), 612.
[30]"Arbeiter" means "worker"; "Gesangverein," singing club; "Männerchor," men's choir; "Sängerbund," singer's society; "Sportverein," sports club.

298   WORKERS

(Sons of Hermann, Harugari, or Odd Fellows) or set up for members of a
particular occupation (*Kranken-Unterstützungs-Verein der Deutschen Mas-
chinisten von N.Y. u. Umg.*) or for immigrants from a specific region
(*Edenkober Kr.-Unterst.-Verein*).[31] Mutual aid funds were often based on
guild traditions, familiar to most immigrants from Germany before the
general system of mandatory health insurance was introduced in the
German Empire in 1883. Not so in the United States—nothing comparable was ever introduced. Most of the health funds worked the same way
as the machinists' fund mentioned above (at least as well as they could,
given their narrow base and shaky actuarial theory). For an annual premium of $2, the fund paid out "up to $500 sickness benefits. $6 per week
up to $300 and $3 a week for the rest and $200 in case of the death of a
member and $75 for his wife. . . ."[32]

Between the Civil War and World War I in the big cities of the Northeast and Middle West, German workers, and in particular skilled workers, developed a remarkably independent way of life within the German
community. Recognizably German in its origins, this working-class
culture had nonetheless adapted to its new environment. A minority was
actively involved in socialist politics and played a major role in shaping
the American Socialist party, which never became a significant force in
American politics. A somewhat larger number—comprised almost exclusively of skilled laborers—was active in organized labor and helped
establish a viable union organization in the United States. Still, to judge
from the evidence cited here as well as the constant complaints of the
working-class press, it would seem that the large majority lacked sufficient loyalty to socialist ideals to withstand the temptations of middle-
class ideology. They exerted no lasting influence on American society to
speak of, except perhaps when workers acted not as members of the
proletariat but as Germans, together with their countrymen of other
social classes, pressing for a more tolerant attitude toward alcohol, for
example, or Sunday as a day of recreation as well as rest.

[31]*New Yorker Volkszeitung,* February 21, 1903, and January 29, 1928; both quoted in Hoerder
(1985), 75–76, 137. "Lodge" was a term often used for a union organization at the grass-roots
level.
[32]Ibid., 75.

9

Johann Carl Wilhelm Pritzlaff (John Pritzlaff)

About some aspects of this letterwriter's life we know almost nothing, although an unusual amount of information is available about others. Johann Pritzlaff was born on March 6, 1820, in the small village of Trutzlatz, Naugard County;[1] when he emigrated he was living in Trieglaff, Greifenberg County, both in Pomerania.[2] Almost nothing is known about his parents or his brothers and sisters. His father is said to have been a master tailor who died in 1839, his brother August was a teacher in Tonnebuhr, Kammin County, and we know the names of two more of his siblings—Elisabeth and Heinrich. Before emigrating to America, Pritzlaff himself earned his living as a shepherd.[3] And that exhausts our knowledge of his family and early youth.

[1] Aikens/Proctor (1897), 556; obituary in the *Sentinel* (Milwaukee), August 17, 1900; Watrons (1909), 777–78; Conrad 1 (1895), 429–30; *History of Milwaukee* (1881), 1, 303–4; Buck 2 (1881), 88–89.

[2] "The shepherd Pritzlaff (went along without permission)" is listed for Trieglaff in the emigration lists; Iwan 2 (1943), 250. The identification of Pritzlaff as this shepherd seems quite certain, when one takes into account both the departure date and the additional lines by the county magistrate von der Marwitz (Greifenberg) of June 29, 1839, when he reported the departure of Pritzlaff's traveling companion, Carl Zion: "On 6/9 a shepherd named Pritzlaff from Triglaff and the former teacher Zion from Swesof," both of whom did not return and probably had traveled to Hamburg with fellow believers (1:131).

[3] Aikens/Proctor, 556. The three villages mentioned belong to three different counties, but they are all located (together with Schwesow, which is referred to frequently) within a few miles of one another—about twenty miles as the crow flies from the Baltic Sea and forty miles east of the present border between Germany and Poland. This area was characterized by poverty, large estates, small villages (average population in the three counties was 244), total lack of industry, and cultivation of potatoes and rye (Keyser 1 [1939], 170–71, 184–86, 204–5; Lucht [1966]; Vollack 7 [1969], 17–26; *Tabellen* [1851], 340–43).

The group of emigrants to which Pritzlaff belonged, by contrast, is one of the best documented for Germany: the Old Lutherans who left Prussia between 1835 and 1854.

After King Friedrich Wilhelm III decreed the unification of the Lutheran and the Reformed state churches into a United Evangelical Church in 1817, bitter controversies developed, despite widespread support for unification, with forces who sought to maintain traditional beliefs and liturgical rites. Following the legal introduction of the union in 1830 and starting in Silesia, dissenting groups formed congregations, which after 1845 were commonly called "Old Lutheran." They regarded joining the Union as deviating from the true faith and insisted on maintaining their own pastors and liturgy; the Prussian government reacted by suspending and imprisoning the clergy and confiscating the churches. The movement continued to spread, reaching Pomerania first. There was considerable dispute about emigration within the Old Lutheran congregations during the 1830s, with one group arguing in favor of freedom of religious expression abroad and the other in favor of standing firm in the face of religious persecution at home.

Between 1836 and 1838 the Prussian government did its utmost to make emigration unpleasant and difficult for the Old Lutherans. Despite the fact that emigration was basically permitted for all, Old Lutherans had to put up with complicated procedures and harassment. Anyone who applied for permission to emigrate had to appear before a commission composed of government officials and clergymen to defend his request. These massive attempts to discourage would-be emigrants from leaving were usually ineffective. As a last resort in the attempt to make leaving Prussia more difficult, it was decreed that every group of emigrants must be accompanied by a pastor.

The idea of emigration nevertheless attracted more and more supporters, and in Pomerania the pastor Johann Grabau from Erfurt offered to accompany a group of emigrants, while a retired Prussian captain named Karl G. H. von Rohr (who later became a pastor in America) worked to organize the mass exodus of 1839. The latter made numerous trips to form an emigration society made up of Old Lutherans from Pomerania, Saxony, Silesia, and Berlin.

In the early months of 1839, the representatives from the participating congregations agreed on a set of articles, according to which community property was not an intended goal of the society, but a common fund was established, to be raised through voluntary contributions and loans, to help pay for the passage of poor families as well. New York was their first destination; they planned to sail from Hamburg on May 1, 1839.[4]

[4]On the development of the Old Lutheran movement and their decision to emigrate see

When it turned out that the direct crossing from Hamburg to New York for one thousand persons would cost about 40,000 talers, but the common fund contained only about 30,000, von Rohr astutely negotiated an arrangement that involved first crossing over to England, then traveling across England to Liverpool, and finally sailing from Liverpool to New York. Von Rohr went ahead across the English Channel and then across the Atlantic to prepare quarters in America, while Pastor Grabau accompanied the emigrants.

The Old Lutheran emigration of 1839, to which Pritzlaff belonged, ultimately included 1,239 persons, of which 570 came from Pomerania (305 alone from Kammin County, 103 from Greifenberg County); the rest came from Saxony, Silesia, and Berlin. This migration to the United States continued until 1854 (reaching a total of some 5,000 persons) but after 1839 there was only one more large wave of emigration, when in 1843 some 1,600 persons arrived, primarily from Pomerania (1,017) and Brandenburg (537).[5]

Pritzlaff joined the group of 176 persons from Greifenberg County who traveled by wagon and arrived in Stettin on May 17, 1839. On May 22 he started off on his overland trip to Hamburg and arrived on June 1; the convoy of wagons, however, was unable to leave Stettin until June 6. In Hamburg he had to wait for the arrival of the other groups, some of which came by way of Berlin and by water. Finally, on June 28 the first steamboat left (the fifth and last did not leave until July 27). Pritzlaff must have been on either the second or third boat, both of which left Hamburg on June 30. Pritzlaff himself reports the further stages of the trip to Buffalo, confirming the statements of Wilhelm Iwan, an historian of the Old Lutheran movement.[6]

In Buffalo, where most of the immigrants were housed in rented warehouses, there was already a small congregation of Silesian Old Lutherans with a pastor named Leberecht Krause. Here it was decided that those who were interested and had sufficient means would go straight on with von Rohr by way of the Great Lakes to the Wisconsin Territory, where government land was available for $1.25 an acre and where they intended to found a small settlement near Milwaukee; the rest should stay in the Buffalo area. Those who were unable to find work in the city were to travel at common expense to Portage on the Genesee

Clemens (1976), 15–56, and Iwan 1:9–157, 2:138–40. It was expected that these loans would be repaid in America, and they were—at least in part (Document "Überfahrts-Kasse" [passage-fund] of April, 1843, in John Pritzlaff Hardware Company Papers, State Historical Society of Wisconsin).

[5]Iwan 1:148–50; Clemens, 55; Iwan 2:294, 297, 291.

[6]See Pritzlaff's letters of June 23, 1839, and April 23, 1842; Iwan 1:130–31, 168–70.

Canal, where work on the canal was paid well and the proximity to Buffalo would permit setting up a daughter congregation. Pritzlaff belonged to this group.

Schools were quickly set up, also in Portage. In Buffalo the first two teachers (before they were dismissed for sectarianism) were Carl Zion and Gottfried Dreyer, whom Pritzlaff frequently mentions. Grabau remained in Buffalo as pastor for both the town and Portage.

In October the forty families who had traveled with von Rohr bought 1,200 acres of government land in what later became Ozaukee County, fifteen miles northwest of the town of Milwaukee. Their land was completely unimproved woodland, and they worked hard to fend off the approaching winter by building log cabins as quickly as possible. During this time, the men lived in tents and the families remained behind in Milwaukee. The settlement received the name "Freistadt" [Freetown]—a conscious contrast to religious persecution at home. Only a few families remained in Milwaukee, mostly fishermen and skilled craftsmen, and they founded a congregation that shared the services of Pastor Krause, newly arrived from Buffalo, with the church in Freistadt.

Milwaukee, where Pritzlaff settled in 1841, was still a true frontier town; in 1835 only 125 people had been living there; when Pritzlaff arrived there were not quite two thousand. Then the town grew by leaps and bounds; in 1850 it had a population of 20,000, in 1860 some 45,000, and at both times a good third were German immigrants. By 1890 the proportion of those born in Germany had decreased—55,000 out of a total of 204,000 residents; but if the second generation is taken into consideration (persons with two German parents, another 55,000, and with one German parent, 15,000), a clear German majority of 125,000 emerges. This high percentage of Germans, stable throughout the nineteenth century, permitted the growth of a many-sided and multilayered German community with a rich supply of cultural, educational, and social institutions. German-language newspapers had been founded in the 1840s. Milwaukee is still considered to be the most German city in the United States, and observers even today see traces of the influence, such as the "Prussian" tendency not to cross the street when the light is red.[7]

The existence of a large German population, together with the pioneer character of the city at mid-century, resulted in good opportunities for Germans to start and develop businesses. Only a few, however, knew how to do this as well as Pritzlaff, after he opened his own store in 1850.

[7]Iwan 1:172–97; Conzen (1976), 14; USC 1890.1, 705–29; Conzen (1976), 184–87; on the German influence on towns in the Middle West see Fawcett/Thomas (1983), 38.

Pritzlaff's letters have been preserved only in typescript; judging from the typeface, the copying was done in America around 1950. Though the transcriber was obviously quite meticulous in marking illegible words or problems in deciphering, the spelling, grammar, and possibly punctuation and sentence structure were probably standardized. Thus it is impossible to establish Pritzlaff's actual degree of literacy.

It is safe to assume that he received only a minimal amount of formal education. But the language he used—though somewhat stilted through his frequent employment of biblical quotations and pious turns of phrase—is clear, precise, and descriptive, expressing acute observation as well as a wry sense of humor. To the reader of his letters in the original, his subsequent success as an astute American businessman does not come as a complete surprise.[8]

Johann C. W. Pritzlaff

Hamburg, June 28th, 1839 / 11 o'clock in the evening. This is a faithful saying: For if we be dead with him, we shall also live with him: If we suffer, we shall also reign with him: if we deny him, he also will deny us: If we believe not, yet he abideth faithful: he cannot deny himself. 2 Tim. 2, 11–13.

Thus will I, as I still live, take up the cross and follow you; my God, make me ready, all things work together for good; help me to fight a good fight, that I may finish my course.
Dearly beloved brother and mother,

[12 ll.: has had no time to write] You dear ones know that we took our leave of you on May 17th, at about half past nine, amid many tears. The evening is still unforgettable for me, especially how we took each other by the hand and kissed and all promised to follow the Lord Jesus with all our hearts. Suppose you all know what happened to us in Stettin; how we had to part from our dear brothers and sisters and how we all lay waiting for almost five days.

Dear brother, mother and sister: time is short; I must close, for we must be on board this afternoon at 2 and load our belongings onto the steamship. As of today we have been in Hamburg already for 4 weeks. We will travel by steamship to Hull in England, from there to Liverpool by steamboats, then we have to go by sailing ship and will perhaps land in Philadelphia. When we have arrived at our destination, I will write more

[8]Typed transcripts are located in the State Historical Society of Wisconsin in Madison, John Pritzlaff Hardware Company Papers.

about our trip. I am, thank the Lord, still quite hale and hearty. How things are with you, I do not know. If in this life we shall never see each other again with our own eyes, oh! may we see each other eternally before God's throne. So, this is the heartfelt wish of your loving and faithful son and brother,

Carl Pritzlaff.

[4 ll.: he is well]

Beloved brother Heitke,[9]

I wanted very much to write to you as well, but time is so short I cannot; please, do not take offense. I will write more when we have arrived at our destination, if the dear Lord guides us to there, about how wonderfully our merciful Father has guided us. [2 ll.: greetings]

I, Zion, send my best to all of you. Remember us in your prayers to the Lord. Hallelujah! Amen. C. Zion.[10]

Give my warmest regards to your dear wife, and pray for us, that the Lord will continue to grant His mercy to us. We have twice received Holy Communion here in Hamburg from our dear Pastor Grabow. Time is up; our things have to be on the steamship. [. . .] I also want to thank you again for the good deed you did for me. Our merciful Father will repay you. May the peace of God be with you, your dear wife and with your poor brother Carl Pritzlaff.

Hamburg, June 29th 1839, 11 o'clock in the morning.

Milwaukee, Wisconsin Territory, April 23rd, 1842

Dearly beloved mother, brother, and sister,

Grace be unto you from God, the Father, and from Jesus Christ, the true and faithful witness, which is, and which was, and which is to come and give unto every one according to his works. [14 ll.: further religious wishes] May the merciful Father bless you with good health and long life, with honor and goods, that your house may be filled with plenty.

Since I have been gone from your midst now for almost three years and in that time have heard nothing from you and you also not much from me, I can no longer refrain from informing you how I have been during this time and how I am now, both in body and in spirit. [4 ll.: should have written a long time ago] I have comforted myself very often with the hope that you had learned from the Tonnebur folks' letters that I am here

[9]This is probably the Carl Heidke in Tonnebuhr, frequently referred to in the letters, who may have helped Pritzlaff pay for his passage (see the end of the letter).

[10]Carl Zion from Schwesow, who is mentioned frequently in the letters, is recorded in Iwan's emigration lists for 1839 as "former schoolteacher" (2:250), and was almost certainly Pritzlaff's traveling companion on the way to Hamburg (see n. 2, above).

in America and still alive. You know that on the 16th of May 1839 I took my leave from your midst, amid many tears and with sad feelings of melancholy, and set out for the emigration to America. Then, after we had safely arrived in Hamburg in less than two weeks after leaving home, we waited an entire month for our countrymen and fellow-believers who had to stay behind in Stettin, as you probably know, because of their passports. The last day we were in Hamburg I wrote a letter to you, which had to be done in a great hurry; I do not know, however, if you received it. On June 31st [sic] we, that is the Schwesow congregation, left Hamburg on a steamship for England, and landed after 3½ days in New Castle. On the third day after our arrival we went from there by train to Carlisle, and from there again by steamship to Liverpool. On July 11th we put to sea from there on a large three-masted sailing ship and after enduring many difficulties, we arrived with God's merciful succor on September 6th in New York in America. The last 14 days of our ocean voyage and the first two weeks after our arrival in New York I was very ill, but the gracious Lord, thanks be to His mercy, saw me through and helped me out like a father. After we went from New York by steamship to Albany and from there, partly by train, partly by canal boats that were pulled by horses, we finally arrived in Buffalo, then the common funds were almost exhausted and there was not enough work available for as many people as we were all arriving at one time. We therefore had to separate. Those of us who were well-off went by steamship another 1100 English miles to Milwaukee and the area, in Wisconsin Territory, and the poor were forced to look for work in and around Buffalo; many of us went 15 German miles away from Buffalo to work on the canal.[11] Here things were not the best for us, like they usually are at the start for many immigrants who have no mastery of the English language. In a short time on the canal we earned enough money that we could travel from one place to another, which I was very fond of doing and still am. After I had worked for one year in New York State, Herman Roggenbuck[12] and I traveled to the state of Pennsylvanien, because wages there were higher than in New York State. After we had worked there for 9 months, H. Roggenbuck moved back to his parents and his relatives in Buffalo, who then left together to hasten after their friends and fellow-believers in Milwaukee. Since I could not get the wages I had earned at the same time as my comrade, I was forced to stay there for another 4 months, when I

[11]To Portage (about sixty miles southeast of Buffalo) on the Genesee Canal. The canal, a southern branch of the Erie Canal, was not finished until 1862 (Taylor [1951], 36).

[12]Herman Roggenbuck, about the same age as Pritzlaff (see his letter of February 21, 1847), must have been the son of the "resident Johann Roggenbuck" from the neighboring village of Schwesow, who emigrated to America in 1839 "with wife and five children" (Iwan 2:249).

then got my wages, and then I set out on September 29th 1841 and traveled partly by train and partly by canal boat to Buffalo and from there after a 3-day stay again by steamship (across Lake Erie, Lake Huron and Lake Michigan) to Milwaukee which is on the latter lake. This long distance of 1300 English miles (or about 325 German miles), which cost me 20 of our talers, I covered safely in 9 days. Great was the joy when I was reunited with my fellow countrymen and fellow-believers, many of whom have already bought land and are building a veritable German *Siedlement* [settlement], since I hadn't seen any of them for 3 years, also hadn't heard much about them. This past winter I worked for an American *Farmer* or *Bauer*,[13] and got 9 dollars a month; but now I've left and haven't yet starting looking for work again. I also want to mention briefly that you shouldn't imagine that the good farming families here are like the ones over there in Prussia, instead they have a much more decent and free way of life. One never sees American women working outside, and they dress very well. They seldom walk anywhere, neither to church nor other social occasions, they ride or drive. And if a farmer over there were to offer such fare like the farmers provide here, one would judge and come to the conclusion that he would go bankrupt in a short time. America is a good country, it blossoms under God's blessing, but it bears thorns and thistles as well. For a man who works, it is much better here than over there; you can earn your daily bread better than in Germany, one doesn't live so restrictedly and in such servitude as you do under the great estate-owners, you don't have to put your hat under your arm or leave it at the door when you want to have the money you've earned. There is quite a fair amount of equality among men here in America. The high and wealthy are not ashamed to associate with the poor and lowly. If one man works for another, he is not tied to any particular time, rather he leaves when he wants to; everyone is his own master. You can also travel freely and unhindered all through America without a passport or anything like that. There's quite a bit of traveling here in general, when a father has a house full of children and they are grown up they are spread out almost all over America. So, with respect to external circumstances, I am, praise and thanks be to our dear Lord, quite hale and hearty and I am doing quite well; I have not been ill for even one day in America, except for the first two weeks. I have clothing and bread as well; I also have money, and as Our Lord Jesus says: If you have food and raiment, be therewith content. How are you, dear brother? How is mother? Is she still alive? Oh, how I long to see her again, and all of you. How are

---

[13]He apparently worked primarily as a teamster for a man named Daniel Richards (Aikens/ Proctor, 557; Conrad 1:429; Watrons, 777).

Heinrich and Elisabeth? Are they all hale and hearty? How happy I would be if Heinrich and Elisabeth came here. Even if emigrating is not a matter of conscience for them, it could still do them good in the future. No one should fear that he is committing a sin if he emigrates in order to make a better living here than over there. For the earth is the Lord's and given by God to mankind, and he can go wherever he will. I also wish with all my heart that my dear mother would come, if it were possible. I would not be afraid of taking care of her here, for it is my duty as a child, and the dear Lord will grant me His grace to do it. If some others emigrate next summer from your area and mother or Heinrich and Elisabeth want to come over here, then I ask someone to advance them the money, especially if C. Heidke or master shepherd Wangerin is along, since I will gladly commit myself that they will get their own back again. If mother does not come, then I ask her not to keep her children back and to consider what a yoke they have to bear over there and what glorious freedom they could enjoy over here. [. . .] The folks from Tonnebur are, as far as I know, all still hale and hearty; they all live 16 English miles from town, except Christian Wilke who lives here and sends his warmest regards.[14] A letter also arrived recently from Schwesow from farmer Wendt, in which he writes that Roggenbuck and Carl Zion are going begging here, which is a shameful lie, instead they make a comfortable living and thank the dear Lord that He brought them out of a land where they would have had to go begging in time, since most of the employers do not want to give a true Lutheran a job any more. Zion works for a tailor and earns 8 of our talers a month, and Roggenbuck works around the town. They send their best to all of you; also Dreier and old Father Wussow and his children, who are almost all married now, except the two youngest.[15]

As far as church matters go, I cannot write much that is good, for the Antichrist has also set up his See in America. But the best thing here is that everyone has the freedom to act according to his own belief. He who follows false teachings here does so of his own free will. We cannot thank God enough that He has brought us to such a country in this hour of temptation, which has struck throughout the whole world. [6 ll.: church matters] But since in America there is freedom of religious belief and expression in the widest sense of the term, Christian congregations have to watch out, on the one hand, that they do not get bogged down in squabbling, and on the other hand that they do not give away the Divine

[14]Apparently they were at Freistadt (see this chapter's introduction); probably the "invalid resident Christian Wilke with wife . . . and three children" (Iwan 2:251).

[15]"Schoolteacher Gottfried Dreyer (37) with his wife Wilhelmine, née Wussow (28), and son August (2)" emigrated from Kammin in 1839 (Ibid.).

rights that they have and allow the priests to set up a dominion that runs counter to the word of God, whereby they fall, becoming mere servants of men, and lose the freedom given them by Christ, according to 1. Cor. 7, 23. And now since the preacher Stephan from Dresden[16] has been infected by the plague of priestly rule against the word of God, along with several others, among others our former preacher Grabau and Krause, a large number of their former parishioners (including myself) have parted from them,[17] and now have formed an Evangelical Lutheran congregation on their own, that is in Buffalo and Milwaukee, under the spiritual supervision and guidance of Pastor Bürger,[18] the former pastor in Lunzenau in Saxony, who with all the power of the Lord and all the strength of his might opposes the Lutheran papacy which P. Grabau and Krause are planning and want to introduce under the guise and in the name of pure Lutheran services and strict church discipline. Pastor Grabau has also published a creed under the name of: *Hirten-Brief* [pastoral letter],[19] in which he cut off all the rights of the parishes, which they have according to God's Word and the Confessional Writings. Thus we do not shrink from rejecting Grabau's pastoral letter for we believe: "That the Lutheran creed is neither deficient nor false, but rather sufficient and perfect," so we do not need a new creed at all. [8 ll.: more about pastoral letter]

Dear Brother August, one thing I ask of you, that you write to me soon again, and do not tarry as long as I have done; write how things are in Prussia and what you are all doing in general, and whether Mother or Heinrich and Elisabeth are inclined to come over here; also what Heinrich

[16]"Bishop" Martin Stephan, spiritual leader of a group of Old Lutherans from Saxony, left shortly before most of the immigrants in 1839 and settled in St. Louis. This group later became the Missouri Synod, which Pritzlaff also joined.

[17]Johann Andreas August Grabau (1804–1879), ordained in Erfurt in 1834. Arrested as an Old Lutheran, he was released from prison only on the condition that he emigrate in 1839. In the United States he took over the congregation in Buffalo and was the leading figure and driving force behind the Buffalo Synod (Iwan 1, and 2:81–94).

Leberecht Friedrich Traugott Krause (1804–1885) was ordained in 1835 in Lobau, Saxony, and persecuted as an Old Lutheran. He emigrated to the United States in May 1839 with a group of sixty Lutherans. In 1841 he took over the congregations in Freistadt and Milwaukee, until in 1848 he transferred to Martinville near Buffalo (Ibid. 1, and 2:67–80).

For several decades the history of the Old Lutherans in America was marked by fierce controversies and the repeated formation of splinter groups based on theological issues of clerical authority and personal differences.

[18]Ernst Moritz Bürger, one of the Saxon pastors who emigrated with Stephan. In 1841, although he was actually on his way back to Germany, he got caught in the middle of the dispute between Grabau and Krause and their parishes, which the two clergymen brought to an end by excommunicating their refractory parishioners. Bürger felt this measure was unjustified and accepted a call as pastor from the excommunicated group (Iwan 2:126–27, 140–41).

[19]Written by Grabau at the end of 1841 to prevent, among other things, the parish in Milwaukee, which at that time had no pastor, from allowing lay elders of the church to administer sacraments in emergencies (Iwan 2:129–33).

is up to. Please be so good, too, and let Wangerin in Trieglaff[20] read this letter; we send him all our best, also his wife and sons. He should write to me sometime; my best also to his two hands, C. Heuer and F. Kurth, schoolteacher Timm, gardener Gentz as well as all who know me and ask about me. Hildemann also sends his best to Wangerin, he would like to ask about his mother, if she is still alive, and what his brothers are doing. [13 ll.: more questions, greetings, wishes] I send many thousands of greetings to my dear mother, and I remain
Your sincere son and your sincere brother,
Johann Carl Wilhelm Pritzlaff.

You should write my address like this: To Johann Pritzlaff in Milwaukee, Wisconsin Territory. North America.

I also want to mention that if some of you do come, don't bring any Prussian money except hard talers, that is better than gold.

N.B. If I have left out or forgotten anything in this letter, please forgive me or remind me in your letter.

Milwaukee, Dec. 21, 1843

Dearly beloved Brother August,
May the love of God the Father, the Son and the Holy Ghost be with us all. Amen.

I received with great joy your long-awaited letter of July 13th of this year at the beginning of October. The carrier of same, however, I have not yet seen, because the emigrants from Tonnebuhr will stay in Buffalo this winter, they had an accident with their ship on the way here from Buffalo and ran onto a *Sandbank,* from which they were taken back to Buffalo by steamboat, and because of the long delay they were thus caught by the winter. As I heard, no one was injured. Herr Heidke sent the letter along with a schoolteacher named Müller who came here from Buffalo.[21] The news in your letter, that you are all still hale and hearty, pleased me very much indeed. [8 ll.: thoughts about death and salvation] I am truly sorry that mother and Elisabeth have not come, or rather, that no one wanted to take them along just because they have not converted to the Lutheran church. My dearest wish and desire now is that Mother, Heinrich and Elisabeth should come over, if they want to, for I think, with God's help, that I can repay the travel costs to whoever brings them

---

[20]Pritzlaff had probably worked for this shepherd until 1839.
[21]The carrier mentioned above is probably the "farmer Martin Friedrich Heidtke (23)," who emigrated from Tonnebuhr in 1843 with his parents, uncle, and farmhand (Iwan 2:268; see also Pritzlaff's February 21, 1847, letter). Iwan mentions a teacher, Friedrich Müller, who taught in the Lutheran school in Buffalo after the falling-out with Dreyer and Zion (1:178).

along. At the end of this letter I have also written a few lines to C. Heidke, in which I have asked him to meet their expenses. I am very pleased to hear that Heinrich wants to learn the carpenter's trade, for that is a good trade here. Dear August, please do everything in your power that Heinrich and Elisabeth come along as well, for it is much better for them here than over there. I still have hopes that we will all see each other again in this life. For someone without means it is of course very difficult to get on at the beginning in a foreign land where he doesn't know the language; but it is much better here for his children. In terms of creature comforts, I am doing quite well; since April 18th this year I've been working in a hardware store and earn 225 dollars a year; but I have to pay for my own board. Board and washing cost 8 dollars a month, which could even support a small family. Thus it would cost me no more (and hardly as much) if mother and Elisabeth were with me, and if the dear Lord grants me good health, I think by next year I will also earn better wages. I have not saved much yet in America; for one thing I have spent quite a lot of money on travel and for another I have also lost 100 dollars to various employers I worked for. I will give you a brief report about the situation with the government, dear brother. There are officials, just like over there, but not ruling ones, like you have; they punish evil and seek to preserve the welfare of the country. One doesn't have to pay heavy taxes here. A person can pursue whatever occupation he wants. For that he doesn't have to pay any fees to the government; they are supported by the Congress of the United States. A farmer who has 80 acres of land pays 3–4 dollars a year, and also someone who has a house or a house lot in the town; he pays nothing for its use. I am distressed by the sad news that you heard about me. But I can see from it how our enemies slander us underhandedly and turn everything to the bad whenever they can. It is true that I wanted to drive some young people to the ball and that our wagon turned over on the way. [3 ll.: drove them for free] But I certainly did not want to attend the ball. It is not true that some of us broke our arms and legs; no one even twisted an ankle. It is also not true that Grünhagen or any people from Treptow were along; it also was not his wagon, it belonged to a German from Bremen instead, who asked me to bring his wagon home again. You can now judge for yourselves if it was worth writing to Germany about. [3 ll.: the letter-writer should have talked to him directly] (I would really like to know who wrote that.) I have mentioned pretty much everything, only one thing I can't say often enough, that you "pray" for me. I can't think of any more news to write you. We here in the town are all still quite well, and as much as I know and hear about those who live out in the country, they are doing well in terms of their physical well-being, and send all their best to all of you. C.

Zion and G. Dreier live here in the town and pursue their professions and also send you their best. C. Zion is married to Wilhelmine Schmeling from Kammin and has already had a son with her. There won't be any space in my letter for him to write a few lines to you. Dear August, your brother-in-law wanted to know how the tailoring business is here. In general it is one of the best professions in America. But now that so many immigrants are all in one spot, work is also fairly cheap, still, a good tailor can earn from 6 to 8 shillings a day, sometimes even more. Give my best to all my friends and acquaintances and everyone who knows me and asks about me. [7 ll.: greetings] May the peace of God be with you all and with,
Your poor—Johann C. W. Pritzlaff
[2 ll.: correspondence]

Dear Brother Heidke,
  I ask you with all my heart, please be so kind and bring my dear mother, brother and sister over with you, should they want to come here. I will repay you the money you will spend for them. Do this merciful favor for me and my loved ones. Our gracious God, who bade us be merciful also promised: that the merciful shall obtain mercy. If you do not come yourself but others with means from your area do, then I ask you to take care of things, go to them and ask them in my name to do me the favor and help my loved ones to come over. Or ask Wangerin from Trieglaff, if he comes, to help out too. Pastor Kindermann is here in Milwaukee; he was very sick for a while, but he has recovered now. Blacksmith Retzlaff from Creitlow sends his best;[22] he was here in our store the day before yesterday and bought some iron. He lives about 5 German miles from the town, where he bought 80 acres of land. He likes it very much in America and wishes very much that you would come sometime. The journey was not half as trying as he had imagined. He asks you to give his best to his brother-in-law in Langendorf and tell him that he is doing quite well here; he will write soon; he hasn't had the time up to now. [12 ll.: advice on exchanging money, rates; wishes, greetings] J. C. W. Pritzlaff.

[22]Kindermann emigrated in 1843 from Kammin as "Candidate Gustav Adolf Kindermann (38)" with wife, two-year-old son, and servant girl (Iwan 2:267). The Pomeranian pastor's son (1805–1856) had become the pastor of the Old Lutheran congregation in Kammin in 1837 and had had to hide from the police for months. In 1843 he became pastor in Milwaukee and in 1844 in Kirchhain (2:100–109).
  The "landowner Karl Gottlieb Retzlaff (32)," with his wife and two children, emigrated in 1843 from Cretlow, Kammin County (2:266). He belonged to the group that bought land in late October for $1.25 an acre five miles north of Freistadt (ca. twenty miles north of Milwaukee) and founded a town named Kirchhain; he was elected head elder of the church in 1845 (1:261; 2:138, 141).

Milwaukee, Feb. 21, 1847

Dearly beloved brother,
  May the peace of God be with you all. Amen.
  [9 ll.: correspondence] We are all, thank God, still quite hale and hearty, and our little daughter can walk and talk.[23] Thanks be to the Almighty for the great goodness and mercy He has shown us in giving us such a beautiful and healthy child. May He continue to keep her under his care and protection and save her from the Devil's wiles and fury. Very often we wish for your presence, and in particular the presence of our dear mother. [12 ll.: wants to pay travel costs for his mother and Elisabeth—a friend should advance the money] The newspapers write about the great dearth in Europe. I would very much like to know if things are also so expensive where you are. We live here in an abundance of foodstuffs. [6 ll.: prices] I have so often said and thought, if the poor people in Germany only had what we have here in surplus. In your letter you want to know: —in what way you could support yourself if it were the case that you came here. I cannot give you any precise information about that. Many people support themselves here, you would also be able to support yourself, and if you had enough money left from your journey that you could buy a piece of land, then you could support yourself in abundance. It could also be the case that you could set up a school in the town, for there are very many Germans living here. Up until now there has always been a lack of decent schoolteachers. But you can't entirely count on that. You also want to know how Friedrich Heidke is doing here. As far as I know, he is doing quite well. At the beginning he was too good-hearted and loaned out a lot of money. He has his land and business in such good shape that he can support himself very well. About two weeks ago he was here in the town with a load of wheat. His brother-in-law Eduard Liesner[24] is also married now to a Saxon girl named Wilhelmine Krimmer. His wedding was on the 12th of this month. With Pastor Ehrenström[25] things unfortunately look dangerous. He came here to Wiscon-

[23]Pritzlaff got married on November 14, 1844, to Sophie Bluhme, who was born April 22, 1822, in Rocksburg, Saxony, and immigrated to Freistadt with her parents in 1839, where they bought a farm. The Pritzlaffs had eight children, three of whom were still alive at the couple's fiftieth anniversary celebration in 1894 (History of Milwaukee [1881], 304; Watrons, 778; Conrad 1:430; Sprengeler [1897], 2). According to MC 1860: Milwaukee, W. 4, #578; 1870: W. 4, #767, Fred Blume (65) (Fredric Blume [74]) lived in Pritzlaff's household. The daughter mentioned in the letter appears in MC 1850: W. 2, #935, as Elizabeth, five years old.
  [24]Probably the "estate manager's son Eduard August Wilhelm Liesner (30½)" who emigrated in 1843 from Moratz, County Kammin (Iwan 2:268; 1:261).
  [25]Karl Wilhelm Ehrenström (b. 1893) was ordained in 1835 in Posen. Like most of the Old Lutheran clergymen, he traveled around serving several parishes and was pursued by the police and arrested. He was let out of prison early under the condition that he emigrate immediately. In America he devoted himself to several parishes near Buffalo but was considered a fanatic. In early 1847 he moved to Wisconsin with his followers (all of five families). In 1848 he went to

sin in the fall of 1845 with some of his followers (who all had long beards) to set up a communistic community. He was about the only one who had any money, though, and so they moved to Watertown (50 English miles from here), bought a piece of land and lived together for a while. Ehrenström gave his followers lessons in Greek and Hebrew with the excuse: —the Bible was not correctly translated and is completely different from the way Luther translated it. They lived like this for a short while; ended in quarrel and discord. He has become contemptuous of God and His Word and fallen into many vices. He moved last summer from here to the city of New York where he was supposed to hold a position as a language teacher. May God have mercy on him and let him not be lost. There are many cases like this in America. Now there is still one question to be answered, and it is the most difficult, namely: why the Lutheran church here in Milwaukee has divided into 4 factions. A whole book could be written about this question. Since I don't have room to put it all on a sheet of paper, I will leave it at that for now. The end of the world is near and I don't believe that a flourishing church-governance can still be achieved, and I believe that Luther's saying is true, when he said: —That at the end of the world only a few households will preserve the Gospel. The congregation I belong to has no pastor now. They have all been exposed and have deceived us long enough with their sheep's clothing. But the Lord Christ said: —inwardly they are ravening wolves, beware of them. I must close now, since I have no more space. Zion and Dreier are both here in the town and pursue their trade. They send their best to you. Also my old comrade Carl Heuer is still quite hale, as far as I know. He bought 40 acres of land right when he came and now works for Ed. Liesner. The current war between the United States and Mexico is not over yet. It seems to me to be an evil war. Here in the West, we haven't been touched by it yet. [2 ll.: correspondence] Once the electric telegraph is laid through the great ocean, we will be able to know what you are doing in Europe in half an hour's time. In Buffalo we know in a minute what happens in New York, a distance of 500 English miles by telegraph. I am still at my old place. On January 28th Herman Roggenbuck was buried at the age of 28 years. Give my best to all friends and acquaintances, especially C. Heidke and shepherd Wangerin. I would like to know if they are coming next summer. [2 ll.: greetings] To my schoolteacher Herr Timm and his family. I thank him for the instruction he gave me. [. . .] [2 ll.: greetings] Please, write again soon and let me know if mother is coming or not, so I can cut back expenses a bit before her

---

New York alone and from there to California, where gold fever had just broken out; he died there before 1852 (Iwan 2:109–23).

arrival. Many greetings from my parents-in-law, my wife and our little Lieschen. Your old school friend August Sülflow[26] also sends his best to you. He also works in a store like I do. [. . .] Finally, I kiss you all in my thoughts.

Your sincere and loving son, Johann Carl Wilhelm Pritzlaff. / [3 ll.: weather]

Milwaukee, Jan. 7, 1849
[almost certainly 1850]
Dearly beloved brother,

The grace of our Lord Jesus Christ, the love of God the Father and the Communion of the Holy Ghost be with you all. Amen.

I received your letter of May 24th last year from miller Bruss (who has settled near my father-in-law and is his neighbor) and was overjoyed that you have come to recognize your sins and have allowed yourself to be convinced by Christ, the Lord, and have gone on board his ship with him; but the waves won't be held off, rather they will rage and roar, and then Peter will start to sink, but he will not go under, Christ the Lord will hold out his hand to him and help him up again. Oh, dear August, that we may be devoted with all our hearts to Christ the Lord and make ourselves ready and prepared to go forth to meet him with joy when he comes, for the signs of the Latter Day are here, and it cannot be far off, so let us watch and attend to the signs of the times and ask for mercy until the end. Dear brother, as we keep reading in the newspapers, you are facing terrible and tragic times over there. Therefore, if you and others with you can get away next summer, do not tarry, for God's judgment and punishment has come upon Europe. Their sins have gone too far; so whoever can should flee. I do not, however, want to say by this that people are better here in America than in Europe. But we can still (in my opinion) live here for some time in outward peace. I also don't want to be too insistent in talking you into coming here, for the Devil never rests here, either. He is busy just like on the other side and causes many here to strive only after riches, may God preserve us from such temptation. He will not suffer you to be tempted above that ye are able; but will with the temptation also make a way to escape, that ye may be able to bear it. If our sister Elisabeth is still inclined to come here without you, I ask again that a good friend pay the travel costs for her. I will pay him back with many thanks. If she stays there (which I do not hope), then I heartily wish

[26]Probably "shepherd August Sülflow," who emigrated in 1839 from Reckow, Kammin County (Iwan 2:251), and later became Pritzlaff's partner.

that someone pay out to her the small present that I already mentioned in my last letter (namely forty talers), since it is better this way than if I were to send the money to Germany, which is fraught with many difficulties. There will certainly be quite a number who trust me enough to pay it back again, even though it has often been the case that people have been cheated this way. I could prove that I am worth it (to pay it) with many signatures if it were necessary. Also please be so good as to bring me (if you come) or send me 2 or 3 hymnals that I mentioned earlier. I am still at my old place; will change jobs next spring (God willing). Either I will move to my parents-in-law in the country, or I will start a small business on my own. I have sold my house and place here in town, for which I will get 600 dollars, but will keep living here until the 1st of May this year. My two children,[27] my wife and I are all still quite hale and hearty and wish the same for you. Please write me in your next letter how large your family is and the names of all your children; also how Brother Heinrich is, whether he is still in the army or if he might not be inclined to come here as well. I would help him out some. [10 ll.: F. Heidke is well, sends regards; correspondence; greetings; spring is the best time to travel] Outwardly we are now living here in peace and the times are good and inexpensive. I can think of nothing else in particular to write. The peace of God be with you and with all who love the Lord Jesus. That is the wish of your loving brother,
J. C. W. Pritzlaff
[12 ll.: postscript—correspondence, greetings]

Because John Pritzlaff, "without means" at the time he emigrated, soon became a wealthy and prominent citizen of Milwaukee, we know quite a bit about his life after the last surviving letter—and a few other details from the time before 1850.[28]

Before Pritzlaff started working in Shephardson and Farwell's hardware store in the spring of 1843, he had worked as a cook on a steamboat on the Great Lakes and as a lumberjack. In 1844 the store was sold to Nazro and King, but Pritzlaff continued to be employed there for another six years.

In the spring of 1850 he set up on his own, as he had mentioned as a possibility in his January 7 [1850] letter, and opened his own store called "John Pritzlaff & Co." His partner was August Sülflow, most probably

---

[27]After Elizabeth, Augusta was born in early 1850 (MC 1850: W. 2; 1860: W. 4).

[28]The information here, unless noted otherwise, is taken from the biographical sources cited in n. 1, the Milwaukee CD, the MC, and Conzen (1976), 116–18.

the Old Lutheran shepherd who had emigrated from Pritzlaff's home county in 1839 (note 26), despite the different spellings "Suelfohn" or "Suelflohn" found in the American sources. His silent partner and creditor (at 7.5 percent) was his previous employer and supplier Nazro. In the first year the sales volume was a modest $12,000, but when Pritzlaff bought out Sülflow's share in 1853 he had to pay $3,300, although both had started out without any significant capital. He now became the sole proprietor of the growing business.

In the 1850 census Pritzlaff was not yet listed as owning any real estate. In 1860, after running his own business for a decade, he listed real estate worth $6,000 and other assets of $4,000, and in 1870, $15,000 and $3,000 respectively. His success in business seems to have been just as great as it was constant. As early as 1867 he could afford to donate land to his parish[29] for the construction of Trinity Church at the corner of Ninth and Prairie streets. By the end of the century, the John Pritzlaff Hardware Co., also active in the wholesale business, was not only by far the largest hardware store in Milwaukee and the surroundings but also one of the three largest in the entire Middle West and West, with an annual volume of business of many hundred thousands of dollars.

In 1884 the business was turned into a corporation. The names of the directors in 1900 are revealing: John Pritzlaff, president; John P. Koch, vice-president; Franz Wollaeger, secretary and treasurer; Frederick C. Pritzlaff, deputy secretary and treasurer; H. August Luedke, manager. The two Pritzlaffs were father and son; the three other directors were all sons-in-law, married to Elizabeth, Augusta and Emma (born about 1852) respectively—an undiluted family enterprise, and at the same time a purely German-American one.[30]

Pritzlaff remained an active member of his Lutheran parish (Missouri Synod) and involved himself in Republican politics, a remarkable choice in view of the fact that the majority of Germans in Milwaukee, especially Catholics and Lutherans, were Democrats. Long before his death in August 1900 his contemporaries were already writing about him in a tone of great respect.[31] He possessed all of the qualities of the successful businessman: honesty, thrift, and good judgment. He ran the largest hardware business in the West outside Chicago and was "very rich." Always self-controlled, never over-excited, he always depended on his own judgment. "There is no other German in this city in whom the German people have as much confidence, or for whom they have as

[29]Iwan 2:140–41.
[30]CD Milwaukee, 1884–1900; MC 1880: Milwaukee, e.d. 119, #350, #351.
[31]As, for example, Koss (1871), Buck 2:88–89, and Flower (1881).

Figure 23. Photo of John Pritzlaff, probably ca. 1895. Photo courtesy of Milwaukee County Historical Society, Milwaukee, Wisconsin.

much respect, and you might call it love, as they have for John Pritz-laff."[32]

This can only be an exaggeration. But there is no doubt that Pritzlaff belonged to the tiny minority of immigrants—and the only one in this volume—who were able to realize the dream of great success. At least once, in 1868, he ran (unsuccessfully) for city council.[33] In an article about Pritzlaff's nomination, the local *Daily Sentinel* said that he was "one of our most highly esteemed German citizens—a business man of long-standing."[34]

Although it is not absolutely certain, it is highly probable that brother August Pritzlaff, the teacher to whom the letters were addressed, emi-grated and came to Milwaukee after all, although only after the end of the Civil War.[35] In 1870 the Old Lutheran congregation of St. Stephanus hired one August Pritzlaff to teach the second grade.[36]

[32]Buck 2:89.

[33]As early as 1844 he became actively involved in politics by joining—as the only German in Milwaukee—one of the Clay Clubs, an election campaign organization supporting the Whig candidate Henry Clay, who ran against (and was defeated by) the Democrat James K. Polk in the presidential election (Koss, 164–65). John P. Koch, his son-in-law and vice-president, was more successful politically. In 1892 he failed in his bid for lieutenant governor, but both in a special election in 1893 and in the regular election of 1894 he was voted mayor of Milwaukee, a city that at the end of Koch's second term in 1896 had a quarter of a million inhabitants (Holli/Jones [1981], 201).

[34]Still (1948), 163.

[35]A teacher of this name appears for the first time in CD 1869–79. In MC 1870: W. 9, #651, the teacher August "Pritzlow" (52) is listed with wife (48) and six children between the ages of seven and 27, all born in "Prussia." August Pritzlaff's immigration would also explain how the letters printed here came to be in the United States.

[36]"He served the parish from 1870 to 1884, and passed away . . . on October 11th, 1884 to the joy of the Lord" (Sievers [1904], 12, 15).

10

Carl Berthold

Much like Christian Lenz, 24-year-old Carl Berthold decided to emigrate in 1852 for reasons that were not purely economic. In his case, too, dissatisfaction with political conditions in his homeland must have been a powerful incentive. Here, however, the similarities between the two emigrants end. In contrast to Lenz, Berthold did not oppose but rather sympathized with the sociopolitical uprisings of 1848. Unlike Lenz, a cowherd's son, Berthold did not come from a poor rural background; his family were burghers. The youngest of three children, he was born in 1828 in Arolsen, the seat of the court of the small principality of Waldeck.[1] His father, Carl Friedrich Berthold, held the post of court huntsman to the princes of Waldeck and Pyrmont and, although perhaps not one of the notables, he was certainly one of the more well-to-do and respected burghers in the town. When he died, only a few months after the birth of his son and not yet thirty years old, he seems to have left at least a modest estate which protected the family from acute material want.[2]

Several years passed after the death of her first husband before Carl

[1] Ev. KB Arolsen. His sisters were named Caroline (b. 1825) and Wilhelmine (b. 1827). In 1825 Arolsen, seat of the court since 1728, had a population of only 1,724, most of whom earned their living either from the court or as tradesmen or artisans. The tobacco factory that had been opened in the early nineteenth century was closed down again after only a short time (Keyser [1957], 53–54; Nicolai [1954]). The character of the town corresponded to that of the principality, not only one of the smallest but also one of the most sparsely populated of the German states (Naumann [1914], 8; see also Curtze [1850] and Martin/Wetekam [1971]).

[2] Ev. KB Arolsen. The father's estate later became a frequent topic in the letters from America.

Berthold's mother, Johannette, remarried in Adorf, a few miles away from Arolsen, in late 1836. The children were by that time eleven, nine, and eight years old. Her second husband, the 39-year-old landowner and gentleman farmer Christian Ludwig Graubner, was a widower with two half-grown children; Johannette bore him three more sons before 1844.[3]

Carl Berthold apparently spent the following years in Adorf on his step-father's estate, until in 1843—one year after his confirmation—he moved to the nearby town of Korbach to be enrolled in the Waldeck Gymnasium.[4] The fact that he was sent to this school points not only to a certain status consciousness and faith in education on the part of his parents but also to their progressive political convictions: the school's staff was known for their liberal if not leftist political views, and one contemporary reported that pupils usually "left the school with free-thinking attitudes."[5]

After only one year, however, Berthold had to leave the school, probably because of his stepfather's desperate economic circumstances: Graubner was heavily in debt and was ultimately forced to sell his estate. Soon afterward (probably between 1845 and 1847) he decided to emigrate to America.[6] It is safe to assume that Graubner was accompanied by his wife and their common children, while Carl and Wilhelmine Berthold moved to Korbach, where their eldest sister Caroline lived with her husband Christian Ludwig ("Louis") Schwaner, a master saddler.[7]

Carl Berthold found employment as an assistant in his brother-in-law's workshop and thus learned the trade of saddler and upholsterer.[8] Aside from this, in his free time he seems to have been an active member of the

[3]Ev. KB Adorf; the marriage records indicate that the bride had been living in Bergheim. Of the seven children from Graubner's first marriage, one daughter (b. 1823) and one son (b. 1825) survived. The second marriage produced Heinrich Carl Ludwig Ferdinand (b. 1837), Georg Friedrich Heinrich Ludwig (b. 1842), and a third son (b. 1844) who died shortly after birth. Located on the Waldeck plateau, Adorf had a population of slightly more than nine hundred in 1880 (Neumann [1883], 6).

[4]Ev. KB Adorf: registration records of the Korbach Gymnasium in Stoecker (1977), 164. With a population of 2,228 in 1840 (although only 273 enjoyed full citizenship), Korbach was the largest and most economically significant town in Waldeck. The town maintained its agrarian character even into the twentieth century (Curtze [1841a], in particular 175–76; see also Keyser [1957], 298–300; Medding [1980]).

[5]Curtze (1841b); Medding, 337; Wetekam (1971).

[6]His application is obvious from the ev. KB Adorf, 1847. Public announcement of Graubner's emigration first appeared on May 10, 1851, in the *Beilage zum Fürstlich-Waldeckischen Regierungsblatt;* by then, however, he had probably been in the United States for a long time (see index in Thomas 2 [1983], list 2, #1).

[7]Ev. KB Korbach (Neustadt); the marriage register indicates that Caroline Berthold's last place of residence was Adorf. Her marriage with Christian Schwaner, eleven years her senior, produced nine children.

[8]Information provided by the contributor.

small Turner group in Korbach, most probably an association with like-minded republican and democratic ideals.[9]

From a political point of view, the ensuing years provided impressions that had a lasting effect on the young man. In early 1848 the revolutionary spirit spread throughout much of Europe, and not even the tiny principality of Waldeck—governed up until then by its rulers as an unchallenged patriarchate—remained completely unaffected. The news of the overthrow of the Citizen King Louis Philippe in February 1848 prompted progressive thinkers in Waldeck to gather for a celebration on top of a hill near Korbach: a victory bonfire was lit, and students from the Gymnasium sang patriotic songs.[10] In March the government, having seen the effects of popular unrest in other German states, was wise enough to propose, on its own accord, constitutional and legal reforms, a reduction in the size of the standing army, freedom of the press, and the repeal of some of the most unpopular taxes. The burghers of Arolsen and Korbach, who saw this as the dawning of a new age, reacted enthusiastically.[11] Only in the following month did revolutionary uprisings occur among the rural population; several hundred farmers gathered, under the leadership of August Wilhelm Wirths, a former theology student from Adorf and the "most fanatical democrat in Waldeck," and marched on the court. On their way, the mob attacked several royal officials who were considered guilty of particularly despotic treatment of subjects. After the princess made a mollifying appeal to the crowd, however, the demonstration quickly dispersed.[12] The following year the revolution flared up once again, a reflection of widespread dissatisfaction, above all in rural areas, with the half-hearted reforms that had hardly affected the relics of the old feudal system at all.[13] Soon afterward, though, in Waldeck as in other German states, the deathlike silence of restoration politics made its appearance.

It is impossible to reconstruct whether Carl Berthold was an active participant in these events or merely a passive sympathizer. His later

---

[9]An official *Turnverein* was first founded in Korbach in 1861, but there had been an informal association since the 1830s, primarily composed of former students at the Gymnasium who had been exposed to the Turner movement during their schooling. Since the movement was politically suspect until the 1850s, they probably refrained from founding an official club (Curtze [1841b], 254; Scheele [1950], 10–13; see also Neumann [1968]). That Berthold was a Turner is indicated in a letter of 1851 not printed here (BABS).

[10]Rörig (1913), 113.

[11]Nicolai, 203 (for quote); Sieburg (1981), 133.

[12]Nicolai, 204–8; this uprising on April 14, 1848, somewhat exaggeratedly referred to as the "Arolsen atrocity" or "outrage," remained the only major revolutionary activity within the principality (Cramer [1971], 258; Sieburg, 136–40).

[13]Nicolai, 210.

letters, however, indicate that after the failure of the revolution, he had few reasons to stay in his homeland, especially since his chances of professional advancement were so slight. In Waldeck, a tiny and primarily agrarian state with little hope of industrialization, artisan trades and industry could provide a secure income for only a few; on top of this came the guild regulations, unchanged and still in force, which placed severe restraints on master craftsmen setting up on their own. Not without good reason were two-thirds of those who left Waldeck artisans, hoping to find better chances of employment either in the United States or in the expanding industrial area around Wuppertal.[14]

Probably in late 1850 or early 1851 Carl Berthold left Korbach and went first to Bremen and then to Hamburg, where he worked in a large saddlery for several months.[15] It is likely that he then returned briefly to Waldeck before embarking at Bremerhaven in March or April of 1852 for the United States with a carpenter from Korbach, Wilhelm Richter.[16] He was already talking with great hope about his "new Fatherland."[17]

Another member of the family followed shortly thereafter: in the fall of 1852, despite the reservations of her sister and brother-in-law, Berthold's 26-year-old sister Wilhelmine also decided to emigrate to the United States with Heinrich Bange—a man whose reputation was apparently not the best.[18]

Spelling and grammar in Berthold's letter are quite subjective, and it is obvious that he tried to write the way he spoke, that is, to adapt the spelling to the phonetics of his dialect. Still, his language is hardly less comprehensible than standard German. Any English terms he throws in are spelled phonetically and idiosyncratically, suggesting that he read very little English.

[14]At the end of the 1830s the emigration rate in Waldeck was only 0.2 percent; in the mid-1840s it rose to an impressive 0.56 percent and only began to fall again in the middle of the following decade. The proportion of artisans among male emigrants during these years ranged from 80 to 85 percent and was some five times higher than in the population as a whole (Thomas 1 [1983], 27, 43; Goebel [1964]).

[15]This is indicated by a letter (not printed here) written by Berthold in March 1851 from Hamburg (BABS); also by the "Meldeprotokolle betr. fremde nicht-zünftiger Handwerker in Hamburg" (StA HH, Meldewesen, A 12, Bd. 6, Nr. 132).

[16]Announcement of Berthold's emigration appeared in the *Beilagen zum Regierungsblatt* of January 31, 1852, indicating that he must have applied for official release and permission to emigrate. The official announcement of the emigration of carpenter Wilhelm Richter from Korbach bears the same date; we can thus be fairly sure he was the traveling companion whose greetings were appended to Berthold's letter from Bremerhaven (Thomas 2 [1983], list 1, #3; 2, #19).

[17]Postscript (not printed here) to the letter of March 23, 1852.

[18]In the official papers there is an announcement of the emigration of one Heinrich Bange, but it is dated May 1850 (Thomas 2 [1983], list 2, #19), so that it can hardly be the same man mentioned above. Wilhelmine Berthold emigrated without official permission.

Carl Berthold

Bremerhafen, March 23rd, 52

Dear sisters and brother-in-law,

I take up my pen to write some lines to you, from here still beloved, because this is now a good opportunity to do so. Because we have been lying here for a week waiting for our ship that isn't here yet. Our ship, called the Liverpohl, is said to be lying in front of the canal and because of unfavorable winds cannot come in here, so we may be lying here several more days before we can get away. They cannot come up with as many ships as there are passengers here, for there are 1200 people here who were set to go on the 15th and already circa 3000 people who have already left. This emigrating is just terrible,[19] most of them are Hessians, Bavarians and Württembergers and Saxons, and the cost of passage is going up every day. We were very glad that we had signed up, otherwise we would have had to pay 40 talers in gold. We want to advise everyone who wants to go to America to sign up at home, and it is the best with N. in Leipzig, where Herr Kümmel is the agent, for there were several here who thought they could cross for 28 talers and didn't have any more, either, so could do nothing but return to their homeland again.

My dear ones, I cannot write much about my journey this far, I liked it very much, although many hardships were involved. [5 ll.: greetings] C. Berthold.

[10 ll.: postscript to his sister Wilhelmine with greetings to various acquaintances]

[2 ll.: greetings from Carl Berthold's traveling companion W. Richter to his family]

St Louis, Mo.,[20] October 13th, 52

Dearly beloved sisters and brother-in-law,

[3 ll.: excuses his long silence] You can easily imagine how things are when you first come to a foreign country and can't speak the language, how things are at first and how one feels. I have tried at times to pick up my pen but just couldn't do it, so I ask you again to forgive me.

Dear ones, the hour of our parting was hard but it had to be, I think God meant it to be so and His Will be done. It is a hard business to be so far apart from brothers and sisters and friends, and to live among strangers, I have only now come to realize that fully. So let us tell each

[19]In 1852 a total of 58,448 people embarked from Bremen and Bremerhaven for North America—more than ever before (Engelsing [1961], 183).

[20]Its population in 1850 was 77,465; ca. 30 percent were born in Germany, ca. 15 percent in Ireland (Kellner [1973], 102; see also the discussion on the German community up to 1860).

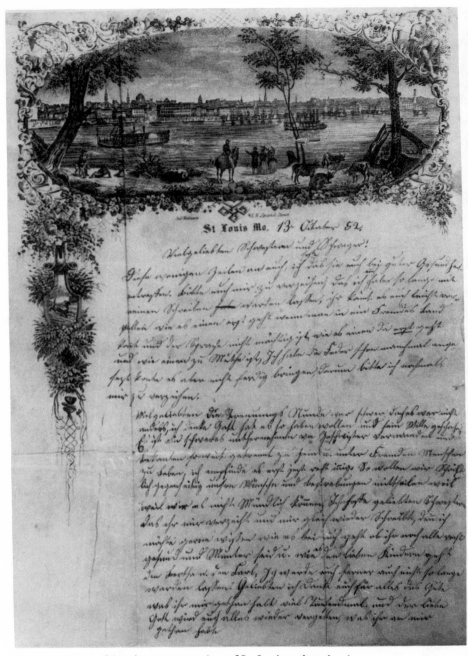

Figure 24. Letter of October 13, 1852; view of St. Louis on letterhead.

other of our wishes and endeavors in writing because we cannot do it in person. [14 ll.: asks for a quick reply; thanks his sister and brother-in-law; news about friends; inquiries about his father's estate]
Do not forget your eternally devoted brother afar
C. Berthold
[7 ll.: greetings; report about various acquaintances]
   Farewell, whether we shall ever see one another again, that is known only by He who guides our fate, when the sun awakes I will pray for this, / may you pray for this as well when it sets over there!
[6 ll.: postscript to his sister Wilhelmine with greetings to various friends; address]

St. Luis, February 23rd, 1853

Beloved sisters and brother-in-law,
   [6 ll: thanks for a letter from Korbach; condolences on the death of relatives] As far as I am concerned, I am, thank God, quite well. You write though that L. Krummel wrote that I was sick, this prompts me to write you back immediately that this is a lie. I do not know how L.K. came to write this, it is not like you think it is in Germany, that we are all living together! We are about 2700 miles apart and he knows nothing about me nor do I about him. My dear ones, don't worry about such stupid writings in the future, if everyone would just mind his own business, he'd be busy enough. There wasn't much other news, hardly any at all, I hope to hear more next time, it is nice to hear some news about what is happening in the old country. I also have no particular news to write from here. [6 ll.: paper partly damaged; weather] We were also facing a fight, but it ended happily. The *Wichs* [Whigs] or *Arestokraten* [aristocrats] as they are called in German, and that's what most Americans are, they wanted to treat the Germans unfairly, they were supposed to have to wait to become citizens until they'd been in the country for 21 years, that's almost like it is in Germany with the princes, they want to rule over the Germans like that, but they got their necks broken. Democracy won out by a great majority, and in a few weeks a true Democrat will ascend the presidential chair.[21] The *Wichs* are now trying all sorts of tricks to get back in, like the big wheels tried to do with the people in '48, but flattery doesn't get you anywhere here.

[21]The "true Democrat" Franklin Pierce, a colorless figure who was regarded even within his own party as a compromise candidate, beat the Whig party nominee Winfield Scott in the 1852 presidential election. The Germans and the Irish, traditional Democrats anyway, virtually closed ranks in support of Pierce, in particular when some of Scott's letters became public, in which he declared himself in favor of extending the residence requirement for naturalization from five to 21 years.

My dear ones, there is much news about Germany in the papers. Everyone is getting ready for an upcoming war, it seems they are all afraid of the new Emperor, he is up to something, he is doing his utmost to prepare his fleet and soldiers for a war that is coming soon, it looks like he wants to start with America, I hope if he comes here he will be well received and keep America in kind remembrance.[22] In a telegraph report this morning we heard that the revolution in Germany is starting again, Kossuth is said to have started in Italy and now to be in Switzerland. May the democrats in Germany do what they can for the revolution and their own freedom, that one day they may be rid of the bloodhounds, for Kossuth is a man of freedom, you don't often find one like him, he's already proved that, and he made a vow here in America to do everything in his power, to sacrifice life and property for Germany's freedom.[23] For it is easier to recognize what someone is really like when you are free like over here, as long as you live in the servitude of preachers and princes they try to keep you in ignorance. Dearly beloved, I have already experienced a lot in this country, but in St. Luis the most, I went there and thought I would meet friends and relatives but I was very much mistaken. I was here for 4 months without work, but no one helped me out at all, that doesn't matter though, I've gotten a job now without them and am now doing, thank God, quite well. [5 ll.: paper partly damaged; asks them not to send any letters to an acquaintance of the Schwaners, whom he has no contact with] Please answer this letter right away, since I am inclined to leave St. L. by May, for there's too much lowdown goings-on here. I'll probably head for Luisville.
[3 ll.: New Year's wishes]
CB.

[22]Berthold is probably referring to reports in the leading German newspaper in the town, the *Anzeiger des Westens,* owned and run by the Forty-eighter Heinrich Börnstein. European correspondents had repeatedly reported that the foreign policy of Napoleon III, who came to power in 1851 as the result of a coup and became Emperor in 1852, would result in a European war. There was no mention, however, of any plans to attack the United States. See, for example, the issue of the *Anzeiger* of February 1, 1853.

[23]Louis (Lajos) Kossuth was one of the leading figures in the Hungarian struggle for independence from the Hapsburg empire between 1848–1849. After the failure of the revolution he fled to Turkey and from there he followed an invitation, issued by the U.S. Senate, to visit the United States. The Americans received the charismatic Hungarian with great enthusiasm at first, but it rapidly cooled when it became clear that Kossuth not only wanted to raise money for the cause of Hungarian liberation but also hoped the Americans would intervene in the conflict. On top of this, the revolutionary made a number of enemies with his hesitant and only half-hearted support of abolition. Among the German immigrants—to whom Kossuth made a stirring speech in St. Louis (printed in the *Anzeiger* on March 20, 1852)—the Hungarian had many dedicated followers; they saw him, too, as a symbol of political change in their own homeland as well (Spencer [1977]; Oliver [1928]; Billington [1964], 330–32; Wittke [1952], 591–92). On February 26, 1852, the *Anzeiger* reported a revolt in Milan, in which one of Kossuth's proclamations was posted. This prompted him to leave for Switzerland to follow events in Italy from there.

[14 ll.: postscript to sister Wilhelmine; greetings to friends and relatives; address; asks her to deliver a letter, probably enclosed]

Heinrich Bange

Bremen, 10/16/1853

Dearly beloved = sister-in-law and brother-in-law,

If I can give you pleasure by writing a few lines, I feel the need to let you know something about the state of our affairs. Although I enclosed a few lines in Butterw.'s[24] letter a few days ago, I feel that under these circumstances it is my duty to write again in greater detail. Unfortunately I learned from your letter, Lui, that my sister-in-law is still very worried about our weal or woe in the distant lands of the Atlantic coast.

Of course I must admit, on the other hand, that it is painful to the highest degree when children who spent their childhood together from early on are deserted by their parents and have to leave their parents' home and then managed to make a harmonious life together among strangers, and have to part then, even if not forever but certainly for a long time, have to call out farewell; but I ask, in this world where no one ever has a heart that is ever completely satisfied, can one ever live together with someone else forever? Certainly not, every man looks with firm inner conviction for what is best for him in the world. If he feels disappointed, it is his own fault.

I am absolutely sure that our existence is secure, because it's actually happened to me, since in the far reaches of Kolumbia's soil I will seek my few days of life with Mina, the only treasure I own in this world. To live happily and content. Or do they doubt these hopes of mine? Then I could also doubt their love for us, but I don't. Although I have been hated and misunderstood by many because of this step that I took hastily and without thinking, I am still convinced that they will always love and keep us in their hearts. [3 ll.: further comments of this kind]

The emigration is heavier here in Bremen than anyone can ever remember.[25] 6000 persons are staying in the harbor in emigrant houses. All are streaming to the places of refuge in America, we will stay here for a few more days, we cannot yet determine our day of departure on the well-known ship Ana-Eilese [Anna Elise], which is to fling us across the waves of the great ocean to the land where we want to establish our home.

[24]Possibly the baker from Korbach, Karl Butterweck, who applied for permission to emigrate in August 1853 (Thomas 2 [1983], list 2, #20).
[25]See n. 19 above; in 1853 the number of ship passengers was just as large as the previous year (Engelsing [1961], 183).

[15 ll.: problems with power of attorney, probably in connection with Wilhelmine Berthold's inheritance; report about friends from Waldeck] We have inquired about how we could be joined in marriage, we were told at the Prussian Consulate or the American, but a suitable opportunity to speak to these gentlemen has not yet arisen, we will do this today or tomorrow morning. [5 ll.: unctuous remarks about forthcoming marriage ceremony; good wishes]
So, with love from your, Heinrich Bange Wilhelmine Berthold
[5 ll: asks for reply; address; greetings]

Wilhelmine Berthold

[Louisville, probably in June 1854]

Dearly beloved of my heart,

With my heart full of longing I take up my pen to report about the course of my life. It has been my duty for a long time, but one must first come to this realization before one can give a detailed account. I am pleased to be able to tell you the happy news that I am very well. [38 ll.: report about the ocean crossing, mostly about the attentions of the captain and amusements on board] In short after 6 weeks and 4 days we completed the journey with great success, on December 22 the heavy vessel Maumaut sailed into the Missisppi. A steamboat tug took us to New Orliens, on Christmas day in the evening we set foot on land again. Business in Orliens wasn't very good, so we decided to continue our journey straight on to Luis Wille, the journey was accomplished in 12 days with great hardship, for the water was so low in the Missisippi that the steamboats could hardly run, the trip cost 10 dollars for each in the first cabin on middle deck, 4 dollars without board, having arrived in Luiswille we met fellow-countrymen enough. Georg Solk, a rich coffee-house owner, took us in and then we found out that it was Korl's boardinghouse too. It was a great relief to see Carl, my beloved brother, again, this happened after two weeks, he was making the journey from Orliens back to Luiwille, you can't imagine how happy I was when I fell into my brother's arms for the first time again. We rented a room in Friederich Butterweck's house, we were living pretty far away from the town where Heinrich found work, so we had to move out of Buterweck's place in Puschertann into the city,[26] we rented 2 nice rooms on the main street, quite a *Plesante* apartment, Carl moved in with us where we now live together, happy and gay. We have furnished our household in

[26]Possibly the carpenter from Korbach, Friedrich Butterweck, who emigrated with his family in 1847 (Thomas 2 [1983], list 2, #19). "Puschertann" may refer to Buechel, a town on the southwest edge of Louisville.

the most elegant way, a courtier over there couldn't have it any better. We celebrated our anniversary here in Luiswille and now we will let our dear Lord God preside and look forward to a happy future. [7 ll.: asks about the financial situation at home probably in connection with her share of her father's estate] Dear sister, I hope you are now content, for if you were here even for only a week you would say, you're doing better than we, because we earn enough money and I am, thank God, in good health too, and I have a good husband, wouldn't want a better one, you can believe me. [9 ll: asks about nieces and nephews and hopes for an answer soon]

A thousand greetings to you all from your sister W B

[8 ll.: more greetings, also from Heinrich Bange; asks for quick reply]

Carl Berthold

Louisville, June 3rd, 1854

Dear sister and brother-in-law,

[3 ll.: standard opening] I hope you won't be angry that I have let you wait so long for a letter, but my circumstances didn't permit it any earlier, for I was never too pleased with the places where I was and thought I ought to find a place somewhere I liked better, so I went from one city to the next, but I haven't found any city any better and healthier than Louiswille and so I have now decided to make my home here, and thus I intend, if it is all right with you, to continue our correspondence undisturbed. As you can see from the small picture, Louiswille is a beautiful city, it lies high on the banks of the Oheuo is quite nicely built up, has good drinking water; the number of inhabitants is 60,000, of which 20,000 are Germans[27] the rest mostly natives, the space within the city limits is 7 miles long and 4 miles wide. That is about as far as from Corbach to Twiste[28] A tenth of Louisw. is now made up of Waldeckers.

[4 ll.: asks for news] This last winter I went on a jouney to the South that I had long had in mind, it is wonderful to take a trip like that, I could tell you a lot about the South, but time is too short. One month ago I came back to L., I didn't know what to say when I saw my sister and all the Corbachers who had arrived, I think when you get this letter another ½ dozen will arrive where you will hear more news, since I think they know more than me.

I must tell you, though, that we Waldeckers gave an extremely elegant ball on Tuesday, May 30th, when we had a pleasant night of music, song,

[27]For a discussion of the German community in Louisville, see the introduction to the Lenz series, Chapter 3.
[28]A town about six miles from Korbach.

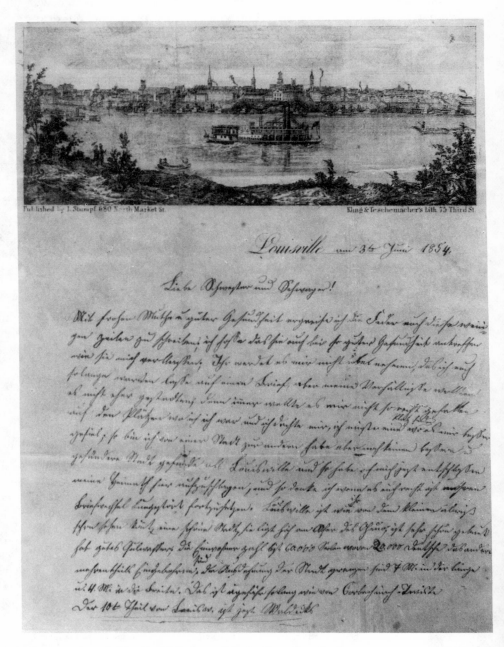

Figure 25. Letter of June 3, 1854; view of Louisville on letterhead.

and wine, where it only cost [75 cents?] each. I wished you could have been there, since naturally it was much grander than anything in Corbach.

[9 ll: greetings, signature, address]

July 17

My dear ones, please don't be angry that this letter wasn't sent any sooner, but circumstances didn't permit, because my sister was always doing poorly, and I kept thinking she would get better, but she still isn't completely well yet, but I hope it doesn't mean anything and she will soon be well again. It is very unhealthy this year, the heat is too oppressive, it's 109 degrees in the shade, that is why diseases are so common. It's not too bad here, but in other cities like St. Louis people and animals have been dying of heatstroke. Now I will close, more next time, all the best from all the Louisville Korbachers and especially from / your loving C. Berthold. [2 ll: his address again]

Dear sister, brother-in-law, children, relatives and friends, my longing to see you grows stronger every day and I think it would suit you as well. I thus intend to make the trip this fall, if I stay healthy. I ask you therefore to answer my letter right away and let me know the state of our property, so that I can make plans accordingly.

I remain your loving brother, C.B.

Louis wille, October 25, 1835 [1855]

Dear sister and brother-in-law,

[8 ll.: thanks for a letter from Korbach; reports about the unhealthy weather and poor harvest] Business is doing fairly poorly, so tomorrow I am going to the South and I think I'll do better business there this winter,[29] for this reason you should not write to me until I have written to you again.

Dear sister, please do not be angry with me for not writing this sad news to you any sooner, our beloved sister passed away on July 3rd and on the morning of the 4th at 8 o'clock she had a decent burial. Dear sister, do not grieve too much, for she passed away peacefully, and thank God, that He called her away from here so gently and didn't throw her into a lengthy sickbed. She was in childbed and she died on the eighth day, the baby died as well a few weeks later.

[29]Berthold may well have been prompted to leave Louisville not only because business was so bad but also because of the events connected with the election in August, which culminated in massive attacks against German (and Irish) immigrants. See the introduction to the Lenz series, Chapter 3.

[6 ll.: words of consolation] Wilhelmine wrote in her letters that I sent you that she was doing very well, that was true, she was doing very well. They arrived here and didn't even have 1 taler, I helped out, I bought everything that belongs in a household as a favor to my sister, and I did what I could, as my countrymen can well attest. That was all fine as long as she was alive, but now the tables are turning. After she lay on her deathbed she had to be buried, but that H. Bange couldn't do it, for it is quite expensive here. I had her buried in a manner befitting our social position and things were fine for a week, then H.B. came by like a pompous fool and wanted to take everything for himself. And that's none of his business, I did it all for my sister and now the things belong to me. For they weren't married, as I just found out recently. Dear sister, if any claims are made on her property then turn them down flatly, because this reverts to the two of us children. My dear ones, I ask once again for your forgiveness and be comforted, for we must all follow this path, may her ashes rest in peace. [10 ll.: more words of consolation; greetings] Carl. Berthold

A few lines about the great swindler H. Bange. — If necessary I can prove it with my countrymen. My dear ones, in my eyes this man is nothing. Cheating the people closest to him out of their own is easy for anyone to do. That's what this scoundrel did. To sell secretly the things I bought for my sister and those that she had brought along. And to almost give them away and to guzzle away all the money, and to spend the rest in such a lowdown way, to end up rolling around in the street like an animal, must one have respect for a man like that? (he is like his father before him) He is the laughingstock of his countrymen and all who know him. He has to avoid the circles where I introduced him and got him accepted, because now they've gotten to know him for what he really is!

My dear ones, you knew what he was like before and I think you will say I am right, but our sister never realized it. I ask you therefore not to reproach her for this and let her rest in her cold grave. And thanks be to Him who called her so early, while she was still doing so well. He loved her too much to let her go through what might have been coming her way! [5 ll.: more consoling words]
All the best from all the Corbachers here in Louisville.

When you write again please be so good as to tell me what the letters cost that I send you, because I always pay for the postage— —
Carl Berthold / Louisville Ky.

Jachsen [Jackson, Miss.], August 9th, 57.
Dear sister and brother-in-law,
[11 ll.: complains that he has had no letters for two years] Then no

hour! and no night passes when I do not think of you in my dreams. Since the death of our beloved sister, I couldn't stand Louisville anymore, and so I left there, most of the time I traveled around trying to find a suitable place, I have found one here, but not for always, I like it here very much. But Missisippi is a slave state and I don't want to live here forever. I went to the South because the wages are much better than in the North. But it is <u>not</u> so healthy here and the heat is much worse than in the North, but I can take the heat pretty well. I am working here in a *Schapp* [shop] where carriages and harnesses are made. Dear brother–in–law you want to know what I earn here, I work by the piece and make only fine harnesses, my average weekly wage is 15 dollars, which is paid out every Saturday. You may think then that one can get rich in only a year. But that isn't so, because everything is very expensive here, my expenses including board amount to 6 to 7 talers a week. I don't know of much news to write about, you should also change your notion of America, you always think when someone comes here from Germany I must have seen him or talked to him, but that isn't so, because things here aren't as close together as Korbach and Lengefeld.[30] One little example here, the city Jacksen in the state of Missisippi is 50 miles from the Missisippi river, is 180 miles from New Orleans, 900 miles from St Louis, 1000 miles from Louisville, 3000 miles from Newyork etc. Think about this and you will be convinced that one can't know how someone is or what he is doing. For 2 years I haven't heard or seen anything of friends or countrymen[31] since here everyone looks after himself, and God looks after us all, the nature of a human being changes completely here, it has to do with the climate, you become more indifferent than you used to be.

The products of the soil are mostly cotton, since cotton grows very well here, also some corn, oats, wheat, potatoes, water and sugar melons. There aren't any apples and peaches this year because they all froze.

Sometimes when I sit alone in my room and think about things, that I am all alone here without any friends and relatives, and that we must live so far apart from one another, I think about the well-known saying, Happy is the heart that finds a friend, it stays young forever [8 ll.: more of the same; asks for news; greetings]
C. Berthold.
[4 ll.: greetings to friends and relatives; address]

If Carl Berthold's first letters are tinged with disappointment, his last letter from Jackson, Mississippi, betrays resignation; the United States

---

[30]A township bordering Korbach.
[31]In 1860 in the entire state of Mississippi there were only two thousand Germans, less than 1 percent of the population (USC 1860.1, 272).

had not become his "new Fatherland" after all. It seems that he suffered much the same fate as many Forty-eighters, whose idealized image of the United States could not stand up to the imperfection of American reality—the existence of nativism and corruption, of slavery, racism, and Protestant domination—and whose democratic zeal and often overly critical attitude toward sociopolitical ills evoked little resonance, indeed often encountered mistrust and rejection, not only among Anglo-Americans but also among their less "political" countrymen.[32] Not all of them were able, like Carl Schurz, to make the move from an idealistic German to a realistic American democrat;[33] many revolutionary refugees preferred to retreat in disappointment from social and political life altogether.

This is what Carl Berthold seems to have done: his originally passionate interest in political events in the United States faded away as quickly as did his enthusiasm for Kossuth, giving way to a more disillusioned and passive stance. In Louisville, where the political scene within the German community was determined, if not dominated, by a large number of Forty-eighters and where Berthold might have had ample opportunity to put his democratic convictions into practice,[34] he seems to have kept up contact only with his fellow countrymen from Waldeck. And after he decided to move to the South, even these ties were abandoned, and he became almost inevitably something of a loner.

The reasons for Berthold's disappointment were probably not only political. It obviously took him years to gain a foothold in his trade: although from his last letter we learn that he had finally found a well-paid position as a saddler, it is very likely that he had earned his living previously in various low-paying jobs.

All of this, as well as his restless nature, contributed to the fact that Berthold was unable to decide to remain in the United States permanently. He returned to Germany, perhaps as early as the late 1850s, maybe only at the outbreak of the Civil War, but he remained there for only a short time. After a three-month ocean voyage, he arrived in the young Australian colony of Queensland in October 1862. The last sign of life that his sister and brother-in-law had of Carl Berthold was a letter written shortly after his arrival in Brisbane; nothing more was ever heard from him again.[35]

[32]Wittke (1952), 60–75.
[33]Oncken (1914), 109; Friedrich (1967), 4.
[34]See Zucker (1967b), 286, 287, 298, 319–20, 330, 345, 350–51; Schem 6 (1872), 637; Wittke (1952), 95.
[35]BABS; information provided by the contributor.

11

Martin Weitz

The bitter poverty of Schotten runs like a leitmotif through the letters of Martin Weitz and also appears in other material about the emigrants from the Vogelsberg. Because of the infertile soil and harsh climate at the higher altitudes of this mountain range, the highest peaks of which reach some 2,500 feet, no agriculture was possible—only cattle raising. As a rule, having a farm was not enough to feed a family; spinning and linen weaving were indispensable side occupations and indeed for many residents the only source of income. Even these occupations, however, could not guarantee a decent living: in the first half of the nineteenth century a weaver working an eighteen-hour day is supposed to have earned 37 guilders a year. Such a low wage meant that dietary staples were limited to potatoes and milk.[1]

Schotten (altitude 850 feet) was only indirectly affected by farming difficulties. Although the most barren areas of the Vogelsberg belong to the county of Schotten, only 15 (including dependents, 117) of the 2,205 inhabitants of the town itself were farmers in 1861. There were almost as many merchants with families, and another 325 persons, supporting 1,174 dependents, made their living as craftsmen. At the time Weitz emigrated, the skilled trade of wool weaver was probably the most important in the town. Of the 220 skilled tradesmen living there in 1830, there were 54 butchers, 97 wool weavers, and 46 in other textile-related trades, above all linen weavers and stocking knitters.[2]

[1]Heßler 1 (1906), 43; Katz (1904), 8–18.
[2]*Beiträge zur Statistik des Großherzogtums Hessen* 1 (1862), 30, 80; 3 (1864), 79, 240; see Wagner 3 (1830), 81, 264, 298–305.

Although the plight of the farmers was aggravated by poor harvests such as those of 1844, 1846, 1851–53, and 1858, the weavers came under increasing pressure from economic crises as well as from competition with cheaper mechanized cloth production both in Germany and abroad. In another Hesse-Darmstadt county seat with a similar occupational profile, Biedenkopf (ca. 35 miles northwest of Schotten), as early as 1826 only 50 out of a total of 130 wool weavers remained independent; the rest were employed as helpers or day laborers. Spinning and weaving were profitable only when done in a factory. What was necessary to make wool weaving show a profit, as it did, for example, in Hersfeld, Eschwege, and Melsungen in neighboring Hesse-Cassel, was considerable capital, mechanization (after the beginning of the nineteenth century), and the establishment of large-scale enterprises. After the 1830s the individual wool weaver hardly stood a chance against the overwhelming power of industrial manufacturers.

In addition to the emigration of the farmers and part-time weavers came that of other craftsmen. Between 1840 and 1843 only about one thousand people officially left the province of Oberhessen to go to America (0.12 percent of the population per year), but in the years 1846 to 1849 this number rose to nine thousand (1 percent per year) and between 1852 and 1855 it reached 14,860 (1.6 percent per year). In the highlands of the Vogelsberg between 1840 and 1861 some 25 townships lost almost 20 percent of their population. The rapid decline of the textile trade, the result of both emigration and occupational shift, had begun in the 1820s and continued into the second half of the nineteenth century: in 1861 there were still 3,407 persons employed in the textile industry in the Vogelsberg; by 1882 only 1,383.

Between 1850 and 1862, 172 persons left the county seat of Biedenkopf with official permission. One hundred sixty emigrated to America, and 128 of these were unmarried. Aside from "helpers, day laborers and others," the group of emigrants included 38 tradesmen. In the years 1852 to 1855 alone, 31 craftsmen turned their backs on their homeland.[3] Emigration from Schotten must have had a similar structure. In any case Martin Weitz, born September 28, 1823, was a wool weaver, he was single, and he left Germany in 1854. Although nothing is known about the exact circumstances of his emigration except that he probably left without official permission, there is little doubt that he was prompted to leave by economic misery at home and by legitimate hopes of a better life—as attested in the letters written by earlier emigrants from Schotten.

Martin Weitz's emigration is a good example of the migration that

[3]Katz (1904), 36; Dascher (1968), 125–27, 158; Huth (1962), 79; Dascher, 126–27; Katz (1904), 31–33; Huth, 99.

occurred as a result of differing degrees of industrialization, despite the fact that technological development in both countries was similar. There were cloth factories in Europe, too, but not enough jobs; and in America, by contrast, laborers were harder to come by, particularly craftsmen.

Although the wool-weaving trade in Europe experienced a crisis and shrank rapidly, with modern factories appearing only gradually, the American wool industry expanded rapidly between 1850 and 1860. Capital investment rose by a fifth, expenditures for raw materials increased by almost half, the number of persons employed grew almost 20 percent, reaching 41,360 (including 16,519 women). Only the number of companies declined, in the face of concentration and increasing mechanization: in 1860 there were only 1,260, whereas ten years earlier there had been 1,817. Of these, 398—with some 25,000 employees—were located in New England, where Connecticut was in third place, following the leading states of Massachusetts and Rhode Island. Here the value of production increased almost 40 percent during the 1850s. The number of employees rose from 3,558 to 4,767, while the number of companies decreased from 109 to 84.

When Weitz found work in Rockville, Connecticut, the town was already an important industrial center because of its abundant supply of water power: the Hockanum River falls some 250 feet in the vicinity. It nevertheless seemed quite rural (see Figure 27, below), and in terms of its population it was also comparable to Schotten. In the spring of 1855 there were 1,980 inhabitants, no less than 39 percent of whom were foreigners: 253 Germans, 247 Irish, 224 English. The town had five churches, five schools, 54 shops (only one of which, a tailor shop owned by John P. Klein, belonged to someone with a German name), and twelve factories, seven of which produced wool fabric, employing 644 (including 259 women) out of 711 workers.[4] The New England Mill, where Martin Weitz worked, was the oldest mill in the town (established in 1841) and required skilled workers for the high-quality production of its "Kasimir." In 1855, 82 men and 42 women were employed in the annual production of 142,000 yards of cloth worth $156,000.

As late as 1846 there were practically no foreigners in Rockville, and almost all of the immigrants living there in 1855 were thus recent arrivals. Of the three almost equally large groups of foreigners, the Germans, mostly weavers, were the only ones who spoke no English on arrival. The group of Germans grew and developed a life of its own. In 1869 in Vernon County (where Rockville is located), there were 96

[4]USC M 1860.1: xxii–xxiii; letterhead of Weitz's July 29, 1855, letter is reproduced in Figure 27. The percentage of Germans in Rockville was disproportionately high: 12 percent as opposed to 1.8 percent in Connecticut (1860) and 4.1 percent in the United States as a whole (USC 1860.2: liii; Vernon Historical Society, Wear, John, Census and Statistics).

German families and 58 other Germans; by 1870 there were 217 families and 63 others, making a total of 621 Germans. It is interesting that although many women worked in the mills, only six of them in 1860 and five in 1870 were married. Geographic mobility was unusually high: only twelve of the 96 families listed in 1860 are to be found in the 1870 census.

Weitz's letters cover the time period that saw the establishment of two singing clubs in 1855 (January 29, 1855), the first German Lutheran church service in 1856, the founding of the *Turnverein* in 1857, and the German mutual aid society in 1858. Among the Germans in 1870 there were seventeen who owned their own businesses, one doctor, one minister, 29 craftsmen, and twenty employed in various occupations (fireman, servant, day laborer). Aside from the 162 factory workers there were also ten spinners and 42 weavers. By 1900 Rockville not only had two Lutheran churches, a reading room for German newspapers, a private Lutheran school, and German language instruction in the public schools, but there were also fifteen clubs and societies, from the *Eintracht-Loge* to the *Liedertafel,* from the Rockville Socialists, German branch, to the Lyra Zither club.[5]

There can be no doubt that Martin Weitz's formal schooling was brief and poor, certainly never going beyond the elementary level. His erratic, frequently phonetic spelling reflects his Hessian dialect and sometimes becomes so exotic as to make comprehension difficult or doubtful. His spelling probably reflects his level of education, but such irregularities occur on an average of about one every five lines, and the rest of the text is no different from what might have been published in a contemporary newspaper—what is surprising is not his errors but how often he is right.

Another striking aspect is his vocabulary. He uses not only technical terms from the textile industry but also words that are normally part of the vocabulary of the educated. The obvious explanation for this as well as for his impressive awareness of current affairs is that he must have been an avid reader, at least of German-language newspapers.

Martin Weitz

Astoria,[6] July 16th, 1854
Dear devoted father, brother, sister-in-law, and children,[7]

[5]The decline of German-American ethnic life, accelerated by World War I, reached its end in 1940 when the last church discontinued services in the German language (Abbott [1976], 1–13, 18–21, 26–27; Vernon Historical Society, Wear, Census and Statistics).

[6]Village on Long Island; its population in 1865 was 3,560 (Schem 1 [1869], 721). Today it is part of the Borough of Queens, New York City.

[7]In the same order: Johann Konrad Weitz (1780–1861), wool weaver in Schotten; Johann Georg Weitz (1810–1858), wool weaver; Anna Margarethe, née Straub (1808–1880); Georg

Thank God I've arrived safely and I want to write a few words and describe to you my whole journey, how it went. We left on April 27th between 11–12 o'clock at night and arrived the next morning at 8 o'clock in Frankfurt, then we walked around in Frankfurt and finished up business with our Agent Textor.[8] I was also at Lotchen's. The next morning at 6 o'clock on the 28th we went by steamboat on the beautiful trip down the Rhine where we saw a lot and in the evening at 9 o'clock in Köln [Cologne] where we were picked up by the innkeeper. [. . .] I don't know his name anymore, there we had free supper and coffee in the morning. At 6 o'clock on the 29th from Köln by train to Bremen till the evening at 9 o'clock, there the innkeeper was waiting again and took us to the inn *"zum schwarzen Roß"* [Black Horse Inn]. There we were well fed, we were there 2½ days, but not for free, we had to pay almost 3 guilders and I didn't have a kreuzer left though I'd still had quite a lot of money in Frankfurt, I had to live off it day and night and had to pay 2 guilders 34 kreuzers overweight, because you couldn't take more than 1 hundred-weight along for free. Dear father, we were lucky, most of the others had to wait for 14 days because so many were there, Textor's people got to go first, that was good, we got to leave. Note, I want everyone to know that whoever wants to go to America should get in touch with Textor and make the journey via Frankfurt to Bremen, that is real service. Then the evening of May 3rd at 7 o'clock we went by boat to Bremerhaven where we arrived May 4th at 12 o'clock midday, we had good wind [. . .] note that we didn't go on the ship Wieland; but on the big ship Johann Lange, and the captain was named Lamke, it was about the most beautiful ship on the sea. It was a three-master, 225 feet long and 42 feet wide the masts 165 feet high above the deck and you can easily imagine what kind of a ship it was, there were 550 persons on it and 35 sailors with 3 helmsmen. On the 6th of May at 3 o'clock in the afternoon we put to sea, on the morning of the 7th the fun started, seasickness broke out for the first time, namely vomiting and dizziness. Dear father I was sick for 8 days when I had no desire to eat.

Every day we got meat, ox and pork meat but I couldn't eat anything but pork. There was rice, beans, peas and barley soup that we had to put

(1839–1911), Margarethe ("Gretchen," b. 1842), Martin (Martin Weitz's godson "Petter," 1848–1858). Martin's mother had died in 1825, and his stepmother died in 1832 (baptismal names and dates from *Deutsches Geschlechterbuch* 98 [1937], 633–34, 660–61).

[8]Carl Heinrich Textor started a commission and shipping agency in Frankfurt in 1852 and published a full-page advertisement in the AB Frankfurt (1876) as "American Passenger and Transfer Agent" as well as the General Agent for Hapag, Lloyd, and Cunard (Ibid., 423, and Anzeige Nr. 154). Textor, who drew up forwarding contracts for the shipping lines, was obviously very successful and well respected by the authorities. See *Amts-Blatt,* October 18, 1883, 310, and letter by Frankfurt chief of police of December 10, 1880, Hs. HStA WI, Abt. 405, Nr. 7755.

vinegar into, otherwise we couldn't eat it. There was coffee in the morning and tea in the evening. Oh my, those with strong constitutions could stuff themselves but I couldn't, it was good that I had coffee and prunes along with me. [7 ll.: shipwreck; storm] If we had had a bit of good wind we would have arrived in 4 weeks but this way it took 6 weeks, we also went by 5 icebergs at a time when that's seldom the case. [11 ll.: accident with the ship; on June 13 the pilot came on board; storm] On the 17th of June in the morning we saw land, they were all shouting land, land, and once again land, at 12 o'clock midday we arrived in the harbor. I had never seen anything like it, it's like you were looking at a forest [of masts], then it was joy upon joy, you can imagine that, now we're getting somewhere.

After we were examined by the doctor, August Reichold[9] went to his brothers and we carried our trunks onto the deck, they were looked at, then the Reichold brothers came, our trunks were loaded right away and delivered to the place, I spent the night at his brother Anton's and Christian's.

Next midday we went to Astoria to see his brother, he wasn't at home. I went on alone and wanted to look for the others, I saw Heinrich Schlörb[10] standing by his house, he caught sight of me, then he was overjoyed and couldn't believe it was me at first. He and his wife received me warmly, I must stay with them, and he said you stay here until you get a job. The next day we went to the factory where Schlörb had to speak for me because he could speak to him, they speak English here. Who could have been happier than me, dear father, here we are at home in America, I had a great yearning for it right away because I found work right away. It isn't for sure that I will stay here: no, but I had to, I didn't have a cent. Elisa Reichold[11] already had to lend me 3 guilders in Bremen, it is sad when

[9]Presumably Heinrich August Reichold, born in Schotten in 1819 (Hs. StA DA, Abt. C 11; duplicate ev. KB Schotten).

[10]Most probably Johann Heinrich Schloerb, born in Schotten in 1821 (duplicate ev. KB Schotten). He was also a wool weaver and before his emigration lived with his common-law wife, Margarethe Gisgen. Their two children, one and four years old in 1853, bore his name.
It was noted in the files of the county officials in Schotten (September 13, 1853) that "he does not want to renounce his rights to the homeland, but only to make the journey on his passport." But the passport could not be issued at first because of unpaid debts. The prison warden claimed twelve guilders "Schließgeld" (lock-up money) (six kreuzers a day) from the time when Schloerb had served a prison sentence (presumably for about four months) for forgery. This obstacle was removed when his creditor reduced the claim to eight guilders and Schloerb's mother agreed to pay half the amount in the summer of 1854 and the rest in 1855. She also paid for his crossing. Schloerb and his family probably emigrated toward the end of 1853. Poverty and the desire for a better future certainly played a decisive role in his decision to emigrate, but the official documents of Schotten County give another reason. In view of his failure to marry, it was noted (September 13, 1853) that "since this illicit relationship can no longer be tolerated, he intends to emigrate to America with Marg. Gisgen" (Hs. StA DA, Abt. G 15, 27).

[11]Most probably Elisabetha Reichold, August's sister born in Schotten in 1826 (duplicate ev. KB Schotten).

someone travels to America and doesn't have a cent and has no friends and acquaintances. I was lucky, because thousands wander around and sleep on the streets, especially those brought over by the towns,[12] Johs Meiski[13] died on the boat according to what we heard. Dear father, I pray to God every day he may keep me healthy, because there are many diseases here, namely cholera, all kinds of fever. Many also die of sunstroke they just fall down dead because it is too warm here, now cool, now hot. Dear father and brothers if I stay healthy then I will earn pretty good money here, since as they say, all beginnings are difficult. I am boarding with Heinrich Schlörb and have to pay 5 dollars every 2 weeks, that's the very lowest here. I like it very much here, because they don't make rugs here like you might think. The looms are set up like at Georg Leuker's, there's no high-speed shuttle, instead they work with their hands like the linen weavers. In one day I had learned it, now it's like we're plowing along. Dear father, we've heard that it's so expensive over there that you can't manage very well, I wish you were all here with me then things would be fine, here we have a lot to eat, it also costs a lot here, when I've been earning for 4 or 6 weeks I'll send you something to help out, I haven't forsaken you, don't think that. I tell you again you should all get along with each other and comfort each other. Dear Georg don't turn your back on your parents and your grandfather, help them as much as you can. Grethgen, be a good girl and hard-working and obedient. And you, dear little Petter, be a good boy too. Dear brother and sister-in-law don't leave my old father and get along with each other. I won't forsake you if I stay healthy.

I can't write any more, when I think about your misery in Germany I start to cry. Dear father, brother, sister-in-law, and children, give my best to all my good friends and acquaintances, all of our friends, and Kaspar Spamer and his wife Grethgen and Johannes Leunig, my godfather's son Georg[14] and his Christigen. [5 ll.: more friends and acquaintances] I can't write any more because I haven't been here very long. Georg Göbel, if you want to come you should but like they say, get some money to-gether. Finally I must say have a good time at the *Sommermark*[15] because here there's no such fun to be had. We don't go out, amusements like that exist only in Germany, they say. Dear father, please write back soon and don't pay for the postage. Letters cost 22 cents here, that's 36 kreuzers in

[12]Passage for the destitute was paid by the town in order to take the burden off local poor-relief funds (Bretting [1981], 102–13; see Bassler [1974]; Fey [1892]).

[13]Presumably Johannes Meiski, born out of wedlock in Schotten in 1822 (duplicate ev. KB Schotten).

[14]Martin's godfather Martin Weitz, master wool weaver, his father's only surviving brother.

[15]*Sommermarkt* is a major fair in Schotten, combined with the annual market, and still held every August.

German money. The address is Martin Weitz in Astoria at the *Kapert-feckterie* [carpet factory] I can't write any more.

Warmest greetings from your son, farewell, I haven't forgotten you. Don't forget me either and keep me always in kind remembrance / Martin Weitz.

[postscript to] Konrad Weitz (V.) on the mountain at Georg Mahr's, I wanted to send something along for you but I can't yet. I would have written a separate letter to you, but I wanted to save you the money. I will also be taking up music in Astoria. There's music here, and it is quite respectable.

You could send a letter along with Leuning's wife's or mail it directly. [4 ll.: is waiting for news; sends greetings from Schlörb and Leuning]

Rockville, July 29th, 1855.
Dear devoted father, brother, sister-in-law, and children,

Should my letter reach you in good health, I will be overjoyed. Finally I have fulfilled my longing for you by sending a small gift, I couldn't do it any earlier since I was doing very poorly. Last year from October until March 16th this year I didn't have any work, the factory in Astoria had stopped work. I had to pay 10 dollars training fee. Every newcomer who comes here has to pay, when I had worked it off there was no more work there. From there we went to another factory, a fur factory, there we had rotten jobs where our hands got all swollen up but it didn't last long. Finally we couldn't get any money then I also lost a lot so I made it through the winter splitting wood for a man in Astoria who wasn't able so I could earn some money. But it wasn't enough. I looked around for work in New York and the area, but all for nothing, if I had been able to speak English I could've gotten a job but I can't. I didn't have any money to move on, you can imagine it was terrible. Thousands and thousands were wandering around without work, without money, without food, dying of hunger. They've set up places where they could get lunch but it isn't enough. They poured through the town in great droves demanding that work be found for them, but all for nothing. All over America it was terrible, many hundreds of *Fektori,* that means *Fabricke,* had stopped work, prices went way up and still are, it should not be called America but *Malerika.* It is easy to say you want to go to America but the hard things they never think about. [6 ll.: dangers of ocean voyage] The second point is when you arrive here and don't understand English, you stand there, eyes wide open, like a calf with its throat cut. You have to be careful, they say, there's a greenhorn. How many hundred are lied to and cheated, no one can be careful enough. In Neu Jork every day there's murder, theft, suicide, lies and cheating, and in any large town in America. If you want to come to America you just can't let that scare you off. You have to think the best, the worst comes later. I don't want to advise anyone not to come, whoever wants to come should come. It's best if you have a friend here who gets you a job in a good state. Dear father and brother, thank God I now have a good job. On March 16th in the newspaper there was a call for 25 weavers in a wool *Fektori* in Rockville in the state of Conecticut to sign up on the 17th at 6 o'clock in the evening. We went there and were accepted. On the 18th we got on the steamboat and went to Hartford, from there to Rockville,[16] first I had to sell my watch otherwise I couldn't have gotten there. When we arrived there in the afternoon they said you have to work nights from 6:30 in the evening till 6:30 in the morning, then we were shocked. I said I didn't care if I only have work, the looms all work by themselves, they are all driven by water, I'd never woven on such a loom. I went to a fellow who taught me during the day, then work started. It didn't go well of course in the beginning, they do difficult patterns. In March and April I didn't earn much, I hardly had enough for *Board,* in July 19½ dollars. Now it's getting better, if you do good work, you earn 18–20 to 24–25 dollars.[17] Dear father, I am now very content with my situation, I'll stay here. Last winter sometimes I just wanted to jump into the water, if you don't have a job in America it's a terrible thing, I can't thank God enough that I have work and am healthy. Here in the *Willischtz* [village], that means *klein Städtgen* or *Dorf* there are almost 250 Germans who work in the *Feckteri,* there are 11 *Feckterie* here. If you don't like it in one you go to another, 3 more are being built. If anyone from Schotten wants to come here, he should come. Springtime is the best, if he has money he can buy land in the state of Wisconsin, it seems to be another Germany, it's healthy there. Where I am in Rockville in the state of Connecticut, 180 miles from Neu Jork, it's also very healthy, the climate seems to me like over there, we had in English 100 degrees of heat, but of course it's not as healthy here in America as over there in Germany. The harvest here in America looks good and there's hope that things will be cheaper than a while ago. There is *Temperes* [temperance] here, that means there's no alcoholic spirits allowed, no beer, no brandy, wine, etc. In many states there's been serious fighting like in the state of Ohio, in Cincinati there was a blood-bath, the Germans won, there were many dead and wounded on both

[16]The trip of about one hundred miles to Hartford, Connecticut, was made via Long Island Sound and the Connecticut River. Rockville belonged to Vernon Township, the population of which was 2,900 in 1850 and 3,838 in 1860 (USC 1850.1, 79; USC 1860.1, 40).

[17]In comparison: according to official sources, the average monthly wage of a farm laborer in Connecticut in 1850 amounted to $12.75 with board; a carpenter's daily wage (without board) was $1.36 (USC 1850.2, 164).

SCHOTTEN

Schotten im Jahre 1646 nach Merian.

Figure 26. View of Schotten in 1646 by Merian.

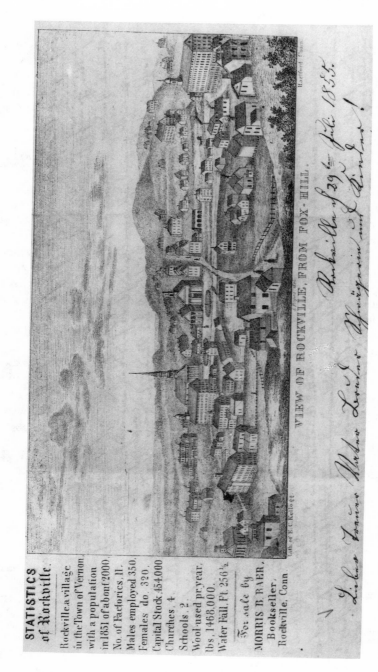

Figure 27. View of Rockville, letterhead of July 29, 1855.

sides. The *Jenkeamerikaner* [Yankees], they call themselves *Nounorthing* [Know-Nothing][18] yankees, they want to have control, but democracy wins, it looks like there's going to be a revolution.[19] Every Sunday you have to go to church, then the factory bosses like you, you don't learn anything bad there, if you understand English or not, that's fine with me. I can go there. With the singing clubs and music, there the Germans in America are on the rise, they earn a lot of respect for that. Even we in Rockville, we have 2 singing clubs. With our German singing we earn great respect. In Neu Jork there was a big song festival that drew a lot of applause from the Americans. I am here in a German *BoardingHaus*, I have to pay 9 dollars a month which is cheap, you may think it's a lot, but you have to remember that the dollar can't be counted as more than the guilder over there.[20] I can't spend any money except for tobacco, I haven't drunk any *Brenti* [brandy] in three months. Every noon there's soup, vegetables and meat, every morning and evening meat, cheese and butter. Every morning we get up at 5 o'clock, at 5 thirty the bells ring, we go to the factory till 12 o'clock noon, at 1 o'clock we go in again until half past 6, at 8 o'clock it's already night. At 4 o'clock in the morning it is already daylight. When the sun goes down it gets dark right away. The difference between you and us is when we get up in the morning it's 11 o'clock over there, it's almost 6 hours. Leuning and I are the only ones here from Schotten, Leuning and his family like it very much here too, we work in one *Fektori*. We hardly see each other all day long, it's so big. His son Adam works in our *Fektori*. We live a mile apart, don't see each other often. What do they say over there about the war, Sebastobel hasn't fallen yet, thousands of people are being killed for nothing, we believe that Germany will be the battlefield.[21]

    Dear father, brother, sister-in-law and dear children, how are you, are you getting along together? Dear brother and sister-in-law, take proper

[18]Weitz is probably referring to the events of April 2, 1855. On this day the mayor of Cincinnati was elected, and the Know-Nothing party (whose candidate was finally defeated by the Democrats) was able to mobilize a mob of people to attack the German quarter, "Over the Rhine." In the face of insufficient police protection, the *Turnverein* and German militia took over the defense by building barricades on the canal bridges leading to the area. They countered an attack of the Know-Nothings with a volley of rifle fire in which two attackers were killed and a large number wounded (White [1980], 355–59). On the Know-Nothings, see the section "Nativism and Politics" in the Introduction.

[19]In contemporary popular German usage, the word "revolution" had a wide range of meanings including uprisings, riots, bloodshed, political change, and the like.

[20]A German-run boardinghouse was usually a simple establishment for bachelors in which food and often lodging was offered on a weekly or monthly basis. In the state of Connecticut in 1850, the average weekly rate amounted to $1.95; $9 per month was slightly above average (USC 1850.2, 164). A guilder was worth 41 cents.

[21]In the Crimean War, the siege of the fortress of Sevastopol began in October 1854, and it was finally captured in September 1855.

care of my father, I ask you dearly, and take care of him like it befits good children, for you see I am so far away from you I cannot be among you, but I will do my duty as far as I am able. I am sending you the first small gift, I'm sending you 10 dollars, that is 25 guilders over there. [15 ll.: transfer; admonitions to his godson, Georg, Gretchen] Dear brother I urge you to stop working at night, you will destroy yourself so that in your old age you will be weak, because working at night doesn't help, it doesn't get you anywhere. Take my advice, for 1½ months here I worked at night and slept during the day, I was happy to have work, but in the end I did get tired. Since the beginning of June I work during the day, on each loom we have 3 gas lamps, I tell you again, father, brother, sister-in-law and Georg do your duty and when it is night then go to your rest. [3 ll.: admonitions] What is the band doing, my faithful colleagues, are they all well, have they kept going or have they given up? Practice properly because there is nothing more beautiful than beautiful music and song. How are my godfather's son Georg and his Christingen, does he have a job and are they married, what is Georg Göbel doing, doesn't he feel like coming over here? [9 ll.: greetings; transfer; asks for acknowledgment of receipt] With the money you should buy food and clothing. If I stay healthy you'll get more before Christmas, I haven't forsaken you, believe me, no day or night has passed when you weren't before my eyes, because you are my only cause for worry, I must close. [5 ll.: greetings, signature]

What I wrote to you is the truth. Write right away, the address Martin Weitz in Rockville in the State of Connecticut.

I have forgotten something else, that in every *Fecktori* there are women weavers. There are *Fektori* where only women weave, they are called *Sassinetmühle* [Satinett: half-wool cloth] with a cotton warp and a wool weft that makes a heavy cloth, you can't see that there's cotton underneath. There is a mill where woollen rags are made over and spun into weft, it's hard to believe that you can make good thread out of rags. In the mill where Leuning and his son and I are, the *Feckteri* is called *Neu-Englandmühle* there they make *Kassemer* [cashmere], beautiful woollen material. I am in the mill where I have made a cross, there's nothing but *Fecktori* where there are many windows. I just read in the *Neu Jorker-zeitung*[22] [newspaper] that last week almost 700 people, of which 150 were children, died of *Cohlerra*. [2 ll.: previous year even more] I could get married any day, but I still want to think it over. So many German

---

[22]See factory statistics in Figure 27. Between 1846 and 1898 there was a German periodical named the *New Yorker Zeitung*, but since it was a weekly and Martin received a daily newspaper (see his letter of April 20, 1856), he is probably referring to one of the German-language dailies that appeared in New York between 1855 and 1856 (Arndt/Olson [1965], 370, 410).

fellows take up with *Ameriganer* and *Eurische* [Irish] you can't play around very much, otherwise they go straight to the *Curt* [court], that means *vor Gericht,* the fellow gets picked up by the court marshal and there they get married, that's the end of the fun. Then they go to the *Fecktori* together and work together and board with other people. No, I'll take good care not to do that for now.

Rockville, December 9, 1855.

Dear father, brother, sister-in-law and children,

I received your letter on October 30 in the evening, but I couldn't eat supper for joy, and have learned from it that you are all well which pleased me deeply. But I have also learned something, that you are not getting along together, which troubles me deeply. [4 ll.: worries about this] Dear father, I will address myself to you first, you are now becoming old and weak and should be understanding, don't be so peculiar, give in a bit, because it can't go on like this, believe me, dear father. Your letter, the words you wrote to me, I will also take to heart and obey, for I have God in my mind's eye and in my heart and guard myself against bad company because here in America it is so much worse than over there in Germany. Dear brother, sister-in-law and you children, I ask you the second question, do you want to get along together in peace or not? Dear Brother, don't be so hard on our dear father, remember, you are the only son living with your father, remember I am so far away from you I can't do more than to send you something from time to time. Dear sister-in-law [9 ll.: further admonitions] I wanted very much to send you something before Christmas but it was impossible because I had to buy myself some winter clothes, since that costs a lot of money here. In Astoria I spent everything on clothes, shoes and boots. Thank God. I am happy that I came to Rockville this spring even if the wage isn't too good, but there's steady work. By the spring two new *Fektorien* will start up, then there'll be *blendi Work* [plenty of work] that means *viel Arbeit.* Dear father and brother, get the fabric for your clothes from Kaspar Spamer or Jacob or Gredchen, because that is sturdy. And you can count on me that I will send you money in the spring, you can count on it, now it's impossible. I am now going to English class, that's the only thing I need, I can already get along a little but it's not enough, because if you know English you can get by. [7 ll.: correspondence] Dear little godson, I am pleased that you always talk about me and that you are going to school. Obey your parents and teachers, when you are grown up then come to America here to me, and Grethchen, you be a good girl too and work hard. Dear brother, you write to me I shouldn't take up with a factory girl, you mustn't think I would marry blindly, remember there's nothing but factory people here, a man can be as rich as can be and still work in the *Fecktori*. I have gotten to know a girl, her father is a shoemaker from Reihnbeiern [the Palatinate] from Lamprecht.[23] As far as I know her, she is a very sweet, good girl and has very good parents. It's just like I was at home, but I'm not thinking of marriage yet. [. . .] Here in America it's better to be married than single, think of all the *Board,* that is *Kostgeld,* both husband and wife can live on that. My godfather's son Georg should write me all the news and Georg Göbel should see that he comes over here because it is better for him here than in Schotten. If he can, he should come in the spring.

[9 ll.: greetings; signature; postage]

Rockville, April 20th, 1856.

Dearest father, brother, sister-in-law and children,

I received your letter only on April 8th, that morning I had just gone to the *Postoffise* and sent a letter to Neu Jork to the agent to send you 20 dollars, that is 50 guilders in your money, only then did I get your letter, I had been there a few times before and asked if there was a letter, he always said no, this is how you ask in English *(Gat ju Lether vor mi dies Män telt mi Nasser)*[24] until finally my letter was in the Rockville *Nusbeber* [newspaper], that means *Zeitung.*[25] *Mister* Leining got his letter on March 16th already, mine lay around that much longer. I was annoyed about it but couldn't do anything about it. Dear father and brother I see from your letter that you are all well which pleases me very much, that's the most important thing. I can well believe that things look bad over there, because I can hear about it every day here just as well as you can write about it. We read the *Neu:Jorker Zeitung* every day, then I read about how things look in Germany or in all of Europe for that matter. Now they want to make peace, but they will keep making peace until everything gets into a mess again, that's how the bloodhounds like it, for they let so many people get butchered for nothing and it didn't even get them anywhere. There is just as much roguery over here, it knows no bounds, the Americans go to *Schochs* [church], that means *Kirche,* 3 times every Sunday and 3 evenings a week, and they think they're so holy but when

[23]Presumably Lambrecht near Neustadt an der Weinstraße.
[24]Have you got a letter for me? This man tells me nothing.
[25]Free postal delivery was first introduced in the United States in 1863, but even then the service was available only in cities with more than fifty thousand inhabitants. The newspapers sought to increase their circulation by printing lists of receivers who had yet to claim their letters and packages.

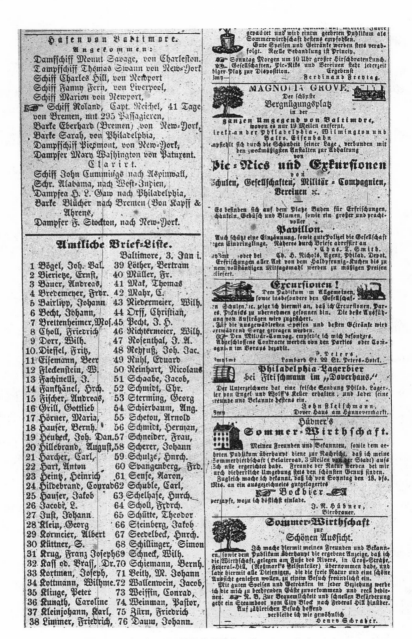

Figure 28. Official letter list, *Baltimore Wecker,* June 3, 1856.

they can take the skin off the back of someone else they don't mind at all. These people just pray to get what they want, that's what the Americans are like, that is the *Neu Northings,* but you mustn't be scared of them, since here they say if you are scared of them, the bogeyman will get you, but otherwise we are free men and you can earn good money if you are healthy, that's what I've wanted for a long time, like I have it, if only the *Luum* [loom], that means *Webstuhl,* ran by itself. My wish has come true, if you have a good job you can go for a walk while it's running. I and Leining's family, we are living here happy and content, though I haven't decided to live here forever, I want to save up some and want to go for at least 2 to 3 months to a barber to get to know the business better so I can set myself up, so I can work for myself later on, because I would really like to go to Central America later, perhaps in 1 or 2 years, it's very good there. [3 ll.: does not want to get married yet] But it will have to happen sometime but I want to wait a while still, for you can't be careful enough. Some marry and afterwards either the wife runs away or the husband, I read about it all the time in the newspaper. That's happened to so many here, but it's the fashion here. Dear father and brother, I'm sending you 20 dollars, that's 50 guilders in your money, you should share it, namely 25 guilders each, and buy yourself some clothes, dear father, and drink a glass to my health and save the rest of it. And dear brother, you should buy food and clothes and use it for the household so that you can get by better. [10 ll.: wishes; money transfer] You write me about Christian Wagner[26] I should find out where he is. It's been a year since I last saw him, in Morosina, 7 miles from Neu:Jork. Then he was working for Christian Kirchner, a baker.

I was at his place twice to get some stuff, and we had a good time together, now I'm about 180 miles away and can't find out anything about him, I think he's still at Kirchner's but in America it isn't easy to find someone if you don't know exactly where he is. — .

It's now 3 o'clock in the afternoon and I was tired of writing. I have to write you today, how things are with me. Today is Sunday and last night I had a dream. [4 ll.: a man wanted to poison him—fight] At 7 o'clock I got up and drank some coffee, got dressed, afterwards I was in the *Willischt,* that means a *Dorf* or *Städchen* to get my hair cut at a good friend of mine, I came home at noon to eat then I wrote the letter till 3 o'clock then I stopped and went to have some beers, good lager. It rained a lot today. My friend Leining tells me Kathringen Damer is coming here, which is good news. Send me one long and one short pipe with a white

[26]Presumably Heinrich Christian Wagner, born in Schotten in 1824 (duplicate ev. KB Schotten).

bowl and *Sottersack* [lower part of a pipe, where fluid collects] as cheap as you can buy it, if you want to, so I have something to remember you by, because a long pipe costs a dollar here, and I do like to smoke. Send me a bit of camomile tea, too. What is Georg Göbel doing, doesn't he want to come over here? And my godfather's son Georg got married and didn't invite you, dear father, the only brother, to the wedding. That is *tu beet* [too bad], but don't worry about it. Give my best to Kaspar Spamer's Gretchen and her husband, and the whole family for that matter. Gretchen should find out about Biehngen from Gedern[27] if she is still in good health and unmarried and if she wouldn't like to come over here, since this girl is so sweet, so good, like no one I've ever met. Grethgen should find out everything and give her my best regards and write me if she'd like to come over to me, because a girl like that is what I'd like to have for a wife. [5 ll.: greetings to the Schlörbs, the band, and all friends; also from the Leining family] Leining is a man everyone respects here, I don't think he'd change places with a statesman, he just wants to be what he is, he's a free man here.

[9 ll.: godson Martin, Gretchen, Georg should be good; good health is the greatest happiness] I'm sending you a newspaper so you can see and read about what's the biggest *Hotel,* that means *Gasthaus,* in Neu:Jork, how many people work there and what they use up every day. [11 ll.: hard winter; shipping and railroad accidents; signature]

[4 ll.: letters via Bremen are quicker] I demand a letter and all the news from you when you get money and every three months. On May 1st I'll be boarding with the Leinings because they treat me like their own child.

It's now 2 years since I left you but I can't count the first year, I didn't earn much then.

Dear father, brother and sister-in-law,

I must address a few more words to you, I keep hearing that you don't get along together. [29 ll.: admonitions to all to live together in peace, as in his February 9, 1855, letter; wants to provide financial assistance and doesn't need any help himself; signature] Take to heart all that I wrote you.

Rockville, September 4th, 1856.

Dear father, brother, sister-in-law and children,

[7 ll.: thanks for letter and pipes] Dear brother you write me I should

---

[27]Biehngen is a diminutive of Philipina. Susanne Philippina Fey, born in 1829, was the fourth child of the master needlemaker Carl Fey and Katharina Christina, née Landmann (Hs. StA DA, Abt. C 11; duplicate ev. KB Gedern, 1829). Gedern is ten miles southeast of Schotten, with a population of ca. 2,000 in 1854. Its important lines of trade were straw weaving and straw hats (Walther [1854], 451; Wagner, 81; *Beiträge zur Statistik des Großherzogtums Hessen* 2 [1863], 30).

Figure 29. Photo of Martin Weitz, probably that mentioned in letter of September 4, 1856.

send you 2 dollars for my birthday, I should put it in the letter. [4 ll.: is too dangerous] One should take care. Dear father and brother, this fall a roommate of mine is going to Germany then I want to send you some money again so you can buy something. If you can't, say a few good words to Gumbel, maybe he'll wait a month or two. [3 ll.: money matters] I'm also sending you my *Protret* so you can see me. I want to see if I can send my godson a pair of trousers if it's not too much trouble, or I'll send 2 dollars so you can buy him some nice clothes and I'll send Georg and Gretchen something later, it's not all that easy. I didn't make too much this summer, we had a lot of *Stappen* [stopping] (that means going for a walk). I also have to do some saving myself, I also have to look out for myself, maybe I'll get married this winter or at the latest in the spring, my wedding is coming up soon, because I'm not getting any younger. I never say I'm as old as I really am, but that I'm turning 28 this month.[28] So drink to my <u>health</u> I have to thank you much for warning me, I might perhaps be in the same misery like some of my comrades, if I hadn't watched out. [3 ll.: Georg Göbel wants money from him; he will get nothing] Give my best to Karl Schlörb, tell him I was pleased about the cloth that Bork got from him, it was fine and good. Sometime I must send you some of our manufacture. I had said something about a girl from Gedern but I haven't heard anything about it, nor news from Schotten, as I've heard things in Schotten have changed a lot.

Dear father, just be content, for the few hours you have left in life, I won't forget you I think of you day and night, all of you; share your joy, suffering, cares and woes with each other, because you just make your own lives more difficult, just be content. Believe you me, America is not paradise. Every person, no matter who he is, has his cross to bear, if not one kind then another, you should all just be content. [9 ll.: admonitions to all] I haven't forsaken you either, but I can't do everything, I don't earn that much since things cost a lot here. Karthringen Dahmer, Michel Burk and his family arrived in good health 14 days ago[29] and they are all still at

---

[28]He was actually 33; in MC 1860: Vernon, Tolland Co., Conn., #654, at the age of 37, his age is listed as 30.

[29]The emigration of Michael Bork and his family is quite well documented. He appeared at the mayor's office in Schotten on May 15, 1855, and stated that he was a full citizen, Old Lutheran, 58 years old, and a stocking knitter. He wanted to emigrate to North America with his wife Anna Maria (53), his son Konrad (26), and his daughter Elisabetha (18). "The reason for my emigration is to seek a better fortune." He would take along assets of 500 guilders.

He had no difficulties in receiving official permission to leave, but on October 13 the county magistrate's office had cause to inquire whether Bork "has revoked his decision to emigrate to America." The mayor then reported that Bork had been unable to sell his house at a fair price and had therefore stayed on in order to find a buyer during the winter. On June 23, 1856, he was apparently still in Schotten; the Borks must have departed shortly afterward (Hs. StA DA, Abt. G 15, 27).

Mißter Leining's. Tomorrow Bork is moving into another house that he has *gerentet* (that means *gezinßt*). Karthringen will stay with us and go with us next Monday to the mill to learn how to weave. Leuning and I will help her. Leining has taken her in like his own child, that's how I am to him too, we live in greater harmony than brothers. Tell *Mißter* Dahmer that his Karthringen will be well looked after at Leinig's.

I also have to write you that this fall is the presidential election, there were two main parties, that's the one for Fremont the other for Buchanan who are the two candidates, Fremont for the Republicans, Buchanan for the Democrats. The election is in November or October, a lot of people will be killed again, since things already look pretty bad, in some states things are already out of hand. We are faced with a great event here, all in all, it's not good no matter where you are. Yesterday on the 3rd I picked up my first papers as an American citizen, that cost me 1 dollar. I must close now. [6 ll.: greetings; signature]

Write me whether your letter costs money, too. I pay for them every time. When you write again use thin writing paper, I had to pay double for the last 2 letters, instead of 22 cents 44 cents.

Rockville, November 13th, 1856.
Dear father, brother, sister-in-law and children,

[5 ll.: correspondence] Dear father and brother, I am sending you 15 fifteen dollars, in your money 37 guilders 30 kreuzers, my father should get 6 dollars of it, my brother 5 dollars, my godson 2 dollars, Georg 1 dollar, and Grethgen 1 dollar, so everyone gets his share, and don't spend it foolishly. Buy yourselves clothing and food, you see now that I haven't forsaken you, that I've done what I could. Up to now I've been able to but when I get married I'll have to save for myself, because it is now high time for me to marry, probably before the spring, since one gets old and has to think of one's future too, for it's a bad proposition when you are old and still have small children. [3 ll.: details] I can't thank God and you enough that I am over here, when I think about you in Schotten and that I might still be over there and I think about my prospects I always get red-hot. You mustn't think that a man can just live here and not think about anything, like living high on the hog. No, it takes hard work and thrift, because if you don't work here you don't have anything. One must not [believe] that when you're in America roast doves fly into your mouth, no, those times are gone here too, but I say if a man is healthy and has work he can make a living, but there are thousands wandering around with no work, no money and no food. It is much worse for people like that here than over there in Germany, because they don't take care of each

other here, here everyone has to look after himself. As far as America is
concerned, things have come to a bad point, here it's all about slavery or
freedom. There were 2 parties here, the Democratic and the Republican,
things always used to be ruled by the Democrats here, but it is no good
any longer, so another party has risen up, namely the Republican party. It
is against slavery and that's a good thing which I worked for too, there
were great public meetings held on both sides. All the free-thinking men
who were leaders in Germany, here they are also for the good cause like
Siegmund Kaufman,[30] namely our neighbor Eisele's son. He also held
meetings in the state of New York, he works for the good cause, he is a
good lawyer, he is respected in the whole region. But many of our
German countrymen who were democratically minded over there, they
say I was a Democrat in Germany, my father was a Democrat and so I
will remain one too. But they don't think very far for they voted with the
slaveholders, because it's all about making Kansas free,[31] since Kansas is
so big that all of Germany could move there. For you also have to think
about your children, there are already 15 states in the South with slavery,
and the slaveholders own 3 million slaves, of which there are many white
ones. In Kansas it is therefore a time of much murder and other shameful
things have happened. When people had settled there the slaveholders
came and chased them off the land they owned with murder and arson,
isn't that a disgrace to future generations, now they have voted with the
slaveholders and James Buchennen is President. Now the Democrats say
Kansas must be free, but the President isn't making it free. I believe it will
end in a civil war. The Republican President is named John C. Fremont
he had endorsed the *Platform* where it says a dam should be set up against
slavery, so it does not spread [. . .] to protect the immigrants, and all in
all to work for the good cause, but no, he didn't become president. The
Negger-Democrats won, but it doesn't mean anything, the good cause is
being worked for every day. In America we have freedom of the press
where all the scandals come to light. If there hadn't been such cheating in
the Democratic party we would have won.

The immigrants can do a lot and they will continue to work for the
good cause and those who wallow still in error they will wake up and say,

---

[30]Sigismund Kaufman, born in 1825 in Schotten, was a book merchant active in the Frankfurt
Turner movement and the Revolution of 1848. He fled to the United States, was admitted to the
bar in 1852, and became a leading figure in the Turner movement, the Republican party,
banking, and the German Society of New York (see Chapter 14, note 10). He died in 1889 in
Berlin (Metzger [1892], 32–35).

[31]According to the Kansas-Nebraska Act of 1854, the decision whether slavery would be
legalized in the future state of Kansas was left to the settlers themselves through their territorial
legislature. As a result, both sides tried to send settlers sharing their convictions to Kansas,
leading to violent altercations between proslavery and antislavery forces.

Long live freedom. There's a lot tied up with the word freedom. Down with slavery. I wanted to write a lot more about the American situation but time doesn't permit any more. If you read the American newspaper, the German newspaper, any newspaper sent to Germany costs 2 cents, that's about 2 kreuzers, that is very cheap, and many are sent to Germany so you can get to know the American news and situation. I think it's useful if you should read them. Tell Kaspar Spamer, he will. Write me about it. Peter Glock came to be with us in Rockville. Leining had written to him. We found him a job 4 hours away in Sauthkawateri[32] in a hat *Fecktori* where we went on Sunday, November 2nd. Glock and I, Leining and his wife and Adam Leining in 2 *Käratsch* [carriage] that means *schäsche* or *Kutsche*. That's where Krämer from Michelbach [one mile east of Schotten] is, he works there too, that was a fun outing that we had there together. Karthringen Dahmer can already weave pretty well. Leining's little Betchen asked if I was writing to Germany, so little Betchen sends her best to Loui and Attel Wengel, Nickalos and little Miena. [4 ll.: further greetings] On Saturday Glock came back to us in Rockville. There where he was working in Sautgamanteri the *Fecktori* went bankrupt. Now he is working with us. As I read *Laastnait* [last night], that means *Gestern Abend,* in the newspaper the European reports I learned that things in France are in bad shape and in all Europe. [4 ll.: revolution?] The revolutionary spirit is still alive and the course of freedom will progress. Kossuth[33] and other free men are working every day in secret, and he is a free man who can get his own will made into law. [28 ll.: won't forget his family; is looking for a decent woman, happy family life; sends photograph; fall in United States the nicest season; acquaintances; wishes; signature; they should write!]

Rockville, August 23rd, 1857.
Dear father, brother, sister-in-law and children,
[6 ll.: correspondence] I am very pleased that you set things up for me. I received the 2 letters from *Mister* Johannes Leining behind the pharmacy in August and I wrote a letter to Philippina Fey from Gedern who is now in service in Ludwigshafen. I wrote her all about my situation and explained everything. I don't know whether she will come now or not, I am waiting with the greatest longing for a letter from her. I want to send you and *Mister* Leining and all my friends my heartiest thanks and I wish and hope that it will work out because I have put all my trust in her. I met

[32]Presumably South Coventry, ten miles southwest of Rockville.
[33]See Chapter 10, n. 23.

her earlier, I know she is a good woman. The time has now come when I want to and must, since I've gotten tired of this life, you can't get very far unless you're married because from what I pay for *Board* alone you can almost pay for 2, if you set things up right. If it doesn't work out with the girl from Gedern then I'll have to look around some more because I have already waited long enough. [6 ll.: everything is expensive in Germany and in America] Since the spring I've been paying 11 dollars for *Board,* that is very expensive but I can't blame the *Boarding*-keeper for that, they don't make much at it either [. . .] that's why I want to be on my own then I'd have more chance to save something. *Mister* Leining has 14 *Boardinger,* that means 14 *Kostgänger,* who board with him. Dear father, this fall I want to send you something so you'll get it before Christmas. I would have sent you something already, but this summer cost me a lot of money. I bought a whole set of clothes, that cost me 30 dollars, and some other things, because when you're single you don't save so much, and when you decide to really save, it costs you even more. But when you're married then you settle down and if you stay healthy and work together then you can really save something. You ask me how Michel Bork is doing, that I will tell you. Michel Bork worked here in a *Fecktori,* and there was an *Eirichsbeu* or in other words an *Irländer Bub,* the fellow never left Michel Bork one day in peace, always harassed him, until finally his anger got the better of him and he threw a piece of iron at him. He was right, that's what everyone said here, if it'd been me I'd have knocked him down, with those people you can't put up with any nonsense. Then the Irish fellow took it to court, then old Bork thought he would be hanged and left Rockville. Now he's a few miles away from us, he works for a farmer, he likes it very much. Therefore I'd like to ask you to find out who wrote that Michel Bork had been stealing here. We want to find out who the lowdown creature was so we can take him to court, because such a creature who writes such mean things to Germany should be strung up right away. And they aren't true, Michel Bork is a good man, and no one in Schotten can say anything against him. [. . .] Dear father I am so very pleased that you are in good health at your age [77], I thought of you on your birthday on August 9, it fell on a Sunday before the summer fair when I would so much have liked to have been in your midst. I would have enjoyed it so much, but nothing can be done, we should be content, we are too far apart. Dear father, I want to arrange it as soon as possible. We have founded a *Turnverein* which has been well received by the Americans, we're also getting a German church and school which is a good thing for the Germans here. It costs me money too, but for something like that I'll sacrifice everything so the young people and adults get some education, they need it badly. Dear father and brother send me 10 to 12 pounds of good camomile when you get the first good chance. I will tell you why, I have a good friend who was a military doctor in the Hussar Regiment in Prussia, now he's here and my roommate, he is a clever doctor, because I'm writing to you he asked me to write you that if you get the chance you should send it, but only good camomile. Whoever brings it will be paid. Otherwise we are all well, many greetings from the Leining and Bork families, Peter Glock is waiting desperately for his family, but he thought it strange that you didn't write anything about them. Write me as soon as possible about what decision the girl makes and what else is being said. Expecting a speedy reply. [3 ll.: greetings; signature]

My best to my little godson and be a good boy. Later when you're a big boy you can come over to me, and Grethgen has gotten a good job in service, but watch out that she doesn't do anything foolish, you know what I mean by that. [3 ll.: weather]

Rockville, November 14th, 1857

Dear father, brother, sister-in-law, and children,

I received the letter you sent along with Peter Glock's wife, and I learned from it that you are all quite well which made me very happy. Dear father and brother I must report an important event to you, that this fall there was a critical situation, namely all at once almost all the *Fecktorien* stopped, many trading houses went bankrupt, so many banks went broke, in short credit and confidence were all gone. We had work the whole time, but 1 month we worked only 8 hours a day, now it is back to full time. We have new machines in our mill, namely the wide *Loom,* that means *breite Webstühle,* where now 2 pieces are woven next to each other. Dear father and brother I wanted to send some money before Christmas, but it is impossible, we haven't had any money paid out for 3 months, now it's already the 4th month. I am sorry but I can't do anything about it, we have to wait and see, but as soon as it's *Gesettelt* [settled] I will send you something, don't worry, the bad times now are just because of the big speculators, in short it's over, things are coming to life again. Dear father and brother, now my wishes and hopes have come true, I can't describe to you how happy I was when I got the letter from my sweetheart, in short it was a great pleasure. It's almost time, because she wants me to come over and pick her up, but I can't do that. It would have been the greatest pleasure for me to come and get my beloved and to see you again, but remember the times and the losses that I've had, I lost at least 3 months besides what it cost me. So I have sent her my portrait she asked for. Since I can't come myself I sent it to her with the greatest pleasure, because her parents don't know me, so they can get to know me. I wrote her that if her parents have any further doubts, they should find out more about my conduct and all my behavior, I wouldn't know of the slightest thing to my discredit, or what I might have done that was wrong. Of course every person has his weak points but one shouldn't pay too much attention to them but pay attention to his virtues, that's the only thing. [9 ll.: thanks for being intermediaries, greetings]

I must also tell you something about the Bork family. Were they also like this in Schotten like they are here, looking down on everyone else since they're here in America? They have so much pride it can't be described. I think they brought along a couple of talers and then they think they're really something special. People don't like that here in America. Here everyone's equal, the rich like the poor and the poor like the rich. Who would have looked up to those people in Schotten, I don't think anyone. They must have thought I would marry their Liesabeth,[34] well, they thought wrong. Whoever takes her won't need to ask for God's punishment, he'll have punishment enough. That's a lowdown bunch. They go around in Rockville, you can read about it in Kathringen Dahmer's letters, the Bork family ran me down so badly it was a disgrace, one can't really be insulted by them, the people know me and they know that lot, I didn't do anything to start it. I don't know anything else new, just keep giving me your help because my sweetheart wants to come over here next spring.

Many greetings from your eternal loving / Martin Weitz

Many greetings from *Mr.* Leining and family, don't worry, I'll take care of things as soon as I can. Don't tell everyone all of what I write you. [. . .]

Rockville, Feb. 1st, 1858

[14 ll.: standard salutation; correspondence; package for his sweetheart] Dear father and brother, following your wishes I did what you asked. When I got your letter I read it and you agree that I should send my sweetheart the money for the passage so I got together 35 dollars right away without delay, that's 87 guilders 30 kreuzers, and will send it to my beloved, so I can grant the wish of my future parents-in-law too and they can see and be really convinced that I don't just want to lure my dear beloved over here and then maybe leave her in the lurch. Heaven forbid that, I'd sooner die, but you know me better than to think I'd do that. But on the other hand I don't blame my sweetheart's parents that they want to

---

[34]Elisabetha Bork, see n. 29 above.

see if I really have a decent living here, that their daughter isn't being taken for a ride, I can support a wife here better than in Germany. [. . .] I'm sending the money to Johannes Leining behind the pharmacy. I'm doing this for a certain reason because I don't have her parents' address, I would have sent it to you, but they should see that I really want her to come over to me. [6 ll.: in case she doesn't come, the money is for the family; is sure she is coming; longs to see her] Dear father, I really wanted to have sent you some money but at the moment it is impossible because the crisis has put me way back too. These haven't been good times, and now I'm settling down, I've bought things for the household that don't cost much money [. . .] as soon as the money gets there write to me right away. [. . .] Dear family, when I read in your letter that my bride came to visit you the tears came to my eyes, how you spent a nice evening together, you can't imagine my joy, oh if only I'd been able to be there too, but it wasn't possible. I ask you to make all the preparations you think are best, I'll write my sweetheart and tell her how she should do everything. I would have gotten the ticket for the ship here, why I didn't is this, so she doesn't have to come with the ship I made the contract with, it is always better to be free. I suggest that she come by steamship, so she gets here quickly, since it doesn't cost much more. [3 ll.: details] Wish we could have the wedding in Schotten, but it can't be, it just isn't possible. [20 ll.: rumors about the Borks; asks for three pipe tips; greetings; signature; Adam Leining sends greetings; signature M. W.; postscript by Adam Leining in English]

Rockville, April 5th, 1858

Dear faithful father, sister-in-law and children,

[9 ll.: death of his brother Johann Georg on February 19, see note 7] The death of my faithful brother grieves me so much. He has it best, he's got it all behind him, he is taken care of, here there is nothing but this world, all is vanity, nothing but trust in the Final Judge, God knows how to guide things best. No I cannot be comforted, dear father, you are now all alone there, with no son anymore with you to help you in your old age. You are now in your 78th year and thank God in good health, dear father, I beg you dearly not to grieve and worry, it can't be changed, I as your faithful son, I will help and take care of you and support you as much as is in my power. [. . .] If I only stay healthy and my plans work out, because I am also all alone here in America, you can't pour out your heart to anyone to relieve the sorrow. [12 ll.: consolation for sister-in-law; should take good care of his father] I will make it all up, dear relatives, you are right that you don't want to keep the business going any longer since the earnings are so poor and my father is too old and weak. You couldn't expect that of him and you have a quiet life. Things always work out better than you think. Dear Georg, it's up to you to do your duty to help your mother and grandfather and brothers and sisters. [23 ll.: admonitions to Georg, Gretchen, godchild; money matters; correspondence] If my truly beloved Philippina is still there give her my love and thousands of kisses, I am waiting with such longing for her. Dear father, if you weren't so old already, you should also come to me, but the trip is too hard for you. If you were in your 50s or at most 60 years old I would say you should come, but it is impossible, so calm down, I will not forget you and all of you. [10 ll.: greetings; signature; weather] I myself haven't done so well, I counted on much more than I actually earned, it is better now, one should not despair.

Rockville, May 2nd, 1858

Dear father and sister-in-law and children,

[30 ll.: correspondence; family should not be irritated that he sent the money to (their uncle) Leuning; reasons as in February 1, 1858, letter] That my beloved was in Schotten and didn't come to see you wasn't very nice of her, but I'm sure she didn't mean it badly, who knows what happened. [14 ll.: details; family affairs] Dear father, I will not forsake you and all of you I will do everything in my power. I am waiting every day for a letter from my beloved, I think she is already at sea, that she will come to me in the next few days. My longing for her is great, when I think about the fact that my faithful brother is dead I don't believe it, it is like a dream. [. . .] I must close in the hope that I will see my bride soon. I want to tell you also that our neighbor Georg Fey[35] is here with us in Rockville and is a roommate of mine and works here for an American as a carpenter (in *Enlichs* [English] *Kapner* [carpenter]), he has a good wage. Joinery and carpentry work that's a good business here, I tell you again don't think anything bad of me, give my best to all my friends and acquaintances and many greeting to you all and always keep your true son in kind remembrance. / Martin Weitz

Rockville, August 1st, 1858

Dearly beloved father, sister-in-law and children,

[3 ll.: correspondence] I would have written to you earlier but time

[35]Presumably Johann Georg Vey, born in 1829 in Schotten. His father was a master carpenter (duplicate ev. KB Schotten).

didn't permit it sooner, I had to write a letter right away to my dear wife's parents, so they would know when my wife arrived, my wife wouldn't have had any peace of mind otherwise. She had a long trip, circa 60 days, from May 4th until July 1st, the best thing about it was that she didn't get seasick. When I got the telegram I went to New:Iork right away and picked up my dear wife, which cost me a lot of money because when you travel here you have to take countless amounts of money along. I was in New Iork for almost 8 days, my wife's friends and acquaintances didn't want to let us go. On July 7th we came to Rockville and on July 8th we got married, and I wish you could all have been here with us. [. . .] We had a good time, Leuning and his family and Glock and his family and Krämer were at our wedding. Fey wasn't at home, he was working 5 miles from Rockville, and I don't want to have anything to do with the others for a particular reason. A lot of other friends were there. I get along with everyone in Rockville, just not with Borks, those people should stay out of my reach. Dear father, we are all quite hale and hearty, thank God, we have set up housekeeping, but it costs me a lot of money, things cost a little more money than over there. Now if God grants us good health we will lead a nice quiet life, because that is the most precious thing in the world. I waited for my wife with great longing to take her in my arms, since she is just the person who suits me and who was destined for me. [3 ll.: details] If my wife hadn't come I had decided to go to Callivonien this fall, and I would never, never have gotten married. I would have forsworn everything. [2 ll.: more of the same] It was 5 years ago at the summer fair when I saw my dear wife for the last time, and have had no other girlfriends, and always weighed secretly, one against the other, if you or you will do, until we finally came to an understanding by writing letters. She really had a lot to fight through at home with her parents, you wouldn't think she could be so steadfast. I can't blame my in-laws for it though, because they don't know me in the slightest, and it's such a long journey to make to America. If God grants us good health, she'll be better off than if she had married a rich man at home or some other friend, you're a free man here and you live free. I'll say it once again, those who belong together, get together, no matter how great the distance. Dear father, I know well enough that my dear brother, your breadwinner, is gone, and that it is perhaps too hard for you, dear father, to work hard in your old age, but be content, things will work out better than you think, you won't go hungry. Dear father, I wanted to send you something now but it is now impossible for me since it cost me too much money to get my household in order. I had already bought a lot but it wasn't enough at all, I never used to believe that everything costs too much, but now I know better. Thank God things are pretty much set up

now, it's so much better when you have your own place and don't have to
be nice to everyone all the time and can even save money besides. The
two of us can almost live on what it used to cost for me alone. [18 ll.: will
send money in the fall; excuses his wife for not coming to say goodbye]
Jacob Spamer is 2 miles from Baltimore, works for a gardener. He wrote
to me, I wrote back, but I don't know whether he's coming up here. [19
ll.: P. Glock will only write again when he's had a reply; happy that his
father is well taken care of; will do his part; admonitions; declarations of
loyalty] Finally the goal has been reached, 2 parts of the world are joined
together, namely the *Theligraph,* we never thought it would be possible
to get news from Europe within a few minutes. [. . .] The harvest looks
good here, food prices will be cheap this winter, I'd never wish for a
winter again like the last one, when many many thousands had to suffer
want. I would have written earlier but I couldn't, we had visitors almost
every evening and every Sunday and I couldn't write very well because
it's hard for me to write until I get around to it, I'll do it as soon as I can. I
must close in the hope that you are all well and getting along together and
    Many heartfelt greetings from both of us and we keep you always in
fond remembrance and remain your devoted son and daughter-in-law /
Martin Weitz / Philippina Weitz
    Dear father, be so good as to go to Gedern sometime and visit my
parents-in-law. They don't know me in the slightest, you would be
doing us a great favor.

                                        Rockville, October 20th, 1859
Dearly beloved father, sister-in-law, Georg and Grethgen,
    [7 ll.: correspondence; money received?] I must tell you the good news
that we have a baby daughter, who was born on the 18th of September
'59 at ¼ past 6 o'clock in the evening. You should see what a sweet girl
she is, she's a bit difficult, she causes us a bit of trouble, a lot of work but
that doesn't matter. My wife had to go through a lot from Saturday
evening 6 o'clock till Sunday evening at a quarter past 6 o'clock. We don't
have any midwives here, the doctor delivers all the babies. We had a good
doctor who is very good in cases like these. He didn't leave her side till
our little daughter was there, so you can imagine the great costs involved. My wife developed an inflamed breast afterwards with three
holes, I got medicine and advice right away, but we have a very good
man here who has healed so many breasts. Now with God's help that's all
over with. [2 ll.: details] My dear wife had to go through a lot, a thousand
thanks to God that she is fairly much back to normal again. You should
just see our dear little girl, how lively she is, admittedly she also cries a

lot, it will make her big and strong. Grethgen can be her godmother, she
has two godmothers here too, Konrad Bork's wife and Frank Adam's
wife. She hasn't been baptized yet, and she won't be baptized until she's
older, here it's not the custom to baptize them right away. [6 ll.: are well;
would like to see his father again] Dear father, I believe we will see each
other in the other world, that means in Eternity. I don't dare think about
my dear brother and my dear departed godson, it makes me want to cry,
but when I think it over, they have the best of things, they are free of care,
they rest from their labor. [19 ll.: further reflections, admonitions to
family members] Your neighbor Kaspar Spamer would like to know
what I earn in a month. It varies, you earn more one month, less the next,
like per month 18, 20, 22, 24, 26, etc. When it goes very well even 28
dollars if you have a good job, because it's a nice job, you sit down at the
Loom, that means *Webstuhl,* and it runs by itself. Jacob Spamer wrote to
me one time, last year, I wrote back to him, *ei to now wat is de mette.*[36] I
always thought he wanted to come over here, but he isn't here yet. [8 ll.:
war[37] has ended; will start up again soon; Georg should get himself
exempted from military service] Also Georg Göbel got married last
Easter and has started working as a weaver. Oh Georg, your troubles and
sorrows won't stop, they'll plague you day and night, you'll have nothing. If you had listened to me, had come over here, you would be a real
man. Give my best to all my friends and acquaintances, thousands of
greetings, especially [4 ll.: names] I can't name everyone by name, you'll
know best. [4 ll.: weather] There's enough news here, but to write it all
would take a year and a day. I close in the hope that our letter will reach
you in good health, we remain with many thousands of best wishes and
kisses from yours truly and we keep you always in fond remembrance. /
Martin Weitz Phillippina Weitz / [10 ll.: wishes, requests]

The available material gives no hint why this should be the last letter
by Martin Weitz that has been preserved. His father did not die until the
end of 1861, and the Weitz family was still living in Rockville in the fall of
1860. They appear in the census in somewhat distorted form—"Witz,"
instead of "Weitz"; Martin 30 years old, instead of 37; "Mary," instead of
Philippina, and 28 years old, instead of 31—but it is undoubtedly the
letter-writer's family. Martin is listed as a weaver, his wife apparently did
not work outside the home, and they had a one-year-old daughter named
Mary and $200 of moveable assets. In May 1861 a son was born; shortly

[36]I (want) to know what's the matter.
[37]Between France and Austria.

before, Martin had changed to a new job in a factory that had just been set up, the Hockanum Mill.[38]

In 1869, at the age of 45, he died of "typhoid pneumonia." He had been quite successful in his career: he ended up working as a loom fixer responsible for keeping a number of machines running smoothly, a job that required considerably higher qualifications than those of the loom operators, or "weavers," and was also much better paid (in 1870 in Connecticut: $2.25 instead of $1.50 a day). At the same time he seems to have become a citizen who was well respected not only by his fellow Germans. The obituary notice in the local newspaper makes it clear that he had been a popular member of the volunteer fire department (Hockanum Engine Co. No. 1), to which both Americans and immigrants belonged.[39]

His daughter Amelia, born in September 1859, was married in Rockville in June 1880 to a weaver who had immigrated from England. Her mother, Philippina Weitz, used German script to sign the letter of consent, written in English.[40] In 1900 Henry Weitz, the son who at the age of nineteen was still a wool weaver working along with his mother and his sister in the Rockville textile factories, was living in Waterbury, Connecticut, (ca. 45 miles southwest of Rockville), had married a woman born in the United States of German parents, and was the father of one child, the nineteen-year-old Philippine. The occupational change dreamed of by the father was accomplished by the son: Henry had become a barber.[41]

[38]MC 1860; birth certificates of both children (September 24, 1859, and May 23, 1861) in Office of the Registrar, Vernon, Conn.

[39]Ibid. for death certificate of May 23, 1869; USC 1880.1, 380; *Tolland County Journal,* May 29, 1869. See MC 1870: Tolland Co., Conn., Vernon town, #311.

[40]Marriage certificate and letter of consent, both June 4, 1880, in Office of the Registrar, Vernon, Conn.

[41]MC 1880: Tolland Co., Conn., Rockville, e.d. 109, #339; MC 1900: New Haven Co., Conn., Waterbury, e.d. 427, #227.

12

Angela and Nikolaus Heck

At least forty thousand people emigrated to North America from the Prussian district of Trier between 1833 and 1884—enough to populate a middle-sized town.[1] This mass exodus from the South Eifel and Moselle regions was primarily due to economic problems: agricultural yields were insufficient to support a rapidly growing population, and most of the farms were small and heavily mortgaged after a series of bad harvests. The iron industry, which had once played a dominant role in the area, experienced a sharp decline after 1850, and the skilled trades—the only alternative to farming—were hopelessly overcrowded.[2] Before the industrial Ruhr valley began to attract more inhabitants from the Eifel, emigration to the United States was for many the only chance to escape a life of poverty and even destitution. This was also the case for the 29-year-old journeyman tailor Nikolaus Heck and his wife Angela née Spoo, aged 28.[3] At the end of February or in early March of 1854 they left their home in Irrel, a village in the southwest Eifel, just a few miles from the

---

[1]Mergen (1954), 3. In comparison, towns with a corresponding population in 1880 include Darmstadt and Münster in Germany and St. Paul, Minnesota; in 1880 both in the United States and in Germany there were only 45 towns with more than forty thousand inhabitants (*Statistik des Deutschen Reichs* 57 [1883], xiii; USC 1880.1, 538).

[2]Graafen (1961), 16–21 and 43–54; see also the introduction to the Löwen letter series, Chapter 5. The causes for emigration are discussed in detail in the county magistrate reports: LHA KO, in particular Best. 442, Nr. 8648, 8649, 9371; see also Brommer et al. (1976), 138–51.

[3]Nikolaus Heck was born on August 13, 1825, Angela Spoo on August 17, 1826, in Irrel (in Bitburg County; its population in 1850 was 712 in eighty-three houses). According to a plat book of 1826, both of their parents owned their own homes (BistA TR, duplicate kath. KB Irrel; Pütz [1975], 28, 31–32).

Luxembourg border. At the end of March, along with other immigrants from Irrel, other neighboring villages, and Luxembourg, they boarded the American vessel *Vulture* in Antwerp. Following a crossing that was filled with hardship and which Angela describes in detail in her first letter, they arrived in New York on May 20.[4]

In contrast to many new arrivals, Nikolaus was lucky enough to find employment in his old profession. He was helped by the fact that the textile industry in New York was flourishing and dominated by Germans: over half of the almost thirteen thousand tailors in the city came from Germany. Only a few, however, were able to work as they had at home, on their own account or in small shops. The majority did piecework at home to supply the ready-made clothing industry.[5] Nikolaus Heck started off (and apparently continued until the 1890s) sewing men's coats and jackets for one of the New York clothiers.[6] It is certain that he earned more money than he could ever have dreamed of earning in the Eifel—as a journeyman with no chance of becoming independent.[7] Angela's rosy descriptions of the material well-being of the family, however, were probably exaggerated: in relation to the cost of living in New York, the wages paid by the textile industry were hardly as high as they seem at first glance. They had also been falling since the 1850s as a consequence of the increasing numbers of immigrants and the resulting pressure on the job market. Wives and children almost always had to work, too, in order to secure a sufficient income; and even then the family income was seldom large enough to permit savings to tide the family over times of economic recession.[8] The fact that the Hecks, according to the addresses provided by their letters, city directories, and the census, moved more than a dozen times during the course of three decades indicates that they were not immune to such income fluctuation.[9] When the family, after fourteen years of living in the overcrowded immigrant neighborhoods in Manhattan, finally moved across the East River to the suburb of Williamsburg, this was undoubtedly a sign of advance;[10] but even so-called "Dutchtown" had the sad character of other lower middle-class neigh-

[4]NYPL. They were married on March 8, 1852, in Irrel (NatA Pension Records). Neither of the two seems to have applied for permission to emigrate.

[5]Ernst (1949), 75–77 and 215; Bretting (1981), 95.

[6]MC 1880: Brooklyn, N.Y., W. 16, e.d. 145, #589; CD Brooklyn 1895.

[7]A journeyman in Bitburg County earned 36–72 talers a year, although Heck's income was probably at the lower end of this scale. Weekly wages for tailors in New York amounted to ca. $8–$10 in the 1850s. Monthly income in the United States was thus roughly comparable to annual income in the Eifel (Mergen [1954], 39; Ernst, 77).

[8]Ernst, 77; Bretting (1981), 94–95.

[9]MC 1880 and 1900: Brooklyn, N.Y., W. 16, e.d. 247, #375; CD New York 1855–68, CD Brooklyn 1868–1900; Nikolaus Heck is mentioned here only sporadically, due to frequent moves.

[10]For a discussion of living conditions in Manhattan see Ernst, 48–60; Bretting (1981), 9–13.

borhoods. It was populated primarily by German immigrants, especially small tradesmen and skilled craftsmen, among them "tailors by the dozen." Most lived in rented accommodations like the Hecks, and only a few could afford to own their own property.[11]

Angela reports only the advantages of life in New York and ignores the difficulties. It is tempting to attribute this to her lack of pretensions, but other facts indicate that she was more interested in impressing her relatives back home than in telling the truth. The letters give the impression, for example, that Nikolaus was distinguished for his bravery in the Civil War and that he had even assumed command of a German regiment in the Union Army, but the military records paint a different picture. A few months after the outbreak of the war, Nikolaus did enlist for three years, and in November 1861 he served in the 52nd Regiment New York Infantry, composed exclusively of Germans, which was posted to Washington.[12] To this extent, Angela's letters tally with the facts. By March 1862 at the latest, however, when the troops were posted to Virginia, Nikolaus was no longer attached to the regiment: he is listed in the muster rolls as "absent." As of July 1862 he was apparently a patient at General Hospital in Mount Pleasant, D.C., he spent the following March in a hospital in Philadelphia, Pennsylvania, and by June he had been discharged as unfit for military service because of "chronic rheumatism and general disability" and was sent home early.[13] And even if the rheumatic tailor did demonstrate remarkable courage in the defense of Washington, he was never promoted—the only military "rank" that Nikolaus attained was that of a private.

Even though Angela tended to portray the conditions of her life as more positive than they really were, she had no reason to exaggerate with respect to one aspect of her life in the United States: religion. Even for German Catholics like the Hecks, in New York it was no problem to "keep up your religion as well as in Germany." Approximately one seventh of the 300,000 to 400,000 Catholics who lived in the metropolis in the 1860s—more than in any other city in the United States—were of German origin.[14] Like their Protestant countrymen, German Catholics organized their own parishes, and German priests celebrated mass in the German language and according to the rites of the old country.[15] When

[11]Of the roughly 24,000 inhabitants of Williamsburg in 1865 about 40 percent were born in Germany; Germans made up ca. 70 percent of the registered voters, a better indication of adult population makeup (State Census New York 1865; Weld [1950], 87; Lapham [1977], 64–66; Doerries [1986], 74–75).

[12]U.S. NatA, Muster Rolls, 52nd Regiment New York Infantry; Kaufmann (1911), 185. For a discussion of the role played by this regiment see Dyer 3 (1959), 1424.

[13]Muster Rolls, 52nd Regiment New York Infantry.

[14]Dolan (1975), 15, 70.

[15]Ibid., 68–86; Lapham, 44–69.

the Hecks came to New York in 1854, there were already five German Catholic parishes in Manhattan, and ten years later this number had increased to eight. When the family moved to Williamsburg in the late 1860s, they were not part of a general diaspora: more than half a dozen German Catholic churches already existed in Brooklyn.[16]

Because German Catholics found themselves in the minority, both in ethnic and in religious terms, they reacted by defending their cultural and religious traditions with particular intensity. The parish, therefore, played an important role and developed beyond its primary religious function to become the central focus of the social life of the group.[17] Angela Heck's letters provide graphic proof of this: the church, which was near their home (both in Manhattan and in Williamsburg), their predominantly German and Catholic neighbors,[18] as well as various church organizations, provided the basic social ties of the family. The Hecks seem to have spent most of their lives in an ethnic and religious microcosm in the midst of a city that—like no other—brought together people from the widest range of national backgrounds and religious or denominational affiliations.

It is quite possible that the letters printed here still exist, but an intensive search for the originals has proved futile. It is certain that the typescript the editors relied on was made in the 1930s by a bona fide historian and archivist, Joseph Scheben, who did not preserve the original spelling and occasionally straightened out a phrase, so that a precise analysis of Angela Heck's language is not possible.

But it is obvious that her style is not fluent, her sentence structure generally very simple, most sentences short, and her vocabulary limited, though not to the extent of garbling the message. Only slight traces of her local dialect are discernible, although it is likely that Scheben standardized the obvious dialect expressions. Angela Heck's simple German shows no influence of English even after ten years, which indicates that she apparently never progressed very far in mastering the language. Her husband's writing, in terms of both style and content, shows considerably more sophistication.[19]

[16]Dolan (1975), 13. The first German-language Catholic parish in Manhattan was that of St. Nikolaus, founded in 1833 in the 17th Ward, an area with predominantly German residents (Bonenkamp et al. [1882], 164–65; Enzlberger [1892], 35–36).

[17]Dolan (1975), 70–71; Lapham, 51–53.

[18]The ethnic and denominational structure of the Hecks' neighborhood can be reconstructed most precisely for the area where they lived after the end of the 1860s. Here they were surrounded almost exclusively by German Catholics, mostly from Bavaria and Hesse (Lapham, 63–66; MC 1880 and 1900: Brooklyn, W. 16).

[19]Carbon copies of the Heck letters are located in Immigrant Letter Collection, State Historical Society of Wisconsin, Madison.

Angela Heck

New York, July 1, 1854

Dearest Relations,

We are writing to tell you that our ship left Antwerp on March 21st. [12 ll.: first days of the voyage; death of four children] Then we sailed with bad winds into Easter week, Maundy Thursday and Good Friday. Then the ship started to roll. Then it was like everyone was drunk. One went running this way, another that way, in order to be sick. Most of the people couldn't face even the mere thought of food. Hauer, Nussbaum, and my husband sat tight on our trunks. The other 8 of us couldn't stand the sight of them eating we were so ill. Then things calmed down a bit until the night of Easter Sunday. Around 12 o'clock there was a noise up on deck that was so loud that everyone awoke. The sailors and helmsman and captain were all on deck for we were now having such a terrible storm that we thought the ship would be torn apart. We all started to tremble and shake. It kept getting worse. We all started praying out loud, all of us in the ship, almost 300 people and all Catholic and almost all from villages near ours, from Luxembourg and from our county. At daybreak things got even worse, that is on Easter Monday. The ship was listing to one side and all the top planks started to break. We had to hold on as tight as we could to keep from falling out. Then we all started again and prayed 17 rosaries before we stopped. All those who didn't know how to pray had to learn. We all called on all the Saints in Heaven and God, the Holy Mother of God, Saint Nikolas,[20] but things kept getting worse and worse. We thought the ship would be ripped apart at any moment. The ship was listing so much that you couldn't lie down, stand up or sit. There weren't any windows in the ship except where the stairs went up. There was an opening there. And also across from our beds. The stairs were then closed off since water was coming into the ship from the deck above and the small trunks started floating around. Our cooking pot and spoon floated all around. Our boys[21] let them float away because they didn't think we would need them. It was so loud, the ship was sailing just like it was in a valley and on both sides it was so high you couldn't see over, just water everywhere. The ship started to crack, two masts broke and their sails and ropes were ripped and torn to pieces. Then the ship sank down very deep and water came into the opening like it was being poured in with a bucket. They couldn't shut this or else we would have suffocated. We were all so frightened we couldn't even pray. We repented our sins and we all prepared to die. Johann and K. Limburg

[20]St. Nikolas was regarded as one of the fourteen *Nothelfer* (saints who are called upon in times of great need) and was the patron saint of bargemen and seamen.
[21]What is probably meant is boys from the village; the Hecks had no children at this time.

were still sitting in bed naked and held on to us as well as we could. We quickly put on our underskirts so we wouldn't be lying there naked when we died. For two days we hadn't put on any shoes and stockings. Our boys lay between the trunks and had tied the trunks down with ropes. For three days we couldn't cook since no one could go up on deck since the water was pouring in over the side. The first day no one ate anything, up to the evening of the second day, then we ate the first bit of our ham raw. On Maundy Thursday we ate the last of the bread we had brought from home. Those who had never believed in God now got a chance to see that He exists. We never forgot Him in our prayers, since we prayed three rosaries every morning and evening. Almost everyone on the ship was unattached, boys and girls, some 30 of them from Konsdorf.[22] Our ship was thrown so far off course by the storm that they hardly knew where we were. We kept hoping from one day to the next but all we saw was sky and water every time we looked. [13 ll.: food ran short] Finally we saw a lot of ships, one after another. Then we were told we would soon be on land. Then finally on May 17th we saw land and cities. But then we still had to wait on the ship until the doctor came.[23] But he was finished quickly. Everyone left the ship, for there were no more people who were sick on board. Then our trunks were taken to shore on a steamboat and we also came on a steamboat. There was a young man there from Hefnig near Echternach who was there to meet his country-men, a real rascal. He then led all of us who were in the ship to a German boardinghouse in New York.[24] There we ate three meals and slept one night. Then everyone had to pay 7 francs.[25] My husband had to pay 14 francs for the two of us, since they had put all the trunks in the cellar and no one could get them back before he paid.[26] The next day most of them moved on to the train. It was all very sad. Most of them didn't have enough money and couldn't go where they wanted. The extra weight of the trunks cost more than they had imagined. [5 ll.: many had to throw away their belongings] We were able to hold on to the money we still had, for one man told us that if you were a tailor you should stay in New

---

[22]Consdorf was a village in Luxembourg ca. ten miles from Irrel.

[23]Before a ship entered the port of New York, a medical officer came on board to make sure that none of the passengers were suffering from a contagious disease. If this was the case, the ship was put in quarantine for thirty days. The examinations, however, were rather cursory (Bretting [1981], 30).

[24]The boy from Heffingen (a village in Luxembourg not far from Irrel) was apparently one of the many "runners," who used methods bordering on the criminal to bring new arrivals to a particular boardinghouse, shipping agency, or employment agency. The runners received a premium for their work.

[25]The French currency was also used in Luxembourg (in 1854 1 franc = ca. 20 cents).

[26]Locking up the baggage of the emigrants was a popular way for innkeepers to force their guests to pay for food and lodging. The prices charged were often exorbitant (Bretting [1981], 43).

York. We had hardly been here for fifteen minutes when they came running to us with cards looking for tailors. [3 ll.: they were able to keep all their baggage] Everyone was very sad when they left but not us because we already knew where we were going. And we also would have had enough money left even if we hadn't found work so quickly, but we were quickly taken care of. When the others from Irrel left on the train, we drove happily with our trunk to our tenement. The first few days we didn't work very much, since we had to buy all sorts of things that we needed. But all that money gives you courage. He started immediately to work for a shop. He earns a dollar every day. He makes nothing but men's jackets. You at home may well think I don't have a job. You mustn't think that; I always help him with the sewing. But there aren't any women at home who have such a good life and it gets better every day. All of the things we need to eat we can buy across the street just like at the market. But this year everything is quite expensive. [6 ll.: examples of prices] The worst bread that they eat here is better than the finest cake at home. We can eat every day for one shilling. We don't need to buy wood; there's enough wood just lying around. Rooms are expensive where we are on the corner. We have to pay 4 dollars a month. But we are among nothing but good people who are all Catholic and German. On Sundays we all go together to church, since there are many German Catholic churches here. I only wish that everyone who has to stay at home and lead a life of poverty could live like we do. Young people who have learned a trade have more here than someone at home who has a fortune of 2000 talers. [5 ll.: greetings] Give my best to Anna Bisdorf and Elisabeth Mutsch too and tell them they should burn up their grape baskets and get themselves some tailors, even if they are windbags. [3 ll.: closing]

[*Nikolaus Heck* continues:]

One other thing I want to tell you: there were 300 of us when we went on board the ship. But when we left, our numbers had increased to the millions. And these countrymen were called lice. The ship was full of them. We didn't have any though. [7 ll.: further comments on the trip; greetings]

Angela Heck

New York, October 26, 1862

Dearest sister, brother-in-law and all at home,

I can no longer keep from writing to you, since I have been in America for 8 years and have only received one letter from you, to let you know how I am. I am still hale and hearty. But these are sad times now in America. I imagine you've heard about it, that is the murderous war that we in the North are fighting against the South, in which almost all the average people, most of them German, are involved. The war has already lasted over a whole year and it has already cost a hundred thousand lives and there's no end in sight. My husband, Nikolaus Heck, is also among them. Since October 1st he's been away from the family for a year. But thank the Lord I am well taken care of. He is a first lieutenant in the 52nd Regiment in Company 2. He receives 60 talers a month. Now, though, because of the bravery he showed in 3–4 battles he has become an *Oberst,* that is a colonel. He has command over the entire regiment. The whole regiment is made up of Germans. They were 1000 men strong when they marched away from here. But now with the hardships they have suffered, though, the cold in the winter and in all the many battles, only half that number remain.[27] The decoration that he received over in Berlin[28] helped him to get this high rank here, and also the large number of Prussian officers who are here fighting in the war.[29] For there are 120 regiments, all made up of Germans.[30] Most of the soldiers had never been soldiers in Germany. Almost all of those who had been soldiers over in Germany have received the rank of colonel. Now as a colonel he earns 100 talers a month, I get my payments every week; that is I get 5 dollars a week. Heck sends me all his money every two months. He gets clothing and food all for free. A common soldier gets 13 talers a month, a *Feldwebel* 30, a sergeant 20 talers a month[31] and the family, every wife gets 5 talers a week until the war is over. They've all enlisted for 3 years. If the war ends earlier than that, they'll all come home. Heck is still in good health. He is now in Washington, the capital of North America. He wrote and told me that I should bring the children and come to see him, he wants to see us so badly. We haven't seen each other for over a year. Now you can well imagine how overjoyed we will be when we see each other again. We will be even happier than we were over there when he returned from Berlin. I receive a letter from him every week, sometimes 2. The state of New York had to supply over 100 regiments. Now

[27]Of the 2,800 men listed in the muster rolls of the regiment, only 200 returned from the war (Kaufmann, 185).

[28]Nikolaus Heck, as a Prussian citizen, had presumably served military duty in Berlin.

[29]There were in fact a relatively large number of former officers—not only Prussian officers—among the Germans who fought in the Union Army (Kaufmann, 131–32).

[30]In fact only ten of the New York regiments were made up exclusively of Germans, three more were half German. Some 36,000 of all the soldiers supplied by the state of New York were born in Germany (Lapham, 201, 207). Angela is probably referring to all of the German-American regiments in the Union Army.

[31]Officers in fact received somewhat more than Angela claims (Nevins 1 [1959], 164). *Feldwebel* and sergeant refer to the same rank.

though they can't get any new people. Now they're drafting until next week.[32] Then it will hit a lot of people before they have their number. When he comes home safely, every man receives 100 talers. If a man dies or falls in battle, his wife receives a pension for the rest of her life, that is 8 talers a month, as well as the 100 talers.

My dear brother-in-law, I have already saved a lot of money. Should Heck be injured, I will be well taken care of. Should he never return, which I hope will not be the case, it can be that we will see each other again. And if Heck returns safely I want to make him happy by letting him go to Germany, even if a few hundred go to blazes. He wrote to me when I come home safely we should travel to Germany. Then we will give a ball and I will invite all our good friends. So you needn't worry about me. I am doing very well. But the dear Lord should bring him back safely. The 8 years that we have been married we have led a wonderful life together and neither of us has made the other angry in the least. My dear sister, I want to let you know that I still have 2 children, a girl named Evchen and a boy named Nekchen [nickname for Nikolaus]. I lost a five-year-old boy to dropsy. Now it's about a year ago, when my husband left. His whole regiment helped bury him. My daughter is 7 years old and my little boy 2 years and three months old. My dear brother-in-law, everything here is very expensive, all the food. [2 ll.: examples] I believe that you in Germany will feel the effects of the war that's going on here. My dear sister, time doesn't hang heavy here. I'm living among nothing but Germans, and the husbands of all the women here have gone off to war. I don't need to do any work but my housework. [27 ll.: asks about health of the family; postal delivery service in New York; relatives should also write to her husband; greetings; address]

New York, October 25 [probably 1863]
Dearest brother-in-law and all at home,

[4 ll.: thanks for letters with news of the family] I'm writing to tell you how I'm doing. My husband has returned home safely, he's been here since the 10th of June. He was very ill, that is from the cold. Those 2 winters lying in the field, that can make the strongest man sick, the regiment he left with was 800 man strong. Now there are only 30 men left.[33] They fell in heaps in the battles or died from illness. We were overjoyed when we saw each other again, as you can imagine. Heck is hale and hearty. But with the war things are still very bad. The people

---

[32]See Chapter 3, n. 29.
[33]See n. 27, above.

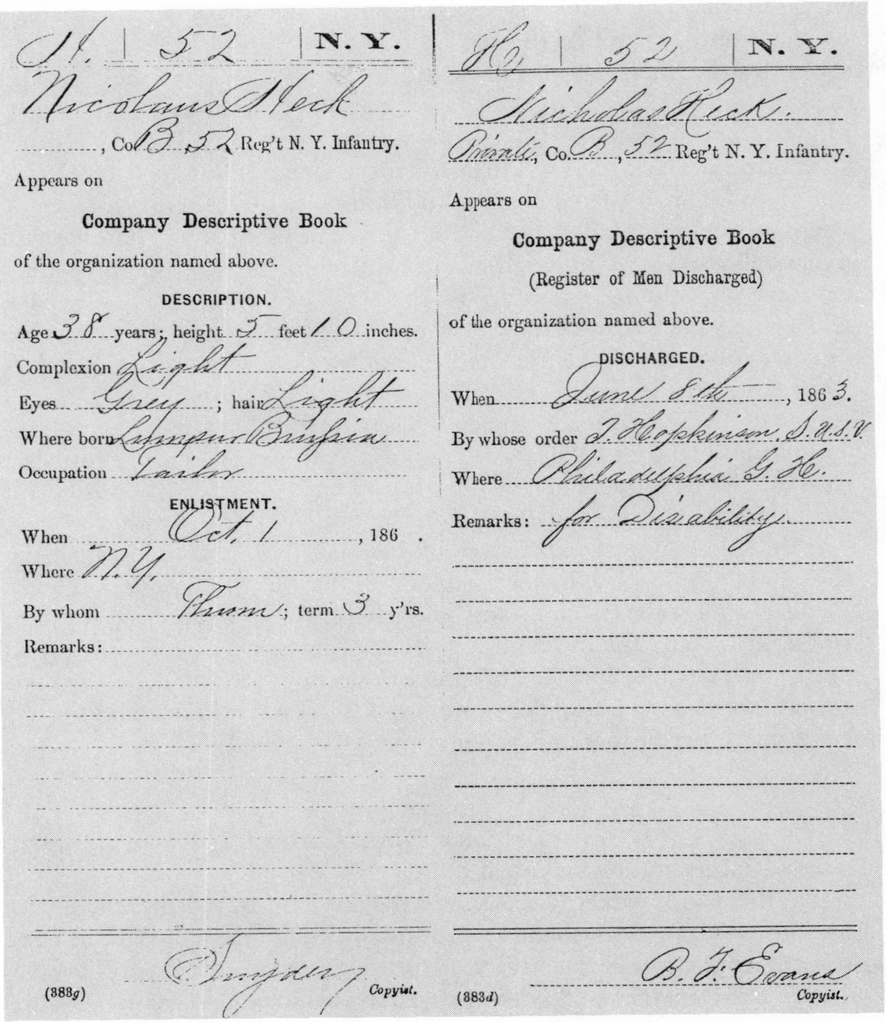

H. | 52 | N. Y.

Nicolaus Heck

........, Co. B 52 Reg't N. Y. Infantry.

Appears on

Company Descriptive Book

of the organization named above.

DESCRIPTION.

Age 38 years; height 5 feet 10 inches.

Complexion Light

Eyes Grey; hair Light

Where born Limpur Prussia

Occupation Tailor

ENLISTMENT.

When Oct. 1, 186 .

Where N.Y.

By whom Thom; term 3 y'rs.

Remarks:

(388g) C. Snyder Copyist.

H. | 52 | N. Y.

Nicholas Heck.

Private, Co. B, 52 Reg't N. Y. Infantry.

Appears on

Company Descriptive Book

(Register of Men Discharged)

of the organization named above.

DISCHARGED.

When June 8th, 1863.

By whose order J. Hopkinson S.U.S.V.

Where Philadelphia G. H.

Remarks: for Disability

(883d) B. F. Evans Copyist.

Figure 30. Civil War muster rolls of Nicholas Heck. *Source:* U.S. NatA.

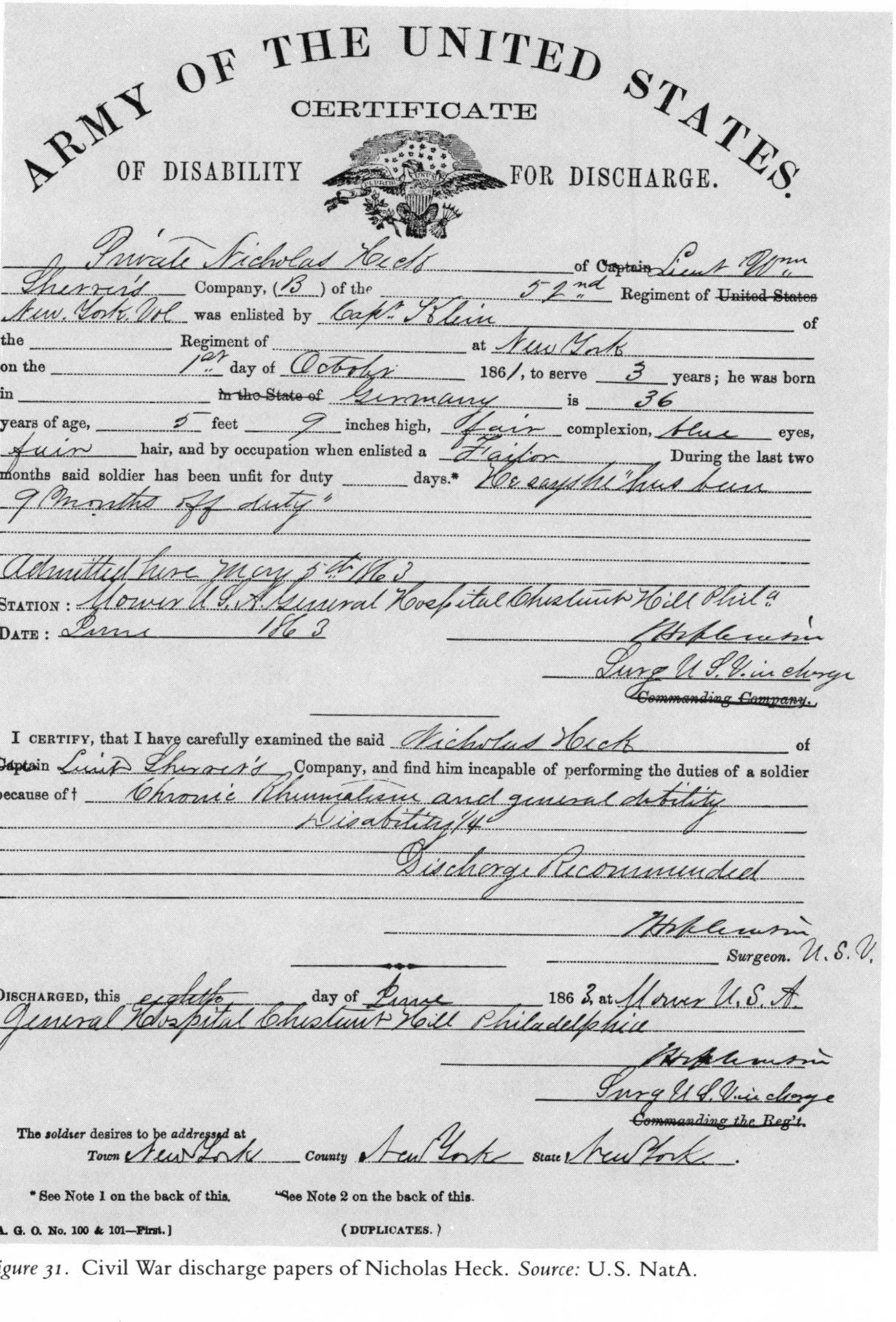

ARMY OF THE UNITED STATES

CERTIFICATE

OF DISABILITY ~~FOR DISCHARGE.~~

Private *Nicholas Heck* of ~~Captain~~ *Lieut Wm*
Sherrer's Company, (*B*) of the *5 2nd* Regiment of ~~United States~~
New York Vol was enlisted by *Capt. Klein* of
the _____ Regiment of _____ at *New York*
on the *1st* day of *October* 186 *1*, to serve *3* years; he was born
in _____ ~~in the State of~~ *Germany* is *36*
years of age, *5* feet *9* inches high, *fair* complexion, *blue* eyes,
fair hair, and by occupation when enlisted a *Tailor* During the last two
months said soldier has been unfit for duty _____ days.* *He says he has been*
9 Months off duty"

Admitted here may 5th 1863

STATION: *Mower U.S.A. General Hospital Chestnut Hill Phila*
DATE: *June* 186 *3*

J Hopkinson
Surg U.S.V. in charge
~~Commanding Company.~~

I CERTIFY, that I have carefully examined the said *Nicholas Heck* of
~~Captain~~ *Lieut Sherrer's* Company, and find him incapable of performing the duties of a soldier
because of † *Chronic Rheumatism and general debility*
+ Disability 7/4

Discharge Recommended

J Hopkinson
Surgeon. U.S.V.

DISCHARGED, this *eighth* day of *June* 186 *3*, at *Mower U.S.A.*
General Hospital Chestnut Hill Philadelphia

J Hopkinson
Surg U.S. in charge
Commanding the Reg't.

The soldier desires to be addressed at
Town *New York* County *New York* State *New York* .

* See Note 1 on the back of this. ‡See Note 2 on the back of this.

[A. G. O. No. 100 & 101—First.] (DUPLICATES.)

Figure 31. Civil War discharge papers of Nicholas Heck. *Source:* U.S. NatA.

who haven't died in the battles are ruined nonetheless. When a man joins up now he gets 500 talers in advance even before he needs to leave. And his family is well supported and the man still gets 13 talers a month. But they can't recruit any more people. Now they are drafting the 18- to 35-year-olds. Whoever is called up and can't send a substitute has to go himself. Now they're even starting to draw the numbers a second time. The city of New York alone has to send another 14,000 men.[34] But thank the Lord that work is going so well. People are now earning one-third more than before. We bought a sewing machine for 100 talers. It sews as much as three men can sew by hand. We can earn 12 talers every week. We always have a lot of work but because of the war food is very expensive. But we don't lack for anything because of this. I couldn't wish for anything more. We have food and drink and what more could you want. I have meat every day and a dear husband as well. You know that. In short, my dear Anna, you can believe me, things are a hundred times better for me than for you. If it should happen that he falls ill, I won't be in need. You can always save enough for times of need. We belong to a mutual aid society. There we pay 10 shillings a quarter. If Heck falls ill, I get 6 talers a week brought to the house. My dear Anna, you also write that I should tell you how things stand with our religion. We go to church every Sunday. We have 3–4 German Catholic churches very near where we live. Our daughter goes to the German Catholic school. But she speaks English as well as she speaks German. I still have only my two children, one girl and one boy. I don't know anything yet about a third. I believe that if you, my dear Anna, could send your Johannes to us for a couple of years, it would be better for you. When I feel sorry for you with so many children, Heck laughs and says I just want to see everyone all together. I still hope I will get to see little Bernhardt again if I remain in good health. His father should let him learn the cooper's trade. That is also good here. A cooper gets two and a half talers a day. You can believe me, really. I imagine that little Bernhardt would never want to return to Germany if he came here, just like I don't want to go back. My dear Anna and husband, if you could see Heck now you wouldn't even recognize him; he is so fat he can't close any of his trousers. I wish Herr Weiler could see him now. Then he wouldn't need to call him the tall tailor anymore. [7 ll.: closing remarks, greetings and signature]

[Nikolaus Heck continues:]

My dear friends, I want to write a few lines so you can see that I am back with my dear family, for as you know, I was away at war. But now

---

[34]In July in New York City there were massive protests against forced induction (above all in the neighborhoods populated by Irish workers); more than one hundred persons were killed (Lapham, 210–11).

with God's help I have returned safely, which thousands of my comrades, who can no longer see their families, have not been able to do. I often told myself, too, that I would never see home again, as the bullets were flying past my head. I was in eight large battles where the comrades in front of me and on both sides were shot down. But I was always lucky. Now though I have had enough of the war. I was away for 2 years, but I would have had another year to serve if I hadn't fallen ill. Now I have my discharge papers. I could write you an entire book about the war, but I don't have enough space.

Angela Heck

New York, September 25 [probably 1865]

Dear brother-in-law,

[6 ll.: a returning emigrant will take this letter along] I also want to let you know that my husband hasn't returned yet. But I expect him any day now, he wrote me that he'd be coming home in a couple of days,[35] since all the warriors who were away are now all home again. Only a few regiments are still in the field. They'll be discharged in a week, since the war here is finally over. [5 ll.: her husband has received no letters from relations] The boy can tell you how things are here and how I am doing. I lack for nothing and am still happy and healthy, as are my 2 children and my husband. But things are very expensive here now. When my husband comes home we'll be able to get good work and earn 20 talers a week. My dear brother-in-law, you can believe what the boy who is coming to see you has to say. He's not an idle prattler. He also tells the truth. Dear brother-in-law, you wrote in your last letter that my husband should come to visit you. I don't object to the cost of the crossing but to the money he would waste over there in Germany. That would be even more and would serve no purpose. [4 ll.: greetings and regards] I don't want to send my regards to Elisabeth Mutsch and Anna Bisdorf since they never write to me. [8 ll.: postal delivery; address]

Williamsburg, January 24, 1869

Dearest Anna and Johannes,

We received your letter, which you sent to us with Herr Oberweis, with delight. The old fellow found us easily, which made us and him very happy. He stayed with us for 3 days. We wanted to keep him here by

[35]Heck reenlisted in the 58th New York Infantry as a private on March 11, 1865, and was honorably discharged on October 1, 1865. Since he was not subject to the draft, he probably reenlisted for economic reasons (U.S. NatA, Muster Rolls, 58th Regiment New York Infantry; Pension Records).

force. But he became restless and wanted to go to Häreson [Harrison, N.Y.] to see the watchmaker, who is a relative of his son's wife. If he hadn't found us, he would have fared very badly. He was out of money. We gave him 5 dollars so he could make the trip. A week later he wrote us that he arrived safely at his destination. But his countryman wasn't at home. He was away on a short trip. He was going to write us later and tell us how he is. That was last year in June. Since then we haven't heard a word from him. It was so hard for him to leave us. He cried like a child and we did too. [5 ll.: other visitors from the Eifel] We had a lot of fun with Oberweis. I told him that in Germany he had been my greatest enemy, when he used to catch us in the wheat or clover. When I heard that he was going to come to visit me, I said [. . .] my folks will have a good time, and my old friend Elisabeth Mutsch too, if she can still remember that he took away our baskets and threw that stick at us. I was beside myself with joy when I saw the old fellow. For I did get to hear news from the old home country. [7 ll.: another visitor from the Eifel] My dear Anna, our daughter Eva had her first Holy Communion two years ago in New York at the church of St. Francis.[36] I wished you could have seen it. Her clothing cost us 25 talers without the candle. She had a white dress and a white veil that came down to the ground, a lovely wreath of rosemary around her head. A girl whose parents are from St. Wendel[37] carried the candle for her.

My dearest Anna and Johannes, since the 1st of August we've been living for over a year in Williamsburg, a town very near New York. We still work for people in New York, we go back and forth in a couple of hours. It is much healthier here than in New York, just like in Germany. All of the small shops are German, 7–8 German-Catholic churches and each one has a Catholic school. We don't have to go further to church than you do at home. That is a church, it's like a cathedral, with three spires on top. Next to it is a small one like in Germany.[38] There's a big school there, with 8–9 teachers, and also that many nuns. The nuns teach the girls and also the little boys until they are grown up. Then they go to the high school until the age of 14. Our little Nikolaus also goes there. We pay 15 cents a week. In the school there are 1500, all with German parents and all Catholic;[39] the priests visit the schools every day and are very

---

[36]Founded in 1844 in the 16th Ward of New York City (Dolan [1975], 13, 16).

[37]County seat in the South Eifel.

[38]Between 1850 and 1860, a new building, which was both costly and imposing, was erected next to the old Church of the Holy Trinity (founded in 1841), which is mentioned here. From the 1860s to the mid-1890s the parish of the Holy Trinity, with ca. eight thousand members, was the largest German-Catholic parish in New York (Lapham, 63 and 66–67; Reiter [1869], 107; Bonenkamp et al., 164).

[39]Reiter, 107; Bonenkamp et al., 164.

strict. We also belong to this parish. We have a pew in the church.[40] For that we pay one taler every three months. My husband belongs to the St. Joseph's society.[41] If he gets sick, he gets 4 talers a week sick pay. And if he dies, he will be collected from the house and taken to the churchyard by the members of the society. The society covers all the expenses. If a new church is built, they have to go there with the flags of St. Joseph. We have three priests in our parish. One arrived here a short while ago. One is a Bavarian, one is an Alsatian.[42] There is confession every Saturday. They are much stricter with confession and sermons here than in Germany. On Sunday the first Mass is at 6 o'clock, the second one for children at 8, at 9 in the little church next door, at 10 o'clock is High Mass in the Church of the Holy Trinity. In all of the churches there are lovely organs and four-part choirs, all German singers. My dear Johannes and Anna, you mustn't think so, we won't lose our religion even though we are in America. There are good and bad people of all nationalities. There are bad Catholics here just like in the big cities in Germany. In short you can keep up your religion just as well here as in Germany. For there are Catholic churches everywhere now. In New York alone there are 42 Catholic churches, English and German. There they sacrifice and beg for thousands for the Pope. We have the portrait of Pope Pius IX. It cost us 5 talers. We receive the church newspaper[43] every Sunday and see everything that's happening in Rome. [2 ll.: address]

The 1870 census shows Hecks renting in a six-apartment flat in Williamsburg. Everyone in the building was of German or Swiss stock, and five of the six family heads were tailors, but the Hecks were the poorest of the lot, worth only $100. From all indications, their circumstances changed little during the rest of their lives.[44] Until the end of the 1880s, Nikolaus Heck apparently continued to work as a tailor. In 1890 he applied for a Union veteran's pension, claiming that he was unable to work due to "rheumatism and piles." Only after he applied again three years later, however, was a pension granted. By then he did not have long to enjoy his retirement—according to the death certificate in his pension file, he died on July 22, 1897, at the age of 71, from a chronic kidney

---

[40]Pew rental was one of the most important sources of income for the parishes (Dolan [1975], 57–58).

[41]Founded in 1843 by Father Rumpler, member of the Order of Redemptionists and pastor of the first German-Catholic parish in New York City (Ibid., 81).

[42]See the information in Reiter, 107.

[43]The *Katholische Kirchenzeitung,* published by the German Catholics of New York, appeared after 1851; in 1877 it had a circulation of 3,500 (Lapham, 69).

[44]MC 1870: Brooklyn, N.Y., W. 15, #187.

infection. It is also clear from the pension file that his widow spent her final years in very impoverished circumstances. Her application for a widow's pension, supported by affidavits from two long-time friends and neighbors, stated that "the claimant's means of support are her daily labor by washing and doing housework by which she does not earn enough for her living," and that she owned nothing "except household furniture." The modest monthly pension of $12 that she finally received hardly covered more than the basic necessities. When Angela Heck died on April 20, 1909, her daughter Eva Gerhold, who had cared for her during her last weeks of life (a doctor was called only the day before she died), had to submit an application for reimbursement to cover the doctor's bill and burial costs.[45]

[45]CD Brooklyn 1880–97; MC 1900; NatA Pension Records.

13

Peter Klein

There is good reason to assume that Peter Klein was illiterate, or at least that he found writing so difficult he preferred to dictate his letters to someone else (the same probably holds for his cousin, fellow emigrant, and occasional co-worker Peter Büch). The letters signed "Peter Klein" were written in no less than seven different hands; some can be attributed with reasonable certainty to one particular individual, but most of them cannot. The signature also varies in each letter. The enclosed letters and postscripts by Peter Büch are written in three different hands.[1]

The fact that the two men from Güchenbach could not write is not surprising. They were miners, as were Klein's two brothers and two brothers-in-law, and their educational opportunities were very limited. Until the 1860s the Protestant children in their village, six miles north of Saarbrücken, had to go to school in Walpershofen, another village about two miles away. Teacher training was insufficient, instructional methods

[1]Originals of the Klein letters are in LA SB, A/4-440 R-1347-90. Klein's first four letters (including Büch's postscript to the fourth letter) were probably written by Johann Gothie, the man who ran the boardinghouse where Klein and Büch lived. The handwriting is the same as in the letter to Klein's father which Gothie wrote and signed at Peter's request on October 26, 1856. Gothie also mentions that he "also wrote earlier in a letter" about the departure of his brother Wilhelm. This is probably the letter dated March 3, 1856, which is signed "Peter Klein."

In much the same way and with the same degree of certainty, Wilhelm Gothie can be identified as the scribe of the four letters Klein sent from California (August 30, 1857, to June 17, 1858). At the end of the letter dated August 30, 1857, Klein refers to Gothie: "and he also wrote this letter."

The letters dated October 24, 1858, to June 28, 1859, were written in hand "C," the seven remaining letters (after October 17, 1859) were written by four different people, in the following sequence: D, E, E, D, F, G, G.

were uninspiring, and attendance was notoriously irregular. Furthermore, formal schooling began "usually in the 7th or 8th year and lasted only until the 10th or 11th year. Such a child attended school four months a year for four years."[2]

Güchenbach, located in the middle of an extensive hard-coal deposit, had had its own mine since the beginning of the nineteenth century. Between 1810 and 1820, however, only ten to eighteen miners were employed in the pit. Then, in 1850 the Von der Heydt mine was opened, about halfway between Güchenbach and Saarbrücken; one year later the Lampennest drift was begun, about half a mile south of the village; and at the end of 1852 the mine was the third in the region to be connected to the railway. In 1853 Von der Heydt employed 746 men and yielded 91,000 tons; by 1860 the mine was worked by 1,532 men and produced 243,000 tons. Growth in the Saar mining industry as a whole after 1850 was less dramatic, but it was continuous and stable: from 4,580 employees and a yield of 593,856 tons in 1850 to 10,095 miners and a yield of 1,956,000 tons (government mines) in 1860. The opening of the Saarbrücken-Bexbach railroad played a decisive role in this development, expanding the markets for coal from the Saar: both the number of mining jobs and the amount of coal produced had doubled by 1855. The significance of the connection to the European railroad system has been described in terms of "an unimaginable boom," "rapid expansion," and a "turning point."[3]

This is clearly not a case of industrial decline, dwindling incomes, or reduced job prospects. The entire region was experiencing a boom in coal mining, and miners were in urgent demand. In the area immediately surrounding Güchenbach, the increase in production and expansion of the work force seems to have been particularly spectacular, and in 1854 the books of the Von der Heydt mine noted a "strong demand for coal and lack of personnel."[4] And just at the peak of the rapid expansion in their industry, two skilled workers, much in demand and in the prime of life (aged 27 and 20), left the Saar to seek work as coal miners in America.

Their emigration was certainly not "typical," but it can nonetheless be explained without resorting to their purely personal motivations for leaving (about which nothing is known). We do know that Güchenbach was a poor village, and the letters written by the two emigrants reveal

[2]In 1845 Güchenbach (usually spelled Guichenbach in the nineteenth century), was located in the township of Sellerbach in the Köller Valley; it is now a suburb of Riegelsberg near Saarbrücken. Güchenbach had a population of 305, of whom 71 were Protestants like Klein (Bärsch [1846], 86; Gillet [1980], 412–19; Beck 2 [1869], 301–11, quote on 307).
[3]Gebel (1980), 227–30; Haßlacher (1904), 111; Haßlacher (1912), 434–47; Gebel, 231–36, 246; Haßlacher (1904), 165, 133–34; Beck 3 (1871), 433–34; Brandt (1904), 13–14.
[4]Gebel, 252; Haßlacher (1904), 136.

that their families were impoverished and that Peter's father, the shoe-maker Johannes Klein (1798–1872), was heavily in debt. Little is known about the local wages in the early 1850s, but it is highly probable that they amounted to less than those paid in 1867, when a "strong, healthy worker" was able to earn 1 taler per shift (twelve hours). It is thus unlikely that the boom in coal mining precipitated by the railroad caused wages to soar.[5]

In Güchenbach and the surroundings, it was certainly known that one could hope to earn higher wages in the United States. Between 1844 and 1853 at least 1,779 persons had left the district of Saarbrücken, many of them for the United States. Even the county magistrate, a strong oppo-nent of emigration, had to concede that "some of the early emigrants, returning with an abundance of financial resources, take their remaining relatives along with them." Their emigration at this particular time may be due to the fact that prices for basic foodstuffs had risen sharply. In Saarbrücken, the prices of wheat and rye (the latter was undoubtedly more important to the Kleins) doubled between 1850 and 1853.[6] Finally, the letters themselves reveal one further point that helps to explain why the two men left: their spirit of enterprise. It takes considerable initiative to leave—without hesitating—the relatively familiar area of eastern Pennsylvania and head off a second time to the wilds of California, to take advantage of every chance to improve one's lot, and to risk one's savings in the hopes of making an even greater fortune.

It was certainly no accident that Klein and Büch ended up in Pottsville, Pennsylvania. The two miners found themselves, one hundred miles northwest of Philadelphia, in the commercial hub of the Schuylkill an-thracite district, an area of growing population in the 1850s—from 7,303 in 1850 to 9,319 in 1860. As early as 1833, people had been moving to Pottsville from villages in the Köller Valley near Klein's home. Upon arriving, he came across people from the villages and towns surrounding Güchenbach, including the owner of his boardinghouse and his new employer. It is clear that the two young men knew about their country-men in Pottsville before they left for the United States.

The extent to which Schuylkill County was dominated by coal can be

[5]Gillet, 414–17; Beck 2:232: The semi-official remarks made by a Prussian civil servant make it clear that even in the 1860s miners had little opportunity to move up in the social system (Beck 2:231–34). See also Brandt, 17–20, 110–13, who also mentions "the sharp increase in wages in the 1860's" (114), and Haßlacher (1904), 162. In the Ruhr District the average wage per shift in 1860 amounted to 1.77 marks (Tenfelde [1977], 292–97, 603).

[6]In the border county of Saarbrücken, the number of persons who did not go to North America was particularly large. Detailed information is available for 1855 to 1862, when a total of 558 persons left the county, 226 illegally, presumably for the United States. Of those who left with official permission, 140 gave North America as their destination, 192 listed other destina-tions (Mergen [1973], 57–58, 74–77, and for the quote, 287; price lists in Beck 2, appendix 2).

illustrated by a few official statistics for 1860. Of the total of 17,607 workers living in the county, 15,053 were employed by the mining industry; and of the ca. $8 million of commercial investments, some $6 million went into the coal industry. Foreigners and immigrants made up a sizable, but for an industrial area hardly unusual, percentage of the population of Pottsville (in 1870, 2,712 out of a total of 12,184) and the whole county (in 1860, 26,140 out of ca. 300,000). Germans (5,823) ranked third after the Irish (10,836) and the British (7,950). There were certainly fewer when Peter Klein lived in Pottsville, but the German colony was able to support two German-language weekly newspapers, both of which were founded during his stay: *Der amerikanische Republikaner* (1855–1909) and *Jefferson Demokrat von Schuylkill County* (1855–1918).[7]

When Peter Klein began his long journey to California in the fall of 1856, hardly nine years had passed since the first discovery of gold. The population explosion that resulted during the Gold Rush was spectacular. In the first months of 1848 only 14,000 people lived in the Territory or (after 1850) State of California, but by the beginning of 1849 the population had already reached 28,000; in 1850 it was 92,000, in 1852, 255,000, and the census of 1860 listed almost 380,000 persons. The structure of the population reveals that gold—above all else—had attracted the new settlers. Compared to the normal distribution in the United States, the number of men between the ages of twenty and forty was very high; women, by contrast, made up only 28 percent of the total population. Some 38 percent of the population were foreigners, of which the largest group was the Chinese (35,000), followed by the Irish (33,000), the Germans (22,000), and the British (17,000). The occupational data, finally, reveal that of the almost 220,000 recorded workers, although 31,000 persons were employed in agriculture (the second largest group), at least half were out looking for gold.[8]

Sutter Creek, where Peter Klein settled when he arrived in California at the end of 1856, had been named after the Swiss immigrant[9] on whose land gold was first discovered—not quite thirty miles away. Sutter Creek, in Amador County, is about one hundred miles northeast of San Francisco and lies to the west of the Sierra Nevada in the area where the

[7]USC 1870.1, 254, 58; Rug/Himbert (1980), 311, 314; Mergen (1973), 42; USC M 1860.1, 528–29; USC 1870.1, 254; USC 1860.1, 526; Arndt/Olson (1965), 586.

[8]Finzsch (1982), 13–14; USC 1860.1, 34; 1860.0, 247; 1860.1, 34. Aside from the 83,000 gold workers identified as miners, most of the 25,000 laborers were employed in gold mines. It is impossible to ascertain how many of the other skilled workers (e.g., 4,000 carpenters, 2,600 blacksmiths) were also employed by the mines (USC 1860.1, 35).

[9]Johann-August Sut(t)er, 1803–1880, from Rünensberg (near Basel) acquired a considerable amount of land around 1840, when California was still ruled by Mexico (see Blümner series, Chapter 2, n. 14). During excavation work at Sutter's Mill (Coloma), the workers discovered gold (*Dictionnaire Historique* 6 [1932], 438; Paul [1963], 12–13).

richest gold deposits were found. When Klein lived there in 1860, the town had 1,214 residents, and of these 13 were black and 179 Chinese. In 1870 the population had risen to 1,966, of which only 72 were Chinese but no fewer than 809 (41 percent) were foreign. It is possible that the percentage of immigrants living in Sutter Creek was even higher in 1860. In 1870, 43 percent of the residents of the entire county were foreigners (in 1880 only 24 percent), but in 1860 there was a slight majority of foreign-born residents.

Amador County, which had been virtually devoid of population twelve years earlier, became dominated by the gold rush. In 1860, 148 local businesses (507 employees)—out of a total of 204 local businesses (805 employees)—were related to the gold industry, producing some $1.27 million worth of gold a year (California total was about 15 million). It is not clear how many persons were partners in these 148 businesses (and if it was registered, Klein's partnership with fourteen other people was one of them), and the number of "free" gold miners—neither employer nor employee—is impossible to establish. The total number of those involved in gold, however, probably exceeded 6,000—out of a total of 7,590 men between the ages of fifteen and sixty—and not a few of the 1,372 women in this age group.[10]

One of the 1,938 men between the ages of twenty and thirty years who were registered as living in Amador County in 1860 was Peter Klein. He was actually almost 33 years old on July 23, 1860, when he was questioned for the census, but he lowered his age considerably to 27. He had assimilated at least in terms of his name, which he gave as Peter Kline. The census, which took place between his letters of June 3, 1860 and September 16, 1860, also reveals that he was living at the time in an establishment called the "Wild Cat Boarding House" and that his savings, listed as $3,000, amounted to more than ten times the annual wage he could have earned under optimal conditions in the mines in the Saarland, if he had stayed.

Peter Klein and his German friends, together with their co-workers from Pennsylvania, Cornwall, and Wales, belonged to the small percentage of experts among the gold miners. They had a distinct advantage over the swarms of amateurs who swept out of the farms, factories, and offices to cover California. It made sense for Klein to go to Sutter Creek and to stay there—despite the proverbial restlessness of gold prospectors—at least until 1862, for the town was one of the three centers of

[10]USC 1870.1, 89; 1860.1, 22–23; 1880.1, 428; 1860.1, 33; USC M 1860.1, 23; USC 1860.1, 22–27. This figure assumes two males for each of the 392 farms that are listed in Amador County in 1860 (USC A 1860.1, 194), along with three owners of each of the 54 businesses (and ca. three hundred workers) that were not related to gold mining, as well as a further safety margin of three hundred men employed elsewhere or not at all.

Californian quartz mining. This method of producing gold, one of many at the time, demanded the most complicated technology, a large amount of capital, and the highest degree of mining skill. This type of mining not only required a considerable amount of staying power, costing months of work before any profit was made, it also meant the end of self-employment. Peter Klein worked in a quartz mine as a paid laborer, but the company in which he was a partner probably mined "deep gravel" or "buried gravel": gold sediment that did not lie on the surface of the earth (as did the first finds) but deeper down below the surface. This gold was normally extracted by means of a shaft (vertical) and a tunnel (horizontal). By 1870, however, Amador County had only 107 companies with 759 workers left, and quartz mines accounted for 78 percent of its total gold production.[11]

Characterizing the language use and degree of sophistication is more difficult for Peter Klein than for any other letter-writer in this volume. We know that since he did not write himself, none of the peculiarities of spelling can be attributed to him—and there are seven varieties. Johann Gothie's spelling is very close to standard German, whereas his brother's and that of scribe C is definitely unusual and sometimes so bizarre as to impede comprehension. The remaining writers are somewhere in between, with the exception of F, who writes such impeccable German that one suspects he went considerably beyond elementary school.

However Klein may have dictated his letters, it seems inevitable that some of the scribe's own language slipped into the written text. Yet it is noteworthy how much of Peter Klein's way of expressing himself survived the dictation process. Some common traits are found in all his letters, no matter who wrote them, and are thus clearly his own.

In a manner somewhat reminiscent of Christian Kirst (their birthplaces were not far apart), Klein's use of language is uncomplicated and direct; his descriptions are practical, colorful, easy to understand. What is more, although it is hard to pin down, Peter Klein's style seems to reflect at least some of the buoyancy, optimism, and self-confidence, along with modesty and matter-of-factness, that appear in the content of his letters.

Peter Klein

Pottsville, March 31st, 1855

Dear parents,
    A few days ago I sent you a draft for 30 dollars.

[11]Finzsch, 33–41; Paul, 29; MC 1860: Sutter Creek, Amador Co., Calif., Twp. 4, #148. On quartz mines see Finzsch, 41–46; Paul, 21, 30–33, 92; USC 1870.3, 760, 770.

And here is a second draft in case the first was lost so you can get the money with this second draft.

Dearest parents, I don't have much time to write today, but I want to let you know that I'm doing very well in America, and we're working in the coal pit, and we're paid by the wagonful and can earn 9 to 10 dollars a week, and pay 12 dollars board a month.[12] All the other things are no more expensive than in Germany.

Lui Dörr and I are working together. And Peter Krebs, and Peter Büch work together in the mine.[13]

In the 3 winter months you can't earn much in America. But we think things will be fine this summer.

When you've received the money write and let me know, and I'll write you later about how things are and will do what I can.

With the best regards, also to all our friends/ your son / <u>Peter Klein</u>. I add my best wishes / <u>Johann Gothie</u>[14]

Write the address as follows— — —

Mr. John Gothie, Pottsville / Schuykill County, Pennsylvania North America.

Pottsville, May 21st, 1855

Dear parents,

I received your letter in the best of health and see from it that you are all well, which pleases me. You write that my sister Elisabeth[15] wants to come here, which I would very much like, for let me tell you, a good woman can have a much, much better life here in this country than in Germany.

You write in your last letter that you want to know how coal is worked here. I can tell you that most of the work is done with powder and the shifts are 10 hours,[16] and the piece rates are like in Germany, and one man digs almost as much coal as six in Germany.

Then you should know that they have coal here that is from 4 feet up to

[12]Ten years later, after a considerable increase in wages, it was only possible to earn the equivalent of six dollars—under optimal conditions—in the Saar mines (Beck 3:232).

[13]Ludwig Peter Dörr (b. 1835) was from Engelfangen, 2.5 miles from Güchenbach (Rug [1984], 173, #375). Peter Krebs was from Güchenbach, married in 1843, and emigrated on October 5, 1854 (Rug [1978], 1–2). Johann Peter Büch (b. 1834) was also from Güchenbach, was a cousin to Peter Klein (their mothers were sisters), and emigrated with him to America on May 23, 1854.

[14]The name was probably originally Gauthier, and he presumably came from the Köller Valley like his brother Wilhelm, certainly from the Saar region.

[15]Born in 1833, married the miner Peter Feld in Güchenbach on November 4, 1856 (Rug [1978] 1–2).

[16]In the Saar mines at the time, usually twelve hours (Brandt, 118).

20 and 30 and 40 feet high. [17] That's to let you know there's only a handful of coal in Germany, compared to here.

You also wanted to know where the people we work for come from, we now work for people from Sulsbach, [18] but you never know for how long, for it's different here from over there, if we don't like it in this place today we go to another one tomorrow, because the coal doesn't belong to any government. [19]

You also wanted to know why Peter Büch and I are no longer together. When Peter Krebs got here, the two of them worked together, and then they left this place and we get together every 3 or 4 weeks.

You also write in Peter Krebs's letter that Peter Büch's family wants to come here, I'll tell you, if they want to work in coal they can do much better here than in Germany. And when they leave for the journey, they shouldn't bring any cloth and only a little clothing along.

The best thing is a good bed, and not too little food, just a lot of potatoes, that's the best at sea.

I should also say be careful on the trip and don't be too good-hearted, so you won't get cheated.

Get yourselves good passports, so you don't get into a mess that costs you a lot of money.

Friedrich Klickert asked me to write what a pair of boots cost, so tell him 4 to 5 dollars, and leather isn't more expensive than over there.

That's all I can think of to write now. [3 ll.: regards] The gold dollar under the seal is for godson Peter / your son, Peter Klein.

My wife and I send you our regards and best wishes. Johann Gothie

Pottsville, March 3rd, 1856

Dear parents,

Since I haven't heard from you in a long time, I thought I would send you the news that I, and Peter Büch, are still alive and well, and we're still in the same place where we were before, at Johann Gothie's in Pottsville.

---

[17]These figures are quite conservative: the official figures for the Schuylkill area are three to 125 feet (USC MI 1880.2, 862–65). Figures for the Saar were one to nine feet (Haßlacher [1912], 8).

[18]Sulzbach, a village with coal deposits, was five miles from Güchenbach.

[19]Through the middle of the nineteenth century, coal mines in Germany were, to all intents and purposes, state-run, that is, run by an elaborate government bureaucracy that decided all management and investment questions as well as determined coal prices and miners' wages. The miners were paid poorly (though always above starvation levels), but were privileged in that they were protected by a comprehensive miner's social security system covering health, disability, and old age and dependents' pensions. Although coal mining was transferred into private ownership during the two decades following 1851, government control remained strict, and miners kept their benefits.

Wilhelm Gothie, and Ludwig Dörr, left here for California in the month of December, 1855. You've probably heard about this gold country, it's 7000 miles away from here.[20]

And the two of us also wanted to go there this spring, that is to California. But since they didn't write like we asked them to, we'll stay where we are.

Things here aren't so good now. All the mines aren't being worked very much, wages are somewhat lower, from 6 to 8 dollars a week, many people are totally laid off.

The winter here, from the beginning of December to the end of March, was colder than you've ever seen in Germany, and the whole time there was deep snow. In the winter here it's generally colder than over there, and more warm in the summer. [4 ll.: letter received from uncle Peter Felt]

Dear parents [so begins P. Büch's letter on the same page; the handwriting is the same]

We don't need to write two letters since we're together and you are too; we wanted to let you know that if you need some money badly you should write to us and we'll help out as much as we can.

We don't have much money at the moment, because we didn't have much work this winter, and we had to pay a lot for board, and a man on his own can't be without money in a strange country, since he never knows what will happen to him, but we hope to do better in the summer.

We hope to hear from you as soon as possible so that we'll know how you are, we're well and healthier than we've ever been in our lives, and we hope the same is true for you.

With best wishes to you, parents, friends and acquaintances, Peter Klein and Peter Büch,
And my regards, John Gothie / we hope to hear from you soon.

Pottsville, June 19th, 1856

Dear parents,

I received your letter of April 27th, and read that you are healthy and well, which I hope you still are.

Then you write that I should come back to Germany, which up to now hasn't occurred to me; I couldn't stand starting all over again in Germany, having to let any foreman or any other upstart push me around and keep my mouth shut. You may think I'm not doing well here, that's not the case, I am healthy and can earn my money and where I'm living here in Pottsville at Johann Gothie's is like being at home with you.

---

[20]He means the distance by sea via Panama.

Then you wrote me I should bring Ludwig[21] a gold dollar, soon I'm going to send you my portrait and then if it works out, I'll send something like that.

With this letter I wish you all the best, and my regards to all of you / Peter Klein / My regards, John Gothie.[22]

Sutter Creek [Calif.] / August 30th, 1857

Dear parents,

father and mother, sister and brothers;

Dear parents you asked me through Johann Gothie to write to you so you'll know where and how I am,

I'm well, thank God, I am in good health and have plenty to eat and drink, in business though I was very unlucky. Wilhelm Gothie worked for seven months at a quartz mine and didn't earn a penny. I thought I wouldn't write until I could send you some money, but I can't now. Dear father and mother, I am well aware of a parent's love for his child, but you should know that my childhood love for my parents hasn't died away, I am in a country where I am sure to become lucky sooner or later. I'm sure I won't leave this country until I can live without having to work, if I have to work it should be in this beautiful country.

Dear parents you mustn't be angry that my help is so long in coming, I think the time will come soon when I can help you again, I hope my brother will help out until I can,

Dear father, this is a wonderful place we don't have any snow in the winter, the frost is very mild, the ice on the water doesn't freeze more than half an inch thick, in the summer it is pretty warm but the heat is easy to take because it's always mixed with cool air, either we have wind from the sea or from the snowy mountains, the nights are very pleasant, even when it's hot during the day the nights are cool.

[21]Peter Klein had two brothers with sons of this name, one born in 1850 and the other in 1855 (see Rug correspondence [BABS]).

[22]This was followed by a letter from *Johann Gothie* to Peter Klein's father:

Pottsville, October 26, 1856

Dear Friend Johann Klein,

On October 2nd we received your letter of September 6th. Your son Peter Klein asked me to answer your letter and let you know how things are. I already wrote in a letter [that of March 3, 1856, for Peter Klein] that my brother Wilhelm left for California in December 1855 and that your son wanted to travel there too; now, since we received your letter, he has already paid for his passage and left on October 3rd for California with my brother's wife and family. It is a distance of 7000 English miles, almost again as far as from Europe to America.

Then he asked me to tell you to write to me, John Gothie, since we receive a letter from California almost every month, so you can find out where he is and how he is. He said we should send his regards to you all, Peter Büch and my wife also send their best, as do I, Johann Gothie.

While I was writing this letter Ludwig Dörr came by and he wants to know why his sister hasn't written even one letter, he wants to know where his sister is and how she is doing.

With these remarks I will close my letter.

I expect an unfailing and speedy answer.

I'm still living with Wm. Gothie and he wrote this letter, Dear father and mother I send my best wishes to you with childlike confidence, my best wishes to my brothers and sisters,

I remain your devoted son— — —Petter Klein

My Address / Mr. Peter Klein / Sutter Creek / Amador Co. Cal. / North America[23]

[5 ll.: no date: regards, money transfer]

[10 ll.: no date (early 1858): sends his father pieces of quartz with gold inclusions; earnings for miners 50–100 dollars a month; Peter Büch will follow when a good place has been found]

Sutter Creek / February 14th / *Anna Domeni* 1858

Dear father and mother, dearest sister and brothers, relatives and friends,

I take up my pen today to converse with you from a foreign land. [2 ll.: health]

Dearest parents I am pleased to be able to do you another favor it is a small gift but people in our situation can't do anything big.

Dear parents I am sending you one hundred talers and hope that you'll be satisfied with this small gift until I can do more, father you want to know if I work for myself or for a master, I work on my own property, father, in America there aren't any masters, here everyone is a free agent, if I don't like one place you go to another for we're all equal here.

I bought myself a piece of land in the town of Sutter Creek and built myself a small house and cook for myself, for food is very expensive here when you board, this way it's 8 talers a week. Dear parents I now have the prospect of being able to help you if you want me to, you just have to write me.

On the above-mentioned piece of land that I bought I dig gold and have enough work for about 3 years on it.

About my brothers I can't say anything at all, they are of age and have to know themselves what's best for them, some like it in America and

---

[23]Johann Gothie wrote another letter to Johann Klein, probably a few weeks earlier (18 ll.: no date: had received a letter from Peter in California; Peter Büch also wants to go there).

some don't. Of course it's a foreign country foreign ways foreign people foreign customs and so forth— —

In the coal mines in America it's normal what you earn in the summer gets used up in the winter, but everyone can save something and live a lot better than in Germany, the average pay is about one taler a day. The trip from Pottsville to California cost me 156 talers sometimes the trip is 200 talers, sometimes the fare comes down to 50 talers so it goes up and down. I wouldn't advise any of my brothers to come to California except my youngest brother, if he wants to come to California he should wait till I write again for he shouldn't be such a burden to you as I, then I'll send him the money. [7 ll.: praises the climate in California, as in August 30, 1857] The wage in Cal. is from 30 to 100 talers a month and food, there are hundreds of people out of work. Lack of water in the summer hampers gold panning it doesn't rain here at all for about 6 months.

About Peter Büch I have no idea where he is, I got the last letter from him in April 1857. [3 ll.: correspondence] It takes about 4 months to get an answer to a letter from Germany since it's a trip of about nine thousand English miles. [9 ll.: requests prompt reply; regards] / Peter Klein[24]

Sutter Creek, March 16th, / *Anna Domeny* 1858
[6 ll.: salutations, sent $100 on February 15, 1858—asks for acknowledgment of receipt] On the 5th of this month I sent one hundred and 30 dollars to Peter Büch in Pottsville and he's probably on his way to Cal. now. [3 ll.: greetings, signature]

Sutter Creek, June 17th, 1858
Dearest parents, I received your letter of April 25th with great joy that you are all well and happy, I received your letter on June 16, 1858.

Dear father you ask me whether we dig gold in the ground on the ground or even in tunnels.

Dear father we dig it on the surface and in the ground on land and on water high and low in tunnels and shafts, the gold has places where it runs through, that's where it pays to work, otherwise there's gold just about everywhere but too little to work, or mixed up too much with dirt and stones. The gold you dig in the tunnels is in a kind of gravel it seems like rivers used to flow through the mountains, it's like this, the rivers naturally were always in the valleys or the lowlands, but it seems like this

---

[24][On the outside of the folded letter:] I received a letter from Peter Büch on February 16th, he is in Pottsville again and he wants to come to me in California.

land went through very large volcanic upheavals, for in this mine there's a *siment* [cement] that is mixed with gravel stones and quartz and burnt by volcanic fire, we also find lava very deep in the ground.

The other mines are on the surface, that is in the valleys and also especially in deposited soil, the gold is usually in the deepest part, when you dig for gold you have to dig up all the dirt and then wash it all, since gold is the heaviest metal it sinks of course to the bottom. In shafts you usually dig out the quartz that is then ground up in these mills, there are a lot of different pieces of equipment that you wouldn't understand even if I described them exactly.

In this letter I'll send you a little piece of quartz there's gold in it and also *sollveretz* [sulfurets] of iron.[25]

That should be a relic of Cal. for you. Dear father I have some money but I'm going to keep it, some new gold finds have been made. I have a mind to go there, it is 800 English miles north of here, and there's supposed to be a lot of gold there. Wilhelm Gothie Lutwig Dörr are going there in two or 3 days, I and Peter Büch will follow. People are moving up there by the thousands,[26] whole villages are empty, my house is built out of boards, and that's how you usually build here.

Peter Biech arrived in Cal. on May 15, 1858 and is hale and hearty and is working in a quartz mine and gets 50 talers a month and free board and I am working in a quartz mine and get four talers and 50 sou a day[27] and have to pay for my own board, food here costs a taler a day but it's very good food for the cooking's not bad here. [7 ll.: correspondence]

Dearest parents I know your situation and I will never forget you even if there were 7 oceans between us. Dear parents I send you my best wishes. [4 ll.: further greetings] Peter Biech says to give his love to his mother. [11 ll.: will send 50 talers by the end of the year]

Sutter Creek, October 24, 1858

Dear father, mother,

[2 ll.: correspondence] I wanted to send you 50 talers, but I am sending 10 talers more as much as 60 American talers that's as much as 75 Prussian talers.

Beloved parents, I am sending you this money for a New Year's present, and I hope that you'll get the money by New Year's, when you

[25]Iron sulfide. Sulfurets referred at the time to metal sulfides with gold inclusions.

[26]Gold was initially discovered in Fraser, British Columbia (as the crow flies, the distance given is correct), in the spring of 1858, and about thirty thousand gold miners, primarily from California, went there. By October most had already returned (Paul, 37–39).

[27]Meaning $4.50; the French sou was common in the Saar.

get my money then don't use it to pay any debts. I want you to use the money as you need it to live on, I've been gone from you for four years, you had a hard time when I left. [4 ll.: hasn't forgotten them] I don't want you to live badly in the few years of old age that you have left to live in this world, I'll send you money from time to time as much as I can, if you need money, I have some money, but I can't send too much of it because in a foreign country you always have to have some money on hand so I can go home again sometime when I want to, and you never know when you get sick and need money. Beloved father I'll send you money by the spring to pay for your debts since I know by chance how much you owe. I have in mind that I and Peter should buy some cattle by next spring since you can make the most money in California in the cattle business. That's the best way to use your money in this part of the country. [6 ll.: cattle find their own food; climate, as in February 14, 1858]

I have a share in a gold mine, there we dug a shaft 246 feet deep and worked a small place down to 260 feet, we found gold there in one wheelbarrow full of dirt we found 1 taler's worth. There are 14 partners here, a claim now costs seven thousand talers. I'm sending my draft to Frankfort to the Rodschield's [Rothschild's] bank, when you get the draft I think you can get it paid out at a number of places everywhere.

You should give my godson Peter Klein 5 Prussian talers of it and extra greetings.
[6 ll.: wishes, greetings] / Peter Klein
Peter Buch sends greetings to you all / [5 ll.: money transfer]

Sutter Creek, March 15, 1859

Dearly beloved father and mother
[6 ll.: thanks for letter and their acknowledgment of receipt of 77 talers] Further I want to let you know where I'm working this summer, I and Peter Büch and another man, we have made a contract for a tunnel 1,150 feet to the shaft, we get 3 talers a foot, it is blue slate which you can dig out with an axe. It's at the gold mine that I already wrote to you about there are 14 men in the company and me and Peter Büch we have one and a half shares of it, if we're lucky we can do it in 9 months and maybe it will take us one year we're working with 6 men. We are provided with the wood and all the material and everything we need for it. There's two foot of gravel on the ground, the gold is in that, where you can wash out pure gold, the shaft is 246 feet deep where we're digging the tunnel.

Beloved parents, I am sorry that I can't keep my promise, since I promised you I'd send so much money by the spring but this gold mine where I have a share costs me too much money so that I can't send you any money. In 3 wheelbarrows full of this gravel we've washed out 6 talers,

Where I and everyone else used to work in the quartz mills, the daily wage goes down every year, last year the daily wage was still between 60 and 80 talers a month and now the wage is from 30 to 50 and 60 talers a month and so the wage goes down every year and there are hundreds of people running around with no work. Dearest sister you wrote me I should send you something too, the next time I can send something to Germany I'll send you something too, with these words I'll close. [5 ll.: greetings] / Peter Klein / [. . .][28]

[on the same page as Büch's letter of May 15, 1859][29]
I put 70 talers in the bank and paid so you should receive 70 talers. [4 ll.: transfer details] / in a short while I'll write you another letter, Peter Klein. [21 ll.: no date, enclosed in the letter of May 15, 1859: transfer of funds— of $70 (see above) for Peter Büch's mother, $20 for Klein's sister Katharina; note by *Peter Büch:* greetings, signature]

Sutter Creek, June 28, 1859
Dear father and mother,
   With these few lines I want to let you know how Peter and I are doing. We are both still hale and hearty and are still working at our claim, we're working with four men at this time, we've worked on it for three months

---

[28][Enclosed letter by *Peter Büch* to his godson, no date; 15 ll.: presents, correspondence, greetings, signature, postscript:] when you write, write what you have to write in one letter, because we're always together. And congratulate Ludwig for me on his marriage, I wish I were too.

[29]*Peter Büch's* letter of May 15, 1859:

Sutter Creek, May 15, 1859.
Dearest brother-in-law,
   I received your letter, which you wrote to me on March 6th, on May 5th in which I see how things are in Germany, that all of Germany is on a war footing, that you're going through hard times, which we can also see all the time in the Californian newspapers and that you think that my brother Conrat also has to go and my brother-in-law too. [3 ll.: mother will be alone]
   Beloved mother, as I see in your letter you are asking me to send you some money. Dear mother, I'm sending you some money as much as I can, I can't send you more than 50 talers now.
   Me and Peter Klein we're working at this place here we have to pay for our own food and we have 2 other men with us one to cook and the other to work. Half of our pay is stopped until we have the job done and Peter and I have 1 and one half share in this place. There are 14 shares in this mine, when we've paid the costs of our share and buy our food there's not much left. [. . .] Dear mother, when you receive my money and you think that my brother Conrat has to go to the army, and he wants to come to America then give him money so that he has enough to come to America. [3 ll.: will send him money then for the trip to Calif.] But he shouldn't go to the coal mines for there's too many layoffs there. [Peter Klein continues; see above]

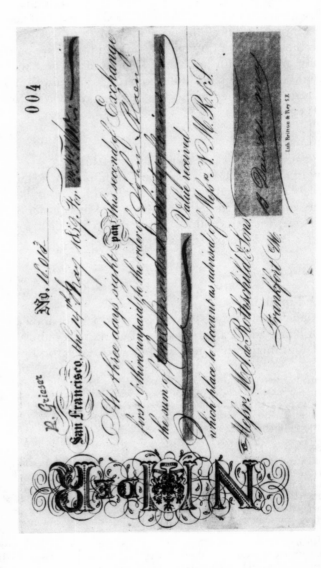

Figure 32. Exchange for 160 fl. (ca. $70) sent by Peter Klein to his father. *Source:* LA Saarbrücken.

already two men work during the day and two men at night, we get three talers a foot and have done 600 feet now and we now have 555 feet left to do we think we can finish our contract in three months.

But we only get half of what we earn every month. [5 ll.: as in Peter Büch's letter of May 15, 1859] I think that we can start to wash by next New Year's, by that time we could have the dirt where the gold is.

A man wanted to give me 1000 talers for my share, but I didn't want to give it up, I think by next year it will be worth more maybe 2 to 3 thousand talers.

I wanted to come home but now I can't because I had Peter come here that cost me a lot of money and so I don't want to come home until Peter has some money too. And when I come home I'm not going to cut out any of my brothers and sisters then I'll give something to each one.

I'd like to see my father and mother again but I can't say when but I'll be home as soon as I can. Times in California get worse every year, the weather is now very hot and dry there's no more water now you can't work anymore in the gold mines there are more poor people running around with no work and no money. [22 ll.: Ludwig Dörr returned disappointed (see June 17, 1858); repeats content of undated letter enclosed in May 15, 1859]

Sutter Creek, October 17, 1859

Most beloved parents
[7 ll.: correspondence; things are fine] I've already done 1000.000 feet in the mountain and we work just like in the *Lamben nest* tunnel [Lampennest; see series introduction] and are still full of hope and think we'll be done here by the 20th of November, God willing, and then I'll write you a long letter about my work. [7 ll.: greetings, is sending a picture] Peter Klein[30]

Sutter Greek, Amad. County. June 3rd, 1860

Beloved parents,
[4 ll.: distressed about illness of his mother] As regards me, I am doing just fine and am in a good situation, make a good wage and have good prospects of making some money shortly. On our contract it's worked out well, we've dug the tunnel 1700 feet and have earned good pay doing

---

[30][Probably enclosed: *Peter Büch's* letter to his mother and brother-in-law, no date; 3 ll.: correspondence] Dear mother I want to let you know that I am living with Peter Klein and think I will stay with him until we can go home, I also want you to know that I have enough work and am having a fine time. [19 ll.: will write more soon; greetings; to his brother-in-law: similar information, correspondence, greetings, signature]

it. But our costs were enormously high even up till now, each single man is entitled to over 1500 dollars already without having been able to use a cent of it. Just about 14 days ago we hit *Zahldreck* [pay dirt],[31] and we now hope we'll have a good chance to get back the money we put in soon, and make some more. [3 ll.: the same] I've helped out my friends Peter and Louis so that each one also has a share of the claim. Peter left from here on May 20th for the United States I bought out his share for 1300 dollars, he'll write to you from New York he didn't like it anymore so much. Dear parents, if I stay fit and our claim pays, like it looks, then I hope to be back with you by next spring and then I'll be able to tell you how affairs are here in California. Here in this country you have to venture and risk to make something, today you can be a rich man and tomorrow as poor again as Lazarus. I for my part, dear parents, have ventured a lot in the last two years [---] have put in almost everything that I earned with hard work, but my prospects are good now and I don't think I've risked my money for nothing, I'm almost sure that I've done outstandingly well to sacrifice my money and work for this business. Two weeks ago now we started to take out pay dirt we're working now day and night, we've hired a lot of people, as soon as we're set up better for more people to work in the tunnel, we want to work with 40 men, 20 during the day and 20 at night, so that we can get the money we put in back out again quickly. Henrich Miller from Rockershausen[32] is going home soon and then I'll send along something for each of my brothers and sisters, I've had rings made, but have never had a chance to send them. Peter's gone to the States but he didn't take along more than 500 dollars, the rest I kept in my hands, you never know what can happen, he might have an accident at sea or something else might happen. He's going to write me when he's found a place, then I'll send him the rest of the money. [10 ll.: family, wishes, greetings, signature]

Sutter Greek Amador County / September 16th, 1860

Dear parents,

I got your letter of July 22nd and see that you're still healthy and well which I am too. I'm still working in my claim, in the summer you can't do much in California because you don't have enough water to wash the pay dirt. It doesn't rain here in the summer, the rain starts up again in December, and I hope that I'll do well in the claim, so that I can visit you

[31]No such word exists in normal German; it is a German-Americanism formed by the literal translation of pay, *zahlen*, and dirt, *Dreck*.
[32]Village five miles from Güchenbach.

next spring. In the meantime I'm sending you a draft of two hundred and fifty guilders (250 fl) 15 kreuzers less than 143 Prussian talers, I'm sending you this money, dear parents, as a New Year's present, and I hope that you do something nice for yourselves and that you will have many more happy years. Give Peter Bieg's[33] mother 30 Prussian talers, and I'll settle it then with Peter. [2 ll.: requests acknowledgment of receipt] Don't save the money use it up and live well in your old days until I come home in the spring. Miller isn't coming home, he's started another business. [9 ll.: friends; greetings, signature, P.S.]

Sutter Creek, April 15th, 1861

Dear parents,

[3 ll.: state of health] Dear parents, I want to let you know too that I am not able to come home as soon as I thought I could, since if I go home I would lose too much that I have worked hard for, but as soon as I can sell out for a good price, I'm coming home. I like it here a lot, I earn 50 talers a month.

And I make 50 talers from the mountain, and that makes 100.00 talers a month, now, dear parents, I must close.

[10 ll.: greetings; will send four gold rings worth 16 talers along with Ph. Froitheim; signature]

Sutter Creek, Aug. 18, 1861

Dear father,

I got your kind letter of June 2nd on August 2nd, and see from the postscript that the rings got there safely. I'm glad to hear that you're all well and healthy. I am also in good health. You shouldn't be sad that I haven't come yet; there are good reasons which I will explain to you. You know that about a year ago I bought out Peter Büch's half share in our mine for thirteen hundred talers, and when I wanted to sell it again, so I could leave and come home to you, I couldn't get rid of it without losing at least half of my money, since our mine didn't turn out as well as we had expected. I had to stay here for a while to get my money back. Now I've sold a half share for sixteen hundred talers, and the buyer has to pay me by May 1st, 1862. If he can't pay on that day, he loses 400 talers, and the share is mine again. That's all drawn up in the court, so I am entirely safe. You see though, that I cannot leave California before May 1st, since I won't get my money till then. By the way, I have a good chance of

---

[33]Despite different spellings, it is always the same Peter Büch.

getting my money, since our gold mine gets better every day. Last year none of the partners could sell out, but now we'd have buyers enough if we wanted. The man who I sold the half share to pays me eighty to one hundred talers every month, I also get 50 talers a month from the company. I like the work in our mine very much. Louis Dörr and I, we're our own bosses, and have as much to say in our gold mine as the foreman in a coal mine. The expenses of our company run to about thirteen to fourteen hundred talers a month. About twenty-five men work in our mine. What's left after expenses is the dividend and it is divided among us fourteen partners. It amounts to about twenty-five hundred to three thousand talers' worth of gold a month. [2 ll.: return delayed] But even if I'm not coming now, I'm certainly coming. If I weren't going to, I would have settled down in Californien long ago and married. Mother should stay well and in good spirits; I won't be long now, I'm hesitating now only because I'm doing so well and it would be a shame to miss this good opportunity. Since I'm doing so well, dear father, do let me know if you need money. I don't want you to be in need when I am doing well. [. . .] Along with this letter I'm sending you a draft for a hundred talers. You can give my brother Ludwig as much of it as you think he needs, and the rest you should keep for yourself. [5 ll.: father and mother should spend the money on themselves, live well, save nothing] I'm not leaving out any of my brothers and sisters, and when I come to Germany, I will do what I can for each of them, but parents come first. [3 ll.: money transfer]

Peter Büch is living in Marietta, Washington County, State of Ohio. He's now married to a Bavarian girl, Lehne Büch, and has bought a twenty-eight-acre piece of land from his wife's brother for four hundred and seventy-five talers. He has a house and two cows there. Just last week I sent him a hundred talers that I still owed him.

As far as the war in America is concerned, I only want to tell you a little bit, just so you know what it's all about. The war or rather the rebellion was started by the slave owners, to overthrow the free constitution of the country and to set up a government by the nobility. These slave owners are great lords who have a hundred and more black serfs and now want to enslave the free white workers, so that the black workers don't take the whites as an example and want to be free too. And that's the real truth of the whole story. And we, free men and honest workers, we don't want to put up with that and want to keep the good and free constitution. And with God's help we will win. For us Germans this war is very good, for since the Germans have shown themselves to be the keenest defenders of the constitution, and provide entire regiments of the best and bravest soldiers and officers, they're starting to fill the native Americans with respect. Now the Americans don't make fun of us anymore since they know that we are the mainstay of their country and their freedom. [5 ll.: commentary on North and South] Here in California, where the population is mixed together from so many countries, the majority (and here the Europeans play the decisive role) is in favor of upholding the constitution and the Union. I don't believe the rebels will dare to raise their heads here. So much about the war in America; the newspapers will tell you the details.

Thousands of greetings to you and my dear mother, and all my brothers and sisters / your true son / Peter Klein

Postscript: When you sign the draft, sign your name "John Kline," and not like usual. In English that is pronounced "Klein," and your signature must be the same name that is on the draft.

Sutter Creek, May 1st, 1862

Dearest parents, father and mother,

[2 ll.: wishes] I am very sorry that I can't keep my promise, but the man who bought the share of the gold mine from me couldn't take it over, because of all the rain we had this winter, from October 20th till March 1st. [4 ll.: details] Everything cost a lot more and work lay still and business fell flat, so our work lay still and that's why the man couldn't take over my share, and now we're starting to work and all the plans that everyone made are ruined and it surprises me that you've never asked if I have some money or not, you mustn't think that I write you lies in my letters, that you maybe think I don't have money enough to come, I could come, but I can't just abandon everything I worked so long to get. I could come since I've saved 1000 dollars but you can't spend everything on travel you have to save for your old age too. I gave Peter 1300 talers cash for his share from my savings, that's put me back a lot, because things cost so much more we haven't made as much as we'd hoped, flour is up to 16 talers for a hundred pounds, which you used to buy for 4 talers. [3 ll.: further prices; not much news to report] You hear as much about the war as we do I think, news gets to you in 14 to 16 days and it takes 24 to 26 days to us, you're closer to the war than we are, and as we hear the southern states [. . .] have almost been beaten [. . .] and every man goes to war of his own free will and fights for lovely freedom, the German regiments have distinguished themselves and won the largest battles. [5 ll.: letter from Peter Büch, he's had a son, is happy and healthy on his farm]

Dear father and mother my situation is uncertain, and the first chance I get to sell I will sell out and come home. [7 ll.: greetings, signature]

Sutter Creek, October 18th, 18[63]

Dearest parents, brothers and sisters, friends and relatives,

I hope that this letter of mine finds you in good health, dearest parents as far as it concerns me I am still hale and hearty and the reason I haven't written was because I still thought I could come home this fall. [3 ll.: correspondence] But I can't come now because things didn't work out like I thought, instead things went the wrong way on both sides, in California and in Brittisch Colombia[34] everywhere you turned you were hit by losses like the wolf chasing the sheep and so all the plans and arrangements that I'd made to come home came to naught, dear parents, and you must be patient till I write again then I'll be able to let you know more than I can now, that will probably take 3 to 4 months, since my partner and I have bought the gold mine, we had to buy it or else we would have lost too much since with the old company we had nothing but trouble and quarrels and so we bought out the other 10 so we wouldn't lose too much, for the sum of 2000 talers, and now we have to attend to the business ourselves and try to put things that were neglected in the disarray back in order again and now we think [. . .] we'll be able to get money from it again in three or four months. [2 ll.: more of the same; correspondence] If I were in New Jork my sister could have come to stay with me a long time ago but if she wants to come she should let me know in the next letter what she has in mind, I like it in this country a lot and the farm girls earn 30 talers a month. If she wants to come I'll send her the money to come or take her in and if she doesn't like it I'll also give her the money to go back that's all I can promise at this point and I think her prospects in this country would be good. She shouldn't imagine that California is so strange since it's an inhabited country and many Germans are here, dear sister if you come to stay with me you won't have to work so hard here as in Germany, I like California a lot. [5 ll.: untouched by the war; last news from Peter Büch in Ohio a year ago] He and his wife and his sister were in the state of Pennsylvania in Schoolkill County Frederigsburg[35] and Ludwig Dörr is in Waschoe[36] Virginia City.[37] [3 ll.: correspondence] I send you all my very best and thousands of greetings

[34]Between 1861 and 1863 large deposits of gold were discovered there (Paul, 38); it is conceivable that Klein also tried his luck there.

[35]Today the only place with a similar name in Schuylkill County is Friedensburg, six miles south of Pottsville.

[36]Washoe and Comstock Lode were names for the area in Nevada—in the Sierra Nevada, one hundred miles from the most important gold deposits in California—where rich deposits of both silver and gold were discovered in 1859. The discovery set off a new wave of migration among the gold miners.

[37]One of the most important towns of the gold rush, ca. fifteen miles southeast of Reno. Its population in 1870 was 11,359, in 1885 ca. twenty thousand (Paul, 72), and in 1985 it was ca. six hundred.

and close my letter now and send the letter enclosed in mine to the address that is on it, it belongs to my partner and we put mine in his and we greet you all, me and my partner your devoted son / Peter Klein Partner to me / Kilian Leuck

It is disappointing that we do not know the end of this fascinating story: did Peter Klein lose everything, or did he become a rich man? Both are conceivable. The only thing we know about what happened to him after the fall of 1863, however, is that he never returned to Güchenbach.[38] In the 1870 census he is no longer listed as a resident of Sutter Creek. There seems to be no plausible reason for the break-off of the correspondence on the part of the German relatives: his parents lived until the early 1870s, and several brothers and sisters much longer. Peter Klein probably died in California—perhaps penniless, or perhaps much richer than he could ever have become in Germany.

[38]Dr. Norbert Finzsch to editors, February 23, 1987.

14

Wilhelm Bürkert (William Buerkert)

Wilhelm Bürkert (born May 17, 1859, in Waldenburg, Württemberg) was the second son of Christine Rosine, née Frank (1817–1869), housewife and midwife, and Johann Georg Bürkert (1824–1875), probably a prosperous and certainly a well-respected farmer, winegrower, town councilor, and church elder.

When Wilhelm Bürkert was ten years old, his mother died. Six months later, his father married one of her younger sisters, Rosine Magdalene Susanne Frank (1835–1928). Two more children who survived early infancy were born to the couple, Carolina Christina (1870–1949) and Susanne Caroline Christine (1873–1932). On August 1, 1873, after finishing elementary school, Bürkert began a three-year apprenticeship as a surveyor. According to the terms of his contract, the master was to receive a fee of 75 guilders, and Wilhelm's father also agreed to pay for lessons in mathematics and languages to be given by the teacher at the grammar school.[1]

At the end of April 1875, his father died, possibly of a brain tumor. Less than six months later, Wilhelm Bürkert broke off his apprenticeship, supposed to run until July 1876, left Waldenburg with 50 guilders and a passage ticket in his pocket, and set off for Hamburg by train via Heilbronn, Heidelberg, and Frankfurt.

Waldenburg, a picturesque town built on a ridge 450 feet above the

---

[1]Information provided by the contributor and the local pastor H. D. Haller; Personenstandsregister der Stadt Waldenburg; contract in possession of the contributor.

Hohenloher plain and around the castle belonging to the princes of Hohenlohe-Waldenburg, had a population of 1,343 in 1875. Many of the inhabitants were court servants or artisans primarily employed by the court, but the majority were farmers. Winegrowing played a minor role; the main sources of income were crop and stock farming. Waldenburg had its own station on the railroad which opened in 1862 between Heilbronn and Schwäbisch Hall, and the town was modestly prosperous, although it did not escape the effects of poor harvests and economic crises. In the 1850s out-migration and emigration were heavy (the population in 1849 was 1419; in 1858, 1254), but in the 1870s when Bürkert left, the town enjoyed a slight increase in population: 1324 in 1871 and 1367 in 1880.[2]

The available sources do not permit any clear-cut answers as to why the 16-year-old Bürkert emigrated. There are certainly no signs of actual or anticipated poverty. A receipt from his guardian, Johann Georg Friederich (1851–1928), a farmer and bookbinder in Waldenburg, indicates that Bürkert's stepmother paid a total of 876.55 marks between August 1875 and August 1876. No record of the guardian's expenditures has survived.[3]

The death of Bürkert's mother when he was only ten years old, the appearance on the scene of his stepmother and his two small half sisters, and finally the death of his father may well have created a family situation in which the young man felt ill at ease or unwanted. The fact that he set off for the United States only a few months after his father died also supports this hypothesis. But apparently there was yet another factor.

According to family tradition, he was guilty of a "small juvenile offense," which had led him to be "deported" by his strict and pious stepmother (and aunt). His frequent protestations in the letters that he had reformed suggest that alcohol abuse, a tendency to shirk, and a "dissolute" way of life sped his departure.

Sending a sixteen-year-old out into the world alone was not unusually hard-hearted or cruel. Parents frequently permitted their children aged fourteen—or even twelve—to travel to America on their own. Adulthood, as opposed to legal majority, came earlier in the nineteenth century than in the twentieth. More important, however, is whether any signs of the illness mentioned in Wilhelm's letters had appeared before he left Germany, and if so, whether he should have been allowed to leave at all, considering the obvious risks.

The fact that his family reacted to his desperate calls for help with

[2]*Beschreibung des Oberamtes Oehringen* (1865), 78, 342–45; *Landkreis Öhringen* 2 (1968), 600, 617; Rauser (1980), 61–62, 120, 218.
[3]Itemized receipt in the possession of the contributor.

almost total silence can be interpreted in only one of two ways. Either they had written him off completely and could not have cared less about his misfortune, or they regarded his hard-luck stories as a pack of lies told by an untrustworthy good-for-nothing. Bürkert's sickbed letter of August 1, 1878, written for him by the German-American farmer Julius Glatt, should have allayed such suspicions: the contents of the letter were confirmed by Foot Hyle, justice of the peace in Blair County, who cited two of the attending physicians as well as his own visit to the patient at the home of Caspar Reesy. All of this was notarized again by the county recorder of deeds.

It is quite unlikely that the family was too poor to offer financial help; at the very least they could have written a few words of comfort. Perhaps they did, and the letters never reached him, which would hardly be surprising, given his propensity for wandering.

As he himself realized immediately, he had arrived at one of the worst possible times imaginable. At the height of the depression of 1873–1879, also very much in evidence in Germany, finding work was all the more difficult for inexperienced newcomers to the United States.

Bürkert's style of writing—presumably like his style of thinking—is rather jumpy, leaving thoughts and sentences incomplete. But he is still able to express himself fairly clearly, though his spelling makes the German reader pause occasionally in order to figure out exactly what the letter-writer means. He obviously had a smattering of education, but no more than that. In all, he seems to be a teenager of a southern German middle-class background whose family situation and personal problems kept him from taking full advantage of the schooling and training opportunities available to him.

Wilhelm Bürkert

New York, IX 29, 1875

Dear mother, grandparents, sisters and honorable guardian,

Praise be to the Lord, etc., that is the first hymn that we can strike up, for you can count yourself lucky to have arrived here safely, especially when you hear that at the same time our ship left, on the same water, no less than 3 ships sank from running into one another in the fog.

So, let us turn our attention to the journey. In Heilbronn there was a one-hour stop, then straight on to Heidelberg. Here there was time to see the main sights. Then on, after refreshing yourself, to Frankfurt. Here, after getting all your things at Mr. Treschof's, the emigration agent's,[4]

---

[4]Probably Christian Emil Derschow, agent for Hapag, Lloyd, and others (Bretting/Bickelmann [1990]).

which cost a lot of money as well, you were taken to an inn, *"zum goldenen Adler"* [Golden Eagle]. Oh, to hell with that food and those beds, bedbug covers, not featherbeds, just a miserable mattress with torn sheets, and awfully expensive. You see, Schröffel in Weinsberg is supposed to put the 12 marks traveling money in your pocket, which he did in Heilbronn, but during the whole of the journey, what with all I had to pay besides in Hamburg, I even used up the 20 guilders that weren't written on my draft (for my 50 guilders) so that here in New=York I only had 30 guilders instead of 50 guilders. [3 ll.: details about draft] So, only the journey was paid for from Frankfurth on, but not the food. If I hadn't had such an honest, Christian, reliable gentleman along with me, looking after me, taking care of me, I would have been, as they say here, cheated blind. But thank God, it is a piece of good luck to have someone along on a damned trip like that. In Frankfurth we left on a Sunday at 8 o'clock in the morning and arrived the next morning at 3 o'clock at a station where we had to spend the night sleeping on the benches in the waiting room, until the train left at 6 o'clock the next morning.

In Hamburg there weren't as many swindlers and pickpockets like there were in that train station where you had to spend the night. You don't dare go to sleep there. We were in Hamburg in 2 hours time. We were brought by coach to our inn, to the *Gasthaus zum süddeutschen Hof* [South German Guesthouse]. Here we spent 2 nights. But better than in that miserable Frankfurth. This innkeeper had been a ship's captain for 20 years and is only interested in taking good care of emigrants.

On Wednesday the 15th of September we had to pay, but all from the 12 marks that were part of the passage contract and which didn't go far at all. On this day we got on a nice small steamship. In two hours we were out of the Elbe. But here we were met by a ship like you can't imagine, with 2 big smokestacks.[5] Everyone jumped for his mattress, assigned by the main agent at the inn in Hamburg, and for his tin ware. It took me an hour to find mine. When I found it, I carried it to the sleeping place I had picked out. But before I realized it, my chamber pot and water bottle had been stolen.

I reported to a steward that they'd been stolen; he said then go steal some yourself. I took one for myself and locked it up in my traveling bag, which was a great help. After 2 hours, the ship started out. We were given lunch.

I was all the way in the front in the first group of berths. I had to eat with 11 others, and carve the meat. Every day, rice soup, potatoes and meat, and meat, potatoes and rice soup, except for the 2 Sundays, when

---

[5] The Hamburg-based steamship *Gellert,* under Captain Darend, which sailed from Hamburg for New York on September 15, 1875 (StA HH, Auswanderungsamt I, VIII A [HPL]).

we had pudding along with it. Oh, I believe that stuff was boiled in sea water, it made me so sick, I ate nothing and drank nothing. In the morning all they had was black coffee, if you can call it coffee, then nothing until lunch mentioned above and then in the evening nothing but tea, which was just as bad as the coffee.

The next morning everyone was already seasick. For on the open sea the ship rolls terribly. It goes as fast as an express train.

I and 2 other friends, among them Herr Ritzer,[6] did not get seasick. Everybody was on top deck. One person puked here, another over there, for in steerage, way down at the bottom, you couldn't stand it. I didn't have to puke. On the 17th of September we arrived in the French city of Havre (Hawer). In this port there was a 24-hour stop. We were allowed to get off. We looked around this really lovely, large and luxurious city. On Sept. 18th at 10 o'clock in the morning, we departed. But then out on the Atlantic Ocean the ship really started to roll and the waves went clear up to the helmsman. On the same evening, on Saturday the 18th of Sept., I collapsed on the deck. They took me to my berth, where I hit, bit, scratched and ripped all the clothes of the sailors who had to hold me down. They gave me chloroform to put me to sleep. The ship's doctor gave up all hope. On the following Monday they were all waiting for me to die.

Oh, how horrible it is when you don't have anyone. My heart was pounding. They put something on it, it was like fire. The doctor said if he hadn't done that, my heart would have burst. I was told never to drink much. It was Wednesday before I was allowed to leave the hospital. During this time I had food from the first cabin, where princes and dukes travel. So it must not have been seasickness since then you have to throw up.

The last few days we had such a storm that you couldn't stand up or lie down. The trunks we had with us were tied down. The last night we had fog. On the 27th of Sept., or on the Monday, you couldn't see anything at all for 2 nights, the ship went very slowly. The steamwhistles were blown a lot. All at once at 9 o'clock they called out excitedly, Hurray, the pilot. He was coming toward us in a small boat. He had to guide us through the reefs off shore and in through the straits. It was a chief helmsman—almost like a ship's officer. At 4 in the morning we heard land–land. And that is a sight, oh splendid. We were in Stett-Neuland.[7]

[6]Immediately above "Bürkert, Wilhelm, 16 years of age, from Waldenburg, Württemberg, surveyor," the HPL lists one "Ritzer, J.," 36 years old, from Winterlingen, Württemberg (ca. one hundred miles from Waldenburg), "brewer" (Ibid.).

[7]Despite the imaginative transformation (Bürkert's version means "Newland Town"), this is certainly Staten Island, which belongs to New York State but lies off the coast of New Jersey and which, together with Long Island (Brooklyn), flanks the entrance to the Upper New York Bay, only a mile wide (The Narrows), and thus the ports in and around Manhattan.

Here the anchor was cast. A doctor came out about 7 o'clock and examined each one to see if he had a contagious disease. Everyone was healthy. We were allowed to go on. We went to the town = <u>Hoboken</u>. Here we had to go on a small ship. And everyone's trunks were inspected, to see if anyone was trying to smuggle something into America. There was a man who had to pay 40 dollars = 100 guilders for 2 silk dresses and 1 gold mark. At 3 o'clock in the afternoon we arrived in New-York.

Here we all went into a garden where a speech was held. It was Castle-Garden,[8] which is set up to take care of the emigrants. Innkeepers came to offer their services. We went to the inn *"Zur Stadt Balingen"* [Town of Balingen], the innkeeper is a Württemberger from Balingen.

<u>The card is enclosed</u>. I got my first job only today, Oct. 2nd, as a waiter and cook. I get food and board and when the month is over, the wages will be decided. Probably 16 dollars = 40 guilders. They won't pay more, that's very little here.

May you all be in good health. You'll write to me soon, won't you? A letter costs 5 cents = 7½ kreuzer. What costs 1 guilder in Germany, costs 1½ dollars here = 3 guilders 45 kreuzer. Here in Newjork things are very bad. Gustav shouldn't come until they're better. Write me where he is, but soon, won't you. All the best to you all. New-Jork is 5 times bigger and nicer than Hamburg, and it has 2 million inhabitants, you can get lost easily.

Your thankful son, grandson and brother. — Greetings, too, to Gustav.

New-York, Bellevue-Hospital,[9] Nov. 5, <u>1876</u>.

My dear ones,

Mother, sisters, brother, grandparents, honored guardian, uncle and aunt [etc.]. For a long time now you have probably been wondering why I've sent no news of myself to you; please forgive me! In the situation in which I was, it was impossible for me to write even a few lines to you. I wrote to my dear brother Gustav last March, in answer to his letter in which he offered me money for the return voyage, which I thought I would take. I thought if I had money I would go back; if not I would get a job as a sailor and go into whaling and travel around the world.

I stayed until the 1st of May here in New-Jork and asked the President

---

[8]Castle Garden, an area of land and set of buildings at the south end of Manhattan, administered by the state of New York, where from 1855 to 1892, immigrants were registered, cleared, and forwarded (after 1892 it was replaced by Ellis Island).

[9]Bellevue Hospital, built in 1826, open to the poor, and part of a walled complex that appropriately enough also contained the poorhouse and a prison, is located directly on the East River at 27th Street. See Booth (1880), 623–25; Bretting (1981), 69.

of the German Society[10] here, in case a letter or money under this or that address should arrive, to send it straight on to the port Rio de Janerio, where we were supposed to unload our catch of whalefish. (The afore-mentioned Rio de Janerio is the capital of Brazil, and the bay of this city is the most beautiful spot in the world, the city itself is very ugly.) But, when we arrived there after 40 days of good sailing, I asked straight away on the 2nd day at the *Postale del Office,* but nothing had arrived, as I had expected. We were there for a week, then we left again. — with the 3-masted "Three-Broders" from here again. This sailing ship is 300 feet (American foot = 12 zoll) long and a tonnage of 1500.[11] I and my other comrades, some men as old as 40 and all unmarried, received blows from the officers and mates like I'd never imagined in all my life, and like you can't imagine, either.[12] We were planning to sail to Valaparaiso Chili, we still had about 20 days to go, when in the evening we caught sight of a colossus, a whale. We stopped, I was one of those on watch that night. About 1 o'clock in the morning the waves started to crash up over the deck, and we had to pump out water for 1½ hours; then a storm came up, like you couldn't possibly imagine. We received the somewhat belated order to pull in the sails, but we had hardly reached the top of the 100 foot high mainmast on our rope ladders when the sail ripped, 8 of our men were swept away into the water and 4 of us were thrown onto the deck. Unfortunately I was one of them, one of the 4 men, 2 of whom lay dead, one broke an arm and I hurt my left foot below the knee. I really wished I were dead. Everyone was crying, screaming and praying. The storm lasted 6 days until a French *Propeler*-steamer picked us up and towed us with great difficulty to Rio de Jenerio. We injured ones got our back pay and were put on an English *Stimer (Dampfer)* and sent back here to New-Jork. I was very lucky that I didn't break my foot. The certificate from my doctor got me out of the hospital. As long as I live I have to keep

[10]The German Society of New York City, although founded in 1784, became a large-scale charitable organization only in the 1830s and 1840s after receiving generous contributions from John Jacob Astor. It worked to provide German immigrants with advice, employment, free medical care, and emergency financial support. The society was supported by donations from its prosperous members and the interest on its endowments (Bretting, 55–68).

[11]The *Three Brothers,* based in New Bedford, Massachusetts, the center of American whaling, was only 357 tons, and no American whaling ship in the 1870s was larger than 400 tons. On October 12, 1875, she set sail for the North Pacific and had not returned by the end of 1876 (Starbuck [1878], 652–53).

[12]The whaling industry, faced with strong competition from Pennsylvania oil, was in sharp decline. In the 1850s the total value of the annual catch still amounted to about $10 million, but by the early 1870s it had sunk to $3 million (Ibid., 660–61). But even before crisis hit the industry, seamen were reluctant to sign on to a whaler; aside from the officers and a few specialists, the crews—miserably paid—were made up of farmers' sons, unemployed immi-grants, and factory workers, as well as delinquents. The treatment on board is described by one historian, otherwise inclined to view his native New England in a positive light, as follows: "Brutality from officers to men was the rule. . . . The ingenuity of whaling skippers in devising devilish punishments surpasses belief" (Morison [1921], 319–24).

pressure off my foot by walking rather crookedly. I don't have any money left, don't know, either, what kind of work I'll be able to get. You can hardly get work even just for meals. I'm unfit for a ship![13] But you dear ones, and especially dear brother, think it over, and save. I would gladly be amidst you again, I am a completely different person, and never forget to pray.

If you want to send me something, be so kind and send it to my doctor, most of all a letter, or even better in care of the German Society. If I had some money I would start a small peddling business, to earn a living and then later set out for Australia, if it weren't possible to be with you again. I don't know what drinking is, except for water. Address. The German Society of the City of New-Jork. No 13 Broadway. To be delivered to William Buerkert. Write Burkert with ue, that is, Buerkert.

Johnstown [Pa.],[14] March 4th, 1877

Dear mother, brother, grandparents, dear sisters and all dear relatives,

You will be astounded to receive yet another letter from me. But do not be angry with me, it is a matter of life and death. Up to now I've been in the coal mine, where I tried to make my living with great effort and hard work and a miserable life. But it was not an accident, a cave-in, no, my long-feared ailment came back slowly, in the coal shaft, the miserable air from 6 in the morning until 6 at night. For lunch nothing but bread and black coffee in my pot, and on top of it the trip beforehand, 400 miles before I got here from New-York. I am really ill, very ill. The company I work for has to pay the doctor, he says: I have sick blood, I have consumption and may well have it until the fall. I won't be taken care of for that long, only 4 weeks. I can do lighter work all right, but where to find it? The doctor says if I have any relatives I should go there, if they'll have me. I will probably not live to see the winter. Oh, I tremble and have to weep when I think of it. As long as I've been in America that is back in New-Jork, almost ¾ of a year, I haven't touched any strong drink. I have a card that I'm not allowed to drink and smoke any more. It's the *Temberenz Ticet;*[15] with which the working class and also big bosses (Americans) swear not to enter any saloons.

---

[13]There are so many incongruities in Bürkert's account of the whaling episode—sailing dates, dimensions of the whaler, distances, etc.—that it may have been simply made up. Still, the evidence does not preclude the possibility that there was at least some truth to the story.

[14]Ca. sixty miles east of Pittsburgh in Cambria County, supported by coal mining and the iron industry. Its population in 1880 was 8,380 (today it is 35,000). In 1880 there were 26 mines and 924 miners in Cambria County; of the almost 47,000 inhabitants, 6,656 were foreigners, among them 2,737 Germans (USC 1880.1, 309, 525; USC MI 1880.2, 666–67).

[15]The temperance ticket was a written oath to abstain from alcohol, sponsored by one of the numerous temperance societies.

Every day I have had nosebleeds, I spit up a lot of blood. Oh, if I were only in Germany; if I could only get better, I would do any kind of work, for I've been taught how to here. I would gladly do the hardest labor. So, please don't let me perish here. Am I not allowed to see you again? Oh, if Father were still alive I would certainly not be here! But it seems as if even my only brother has deserted me. Oh—I don't want any money, no, that did hurt me, even to accept the 25 dollars or to have to accept it. If I had only been in a position to save one cent. So I ask you please to pay for a passage ticket, so I can come back to the German shores. I will gladly repay you if I get well again. Don't send me anything, I have 1 good jacket and work pants. Once again, please be so good and write back right away. I'm having myself sent to the hospital in New-Jork. To the charity hospital. Please send me an answer care of the German Society of the City of New-Jork No 13 Broadway New-Jork, to be delivered to Willie Büerkert. Please be so good and do it, won't you, I'm going under here.

Hoping, thanking / your / reformed / Willy

Julius Glatt

[Martinsburg, Pa., August 1, 1877]

To the honorable office of the Mayor / of the town of Waldenburg.

William Bürkert, son of the late farmer Georg Bürkert from Waldenburg, Oehringen County, Kingdom of Württemberg, fell seriously ill on June 20 and his recovery was doubtful. His illness is quite unknown to the 3 doctors attending him.

After he had gotten somewhat better, he himself claimed that it was a family illness, his father died of it. Water on the brain. The attacks which he had during his illness every 10 minutes were such that 3 men had to be kept in attendance to hold him down.

But the doctors have treated him, although they were not at all certain they would be paid, with a degree of loyalty and persistence that has astounded everyone. They came to see him three to 10 times a day, for several hours, although the farm where he worked and then fell ill is 1 mile away from the town.

My request directed to the town mayor's office is that the necessary money be provided from the ward's fund for the aforementioned Wilhelm Bürkert, to pay for the costs caused by his illness as well as for his journey home. Which in the opinion of the doctors would be the best for him.

I am performing this duty, since Wilhelm is still too weak to write himself.

The sum which Wilhelm must request is 150 dollars and the money should be sent to the Bureau listed below of the official authorities of the town of Martinsburg.[16]

This letter is authenticated by the signatures of the attending physicians, the local authorities and the patient himself.

Yours faithfully / Julius Glatt[17]
Martinsburg, Blair–County
Pennsylvania, August 1st, 1877.

Yours faithfully W Bürkert.

Address of Fred. Hyle[18] *Justice of the Peace* Martinsburg Blair County Pennsylvania

[11 ll.: repetition of address; asks for notification of money sent to Wilhelm Bürkert; the latter's address]
Mr William Bürkert
in care of Mr Caspar Reesy[19] / Martinsburg / Blair = County = Pennsylvania / North-America

[22 ll.: notarization in English of the statements above, with reference to the two attending physicians, Dr. Bloom and Dr. Crawford, by Justice of the Peace Fred. Hyle along with a stamped certification of the latter's official status until 1881]

Wilhelm Bürkert

Martinsburgh [Pa.], *the* 15 October, 1877.

Dearest mother, brother, sisters, grandparents and honored guardian,

Two months have now passed since I've been cured again, and since a friend wrote on my behalf, because I was too weak then to do it myself; but now I am here, pretty much back on my feet again and work for the man at whose house I went through my serious illness and who took care of me. But now I am in the lurch and don't know what to do. I still have about $100 of debts at the doctor's, which was in the letter sent to the town hall in Waldenburg with his signature and the court's notarization.

[16]A small town ca. thirty miles east of Johnstown; its population in 1880 was 567. Of the almost 5,300 inhabitants of Blair County, 3,858 were foreigners, among them 3,258 Germans (USC 1880.1, 308, 525).

[17]According to MC 1880: Blair Co., Pa., North Woodbury Twp., e.d. 174, #156, a 28-year-old farmer born in Baden, who lived with his Swiss-born wife and a farmhand, also from Baden.

[18]He appears as early as MC 1870: Blair Co, Pa., Borough of Martinsburg, #64, as a retired farmer (46) with four children and property totaling $3,600; in MC 1880: e.d. 175, #47, as justice of the peace.

[19]Apparently the farmer who lived one mile from the town employed Bürkert and took care of him during his illness.

If I don't pay him very soon I'll be out of work today. I also owe the man where I work, but I want to work that off. I have 4 months to go. The doctors are screaming for their money and I either have to pay or get out of the area completely. I said that I had 2000 marks and they said they wanted to treat me, so I had to swear it in front of the court and so they sent the letter to the mayor's office.

So please help me out, otherwise I will starve this winter, or freeze to death. I left here 4 weeks ago, since no letter came at all, but I had to come back and calm down the people, since it is hard to find work. All over America there are (*Stricke*) [strikes] that means revolution, and you can't even get a piece of bread by working for it. In New Jork, Boston, Baltimore, Washington, Cicago, Pittsburg, Philadelfia, and St. Louis, there are more than 150,000 workers out of a job and many even have families.

Yes, mother, it is hard, you don't need to be angry with me, I like to work, and I don't drink, and I don't lead a lowdown life, either. If I were at home I would surely earn my own living, but here, here it's all over. I am among Americans, if I were with German-Americans I would have been chased away a long time ago, and wouldn't be allowed to show my face. Oh, I am leaving this country, even if I have to smuggle myself onto a ship. If it hadn't been for the doctors, I would already be resting in peace. I have found out what that is. Dear mother, please write back to me immediately and dear guardian please see to my best interests. Don't think I will ever be too well-off here. Dear mother, write me above all about how my brother is and give him my address so he'll write to me after all; it is hard not to hear anything from your brother for such a long time.

Give my best to my little sisters and they shouldn't think badly of me, teach them to love me. [3 ll.: details] Oh, give my dear grandparents all my love. And all my best and loving wishes to you, too, I dream of you and my dear father every night, and I must weep for hours when I awake!

Please be so good and write straight away. / Loving you and all of you with all my heart / William.

Martinsburg, December 8th, 1877

Dear grandfather and grandmother,

It has now been a long time since I sent off word that I was so dangerously ill. But no one finds it worth the trouble to send me an answer. In the entire last year I have only received one single letter.

I have sent off a letter several times, but never gotten an answer. Now I turn to you, dear grandparents, perhaps you think better of a poor orphan in America. All that I want is just to know how you, my dear ones, are. I don't even know how things are, are you still alive, or not. Oh! May these lines reach you in good health. Oh! If only I could see you once again. How are my dear good mother, my good brother and worthy sisters? Please write me about <u>everything</u>; oh, you have no idea what it is like when you don't hear anything from your loved ones for years on end. I am living here with good people, but without work. I haven't heard a word of German for half a year. Oh, if I had the means, I would come to you bravely. But it won't work out like this. I often think I've been deserted. Please be so good and don't make me wait long for an answer. Oh, give my best to everyone and wish them happy hearts. Farewell, may God keep you in good health / your / loving devoted / grandson, son and brother / William Buerkert

Jamestown,[20] Missouri, *June the 27th,* 1880

My dear mother,

Once again I take up my pen to call out greetings to you across the ocean. I wrote to you 3 times after I got your last letter, without ever getting an answer back. I wrote you then that I was planning to travel to California. I went out there, as I thought, to make my fortune. My savings then amounted to 125 dollars. I and two others bought a piece of land for $300 and started to *minen.* But there was very little gold to be found and also we were dogged by the rough miners and mine owners. Then we were forced to sell our land for $175 after 4 months of hard work. We lost about $35. We took off for Oregon and went on from there eastward, until we came to Colorado. There we worked as guides for the trains of immigrants which move from the eastern states to the West. This job was very dangerous, we had to fight too much with bands of Sioux Indians and with the so-called (*Outlaws*) (that means with white men who break the law). I stayed there about 7 months. Went through the *Indian Territory* [now Oklahoma], where we earned a few talers with *trapping,* that means catching beaver, by selling the furs in Texas and from there I came back to the state of Missouri 3 weeks ago,[21] and since the harvest had just started I worked through it, earning from 2 to 2½ dollars a day; if I wanted to move on with the harvest I could, if I kept going

[20]This village's population in 1880 was 185, and it lay halfway between Kansas City and St. Louis, just south of the Missouri River in Moniteau County. The county population of 14,000 included 1,170 foreigners, 728 of whom were German (USC 1880.1, 243, 517).

[21]There is one common denominator to this Wild West story: the various episodes might easily have occurred about a generation earlier. In 1880, however, they could be found only in dime novels, not in real life. It is almost certain that Bürkert made them up.

north I could still do 4 weeks of harvest work, but first of all I want to rest up a bit and second of all, some *Farmers* have asked me to plow their corn. That's an easier job; of course only 1 dollar and 25 cents a day; but much quieter, and when you do harvest work for 3 whole weeks that is as much strain as you can take. It's now 87 degrees in the shade here. It's only 10 o'clock and 26 minutes. *Well,* dear mother, how are all of you? It's tough when you are begrudged writing home, are my dear grandparents still doing well, and you, dear mother, do you have a comfortable life? What are the dear little ones doing? Have them learn some English. When I buy a small place here, about 100 *Acres* or morgens, which I plan to do this fall, I won't be visiting you this year but will wait until next year; but I could also visit this fall and settle down when I come back from Germany. I can get good land here for 5 dollars an *Acer,* of course uncultivated, but after a few years the *Acer* is then worth 50–60 dollars. I have enough to buy a small place. I want to live and die in America. Oh mother, if you could come back with me here, I'd like to [-----] the days [rest missing].

High Point,[22] Moniteau Co: Missouri
March the 27th [1881].

Honored Guardian,

I received your letter of 20.II and learned to my great dismay that all of my expenses, lost time and hopes of being independent were for nought. But that doesn't help, you just keep power of attorney. I can't and couldn't serve in the army. First of all I couldn't because I didn't have the means then to travel to Germany and secondly I was ill and I also didn't know, since I was never asked to serve, that I had to in the first place. I lost my passport on the steamship *Three Brothers* when I was taken off board during a whaling trip from New York to Rio de Jeneiro, on which I nearly broke all my ribs along with legs and neck. And then it would have been completely unnecessary to report, since I wasn't fit or able, to which the doctors can bear witness. I still have to take medicine. I bought some woodland on February 1st from my boss[23] and thought I could cut the wood next fall and haul it for the railroad company since a railroad is being built nearby. I've paid all but 45 dollars, which I'll work off. I still owe about 25 dollars to the doctor which I will have paid off by the fall. So in other words I have 70 dollars of debts and I have to see that I keep

---

[22]A village whose population in 1880 was 128 and which was ca. eighteen miles south-southwest of Jamestown (USC 1880.1, 243).

[23]There is no evidence of this alleged land purchase in the Moniteau County records, nor in the records of the neighboring counties Cole, Miller, and Morgan.

my health so I can work and pay them back. So I can't travel to Europe and if I were to go there I would have to work for a while and earn some money. I don't want to sell my woods, nor can I. Woods are worth next to nothing here unless there are good prospects to use the wood for railroad construction, but if I don't get my money or property by next fall I won't be able to buy a team and tools and wagons; so the price for my woods would be almost nothing and I would be broke since I paid 175 dollars for it. I had 200 dollars and a horse, but I wasn't able to work the last two months, so I had to pay the doctors and when I saw it would cost my savings I sold my horse. So now I have nothing, but I am hale again and will start to plow next week. We had the hardest winter ever seen in America. When a man here gets sick for a few weeks and needs doctors and nurses he is in a bad way, and 100 dollars is nothing to him and doesn't go further than 25 guilders in Germany.

Dear guardian, do the best you can, try to get me my complete emigration papers. I am an American citizen and have no need to be a German citizen, so I'll manage without [rest missing].

Wilhelm Bürkert's letter of March 27, 1881, is the last sign of life that we have. He could not be found in Missouri in either the 1880 or 1900 census, and there are no other clues as to his whereabouts. The nature of his illness, too, remains unclear. Four different medical specialists were kind enough to attempt a "historical diagnosis" based on the symptoms described in the letters. Apparently, there is only a slight chance that he suffered from tuberculosis or a brain tumor. Instead, it is more likely that Wilhelm Bürkert suffered from epilepsy or "cerebral seizures" combined with alcohol abuse, and the latter may well have been exacerbated by his unfortunate family circumstances.

15

Matthias Dorgathen

Matthias Dorgathen is the only one of the letter-writers in this volume who left the United States and returned to Germany permanently. Return migration, usually the product of a wide range of factors, is a phenomenon that is quite difficult to assess; at the same time, it certainly played an important role in the migration process as a whole. Much too little is known about this phenomenon—at least for Germany.[1]

In the early 1880s Matthias Dorgathen's hometown of Styrum, today part of Mülheim on the Ruhr, had a population of approximately 7,500, almost half of them Protestant like the Dorgathen family. The only factories located in the town itself produced firebrick and glue, but coal mines and other industries in the immediate surroundings provided many jobs.[2]

The Dorgathens were obviously not among the poorest residents. The father, Heinrich Dorgathen (born in 1821), had originally been a barge-

[1]Not even reliable figures are available: contemporary statistics are lacking and other sources are unreliable because returning emigrants were not recorded systematically. The official (American) figures begin as late as 1908–1910 and include the total number of immigrants arriving and leaving the country, along with the percentage of returning emigrants, which, according to this definition, amounted to some 20 percent of Germans (Irish: 7 percent, North Italians: 62 percent) (*Reports* 1, [1911], 113). Throughout the nineteenth century, the overall rate of German return emigration certainly lay below 20 percent; in the 1830s it could hardly have surpassed 5 percent, and in the course of subsequent decades it probably rose. The tendency to return depended not only on the particular year and economic situation but also on the age and marital status of the emigrant. The two most informative recent studies on this topic are Moltmann (1980) and Kamphoefner (1986b).

[2]Neumann (1883), 1203.

man, which normally meant that he owned at least one barge on the Ruhr, but shipping, and in particular coal shipping from the central Ruhr District to the Rhine, was gradually brought to a standstill between 1865 and 1880 by the overwhelming competition of the railroads (in 1889 shipping operations were closed down completely).[3] At the time Matthias Dorgathen emigrated, his family—his parents, two married sisters, and two brothers, Wilhelm and Heinrich, who worked in a mine and a factory, as well as the latecomer Karl—was also engaged in farming and even employed a servant girl.

Matthias was born in 1852 and experienced firsthand the breathtaking boom of the Ruhr District, based on the coal and iron/steel industries. Given where he lived and what was in demand, it was only logical that he should become a miner. Before emigrating, he probably worked in the Alstaden mine less than two miles from the center of Styrum.[4] Mining companies in the Ruhr District could still meet their expanding labor needs locally until mid-century; a sizable influx from other areas began around 1860. Of the 13,693 migrants who moved to nearby Borbeck between 1865 and 1870, 82 percent came from the Rhineland and Westphalia; the rest were from other parts of the country and abroad.[5]

Thus it may be surprising at first glance that in 1881, Dorgathen, with an occupation that was in great demand and living in an area that was itself attracting migrants, left for the United States—and he was by no means alone. But in view of the overall economic situation, his decision was quite understandable. The profound depression of the 1870s, lasting from 1873 to 1878–79, had hit the Ruhr District hard. Year by year, the average wage for a shift in the coal mines of the Ruhr continued to sink, from a high of 3.75 marks in 1873 down to 2.33 in 1879—no less than 38 percent. The decline was somewhat milder at the Alstaden mine—from 3.75 in 1875 to 2.49 in 1879—but the trend was much the same, and the number of men employed by the mine decreased over these six years from 553 to 425. Even the slight recovery in 1880 and 1881 (Alstaden wages averaged 2.63 marks and 2.69, respectively) did not leave much room for optimism.[6]

The district governor in Düsseldorf reported on April 19, 1881—two weeks after Dorgathen's departure—that a "spring lull" had led to a drop in shifts and increased layoffs at many mines. He continued, "The desire

[3]Fischer (1965), 134–44; Barleben (1959), 255–65.
[4]Aside from several vague hints in the letters, his employment there is supported by the fact that the first letter of the series was written on stationery he had brought along with him with the letterhead "Alstaden: Actien Gesellschaft für Bergbau."
[5]Massive migration from the eastern areas of Prussia did not begin until the 1880s (Fischer, 252–54).
[6]Tenfelde (1977), 603; Fischer, 52–53.

to emigrate has unfortunately spread, especially among the most hard-working and best miners." Half a year later, on September 30, 1881, he provided more details:

> The shift wages of a hewer amount to an average of 2.50 marks. The result of these low wages has been heavy emigration, which has carried off many of the best workers among the miners during the summer, to North America. Ohio was the destination given by many miners, in particular from the Rheinpreußen mine in Ruhrort and Dahlbusch near Gelsen-kirchen. Agents from companies there drew up contracts with the miners and advanced them the money to travel via Antwerp. The insistent warn-ings issued by officials and mine owners remained largely unheeded.

In 1881 a total of 1,700 laborers, mostly miners, left the Ruhr District for North America.[7]

Dorgathen's letters make it clear he was not recruited and supplied with travel funds by an agent; instead, he struck out on his own (although he did borrow some money), in response to favorable reports from friends from the surrounding area who had emigrated earlier and who were also well known to his family in Styrum.

At about the same time as in the Ruhr District—the late summer of 1879—the American bituminous coal districts began to experience an economic upswing, characterized by larger wage increases and a greater demand for labor than in Germany. This was particularly true of the mines in eastern Ohio,[8] which, along with sections of Pennsylvania, West Virginia, and Kentucky, tapped the largest contiguous coal deposit in the United States. These favorable circumstances may well have attracted the first emigrants from the Ruhr District to Ohio and given rise to their positive reports, later criticized frequently by Dorgathen.

First Dorgathen went to live for almost a year in Stark County, one of the four leading coal counties in Ohio both in terms of coal production and number of miners (1,381 in 1880 and 1,179 in 1890).[9] Navarre, a place mentioned frequently in the letters, was still a village, but Dor-gathen located in Massillon, a rapidly expanding industrial town. In 1880 the town had a population of about seven thousand and in 1890 more than ten thousand.[10] During the 1880s, population growth in Stark County as a whole was equally impressive—from under 65,000 to al-

[7]LHA KO, Best. 403, Nr. 8319, Bl. 534, 535, 604–5, 651 (report of October 13, 1881); Tenfelde, 236.
[8]In 1880 Ohio produced one-third as much coal as Pennsylvania (USC MI 1880.2, 662, 666).
[9]USC MI 1880.2, 662–63; USC MI 1890.1, 396–97.
[10]USC 1890.1, 475; 1890.18, 329.

most 85,000, including over 12,000 immigrants, almost half of them German.[11]

When Dorgathen moved about ninety miles southwest to Buckingham, Ohio, he settled in a county with a social and economic structure that was quite different. As of 1880 only 28,000 people lived in Perry County, and its population grew by a mere three thousand in the course of the decade. Barely 10 percent had been born abroad, the majority British (57 percent), followed by Germans (22 percent) and Irish (17 percent). In terms of coal production and number of miners (1,505 in 1880 and 2,448 in 1890), however, Perry County led the state.[12]

Despite these differences, both areas contrasted sharply with the scale and structure of mining Dorgathen had known in his previous home in the Ruhr District. Although there were some mines in the Mülheim-Essen area (such as the Humboldt), where about two hundred miners worked to produce sixty thousand tons of coal, in 1880, more typically, mines employed five to six hundred men and the annual production ran from one to two hundred thousand tons (among them his old mine Alstaden, as well as Roland, Sellerbeck, Concordia Oberhausen, and others). At least one mine (Oberhausen, owned by the Gutehoffnungshütte) had 1,670 employees and produced almost a half million tons annually, thus surpassing the total number of miners in both Stark and Perry counties and producing considerably more coal than all of Stark County and almost half as much as Perry County.

Of the 69 mines in Stark County, one produced 58,000 tons in 1880 and seven others between 25,000 and 33,000 tons a year. Among the thirty mines in Perry County, there were four with an annual production of between 93,000 and 121,000 tons. On the average, twenty miners produced about five thousand tons a year per mine in Stark County, and in Perry County the ratio was fifty men to thirty thousand tons.[13]

During the first few months of recovery after the depression, the Ohio miners' union was successful in its fight for higher pay. The miners in the Tuscarawas Valley, including Stark County, led the battle. In October 1879 they forced through a ten-cent increase in the tonnage rate, but a four-month strike against the companies dubbed "the seven" by Dorgathen was unsuccessful and had to be broken off in April 1880. In early 1882 miners throughout the entire state organized to form the Ohio Miners' Amalgamated Association.

[11]Including the Austrians and the unusually large number of Swiss and Alsatians, German-speakers accounted for more than two-thirds of those born abroad, far more than the 21.5 percent British and 5.5 percent Irish (USC 1890.1, 35, 650).
[12]USC 1890.18, 326; USC 1890.1, 35, 650, 397; USC MI 1880.2, 663; USC MI 1890.1, 396.
[13]Fischer, 43–59; USC MI 1880.2, 662–63, 907–9.

Partly in reaction to this, some fifty Hocking Valley mines (Athens, Hocking, and Perry counties) joined forces in the spring of 1883 to form two larger associations, the Ohio Coal Exchange and the Hocking Valley Company, mentioned frequently by Dorgathen. The latter, in view of a slump in the coal market, announced the following June that as of the end of the month, the rate per ton would be reduced from 70 to 60 cents. The miners—over three thousand men in 46 mines—promptly went on strike, at which point the piece rate was cut another 10 cents a ton and the miners, in order to be allowed back to work, were required to sign individual contracts that would effectively rule out further militant action on the part of the union. The mining companies went even further: agents were sent to the South and the East to recruit blacks and immigrants from southern and southeastern Europe. They arrived under the protection of heavily armed Pinkerton detectives; even a unit of the state militia appeared on the scene.

In January 1885 the Ohio State Assembly appointed a committee to investigate the Hocking Valley strike. On March 18 negotiations between the two sides led to a compromise settlement that ended the strike: the miners accepted piece rates of 50 cents a ton, and the mining companies withdrew their contracts. An extremely well-organized campaign to support the strikers had managed to collect and distribute some $125,000 in goods and cash;[14] Matthias Dorgathen also contributed a considerable share of his wages to the fund.

Dorgathen did not stay in Ohio long enough to see the end of the strike, a settlement that represented a bitter blow to the miners' union. Two weeks earlier he had finally given up, partly because his earnings continued to shrink with each payment into the strike fund, and started off on his way back to Germany.

During the less than four years Matthias Dorgathen lived in the United States, he wrote considerably more (and longer) letters to Germany than any other correspondent in this edition during any four-year period. The correspondence list[15] he kept from August 14, 1881, to January 3, 1885, includes 27 letters, copies of which are in the Bochum collection and are printed here, 25 letters "home," which have not survived, as well as 48 more addressed to fourteen different friends and relatives. The list does not include five letters from the same time period as well as seven written before or after, all of which are included in this edition, and probably some more addressed to relatives and friends. His unusually close connection to family and friends, as evidenced by his dedicated letter-writ-

[14]Roy (1905), 190–97, 230–41.
[15]In the same notebook that contains his "My Travels to America" (see n. 45, below).

ing, may very well have contributed to his decision to return to Germany.

Dorgathen is not only the most prolific letter-writer in this volume; he is also the one who gives the reader the most trouble, owing to his wildly erratic spelling; his virtually complete disdain for punctuation, resulting in endless run-on sentences; and his use of the Ruhr dialect, naively put into writing side by side with the High German he learned in school.

Yet for someone struggling so hard with the written language, it is impressive how well he can get the colorful story of his American years across, how lively the images and episodes he describes come through, and how neat and orderly his handwriting is, compared to his chaotic spelling.

By 1883 he seems to have acquired at least a rudimentary English, and his letters contain progressively more untranslated English terms, but no English elements of sentence structure. It appears that the use of his restricted English was confined to comparatively rare contacts with Americans or Irish, while most of the time he spoke German—though a German studded with loan words like "buddy" or "trouble," which became so familiar that it did not occur to him that such terms would be lost on the recipients of his letters.

Matthias Dorgathen

Navare, May 7, 1881

Dear parents, brothers and sisters and brother-in-law,

I just want to let you know how I am and how I've been. So we arrived on Sunday, April 24, in Nevjork in the harbor and stayed on the ship until Monday morning 10 o'clock then we got off the ship and went to Kastele Garden[16] and from there we went to Möller's *Hottel.* Kastele Garden, that's a place, the emigrants all get together there. We stayed in Nevjork until Tuesday, April 6,[17] at 7 o'clock in the evening and then we went by train to Navare[18] and arrived Thursday the 28th at 11 o'clock in Navare. Then we walked all around the town until we finally came to Schlösser and Fossing's, there we were well looked after. They did everything they could, but dear family, it's not quite like what we'd imagined. Work is scarce at the mines here, you can't get a job now, we're now working on

---

[16]See Chapter 14, n. 8.

[17]April 26 is certainly what he means.

[18]The village population in 1880 was 867, in 1890, 1010 (USC 1890.18: Stark Co., Ohio, Bethlehem Twp., 328).

the railroad, but the wages aren't as high as the others always wrote, here on the railroad you earn 1 dollar and 23 cents, that is 5 marks of our money, but you have to pay 14 dollars, or 56 marks in our money, for board,[19] but if you have your own household you can get by with half that, since food is cheaper here than at home, except potatoes cost more here, eggs only cost 4 pfennigs apiece. The Americans only work half the time, when they have money they don't do any work until it's all gone. Here they much prefer Germans to the English.[20] And the people are so kind you can't imagine, we've rented ourselves a room for 5, me and Emil Klewer, Böhkel, Heisterkamp, and Goltschmied, Bö Heist and Golt are from Dümpten,[21] we do our own cooking, then you live more cheaply. At first we couldn't find any work at all because the railroad was at a standstill, it was sold to another *Combanie* as they call it here. The countryside here is beautiful, there are birds like you've never seen, it's hilly but the land is good, we've already been all over the area, we walked 7 to 12 miles every day, but a mile here is only 20 minutes,[22] the village where we are is called Bethlehem,[23] it is near Navare, here you can go fishing and hunting as much as you like, we've already done some fishing since we are near a stream, it's called *Rebbe* [river]. The land is good here, it's the best land for wheat in all America, an acre costs 100 dollars here, an acre is also a lot more than a morgen at home, but farther into America the land doesn't cost so much; if anyone can't stay away from drinking liquor, he should come to America, there schnaps is very expensive and even more awful as they say, I haven't drunk any, but here they have apple wine, that is very cheap and good, for 5 cents you can get a couple of liters. Tell Herman Luthenbrink I've often thought about his good schnaps, since you miss that here, but I've gotten used to it, I can put up with it fine. But everything does seem different than at home, you can't understand the people and then you're completely stumped. When they start taking on miners again then we'll go back to the mine / here they call it / *Bänk,* since here they work differently than at home. It's all done by percussion drilling, the coal is so hard here, that would be something for you Johann and Heinrich, you can really say Heaven help me, like Johan

---

[19]In the Ruhr District in the 1880s, board cost an average of 45 marks (Tenfelde, 317).

[20]Though one can never be quite sure if German immigrants actually do mean English or British when they write "English," the term usually stands for "English speaker," i.e., American.

[21]Dümpten, in Mülheim County, two and a half miles east of Styrum, had a population of ca. 4,100, and the Roland mine was located there (Neumann [1883], 231).

[22]One hour as a measure of distance was the equivalent of three American miles. The old German mile, which was still in some use in the 1880s, measured about 4.7 American miles.

[23]Bethlehem Township in Stark County, which included Navarre, had a population in both 1880 and 1890 of ca. 2,300.

said when we first bought the guitar. We play every evening and sing along, here you can live well if you only have work, if you go to ask for a job here you say to the foreman or the master, tell me, do you have any work, here they aren't as proud like at home, you don't have to go cap in hand like at home, they'd just laugh at you here, here you're free to do anything, you don't have to register with the police when you move in or out, you also don't have to pay any taxes. If you rent a house here, you can move out any day, you just go there and say, I'm moving out tomorrow, that's all, but as long as I pay my rent I don't have to move out, for that time the house is mine. It's the same at work, when I have a place in the mine no foreman can boot me out unless I do something no good, for example stealing, that's punished hard here, otherwise the job is mine, but I can leave whenever I want to, if I want to quit then I just pick up my tools, that's all, and I can go wherever I want.

I'll close now since I don't know much yet, when I've been here longer I'll be able to write more.

But I do want to write one more thing. You brothers and sisters, treat our parents well and don't give them a rough time, and don't let mother peel potatoes in the evening and get up early in the morning, spare her as much as you can, for when you're in a strange place you really miss your parents. [5 ll.: the same; is well; cigars he brought along are good] Everything I brought along was useful, but if I had known, I wouldn't have brought so much clothes along since they don't cost more here than at home, and aren't any worse. The trip cost me a lot more than I'd counted on, when I got to Navare I only had two dollars left, the trip to Ackron cost 115 marks without baggage, in Antwerp it cost 4 marks 80 pfennigs for a room and carting the bags from the train station, and in Nev jork a room cost 8 marks and from Ackronn to Navare it also cost 4 marks and when I changed money in Halfay [Halifax, Nova Scotia] I lost 1 mark 12 pfennigs for every 10 marks. [8 ll.: loss on exchange rate in New York; expensive to stay in London; cost of food on the trip overland] Write back right away how things are going at home, if you are all still in good health and if there's any other news, how Heinrich is doing at the mine and Wilhelm at the factory, my father in Duisburg and mother and sisters should also write me a few lines. [10 ll.: greetings to eighteen friends and relatives listed by name, including the "Schlössers in Alstaden" as well as the "Verein Hoffnung" (singing club), they should all write]

From afar, thousands of greetings from your son, brother and brother-in-law, I remain forever grateful to you, I'm already awaiting an answer.
[. . .]

Masillon, May 15, 1881

Dear parents, brothers, sister and brother-in-law

I want to let you know that I am no longer in Navare but in Masilon[24] that is 2 hours from Navare, in Navare we couldn't get a job for now, so we had to go to Masilon. Here we're working in a quarry, me and Goldschmid Vos and the two Hintes, it's already so hot here like it never is at home even in August. We earn 1 dollar and 25 cents, or 5 marks a day, we work from 7 in the morning to 12 noon, then from 1 in the afternoon till 6, or 10 hours, but there's no coffee break in between like at home. [. . .] It's no fun at all to work 5 hours straight in the heat but it doesn't matter, I'm in good spirits, it won't take much longer then I'll get a job at the *Bänk* (mine) there you earn more than in a quarry. The thing to do here in America is to be a foreman or *Bas* [boss] as they say here, they earn 150 dollars, or 600 marks, that would be ideal. We've gone into boarding close to where we work, they are good German people, Protestants too, but we have to pay 14 or 15 dollars for board, the food is good, too, but you only get something to eat three times a day [. . .] that seemed strange to me at first but you get used to everything here. You also have to get used to doing without Sunday revels because Sundays everything's shut, saloons and all businesses in general. Whoever sells or serves liquor and beer has to pay 50 dollars, but if one of us gets drunk and makes a ruckus he gets put behind bars and has to pay 5 dollars, not only on Sundays but every day of the week. Here in Masilon the countryside is beautiful, everything is green, lots of hills and even more woods. God knows how many fruit trees there are here, the livestock, especially cattle, wander around in the fields and the woods as if they had no owner and there are birds so beautiful you wouldn't believe, but they sing very badly, not nearly as nicely as at home in Germany. Here there are black ones with blood-red wings and ones that are all red, and green ones with red wings, too beautiful for words. We don't do anything on Sunday, we go for a walk in the woods, the birds there are so tame, if you throw a rock they don't even know if they should fly away or not. This would be a good place for someone who likes romantic scenery, for Uncle Heinrich it would be the best spot anyone could imagine. Anyone who knows a trade, for example, cabinetmaker, shoemaker and mason, is in demand and well paid. Putting new soles on a pair of boots, for example, costs 1 dollar, and it's the same with everything else. I will stop now since the paper is almost full. [6 ll. greetings, friends should write]

---

[24]Massillon, Stark County, Ohio, was a transportation, industry, and trade center, with a population in 1890 of some ten thousand, including almost two thousand immigrants (USC 1890.18, 329; 1890.1, 475).

Many greetings from your son, brother and brother-in-law / Matth
Dorgathen
But write back right away, since when I get a letter it's just as good as
talking to you.

Massillonn, May 26, 1881
Dear parents, brothers and sisters and brother-in-law,
[7 ll.: good wishes, correspondence] Today is Ascension Day but it
isn't celebrated here by the Americans, it's a normal work day like any
other, it's just the same with the second day of Pentecost, they work then,
too. We only have two holidays here, aside from the normal Sundays,
that's coming up on May 30. [4 ll.: Memorial Day] The second holiday is
on July 3, that's when the battle for freedom was fought. Dear relatives,
you wouldn't believe how many immigrants are coming here, every day
whole trainloads go by and many stay here too, that's why things here are
getting so bad. Many say if they had the money they'd go home again.
That's how one fellow came to us on Thursday the 26th in the evening,
we happened to be in town, he'd just arrived and didn't know his way, he
wanted to go to his brother who lives two miles from here. I knew where
his brother lived, I'd been to his house, but it was already too late so he
had to stay in a *Hottel*. He is from Speldorf, he also said if he had the
money he'd go back to Germany and Sunday the 29th Fischen, or (Ficks)
from Broich[25] also arrived here, but there's not as much going on here as
they always wrote, it's all over with the 9 and 10 marks that were earned
in the mine, here there's no work at all in the mine, they only work 3 or 4
shifts and when you start out you have to have 20 dollars worth of tools.
In the winter things are supposed to pick up at the mines, but in the
summer there's nothing going on, everyone who comes has to do other
work if they can get it, and otherwise they have to move on or go back,
since in Nev jork there's more work than here. If it doesn't get better
soon I'll be leaving, because if you work for 5 marks a day and then only
if it doesn't rain, and it often rains the whole day here, then you don't
have much left over, because everything costs a lot here, except shoes and
boots and clothes, a pair of work shoes costs 6 marks, they last as long as
two pairs back home and the same with boots, but repairs cost a lot here.
I wore my buckled shoes for less than 2 weeks in the quarry before I was
walking on the insoles, I had them fixed, that cost 1 taler and 60 pfennigs

[25]Speldorf, Mülheim County, had a population of ca. four thousand, and was about two miles
southwest of Styrum. Broich, Mülheim County, had a population of ca. three thousand, and
was three miles south-southwest of Styrum (Neumann [1883], 1164, 150).

or 85 cents and a cent is 4 pfennigs, but you can get a whole suit for 5 dollars. They hardly ever wear shirt-fronts here, almost everyone wears pleated shirts, they are very cheap here, hats are cheap here, too, I bought myself one, a white straw hat for work since otherwise you can't take the miserable heat. It's already much warmer than over in Germany and they say it will get much hotter. I'm already all yellow, burned by the sun. On April 15 snow was still lying on the ground and in July the apples are already ripe, it's that hot here. So, the hat cost me one mark, in Germany it would surely have cost three, you can also get as many apples as you want, they are still cheap now, and the nuts are cheap, you can get coconuts here, they are as big as a baby's head. Here Saturday night is Sunday, on Sundays there's nothing going on. Write and tell me if it is true that there's a war in Germany, they talk a lot about it here, they're always going on about it that France declared war on Germany, if need be then I'll come back to Germany and help beat up the French, for we are still Germans here in America and German-minded, when we go to a saloon here in the evening and sing songs then we don't have to pay for anything, they like to listen to German songs so much here, they can all understand German here, too. They've also asked us to start a men's singing club, since a lot of gentlemen and bosses want to join, they also want to find us a director, we're going to get together this week with them, then we'll see what happens, since we all have a good time singing. We are a group of 12 men here in Massilon, I knew them all from home, that is me and Keffen, Vos, Goldschmid, 2 Hinde, Böckel, Heisterkamp, Brus and Kiphen from Alstaden,[26] Ers and Gißen and many more that have come. I will close since my sheet of paper is full. Give my best to all friends and relatives and all the neighbor girls and tell them they should just come on over to America.

Massilonn, July 3, 1881

Dear parents, brothers and sisters and brother-in-law,

I want to let you know that I got your letter of June 5 and learned from it that you are all still hale and hearty. I was very pleased to hear that, because there's nothing more important than good health. I am, thank God, also still hale and hearty, as long as that is the case I am satisfied, for here you really can live better than over there in Germany, especially if you're married. Dear family, you wrote me that I should tell you why I am not in Bethlehem any more, I'll tell you about that. In Bethlehem we

---

[26]Alstaden, Mülheim County, had a population of ca. four thousand and was the site of the mine of the same name (Ibid., 16).

couldn't get any work, we went around from April 28 to May 9, for 11 days and couldn't get a job anywhere in Bethlehem, so we had to go to Massilonn, I wrote that I was working on the railroad in Bethlehem, but I wasn't working on the railroad there, how I came to write that was this— I didn't want to write until I had work, and the day before I wrote you they had said tomorrow we could start working on the railroad so I thought now I could write I had found work, but there wasn't any so I went to Massilon and got a job in the quarry. You write that I should tell you why I am not working in the mine with Schlössers, I'll tell you why, in the mines here things are very bad in the summer, they only work a couple of shifts a week, sometimes there's no work for an entire week, so you can't even earn enough to pay your board, so I'd rather do something else than lie around at home and go into debt. Dear parents and brothers and sisters, how are the broad beans and peas doing, did they turn out well, we can't get any here and I like to eat them so much. Please send me over a meal of beans and peas, and how are the potatoes doing? They are good here, but if you want to see Colorado beetles then you should come over here some time, the bushes are so full of them that you can hardly see any leaves. The wheat is already being cut here, when we started work on May 10 it was hardly two inches high and now it's already ripe, everything here ripens much earlier than in Germany. That's because of the heat and the rain. The wheat harvest is mostly done by the men here, it goes much faster than at home. Another time I'll write more about that, they've just started here, during the harvest they pay 2 to 2½ dollars per day plus board, if I could only do good binding work I'd also go to work for a farmer. Dear family, tomorrow the 4th is a holiday, nobody will work tomorrow, the 4th of July is the biggest holiday in America, every year they celebrate, on that day America fought itself free from England, there's music everywhere. I'll write and tell you how it was in another letter. On Friday they shot our President, from what they say he is badly hurt, an Italian is supposed to have done it,[27] when I hear more I'll write you, from now on I'm going to write a letter every week if it's at all possible. With this I will close, regards from your son and brother Matthias. [10 ll.: correspondence] Give my best to all relatives and friends and all the girls, send me one soon, because I want to get married, since then you can live much better than when you're single, but she should be nice and pretty, there are enough of the other kind running around here, just kidding. [4 ll.: greetings]

[27]On July 2, 1881, a Saturday, President James A. Garfield was shot in a train station in Washington, D.C. He succumbed to his injuries on September 19 and was succeeded by Vice President Chester A. Arthur. The assassin was a half-crazed office seeker, a Chicago lawyer named Charles Guiteau (1841–1882). He was not an Italian but in fact an old-stock American of Huguenot background.

Massillonn, July 13, 1881

Dear parents and brothers and sisters,

[29 ll.: correspondence; is healthy; heat; sunstroke casualties; money matters; artisan wages; no broad beans, no black bread; baggage damaged during crossing] My clothes and hats are still fine, they came through pretty well, but if I'd have known, I wouldn't have brought so much along, for here everything is cheaper than at home and not more expensive like they always said, and you don't dare wear a cap here, you get laughed at, here everyone wears hats, they're also cheap here. Dear sister, you're in a mixed choir, well, keep it up as long as you like, since there's not much else going on in Styrum, you write that you'd like to come over with several girls, go ahead and do it, things are very good for girls here, they earn 10–8–12 marks a week and don't have to do much work, out in the fields it's mostly the men who do the work, the girls have it really good here, but things look bad for a prepaid ticket, but I'm just kidding anyway, you have to stay at home and help mother with the work. Dear parents, if I move on I'll let you know early enough. Dear Brother Heinrich, you write you want to come over and help us sing, go ahead and do it, it's much better here than in the Alstaden mine but we don't have a club yet, here there are mixed choirs, 1 Lutheran and 1 Evangelical, I think I'll join that one. That's all for now, best wishes from your son, brother and brother-in-law / M Dorgathen

[15 ll.: correspondence; greetings; is sending photograph]

Massillonn, July 31, 1881

Dear parents, brothers, sisters and brother-in-law,

[10 ll.: correspondence; advice to his brother about his foot problems; is well]

Dear parents and brother, sisters, you write that nothing much was going on at the Styrum fair, here there's nothing going on, nothing at all on Sundays, if we don't do anything ourselves, there are God knows how many meetings every Sunday, and how many houses of prayer and churches there are here. You write that there's a big *Turnfest* [Turner championship] in Mülheim,[28] I wish I were there with you, then we could really have a good time. So Hermann Kempgen and Johann Stemmer have to go into the army, then tell them they should come to America, no one has to be a soldier if he doesn't want to, no one who is a

---

[28]Mülheim, an industrial city in the western Ruhr District, had twenty-two thousand inhabitants in 1880, and was known mainly for its iron, steel, machinery, and coal trade (Neumann [1883], 796).

Figure 33. "I'm also sending a little picture we had taken of ourselves, 2 pictures 2 marks. I and Christian Hinte sitting, then the first is Matth Brus, the second Friedrich Goltschmit, 3 Heinr Kiphan and 4 Heinrich Hinde" (unpublished passage, letter of July 13, 1881).

soldier here has to suffer, they're all volunteers, they get 16 dollars a month and free board and when they've served their time they get a lot of money and a lot of land, there's a fellow living here who was a soldier and doesn't need to work. Dear brother, you write that you want to know why Heisterkamp Bröhkel and Kleber aren't here any more, they were out of work for the time being so they went along with a *Baas* [boss] named Vogt to Cristline,[29] there are new bridges being built there, that's 80 English miles from here. Emil Kleper and Heisterkamp went on from there to the state of Illinois, that's still farther, there Emil's working for a butcher and Heisterkamp is also working there. I and I .derich Golt-schmid are still at the quarry we weren't [---] able to work up until 5 days ago because of the heat. Now it's not so hot anymore, the wind blows through the oat stubble. [5 ll.: comments on how friends are get-ting along and best wishes] Dear brother, nothing will come of the club here, that all petered out, people can't agree on things like that, write and tell me how things are at work, whether you are all still at the same place, Johann I know is back at the mine, how did that happen? [4 ll.: questions; is pleased with the presents] All the best from your son, brother and brother-in-law. [18 ll.: about friends; wishes; quality of cigars]

Massilonn, August 22, 1881

Dear parents and brothers and sisters,

[3 ll.: correspondence; is well] As long as I stay healthy I'm satisfied, there's a lot of cold fever going around, many people are lying sick with fever, some get well quickly some have it for a long time. [8 ll.: corre-spondence; should not send any broad beans; weather] Dear parents and brothers and sisters, I was very glad to hear you got the picture and that you liked it, that makes me very happy. Matth Brus and Hermann Kihpen aren't here anymore, they are in Schickajoh [Chicago]. How they are doing I don't know, they write they are all right, I don't know whether it's true. You write that you got the rye cut and threshed quickly, I'm glad to hear that, as you can well imagine. [15 ll.: news about friends; greetings]

You thought I didn't have any more paper, I thank you for being so thoughtful, but paper, pens and ink are very cheap here, paper is cheaper here than in Germany or in Mülheim, little things don't cost as much as they always say. I'll close for now since it's getting dark, I've been writing on this letter for 3 evenings, it gets dark so early here. I hope my letter

[29]Probably the railroad junction Crestline in Crawford County, Ohio, sixty-six miles west of Massillon.

finds you in the best of health as it found me upon leaving. All the best from your son, brother and brother-in-law Ma Dorgathen

Dear parents, brothers and sisters, write again soon, I'm already waiting for a letter, that business about sending the girls was just a joke, but give my best to all the girls that I know and tell them I'm coming back soon and want to bring one back to America with me. [7 ll.: correspondence; greetings]

Massillonn, November 7, 1881
[almost certainly September 7]

Dear parents and brothers and sisters,

I received your dear letter of August 18 and was very pleased to learn from it that you are all hale and hearty. I am, thank God, also still in good health. It is very hot again here, yesterday Tuesday the 6th, we only worked until 11 o'clock then we stopped because it was too hot, it was 120 degrees, here 3 degrees are as much as 1 degree in Germany, you can figure out how hot it is here. They are now cutting the corn it is 8 to 10 feet high and between the Turkish wheat they planted pumpkins and bottleneck squash, they are ripe now too, they are as big around as buckets and so heavy a man can hardly pick them up, there are whole patches of 10–12 morgens and even bigger with nothing but corn and pumpkins on them, that's quite a sight, you can believe me. Dear parents and brothers and sisters, you wrote me in the letter I should write what it costs here at the post office when I send off a letter, it costs 5 cents or 20 pfennigs just as much as at home when you send a letter to here. Dear sister Julchen, sometime when the weather is nice and I have time I will have myself photographed and send you a picture for your locket, here you can't get a picture taken on Sundays, Sundays everything is closed. [2 ll.: illness and deaths at home] There's so much hot and cold fever going around here it's terrible, lots of people are sick, and mostly the ones who've just arrived in the country, they can't take the climate and are down suffering from fever for months, some even for 1 whole year, as some people here say. [5 ll.: accident at the Sellerbeck mine; asks for details; asks for report about the founding anniversary and the songs that were sung; is not in a choir] And whether washing and ironing cost a lot here, yes, that costs a lot here. But it comes with my board, it has to be or is done by the woman at the boardinghouse, Cristian Hinde's wife. Dear brother Wilhelm, you write that you don't have a good job and want to work in Oberhausen, you're right about that, you have to work where you get paid the most, but you have to watch out that you learn a trade, too, the factory workers who know what they're doing earn a lot of money here, 16 to 20 marks a day. And you, dear parents, I was very pleased that you wrote yourself, I could read it fine, just keep well. And you, dear mother, just don't wear yourself out or worry, so you'll still be healthy when I come back. [3 ll.: Karl should work hard; wishes] All the best from your son and brother / Matthias / [. . .]

To Uncle Heinrich Antroch
Dear uncle, cousins and nieces
[12 ll.: about corn, pumpkins, birds: as in earlier letters] It is still hard to get a job in the mines, there are enough mines but enough miners too. Here they call a mine a *Bänk* and a miner is *Kohl dicker* [coal digger]. Here the mines are 50 to 70 feet deep and it's much healthier work than at home. If only I could lay bricks, since masons earn 10 to 12 marks, the carpenters also earn a lot of money. I am still at the quarry and earn 5 marks. [4 ll.: doesn't know if he will stay in Massilon in the winter] All the best from your cousin / Matthias / please write back

Massillonn, November 18, 1881
[almost certainly September 18]
Dear parents and brothers and sisters,
[2 ll.: is well] It gets dark very early here, we get off work at 6 o'clock and have to walk for a quarter of an hour. If we don't hurry up a bit then we have to eat by lamplight, at 6 thirty it is already dark, then you sit around for a bit, at 8 o'clock or 8 thirty we often go to bed, here you can sleep long in the mornings, we don't have to get up until 6 o'clock in the morning. So from 9 to 6 that's 9 hours, you don't sleep that long at home. [11 ll.: weather—long spell of hot, dry, dusty weather, made work difficult; now rain, cooler] we also got very thin, as you can well imagine, from sweating so much and drinking so much water and not eating very much, you can't get fat from that. Now it should be different, I think, if I stay healthy, that's the main thing here in America, and I keep working then we should do all right, but otherwise the streets aren't paved with gold here like people always write, more lies are written home than truth. Heisterkamp doesn't earn all that much, either. The others, Böhckel, Klehwer, Giesen and some more who left here with Heisterkamp have come back, they want to work in Betlehem, they say things out there weren't any better than here, either, and Heisterkamp earned one and a half dollars at the most. If they could earn so much there, they surely would have stayed, they love that money too. [5 ll.: Johann Bierbroth's wife from Altenessen came to join her husband, four

days after arriving she gave birth to a baby girl] Saturday the 17th it rained all day again, we couldn't work the whole day. [11 ll.: will leave when work at the quarry is finished; greetings; signature]

I'm sending a picture with a real curly-head, you can give it to Karl or little Heinrich, you should give it to the one who's best behaved. In the next letter I'll send a picture, I bought one already but I first have to know what the text on it means.

Massillonn, October 12, 1881

Dear parents and brothers and sisters,

[31 ll: correspondence; is well; weather is now cold; friends; presents] But I didn't get the letter from sister Julgen with the picture, that must have gotten lost, many letters get lost in the mail. Dear parents and brothers and sisters, you write that agents are running around at home, trying to collect people to take them along to America, don't anybody be fool enough to go with agents like that, because I believe it's all a swindle. Here in Massillonn and Navare we can't even get on at the mines, the Schlössers, Damers and everyone are working on the new railroad, they couldn't even get work at the mines, we went all over the place, couldn't get a job anywhere, everywhere people, miners aplenty. [7 ll.: the same; waiting for letters; Karl should work hard] I am still at Christian Hinte's, both of the Hintes had a bad fever, I also couldn't work for 5 days, 2 days we had to take off because of the boss's wife, you can read about that in Johan's letter, and for 3 days I wasn't fit to work I had such a bad cold. But I didn't have the fever, now I'm fine again. So I'm sending this letter with the small pieces of paper. [5 ll.: correspondence; greetings; signature]

Massillon, October 23, 1881

Dear parents and brothers and sisters,

I received your kind letter of September 27 last Saturday. When I came back from work Heinrich Hinde's wife brought along 2 letters for me, 1 from Johann and 1 from you, and I see from it that you are all hale and hearty, I am well again, too, thank God. I had to take off a week, I wasn't fit to work. Now I'm working on the railroad and earn 1 dollar 75 cents or 7 marks. If I stay healthy, I'll have my picture taken. A lot of people are still sick here, it is an unhealthy year and this is not a healthy area. Dear brother, you think I should also go to Pittzburg in the winter. Pittzburg is not far from here, about 70 miles, but I don't think things are any better there and board is so expensive, 4 dollars a week or even more, and I also don't want to go back, since Pittzburg is closer to Nev Jork, you can always go back if there's nothing to be had. [3 ll.: correspondence] Workday evenings you're so tired, on the railroad you have to work hard and straight through, but for 7 marks it doesn't hurt to work a little and if the weather is nice then it's not bad. I wrote in Johann's letter about why we left the quarry and anyway I earn 2 marks more, that's also worth something. [10 ll.: family, wishes; warning to brothers and sisters to behave well toward their parents; signature]

Dear Sister Julchen, you mustn't get angry, but you should be kind to our parents, especially mother since she is at home all day long, she also hasn't got anything, and I'll be coming home this year. I don't want our mother to trouble herself, she has had enough troubles in her life, you should all keep that in mind, since father is always in Duisburg.

Massillonn, November 8, 1881

Dear parents and brothers and sisters,

[14 ll.: correspondence; has had fever; symptoms] Today I'm better, but I was at the doctor's, there I got some powders and he said they would get rid of it fast, but I can't work yet. I think I got it on the *Rigelweg* (new railroad) there you have to sweat even when it's cold and at lunchtime you have to eat outside, and cold food, so you get so cold that you shiver. They work hard here on the railroad, and everywhere else here, too. On the railroad they're almost all English and Irish and those are rough people, the bosses are also Irish, they cheat the Germans whenever they can, that's how it is in this blessed America. I had to put off writing again, because yesterday, Thursday, I came down with fever again, I stayed in bed until this morning, Friday, now I can move around again, I started to write this letter 3 times, I won't be able to work this week, I think I'll go away from here, here it is so unhealthy. The fever is almost everywhere in all of America, they always wrote that it was so healthy in America, that's what the Schlössers and Damers wrote home, but that isn't the case. At home in Germany it's much healthier than here, Wilhelm Schlösser also had a bad time with the fever, 3 men from our house can't work now, me and Herm Billtstein from Alten Essen, he also boards with Crist Hinten, and Frid Goltscheid, I wouldn't have written you about that, but why should I write lies, but you shouldn't worry about me since everyone who comes to this country gets the fever, I think I'll be getting better soon. [. . .] I think that when I am well again, which won't take very long, then I want to leave Massilonn and go where there are more mines. [5 ll.: prices of grain and flour] But traveling isn't any more difficult than at home, not at all, there's a railroad through the wilderness, I've been on it, but if you really want to see wilderness then you have to go to Teckzas, there are still a lot of wild Indians there, that costs about 20 to 25 dollars, I thought I might go there. But here you can't work on dry bread alone because here you have to work hard. Dear brother, I hope you'll have a very good time at the foundation anniversary in Oberhaußen, give my best to the whole Verein Hoffnung and tell them if I stay healthy I'm thinking of singing along with them next year in the fall, since this place isn't any good. The miners who the agents brought here are not doing very well either, as I heard, they're supposed to work where the others are striking, lots of miners are still on strike here, I wouldn't advise anyone to work when there's a strike, then the miners stand outside the mines with loaded rifles, they did that here in the Massilon area too. Here in this strike they wanted to set fire to the Lüher mine, we went down to the mine once and there they were standing with guns too and said we should not think of going to work, but we didn't want to anyway, when someone does go to work, he's in a bad way. I know some who came with an agent who haven't gotten any work at all yet, that's not far from here, I know one fellow, he said that was why they were brought here, because of the strike, they were supposed to work and they don't want to and aren't allowed to. The miners here got 10 cents a ton more, they want more than [---] more. [23 ll.: pictures; greetings; correspondence; wishes; signature]

Massillonn, November 20, 1881

Dear parents and brothers and sisters,

[7 ll.: correspondence; had fever, went to the doctor; is well again] I and Friderich Goltschmidh wanted to leave here for Orangwihlle[30] where the Dorfels are, where Johann Vanscheith wanted to go. They'd written we should come there, there we could earn a lot of money, so Friederich Goltschmid went there, I wanted to follow later, I couldn't go with him right away because I had fever. But yesterday Friederich came back again, there's nothing going on there, we could certainly get work but he couldn't promise that we'd be able to earn enough for board, those are fine countrymen, the widow Dorfelt wrote so glowingly about everything, that they have more than enough of everything, but when you go there you find out the truth, she lives in an old house and is happy just to have enough to eat and it's the same with Karl Dorfelt, her brother-in-law. He has 7 men working for him and still has to work himself, too. There is hardly any work at all and they cheat us into

[30]Orangeville, a village in Trumbull County, Ohio, sixty miles northeast of Massillon.

coming there (the highest wages are 25 to 30 dollars) and make us shell out 6 dollars for the trip, since I have to pay half of it, now when I need the money so badly, that pack of liars. [21 ll.: correspondence; comments; brother Karl's illness; greetings; his family's potato harvest; prices in the United States; friends; correspondence] And you, Brother Wilhelm, so you're not at the factory any more but at the Konkordia mine,[31] you're right, you should go where you can earn the most if the work isn't too hard, you turned 18 in October, 2 more years till you have to go to the army, I'll be curious to hear, Heinrich, how you get along as a soldier. [3 ll.: correspondence; photograph] I think if it is God's will then I'll stay here in America till next summer if it's at all possible. I will stop now, I am healthy again. All the best from America to Styrum from your son and brother Matth Dorgathen. Give my best to brother-in-law Johann and Maria and Heinrich. If I get the fever again and have enough money then I'm coming home. But I still would like to stay here, otherwise everyone will say he hardly left and now he's back again. But I'm over the fever now, I think, and so I still can hold out here. My best to Gottlib Nebel, I'm in good spirits again now

Pitter, don't lose heart, let's drink a schnaps together instead, God doesn't forsake a German. [2 ll.: greetings]

[. . .] Massillonn, December 10, 1881
Dear parents and brothers and sisters,
[2 ll.: is well again] I can now eat well again and we have slaughtered a hog and also have sausages and *Banas* [*Panhas:* Westphalian head cheese] and fresh meat, the two Hindes bought a hog together that weighed 360 pounds, each one had to pay 10 dollars, 40 marks, but then they got it already slaughtered and the sausages already made, there wasn't anything that they or we had to do, their son is a butcher and has his slaughter-house some 20 paces from our place, that's where they bought the hog.

Dear parents, brothers and sisters, I want to tell you that I am no longer working on the railroad but at the *Kohl Bänk* [coal bank] or *Zeche*. On the railroad they cut 1 mark and with only 7 hours work most of the time, then they have 5 marks 40 pfennigs and when the weather is bad you can't work at all. I had to buy my own tools and if you're new at the mine you don't get the best place to work, but it's still better than on the railroad. Here the coal is sifted and then it's paid by weight, you don't get anything for the dirt, and 95 cents or 3 marks 80 pfennigs a ton for the

[31]The Concordia mine in Oberhausen employed 735 men in 1881, produced 204,000 tons, and paid a shift wage of 2.66 marks (Fischer, 56).

lumps, 1 ton is 2000 pounds or 20 scheffels. My comrade that I have with me is from Alten Essen, named Johann Bierbrod. Heinrich Fischdik and Diederich Huth have also written me. [6 ll.: correspondence; greetings; signature]

[undated; probably December 19, 1881]
Dear parents and brothers and sisters,
[5 ll.: is healthy; happy to hear his mother is recovering] Here the weather is so changeable, frost, then snow and then rain but it is so cold in the old plank houses here you wouldn't believe it. [10 ll.: hundreds of people out of work; has not earned much, has spent a lot] Here there is a lot of riffraff running around without work who steal everything that isn't nailed down to the ground, not even far from here, they've held up trains and plundered them. [7 ll.: correspondence; greetings; signature; postscript, will send his mother $10] I had to buy a lot, mine boots for 4 dollars 25 cents and a new suit [. . .] and 2 dollars for our church and 50 cents for the Catholic church and a lot besides and all those damned celebrations, otherwise I'd have earned 40 dollars this month. [9 ll.: work; wishes, greetings, signature]

[. . .] Massillonn, January 12, 1882
Dear parents, brothers, sisters, and brother-in-law,
I received your letter of 23 December today on January 12 and since we aren't working in the mine today I am writing right back. [7 ll.: well again, has an effective medicine for fever; get-well wishes for his mother] Dear brother-in-law Johann and sister Marie, you write you haven't had a letter from me for such a long time and think maybe I can't write because of my hand, I've written almost every week. I'll tell you from October on how many letters and on which days I wrote since I always write it down when I send off a letter, at the end of the letter I'll write them all down. Dear brother Karl, so you don't have school until January 2 and you will get a new reading book [. . .] write me what stories are in it. [2 ll.: greetings to his teacher Ricken] Dear brother Heinrich you wrote that your play went well write me what play it was and who all played in it and if you were in it too. [4 ll.: friends; travel plans] Dear brother, work is bad here at the moment, both in the mines and above ground we've only worked 3½ shifts this month so far, we don't know yet if there'll be work tomorrow. We sometimes work even if there's no coal to be dug, then you go in and get your blasting done since when they dig things usually go very fast here, in general work is very different than at home and with

the blasting, you can't blast when you want to, it starts at four-thirty in the afternoon and then one place after the next then it's one blast after another and the explosions are much bigger than at home, we drill most of the charges 7½ to 8 feet and then the bore hole is much bigger than over there and we put in the charges, 3½ to 4 feet of powder or even more, that really makes a bang each time in the hard coal. Give my best to all my friends and the Verein Hoffnung. Dear sister [2 ll.: correspondence] you ask if I also get letters from Styrum where they were running you down, no, no one from Styrum but you has written me except Gottlieb Nebel, Diderich Huth and Heinrich Fischdick and Vanscheith and Bungert. But they all wrote good things about you. No one has written anything bad about you. Now I'll write you when I wrote the letters. [21 ll.: correspondence;[32] friends; wishes, greetings, signature]

Didn't you get the letter with the new penny and the pumpkin seeds? [3 ll.: greetings]

[. . .] Massillom, 3/5/1882

Dear parents and brothers,

[4 ll.: is well; hopes they are too] I think I'll be leaving Massillom since like I wrote in the last letter, Kristian Himde went to Corning three months ago, that is the place that was written up in the newspaper you sent me. Cristian will be gone 3 weeks tomorrow and wrote that things were pretty good there, better than in Massillonn, and he's having his wife come to Corning and wrote that I should come too, there's no place for Heinrich Hinde to live yet. I wrote him back that if I get work right away I'll come along, I'm now waiting for a letter. [5 ll.: correspondence; possible change of address] Here things are bad again at the mines and I think we'll be going on strike again soon since the bosses want to cut 10 cents a ton, from 95 to 85 cents a ton. Now we've already lost 4 shifts this week because of this, tomorrow is the meeting to decide if we'll work for 85 cents a ton or if we go on strike, if the weather stays good there's enough work above ground and better for us Germans than in the mine, here in the mine where I am the Germans get put down too much, a few days ago we went in to the boss, he should let us blast the overhang[33] that day since it takes three of us men to push the carts up. He lets the English blast the overhang so a mule can pull up the carts. So we said to the boss he should let us blast the overhang too, then the bastard said *det et guth nov vor dötschmän. Gott däm dötschmän kent puschen de Senewebitschen.*[34] That

---

[32]List of fifteen letters, each with date and addressee. Two are not in BABS; four other letters printed here are missing from the list. See n. 15, above.

[33]Layer of stone above the coal seam.

[34]That's good enough for Dutchmen. Goddamn Dutchmen can push the sonofabitches.

means in German *das ist guth genug vor die Deutschen Gott verdamen der deutsche kann noch drücken die Huhrenkinder.* That's what it's like for us Germans. [8 ll.: package too expensive; his brother should learn to play the guitar; greetings, signature]

Backinhamm, April 10, 1882

Dear parents and brothers,

[18 ll.: is well, good wishes; correspondence—many letters get lost; Easter unimportant in the United States; his ocean crossing last Easter] Here they wanted to work on Good Friday since there aren't many Protestants here but we didn't want to work, then the sensible Catholics came and said we aren't going to work on Good Friday, so no one worked, otherwise the English, Irish and Americans all worked, they don't keep any holidays, they're even working today, but we aren't.[35] Dear parents and brothers, work here is going better than at first. But it's not like all of them write. When things really get going, you can earn 2 to 2½ dollars, but after things go well for 1 month then they go bad for 2 months, and the people who came with the agent they also don't get things the way they want, they all have a lot of debts with the *Combanie,* they get 2 dollars cash a month to do what they want with, and when they earn more than what they bought from the *Stor,* it's kept back until they've paid off their debts, that's the way it is here in Backinghamm, and still fresh Germans keep coming here every day, since the people wrote such good things about this place, when work is brisk you can certainly earn good money but the *Truchel* [trouble] is, it's hardly ever brisk, and there's no other work except in the mine. If I leave this place I'll never go anywhere where there's no other work but mine work. Anyone who only wants to be a miner here in America and doesn't want to do any other kind of work just can't make it here, you have to be able to do all sorts of work. Today this job is closed down; tomorrow that one. Dear parents and brothers, I've been away from home for more than 1 year now, the next time we celebrate Easter I think I'll be home again. [3 ll.: correspondence; greetings; signature, wishes]

Dear brother Heinrich, either you should do it or it doesn't matter who, but pass out the cards, and the one card with nothing on it belongs to the girl who works in our house, I've forgotten her name, if there's anyone else who wants a card be so good and write me. Give my best to all the boys and girls in Styrum and tell them I'm coming back soon.

[35]April 10, 1882, was Easter Monday. Easter and Pentecost were (and still are) "double holidays" in Germany: the Sunday and the following Monday are both official holidays.

Bakinghamm, 5/6/1882

Dear parents and brothers,

[3 ll.: correspondence; is well] Things at work here are much worse again. We've been working since the first of May, and they say it'll go on until the 15th, only half a shift a day, from 7 in the morning until 12 noon and yesterday, Saturday and Monday, that's tomorrow, not at all. If it doesn't get better after May 15th then I'll be leaving, since you can hardly earn enough money here for board and that costs a lot here. I am back at Crist Hinde's again and have to pay 16 dollars for board. Everything costs a lot here and nothing is even available. Yesterday the *Supretenter* [superintendent] or in German *Supresendent* from the mining company, we told him that everything in the *Stor* costs too much and that most of the time there's no food there, and then the goddam bastard said that in Corning and Schawene, Schwawene is 5 miles from Backinghamm,[36] that there's where the best *Kohlticker* [coal diggers] in all Ohio are, they *deckten* [dug] coal on bread and water and that's what we should do, too. We never heard anything like that in Germany. Dear parents and brothers there are now so many fresh Germans, Irish, Italians, Saxons and Bohemians and Chinese coming into this country, there are already many more than twice as many as last year, and every day so many keep arriving in Nev Jork that they can hardly all find a place to stay. They write here in the newspapers[37] that we should write home about the truth so that all these people don't all rush into disaster. But there are still too many lies being written, the people who do that can't go back to Germany, they like to have their relatives or friends nearby, then they borrow the money from the *Bas* where they work and send tickets over and then on top of it they lie about having saved the money themselves. There are many people who are 100 dollars in debt and send 2 or 3 prepaid tickets over, but that won't keep on much longer, the *Combanie* and the *Bassen* get cheated too often, yes, that's the game in America, the poor immigrants. Dear brother, you write that Hermann Ludwigs and Gerrad Stollen are back in Styrum again, things aren't nearly as bad here as they were out there. [7 ll.: Hermann Ludwigs should write about his stay in Russia; weather; correspondence] Easter went by like a normal Sunday, then you play cards and sleep. We had quite a lot of eggs. I'll close for now, give my best to all my relatives and friends, brothers-in-law and sisters. All the best from your son / Matth Dorgathen
[4 ll.: greetings to seven friends and the Verein Hoffnung]

[36] The three villages lie close to one another in Perry County. Populations in 1880: Corning, 270 (in 1890, already 1,551); Shawnee, 2,770; and Buckingham, probably less than two hundred (today, forty-five) (USC 1890.18, 326).

[37] In 1882 there were no German-language newspapers in either Stark or Perry County, but several were published in nearby cities such as Cincinnati, Cleveland, and Pittsburgh.

Bakinghamm, 5/28/1882

Dear parents and brothers,

[7 ll.: Pentecost, like Easter, unimportant in America; storm] Write me how Pentecost and the fair went over there. Dear parents and brother, things have still not picked up here, they're still going *slo,* for quite a while we've only been working half days, and if we work a whole day it doesn't go smoothly either and now we have a Irish boss again. There are just too many people here in Bakinghamm, and every day fresh Germans and people from other countries still keep coming. But no one is being taken on. Dear parents and brothers, I think that in 2 weeks I'll be leaving here, first of all because I don't like it here and secondly I want to know now if things are this bad all over America. [. . .] I want to know this, if I come home again then they shouldn't be able to say, he always stayed in one place. I don't know yet where I'll be going, if I leave shortly I'll write you right away. [3 ll.: correspondence; Verein Hoffnung] Go over or ask Stöckman or someone about my passport. I only have a passport for one year and that year is already over, so find out about it. One person says I have to write to Neu Jork to the German Consul, the next says something else, so you should ask about the matter. Dear father and mother and brothers, I think I'll be staying in America this year too and will come back home next year, God willing. [3 ll.: wishes] Last week a fellow arrived here fresh from Oberhausen, Herm Brinkmann, his father is the Protestant sexton in Oberhausen, he boards together with me, he also wants to go right back home, he didn't believe our letters, either, now he can see for himself that we wrote the truth. That's all for now, give my best to all friends, relatives and all the boys and girls in Styrum. Greetings from your son and brother Matth Dorgaten. [2 ll.: greetings]

Bakinghamm, 6/8/1882

[30 ll.: to parents and brothers; birthday wishes; thanks for presents; correspondence; friends; shouldn't allow everyone to read the letter]

Bakinghamm, 6/29/1882

Dear parents and brothers,

[8 ll.: correspondence; fever is going around, but he is still in good health; weather] Work is going well at the moment, this month I earned 40 dollars clear, it's a good thing, too, because I didn't have much money anymore, everything is so expensive here and as long as I've been here, things have been going badly, except this month. But you have to work, work like a mule here, you'd better believe that. Our shift is from 7 o'clock in the morning till 12, afternoons 1 to 5 and 6 and in the evening you usually work another 2 to 3 hours. If the blasts miss, you don't have anything, you have to keep working until you can make another blast and you can't cut the coal much here either, and if you don't blast the coal then you can't do much with a *Pick,* the coal is too hard. [2 ll.: Pentecost] But write me about how the Styrum fair was and the foundation anniversary and what songs you sang at the Hoffung. I hope you had a good time at the fair and that you, Heinrich, had a good time at the founding anniversary, and a lot of fun. [8 ll.: correspondence] I don't have much other news, but I will write you that we've gotten a German doctor, we pay him 50 cents a month, then everything is free, the *Combanie* had sent an English doctor to drive away the German doctor. But when we all went to the German doctor, they sent him a letter last Saturday that if he didn't leave in a few days Negroes would come Saturday night and kill him. And we got wind of it and so last Saturday we set up watch with revolvers, shotguns, axes, and hoes to greet the Negroes, they were on their way, but they didn't get as far as here, they were warned that we were standing guard. And God help them, too, if they had come. When we find the real ones behind it all they'll be strung up. Two fellows from here have already taken to their heels, English people from the *Losche* [lodge: (here) union]. We are also all in the *Losche,* they are firmly on our side, everyone's afraid of the Germans here, they say they are not to be trifled with, they all stick together like brothers are supposed to. [3 ll.: greetings; signature]

Bakinhamm, July 30 [probably 1882]

Dear parents and brothers,

I just want to let you know that I am still, thank God, hale and hearty, oh but not really hearty for here you have to work like a mule these days, things have really been going this week. Last week we had three days of Sunday, we stopped up the hole (didn't work) because they wanted to cut our coal illegally. They took 500 and 1000 pounds off the cart and said there was too much bone coal in with it. Bone coal is bad coal, they don't want to have that, there are bits of stone in it. If they ever take something out of the cart we have to take the next shift off, the second time 2 shifts, the 3rd time 3 shifts and the 4th time the whole month off, we didn't like that. It used to be like this, if they *docken* [dock], *docken* they say for *streichen* [cut], if they *docken* us 4 times in a month then you had to quit altogether, we didn't like that either, so we didn't work for days, now it's like this, if we get docked we only have to take one shift off for each time. [10 ll.: details; weather; doesn't know when he'll be coming home]

Dear brother Heinrich, you write me you have to be a soldier for 10 weeks, oh that doesn't matter, you shouldn't worry about that, I'd like to be a soldier for 10 weeks sometime, and 10 weeks go by quickly, look how fast the time has passed since I left home and have been in America, the land where milk and honey flow like some people think. But they're making a bad mistake, here you have to work like *Häll* [hell]. But it doesn't matter, I still can all right. [18 ll.: correspondence; hopes his parents are in good health]

That's all for now, because they're raffling off a shotgun near here, and I've bought a ticket. Keep yourselves hale and hearty till we meet again, God willing, and give my best to friends and relatives, but greetings to you all in Styrum from America across the great ocean from your son and brother Matth Dorgathen. [4 ll.: friends]

Dear brother-in-law, sister and Heinrich [23 ll.: family; alcohol; broad beans; greetings; signature]

Bakinghamm, August 27, 1882

Dear parents and brothers,

[3 ll.: is well] We are now working again, we had to take off 14 shifts because of a cloudburst, now everything is halfway fixed, things are moving along again now as long as it lasts, if you think things are going to go briskly then something comes along and gets in the way. Things never go smoothly for a whole month as long as I've been here in Massilon, if things don't go smoothly, then soon all the coal mines stop. Here it's still the best on the coal *Bänk*. [7 ll.: asks about friends] Our Heinrich must be a soldier now and he probably doesn't like it very much, but it's only for 10 weeks, write me if there's still a war going on, then I'll go to the German consul and tell him he should send me back to Germany, that I want to help beat the enemy, that I am still a German, and by God I am, too. Dear parents and brothers, we want to build a church here, we all have to give something, I gave one and a half dollars, and we've made up raffle tickets, we bought a watch and a clock that we want to raffle off, a ticket costs 50 cents, and we want to write to Germany, maybe to Mülheim and Styrum a sheet of paper with all our names on it, and here to the Ohio Synod[38] then we should get enough money together. Now we hold some religious meetings on Sundays at one of our comrade's. Sunday morning there's singing and reading from the Bible, and then there's a short prayer and then we all go home. This

[38]One of the Lutheran denominations, founded by clergy from Pennsylvania in 1818 (Owen [1947]).

afternoon a pastor wants to come from Lecksintonn[39] 15 miles from
here, he wants to hold a service here this afternoon. But I don't think he'll
be coming, it rained all night and then it's so muddy here. [3 ll.: greetings, signature]

Backing hamm, October 1, 1862 [definitely 1882]
Dear parents and brothers,
   [5 ll.: correspondence; address] If you would be so kind, please send
me a translator, a book where English is translated into German, but
something different from the other one, but not expensive, the other one
got away from me. [4 ll.: greetings, signature, address]

Bakinhmamm, December 17, 1882
Dear parents and brothers,
   [13 ll.: correspondence; is well] A few Sundays ago we went to Logen.[40] That was quite a trip, first we went by wagon to Stretzwille[41]—6
miles, and then by train from Stretzwille to Logen, a new Lutheran
church was being consecrated there, they'd separated off from the others,
the Lutherans say they don't keep the true faith and the ones who have
the new church say the old church doesn't teach or have the true faith, it's
really something here with religion. We drove from Bakinghamm in an
old wagon and what a road, up a steep hill and then down again, we were
mighty glad when we got to Stretzwille, since the wagon was so full we
kept expecting it to turn over any minute. But it went fine, then we got
on the train from there to Logen, the celebration was very nice, first there
was singing by a mixed choir, German, and then a sermon in German,
then a sermon and singing in English, then we went to a hotel for lunch,
in the afternoon back to church and then back from Logen to Stretzwill.
On the way back the English got into a fight on the train. [5 ll.: return
trip]
   Dear brother, you write that you are back home again and heartily sick
of the soldier's life, that I can well imagine. [5 ll.: details; pipe bowl] But I
think that on payday in April I'll stop working for now in America and
will come home again. [6 ll.: details; happy about the good news from
home] Things here are very bad now, and at the moment, there's nothing
going on, last week we went on strike, now the *Companie* has stopped
production, we haven't earned anything in almost 2 weeks and it could

[39]New Lexington's population was 1,357 in 1880 (USC 1890.18, 326).
[40]Logan, in Hocking County, had a population of 2,666 in 1880 (USC 1890.18, 320).
[41]New Straitsville, in Perry County, had a population of 2,782 in 1880 (Ibid., 326).

be a long time before we go back to work again. Tomorrow we've got a meeting, then it'll be decided when and how. If it turns out bad we'll still have months of Sundays, but I was lucky to get a letter last week from my old comrade from Massilonn, he's in the state of Illinois, that's in the West, very far away, it costs 16 dollars from here. I can get good work there, if they break the strike here then I'll be going there. [4 ll.: greetings; signature; asks for an answer soon; regards from a friend]

Bakinghamm, December 25, 1882

Dear parents and brothers,
[8 ll.: correspondence] We are back at work again, but work is going very badly, it's never been as bad as this, if I weren't thinking of coming home in the spring then I'd go somewhere else, but I'll stay here as long as I can manage to get by until I come back to Germany. If it gets too bad then I'll have to go somewhere else. Dear parents and brothers, today is Christmas but days like that here are nothing special, we've had so so many Sundays and now the three Christmas holidays, it's hard to know how to pass the time. [17 ll.: Christmas wishes; expresses sympathy to Karl for his toothache; glad to receive a letter written by his parents, replies to its contents; wishes, greetings; signature]

Bakinghamm, January 7, 1883

Dear parents and brothers,
I want to let you know that I received your kind letter with the lovely present yesterday. I was at a baptism at Crist Hinte's, and then I said I want to go to the post office, I think there's a letter for me, and I was right, there were two there for me. I got the first one from brother-in-law Jann, then the *Post Clerk* said *ist det aut ju Letter,* is that also your letter, and he showed me the package, I said: *Jes* and took the package too. [3 ll.: thanks for presents] Thank you, too, for the others that were with the book, I was very pleased with that. Dear brother Karl, I am very glad you wished me luck and blessings, you should keep on like you wrote me and study hard and be obedient, when I come back to Styrum and if we don't like it anymore in Germany then we'll all go together to America, I know of enough jobs now, you should buy yourself a small translator and learn English, for the language here in this country is better than everything, that's what you should do, Karl. Dear parents and brothers, I thought Uncle Heinrich got 150 marks from me and on the receipt he only wrote down 75 marks, how did that happen, did he only lend you 75 marks for my journey to America, dear Mother, then it's all right, then the other

money is for you. [3 ll.: wants information] I am glad that I could do something nice for you with the money, I'm glad to do it. Dear parents and brothers, things here are the same as always, except that things are moving again and it's a good thing, too, so I can get together enough money in case I want to come home. That's all for now, since this is the second letter I've written this morning, this one and one to Peru La Salle in Ilinois,[42] I can get a job there anytime, too. [9 ll.: greetings, signature; asks for an answer soon]

Bakinghamm, Jan. 30, 1883

Dear parents and brothers,

[14 ll.: correspondence; lost letters] Believe me, dear parents and brothers, a lot of ships go down and then the letters go down with them. [5 ll.: Christmas tree back home] Dear parents and brothers, Fridrich Goltschmid and I had been planning to come home in April, but now people write from Germany and also the newspapers here write that things are so bad in Germany because of the flooding, that everything is going badly, everything is so expensive and it's bad with work, too. Write and tell me how much of all that is true, if it's true then I'd rather stay here for a while. [13 ll.: good prospects in Buckingham for the summer, should he stay or go back] You write me that Friederich Töpp is also back home again, what happened, didn't he like it in America, or didn't his wife want to come, and where was Friederich last living in America, you should go see him and give him my best regards. [4 ll.: should find out what line he traveled and how much it cost] They sent me a notice that there was a money order for me at the post office, I had to pick it up myself, but I thought it was a registered one, then you have to pick it up and sign for it, I went to the post office and asked Scharlie *ist Ee Register Letter her fer Mie,* in German *Karl ist ein Eingeschriebener Brief hier vor mich.* Scharlie or Karl is the name of the post office clerk, then he said *Jes (ja)* then I had to sign for it and then it was *Oll Reith.* That's all till next time. [11 ll.: greetings, signature; regards to friends; is sending along the lyrics of a song]

Bakinghamm, March 1, 1883

Dear parents and brothers,

[3 ll.: correspondence; is well] But I'm off work again, they're changing the scales and the sieve the coal goes over, we didn't work yesterday,

[42]Peru, La Salle County, a town with coal mining and metal industry, 420 miles west of Buckingham.

and they say it can take the whole week. Here in America you sure have a lot of Sundays, but when things get going then you have to work very hard. Otherwise things are much the same, except that on payday there was a fight here in Bakinghamm between two English and one of them, our driver who drives our carts from the face cut up the other one's arm so badly that it had to be taken off, they say he's going to be convicted today at court. The English are mad at our driver because he used a knife, they don't usually use knives. Dear parents and brothers, I am sorry about Cristian Röschen that he lost his life like that. After all, in Germany more people die in the mines than here in America. [9 ll.: correspondence] So, Friederich Töpp is now working at Alstaden and told you that if he hadn't loved his wife and children so much he wouldn't have come back to Germany. He's not far wrong about that, if I had a wife and children here I wouldn't come back to Germany so soon, either. But I'm glad now that I don't have a family, so I can come home when I want to, and if I have money and things are going well at home then I'm coming home, God willing, this spring I think. But I don't know if I can still get along with work there, but I think I can, and if not, I'll go back to America if I can. Man proposes, God disposes. [16 ll.: Karl should pay attention at school; John Bierbrod writes from Illinois that there are good jobs there; his parents should write if they need money; greetings, signature; regards to friends; weather]

Bakinghamm, April 22, [probably 1883]
Dear parents and brothers,
   I just want to let you know that I am still hale and hearty, and that it has almost been 5 weeks now since I got a letter from home, 5 weeks ago on Wednesday I got your last letter. [4 ll.: worried about his mother's illness] The Goldschmids and Hintes don't get any letters anymore at all, I think the letters keep getting lost. Every time the mail comes, it always comes every other day, then we go down to the post office, but there's never anything for us there. Yesterday I got a letter from the state of Illinois from Johann Bierbrod, he writes I should move to Ilinois, but things aren't going all that well there, either. Here things have been very bad up to now, I only earned 14 dollars last month, I was lacking 3 dollars to pay for my board, and if I want to earn enough for board this month then things have to get better than they've been. It's good that I'd saved a few dollars, otherwise I'd have had to go into debt, but if I can't earn enough for board this month, either, then I still won't have to go into debt. They all say the next month will be better, last year things really got going in June, when things really get going here then you have to work almost all

day and night, but that doesn't matter, then you also earn *Moni* (*Gelt*) we've been having an easy time of it for quite a while, so when things get going you're able to work hard again. [7 ll.: weather] A lot of Germans are leaving, this month a lot of them left, the English take their places, the *Bas* doesn't like us Germans. Before a year is out there won't be very many Germans here in Bakinghamm, they'll all be gone. [. . .] I have a great plan in mind but I'll write you about it some other time, that is to go west and buy land. I'll write more about that the next time. I'm going to school every evening, with the last teacher I only went to school two evenings a week, but he left, now we've got another teacher, last week he started up evening school again in English, speaking, reading and writing. That's all for now, I hope our dear mother gets well again soon. [5 ll.: greetings, signature; correspondence]

Bakinghamm, April 30, 1883

Dear parents and brothers,

[4 ll.: correspondence; is well] Work is going somewhat better, I'll earn enough for board this month after all, and they say that after May 1st things will really get going, that would be good. Dear parents and brothers they write here in the newspapers that the workers in Germany want to strike, write me the truth of the matter, I don't believe it yet, they aren't so quick to go on strike in Germany as they are here. Here in Stretzwille, that's the name of the place, it's 5 miles from here (I have often been in Stretzwille) anyway in Stretzwille they've docked the teamsters, the mule drivers, of one of the mines 25 cents, they used to get 2 dollars and now they're supposed to get 1 dollar 75 cents, the teamsters don't like that and because of the teamsters all of Stretzwille is at a standstill and that's a lot of mines, it's been almost 3 weeks now and no one knows how it's going to end. They are very quick to go on strike here. [12 ll.: friends; weather; the soldier's life is unpleasant; best wishes for the foundation anniversary and Hoffnung] It won't work to come home yet, things have been going too badly and I don't have enough money anymore, and in my last letter I wrote you about buying land, in Teksas. Teksas Statth or Statdh Teksas is far off in the west, near Colifonien, that's a ride of about 3 days and 3 nights. There's still a lot of good cheap land out there, they want to start a German colony there, our German doctor wants to go there and buy 42,000 acres of land, and next spring we'll go out there. An acre costs between 1 dollar and 3 dollars an acre, a lot of people have signed up with the doctor, I have too, and the land doesn't have to be paid for immediately, you get years to pay it off, everyone gets about 80 acres, you can get more, too, and the farm equipment doesn't have to paid off right away, either, the doctor will get a better price for buying so much all at once [. . .] and livestock is dirt cheap out there. In another letter I'll write what it all costs, and Teksas is the healthiest place there is. Write me right back what you think of all this. [7 ll.: greetings, signature; asks about his uncle's wish to emigrate]

Bakinghamm, June 1, 1883

Dear parents and brothers,

[3 ll.: correspondence; is well] Work went fine from May first to May 23, after that we didn't have any work, they say it'll start up again on Monday, there was a storm on the lake our coal gets taken across, the storm ruined the loading bridge[43] and a lot of other things and many people say the coal loaders were on strike, we don't know ourselves exactly. But this much we do know, that we've already had 6 days off and that there won't be any work until Monday, it's a shame, otherwise we'd have made a good wage, but we still made 30-odd dollars in the month of May. I think things will start up again on Monday. [14 ll.: hasn't received a letter for four weeks; complains about friends not answering his letters; birthday greeting to his parents] I think if things go well for a couple more months then I'll be coming home. I don't have enough money yet, things were too slow this winter, I think they'll get better now here. In the state of Ilinois they're on strike and they say strikes are starting up in Panselvanin. It is terrible with all the strikes here in this country, if you want to get somewhere you have to work in the country, in farming, that's still worth a lot, there's always a lot of *Trubel* at work in the mines and factories. Either this month or next the German doctor is leaving for Teksas and maybe another German as well to look at the land we signed up for and see where the German colony should be. [3 ll.: pleased at Karl's success at school and his mother's recovery] I'll be coming home when I can, and if things are good in Teksas then we'll all move there. That's all for now. All the best from your son and brother Matth Dorgathen. [2 ll.: greetings]

Bakinghamm, June 20 [probably 1883]

Dear parents and brothers,

[4 ll.: correspondence; is well] But things at work are still not going well, production is slow. There are too many *Minners* here and we have to

---

[43]The lake Dorgathen mentions is Lake Erie, and the loading bridge was at the port of Cleveland.

stapen [stop] a lot (take time off) and in other places they're on strike a lot, almost all of Ilinois is on strike. Ilinois is the state after Ohio, there the companies have brought in *Pläklinge* [blacklegs] to work where the others are on strike, *Pläklinge* are real riffraff, when the others are striking for their fair rights then they do the work. They aren't in and won't join the *Union* (*Losche*). Anyway, the *Bläk linge* wanted to work, so the women and girls came and chased them away and took over the mine and then the army came and then they fought with the *Minners*. But the strikers were defeated. The newspapers and magazines are full of the story. All Ilinois is in an uproar, in many places the workers have won, that's good, people here usually stick together more than in Germany, even though now and then there's a *Pläckling* among them. The word *Pläkling* comes from *Neger* [Negro], the Negroes are sent everywhere where there's a strike, *Pläck* means *schwarz* [black] in English, so they compare the whites who work here when there's a strike with the Negroes, *Schwarz ling* in German, and here *Pläckling*. [5 ll.: didn't buy land in Texas, only an option] Anyway I'm coming home and if I'm going back to Germany, I could forget it anyhow. But my dear family, if I could have forgotten about you then I'd have left Bakinghamm a long time ago. But this way I'll be staying here and see to it that I get the money so I can come home again, otherwise I've had a lot of letters from America saying I should go here or there but it costs a lot to travel here. [4 ll.: when you arrive at your destination, you don't have any more money] I thought a lot about it before I wrote, you write that you want to send me the passage money, but I'd rather wait a bit until I have enough myself, for what would people say if you sent me the money and dear mother, you've already bought me a lot of things, that is very nice. I'm coming home soon, and dear brother, I was glad to hear that your foundation anniversary went so well and the singing was so good, and write to me sometime. [9 ll.: weather; greetings, signature; is sending a few potato bugs, of which there are vast numbers]

Bakinghamm, July 29, 1883

Dear parents and brothers,

[3 ll.: thanks for letter, best wishes; is well] Me and Goltschmid, we wanted to leave Bakinghamm because things were so bad here, we wanted to go to Baltimore, that is a port town, we wanted to go there and work there and see if we couldn't get across the ocean for free or for half the money, we decided on tomorrow, June 30, so I thought I wouldn't write any earlier and would write from Baltimore, but now production is up, now we still want to stay here. [8 ll.: details about work] But we're still earning money even though work is so poor but we're using up a lot of blasting powder without getting much out of it. Yesterday morning at 12 o'clock we set off a charge that had 44 inches of powder that brought us 8 tons of coal. When we went back to work at 1 o'clock after lunch we wanted to load the cart then I said to my *Bodie* [buddy] listen, Julius, what's that noise, we listened and there it was again, *All Recht,* we had to run away with our cart and our nice 8 tons of coal got buried and we couldn't work all yesterday afternoon, rocks were still falling down. Tomorrow I'm going in to the *Bas* to see if he can't give me another *Schapp* [job] or we'll start closer to the face, there the over-burden ceiling is better. Dear parents and brothers, last Monday there was another real *Feith* [fight] day, *Fecht* day, there were two men playing for 100 dollars, the game is throwing with big heavy rings, they stick a kind of iron rod into the ground, but all the way into the dirt so you can't see it and they put a piece of paper where the *binn* [pin] is and then they start pitching 20 to 30 feet away and even farther. Whoever pitches the most onto the iron pin wins. They pitched from morning till night, then one of them, a Scotsman, won the hundred dollars, there was one English and one Scott, also a coal *miner,* and in the evening the fighting or boxing started up between the two sides, they boxed each others' faces more black and blue than ever before. At the end they even pulled *Rewolwers,* but there wasn't any shooting. The brawl went on far into the night. Dear parents and brothers, didn't you get the letters of June 1 and of June 20? In one I sent along 3 Colorado beetles. [. . .] Dear parents and brothers, on the 4th of June [*sic*], the biggest holiday in the North American Union, there was a photographer here, we all drank one too many, it's like that here on the 4th of July, and I had my picture taken, but it's a very poor likeness. [5 ll.: greetings; signature; photograph] It's not a good picture, I think you could use it to scare cats with, but I do want to send you a copy.

Bakinghamm, August 26, 1883

Dear parents and brothers,

[3 ll.: correspondence; is well] Work is going quite well now, if I stay healthy I can earn a good wage this month, but now you have to work day and night and like a mule, but that doesn't matter, then you also earn *Moni,* then I and several other comrades will be coming home perhaps before the winter. They say next month they won't pay 80 cents, on September 18 then the half a year for 70 cents will be over and then there will be another half a year for 80 cents. Many people say the *Companie* won't pay 80 cents and others say the *Kompanie* will pay it, we'll just have to wait and see, you can't believe anyone here, here the babes learn to tell lies when they're still lying in their cradles. [12 ll.: correspondence; weather] They want to start a German singing club here today, the first rehearsal is tomorrow, they asked me to come and sing too, I want to stop by and see what the singing is like. I don't know if I'll join since I want to come home anyway. Dear Brother Karl, I am glad that you are studying so hard. [3 ll.: should buy himself an English dictionary—perhaps they will all come to America] I can't go to school now, we don't have the time for it, and if I come home this year I won't be going anymore, otherwise I will. Dear parents and brothers, you write that your church will be finished soon. We don't have a pastor anymore, he went to the state of Indiana, I don't know when we'll get another one. [6 ll.: good wishes, signature, greetings]

Bakinghamm, September 23, 1883

Dear parents and brothers,

[4 ll.: correspondence] If there had been a strike I would have gone to Baltimore and worked there and would have come home, but the *Companien* here are paying 80 cents and work is going well; so I think I've lived here through all the bad times and for 70 cents and now we get 80 cents a ton and it's going well, as long as it lasts I'll stay here, then if I stay healthy, I can bring a few dollars with me when I come home. [2 ll.: nothing new] Except now we have a glee club, yesterday the books arrived from Cinzinatie. We have the *Regensburger Liederkranz* [songbook] that we had at the Gesangverein Hoffung in Styrum, this afternoon we're going to sing it for the first time. I'm curious to see which song we'll sing. Our director is a German teacher and an excellent fellow and I think a good director, we'll see. [3 ll.: work] Day before yesterday we had a bad thunderstorm, it rained very hard. When we got to work yesterday morning it was all full of water, it all came in from above through the shaft, so yesterday we worked for wages, the shift wage for a *Minner* is 2 dollars here, that is good money. This month we've already worked several days on daily wage, when something breaks then I go to the boss, then he says (*Oll Reiht ju fikset*) *Oh schon guth mach es wider guth oder Recht.* [14 ll.: friends; good wishes; signature; greetings]

Bakinghamm, October 7, 1883

Dear parents and brothers,

[11 ll.: is well; thanks for letter of September 9; friends; earthquake in Panama; correspondence] You asked if I still had the guitar, oh yes, I still have it and still play it, but soon I'll have to sing, we have a good glee club, it's called Sangeslust, we sing twice a week, Wednesdays and Sundays, we're singing the song *Schlesswig Holdstein Meer umschlungen* [Schleswig-Holstein surrounded by the sea], No. 79 in the Regensburger Liederkrans. We can already sing it pretty well. Today we're going to get a new song. I sing my old part again, *först* tenor and still enjoy singing. Dear parents and brothers, now it's all over with our dangerous work. When we went to the mine on Wednesday everything had caved in all the way to the entrance, our boxes and tools lay underneath in the front and we had to dig for three hours until we got them back again. Now we have to open up a new *Rum* [room], the first 6 shifts you don't earn anything, you have to go in at first 12 feet narrow and when we're 15 feet in then we widen the *Rum*, then it'll get better again. [4 ll.: details] Dear parents and brothers, we have a pastor again from Logen, he comes to Bakinghamm twice a month and holds a service, and otherwise I still have books, for example I have two Testaments, one from home and one from Piladelvia and the hymnals they have here, there are a lot of godly texts in them, I also have a lot of good papers from London and Nu Jork. You write me *jur leik no de-Worken op de Peicknick ei ges jur gett Lessi ower der,* that is you don't want to work, I think you must have had a good time at the Oberhausen fair. [7 ll.: greetings, signature, greetings]

Bakinghamm, December 2, 1883

Dear parents and brothers,

[21 ll.: is well; concerned about lack of letters; Goltschmid has left for home; work is hard] By God, the coal is hard, that is the *Meinen* (cutting), it's almost like iron pyrite in the dirt. I had to buy new picks and even they aren't good enough, they go dull all the time, then I have to go out to the smith's and have them sharpened and work like a *Miul (Esel)*. But now my *Rum* has gotten a bit better, there's not so much rock sulfur and when that gets cleared away, then the coal will be good, when I've gotten in further then the coal will be good. We have two singing rehearsals this week, I didn't go to the last rehearsals last week since I had a cough, but this morning I sang along, a new song from the Regensburg *Helden Gesang in Wahala*. We also sing the *Schmidelid* and *Bundeslied* from the Regensburg [songbook], and *Schleßwig Holtstein, Was hab ich denn meinem Feinsliebchen gethan,* and *im Pokal deutschen Wein,* that's the best one, and *Nun schläft der Sänger* and *Brüder last uns lustig sein,* we've practiced all of these, but I like *im Pokale deutschen Wein* the best, that is a nice song and easy. [8 ll.: greetings, signature; asks about Goltschmid]

Bakinghamm, January 25, 1884

Dear parents and brothers,

[42 ll.: thanks for letter; hard winter; angry that Goltschmid kept 50 cents of his present to the family] I am glad that you have a servant girl again, so mother doesn't have to do all the work alone, I am sorry to hear that brother Wilhelm's foot is infected, it should get better soon, God willing. [6 ll.: greetings, signature]

Bakinghamm, August 17, 1884

Dear parents and brothers,

[6 ll.: thanks for letters; is well] These are bad times now for the other companies, in the ones in Schawnee, Stretzwille and Longstreth and Maunddenzitti[44] and other mines besides, the *Minners* are still on strike, now we have to pay 1 and a half dollars a week for the strikers and then there's a kind of collection, things are very bad there, there are about 5000 *Minners* who are striking and some are already going hungry. But they aren't giving in, anyway they're getting support from all corners, bars and stores and in fact all the business people have to give something, there are two in Corning, one has a big *Stor,* a *Stor* is a shop where you can buy everything and the other one, a Jew, also has a big business, the two of them didn't want to give anything, so everyone said right away, we don't want to buy anything from those scoundrels, they hung up public notices at the mines that they didn't want to do anything for the Hocking Welli strikers, now nothing's being bought from those two goddamned pigheads. And secondly there are two men working here with us at 19 who didn't want to give anything, so we held a meeting and it was decided if they didn't give something they'd have to leave, we went to the *Bas* and told him that, he said *Oll Reiht,* so he talked to the fellows, and then they wanted to pay after all. You can't kid around with the English in things like that, since there aren't many Germans here any more. Last week on Saturday we were all called out of the mine at about 11 o'clock for a meeting, they said that our *Companie* was sending coal to the Haking Welli *Compani,* and a lot of people wanted us to *stopen (Aufhören)* work immediately and send two men to Corning to the *Supresendent.* But work started up again in the afternoon and a committee was sent to Corning, it turned out that it was all a mistake. If it'd been true, we'd have stopped work immediately. A lot of goddamned *Bläck-*

---

[44]The towns of Shawnee and New Straitsville (each ca. 2,800 inhabitants in 1880) and Monday Creek Township (1,100 inhabitants in 1880) in Perry County and Longstreth in Hocking County all lie within a ten-mile radius of Buckingham (USC 1890.18, 326).

linge who want to work cheaper keep coming, but then after a couple of days they go away again, they don't have the knack, and things get bad if a lot of them show up. [. . .] I'll be curious to see what happens next September, then the half year for 70 cents is over and we're supposed to get 80 cents, I'll be curious to see if that happens without trouble, I don't think so, things look bad. That's all for now till the next time. All the best from your son and brother Matth Dorgathen. [4 ll.: money matters]

Borkinghamm, August 30, 1884

Dear parents and brothers,

[3 ll.: correspondence; is well] You wrote I should write about how the children are confirmed here. Oh, that's almost just like in Germany, except that the pastor is nicer to the children. I liked it a lot better than at home, the pastor did a much nicer job, in fact all the pastors here aren't so stuck up, a lot more plain than at home, not so proud. After he gives the sermon then he goes to a house in the parish and then they send out for 10 cents worth of beer, then we talk about everything, about Germany, about work, and every now and then someone tells a story, he's not a hypocrite like most of them are, he's hardly older than I am, but he is a good pastor, that's the best thing. Dear parents and brothers, you write me that work at home isn't going very well, that's too bad, and that you have to take time off, and from Essen and Borbeck they write that things are even worse, I don't know the names of the mines, they've let almost all of the workers go, is that so? Then things there must be even worse than where you are. You wrote I should write about the two who were killed in the accident. One died immediately [. . .] he was from Borbeck, just a boy of 16 years and not in the union, and the other's name is Joseph Sons, from near Borbeck, he belongs to the union but he isn't dead yet, he's in the hospital in Kolombus. He broke his back, but the people who've gone to visit him say he'll get better. He's lying in a rubber bed filled with water, so he won't get bed sores. Dear parents and brothers, things look very bad here at the moment, yesterday we did our last work for 70 cents and they say the *Compani* doesn't want to pay 80 cents. We had a meeting the day before yesterday about what we should do, two representatives were elected and sent to Coring to see what they're doing there. It was decided that we should keep working until September 11, then there's a convention in Kolombus then they'll decide what will happen, whether we get 80 cents or whether we should work for 70 cents or whether we should go on strike, and the last one is the most likely, I think. The others, the Haking Welli I wrote about, they are still on strike, knocking over trains and telegraph poles and beating up *Bläcklinge*.

That's all until next time, then I'll write more about it. All the best from your son and brother Matth Dorgathen. [3 ll.: thanks for letter written by his parents]

Bakinghamm, September 28, 1884

Dear parents and brothers,

[3 ll.: correspondence; is well] But as far as work goes things are absolutely terrible. Dear parents and brothers, I should have written earlier, I certainly had enough time, but I wanted to wait and see first what would happen, because since the beginning of the month all the mines of our *Companie* are at a standstill, we worked for 6 days, then the *Companie* closed all the mines and everything is still closed and we don't know when things will get going again [2 ll.: the same] and the other *Companien* only pay 70 cents and the *Minners* are working for that, that was decided in Colombus at the convention until the coal price goes higher. Here the *Meiners* are all spread out in the other mines, all the bad shafts are now being worked where no miners used to go. Last week a German from Borbeck was killed in an accident in No. 12, he is the first one to go into our Protestant cemetery. The ones who aren't married here have a hard time getting work, in most mines, if they find out someone is working there who isn't married and he hadn't worked there before, he has to quit. So, dear Brother Heinrich, if you want to come over here, if I were you, I would wait until the bad times are over, because in many places over here things are even worse than here in Bakingham. That's because of the presidential election, that's next month, when that's over, then things will get better. Every 4 years a new one is elected and here the English say it's always like this before an election. As I said, I don't advise anyone to come to America now because at the moment things are pretty bad. The Hocking Wellie miners are still on strike, they're supposed to get only 50 cents a ton, they won't do that. Several fights between guards and *Minners* have already broken out, guards and miners too have been shot dead and one mine has been burned—

Dear parents and brothers, tomorrow morning I'm going out to look for work, since I'm so tired of lying around, 20 miles from here there are coal mines. Yesterday I talked to some English, they want to go there tomorrow and I'm going along, there is an awful lot to carry with all the tools, when you go from one place to another. Dear parents and brothers, I wanted to come home, but when I got your letter that things are so terribly bad I decided not to. [. . .] I thought, then it's better to stay here and rest a while. But I'm tired of that, too, now. That's all until next time. Thousands of good wishes from your devoted son and brother Matth. Dorgathen. [2 ll.: greetings]

[enclosed on a separate sheet:]

Dear parents and brothers,

Two fellows from Oberhausen are coming home, named Heinrich Eng and another one named Haas, neither of them were in the country for very long, but they're both a couple of liars and braggarts. They don't know anything about work here. The few months Haas was here, he had the best job, in the pillar, and now he boasts that no one has to work hard over here, but we work harder and longer than at home. [6 ll.: details; correspondence] Don't let anyone read this page.

Bakinghamm, November 23, 1884

Dear parents and brothers,

[7 ll.: correspondence; is well; work is not going well; his brother should not come] The other mines in Hocking Wellie are still on strike and we still have to pay 6 dollars and more a month, but I think the *Minners* are going to win, since the *Companien* will have to start up again or else they'll go broke. All together they've already lost almost five million dollars and the miners can hold out since they get support and the *Companien* can't hold out much longer, the scoundrels. Dear parents and brothers, I am glad the potatoes turned out so well at home and that the grain is growing again and that you've slaughtered a hog and still have another one in the pen. Things are better at home at the moment than they are here. You can make enough for board and some extra money, and when the month is over you break even, but it doesn't matter, it should get better soon. [10 ll.: his brother Wilhelm's birthday; relatives] I wrote you in my last letter that I wasn't out of work for long, that we left Londdelle right away and that I'm now in Coring in N 11 with Schmitz and Schlinemann, working for foreman Schlingeman's brother. August Schlingeman asked me to ask you to give his best to his brother the foreman. We're getting another president from the other party. The Democrats, mostly workers, have carried the day, now things should get better soon. I'll send the future president in the letter. [8 ll.: greetings, signature; pleased to get letter from his parents; reunion]

Corning, January 4, 1885

Dear parents and brothers,

[4 ll.: correspondence; is well] But as far as work goes, things are still very bad. The old mines are still at a standstill and there are lots of people without work and the Hoking Wellie miners are still on strike. Here the mines are overcrowded and you can't earn much and you still have to pay one and a half dollars every week for the strikers, they aren't giving in, the strike has lasted 6 months already and can still go on for a long time. That won't matter if only they win, otherwise we'll have to work for less and we won't be doing that any too soon, that's for sure. [6 ll.: weather] Christmas and New Year's went well, we sent out for some beer at New Year's and had a bit of fun, I would have liked to have sent over a small Christmas present but times are too bad, you can't earn much more than enough to cover your board. I had saved a bit but then I didn't work for two months and I traveled around looking for work, and then I didn't have any more money. But I still have enough so I can pay for my board for a couple of months and I'm still earning money every day, though not very much. Things have gotten better, the good old Lord still lives here in America like in Germany. If I'd known how it would be this winter I'd have come back to Germany. But no one wants to go with their hands completely empty and so you keep on going, [. . .] when I've been here for one more year or stay here then I'll get my second papers. I have the first ones already, you only have to be in the country for 5 years then you're an American citizen. When I come home I probably won't even recognize Styrum anymore, you write it's so built up. No single day goes by without my thinking a hundred times about my dear old home, you can believe that. [11 ll.: New Year's and birthday wishes; signature; greetings][45]

[45]Undated entry in a notebook (BABS): In the year 1881 / My Travels to America

I, Matth Dorgathen, departed from Oberhausen on April 5, 1881, at 6:25 in the morning, arrived in Antwerp at 1 o'clock in the afternoon, departed from Antwerp on April 6, at 4:30 in the afternoon with the ship Kauta Hamiltonn for Harwich, arrived there on April 7 at 5 o'clock in the morning, then traveled by train at 6 o'clock to London and arrived at 8:15 in the morning in Londonn. Stayed in Londonn from April 7 to April 10, then traveled by train on April 10 at 12 o'clock in the morning to Liverpool and arrived there about 2 o'clock and from there embarked on the ship Viktoria and sailed from Liverpool on April 10 at 2 o'clock in the afternoon and landed on April 21 at 6 o'clock in the morning in the state of Kanada, the town of Hallifacks, stayed there until April 22 and went from there at 9:30 to Neu Jorck. [5 ll: trip from New York] We arrived in Navare on Thursday, April 28 at 11 o'clock in the morning. We remained out of work until May 9, on May 10 we went to Massillonn and worked there in a quarry until October 10, and then I was sick until October 15, and then worked on the Rellroth (Bahn) until November 5 and then was sick until November 24 and started work again on November 25 until November 27, was sick again until December 2 and started work on December 3 at Rossels Kohl Bänk. In December we worked 12 shifts and in 1882, 13 in January and 17½ shifts in February. Thus I worked at Rossels Bänk until February 28, 1882, and then quit working there, since they went on strike, they wanted to cut 10 cents off the price of the ton, instead of for 95 cents we were supposed to get 85 cents. I stayed in Massillon without work from March 1 to March 15 and left for Backinghamm near Corning on March 15 at 4 o'clock in the morning, and arrived at 7 o'clock in the evening, 225 miles from Massilon, and started work in Mine 19 in Backinghamm on March 17, 1882. I worked there until August 1884, then Mine 19 was shut down and I went without work for 3 months. At the end I got a job in Corning in Mine 11, I worked there from November 26 until last February, then I stopped working there, since we got a 10 cent cut per ton and had to pay 10 cents a ton for the strikers in the Hocking Welli. Thus it had been 70 and 80 per ton and now 70 and 60 cents and 10 cents per ton for the strikers in Hocking Wallie Thal, so now only 50 cents per ton. Then I got everything ready to come home, and left Corning on March 5, 1885, at 7 o'clock in the morning and arrived in Kolombus at 11

Matthias Dorgathen's wish to return to America was not to be fulfilled. He returned to Styrum in March 1885, and the following January
he married Anna Trautmann (1854–1924). At the end of October, a
daughter was born. But then, according to family tradition, he contracted stomach cancer, and he died in April 1889 at the age of 37.[46]

o'clock in the morning, left Kolombus at 1 o'clock and arrived at 8:30 in Pittzburg and left
Pittzburg at 9 o'clock and arrived the next day, March 6, via Pihladalvia in Nev-Jork, stayed
there until the next day, March 7 and left for Germany on March 7, 1885, at 1 o'clock in the
afternoon, on the ship Lerdam from the Dutch-American shipping company. [7 ll.: ocean
voyage; Rotterdam–Oberhausen] That is my journey from and to America, and if I stay healthy
and God is willing, then I will go back to America again. I left Germany on April 5, 1881, and
returned to Germany on March 22, 1885. / Matthias Dorgathen
    [46]Ev. KB and Standesamt Mülheim on the Ruhr.

16

Christian Kirst

The peasant farmer Christian Kirst was 54 years old when he left his village of Züsch, near Hermeskeil (fifteen miles southeast of Trier), to emigrate to North America together with his wife Carolina (48) and two children, Peter (10) and Wilhelmina (7), in the summer of 1881. In Züsch Kirst owned a house and probably some land, which he had inherited after the death of his father in 1873. His father, who was a baker, tavern keeper, and brewer, had achieved modest prosperity and prestige, but Christian's holdings probably amounted to the village average of eleven acres, two-thirds of which were meadow.[1]

During the eighteenth century an ironworks had flourished near Züsch, attracting hundreds of workers to the area. In 1835, however, the works closed down for good. The population of the village doubled between 1811 and 1841 to reach 679, and it began to decline only after 1864 (from 734 to 595 in 1900). Partible inheritance led to a decrease in farm size, and agricultural yields, never very high due to the poor soil and mountain climate of the area (elevation is 1,640 feet), were reduced. In 1873, 648 people lived in Züsch in 133 households, of which 118 owned livestock; 225 cows and only 13 horses are listed for the entire village.

In the light of all of these factors—population explosion, diminutive farms, paucity of livestock, decreasing land productivity, rough climate, and loss of jobs—it is hardly surprising that a report on the forest

[1]Letter by Peter Kirst in Züsch to his brother Christian, dated and begun September 4, 1881, finished and sent between March 18 and April 4, 1882 (BABS; Petto [1985], 224; affirmation of the mayor of Hermeskeil, August 16, 1854 [BABS]).

settlements near Hermeskeil, written in the late 1840s by the district governor of Trier, contains the following passage: "The daily diet consists of potatoes, rarely of bread. Only a few families are in the fortunate position of being able to slaughter a small pig every year."[2]

Under such conditions it is understandable that a report written by the mayor of Hermeskeil in March 1840, submitted to the county magistrate in Trier, begins with the rather terse comment: "The obsession with emigration to the American states is spreading with a vengeance, particularly in Züsch, Damflos, and Reinsfeld." In 1854 the county magistrate in Trier, in a report to the district governor, provided the following clear-sighted analysis: "The prospect of high wages in America and thus the chance to accumulate savings, as well as information about the good quality of life there, whereas most emigrants here must live on a very simple diet and often suffer from a lack of even the most necessary things, are all circumstances that awaken and increase the desire to emigrate." The corresponding report of 1872 explains: "The causes for increasing emigration are reductions in the size of holdings, as a result of population increases, low profitability of land, and the increase in local taxes. . . ." In the year in which Kirst emigrated, the county magistrate reported to the district governor:

> With regard to the general causes, adverse circumstances and poor harvests have befallen the farmers in this area . . . in recent years. Many of them have fallen into grinding poverty and debt as a result. Emigrants are recruited primarily from the ranks of peasants . . . who cannot make ends meet or believe that they cannot make ends meet and hope for a better living in America. Some have relatives who have already emigrated and have painted a favorable picture of conditions in America in their letters.[3]

All of this certainly applied to Christian Kirst.

The Roth and Kirst families were closely tied together by a double wedding in 1859. On January 6th, Christian Kirst married Carolina Roth, and at the same time Carolina's brother Franz Peter (22) married Christian's sister Sophie (27). Jakob Roth, the brother of two of the newlyweds, had already emigrated to the United States in 1850 at the age of nineteen. His father had applied for emigration permission for his son, a minor, saying that he wished "to seek his fortune there, if possible," a common phrase. Without hesitation, the government of the Grand Duchy of Oldenburg (to which Birkenfeld including Hujet-Mühle near

---

[2]Edelmann (1920), 166–67; Backes et al. (1970), 115–18; Edelmann, 150; Prüm (1978), 81–82; Edelmann, 129a, 155 (for quote).

[3]March 14, 1840, LHA KO, Best. 442, Nr. 9371, 215; March 14, 1854, ibid., Nr. 6722, 185–86; March 16, 1872, ibid., 308; May 27, 1881, ibid., 376–77.

Abentheuer, the place of residence of the Roths, belonged) agreed to grant the requested permission to emigrate to North America and release him from all rights and responsibilities of citizenship.[4]

The correspondence between the emigrant and his relatives in the Hunsrück continued for 31 years after 1850. When the Kirst family arrived in New York shortly before August 7,[5] they went directly to their well-established brother and brother-in-law Jakob Roth, now a tavern keeper in Pittsburgh, Pennsylvania. They received a warm welcome not only from close relatives: the more distantly related and earlier emigrant John M. Hammel, also a saloonkeeper, did the Kirsts a number of favors, as did "Bien from Birkenfeld."[6]

Jakob Roth provided the Kirsts with lodging in his own house (and may have advanced part of the travel costs; see Kirst's letter of March 20, 1883). He and other friends looked after the needs of the new arrivals. Thus the Kirsts—like the majority of German emigrants—profited from the fact that they were not the first in their family, their village, or neighboring villages to immigrate. Earlier emigrants supplied those who came later with news and information, sometimes with passage money, and with lodgings, jobs, advice, and help once they arrived in the country—at least most of the time.

Züsch and Hermeskeil had a long tradition of emigration, so that not even Jakob Roth could count as one of their earliest emigrants. Prior to 1840 at least twenty persons or families left Züsch for North America. Bad harvests like those of 1842, 1845, and 1846 led to an increase in emigration, which reached its peak in the county of Trier in 1846. Despite the steady general increase from 1848 to the mid-1850s, the number of emigrants in 1846 was never surpassed.[7]

Emigration from the county of Trier and in particular from the township of Hermeskeil remained at a high level during the twenty years after 1855, then came almost to a standstill at the end of the 1870s. The last large wave of emigrants was registered by the county of Trier and the township of Hermeskeil in 1880–1882, probably as a result of the series of poor harvests that affected the area after 1877.

[4]Ev. KB Züsch; application of June 1, 1850, permission granted June 11, 1850 (LHA KO, Best. 393, Nr. 877, 29–31).

[5]Peter Kirst acknowledged receipt of Christian Kirst's letter of August 7, 1881, from Pittsburgh (see n. 1 above); this must have been the first letter sent by Kirst shortly after his arrival.

[6]In the Pittsburgh CDs from 1879–80 to 1885 Jakob Roth is listed as a saloonkeeper, and his address is given as 1221 Carson Street. Hammel is also listed and lived next door at 1207 Carson Street (Ev. KB Züsch). As early as MC 1870: Birmingham, Allegheny Co., Pa., Pct. 2, #725, Jakob Roth (according to CD 1869–70 a beer saloonkeeper) reported total assets of $8,000.

[7]Backes et al., 138; see n. 3 above, mayor of Hermeskeil to county magistrate Trier, March 14, 1840; Prüm, 81. The number of persons who emigrated in 1846 from the county of Trier—with official permission to leave and only between the months of March and December—reached 653 (Mergen [1953], 99; for 1853 see n. 3 above, county magistrate to district governor of Trier, March 14, 1854).

Christian Kirst, in particular, must have been affected by the conditions reported in a study of the region of Hermeskeil: "Even in good years, the farmland barely provided only for the basic needs of potatoes and grain. Necessary cash had to be earned during free time by work as a day laborer or in cottage industry. . . . If a farmer suffered an accident, loss of livestock, or a poor harvest . . . his situation became precarious."[8] Christian Kirst was one of the last of the 79 residents of Züsch listed in the files as having left the village to go to America between 1854 and 1897.[9] Almost half of these emigrants left with official permission and half without. When the Kirsts left, 55 persons had left the immediate surroundings (township of Hermeskeil) the previous year, ten persons in 1881 with official permission and 34 who—like the Kirsts—had not taken the trouble to apply for official papers. A number of the 54 emigrants who left in 1882 are mentioned in the correspondence—above all Karoline Kirst, the 21-year-old daughter of the Kirsts, who remained behind in Züsch at first.[10]

The reason she did not go with her parents remains unclear. Perhaps they did not have enough money; in February 1882 Kirst was able to send her money he had earned for her passage. The successive arrangements made for her passage indicate how intensive the emigration from the area of Züsch had become. In November 1881 her father suggested with whom she should travel, in March 1882 her uncle made other arrangements; she finally came with yet another group of people on July 16, 1882. Intended and actual traveling companions came from Züsch, Abentheuer, Thiergarten, Reinsfeld, and Schwarzenberg (three to seven miles from Züsch).

Numerous countrymen lived in Pittsburgh. The city, molded by the iron industry since the middle of the century, had experienced a breathtaking boom since the Civil War as a center for the production of steel, iron, and glass. It had accordingly attracted both domestic and foreign laborers, particularly those with skills in iron manufacturing. But industry produced not only riches and jobs. The iron city was known as the "Smoky City," and smog often plagued the inhabitants.[11]

In 1860 the population of Pittsburgh was only 49,000, but by 1880 it

[8]For the years from 1856 to 1875 the county of Trier lists an annual average of 44 emigration cases or about one hundred persons who emigrated with official permission, while the township of Hermeskeil averaged 32 persons who emigrated with or without permission. The number of emigration cases from Trier County reached 109 in 1880 and 149 in 1881 (Mergen [n.d.], 19; Backes et al., 140; quote: Edelmann, 177).

[9]Actually, 1854–1882, since in the years following 1882 only thirty (out of a total of 927) persons emigrated from the township of Hermeskeil (Backes et al., 140).

[10]Ibid. One year before they emigrated, their 11-year-old son Jakob died of "cramps," five years earlier their 14-year-old son Karl had died of "brain fever"; three other Kirst children died in infancy or early childhood (Ev. KB Züsch).

[11]Baldwin (1937), 218–47, 326–51.

had tripled to 156,000, including 45,000 immigrants: among them were 16,000 Germans, 17,000 Irish, and 8,000 British. In 1890 the population reached 238,000 (through immigration and annexation), of which more than one out of ten (25,000) had been born in Germany, and approximately the same number were second-generation German-Americans. When Christian Kirst arrived, he had the choice of four local German-language daily newspapers, the *Pittsburger Abendblatt,* the *Pittsburger Beobachter,* the *Freiheits-Freund,* and the *Volksblatt.* There were also two dozen religious, political, and business publications in German which appeared weekly or monthly.

Kirst must have also had considerable contact with his countrymen on the job. The 1880 census lists a total of 4,709 iron- and steelworkers: 2,273 Americans, 966 Irish, 742 British, and 603 Germans. Among the saloonkeepers (such as Hammel and Kirst's brother-in-law Jakob Roth), the Germans predominated: out of a total of 806 persons in this occupation, 287 were German, 267 American, and 171 Irish.[12]

The fact that Christian Kirst emigrated at the age of fifty-four suggests that he felt his economic prospects at home were hopeless.[13] His advanced age also presented a considerable handicap, as he testifies in many passages in his letters, both in his attempts to adapt to the new country and to his earning prospects. In general he describes his daily life in a realistic manner, without trying to gloss over his difficulties. Many aspects of his existence in America are left out, such as his work and the German community; but his interests and observations are quite varied, and they reveal a certain flexible and practical turn to his personality. He may describe difficult and unpleasant conditions, but he never creates the impression of being helpless or distressed. Perhaps he benefited from a certain degree of fatalism—and the memory of the privations and hopelessness of life in his village back home in the Hunsrück.

Since it is almost certain that Kirst never went beyond elementary school, and there are good reasons to assume that even the little schooling he received was not of high quality, the standard of his written German is quite surprising. Spelling mistakes are rare, and even his punctuation is passable and rarely makes reading difficult. On the other hand, some of his sentences tend to run on in a stream of consciousness, and his syntax

---

[12]USC 1860.2, xviii; USC 1870.1, 380; USC 1880.1, 536–41; USC 1890.1, 478, 670–73, 432–33, 800–803; Arndt/Olson (1965), 579–85; USC 1880.1, 895.

[13]Several passages in the letters, particularly toward the end of the letter of November 29, 1881, seem to suggest that Kirst had something to hide, but it was probably unpaid debts rather than any punishable offense. His brother replied on September 4, 1881, to Christian's first letter: "You write that you don't like it very much in America—when you've been there a while it'll be better. Just think back on Züsch where it's bad in every respect. And keeps getting worse. . . . Here you wouldn't mind working if you could earn anything" (see n. 1 above).

does not always conform to that of High German. Traces of his regional dialect are noticeable in his syntax, spelling, and the use of about a dozen dialectal words a modern German reader not raised in the Moselle area would have a hard time understanding. Yet these limitations do not seem to impede the liveliness of his style, based on his down-to-earth concreteness and spontaneity, perhaps even a certain narrative talent.

Christian Kirst

[Fragment of what was probably the first letter written shortly after their arrival in Pittsburgh, August 7, 1881; see note 5]
No. 8. The whole circle of friends have showered us with gifts. Jakob gave us flour, salt, coffee, rice, barley, lard, bacon, eggs, soap, pepper, china, straw for one bed, 1 bed frame, table, clothes cupboard, kitchen cupboard, 2 chairs, 1 stove. The furniture belongs to the apartment, I don't yet know if I own it. Mienchen[14] got 1 pair of shoes, 1 set of clothes, 1 pair of underpants, 1 slip, my wife got three sets of clothes, I got a pair of trousers, 1 vest, Peter got 1 jacket.

Bien from Birkenfeld bought each of the children a straw hat, Lottchen made my wife a pretty hat, wants to give us pots and pans, potatoes and vegetables. Whenever I go to Hammel's there's 1–2–3 glasses of beer, that is the custom here in this country. It's like that here at Jakob's, his wife is also very good, can give you everything. Write and tell me how things are back home with my house or what will happen. [3 ll.: harvest, relatives] What is happening with Hirsch's house and land and with the baker or if anyone is leaving in the fall. Write to me soon, I think about the old homeland every day and always long to know how things are there.

No. 9. I've numbered the pages see above there are numbers from 1 to 9. [ca. 12 ll.: simple geographical diagram of Pittsburgh, Allegheny, and Birmingham with the three rivers]

You have to imagine yourselves standing near Trier on the Franzen Knippchen[15] and the Mosel flows from the Ruwer to Trier, then Trier would be Birmingham, the Mosel the Monogohela, where the Marxberg [Markusberg] and the town of Palien are would be Pittsburg, beyond it the Alligeny river, beyond that the city of Alligeny. There are 4 bridges over the Monogehela river, one is a railway bridge to Pittsburg. 5 bridges go over the Alligeny to Pittsburg but it's all steep mountains around Pittsburg and from Baltimore to Pittsburgh it's all mountains.

[14]Diminutive of Wilhelmina (English equivalent is Minnie).
[15]Lookout point near the modern television tower.

Figure 34. Lithograph from 1871 which Kirst sent to Züsch.

The ship we took was called the *Straßburg,* had 63,180 cubic meters, was 153 paces long, 20 wide, 1750 passengers with the officers, sailors, servants 1800 persons. We were fed pretty well also had no storm except 2 times but then it rocked so that everything that wasn't tied down fell about. Also no ship goes down in a storm unless it runs into a rock.

Pittsburg, November 29th, 1881

Dear brothers and sisters[16] and daughter Carolina,

I hereby let you know that yesterday on Nov. 28th I deposited 10 dollars in the bank here in Birmingham as a Christmas present for you, dear brothers and sisters, one taler for each and with the rest Carolina should get herself ½ dozen undershirts, of cheap linen from a peddler or in a shop, shoes and stockings, for wool is more expensive than over there. She should buy some shoes or have them made, but not work shoes with nails, rather clean Sunday shoes for here that is the fashion among women. The shirts should be made with short sleeves [. . .] she shouldn't buy any other clothes because the fashions here are much different from over there—a slip or 2, flannel or homespun if there's enough money.

Karl from Sulzbach's[17] three boys are here, Carl is at a brewery, Johann at a butcher's and Fritz is near Philadelphia and works at his trade on a metal lathe. They want to have their mother and the rest of the sisters and brothers come in the spring, and then our Carolina should come with them, we've set it all up: when they send their mother money, then I'll send money too, when they sign up here for their mother's passage I'll do it too, so they can come together on the train and on the sea, then she'll be with trustworthy people for Marie is a hearty person, she'll watch over Carolina.

[7 ll.: travel arrangements] I've been working every day of the week and Sundays and even nights, you know when you have nothing everything costs a lot. [4 ll.: high prices, drought, heat] Potatoes per bushel 1 dollar 25 cents about 60 pounds, butter ½ dollar a pound, eggs 30 cents a dozen, bread ¼ dollar about 5 pounds, cabbage 12 to 15 dollars for 100 heads, meat 10 to 18 cents a pound, coffee 18 to 30 cents a pound. [7 ll.: further food prices] We buy the cheapest things and cook like over there, the good life you have here as they say, they spend everything they earn

[16]His father (1792–1873) and mother (1798–1867) were deceased. In 1881 the following siblings were still alive: Carl (1822–87), a farmer; Elisabeth (b. 1829), married to H. Hintze, a forester in Trier; Marie (b. 1830), who lived until 1887 with Carl and Peter on the farm (December 27, 1887, letter from Franz Peter Roth to Christian Kirst, BABS); Sophie (b. 1831), married to F. P. Roth, sawmiller; and Peter (1838–87), farmer (Petto, 224; ev. KB Zürch).

[17]Presumably Sulzbach near Idar-Oberstein (18 miles north of Züsch), but possibly Sulzbach near Saarbrücken (24 miles south of Züsch).

and can't pay their monthly house rent 2 rooms 6 to 9 dollars a month.
The Americans don't live like the Germans, no one saves for the future,
shoes, stockings, and clothing aren't mended, bread, meat and food lie
around on the streets, if people in Germany had that they would be so
satisfied, what is left over or they don't like is thrown away or burned in
the stove, here there are people when they earn 10 to 12 dollars a day they
don't even have their own place to live, eat up and drink up everything, 1
shot of whisky 5 cents, over there 5 pfennigs. 1 glass of beer 5 cents, 1
glass of wine 10 cents, the bars are completely different from over there,
the saloonkeeper stands behind the counter, like in the shops in Germany,
here they drink everything standing up, all in one gulp, you can imagine
how that hits you over the head. Like all those here who guzzle away
their whole day's wage in one hour, that's how the Americans work,
when they really get going you can't beat them but when the heat is off
they are so lazy. Over there they say the language isn't important, you
can get along everywhere what with so many Germans there, that isn't
true, it is the absolute worst if you can't speak the language, then many
Germans get double-crossed or cheated and stand around and have no
idea what's going on. How many Germans and Americans have I met
here who didn't speak a single word of German, then after a while they
speak better and more clearly than me, not all do this however, there are
also decent people here. About farming I can only write what I've heard
from others, if you work from half past 6 in the morning to half past 5 in
the evening then you can't really say, but Lottchen from Birkenfeld they
have a farm about 1 hour from Allegehny with 2 houses and 2 houses in
the city, she told us she had made 1,050 dollars on vegetables this year at
the weekly market in Pittsburg and still planned to sell celery for 700
dollars, I take it from this that if a man has a bit of land he can do good
business. I spoke with a German who lives a few hours from here he has
rented a farm of 60 acres for 600 dollars a year and still does good
business. Running a saloon here in the city is the best business. Now I
want to write you why the Germans don't like it here: 1, the language, 2,
change of occupation, 3, you don't get to know people as easily here as
over there, here you're always an outsider, you work all week, Sundays
everything is closed, bars and shops, over there it is customary to go out,
here you stay at home, over there they say the miners earn 4 to 5 dollars a
day but they don't mention the bad things, here there are all private
mines and factories and if a man has an accident he doesn't get a pension,
if you're sick you don't get any sick pay,[18] the miners only work in the
winter when the water is high and the ships can run, but in the summer

[18]Coal mines in Prussia, including those close to Kirst's home, had been government property
until the middle of the nineteenth century. After 1851 they passed into private ownership, but

when it isn't then they use up what they've earned in winter, it's like that in all of the factories today they hire 50 men tomorrow they fire them. Schools here are free, but you have to buy the books, it's like over there. If you don't have any money you don't have to pay. The people here who own property have to pay for everything, doctors and pharmacists are more expensive than over there, every visit costs 5 talers, pharmacists are 3 times more expensive than at home. There are more religions here than over there: Benetists, Baptists, Puritans, Catholics, Evangelicals, Lutherans, Reformed Lutherans and I don't know what else, I haven't been to a church. There aren't any *Schandarmen* [constables] here but instead there are *Polismänner,* or *Polizei* in German, over there they say you can hang at the drop of a hat, that is also not true, here you are punished according to your crime like over there, as a man here things are the opposite from over there here the woman rules the roost, if a man comes home drunk and his wife reports him he gets put in *Prisong,* the first time for 5 days and then longer and longer if he does it again, if he beats her and she reports it he gets punished and she doesn't need any witnesses. The government is trying to give women the vote,[19] whether that will go through is not yet certain. The children of the poorer classes are very badly brought up, some don't go to school at all, are cocky and rude, run in the streets until 10, 11 o'clock, some can't write their own names, at 9 to 10 they go to work in the factories, girls and boys you can imagine what kind of mess that is. I must close I hope when I write again I can write you more I worked all last night and didn't sleep and you know what it's like to write then, your fingers and head don't feel like it, something else occurs to me, on the 2nd of July Garfield, the President of the United States, was shot by a lawyer named Guitau in Washington and died on the 19th of Sept. up to now he hasn't been sentenced. The whole country mourned him all the saloons and stores were closed the day he died.[20] [8 ll.: black crepe bands, flags; they are healthy, asks for news] At the end of October I dreamed a lot about you several nights perhaps something has happened to you, write me about everything how my affairs are over there, how sister Elizabeth is getting along with her land and the crops, did you take everything out of my house before anyone else showed up,[21] what happened to the garden and to the meadow, write

---

many of the traditions remained alive: government regulation of operations, especially safety rules, was particularly strict, and miners remained covered by a rather comprehensive mandatory scheme of social security, including medical insurance financed by contributions from both miners and employers (Tenfelde [1977], 177–91, 282–83).

[19]Agitation for women's suffrage was strong, but at that time it existed only in Wyoming and Utah Territories (introduced in 1869 and 1870, respectively), but not in any state. It was introduced across the nation in 1920.

[20]See Chapter 15, n. 27.

[21]The house and the furniture had not yet been sold at the beginning of September 1881,

me what people said about me and how long it took till word got out, who said the nastiest things. Answer all the questions for I would like to know everything, how Christian and Karl Hirsch are doing, what does he write, hasn't anybody decided to emigrate to America, did you have a good fall, did you get the second cutting of hay and the potatoes in and how much. Now I will close and send you all dear brothers and sisters and daughter Carolina a thousand greetings. Many thousand greetings to you from mother, Peter, and Wilhelmina. Fare thee well in the old country, God willing.

Your devoted brother and father / Chr. Kirst

Write me if the money got there. [. . .] When you write about my affairs, write on a separate piece of paper, for the people here in America are very nosy and prying, not everyone needs to know about that. We are still living with brother-in-law Jakob the address is the same.

Pittsburgh, February 26th, 1882

Dear brothers and sisters and daughter Carolina,

I wrote you a letter on the 12th of the month and reported that I have sent 55 dollars for Karolina, and listed everything she should bring along: I forgot the following things, bring also the 2 straight awls that were always behind the door on the shelf in a little box, the meter-stick, the little potato scoop, for taking boiled potatoes out of the pot, the little hammer for nailing in shoe nails, if you can buy a little set of shoemaker's pliers like we used to have [. . .] your confirmation certificate and smallpox certificate if you still have it [. . .] also Peter and Mienchen's smallpox certificates if they're still there, if they aren't anymore you don't need to get any, you don't have to have them here.

Bien from Birkenfeld has bought herself a house on the hill for 4000 dollars, which I already said in my first letter. She would like a few shoots of our fat red currants and gooseberries [. . .] her double lilacs. Before you leave write me with whom and with which ship and which crossing you are coming on and how much it costs.

When you get to Pittsburg ask at the train station for a *Straßen Car,* or *Street Car,* in (German *Omnibus*), which leave every 7 minutes from the south side for Pittsburg and back, it costs 6 cents, in every car there's a *Condokteur* in the back, give him the address of your uncle: Jakob Roth, Carson St. No. 1221 south, then you get off in front of his door. If the *Condektor* can't speak German there are always Germans in the car, so you'll be all right, should you arrive at night after 12 o'clock then stay in

"because the people have no money"; the meadow was possibly auctioned off in 1882 (see the letter of Peter Kirst to Christian Kirst, September 4, 1881, mentioned in n. 1).

the waiting room until 6 o'clock in the morning then they run again, we'll come and pick you up at the train station but you can't depend on that, one ship is more days at sea than another, one train is delayed another isn't, that's not a sure thing you can't tell what day or hour you'll get here, we were supposed to get here at 6 o'clock in the evening and it was 10, the train was delayed so long. [10 ll.: luggage; question about a horse; greetings]

Your devoted brother and father / Chr. Kirst

Bring a small ball of white and small ball of blue linen thread you know what kind, the one we always had. Bring along a woolen kerchief for yourself for the winter like the ones Karlin Lehrche makes with green edging. You don't need to bring any books along except the Bible. When you get to this side of the ocean, whether in New York, Philadelphia or Baltimore you can telegraph us from there, then we will know what time the train comes to pick you up. [12 ll.: she should find out arrival times of trains; measure Prussian ell with the meter-stick, weigh an object in the luggage in pounds] Here the measures and weights aren't the same as the German ones, the foot seems to me to be shorter, and the ell longer than over there, and the pound lighter.

Pittsburg, June 11th, 1882

Dear brothers and sisters and daughter Carolina,

We received your letter of April 4th on the 24th and gather that our Carolina is not coming on the ship *Belgenland,* we would like to know why she is not coming or did something else happen, for over two months have passed since you wrote me, we can hardly wait till she comes, she is supposed to go to work for Bien from Birkenfeld, who'll be glad when she gets here, she'll get 2½ dollars a week, she has a farm on the hill and one here on the south side. She has Clara, the daughter of sister-in-law Bien, as a servant girl, she needs to have 2 girls, she also has a hired hand named Ettmann Grim from Saarlouis and another servant from the town and her mother my wife has to go almost every day to help up on the hill, it's the same kind of arrangement as our Liesbeth had at the forester's lodge, but it's only ¼ hour from the city. [. . .] I've told Carolina all about what she should do on the trip so if she doesn't get a chance to travel with close friends she should start off anyway, there are good and bad people everywhere, it isn't as dangerous as you imagine over there it's a pleasure trip if you can only stay healthy. [12 ll.: sons of Carl from Sulzbach (see Kirst's letter of November 29, 1881) now all in breweries, one visited him; all are healthy; greetings]

Your devoted brother and father / Chr. Kirst

Pittsburg, July 16th, 1882

Dear brothers and sisters,

I must let you know that our Caroline arrived here last Sunday the 9th in the afternoon between 1 and 2 o'clock. She didn't telegraph us from Newjork, but we had figured out that she'd be coming on the 9th. I, and brother-in-law Jakob, and his son Ernst went over to the train station to pick her up, but while we were inside the emigrant train arrived and she was one of the first to get off and when we asked about her a man had directed her to a street car and when we got home she'd already been at the house for half an hour.

The next day her aunt[22] went with her to a shop and bought her a hat for 5 dollars; and 2 dresses and 2 aprons, I don't know how much the dresses and aprons cost. She and we were all glad when she got here, she likes it very much and the crossing went well, they didn't have any storms; she left Neujork Saturday evening 8 o'clock and arrived here Sunday between 1 and 2. The Hermann Weber family from Züsch and the Becker family from Reinsfeld and a woman from Landweiler, her husband named Bouillon from Thiergarten and Karl Roth Pitters Fritz's second son from Abentheuer were with her until Newjork there they separated each going to their new homes on different trains. The Becker family from Reinsfeld was with her all the way to Pittsburg. Bien from Birkenfeld wanted to have her on the first day but my sister-in-law didn't allow it, she should have 8–14 days to rest and get all her clothes altered to American fashion. She wants to buy her a second hat this week for work days, I can't tell you how much they've already done for us, they pay ¼ dollar a week for our Mienchen to learn how to crochet and knit, and Peter is *all reit,* in German *was er thut ist recht.* Things here are quite different from over there, here it doesn't matter who you are, here everybody's equal, here the banker knows the beggar, even our Peter has the son of a banker as a friend and when you walk down the street with him they call out from all the street corners *Hello Pitt!* in German *Willkomm Pitt,* everyone likes him, even a *bas* [boss] in German *Meister,* from a glassworks went out with him. He could have had 3 dollars a week but I didn't let him, he should learn something at school first for there are many thousands here who can't write their names and can't get any further than day labor. Peter speaks English as well as he does German, the children learn it so easily, Mienchen too, she has grown up a lot, if you could see her you wouldn't recognize her, she goes around every day wearing hats and stylish clothes, didn't cost me anything my sister-in-law did it.

[22]According to MC 1870: Birmingham, Allegheny Co., Pa., Pct. 2, #725, the wife of Franz Roth, Elizabeth, born in Pennsylvania in 1837.

I'm still at my first job, get 1 dollar 25 cents a day.[23] My brother-in-law Jakob spoke with a smith last night who makes steel into tools, when he needs someone I'll go there and get 1 dollar 60 cents a day and not have such hard work as here. Since the 1st of June work at all the ironworks here has stopped, because of the unions that they have in this country, the workers want more money and the factory owners don't want to pay, who knows how long it will take before they settle it. But so far I've still always had work. [8 ll.: heat, thunderstorms, floods]

Carl from Sulzbach's 3 sons are here, Carl is in Pittsburgh has his second job gets 55 dollars a month without meals, Fritz in Allegeny also at a brewery, Johann on the south side of Birmingham at a brewery both get meals I don't know exactly at least 24–30 dollars a month. They're expecting their sister Lina today, she was supposed to have left from Antwerp on July 1st. There isn't any other news to write except that the President's murderer Guiteau was hanged on June 30th. [14 ll.: greetings, signature; correspondence]

Peter Arend Müller told our Caroline I should write and tell him what things are like here, so I have enclosed a letter and left it open so you can see what I've written. [. . .]

Pittsburg, July 16, 1882

Dear Peter Arend Müller! [a miller in Züsch]

My daughter Caroline told me you wanted to know how things are here in America: therefore I want to write the truth to you. The baking trade here is very brisk, but the journeymen receive the least pay of all the occupations, 2 to 3 dollars a week, and have to work almost day and night, a servant girl earns more, and if she can sew and iron she can even make more than 3 dollars a week. The best craftsmen here are: blacksmith, locksmith, carpenter, cooper, tanner, brewer they usually earn 12 dollars a week, and even more if he knows his trade well for they mostly do piecework, if he works hard and is thrifty he can save more money in a short time than he could in a lifetime in Germany, but if he is no 'count he can guzzle away his day's wage every evening without even sitting down since the drinks here are more expensive than over there. [. . .] It's hard to give anyone advice for or against since no one likes it here at first—you have to decide on your own since if you don't know the language you can't understand anyone, that's the hardest thing to go through, the children learn it very easily but it's hard for the old folks—I know people

[23]This was slightly below the average wage for an unskilled laborer in Pennsylvania in 1882 ($1.34) and much less than the puddlers he mentioned in his January 1, 1884, letter ($3.06) and less than skilled workers at the rolling mills ($4.78) (History of Wages [1934], 257, 246, 242).

here who have been here for 10–12 years and still can't speak perfect English. If a man comes here who has some means he can do a good business, here it isn't like over there, here you can do what you want, here it is a free country, here is the land of Canaan where milk and honey flow! Here officials don't decide who pays their salaries as they see fit, here you can give what you want, here the church and schools are free, I am already in my 2nd year here and haven't paid a cent don't need to either. I've already saved more here and lead a better life with my family than even the best is able to over there, here you make more in the clear in one year than you can make in debts over there in five years. Here you work harder than over there, but when it's payday and you get those lovely dollars counted out in your hands, the hardship is forgotten, you get fresh courage, here they always say *Gohätt* [go ahead], *Vorwärts* in German. I'm only sorry that I spent the best years of my life in the German land of Egypt so miserably and painfully, for nothing. [. . .] I know that most live in the same circumstances as I did, but heartily wish that they were all here and could see for themselves then they could say with me: it is much better here than in Germany. Give my best to all the friends and acquaintances who ask about me. [3 ll.: names and comments on two] I have often thought of the poor suffering women of Züsch, my wife says I wish they all had it so good as me. Instead of having to go into the woods to get a load of fodder or straw in Züsch, I get my children and go for a walk in town; if I pay 5 cents for the *Street Car,* in German *Pferdebahn* [horse car], I don't even have to walk.

Here is what our Carolina has to say to your daughter Philippina:[24] I wish you were here with me even if it were only for a day, then you would see how nice it is here in this country, otherwise you won't believe it. I got here Sunday the 9th of July and my parents and friends were very glad to see me. The next day my aunt went with me to a shop bought me two hats and two dresses and 2 aprons is having all of my clothes altered to American style and is keeping me with her for 3 to 4 weeks, before I start work. [2 ll.: sea voyage calm; greetings] / <u>Karolina Kirst</u>

Pittsburgh, May 20, <u>1883</u>.

Dear brothers and sisters,

I can't help writing to you again, for you don't forget the old home-land, no matter how it was back there. [5 ll.: it's all the same wherever you are] The Germans in this country are always homesick, I am doing

---

[24]Born in 1862, two years younger than Carolina and also confirmed two years later (ev. KB Züsch).

quite well and have enough money, I've paid back my brother-in-law Jacob, have sent our Carolin money for the trip here, have bought all the furniture and lived well besides, and still have money saved up. Here you can make money if [you] work hard, are healthy and thrifty you can earn a living. But here it's *Gohätt, Horriab* [go ahead, hurry up], in German: *Vorwärts, Hurtig,* that's all you ever hear here, that's the password and battle cry, those who never learned to work with their hands at home don't like it here either, those who didn't have anything over there and had to work with their hands they like it here. You just can't imagine what this country is like, and I can't tell you about everything you have to tell me what you want to know for it's hard to think of everything when you're writing. [5 ll.: correspondence] I've been hoping every day for a letter, but in vain, here you always want to hear something from the old country, when Germans get together they only talk about the old country. Here there are people from all the nations on earth how can you learn the English language when each speaks his own language. I'm still living with brother-in-law Jacob pay 5 dollars a month rent since April last year, we've been kindly received by him and done well by him, he is a rich man, not tightfisted, he also has a very good wife who is very generous, she still pays for all of our Mienchen's clothes also sent her to crochet-school and paid for everything, Peter gets all of his work clothes from her which her son Ernst doesn't use anymore, most of the time he's at our neighbors' the Miller brothers they have a *Liebertestall* [livery stable] or *Leihstall,* they have about 30 to 40 horses. They are undertakers, here in this country it's different from over there, when someone here is buried, depending on how rich he is, he hires 100 to 150 coaches to take all the people to the funeral, each coach costs 5 dollars, the coffin 5–10 dollars. The rich people have their own graveyard plots for their families, the poor people have to pay for their graves too and have a smaller funeral, the undertakers arrange everything. Peter is doing very well there he has his horse in the stable, when he does a job for them then he rides, that is the custom here, he rides into the town to the mayor's office, takes the death certificates, rides to the veterinarian when they need him, in short he has to ride his horse every day. They also taught him how to ride, <u>Willi</u> led the horse by the bridle and <u>Säm</u> had the whip in his hand, they taught him how to ride, he rides as well as a Hussar. At Christmas <u>Säm</u> bought him a whole set of clothes 1 jacket, 1 vest, 1 hat, 1 pair of trousers, 1 woolen shirt, 1 pair of suspenders, the suit cost 10 dollars and then he introduced him to his mother who likes him a lot too because of her <u>Schorsch</u> [George] who died in May last year, Peter was his favorite, she also gave Peter ¼ dollar and said he should also have money in his pocket, he speaks English as well as a native-born American, if you didn't know it, you'd never believe he was born a German, Mienchen also speaks so well, but the language is so hard for the older people. I also have to tell you what we received for Christmas from brother-in-law Jacob: I got a bottle of German wine, 1 knitted wool jacket, 2 handkerchiefs, mother got a brown dress and 2 woolen spreads to fold over and put on the beds, Peter got a rubber raincoat, Mienchen got a red-brown woolen dress and a hat the same color, Carolina a white lace scarf and 2 aprons.

From the Hammels we received: I received a bottle of the best *Wisky,* mother 1 black velvet hat, Carolina 5 dollars, that's what they do here at Christmas or birthdays they give out presents. Please be so good and answer this letter for I would like to know what has happened since I left and what has happened with my house and all my affairs, write me about the other people from Züsch who've moved to America, how they like it, where they are, and what they write.

Now I want to tell you the names of the ironworks: the following ironworks lie along the banks of the Monengahela and how many men are employed and how much pay they get every 14 days.

Name of owners
1. Freind, employs   400 men   wages 8,000 dollars every 14 days
2. Pointer Comp. Sons 900   "   "   25,000   "   "   "   "
[16 ll.: fourteen more works]
17. "Kloman Superior Rolling Mill Allegeny" 600 men 9,000 dollars born in Marihütte or Buß.[25] [. . .]

The following ironworks lie along the banks of the Allegeny
[6 ll.: six more]
7. Union Iron Mill from Carnegi Bros. Comp. 1,150 m. 31,000 dollars [4 ll.: four more]
Iron means: *Eisen, works* means: *Fabrik, Bros.* means: *Gebrüder, Rolling Mill* means: *Walzwerk, Nail* means: *Nägel*

That's 27 [actually twenty-nine] *Walzwerke* (called *Roll Mill)* who knows how many glassworks (called *Glashäuser* here). [4 ll.: many more factories; no more space to write] I am enclosing a map of the United States with information about the religions, population, income and size of the states on the back.

Many thousands of greetings from me and my family to you all. Fare thee well, God willing / Your devoted brother
Chr. Kirst.

[25]Mariahütte is four miles south of Züsch; Buß is near Schwalbach, Saarlouis County. The brothers Andreas and Anton Klomann, blacksmiths, probably came from Trier or the surrounding area. In 1858 they opened a small forging mill in Allegheny which primarily produced axles for railway cars. Andrew Carnegie acquired a share in the company in 1864, marking the first step toward the creation of his steel empire (Baldwin, 326–29; Cronau [1924], 384).

Dear brother,

Be so good as to answer me immediately, for I would like to know about my house and the whole business. Did you receive your money or not? If not write me then I'll pay you. Everything I left behind you can keep for yourself, add it all up and if you don't have enough let me know. I will make good for it. Did you get the money for the IOU I signed or not? In short write me about how things are or what has happened.

Write me about whether my brother-in-law Peter from the Hujet sawmill sent a letter here to my brother-in-law Jakob, don't forget to write, you know why! Write me about what my sister Elisabeth and her family are doing in Trier?

[2 ll.: greetings] / Your devoted brother / Chr. Kirst.

Explanation of the English words on the enclosed map of the United States [dated 1848]

Farm Animals	= Viehzucht	Mistellaneous	= Vermischt
1. Scheep	= Schaafe	1. Coal	= Kohlen
[24 ll.: translations of other farming terms]			
Males means	= Männlich,	3. Females	= Weiblich
4. Native	= Innländer	5. White means	= Weisse
Foreign	= Fremdlinge	Colored means	= Schwarze . . .

Pittsburgh, January 1st, 1884

Dear brothers and sisters,

We received your letter, dated September 30th but posted on the 19th of November, on the 5th of December and from it we can see that you are all still healthy, as are we thank God you write that you had a bad and rotten year last year, we read in the newspapers that the water of the Mosel and Rhein caused very great damage. [. . .] They collected here in all of North America for the victims all of the cities sent huge sums of money to Germany, I can still remember the following cities: St Louis 30,000 marks, Cincinati 40,000 marks, Chigago 60,000 marks, Pittsburg 50,000 marks, New York 100,000, Louisville 16,000 m., Detroit 12,000 m. I enclose a poem that I cut out of the newspaper so you can see that we hear about all major events. On the 8th of October the Germans celebrated the 200th anniversary, that 200 years ago the first Germans immigrated into this state, I am sending a page from a newspaper which describes everything; as regards agriculture I can't describe it to you, I am sending you a book where you can see everything: the title of the book: *Wegweiser nach Süd Minnesota und Ost Dakota* [Guidebook to southern Minnesota and eastern Dakota]. You want to know what the laws and rights are like here: most of them are like over there: churches and

schools are free of charge, you can go to church or not when you die the
pastor buries you anyway, and gives you a better sermon than Pastor
Mertens in Züsch, you can baptize the children or not, send them to
school and have them confirmed or not, that is freedom, it's the same
with marriage: you can be married by the pastor or the justice of the peace
or not, that is freedom. [5 ll.: women, justice: as in his letter of November 29, 1881] With regard to law and order is the following: at every
skwär [square], or *Kreuzstrase* in German, stands a policeman since we
only have [3]84 here in Pittsburg, the barkeepers, businessmen have to
pay taxes like over there, but the barkeepers can serve beer as long as they
want to at night, here there's no closing time, here it's not like at Kunzen
Bäcker's when you stay later than 10 o'clock it costs 5 marks here you
stay as long as you like, also the barkeepers aren't supposed to serve on
Sundays, or draw beer, the bakers and shopkeepers aren't supposed to
sell, then they close the front doors then you go in the back door,
everything's not as strict, here money is everything, here you can get so
drunk that you fall from one side to the other, if you get up again quietly
or if someone else helps you up, if you don't bother anyone the police let
you go, but if you make a ruckus, or swear or hit someone the police take
you along and put you behind bars till the next morning then you have to
pay the police a fine of 1 to 5 dollars depending on what you did that is the
police in America. The courts are like over there, there is no mayor, a
justice of the peace but he doesn't have a court clerk or marshall he does it
all himself.

[2 ll.: penal code is like "over there"] You can get citizenship when you
can prove that you've been in the country for 5 years and have paid
Taxen, or *Steuern* there are many thousands here though who have been
here 20–30 years already and still aren't citizens, and don't want to be,
since a citizen has no more rights than someone who isn't a citizen, except
he can vote for Congress or for President,[26] that is the right of a citizen,
you can also get a minor post like policeman, you have to know the
English language though. No one has to be a soldier, they're all hired,
there a man gets 14–16 dollars a month clothing and food, that is a soft
job for those who don't want to work. You can hunt where you want,
but it's forbidden during the closed season the same thing with fishing
only the big gentlemen do it or sluggards, it's not [worth] it. The
factories and mines here don't have a relief fund, but here they have
associations, called *Losche* [lodge], you pay 25 cents a month and when a
man from the lodge dies you have to go to the funeral and pay a dollar

[26]In many states, aliens had the right to vote in state or municipal elections after they had
received their "first papers."

from which the deceased is buried, also when you are sick you get 5 dollars a week sick pay, you can double it, when the husband dies the wife gets it, and if the wife dies the husband gets it you can get as much as you want depending on how much you pay in up to 1000 dollars. Here they also have other associations, called building societies. [7 ll.: explanation of building societies] Now I have to write to you about how wages are at the moment, since the month of Nov. the rolling mills have had 10 percent of their wages cut that means the day laborers and the ones that do piecework; but not the puddlers and rollers, *Wälzer* in German, since they are paid by weight, their wages can't be cut until their contract runs out, that will be next summer, then it may be different, or there will be a strike, that means in German laid off, until they get their old wages back. The glass factories have been on strike since the month of May, the factory owners wanted to cut the raise they agreed on 3 years ago, so they stopped working and it hasn't been decided yet; now you will think that the people must be starving, but that is taken care of by associations or *Unionen*. There the needy are supported, but it's still pretty bad when a strike happens; last summer our *Compagnie* did major repairs or a change-over in their factory, it cost 55,000 dollars they put in single puddling ovens, before they were double, they now have 34 they are set up with an air blower that blows the air on the fire underground, so they can burn the small coal that falls through the grate, who knows how much that will save every year, because of the changes we didn't work for 4–6 weeks this summer and are still working less, sometimes only 3 days a week, but they say after New Year's it will be like before; they are also building another steel works where all the steel tools will be made and a grinding shop where all the tools will be polished, the buildings are finished except for the roofs and the inside fittings; when times are bad here it is still better than when times are good over there, if you work and stay healthy you know no want, you can always save something and lead a good life, I get a poor wage but live like on holidays over there, we have meat and vegetables for lunch every day; bread here is like cake, we don't overdo things, we could spend everything and more, but that's not what the Germans tend to do, they still save for the future or for their old age; most of the Americans have to spend everything, here it's easy come easy go! They are always merry and gay; if I had stayed over there I would have always had a poor, wretched and miserable life, we've seen enough examples of that over there, but here the rules are the same for all, here there are no differences, except for all the Germans who usually came here as beggars and now have something, they are stupidly proud; not the Americans, they just always ask: *Hei de du?*, *Wie gehts* in German. *Werri Well!*, *sehr wohl* in German, is the answer. Dear brothers and sisters,

you wrote about the people from Züsch who have emigrated that Frü-
hauf and Carolina Jost like it here, I believe it, those are people of means,
if they are thrifty and hard-working they won't have any trouble; and
that Gemmel and his son-in-law don't like it, I believe that too; they're
having the same problems like everyone who comes here at the beginning with no money and wants to get rich in one year, but all that passes
with time. I know from my own experience, that's how I felt at the
beginning too but now I wouldn't like to be over there forever anymore;
now I'll also write you about the reasons no one likes it here at first; it's
very easy to understand: when you first come here and can't understand
the language, you have to talk with your hands and feet, when you see
the clumsy, heavy American tools you lose heart, and then with homesickness on top of it all, that's really a burden, that's why they say: all
beginnings are difficult, and there you are with empty hands, then you
have all sorts of thoughts. [. . .] There's only one thing I regret, that I
spent so many years over there, if I had come here 20 years ago then I'd
probably be a rich man by now, but now it's too late to get rich, I'm too
old for that, but I still have a good life. Oh why should I mention the past
to you, you know yourselves as well as I can tell you, you know how
things were for me over there anyway. [7 ll.: questions about relatives]

I still want to let you know what presents we received from brother-in-
law Jacob. [4 ll.: as above] Caroline is no longer in service at the Rath-
mann's, she works since Dec. 17 for an Englishman [English-speaker]
named Willi Beck, partner in a glassworks, lives on 7th Street, gets 2½
dollars a week, but she likes it fine, already got a cotton dress and an
apron as a Christmas present.
[2 ll.: wishes, signature]
[Postscript on new sheet of paper:]

[. . .] You shouldn't believe everyone, anything can just be written in a
letter, like for example Karl Hirsch I didn't want to mention him in my
letter here I can tell you what I think: he writes that he trades in cattle and
wood, now Carl Hirsch is much too poor for that, it's different over here,
here they do everything on a big scale and you have to have untold sums
of money, that's just like if I were to write that I was trading in cattle and
wood, he had perhaps as much as I did to start? First of all you have to
know the English language for here everything that has to do with
business, reading and writing is done in English. Secondly, if you don't
have any money who sponsors you then? For in America they also
demand guarantors, they aren't as easygoing as it's said over there, if he
had said he was a cattle driver you could have believed that, you know
yourselves what he used to be over there, that's what he is here, too. [18
ll.: correspondence; enclosed newspaper articles about the bicentennial

celebrations and great fire in Pittsburgh; will write again only when he gets a reply]

You wrote that my house was auctioned off for 360 talers was the meadow included? Did you receive the money that you signed bond for me? and how are things with Kälberhennes, Fräulein Herbings in Börfink and sister Elisabetha in Trier.

Your devoted brother / Chr. Kirst

With the long letter of January 1, 1884, the series breaks off. The census data from 1900, however, permit us at least a glimpse at the subsequent life of the Kirst family. The head of household was first listed in the city directory as a "laborer" in 1885. In 1900 Christian, now 73 and retired, lived with his wife (66) in the house that belonged, free of debt, to their forty-year-old daughter Caroline. Her name was now Miller; she had perhaps married Willi or Sam from the livery stable next door (see the May 20, 1888, letter) and been widowed. Wilhelmina, still unmarried, also lived with them in the house, and she is listed in the census as "Minnie" (25), a "salesgirl" (in CD 1998–99, "cashier").

Their son Peter (29) remained true to his early fondness for horses and wagons: his occupations in the 1890s include driver, hostler, and streetcar motorman. He lived in a rented house, and in 1886 he had married a woman named Wilhelmina who was born in Pennsylvania (as were both of her parents) in 1874. Their three daughters were named Catherine, Caroline, and Margarethe.[27]

[27]MC 1900: Pittsburgh, Pa., e.d. 303, #164; e.d. 279, #130; CD Pittsburgh, 1891 through 1900–1901.

17

Ludwig Dilger (Louis Dilger)

Ludwig Dilger—who called himself Louis in his first letter from America that has survived—was born on January 30, 1863, in Witten, Westphalia. His father Gustav (born in 1834) was a glassmaker employed in the Müllensiefen glass factory (now DETAG), which was founded in 1825 in Witten, a rapidly growing industrial town on the Ruhr (coal, steel, machinery, railroad shops) with a population that grew from 8,000 to almost 24,000 between 1861 and 1885.[1]

Ludwig Dilger had eleven brothers and sisters. The occupations of his four brothers are known: Gustav was a locksmith, Albert became a carpenter and worked for the railroad, Hugo was a civil servant, Wilhelm a policeman. Ludwig was apprenticed to a baker and worked in the baking trade when he first arrived in America. His postcard of August 1880 from Hagen, Westphalia, indicates that his decision to emigrate—obviously against his father's will—was partly prompted by problems in finding a job.

Friends who had gone to America earlier may well have encouraged him to follow, and several passages in the letters suggest that tension between father and son also played a role. Ludwig Dilger emigrated in late 1881 or 1882, probably via Antwerp and without official papers, since he was still liable for the draft.[2] The letters contain only some of his

[1] Ev. KB Witten; Wüstenfeld/Wüstenfeld (1969), 16, 17. Information about the individuals, unless noted otherwise, was provided by the contributor or taken from documents in his possession.
[2] In 1882 he appears for the first time in the St. Louis CD (no occupation given). MC 1910 says 1892 but clearly means 1882 (St. Louis, e.d. 182, #77).

many occupations. The St. Louis city directories are more complete: 1885–86, driver; 1888, laborer; 1889–91, machinist; 1892, grinder; 1893–97, laborer; 1898–1904, grocer; 1907, [pipe] fitter; 1909–11, car [builder]; 1912–17, repair[man]; 1918, machinist; 1919, laborer; 1922, tester; 1925–29, clerk; 1930, freight handler; 1931, park laborer; 1932–33, city laborer. Although it is not correct to speak of him as a downright failure, it is clear that nothing he turned his hand to was an overwhelming success. We can only speculate about the extent to which this may have been due to force of circumstances, his personality, or his political activities.

Politics takes up considerable space in the letters. It is unclear how much of his socialist ideology he brought with him from Germany; his family's political orientation, however, was more nationalistic—perhaps yet another reason for his estrangement from his father. After 1886 his own comments on his political views speak for themselves, but the letters do not give a clear account of his political and union activities.

During the fifty years spanned by Dilger's letters, the development of the political groups and unions labeled "socialist" was complex, contradictory, and locally varied. We only know with reasonable certainty that in the early 1920s, Dilger belonged to the left-wing group in St. Louis associated with the weekly publications *St. Louis Labor* and *Arbeiter-Zeitung*, both of which supported Eugene Debs, the presidential candidate of the Socialist party from 1900 to 1912 and again in 1920.

In 1920, as he wrote himself, Dilger was a delegate to the Farmer-Labor party convention, at which a candidate was nominated to run against Debs; the party's platform was tailored more closely to agrarian interests, and the party was less radical than the Socialists in demanding nationalized industries. His more moderate position may have been related to his union activities; during the railroad strike, he seems to have been the chairman of one of the local repairman unions affiliated with the AFL.

His reputation as a socialist, however, does not seem to have suffered. When public meetings in preparation for upcoming local elections were announced for the 28 wards in the city, he is listed as the chairman for the 13th ward. It is worth noting that out of the 28 ward chairmen, eight had English names, four were possibly German, and sixteen more were definitely of German origin. In other lists of candidates and supporters, even in English-language party publications, German names were still more predominant.[3] These figures indicate, and provide a more graphic

[3]*St Louis Labor,* January 27, 1923. Of the Socialist candidates in the 1922 elections in Missouri, five had English names, four could not be clearly determined, and 31 were German. Of the fifty-one names of donors to the election campaign funds, only four were definitely not German (Ibid., October 21, 1922).

illustration than is found in most of the literature on the subject, that socialism in the United States was largely a German import in its beginnings, and that even at its height (in terms of number of votes in presidential elections: 920,000 in 1920), its primarily German character had not been lost—at least not in St. Louis.

Considering that by 1920 the number of city inhabitants born in Germany had dwindled to 30,000 (in 1890, the 66,000 German-born residents accounted for well over half of the immigrants in St. Louis), it is remarkable that the Socialist candidates in the 1923 local election (with a 28 percent turnout) received almost 5000 votes (Republicans 42,000, Democrats 26,000).[4]

Much like Milwaukee,[5] St. Louis had been regarded as a "German" city since the mid-nineteenth century. In 1880 St. Louis, with a population of 351,000 the fifth-largest city in the United States (after New York [including Brooklyn], Philadelphia, Chicago and Boston), listed 55,000 German-born inhabitants, and including the second generation, Germans made up about one-third of the total population—a share that then began to decline steadily. In 1920 St. Louis had a population of 773,000, of which 30,000 had been born in Germany and almost 120,000 were German-Americans of the second generation.

Since mid-century St. Louis was a booming Mississippi Valley metropolis, an industrial town (iron, lead, zinc, shoes, beer) as well as a center of trade and transportation. German immigrants and their children made a significant contribution to this commercial growth. By the 1850s, too, largely due to the influx of intellectuals in the 1830s and after 1848, the city became the hub of German-American culture in the Middle West. In 1897 a total of five German-language dailies were still being published, including time-honored papers such as *Die Westliche Post* and *Anzeiger des Westens*. As late as 1910, two of them with a combined circulation of about 55,000 were still in existence.[6]

The German community was well integrated in the city as a whole. Their residential areas were widely scattered, with the highest concentration of German-born residents in 1880 reaching only 28 percent in one of the twenty-eight wards; in 1910 it had decreased to 14 percent. Germans remained intellectual and cultural leaders well into the twentieth century. In 1900 the professor appointed to the chair in the German Department at Washington University in St. Louis, endowed by the brewer August Busch, proudly announced that almost half of the students were attending classes in German language or literature.[7]

[4]Ibid., April 7, 1923.
[5]See the introduction to the Pritzlaff series, Chapter 9.
[6]USC 1880.1, 538–39; USC 1920.2, 745, 758, 752, 926–27, 946; Detjen (1985), 12.
[7]Olson (1980), 50, 77.

St. Louis was particularly hard-hit by the anti-German movement of 1917–18. Robert Prager from Dresden, the only person killed during the nationwide persecution, lived in St. Louis from 1914 to 1917 and in April 1918 was lynched across the river only a few miles away from the city. German disappeared from the schools and from Lutheran church services, German books were removed from the city library, martial patriotism led to the renaming of Berlin Avenue as Pershing Avenue,[8] and last but not least, in April 1917, fifty full-time employees of the semiofficial American Protective League started work in St. Louis, investigating about eleven thousand cases of suspected espionage, pro-German propaganda, pacifism and radicalism, draft dodging, disloyalty, and activities of enemy aliens.[9]

Considering his limited school education, Dilger's writing is remarkable. His German is correct in all formal respects, he has no trouble expressing himself, and in the rare instances when he uses Westphalian dialect, he does so deliberately and sets it apart. One can find fault with his language in only two respects: his sentence structure is very simple and somewhat repetitious, and his descriptions as well as his value judgments tend to be black or white, with little room for nuances or shades of meaning.

What has just been said holds true for the twenty-five years after his emigration. From about 1908 on, Anglicized spellings can be found in his letters, like "yetzt" for "jetzt" [now]. At the same time, more and more uncommon phrase patterns appear, and it is never hard to find the English idiom that had served as a model. Similarly, English words creep in; unchanged or Germanized, what they all have in common is that a German reader would not understand them unless he knew English fairly well.

Ludwig Dilger

[postcard with no date,
postmark Hagen, Westphalia, August 12, 1880]
Dear parents and brothers and sisters,

Just to let you know that I still don't have a job. Since Sunday I've been staying with the Rechenbergs and have looked and tried to get a job in Barmen-Elberfeld, Ronsdorf, Remscheid, Schwelm and now in Hagen, but with no success. If I don't get a job by Sunday, I will be forced to come home, because I'm out of money.

---

[8]General John J. Pershing (1860–1948) commanded the American expedition forces in Europe, 1917–19.
[9]Luebke (1974), 5–15; Olson, 204–5; Detjen, 151–52.

Many greetings from your Ludwig
Please have a look in the Dortmund newspaper.

[no date]
Dear parents and brothers and sisters,
    I'm sending you this poem[10] as a belated Christmas present and re-
main, sending you all the best / your son and brother / Louis Dilger
Please let me know what you think of this poem in your next letter.

St Louis Mo., Oct. 13th, 1885
Dear parents and brothers and sisters,
    You must excuse my long silence, since up to now I've been waiting in
vain for a letter from you. In my last letter of May 17th, I wrote that I am
working again for my old *Boss* F A Dreste & Son and I'm still there now,
too. Dear parents, I am still, thank the Lord, quite hale and hearty and
hope you are as well. Times here are very bad at the moment and wages
are very low, on top of that a poor harvest, makes the prospects for the
coming winter very bleak. In my last letter I mentioned that the St Louis
Patent Bread Co. went bankrupt and I was therefore out of work. I am
now earning only 20 dollars and have to work very hard. [6 ll.: asks about
their health; birthday greetings for his father] Do not be angry with me
for not writing so long, my head was turned by the girls, but that's all
over now and from now on I will be prompt in answering every letter
again. In my next letter I will send your birthday present. I would have
liked to have sent one now, but I have bought a new supply of clothes
(clothing here is very bad).

[10]The great respect that you now hold
  In your new sphere of action
  Is thanks to German ways of old,
  Work provides great satisfaction.
  What's had the chance to bloom and grow,
  Your goals and your achievements,
  Are nourished by the German soul,
  Which is unique, knows no appeasements. [4 ll.: holidays]
  With a German oak together,
  You plant anew a Christmas tree,
  Its branches reach out, high and nether,
  Enfolding sweet and youthful dreams. [8 ll.: memories of the homeland]
  Oh, German faith's eternal here,
  That time cannot undo,
  Uniting both the hemispheres,
  The homelands old and new.
  The end.

How are my married brothers and sisters getting along? Is Ida still single or has she also been sold? I am still single, thank the Lord, and intend to stay single until the times improve. I don't pay any attention to my countrymen here, because the farther away you are, the better friends you are. I must close here, since my time is very limited and I'll tell you more news in my next letter.

All the best from / your son and brother

Louis Dilger

[11 ll.: correspondence][11]

St. Louis, March 26th, 1886

Dear parents and brothers and sisters,

Finally, after 5 months of being ill I am able to send you a sign of life. Since the 24th of the month (Wednesday) I have been boarding with Albrecht Nettmann[12] and his wife and I'm not yet fit to do any work. I was in the Alexianer Hospital[13] from November 10th last year until March 24th this year and paid 5 dollars a week. That took all the money I had saved and now I am completely without means and too weak to work. Thus I ask you, dear parents, if it is possible, to help me, I will gladly pay you back as soon as I can work again. I don't know what the actual cause of my illness was, nor does the doctor, so I will just tell you how it was. It started so suddenly that on the one evening I went to bed,

---

[11]The following letter from Louis Dilger's employer Joseph Dreste (baker, according to CD 1886) to his father follows chronologically:

St Louis, Feb. 1, 1886

Honorable Herr Dilger,

Once again I take up my pen to inform you about your son Louis. In my last letter I wrote that your son was on the path to recovery, but his fate has changed. He was already back on his feet, then the doctor discovered his wound had not healed properly and he would have to undergo another operation. And now we don't know if he will live through it or not, but we're hoping for the best, and when he has recovered, or is well enough to leave his bed, I doubt that he will be able to work for an entire year, and he has already run out of money, since he has been ill since November 10, 1885, already three months. I have already given him all the assistance I can, since I had an unfortunate year myself last year, I lost my wife and I had just taken over the business myself, which set me back quite a bit. I think that when your son has recovered somewhat, he should journey back to his homeland. Hopefully you will help him so he can make the trip. Your son knows nothing of this letter, since I thought it was my duty to inform you how things stand. I hope that if you can provide some help, you will do so as quickly as possible. I must close in the hopes that you do not think this is not the truth. Your son is in the hospital and is being cared for very well, as he told me himself. Please write back as soon as possible. I have not yet received an answer to the last letter I wrote you.

Respectfully yours / J. Joseph Dreste / [2 ll.: his address]

[12]Nettmann is listed in St. Louis CDs for 1882–93 as a "machinist."

[13]An order of primarily German lay brothers, founded in 1350, and dedicated to the care of the sick and burial of the dead. The order supported hospitals in St. Louis, Chicago, and Oshkosh, Wisconsin (Bonenkamp et al. [1882], 330).

hale and hearty, and next evening I could neither lie down, sit or walk. During the night, my anus had swollen shut so that I couldn't relieve myself, although I felt a constant need to. There was a tumor deep under the skin of my buttocks. [2 ll.: details]

As soon as I was admitted to the hospital I was operated on and 3 more times later until all the poison was out of me. The wounds have hardly healed. [. . .] The doctor regards my recovery as a miracle and is not a little proud that he brought me through. [. . .] I am eternally grateful to the Catholic order of the Alexianer brothers for their more than motherly care. Dear parents, I would have liked to have sent you a Christmas present as I promised, but you can see that I couldn't. Don't ask me to come home because I can't. If I had been able to, I would have come last fall, I asked all around and everyone advised me to stay here. I am very grateful to Mr. Nettmann for taking me in as he did. He often sends his best to you. Dear parents, yesterday the great Gould railroad strike was decided in favor of the *Knights of Labor*[14] (*Arbeitsritter*). The monopoly had to bend in the face of organized labor.[15] A great victory. The local social labor party[16] is very active here, Nettmann is the treasurer, he is a hard-line social democrat.

[13 ll.: unions; boycott as a strategy in labor disputes; greetings, signature, address]

St Louis Mo., 1886 [before August 29]
Dear parents and brothers and sisters,

I received your dear letter safely and the money as well. I was over-joyed that you helped me in my time of need, because if I've ever needed money then never more than now. Dear parents, I am pleased to let you know that I am now so far recovered that I can do light work and have gotten an easy job, that is as *Barkeeper* or *Kellner* in German, I only earn 10 dollars per month and food, but that is better than nothing. Dear parents, I thank you for your help from the bottom of my heart and hope that I

[14]Established in 1869, its influence and membership grew rapidly during the 1880s (in 1886 it reached 700,000). Unlike the AFL, which succeeded it as the leading labor organization around 1890, the Knights of Labor admitted unskilled laborers and pursued reform objectives that went beyond improved wages and working conditions.

[15]Jay Gould, 1836–92, was a railroad magnate who controlled some ten thousand miles of railway lines, primarily in the Southwest. On the strike see *The Greenwood Encyclopedia* (1977), 167.

[16]More correctly, Socialist Labor party, which adopted this name in 1877 and, by the end of the 1870s, had achieved local and state election victories and had attracted about ten thousand members in 25 states. Most of the party members, however, were Germans and other immigrants. After a series of catastrophic defeats, membership dropped to a low of 1,500 in 1882, 90 percent of them immigrants. In 1883, despite internal disputes, the party started to gain momentum again (Bell [1952], 233–42).

will soon be in a position to repay you. For the time being, I cannot. Now I am really tired of this place and if God is willing, I will see you once again. Albrecht Nettmann is also out of work at the moment because jobs are hard to find, he has also been through a lot and can tell you a thing or two about America. I would have liked to have come home a long time ago, but it's hard to get the money together and when you do, some illness comes along and takes away every hard-earned dollar. Dear parents and brothers and sisters, you ask if there are no health insurance companies here, yes, there are some but like all the other American institutions, they are nothing but *Humbug*.[17] [4 ll.: asks for address of Uncle Felix]

How are all my married sisters and brothers, are they all hale and hearty, give them all my love. Oh, how much I would like to see my twin sisters, have they grown a lot? I feel very much alone in the world and would very much like to be with you at home, I didn't want to make you angry, dear parents, and forgive me for what I did before. Dear parents, perhaps you already know that Jay Gould has gone back on his word with the *Knights of Labor* here and now the people have had to give up the strike, otherwise they would have starved, but the hour of revenge is not far off. The *Knights of Labor* (*Neihts of Leber*) are growing stronger every day in number of members and will secure their rights at the next election. [2 ll.: details] Witten must have grown a lot, as I see from your newspaper. [10 ll.: correspondence; greetings, signature; address][18]

St. Louis, Nov. 5th, 1886

Dear parents and brothers and sisters,

I am very pleased to be able to inform you that today, after 3 months of

---

[17]Mandatory health insurance for industrial workers, later expanded to other occupations, was introduced in the German Empire in 1883. Half the premium was paid by the wage earner, half by the employer.

[18]The following letter from Albrecht Nettmann to Dilger's father follows chronologically:

St: Louis, Aug. 29, 1886

Dear friend,

Due to circumstances which I will describe in greater detail during the course of this letter I am forced to inform you about your son Louis. The latter was of late, as you will have seen from his letter addressed to you, boarding in my house, and had a place here in the house as a *Baarkeeper* or in German *Kelner*. But about 4 weeks ago he quit this post in order to take up another, namely as *Treiber* [driver] for a baker named Kämmerer, where he receives $25 a month and *Bording*, in order, as he said, to save some money for the crossing to Germany to his dear parents. But unfortunately, after hardly a week there, his great plans were dashed in the most painful way. For the old trouble, the illness that has befallen him here in this country, made its appearance once again. [2 ll.: life was in danger] But after the operation, which was carried out on him here in the local city hospital for the second time, he has improved somewhat, given the circumstances, in this institute where he still is at present and where my wife and I take turns visiting him once a week. [2 ll.: recovery will still take months] Louis asked me to tell you this, since up to now he has not been able to do so himself. [23 ll.: wishes, correspondence; greetings; signature; address]

illness, I am well and have been released from the hospital. But I will have a scar as wide as a finger for the rest of my life, the result of six (6) operations. I am back at Mr. Albrecht Nettmann and his wife's, who send their best, too. As soon as I am able to work, I will look for an easy job. And since smoking and drinking is strictly forbidden (by the doctor) I hope to have saved enough money by next spring that I can come home. As I see from your kind letter, you want to send me the money for the journey, but please don't, for as long as I can't earn enough money myself I'm not coming home, even if it takes 10 years. But the fact that you offered it is further proof of your love for me, for which I thank you from the bottom of my heart. But I couldn't possibly let you spend your last dollar on me. I will see you again, hopefully next spring. How are you, dear parents, brothers and sisters? All well? [2 ll.: further questions, greetings] I have been through a lot, a lot in this country of whore-freedom. Freedom, it sounds ridiculous to hear a man speak of freedom here, when he is still enslaved by a *Corporation* as he was not in Germany. But the worker will soon realize what his freedom is all about, since in the elections yesterday, labor candidates won all over the country, and the next election will bring even better results. Henry George, the Labor candidate for the *Mayors office* received 69,000 votes in New York. The Democrat, Hewitt, 80,000 and the Republican, Roosevelt, 58,000. So the Democrat was elected, but they used every means, good and evil, to beat the Labor candidate. The Social Democrats are making great progress here and I predict that in 15 years we'll have a Socialist president and *Congress*. So much about the Labor movement.

I have a lot of friends here and will soon have a job again and it's not long till then and till my departure from here. Otherwise I can't think of any other news, I live very well at the Nettmann's. Will write often. I send you thousands of greetings and remain
Your loving son and brother Louis.
[10 ll.: enquiries, address, greetings]

Pullman,[19] Ills., Jan. 20th [probably 1890]
Dear parents and brothers and sisters, dear father,

As I cannot ignore the earnest request of my dear mother and brother Hugo, and because the birthday greetings from my dear sister Emily have put me in a more gentle frame of mind, I will therefore kneel down before you, dear father, as a son, and if I ever did you wrong, then I ask

---

[19]Company town founded in 1880 by the inventor of the railway sleeping cars of the same name, with a railroad car factory and housing for the workers, annexed to Chicago in 1889.

you, as your son, for forgiveness, and I hope that you will find a place in your heart for me, like the prodigal son. At the same time I ask you, dear father, to believe and trust in me in future, more than in other people, then this sad episode will never repeat itself!

[4 ll.: thanks for birthday greetings] At the moment I am very hale and hearty, and I've been working for the last 3 weeks with my friend Gustav Korthaus here in the *Pullman Car Shops* and for the time being I only earn 1½ a day, but the work is nice and easy. I'm working as an axle turner on a lathe, spoiled machinist, and now I'm learning it first. The foreman is an Irishman and he likes me a lot because I'm the only German who speaks perfect English. In two months I'm getting married, because my future father-in-law broke his leg, so I couldn't do it this month like I wanted to, since he wants to dance at my wedding, because it's the eldest daughter that I'm marrying.[20] By the way, he is said to be worth 15,000 dollars and is paying for the wedding, since I have nothing, he also showed me his will in which he's leaving me one of his houses, in fact the nicest one. That's how things are for the "good-for-nothing with no character and fly-by-night without childlike feelings," that's how I am in their books here. Young men who are better looking and better off would have liked to have had my bride, and if that rascal Nettmann goes to her father and slanders me, then something terrible is going to happen to him. [7 ll.: greetings from friends; correspondence; asks parents for a photograph] And thanks again to Sister Emilie for her charming New Year's card, and as soon as I can, I will send her 20 marks for a new dress. [4 ll.: greetings, signature]

St. Louis, April 27th, 90

Dear parents and brothers and sisters,

I should almost feel ashamed for having made you wait so long for an answer, but because since the arrival of your letter I have entered the state of "patched trousers," I am sure you will gladly forgive me. Did you get my invitation? My wife and I would have been pleased if you could have come to the wedding. My wife is very enthusiastic in her praise of your picture. [4 ll.: details]

Dear parents and brothers and sisters, my only wish is to see you again, and my wife would very much like to accompany me, but it will take perhaps 3–4 years, then we'll both be coming (perhaps even three of us). I

[20]Emma, born in November 1870 in Missouri, was the daughter of Wilhelm Burmeister, born in 1836, who immigrated in 1859. St. Louis CD lists Burmeister simply as a "teamster," but the 1900 MC indicated that he rented out teams (MC 1900: St. Louis, e.d. 134, #52). In 1902 his assets amounted to $6,620 in real estate (*Barr & Widen Co.'s Credit Guide* [1902]).

have made a good match, two weeks from now I'm moving into my father-in-law's house, which will be mine later. My furniture and carpets and everything cost 1,200 marks all together, half of which was paid for by my father-in-law, he also gave my wife an elegant wedding dress, paid all the bills for the large wedding and gave me 20 dollars on our wedding day to pay for the music and the carriage. In my next letter I'll send you and all the adult brothers and sisters a picture of me and my wife in our wedding clothes. [16 ll.: asks for his brother Albert's address; W. Fiege in Chicago; family; greetings, signature; address]

St. Louis, Mo., Aug. 25th, 1891

Dear Brother Wilhelm,

[4 ll.: correspondence] My daughter will be one year old on the 30th of this month and is starting to walk now. I am still working in the *Medart Patent Pulley Co.* and am earning 2¼ dollars a day or 9 marks in your money. Now you'll probably think that I must be getting rich with a wage like that, but that is not the case, because everything here is more expensive than over there, primarily the rent. I pay 10 dollars a month for two rooms and a kitchen, or 40½ marks in your money. [3 ll.: photographs]

Dear brother, you sound like you would like to come over here, but I don't advise you to do so. If you can earn 50 to 60 marks every two weeks over there, then for God's sake stay there, because painting has gone to the dogs here. Anybody can pick up a brush here and just splash some paint around. But if you can do especially good and fine work, then come on over, before the winter, you'd be very welcome.

I'd very much like to have Brother Albert here, he could earn a good salary in his business. Cabinetmakers earn 40 cents an hour (1 mark 62 pfennigs) and work 8 hours a day.

[18 ll.: correspondence; W. Fiege's whereabouts unknown; family; greetings, signature]

St. Louis, Mo. Oct. 15th, 1891

Dear Brother Albert,

Please forgive me that I have kept you waiting so long for an answer, you know that I hate writing. My hands are so stiff from hard work that as you can see I can't write decently any more. [4 ll.: health, photographs] Dear brother, you asked in your letter if my wife is German. Burmeister is certainly not an Indian name, nor an English one. Of course she was born here, her parents are Low Germans. [. . .] She doesn't have any relatives in Langendreer. She would have liked to have written you, but she can't write German because they don't teach German here in the public schools.[21] Dear brother, my wife would very much like to have one of you brothers here. If you want to come next spring, you'd be a thousand times welcome. I have found out that you are thinking of getting married, but then it wouldn't work out for you to come here, for you ought to know that getting started here is harder than anywhere else. You can't expect to get the same wage here at first as someone who's already had experience, the additional costs are higher, furniture is expensive here. My furnishings cost almost 1000 marks and aren't even anything special. [9 ll.: W. Fiege's whereabouts unknown; greetings, signature; address]

St. Louis, Mo., Oct. 15th, 1891

Dear Brother Wilhelm,

[24 ll.: family; photographs; his wife would like his brother to come] If I have enough money later and there's no danger of my being drafted into the army, and our parents are still alive, then I'll come for a visit with my whole family.

Why do you keep asking if my wife is German? The name is enough to say so. Of course she was born here, but she speaks German just as well as any of you and is proud of her German heritage. Her father came over here in the year 1860 from the Duchy of Lauenburg near Hamburg, and fought in the Civil War here on the Union side, and now he receives 12 dollars a month pension.[22] On the side he has 11 horses in his teamster business, then he also has 3 houses here and a farm of 108 morgens, 35 English miles from here, which he has rented out. [9 ll.: best wishes, greetings, signature, address]

St. Louis, Mo., Feb. 25th, 92

Dear Brother Wilhelm,

[24 ll.: correspondence; has found a good match for Albert; comments on the news from Witten; in America everyone has to help himself] So

[21]German had been taught as an optional subject since 1864 in the public grade schools of St. Louis, but it was eliminated from the regular curriculum in 1888 (Olson, 95–106).

[22]Burmeister served three months as a volunteer in the early summer of 1861 in the Second Missouri Regiment and from August 1861 until August 1864 in the First Missouri Cavalry Regiment. When he was kicked by a horse, his ankle was broken, and he first received a pension of $4 a month. After countless petitions, this was raised to $12 in July 1890 and $15 on February 24, 1908; he died on April 23, 1908 (NatA, Pension Records, Union Army, William Burmeister).

only a few more weeks and then you'll be up for the draft, if they take you, then pack your bundle and come on over to me, you'll be very welcome. There's more than enough work here for you, you needn't worry about that. [3 ll.: correspondence]

Is Father still so angry with me that he never sends along any word of greeting? I am not angry with him and even if he never writes, he's still my father, he is a bit too hotblooded all right, that's because of his South German–French background, but he worked hard and brought us up honestly, and therefore we owe him our respect and love, even if he does us wrong.

Give Mother my very best and tell her that I am very sorry I couldn't send her a present for her birthday. I would so very much like to see her again, dear old Mother. Wilhelm, be good to your mother, you may have 10 women in your life, but only one mother.

[6 ll.: greetings, signature; address; greetings]

St. Louis, Mo. 1/28/1894

Dear Brother Wilhelm,

[2 ll: correspondence] As I see from your letter, you have already achieved military honors by becoming a private first-class, a somewhat empty honor, but still a sign of your good behavior. Dear Brother, I am glad that you are doing your duty, because if you want to come here later and the circumstances here do not come up to your expectations, you will at least be able to return home, without being bothered. [2 ll.: he cannot]

But still you mustn't think that I am homesick, because I'm an American through and through (naturalized citizen) and am well satisfied. I wouldn't want to live in Germany again, I'd just like to see you all once more. [8 ll.: would like news of the family; asks about his sister Emma in Brazil, relatives, friends, wages]

Dear Wilhelm, times are worse here than I've ever seen before in the 13 years I've been here. All work and business at a standstill, hundreds of thousands without any income, but provisions are still very high except for flour.

Still, I've been lucky so far because I still have work. We had to agree to a wage cut of 10%, and we only work 8 hours a day. But I still earn a good living. I now get (2 dollars a day for 10 hours) or 8 marks a day. [11 ll.: all are well; expecting another baby, hoping for a boy; greetings]

St. Louis, Mo., Dec. 18, 1896

Dear parents and brothers and sisters,

[7 ll.: Christmas—a holiday for the children; thinking of home] I would have sent you a little surprise a long time ago, but I was always lacking the means and still am now, the last three years I've been suffering from bad times, and if my father-in-law hadn't been generous in supporting me, I might have gone under. The times have never been worse as long as I've been here. But that's what is called a "Democratic government." Nettmann has also been out of work for 9 months and he is doing very poorly. But now we have a Republican again for president, and things will get better in the future. [2 ll.: tornado] It didn't hit us badly, and I was glad, because my father-in-law was off on a visit to his brother's in Germany and he had left me in charge of his business. [10 ll.: asks about the economic situation in Germany; all well, also second child]

Dear parents and brothers and sisters, since I am out of work again at the moment, I have decided to buy a small grocery store, I also have a good opportunity to buy one at the moment, since the owner is sickly and his wife can't run the business. The business has been running for 23 years, very profitably, and within a few years it should enable me to live as well as the present owner does. But since the business has to be paid for in cash, 750 dollars, and my father-in-law is only willing to give me 675 dollars (all the cash he has) I ask you please, dear parents, to lend me 75 dollars, just for a short time, and help me make my fortune. I don't want my father-in-law to go into debt on my account, otherwise I wouldn't need to ask you, but he has already done more than enough for me. I hope you won't refuse to do me this favor, I will be eternally grateful. [22 ll: greetings; address; birthday greetings to his mother; signature]

St. Louis, Dec. 9, 1906

Dear father, brother, sisters, brothers-in-law, sisters-in-law, grandchildren, and all relatives and friends,

[10 ll.: is thinking about Christmas and his youth; asks about the family] I and my family are doing very well at the moment, my family was enlarged by one member/girl 2 months ago.[23] I've given up my business, after I lost 1200 dollars.[24] I'm now working in the *"American Refrigerator Transit Co."* as a *Pipe-fitter* on air brakes, and earning 2 dollars and one quarter (2¼) a day, and in addition my eldest daughter (Clara) earns 1 dollar a day as a *Press-feeder*.

[23]After Clara (b. 1890), Florence (b. 1894), and Oscar (b. 1902), Adele was born (MC 1910: St. Louis, e.d. 182, #77; see also MC 1900: e.d. 139, #176).
[24]His father-in-law was his partner, at least in 1898 and 1899; from 1900 to 1903, Dilger appears as the sole owner (St Louis CD). The decline of the business is documented in the credit-rating books of Barr & Widen, St. Louis, for 1902 and 1903, as well as Engel & Foote Co., St. Louis, for 1904. In 1902 his credit limit was set at $3,000, one year later it was reduced to $1,000, and in 1904, it was noted that he was a "very slow" payer.

There's certainly plenty of work to be had here, Polacks and Italians earn 2 dollars a day with a pick and shovel. But housing is terribly expensive, 2 rooms and a kitchen go for 12 dollars a month in the poorest neighborhoods. Food, too, is very expensive, so you can't save anything, in spite of the high wages. I belong to a *Loge*[25] and in the event of my death, my family will receive 1000 dollars [2 ll.: questions about Germany, family] My son Oskar is almost 5 years old. He's a big strong boy, a true Dilger—hot-tempered but good-natured.

With this I will close for now. From now on I won't be so slow in writing, and I wouldn't have been so slow in writing if every time I asked for support, I hadn't received "no" as an answer. I wouldn't have lost my business if I had received help immediately when I asked for it. Of all your children I've made the fewest demands and cost the least. Not once has one of my children received a present (no matter how small) from their grandparents in Germany. But let bygones be bygones. [8 ll.: greetings; signature; address]

St. Louis, Jan. 17th, 1907

[38 ll.: salutations; correspondence; asks about Emma; wishes his father a long life; no presents for his children: as in February 19, 1906, letter; doesn't believe his father's claim that he is poor; asks about relatives]

We only work 9 hours a day. Wages keep going up here. A wheelwright earns 20–25 dollars a week. A mason earns 75–80 cents an hour or 6–6½ dollars for an 8-hour day. A carpenter 4½–5 dollars a day and so on. America, I love you, no longing for Germany at all. It's the richest country in the world. It's the best country for a poor man. Our city of St Louis now has 750,000 inhabitants. I'm surprised that so few Germans are coming here now. Polacks, Italians, Greeks and Russians are coming by the hundreds of thousands.

[7 ll.: greetings; signatures of all the members of the family]

St Louis, Mo., Sept. 28, 1908

Dear brother, sister-in-law, and children,

[5 ll.: correspondence] Today is my youngest child's birthday (Adele). She is now 2 years old and won the first prize in a beauty contest. So you can see that I've learned at least one trade well. 10-minute break, for drinks!! Here's to your health and that of your family! Cheers!!

Now we turn to another subject, that of the great inheritance. If you would like to do me a big favor and at the same time save me 40 marks,

---

[25]Lodge: mutual aid society (see Introduction to Part II, above).

then send me my entire share (if you can). The notary public charges 10 dollars for his efforts, whether I receive 50 or 500 marks.

Dear brother, as you've probably heard already, I lost my wife's inheritance in business. For 9 years and 4 months I was in the grocery and produce business. For the last 2½ years I've been working as an air-brake inspector. Since the panic we've only been working 8 hours a day. [2 ll.: ages of the children] Business here was absolutely terrible last year. And food prices are higher than ever. So you can probably well imagine the misery and distress among the poor people. Up until now, my family and I have managed to muddle through. [11 ll.: has rheumatism, is fine otherwise; greetings; signature]

                                              St. Louis, Nov. 12th, 1908
Dear brother and sister-in-law,

I am in possession of your kind letter and I am pleased that you and your family are hale and hearty. I also received your bank draft. Do you have any idea how much I received? Let me tell you! All of 59 dollars. But it's not your fault. It only goes to show how little it takes to be a millionaire in Germany. There's a man here named Rockefeller who has 1000 million dollars, just as much as the entire war reparations that France paid to Germany. [4 ll.: memories of his youth]

Dear brother, I also want to let you know, by the by, that my wife has unexpectedly come into possession (with her sister, as joint owner) of a two-story house, next to a nice lot, according to the terms of my deceased father-in-law's will.

If nothing unexpected happens to prevent me, I will come to visit you in 2 years' time, that would be in 1910. I actually wanted to surprise you, but since I've been assailed from all sides, I've had to give in. [. . .] So don't tell anyone what I've told you, it will make the joy of seeing one another again even greater. What would you say if I came unexpectedly and knocked on your door and asked in perfect English for a place to stay?

Dear brother, I'm enclosing the receipt and would like to thank you for having been so prompt. We now have a Republican for president again; and the moneybags keep the power. We'd be much better off if we had an honest government like you do.
[6 ll.: greetings, signature, address]

                                              [letter badly damaged]
                                              St. Louis, Jan. 30th, 1909
Dear brother, sister-in-law, and children,

Today, on my 46th birthday, I am moved by memories of my childhood to answer your kind letter of the ninth of this month. First of all, my heartfelt thanks for the wonderful album and postcards! You couldn't have given me a nicer present. All of my relative and friends admired them very much. It goes to show the people who were born here that we didn't grow up on a manure pile and that there are [---] a lot of things worth seeing there. [6 ll.: mentions his plans to visit] All of what I've experienced and seen [---] fill a big book.

In terms of ships, it's well known that Germany [---] surpasses, or exceeds, all other countries in the world.

Many thanks, too, for your kind offer of 20 marks to cover travel costs, I know your intentions are the best, but an American stands on his own two feet, since here the saying is *"help yourself!"* [22 ll.: correspondence; relatives; lists all his children; his second daughter Florence is being confirmed; asks about friends] You are surprised that I haven't forgotten my native tongue, although I never hear a word of Westphalian, the reason is that I don't want to forget it. St Louis has about 300,000 Germans, but up to now I haven't met even one Westphalian.[26] Here there are mostly High Germans, Bavarians, Swabians, Badenese, Hessians, Saxons, Swiss, Hungarian Germans and so on. [14 ll.: correspondence, thanks, greetings, signature, address]

St Louis, March 23rd, [probably 1913]

Dear Brother Albert and family,

[10 ll.: correspondence; in memory of his deceased brother Gustav] Dear brother, as far as my circumstances are concerned, I can't complain. I have steady work for a relatively good wage, have my own house[27] and am quite well. Otherwise worker's conditions here are probably much the same as over there. No chance of savings, since the food prices are too high. What good does it do me to earn 3 dollars a day, when it takes every cent to keep on living. This country is ruled by priests and petticoats. The whole pack of Jesuits that Bismarck chased out of Germany have made themselves at home here and are living high on the hog, rolling in clover.

They rule via the women, whose bodies they "bless." Beautiful daughters turn into "brides of heaven." Dear brother, I can well imagine that Germany has grown in leaps and bounds since the war of 1870–71. I would like very much to witness this boom in person myself. But it isn't possible. I won't travel on alms. [4 ll.: too expensive—$350]

[26]Even if all German-Americans with even one German parent are taken into account, there were only 186,404 living in St. Louis in 1910 (Detjen, 9). Westphalians, however, were far from being underrepresented (Kamphoefner [1987], 70–105).

[27]In MC 1910 he is still listed as a renter; all four children lived at home, 3819 Marine Avenue. Clara (19) worked in a factory, Florence (16) in a laundry.

You may have already heard from brother Wilhelm that my eldest daughter got married. Her husband is an electrician. My son Oscar is 11 years old and strong for his age. My 2nd daughter Florence is 18 years old and works in a printer's shop, she earns 8 dollars a week. [. . .] My youngest daughter is 6 years old and goes to school. She is a very clever child and the family favorite. [9 ll.: greetings, signature, address]

St. Louis, 12/6/14

Dear brother, sister-in-law and [---], as well as all friends and relatives,
[3 ll.: correspondence] Aren't my letters getting through to you at all? If that's the case, I will complain at the postmaster's. [11 ll.: correspondence; Christmas greetings; questions] How are brother Hugo [---] Wilhelm doing? Have they been drafted into the army? We've all been doing very well up to now, and are all working, even though times are bad. Here in St. Louis we have 60,000 unemployed. [. . .] Dear brother, since it is almost impossible to find out anything definite about the war in Europe, please, dear brother, write me the real truth, because the English newspapers only write about German defeats, and the German newspapers only about German victories. You can't believe either of them, since no war has ever been fought without losses. [. . .] Every day I think about the poor soldiers of all nations who are lying in the trenches in this terrible weather, trying to kill each other. But one thing is for sure, and that is that Germany is not to blame for this war and that after it has paid this high price, it will emerge victorious from the fight. What is right should and must triumph.

The American people, with only a few exceptions, are anti-German and openly show their friendship for the English. If Germany loses the war, we would have a hard time of it here. So, cost what it may, you must win, in order to exist at all. Because if you lose, Germany will be torn into pieces.

There's not much news to report here, all we read about is murder, robbery, suicide as well as divorces. [8 ll.: greetings, signature, address; apologizes for his poor handwriting]

St Louis, Feb. 7, 1915

My dear Albert and family,
[2 ll.: correspondence] First of all, many thanks for the beautiful postcards, and especially for the puzzle-picture "who remains the victor," which all our friends and acquaintances admired very much. [2 ll.: correspondence] Dear brother, nothing that Germany has done up to

now has caused such a sensation and so much respect as the "blockade declaration" off the coasts of England and France.

That will badly hurt the pocketbooks of our infamous American hypocrites and bigots. And that's the only spot where these "assistant Englishmen" have any feelings. Hopefully the blockade will be strictly maintained. For our hypocritical government just sits there and watches all the grain and meat being shipped out, in order to keep this disastrous war going on even longer, and those of us here who have no part in it, have to pay twice the price or starve. [4 ll.: prices of flour and horses are far too high] Dear brother, I am certainly against all wars, since the people who always suffer the most are ultimately the poor, but I am firmly convinced that this war was not provoked by the Germans, and that it's a fight for the existence of the German Empire, and so I say to you all "keep holding on, boys" and "beat 'em back," until they grow sick to their shivering bones, and may the Lord be with you and bless you, Amen! If I were over there, I would have volunteered a long time ago and would have died happily after having sent a ½ dozen Englishmen before me into the hereafter. If that nation of shopkeepers ever tried to attack this, my new homeland, I wouldn't hesitate long to shoulder a gun.

There's a lot of stupid talk here about militarism etc. but what about "*Navyism*" that played the "*Bully*" for hundreds of years, claiming all the oceans in the world as its own private property. [. . .]

Dear brother, write me right away in case any of our relatives is wounded or killed, which I hope won't happen. [6 ll.: four million unemployed, food prices high, misery; newspapers full of crime]

Up to now we've been doing fairly well, I have a steady job and decent wage, but no chance of saving anything. [4 ll.: greetings, signature]

St Louis, Feb. 26, 22

My dear Albert and family,

[20 ll.: correspondence; thanks for photographs] Albert, how are you and your family, write and tell me how you really are. You are certainly happy to still be alive. Up to now we've been doing fine, but it looks like bad times are coming. Business has almost come to a standstill, wages have been cut back sharply, and the cost of living remains high, and then these horrible masses of unemployed! Hopefully it will all turn out for the best. The Germans were almost forsaken even by God himself. You have a hundred years of hard times ahead of you. If the Lord God is to blame for the war, like the preachers keep claiming, then the Devil is quite a decent fellow by comparison, isn't he? [6 ll.: photographs]

Dear brother, you write that Germany wants revenge! You should get that idea out of your heads. What all didn't Germany have on its conscience before this war? Just think back 150 years, to Poland, Schleswig-Holstein, Elsaß-Lothringen [Alsace-Lorraine], Kiao-Tschau [Kiaochow], etc. Now don't start crying if Germany's in for it now, if you want peace, stay peaceful! The Hohenzollerns, with their eternal sabre-rattling, are the real cause of your misery. The peace of Versailles is very severe, perhaps unjust, but it was specially set up that way to get rid of that damned German militarism forever.

Dear brother, I thank you very much for your invitation to come for a visit; but you don't know how things are. [3 ll.: a friend who is visiting Germany will explain] In three years my son will be finished with his training, then he'll earn 45 dollars a week and I won't be missed.

Hopefully Germany will have recovered somewhat by then.

I can well imagine [. . .] that things have changed dramatically; and I would very much like to see these changes myself. [8 ll.: hopes it will be possible; family] I must close now, brother, [. . .] and I ask you not to criticize my poor handwriting too much, since I always write English. English is as natural to me as lice are to a beggar. I'm not exaggerating when I say that I speak English better than German. Two years ago I was a delegate to the national convention of the *Farmer Labor* party in Chicago.[28]

[5 ll.: signature, greetings]

[letter badly damaged]

St. Louis, Mo., J[---] 11th [----] [probably 1922]
My dear Albert and family,

On June 4th (on your birthday) I was very pleased to receive your kind letter. [4 ll.: best wishes] Your letter was held up here at customs and I had to take off 2 hours from work to pick up the letter personally and open it in front of the customs officer. Do you [----] that kind of prying? So please don't send any newspaper clippings in the future. [5 ll.: thanks for picture of his parent's house; would like to see his homeland again]

Dear brother, the political situation in Europe seems to stay much the same. The French (that bunch of swine) are still sitting on their high horse [16 ll.: France has war debts of $11 billion and doesn't want to pay; prices and taxes are rising, wages sinking, but he's getting by]

[28]May 5–10, 1920. The party had just been formed by numerous radical farmer, union, and socialist groups, primarily in the Middle West. The 1920 results of the presidential election: sixteen million votes for the Republican candidate, nine million votes for the Democrat, 920,000 for the Socialist, 265,000 for Farmer-Labor. In Missouri the Socialist candidate Debs received 21,000 votes, the Farmer-Labor candidate 3,300 (McCoy [1971]).

Dear brother, I was glad to read that you are well again, I can well imagine how this disastrous war has weakened the poor German nation, physically, economically, financially, but hopefully not morally. My grandchild was seriously ill for 2 weeks but is now recovering. [3 ll.: greetings, signature]

St. Louis, Feb. 4th, 1923

My dear Brother Albert and family,

First of all, many thanks for wishing me a happy birthday. The same longing for a reunion also fills my heart, but I can't afford it at the moment, since I am still on strike. It's now been more than 7 months that we've been on strike[29] and if we were to give up now, we would lose everything we've gained in the last 10 years, and turn into wage slaves, that's why our motto is *"stick tight" give me Liberty, or give me death (gieb mir Freiheit oder gieb mir den Tod).*

Dear brother, I read in our papers that France has taken over the whole Ruhr District, and the screaming from Berlin. I can't understand what the difference is between a French capitalist and a German one, as far as the workers are concerned. Maybe the French will pay you better than the Germans. I have lost all respect for patriots, because there's usually a purse behind it. In this country it doesn't matter what the nationality of an employer is, what counts is the man who pays the most. What did Hugo Stinnes or Adolph Thyssen[30] ever do for you or your country? Self-enrichment was their only goal. Capital knows no borders, it is *international.* If capital is now internationally organized, then the workers, logically speaking, must do the same. Sitting around and moping won't get you very far. The Americans say, *help yourself (hilf Dir selbst).* That's what makes this country independent. The French *Invasion* is the natural result of losing a war. But enough of that. [10 ll.: memories of his parents; greetings; signature]

St Louis, Mar. 22, 23

Dear brother and family,

I received your letter, as well as brother-in-law Emil's, and was very pleased to hear that Sister Lina received the 5 dollars. I would have been

---

[29]An unsuccessful strike conducted by more than 400,000 railroad workers was in reaction to, among other things, a 13 percent wage cut. It began on July 1, 1922, but lost momentum in September. On July 1, 1923, some 150,000 workers were still on strike (see American Federation of Labor [1924], 250–53).

[30]Two prototypical captains of industry heading business empires centered around coal and steel in the Ruhr District.

very disappointed if the money had fallen into the hands of the French. I would like to send her some more, but we are still on strike. But now it looks like the strike will soon be coming to an end, and in our favor. Up to now more than 200 railroads have signed agreements with their workers. If we had lost, it would have been the death of all the other agreements.

That is why we have to keep going. We railroad unions are the strongest unions in the country and have more than 2 million members, but only 417,000 went out on strike. There are still 150,000 of us on strike. This strike is the biggest and most bitter ever held here. I am a member of the *Central* strike committee for the St. Louis *District.*

Now, dear brother, as I see in our newspapers, the French are behaving like barbarians, like cowards usually do toward people who are unarmed, but the bell will soon toll for this band of robbers, too, and it may happen sooner than they ever dreamed. Your biggest threat, however, lies with the capitalists, they are already starting to found a kind of *Fascity,* and arm them, so be careful.

Because that gang is even worse than the French, they'll take away all the freedom you still have now. Surely you've read about how the *Fascity* in Italy are carrying on. [13 ll: greetings; well-being] Many thousands of greetings from Louis and family / write back soon.

St. Louis, Mo., Feb. 5th, 1925

Dear Brother Albert and family,

[3 ll.: correspondence; thanks for birthday greetings] I have given up hope of coming to see you again, ever since we lost the big strike. I had 500 dollars in the bank for that purpose but I had to use them to live on. The strike also cost me 2000 dollars in wages and my job, so that now I am still out of work. My youngest and prettiest daughter Adele (18 years old) has also been sick for 5 months. So the whole burden has fallen on the shoulders of my son Oscar (23 years old). Unemployment is high here, and anyway if you're already gray, you don't have much chance of employment here. Robbery and murder have been running rampant since the war. And on top of that, the dishonesty of the public officials. God only knows where all this will lead. I've been following events since the Versailles bandits' peace, feeling great sorrow for the German people. A disgrace to modern civilization. A peace treaty like that can only breed new wars.

[. . .] Dear brother, the great railroad strike has taught me a lot. I have lost all trust in mankind, and now I no longer trust even my closest friends. For 26 years I worked for the labor movement. I was a delegate

to the national convention of the Labor party, chairman of my union in
St. Louis, etc. Now I'm through with all of that, and from now on I'm
only going to look after my own best interests. I'm through with all
those progressives. [13 ll.: health; signature; greetings]

                                        St. Louis, Nov. 7th, 1925
Dear brother and sister-in-law and all relatives,
    [8 ll.: correspondence] A whole year without work, as the president of
my local I couldn't do anything but lead the strike, much less look for
work. After two years we lost the strike and I lost 2500 dollars in wages
and 1000 dollars in cash that I had in the bank and that I had saved for a
surprise visit to the old country. But what's done is done, let bygones be
bygones. Now I am working at the *Merrell Drug Co.,* but I earn only half
as much as on the railroad. I would have been more than glad to help you
out financially, but I couldn't, since I received no salary as president of the
local during the strike. They boast a lot here about the great prosperity of
the people, but wages are low, except for construction workers, and the
cost of living is terribly high.
    Every day the rich get richer and the poor get poorer. [4 ll.: inflation
would not have made trip to Germany any less expensive]
    You also seem to be suffering under the mistaken impression that I
have lost everything. I still have my nice house, for which I was offered
8000 dollars. So I don't have to rely on my children. Still, I don't deny
that my daughter (the youngest and prettiest one) earns 20 dollars a week
as a *Telephone Operator,* and that helps. [5 ll.: expresses sympathy on
several deaths in the family]
    I can well believe that you are overjoyed to be rid of the red legs,[31] even
the sympathy of the American people is more and more with the German
people.
    I don't believe that America can ever be dragged into a European war
again, one bad experience is enough. [13 ll.: unpaid war debt of the
Allies, therefore high taxes; family; greetings, signature]

                                        St. Louis, Feb. 12, 1926
Dear brother and family,
    [7 ll.: birthday greetings to Wilhelm; Albert's illness] I am still feeling
very good at the moment, despite my 63 years and hard work. The same
is true of the rest of my family. [5 ll.: sister Emma in Brazil]

[31]Common nickname for French soldiers, from their uniforms during the Franco-Prussian
War of 1870–71. His reference is to the French occupation of the Ruhr, which ended in August
1925.

You spoke of unemployment in Germany. That's no new disease here, here it's a chronic illness. We always have 1½ to 2 million men out of work here. And at the same time the newspapers keep blathering about the great prosperity here. Of course it's true that the millionaires have never made as much money as they do now, but the working people, with few exceptions, now earn less, compared to the cost of living, than ever before. If I weren't so well known here, I wouldn't have gotten a job again so soon after we lost the strike. I am now working in a wholesale drug store (medicine) and only earn ⅔ as much as I earned on the railroad. My daughter Adele earns 2 dollars a week more than I do. She is a *Telephone Operator.* [12 ll.: family; newspaper reports of murder and robbery; greetings, signature]

[26 ll.: April 11, 1926, to Brother Albert: condolences on the death of his son Alfred]

St. Louis, Sept. 26th, 1926

Dear brother, sister-in-law and grandchildren,

[15 ll.: was ill; state of health] How are things over there really? All the Americans who have visited Germany say that Germany is in better condition than any other country in Europe.

[2 ll.: family] I don't feel as strong as I used to, I used to be a husky fellow, but at least I'm still able to do a good day's work. And believe me, you have to work a lot harder here than over there. Murder and robbery are running rampant here, as a result of the war. In Chicago and Detroit, the streets aren't safe for young girls and women. Our court system has collapsed. [. . .] 68% of all criminals are Catholics, mostly Irish and Italians. [3 ll.: details] We want to keep the papist gang in check. [4 ll: greetings, signature]

St. Louis, Nov. 22nd, 1926

Dear brother and family,

[17 ll.: correspondence; all are well; on "prosperity," wages, and prices, as in letter of February 12, 1926] The same gang of capitalists that robs us does the same in Germany, since capital is international.

They are the best of friends. It's only the poor workers who hate one another, and that is just what the capitalists want. And at the same time, these traitors boast that they are superpatriots. [9 ll.: crime; streets not safe for women; greetings; signature]

St. Louis, 5/22/28

Dear brother and family,

[15 ll.: family] In terms of the job situation, things over here look no better than other there. We have 5 to 6 million unemployed, and at the same time the big capitalists sneak 700 to 800,000 Poles, Greeks, Mexicans and Chinese into the country every year, because they work for lower wages. Capitalists are the same in every country, namely "thieves." That's the gang that incites all the wars and then when peace is concluded, they're the best of friends again.

Your flyers were here in St. Louis and received a big welcome. They had more luck than sense, too, they all almost fell into the ocean.

You say "German swords and German songs, both have good resounding tones." That used to be true, but the good sound has been lost, they still hate the Germans a lot here. [8 ll.: friend reported after a trip to Europe that:] The morality in your cities is much lower than here. Before the war, the virtue of German women was world famous. [21 ll.: hates wars; greetings, signature; postscript to his nephew: he's welcome to come for a visit; Adele has ulcers; she doesn't speak any German; greetings, signature; asks for musk seeds]

St. Louis, 6/14/28

Dear brother, sister-in-law, and grandchildren,

[14 ll.: best wishes; house repairs; family] My dear ones, I and mine are fairly well, I won't be getting any richer over here any more than you will over there, I make a decent living and I am satisfied. My son earns 40 dollars a week and pays me 10 dollars for board. A year ago he bought a fine automobile that cost him 932 dollars and has driven it 12,500 miles so far. He sends his best regards to you all. Your flyers were here for a visit, and they got a big welcome. But our Lindbergh is still way out in front as the best pilot in the world. He flew alone and landed where he had intended to.

[9 ll.: wars—the fault of the rich robbers; unemployment for seven million; war debts, priests] I will stop now and enclose a few words in English for your son. With many thousands of greetings from your loving brother Louis and family. [. . .]

My dear Nephew Al. jr.

[4 ll.: Adele is off on a trip; visitors] *You are welcome but I would not advise you to quit your Job over there, because work is very scarce here at present, besides, I am sure you would not like it over here. You are better off over there, where a man can get a good glass of Beer or Whiskey.*

[. . .] with best wishes / Your Uncle Louis

St. Louis, Sept. 23, 1928

Dear brother, sister-in-law, and grandson,

[12 ll.: thanks for musk seeds, is sending $1] Big capital is just as heartless here as over there, and American capital rules the world. [7 ll.: work is scarce; self-interest rules] Revolution, religious war and only then comes the day of the poor man. [13 ll.: all the empires in world history were brought down by greed; greetings, signature]

St. Louis, Nov. 29th, 1928

My dear brother and family,

[7 ll.: health; weather] Dear brother, you are being unfair to our late father when you describe him as hardhearted. It was a hard struggle for him before he agreed to my emigration, especially because I got my passage ticket and train ticket, before he had any idea what I had in mind. And on the day of departure, he took his watch out of his pocket, gave it to me, and said "be honest and good and bring me no shame, and should you come home again, do not forget that you have a father." He couldn't have done anything more. Thank God I never brought him any shame.

When I came to this country, it was a free country, not only in theory but in practice. The World War, however, changed all that. England with its horrible propaganda of hatred of everything German is to blame for it. Hatred of the Germans has died down in the last years, but it still exists. No one is likely to bother me, since I have a good command of English, better than thousands who were born here, because I don't have a German accent.

So, dear brother, once again Germany has shown the world what it can do, since Graf Zeppelin not only flew over here but also back again, and that is what they really admired here. Now they even admit that Germany has outdone all the nations in the world. We've now elected a new president here. It was the most important election that I've ever taken part in. It was the first time that the Catholic Church had a candidate in the running.[32] As you well know Rome works on the quiet, but it didn't do any good, for Rome's candidate suffered the worst defeat in the history of this republic. The holy baldpate won't be allowed to rule this country.

As far as labor is concerned, the election was meaningless. The money-bags rule both parties.

[7 ll.: high taxes, import duties] Dear brother, I am very glad that I won't be alive much longer. The entire world has changed so, there's no

[32]Alfred E. Smith (1873–1944) was defeated by Herbert Hoover, 15 million to 21 million votes.

brotherly love anymore, it's every man for himself and the devil for all. The women have taken over, especially the young ones, they smoke, drink, swear, show all they have and what you can get very cheaply; where will it end. [4 ll.: greetings, signature]

St. Louis, Feb. 3, 1929
Dear brother, sister-in-law and grandchildren,
[7 ll.: thanks for birthday greetings] I am doing fairly well, have enough to eat and drink, good clothes and good friends and I am quite satisfied. Only with drinking things look bad in this <u>free</u> country. We make our own beer at home here in the cellar. [. . .] The rich people here can have everything their <u>heart</u> desires, liquor, beer, wine, champagne, cognac. [. . .] The bloodsuckers, who produce nothing, have Heaven on earth. [2 ll.: camel and the eye of a needle] Now it has its Heaven here. From year to year, the middle class gets smaller and the capitalist class gets bigger, here just like over there. [6 ll.: greed destroys empires; billionaires in the United States] Enough of that.
You at least have a pension fund. Here you get a kick in the backside when you get old. A disgrace for the richest country in the world. Things keep getting better and better. A couple of days ago they hanged 2 murderers and on the same evening we had 24 robberies in 3 hours, that's what you call "higher civilization." [7 ll.: greetings, signature]

[27 ll.: April 19, 1929, to his brother Albert: correspondence; storms; family's health; Zeppelin; hatred of the Germans; unemployment—as in earlier letters]

[17 ll.: January 18, 1930, to his brother Albert: grief over the death of their sister Lina; life not worth living, particularly in America; no pensions]

St. Louis, March 10th, 1930
Dear Albert and family,
[3 ll.: correspondence] My wife has been suffering from rheumatism for two months, and my youngest daughter has had a stomach and gall bladder ailment for 9 months, and I don't believe she'll ever be completely healthy again. Besides that, my eldest daughter has left her husband, a hard-working electrician but just as hard a drinker. And to fill up our cup of woes, a half dozen comrades and I are expecting to be dismissed. The corporations in this country keep consolidating, and the

first step is always to get rid of workers. And what's more, it is almost impossible to get a job, especially for a man my age. [. . .] Almost 50 years ago, when I landed here, this was a wonderful country. If I had had my parents here, I could have really gotten somewhere. We have wonderful schools here, where you can learn any trade for free. I couldn't take advantage of this opportunity, since I had to feed and clothe myself and earn the money myself to pay the doctors. [2 ll.: children are good to him]

I am also very grateful that I have my own lovely home. The taxes are quite high, of course, I have to pay 90 dollars a year, along with the repairs. I also have it nicely furnished, have a furnace, gas and electricity, *Piano, Radio* and *Phonograph,* so no lack of music. Besides that I have an inside bathroom with hot and cold running water. My house has 5 big rooms, along with the hall and bathroom. My son Oscar has a nice car and I ride to work in it every day. Dear brother, you asked if I didn't teach my children to speak German. Yes, I certainly did. But they don't teach German in our schools, and in general, since the war, not much German is spoken here, and the children forget German very quickly. And by the way, my wife was born and brought up here, and I only speak English with her. I will try to convince one of my children to write a letter to you, you could have it translated over there. [7 ll.: is in good health again; best wishes; signature; greetings]

St. Louis, Aug. 10, 1930

My dear Albert and family,

[2 ll: correspondence] As you may have read in your newspapers, we've been having the hottest summer we've ever had. Since I am now employed in one of the city parks (*Marquette Park and Bathing Pool*) and since I always have to work in the hot sun, you can imagine that I don't feel like writing letters when I come home all sweaty and tired in the evenings. [21 ll.: heatstroke casualties; drought, crops are suffering; health; prohibition; crime]

My job goes until September 15th. Taxes keep going up every year. I now pay exactly twice as much as I did in 1911 when I bought my house. Time will bring an answer. [11 ll.: greetings, signature]

St. Louis, Dec. 5th, 1930

Dear brother and family,

[4 ll.: correspondence; health] Up to now we've been doing fairly well, despite the bad times. I work 4 days a week, enough to get by. But there is such misery and starvation among our poor! And our big millionaires live it up. [. . .] Our big "fatnoses" are scared stiff. They are trying everything to get business going again. The government is building 50,000,000 dollars' worth of new buildings, thousands of miles of new roads are being built, 35,000,000 dollars worth, shipping on the Mississippi River is being improved, etc. Robbery, murder and theft are running rampant. And anyone who knows the Americans knows that they stop at nothing. The day before yesterday two capitalists were stopped in their cars and robbed during broad daylight. Stores are robbed every day. If they don't turn over the money fast enough, they're shot dead. Ours come in gangs, with revolvers, guns, machine guns, bombs, and everything you need to go to war.

Dear brother, thanks very much for the picture of your city of Witten, it must have gotten much larger and prettier. [12 ll.: Adele and Oscar are getting married soon; greetings, signature]

St. Louis, Jan. 17th, 1931

My dear Albert and family,

[29 ll.: thanks for letter; Adele got married on December 30, she now lives in Boston; family events; New Year's greetings; the Depression; criticism of religion] Thus there is only one cure for the current situation, namely the "Russian" one. Our capitalists, and yours, too, don't allow the truth about the situation in Russia to get out, they control the press and are scared stiff that the poor people might revolt. Capitalism is standing on the edge of its grave. [2 ll.: Jesus preached brotherly love] I feel sorry for your fascists, they are tied to the yoke of the Pope but they don't know it. And what is the Pope? Antichrist. But enough of this misery.

Come what may, Germania stands firm. [21 ll.: anecdote from their youth; greetings]

St. Louis, Feb. 12th, 31

Dear Albert and family,

[5 ll.: thanks for birthday greetings; health; flu epidemic] Business is still languishing. Wages are cut every day. I only work 4 days a week, hardly enough to stay out of debt. Oscar is still living at home and is in no hurry to get married until times improve. My daughter Adele got married on December 30th and is living in New York. My wife can't get over her having married a Catholic. I didn't like it either, but what can you do? It's too late now. He is a good boy, thrifty, and good to her. He earns 300 dollars per month with the chance of a higher position in a few months with a salary of 500 dollars per month.

[43 ll.: Witten; description of an experience with his father—surprise visit of his Uncle Alois, whom he didn't recognize at first, his father's youngest brother, a restless, widely traveled fellow; greetings, signature]

St, Louis, Aug. 18, 1931

My dear brother and family,

[46 ll.: the Depression; memories of his youth; family history; Witten] Have you ever heard of our *Municipal* opera in beautiful *Forest Park*? It is famous throughout the whole world, we often go there. The *Park* is 1368 acres in size. Dear brother, I do not understand your enthusiasm for the Hohenzollerns with their steel helmets.[33] If they take over, they will plunge Germany into war again. No one hates the German people, but the Hohenzollerns have no friends. [19 ll.: no news from Emma; murder, dishonesty; best wishes; signature; English p.s. for his nephew Albert]

St. Louis, Dec. 11, 1931

My dear Albert and family,

[17 ll.: correspondence; family; the Depression; the poor start revolutions but never wars; family] As I see in the papers, the European powers do not want to pay their debts, they owe us 11 billion dollars, but they always have enough money for preparations for a new war. Germany owes the United States 2½ billion dollars that it borrowed for war reparations. Why should we pay twice as much taxes in order to help the Europeans start a new war. But enough of that!

The economic situation here is very sad, businesses go bankrupt every day. One bank after the next closes its doors. Here in St. Louis, there are 125,000 unemployed. Hopefully the new year will bring an improvement, if not, then there will be a revolution, and may God protect us from that. [10 ll.: family; greetings; signature; correspondence]

St. Louis, Feb. 3rd, 1932

Dear Brother Albert and family,

[26 ll.: thanks for birthday greetings; family; international bankers are cheating the people; unemployment—not in Russia; communism keeps getting stronger; capitalism on its deathbed] And your bankers work hand in glove with ours. Now our big capitalists are trying to plunge us

[33]The Hohenzollerns were the Prussian kings and German emperors, the last of whom, William II, abdicated in November 1918. The strongest force working for a restoration of the German monarchy was *Der Stahlhelm* [Steel Helmet], the national German World War I veterans' organization.

into war with Japan, but no one here wants anything to do with it. The rich "patriots" stay home, and the poor devils have to pay for their patriotism with their lives. [10 ll.: family; greetings, signature]

St. Louis, May 10th [probably 1932]

Dear Brother Albert and family,

[10 ll.: correspondence; has gallstones; family is well; bad times] Gold rules the world. Gold is also the cause of your reparations. But these men are playing with fire, one spark can set the whole world on fire. Hopefully I won't be alive by then. [8 ll.: conditions in Russia not as bleak as they are reported to be]

Dear brother, I've received a *Copie* of the Köln [Cologne] newspaper, but I haven't found anything in it to convince me to subscribe to it. The less you read the papers, the calmer your nerves stay. Capital rules all newspapers. [12 ll.: Witten; will send photographs of St. Louis later; greetings, signature]

St. Louis, October 10, 32

Dear Brother Albert and family,

[2 ll.: correspondence] There's a lot of illness in my family. My second daughter (Mrs. Karl Boos) had an operation for (*Appendicities*) two months ago and is still very weak. [3 ll.: further illnesses] The economic situation is very unfortunate here too. We have between 10 and 12 million unemployed here. And the taxes keep going up. Thousands have lost their property because they weren't able to raise the money for the high taxes. That's the result of the calamitous World War. And who is to blame. Our great millionaires. [15 ll.: the poor never start wars; war debts unpaid, but new armaments, particularly in France; his brother is probably better informed about Russia; Witten] All in all, I've been a citizen of this country for 42 years, and this is my home and that of my family. I wish Germany happiness and prosperity, but I never want to live there again. To come for a visit, I'd love to. [9 ll: greetings; signature; correspondence]

St. Louis, Dec. 12th, 32

Dear Albert and family,

[7 ll.: Christmas greetings; is to have an operation] Thank Heaven I have such good children, one tries to do more for me and my wife than the next, my son Oscar will pay all the costs of the operation and hospital, between 300 and 400 dollars. [5 ll.: family] I always intended to surprise you with a visit, but the last 3 years have ruined everything. I've had to take every dollar out of the bank. And besides that, we only work 10 days a month. [9 ll.: symptoms of illness—prostate] One thing is certain, we're going to be rid of our *Prohibition*. The Democrats will make sure of that. As you've probably read, they beat the Republicans in the last election. Hopefully the industrial situation will improve in the next years. [3 ll.: murder and violence in the newspapers] One thing is certain, America won't be that quick to get involved in European affairs again. "Peaceful" France has billions for armaments, but not a dollar for war debts to America. Hatred of the Germans (caused by England) has almost disappeared here. How did you end up with so many different parties in the *Reichstag*? The Germans were always known as clear-thinking people, but it doesn't look that way any more. Hopefully you won't let your republic go under. Hitler, an Austrian, didn't you have anyone in all of Germany who could lead you? For God's sake keep the Hohenzollerns away from the throne, otherwise it won't be long until you are at war with some country. Take Switzerland as your example, it stayed neutral in the midst of the fray. Keep a sharp eye on your ammunition manufacturers and bankers, those are the crooks that push a country into war.

Dear brother, I will close now and ask you to forgive me for my poor handwriting and use of a pencil. [3 ll.: greetings; signature]

St. Louis, Jan. 13th, 1933

My dear brother and family,

[3 ll.: correspondence] It affords me great pleasure to report that my operation was very successful and that I will have sufficiently recovered in 3 to 4 weeks to take up my duties again in the city park. It cost my son Oskar 300 dollars. In this area you are 50 years ahead of us. With regard to pensions, various states have made a start, but the restrictions are so strict that you have to be completely unfit for work and 70 years old before you get even a little support, and you must not own any property to qualify. [30 ll: illnesses; expensive medicines; England is mainly to blame for the World War; the United States was on the wrong side, hatred of the French is increasing; the workers must unite against the rich; greetings, signature]

St. Louis, April 15th, 33

Dear Brother Albert and family,

[6 ll.: thanks for best wishes; family; health] As you know, I am a city employee. In the recent city elections, my party (*Republican*) lost, after having been in power for 20 years. As a result, 7000 city employees will be losing their jobs. We expect to be dismissed on May 1. Work can't be found at any price here. Thank God I don't have any debts on my house, and don't have to pay any rent. My taxes amount to 85 dollars a year for the house, 9½ dollars for water, 10 dollars for insurance. My monthly expenses are 3½ dollars for gas, 2 dollars for electric lights, 3 dollars for the telephone. I pay 5 dollars a week for life insurance for my family. The current living conditions make me tired of living. Has your situation improved or gotten worse since Hitler took over the helm? As I see from our newspapers, Hitler and von Papen were in Rome to see the Pope and have signed a pact against the Protestant Church. Whether that is English propaganda or not, I can't judge. This much is certain, Germany lost its best friend (America) when it made Hitler dictator. Dear brother, in our presidential elections in November we threw out the Prohibitionists. Since the 7th of this month our breweries have been going full steam again. They are working 24 hours a day and still can't brew enough beer. Thousands have gotten jobs. But our capitalists are not in a position to provide work for all the unemployed. The machines and new work-saving devices don't permit it. Capitalism is bankrupt. [12 ll.: nationalization is the only solution; bankers; middle class destroyed; war; greetings]

St Louis, Dec. [probably 18th, 1933]

Dear Albert and family and all brothers & sisters,

[10 ll.: Christmas greetings, thanks for newspapers; was unemployed and sick] I am now employed as a boilerman in a straw hat factory, where my son-in-law is the *Superrindent*. It was impossible to get a job in St Louis. I am stationed in a small country town 35 miles from St Louis. I see my wife and son only once every two weeks. Times are getting noticeably better here under *President* Roosevelt and I hope next year will bring better times. I am very pleased, dear Albert, to hear that you've managed to get through these hard times fairly well. [2 ll.: asks for Emma's address in Brazil] Dear brother, what is your son? On the picture it says "*S.A. Mann*"?[34] [5 ll.: correspondence] I am proud of my children, without their help I would have lost my house and everything. But I've never given up hoping for better times. [8 ll.: correspondence; best wishes, greetings, signature]

---

[34]S.A. stands for *Sturmabteilung,* or stormtroopers, the paramilitary branch of the Nazis during the 1920s and early 1930s. After Hitler's rise to power, the membership of the S.A. "brown shirts" rose dramatically, and its function shifted from street brawling to political and social activity as well as military training.

St. Louis, April 27th [probably 1934]

Dear Brother Albert and family,

[9 ll.: illness; family] The richest country in the world cannot afford pensions for its poor, but all the high officials and their wives have pensions. Dear Albert, if you think I made a mistake by immigrating here, then you are mistaken. The difference in way of life between here and there is so great, it is impossible to compare the two. I have a nice house here with 5 rooms besides bathroom and hall, *Furnace* heating, hot and cold water, electric light, gas stove, radio, telephone, lovely garden, live on a pretty street with shade trees and flowers, eat and drink of the best, have 1750 dollars in life insurance, that is more than I could ever have owned in Germany. Work makes life sweet, when I'm out of work for a month, I feel lazy and nothing tastes good. I like to work and I have an easy job, my son-in-law is the only *Baas* I have. Now, dear brother, something about today. Since President Roosevelt has been in office, business has gotten back into swing. He is really a man with a heart for the poor, even though he's a millionaire himself. I can't tell you my opinion about Germany, for it's been 53 years since I left home and in this time the entire world has changed greatly. Your Hitler is hated a lot here and all over America, but not the German people. [5 ll.: France and England unpopular] If Europe must have a war, that's your problem, we will never again be drawn into it. But if any nation dares attack this country, beware! The Americans have shown the whole world who's the best fighter. Your son, I think, should defend Germany and Hitler, although I haven't the slightest idea what the situation is over there.

I am proud of my German heritage, but American from head to toe. [9 ll.: thanks for Emma's address; best wishes, signature]

St. Louis, Nov. 12, 1934

My dear Albert and family,

[3 ll.: correspondence] Now, don't you believe that I have lost my love of the old homeland. I am very proud to be an American citizen, but I never forget that I was born in Germany. As far as the lies of the Jews who've been driven out are concerned, I am completely unmoved, since the time will come when they'll await the same fate here. Not all Jews are despicable, many of our benefactors are Jews. At the moment here Germany is the country that is hated most in all the world, but that will change in time. [3 ll.: death of his sister Elfriede]

Dear brother, you write in your letter that I made a mistake in coming to America. Don't you believe that, for here I live like a capitalist lives in Germany. Even though I still have to work (I've been idle for 4 months, our factory is opening again on December 1st) I still live better than your working class can afford. And my children make sure that I always have money. The husband of my youngest daughter (Adele) is vice president of a rubber factory with a salary of 325 dollars per month. My second daughter's (Florence) husband is a manager in the Langenberg hat factory here in Maskoutah [Illinois], with a salary of 185 dollars per month, my son Albert is an inspector for the *St. Louis Cold Storage and Refrigerator Co.* with a salary of 35 dollars a week, and my eldest daughter (Clara, a widow) is a housekeeper with a salary of 32 dollars a month plus board and lodging. These children make sure that my wife and I suffer no want. Since we've elected Mr. Roosevelt as president, the business situation has improved considerably. Our Congress, which will be in session as of January 3rd, is committed to setting up a pension plan, then I'll stop working. America loves peace. The European cutthroats drew us into war one time, but never again. [19 ll.: war debts, neutrality; family, greetings (some in the local German dialect), signature; address]

St. Louis, Feb. 10, 1936

My dear Brother Albert and family, as well as all brothers and sisters,

[10 ll.: correspondence; health; best wishes] Dear brother, last summer my wife and I went to visit my daughter and son-in-law for 3 months, and in the course of a conversation, I asked my daughter to write to you, I gave her your address, knowing that she can't write German. You can well imagine how surprised I was to hear that she sent you a Christmas card. Soon you'll be hearing from my granddaughter Eileen Boos. She goes to high school here and is taking German, so watch out, my boy. Dear Albert, you asked me if you'd insulted me in your last letter! Not in the least, I just didn't know what to do. You write that I, as a true-born German, should promote German culture in this country, which as a true American would be impossible for me to do. But let's not be enemies because of that. [3 ll.: get-well wishes for son Albert] How are the times over there? Everything here is in a state of great economic uncertainty, we are coming up to another election again, and our great barons of finance are trying their utmost to beat President Roosevelt. That is the same gang that drew us into the war against Germany. [6 ll.: war debts; greetings, signature]

[30 ll.: letter fragment, no date: family, wages, prices; greetings, signature]

Figure 35. Photo of Louis Dilger and his wife Emma, ca. 1935. *Source:* Lieselotte Ohngemach.

Louis Dilger died on June 28, 1943, at the height of the war he had warned against for so many years. His children achieved modest prosperity, with one exception: his Catholic son-in-law, whom the Dilgers did not approve of when he married their daughter Adele, had a highly successful business career. The couple put the world of the "simple folk," in which Adele had grown up, far behind them. They apparently took up an appropriately conservative stance; in their eyes, Louis Dilger's political opinions must have seemed like the unfortunate and somewhat embarrassing aberrations of an otherwise amiable man.[35]

[35]Newspaper clipping (obituary) attached to the last Dilger letter; Mrs. C. J. Wibbelsman (née Adele Dilger), San Diego, Calif., to the editor, January 26, 1987. Clemence J. Wibbelsman, born in 1904 in St. Louis, graduated from St. Louis University and became a top executive in a number of major companies, including Johnson & Johnson (*Who's Who in America* 32 [1962–63], 3,370–71).

III. Domestic Servants

Introduction

Even though girls and women made up only a minority of German immigrants, in numerical terms it was a large one: after the first third of the nineteenth century they made up an average of 40 percent, a higher percentage than in most other ethnic groups.[1] The overwhelming majority of women emigrated with their families or followed other family members—their parents or husbands—who were already living in the United States; relatively few went to America on their own.[2] The situation of these unmarried female immigrants hardly differed from that of their male counterparts, since—in contrast to most married women—they needed to find employment as quickly as possible in order to earn a living.[3] In their search for employment their choices were severely limited. Up until the end of the nineteenth century, employment possibilities in industry hardly existed, and the few other occupations open to women almost always required qualifications and language abilities that the immigrants did not possess. For most of the female immigrants, taking a

[1]Ferenczi/Willcox (1929), 401–22; Marschalck (1973), 72–73.

[2]More precise information about the percentage of female emigrants who left on their own is available for only a few regions: in Württemberg between 1855 and 1870, for example, only ca. 30 percent of the unmarried emigrants with permits were women (Hippel [1984], 217). In Osnabrück between 1832 and 1859 they similarly made up only 34 percent of those traveling alone (Kamphoefner [1982], 63).

[3]Female German immigrants who were married almost never worked outside of the home; at most they contributed to the family income by taking in boarders, even more rarely by home industry (Harzig [1986], 118–19).

position as a servant girl thus remained the only chance to enter the American labor market.[4]

In some respects, it is true, work as a domestic servant, cook, or nursemaid also met the needs of the unmarried immigrant: accommodation in the employer's household spared her the difficult search for appropriate lodgings and at the same time reduced the insecurity and danger of the strange surroundings; since servants were also fed by their employers, they could often save a considerable portion of their earnings.[5] Furthermore, work in the household corresponded best to the experience these young women brought with them from Germany—a large number of them had already worked there as a maid or servant girl.[6] Finally, most of these women regarded the years of employment only as a transition stage to marriage, and work in someone else's home, in contrast to other occupations, could be seen not only as a way to earn a living but also as preparation for running one's own home in the future.[7]

Jobs were plentiful for domestic servants, for as the urban middle class continued to grow, so did the number of families that could afford to employ domestic help. In the United States at the beginning of the nineteenth century only roughly forty thousand servants were employed, but by 1870 the number had increased to nearly one million, and in the following four decades it reached well over two million.[8] Around mid-century an average of one out of ten—and by the end of the century one out of eight—households in the United States had a servant girl. In 1870 in New York there was one domestic servant for every fourth, in Chicago for every fifth, and in St. Louis for every sixth household.[9]

Even in the land of democracy (as in Germany, England, or France), the employment of domestic servants became a requirement for and an expression of bourgeois lifestyle: the servant girl relieved the housewife of hard and dirty chores and gave her time to pursue her "proper" duties as wife and mother or to become engaged in social work or social life. At the same time, a servant girl functioned as a status symbol; wearing a little cap and a spotless white apron—as a substitute for livery, which

[4]Private households provided about 70 percent of all jobs for women in 1840, industry only 25 percent; even at the turn of the century one-quarter of all working women were employed as servants (Kessler-Harris [1982], 47–48; Dickinson [1980], 96).

[5]Katz (1975), 256; Dudden (1983), 60–61.

[6]As did almost all of the writers of the following letters. Occupational information for women in the emigration lists is exceedingly rare; results from the Osnabrück materials, however, may well be typical: three-quarters of the women traveling alone (1832–59) gave *Magd* [maid] as their occupation.

[7]Katz (1975), 256; Dudden, 210–11.

[8]Sutherland (1981), 45; USC 1870.1, 686–87; USC 1910.4, 54.

[9]Sutherland, 10, 46; see also the data in Katzman (1978), 286. By contrast, even in Berlin at the end of the nineteenth century there was at most one servant in one out of eight households.

only very wealthy families could provide for their domestic staff[10]—she was a living symbol, either when opening the door or while shopping, of the fact that her employer belonged to the middle class, and she conspicuously set the family apart from lower-class or working-class families that could not afford to employ domestic servants.

In the South nearly all servants were black (a fact that remained unchanged after emancipation), but domestic service in the North, after the first third of the nineteenth century, increasingly became the domain of female immigrants. In 1840 the proportion of immigrants had already surpassed that of American girls, and by the end of the nineteenth century it was almost twice as high.[11] Irish girls, after mid-century, provided the largest contingent of domestic servants (above all in the large cities of the northeast). Even though their predominance was not as strong outside New York, where in 1855 about four-fifths of all domestic servants came from Ireland, they determined the image of servant girls to such an extent that for many Americans domestic service and Irish background were inseparably linked: *Bridget* became a symbol of the typical servant, whose shortcomings and ethnic idiosyncrasies provided endless material for jokes and caricatures.[12]

Although the total number of female German immigrants who worked as domestic servants was far less than the number of Irish girls, in terms of the percentage of total employed persons, German-born women were also overrepresented in this occupation. After the middle of the century, Germans made up the second largest group of servants in a number of middle-sized and large cities.[13] In contrast to their Irish colleagues, the Germans did have to fight the language barrier. As the letters by Wilhelmine Wiebusch show, however, the barrier was not insurmountable. Immigrants often found their first jobs (as did Marie Klinger and the Winkelmeier sisters) in the households of countrymen who were already established and prosperous.[14] German servants did not seem to encounter

[10]Katz (1975), 141; Sutherland, 10–14; Dudden, 104–8; see also Hobsbawm (1968), 131, for whom the employment of servants is a central indicator of a family's status as part of the middle class.

[11]Sutherland, 48–49, 58; Katzman, 289; USC 1890.2, 484–85, 502–3, 530–627. In small towns and rural areas, however, American-born servants continued to predominate (Katzman, 63).

[12]Ernst (1949), 66; Katzman, 66–67; Dudden, 60–61; Diner (1983), 70–94. In contrast to other emigrant groups, the number of Irish women outweighed that of the men; the majority of Irish female immigrants were young, unmarried women (Diner, 30–42).

[13]In 1870, for example, the Irish were the most strongly represented among foreign-born servants, with a total of 145,000, followed by the Germans, with a total of only 42,000 (USC 1870.1, 705). On the proportion of servant girls among working female German immigrants see Hutchinson (1956), 104. See also the case studies by Ernst, 66; Kleinberg (1973), 181–82; Conzen (1976), 93; Griffen/Griffen (1978), 233–34, 244–50; Glasco (1980), 94, 205–8.

[14]Ernst, 66; Conzen (1976), 92; Griffen/Griffen, 249.

as much resentment from their American employers as did their Irish colleagues. Catholicism as well as other ethnocultural characteristics of the Irish seemed strange and often threatening to many employers. German girls, on the other hand, were mostly Protestant, and to many Americans that characteristic spoke of sobriety, modesty, cleanliness, and a willingness to work.[15]

An immigrant could find her first position as a servant in a variety of ways. On occasion young, single girls were even engaged by agents in Europe or on the ship, but German girls apparently found employment only very rarely in this relatively risky way. It was safest and easiest for the new arrival if she could turn to relatives or acquaintances already living in the United States for help in finding a position. Women who did not have such helpful contacts could always go to the appropriate employment agencies. These existed in almost every town of over five thousand inhabitants and there were dozens of them—some specializing in female immigrants (and even specific nationalities)—in the larger cities.[16]

What was the average workday for a servant girl in the United States like? Ultimately it was much the same as in any large city in Germany,[17] and typically it went like this: the day's work usually began early, around six or seven o'clock in the morning, with the dirty but unavoidable job of cleaning and lighting the kitchen stove. After breakfast had been prepared and served, the traces of this meal had to be removed from the kitchen and dining room; afterward the agenda included making the beds, dusting, possibly shopping—jobs that more or less occupied the entire morning and had to be finished at the latest when it was time to begin preparing lunch. The amount of effort expended on lunch depended not only on the culinary standards and expectations of the family but also on whether the housewife cooked the meals herself or whether— which was frequently the case—she turned the actual preparation of meals over to the servant, merely deciding on the daily menus or perhaps demonstrating her housewifely competence by checking the seasoning of the finished dishes. When the kitchen had been cleaned up after lunch, the servant had perhaps enough time to catch her breath before turning to her afternoon chore of cleaning one of the rooms. Toward evening she then began the preparations for dinner, which in most American families was the largest and most extensive meal of the day and which was often eaten relatively late. It could easily be 9 P.M. before the cleaning up was finished and the servant could finally think of calling it a day.[18]

[15]Sutherland, 39; Dudden, 167–71.
[16]Conrad (1908), 12; Katzman, 97–103; Sutherland, 16–22; Dudden, 80–85. See Figure 36.
[17]See the introduction to the Wiebusch series, Chapter 20.
[18]Katzman, 120–22; Sutherland, 94–99; for Germany see Wierling (1983).

SITUATIONS WANTED.
FEMALES.

THE UP-TOWN OFFICE OF THE TIMES.

The ONLY up-town office of THE TIMES is located at No. 1,269 Broadway. Open daily, Sundays included, from 4 A. M. to 9 P. M. Subscriptions received and copies of THE TIMES for sale.

ADVERTISEMENTS RECEIVED UNTIL 9 P. M.

A—NO. 1,252 BROADWAY.—FIRST-CLASS French cook, excellent laundresses, waitresses, chamber-maids, and house-workers; all certified reference.

A—GOOD PROTESTANT SERVANT girls, German ..., 140 Sixth-av., above ... No charge until suited at the largest new employment house.

—GRIMMKOLD & BROLUND'S SWEDish servants; City or country. No. 1,140 Broadway and No. 154 East 20th-st.

A T LONNBORG'S SWEDISH EMPLOYMENT Office, No. 408 4th-av., a number of select Swedish help.

CHAMBER-MAID, &c.—BY A RESPECTABLE German girl as chamber-maid, waitress, and assist with washing and ironing; best City reference; City or country. Call at No. 101 East 10th-st., corner 3d-av.; no cards.

CHAMBER-MAID.—BY A YOUNG GIRL as chamber-maid or parlor-maid, or would do chamber work and waiting in a small family; City reference from last employers. Call No. 647 3d-av., between 41st and 42d sts.

CHAMBER-MAID AND ASSIST WITH Sewing or Children.—By a young woman, understands her business thoroughly; good City reference. Call at No. 213 East 29th st., between 2d and 3d avs., first floor.

CHAMBER-MAID AND WAITRESS.—BY a lady leaving New-York end of May for her thoroughly ... and competent chamber maid and waitress. Call for two days, between 11 and 10 o'clock P. M. at No. 157 West 34th-st.

CHAMBER-MAID.—BY YOUNG GIRL; assist with waiting or washing in private family; no objection to country; best City reference. Call, after 11, at No. 210 East 17th-st.; no cards.

SITUATIONS WANTED.
FEMALES.

COOK—WAITRESS.—BY TWO GIRLS together, to go to country with small family; one first-class cook; would do coarse washing; other first-class waitress and assist with chamber work; best City reference. Call at No. 410 West 50th-st., third floor, back.

COOK.—BY A RESPECTABLE WOMAN AS FIRST-class cook with kitchen-maid; understands French and American cooking, including all kinds of entrées, pastry, and desserts; best City reference. Call at No. 409 9th-av., first floor; Newport preferred.

COOK, &c.—CHAMBER-MAID, &c.—BY two girls together; one good cook and laundress; other excellent chamber-maid and waitress. City or country; good City reference. Call at No. 236 West 41st-st.; hats or cards not noticed.

COOK.—BY RESPECTABLE GIRL, AS GOOD plain cook; first-class baker; or as chamber-maid and assist with the washing and ironing; or would assist in the care of children; City or country; good City reference. Call at No. 349 West 32d st., rear ones.

COOK.—BY SCOTCH PROTESTANT YOUNG woman as excellent family cook; understands soups, fish, meat, and pastry thoroughly; good baker; highest references. Call at No. 145 West 24th-st., third floor.

COOK.—LAUNDRESS.—BY TWO GIRLS together; one first-class cook, the other first-class laundress; best City reference from last place. Address M. D., Box No. 236 Times Up-town Office, No. 1,269 Broadway.

COOK, WASHER, AND IRONER.—BY young woman in private family; good bread baker; City reference. Call at No. 558 7th-av., near 40th-st., first floor.

COOK.—BY RESPECTABLE GIRL AS GOOD COOK in private family; would do coarse washing; best City reference from her last place. Address R.C., Box No. 311 Times Up-town Office, No. 1,269 Broadway.

COOK.—BY RESPECTABLE WOMAN AS GOOD COOK; will assist with coarse washing; good City reference. Address H. G., Box No. 312 Times Up-town Office, No. 1,269 Broadway.

COOK.—FIRST-CLASS, BY THOROUGHLY COMPETENT woman in private family; City or country; very excellent City reference. Address A. C., Box No. 290 Times Up-town Office, No. 1,269 Broadway.

COOK, &c.—BY PROTESTANT YOUNG WOMAN as cook, washer, and ironer, or house-work, in ...

SITUATIONS WANTED.
FEMALES.

LADY'S MAID.—BY A MIDDLE-AGED NORTH German as lady's maid; would like to travel to Europe; has been there before as guide; speaks four languages; experienced hair-dresser and dress maker; excellent City reference. Address H. B., Advertisement Office, No. 354 3d-av.

LADY'S MAID.—BY A COMPETENT PERSON as maid and seamstress or would take care of children; understands dress making and fine sewing; willing to travel; four years' first-class reference. Address B. A., Box No. 293 Times Up-town Office, No. 1,269 Broadway.

LADY'S MAID.—BY FRENCH PROTESTANT girl, speaking English and German, as maid, seamstress, or nurse; good references. Address, for two days, Marie, Box No. 324 Times Up-town Office, No. 1,269 Broadway.

LADY'S MAID AND SEAMSTRESS.—BY intelligent German girl, or to growing children to travel; City reference. Apply at No. 993 2d-av., one flight.

LADY'S MAID.—BY COMPETENT GERMAN person; fully understands her duties; hair-dressing and sewing; speaks French and English; best reference. Call at No. 210 East 83d-st.

LADY'S MAID.—GOOD SEAMSTRESS & DRESS-maker, and hair dresser; thorough in all branches; good City reference. Address L. K., Box No. 279 Times Up-town Office, No. 1,269 Broadway.

LADY'S MAID.—BY A FIRST CLASS FRENCH lady's maid; cut and fit; good hair dresser; first-class reference. Call at 160 West 34th-st., second floor.

LADY'S MAID.—BY A SWEDISH LADY'S maid; best of references from diplomatic families. Call at 215 West 105th-st., care of Mrs. Cottle; no cards.

LAUNDRESS.—BY A RESPECTABLE WOMAN as first-class laundress, who understands her business thoroughly and would go to the country for the Summer; best of reference, and has lived in last place four years. Call at No. 326 East 51st-st.

LAUNDRESS.—BY A RESPECTABLE GIRL, IN a private family; would assist with chamber work; best City reference; would go to the country for the Summer. Call or address No. 145 West 51st-st., third floor, front room.

LAUNDRESS.—BY A LADY FOR A FIRST-class laundress, whom she can thoroughly recommend, with a family going to country for Summer. Address, for two days, M., Box No. 323 Times Up-town ...

Figure 36. This "situations wanted" section from the *New York Times,* May 8, 1883, reflects the prejudices in favor of northern European Protestants which benefited many German women. Along with seamstresses and waitresses, these were the most common lines in which women sought, and found, urban employment.

Aside from this daily routine there were other jobs that had to be done once a week, as they are reported in one of the letters by the seventeen-year-old Margarethe Winkelmeier: "Monday washing, Tuesday and Wednesday ironing or knitting, Thursdays I have my day off, Friday and Saturday scrubbing and cleaning." Above all the exhausting ordeal of doing the laundry, which usually took all day (and sometimes even two days), was the nightmare of every servant girl. But the next day's ironing was only slightly less strenuous than washing.[19]

In most American households things were somewhat easier than what the immigrants had been used to in Germany, but the blessings of modern appliances were hardly known by the majority of servants during the nineteenth century. At least as long as there was a sufficient supply of labor, the Americans—otherwise highly enamored of innovation—showed little interest in allowing progress to invade the home in the form of time- and energy-saving household devices. Widespread use of washing machines, vacuum cleaners, and refrigerators began only after World War I. After the 1880s, it is true, wood and coal stoves disappeared along with petroleum lamps; gas lines provided homes with energy that was clean and efficient. And although in the first half of the nineteenth century many commodities—from bread and soap to clothing—had to be produced in the home, the following decades saw a steady increase in the supply of finished products.[20] Despite such improvements, however, housework continued to remain a time-consuming and back-breaking business. Many of the immigrant women, however, had been used to far worse, especially those who came from a farm, where they had done hard physical work not only in the house but also in the field or barn.

In addition, relatively high wages compensated for many a hardship. Around the middle of the nineteenth century, a servant girl received between four and six, and by the end of the century ten to fourteen, dollars a month. This was at least twice to four times as much as a maid or servant could earn in a German town during this period.[21] In American households even beginners were seldom paid below average. New arrivals who first found work in the homes of their countrymen, however, often discovered that German-Americans exploited their lack of experience and inability to speak English and paid them lower wages.[22] Even in

[19]Ibid.

[20]Katzman, 123–30; Sutherland, 191–95; Kessler-Harris, 110–12.

[21]USC 1850.2, 164; Kleinberg, 220; Conzen (1976), 92; Schneider (1983), 148. By the end of the nineteenth century, servant girls in German towns and cities received an annual wage of 120–240 marks, which amounted to a weekly wage of ca. $2.50–$5.00 (Schulte [1978], 889; see also Conrad [1908], 13).

[22]Sutherland, 107; see the letters by A. M. Klinger, Chapter 18, and the Winkelmeier sisters, Chapter 19.

comparison to women who worked in other occupations, the servant girls were often better off. The wages of seamstresses or female factory workers were roughly equivalent, and sometimes slightly higher; but these women had to pay for their own room and board; consequently their real income was always lower than that of a servant girl.[23]

Board and lodging, which the servant girl received in addition to her wages, varied from household to household. At best, a girl had her own room, albeit small and sparsely furnished, usually situated near the kitchen and clearly separated from the living room and bedrooms of the family for which she worked; at worst she had to make do with a bed in the storeroom or even the kitchen.[24] Compared to the standard of living of her employer, a servant's quarters were certainly spartan; but compared to the living conditions found in the homes of lower-class families in Germany or the overcrowded tenements in the immigrant neighborhoods of large cities, they were positively luxurious. Much the same can be said of the food. Although some housewives may have jealously guarded or even locked up their provisions, and some servants may have had to serve delicacies that they themselves were not even allowed to touch, in most households the servants ate as well as their employers. Even if they usually had to eat their meals in the kitchen, the food was almost always more plentiful than in Germany, where for many the daily diet consisted largely of bread and potatoes.[25]

Servants in the United States usually enjoyed a greater degree of freedom and were less frequently patronized than was the case in Germany—most male and female letter-writers agree on this point.[26] When the author of an emigrant guidebook declared that the treatment of servants was first-rate and that "the distance between master and servant is almost unnoticeable, both in name and in conduct,"[27] he certainly exaggerated. Class distinctions were perhaps less clearly evident in the United States than in Europe, but middle-class Americans were particularly sensitive with regard to their own social position. As a matter of course, they expected their servants to respect their superiority, real or imagined, and to behave appropriately. This social distance did not necessarily exclude the occasional housewife from seeing herself as the guardian and mistress of her servant, in a maternalistic and solicitous sense—as is shown in Margarethe Winkelmeier's description of her two

[23]Katzman, 141–43; Sutherland, 109.
[24]Katzman, 108–10; Sutherland, 113.
[25]Katzman, 110; Sutherland, 113; Dudden, 193; on nutrition in Germany see Teuteberg/ Wiegelmann (1972).
[26]Aside from the letters in this edition, see also the letters published in Helbich (1985a), 115, 130–31.
[27]Bromme (1848), 415.

employers: one taught her sewing and the other cared for her during a long illness "like a mother." Others, however, regarded servants as nothing more than an irritating appendage to the family—a stranger, impenetrable and unfaithful, spoiled by being treated too well and paid too much.[28]

In contrast to many of their Irish colleagues, German immigrants seldom remained servants for many years. Most of them found a suitable marriage partner within a relatively short time and withdrew from domestic service.[29] In view of the large number of their young and unmarried countrymen, there was hardly a lack of potential husbands. "Hardworking and active girls, who are passably attractive, can be sure to receive marriage offers in the first year," extolled the author of an emigrant guidebook—but he did not neglect to add the warning that it was better to "remain a few years in service to a good master" and "to first save up a couple of hundred dollars" than to marry the first suitor who came along.[30] Here he must have severely underestimated the rational decision-making abilities of young women who were usually well aware of their various options.

It was not only the modest savings many servant girls accumulated that made them particularly attractive for men who were seeking a wife. Because of their duties in the household, they also seemed almost predestined for the role of the hard-working and thrifty housewife, and also they were often more sophisticated and better dressed than others of their sex. Another advantage was pointed out by a German-American in his *"Winke für Auswanderer"* [Tips for emigrants]: women who had worked in Yankee houses, he claimed, not only had a better command of the English language, they were also more familiar with the customs of the Americans—abilities and knowledge that could prove to be extraordinarily useful (also for the husband!).[31]

The years spent in domestic service undoubtedly promoted the acculturation of immigrant girls, although it would be wrong to overemphasize their "Americanizing" effect. Most of the young women of necessity learned the new language relatively quickly, and they adopted American dress as well as the occasional custom they had come to know in their employers' homes. On the other hand, the amount of time they spent in a predominantly American environment was relatively short; anything more than basic learning and adjustment processes were restricted by the social barrier between master and servant, and the most

[28]Katzman, 172; Sutherland, 26–29; Dudden, 85.
[29]Glasco, 208; Conzen (1976), 93; Dudden, 211.
[30]Bromme, 416.
[31]Haas (1848), 57.

important social contacts of the servant girls almost always remained those with their German friends and acquaintances.[32]

Conversely, one can ask to what extent the employment of a German, Irish, or Scandinavian servant girl contributed to a revision of her employer's prejudices and clichés about a specific ethnic group or about immigrants in general. For certain individuals it may well have helped, as Wilhelmine Wiebusch's letters indicate. It is somewhat unlikely, however, that many employers were as enlightened and understanding in their reactions as her first employers, Mr. and Mrs. Moses.

[32]Dudden, 227–31. Dudden also points out that employment as a servant girl—as is frequently assumed—did not necessarily promote entry into the middle class.

18

The Klinger Family

The importance of close family ties in deciding to emigrate, making a new start, and living in the United States is well documented in the following series of letters, written by six children who crossed the Atlantic, one after another, over a period of ten years.

Their father, the winegrower Eberhard Ludwig Klinger, had settled in Steinreinach,[1] a hamlet in Waiblingen County in the Neckar District of Württemberg, at the beginning of the nineteenth century. When in 1824, at the age of 41, he married a winegrower's daughter, Barbara Durst, the couple already had four children[2]—seven more were born in the years to follow.[3] That Barbara and Eberhard Klinger married so late does not reflect moral laxity on their part. Instead it should be attributed to the numerous measures introduced by the local Württemberg authorities to prevent marriages that were undesirable, that is, financially shaky, and hence to protect local poor-relief funds from being overburdened.[4] Despite the fact that the legal "right to marry" had been in effect since 1809, the next generation of Klingers was still affected by this policy. Designed to keep the unpropertied have-nots from marrying and having large

---

[1]The population in 1850 was 552, mostly engaged in winegrowing. Steinreinach belonged to the parish of Korb, but a school was opened there in 1825, which the Klinger children probably attended (*Beschreibung des Oberamts Waiblingen* [1850], 172).

[2]Georg Eberhard (b. 1819), Anna Maria (b. 1821), Jacob (b. 1823), and the fourth died in infancy (Ev. KB Korb).

[3]Of these, Daniel (b. 1827), Barbara (b. 1830), Gottlieb David (b. 1833), Elisabeth Katharina (b. 1835), and Rosina (b. 1838) survived (ibid.).

[4]Matz (1980), 36.

families, its main, dubious accomplishment was a growing number of illegitimate children.[5]

Eberhard Klinger's financial situation seems to have stayed precarious all the rest of his life. He never amassed enough money to qualify for full citizenship and so, like many others, remained an underprivileged resident (*Beisitzer*).[6] Despite regular financial support from their children in the United States, as can be seen from the letters, the Klingers spent the last years of their lives in impoverished circumstances.

The Klingers were hardly unusual. The economic situation and prospects of the rural lower classes[7] in Württemberg continued to worsen until the middle of the nineteenth century. The majority of winegrowers lived on the verge of starvation, and a single crop failure could mean total disaster.[8] Artisans were no better off; most of the common trades were overcrowded, and incomes were so low that it was hardly possible to earn a living.[9] The effects of growing population pressure and increasing poverty were visible in the number of emigrants from the kingdom at an early date;[10] emigration from Württemberg reached its peak between 1846 and 1855, however, when a series of crop failures and poor grape harvests led to a crisis. During the "winter of hunger" in 1852, almost one-quarter of the population had to be supported by the government, and the annual emigration rates reached 1.5 percent. Only after 1855, in the wake of early industrialization, did the emigration rate begin to decline.[11]

In 1848, in the midst of the crisis, the eldest daughter of the Klingers applied to the local authorities for permission to emigrate to North America. The latter attested to her good conduct, the fact that she could not expect any money from her father, but that she had (according to her

[5]Between 1831 and 1871, the rate of illegitimate births in the kingdom of Württemberg lay between 11 percent and 16 percent; no reliable figures are available for the years prior to 1831 (Ibid., 303–5).

[6]According to the civil rights law of 1828, citizens and Beisitzer were equal with respect to the right to settle somewhere, to receive welfare support, and to marry, but only citizens were allowed to vote, hold public office, and enjoy local privileges (e.g., use of the common lands) (Klein [1933], 27).

[7]This class includes smallholders, winegrowers, artisans without their own businesses, and day laborers, although the boundaries between these groups were indistinct.

[8]Throughout the nineteenth century, more than 50 percent of the population was employed in agriculture (Hippel [1976], 303). In the county of Waiblingen (population in 1822 was 5,484), farmers and winegrowers (2,407) made up the largest group, as opposed to artisans and persons employed in other sectors (1,533) (*Beschreibung des Oberamts Waiblingen* [1850], 32). Dwarf operations of four acres or less were predominant (Hippel [1984], 180–81).

[9]On the average, artisan families in Württemberg had to pay 80 percent to 100 percent of their income just for food (Hippel [1976], 350).

[10]Hippel (1984), 139.

[11]Hippel (1976), 362; Hippel (1984), 143. Württemberg emigration rates were some 60 percent higher than the German average (Marschalck [1973], 35).

own account) "100 guilders in cash and 100 guilders in clothing and the like." In addition, the authorities stated that she did not suffer from "any of the defects listed in Article 19 of the civil law code of 1833" and that there were no objections to her emigration.[12] Less than one month later, she received her official permission to leave the kingdom of Württemberg.[13]

From Anna Maria Klinger's first letter we learn that she arrived in New York after an unusually long voyage and apparently found a job on the same day as a servant girl working for a German-American pharmacist. Soon thereafter she must have met her future husband, Franz Schano,[14] who—according to a later letter—had taken advantage of home leave to desert from the Bavarian army and emigrate to the United States with his father and brother.

In the following years Anna Maria and Franz Schano systematically arranged the emigration of five more Klinger children. In 1851, provided with detailed instructions, a prepaid ticket, and 15 guilders for provisions, the twenty-year-old Barbara ("Babett") was the first to arrive in New York.[15] Brother Daniel, however, was told to be patient: Maria and Franz Schano repeatedly wrote to say that he would not have a chance in his current trade (he was probably a carpenter) and should first learn a new "profession." It would thus be better to let his sisters come first, since they would be able to find a job immediately and then help finance his ticket. Actually, two more younger siblings arrived before Daniel, also with financial support from the Schanos: the twenty-year-old Gottlieb, a day laborer in Korb or Steinreinach, and Katharina, who was eighteen years old and had been working as a servant girl in Stuttgart.

Gottlieb Klinger had received official permission to emigrate in May 1854, but in his application he had falsified his year of birth;[16] after his departure it was discovered that he had neither registered for the draft nor done his military service. Following an order of the high court in Waiblingen in August 1854, his modest property holdings were confiscated (at least temporarily), a move that probably disadvantaged the family more than the emigrant himself.[17]

[12]StA LB, F 210, Bü. 411, Nr. 277. The so-called "defects" included prior convictions or being a minor (*Regierungsblatt* 56, December 27, 1833, 516).

[13]Anna Maria Klinger was not the first member of the family to emigrate; a cousin named Gienger (mentioned several times in the letters) had already gone to the United States, and his brother Christian Gienger followed later (StA LB, F 210, Bü. 411, Nr. 277; Bü. 412, Nr. 250).

[14]MC 1850: New York City, W. 5, #264; MC 1860: Albany, N.Y., W. 9, #94.

[15]The Waiblingen files do not contain an application for permission to emigrate in her name; she probably left, like her brother-in-law, with only a passport or certificate of citizenship.

[16]StA LB, F 210, Bü. 414, Nr. 587. In the report from Korb to the Waiblingen County authorities, it was noted that Gottlieb Klinger had already booked his passage via the Müller agency in Stuttgart. Local officials attested to his good conduct and assets of 140 guilders. No application was filed for Katharina Klinger.

[17]GA Korb, Kataster Korb–Steinreinach 1842.

Finally, in early 1857, the Schanos and Gottlieb Klinger sent a draft for 75 guilders for brother Daniel, leaving it up to him whether to use the money for the tools required to set up his own business or to pay for his passage to the United States. Daniel decided on the second plan of action and set off shortly afterward, together with his common-law wife, Marie Friederike Kaiser, pregnant at the time, and their two children.[18] It is likely that Daniel Klinger, like his parents before him, had not been allowed to marry because of his poor financial situation: the new civil law code of 1852 called for a minimum of 150 guilders as a prerequisite for legal matrimony.[19]

In her home village of Kleinheppach,[20] Friederike Kaiser hoped to follow Daniel by applying to the local authorities for 45 guilders to help pay for her passage. According to the council minutes, the sum was approved quickly on the grounds that she and her children "would shortly become public charges" anyway.[21] But the family still ran out of money on the trip. On July 15 the village council in Kleinheppach was confronted with a letter from Friederike Kaiser, stating that she had arrived in Le Havre with her children but did not have enough money to pay for the food for the voyage. If she did not receive another 25 guilders immediately, the ship would leave without her, and she would have no choice but to return, penniless, to her old village. After lengthy debate, a committee of local citizens and village councilors decided the same day to "sacrifice from the treasury another 25 guilders, as well as 15 kreuzers for postage, for the loose creature," in the hopes that this additional payment would rid them of the "creature" and her children once and for all.[22] As paradoxical as it may sound, the prominent citizens of Kleinheppach were influenced in their decision by a crisis in the local poor-relief fund: the illegitimacy rate in the village was the highest in the kingdom (at mid-century, sixteen out of one hundred births were illegitimate);[23] and the large number of persons living on welfare caused a considerable drain on local resources. In the long run, financing a trip to America, even though in Friederike Kaiser's case it cost more than 70 guilders, proved to be a more economical solution to the poverty problem.

[18]Daniel (b. 1849) and Gottlieb (b. 1852–53); MC 1860: Albany, N.Y., W. 9, #335.

[19]Matz, 188–89. Possession of sufficient household furnishings, or enough money to purchase same, was also required. "Poor housekeepers" and persons of ill repute could be denied permission to marry.

[20]Village near Korb whose population in 1850 was 574 (Beschreibung des Oberamts Waiblingen [1850], 165).

[21]GA Kleinheppach, Ratsprotokolle Bd. VIII, Bl. 312, 394.

[22]Ibid., Bl. 313, 396; village account book of 1856–57, Bl. 38; only excerpts of the relevant passages of Friederike Kaiser's letter are preserved. Neither Daniel Klinger nor Friederike Kaiser seems to have applied for official permission to emigrate—even though they received financial support from local authorities (see also Hippel [1984], 140).

[23]Beschreibung des Oberamts Waiblingen (1850), 166; see Matz, 249–50.

One year after Daniel and his family left, Rosina Klinger, the youngest member of the family and now twenty years old, arrived in New York. She had been urged to emigrate by sister Katharina and her husband, who were obviously counting on her assistance in their business, whereas the other brothers and sisters had hoped she would take care of their aging father, now that their mother had died.[24] Although her assets were limited to 25 guilders, permission to emigrate was granted immediately, since "the would-be emigrant has several brothers and sisters already in America who have sent her money for the passage."[25] Had this not been the case, a larger sum would have been required, according to regulations in the other countries she would be traveling through.[26]

The letters themselves tell the rest of the story up until 1883, the year all contact with Germany seems to have broken off. At this time, the head of the Klinger family had been dead for seventeen years and brother Jacob for sixteen years;[27] whether brother Eberhard, who had moved to Stuttgart-Zuffenhausen in 1864, was still alive is unknown.

Fortunately, there is no need to characterize the language of each one of the letter-writers in this series, since all except Gottlieb write alike in most important respects: with a good deal of spelling and punctuation errors but largely acceptable grammar, with a rather simple structure and a limited vocabulary. Still, they are able to get their messages across and even to make some successful attempts at wry humor.

There is fairly little influence of Swabian dialect, and even in the later letters, few English words and hardly any English influence are to be found.

Anna Maria Klinger

New Jork, March 18, 1849

Beloved parents and brothers and sisters,

Out of filial and sisterly love I feel obliged to inform you about my well-being in America. After a long and trying journey I arrived in New Jork safe and sound after all, and until now I have been quite well. [3 ll.: hopes her parents are well, too] Now I want to tell you about my situation, that is that on the same day I arrived in New Jork, I went into service for a German family. I am content with my wages for now,

[24]Barbara Klinger had died a few months earlier, in May 1858 (Ev. KB Korb).
[25]StA LB, F 210, Bü. 416, Nr. 31. In contrast to her sister Anna Maria and brother Gottlieb, the authorities attested to her "orderly"—not "good"—conduct.
[26]Hippel (1984), 133–34.
[27]Eberhard Ludwig Klinger died in 1866 at the age of 83, Jacob in 1867 at the age of 44 (Ev. KB Korb).

compared to Germany, I make 4 dollars a month in our money [10]
guilders,[28] if you can speak English then it's considerably better, since the
English pay a good wage, a servant gets 7 to 10 dollars a month, but if
you can't speak or understand English you can't ask for so much pay. But
I hope that things will get better, for it's always like that, no one really
likes it at first, and especially if you are so lonely and forlorn in a foreign
land like I am, no friends or relatives around. [3 ll.: but her parents should
not worry] The dear Lord is my shield and refuge. [10 ll.: wishes her
parents and brothers and sisters could be with her in America, where they
would have a better life] I keep thinking you are fearful and worried
about me because you have not received a letter for so long, first of all,
we were at sea for one hundred and 5 days,[29] 7 weeks we were docked at
Blümuth [Plymouth] before our ship was done. You probably read in the
letter I wrote to the mayor about the bad luck we had. From England to
America things went well, we still had one big storm, but we suffered no
more misfortune, there were 200 and 60 passengers on the ship. My
journey from Stuttgart to Antwerben went well, I met up with those 3
girls who were also going from Stuttgart to America in Maintz, but
they'd already met up with companions on the way, they started behaving so badly on the journey already, and at sea there were two tailor boys
with those girls, I got annoyed because I couldn't stand such loose
behavior, one of them went to Viladelfe [Philadelphia] and another in
New Jork. [13 ll.: asks for addresses of some friends; asks her parents to
thank the mayor for the money that was sent to her in Plymouth[30];
reports about the number of immigrants this year]

The city of New Jork is the largest in America, it is so big you can't
walk around it in one day, the religious institutions are like in Germany,
there are 182 churches here, but belonging to different religions. Here
you can find people from all corners of the world, there are about 4,000
German residents alone.[31] I will be able to write more in the future when
I have been here longer. But I do want to tell you this [that so many
deserters] from the army have arrived here.[32] [16 ll.: advises her brothers
to emigrate; asks for an answer soon; greetings] Gottlieb should give my
best to his cook where he was when I left, she only needs to come to

[28]In Waiblingen County, a servant girl only earned 8–10 guilders in an entire year, along with
a few yards of cloth, a dress and a pair of shoes (*Beschreibung des Oberamts Waiblingen* [1850], 49).
[29]In their report of 1861, the Commissioners of Immigration listed a voyage of 106 days as the
longest crossing ever recorded from Europe to New York (*Annual Reports* 5 [1861], 82).
[30]Anna Maria Klinger apparently ran out of money during the long unexpected delay in
Plymouth, and she had written to the mayor of Korb. Obviously, her request was granted, and
money from the treasury was dispatched.
[31]In fact there were fourteen times this many, that is, about fifty-six thousand (Bretting
[1981], 179).
[32]This comment may well refer to her future husband, Franz Schano.

America, it's very good for girls who have to work in service. I haven't regretted it yet. Write me, too, about what's happening in Stuttgart. Dear parents, my next letter will make you happier. [7 ll.: asks for reply; address]

Anna Maria Schano, née Klinger

[New York, probably mid-1850]
[Beginning of letter missing] I've saved up to now in the time we've been married[33] some 40 dollars in cash, not counting my clothes. Dear parents and brothers and sisters, I certainly don't want to tell you what to do, do what you want, for some like it here and some don't, but the only ones who don't like it here had it good in Germany, but I also think you would like it here since you never had anything good in Germany. I'm certainly glad not to be over there, and only those who don't want to work don't like it here, since in America you have to work if you want to amount to anything, you mustn't feel ashamed, that's just how you amount to something, and so I want to tell you again to do what you want, since it can seem too trying on the journey and in America as well, and then you heap the most bitter reproaches on those who talked you into coming, since it all depends on whether you have good luck, just like in Germany. Dear parents, you wrote me that Daniel wants to come to America and doesn't have any money, that is certainly a problem. Now I want to give you my opinion, I've often thought about what could be done, I thought 1st if he could borrow the money over there, then when he has saved enough over here then he could send it back over, like a lot of people do, and secondly, I thought we would like to pay for him to come over, but right now we can't since it costs 28 dollars a person and I also want to tell you since my husband wrote to you, the money we want to send you, whether you want to use it to have one or two come over here or if you want to spend it on yourselves, you just have to let us know so we have an idea how much you still need, and you'll have to see to it that you have some more money, too, since we can't pay it all. [. . .] Things in Daniel's *Profesion* are not the best, he shouldn't count on that, it would be better if he were a tailor or shoemaker, but it doesn't matter, a lot of people don't work in their *Profesion* and learn others or other businesses, since you don't have to pay to learn a trade in America. Dear parents and brothers and sisters, if one of you comes over here and comes to stay with us we will certainly take care of you, since we are now well known, and you

---

[33]The exact date of Anna Maria Klinger's marriage to Franz Schano is unknown; they were already married when the 1850 census was taken (MC 1850: New York City, W. 5, #264).

needn't be so afraid of America, when you come to America, just imagine you were moving to Stuttgart, that's how many Germans you can see here.

And as far as the Americans are concerned, whites and blacks, they won't harm you, since the blacks are very happy when you don't do anything to them, the only thing is the problem with the language. It's not as easy to learn as you think, even now I don't know much, and there are many people here who don't even learn it in 6 to 8 years, but if you start off working for Americans then you can learn in one year as much as in 10 years living with Germans. Dear parents and brothers and sisters, I'd like to be with you, you will surely be pleased to get the picture of us, to see me again, and I would also be so happy to see you again. In my dreams I've often been with you and also in my old job in Germany, but when I woke up, it wasn't true, but still I am happy in any case that I am in America. [30 ll.: more details, description of the enclosed photograph; regrets her parents' financial straits and complains about her brother Eberhard's ingratitude; news about acquaintances from Steinreinach] We would have liked to have sent a few dollars along with this letter but at the moment we don't have much money, since I can well imagine you could use it now, but things go slowly the first few years, you have to take care of yourself, since the motto in America is help yourself. [8 ll.: complains that none of her sisters and brothers have written; greetings; signature]

Franz Schano

New Jork,
[date missing, probably late 1850]

Dearest parents-in-law,

[8 ll.: thanks for a letter from brother-in-law Eberhard; excuses his delay in writing] We had a lot of things to take care of, as young beginners, especially since it will be winter soon and we don't have any potatoes or other crops to harvest, so we had to buy food and fuel and other things that go along with them, all with hard cash, and just on the same day we got your letter I lost my job and was without work for three weeks and so all of this kept us from writing. But I have given up my *Profesion* and have taken up another that should be of greater advantage to me, I'm now learning the sculpting trade,[34] but I can't expect to earn very much the first half year, it will get better after that. [4 ll.: he and his wife,

[34]In MC 1850, Franz Schano is listed as a "stone cutter," in MC 1860 (Albany, N.Y.) as a "wood carver."

however, still want to send 23 guilders] As for the rest, we need more information about the best and cheapest thing to do, because it's like this, we don't think it is a good idea for Daniel to come over first, since Daniel's trade isn't good for anything over here and so he has to learn a new one. Instead it would be better if the two girls [i.e., Barbara and Katharina] came over first, because within a few days we could get more work for them than they'd want. For the girls earn a lot more than he does, and he can be sure that after the girls have been here for just one month, we can then take care of his passage. We can set it up here so that the girls come over for the price of one and a half persons, since if you're not over twelve years old you're only charged as half a person, but it doesn't matter if you are already over 13 or 14 years old, if you just say you're 10 or 11 years old, that's how I arranged the passage for my mother and three brothers and sisters. [5 ll.: details] Now we would appreciate it if you could find out what the price is with food and without food, but you should just say it's for one and one-half persons, we can pay to have them come over for forty dollars, but without food, if it turns out that passage is cheaper over there, then we want to send the money, so please find out how things can be arranged the cheapest and safest, since we are not overflowing with money and it's not like we don't have to watch out, and we have to sweat for every dollar we earn, and my wife (your daughter) puts up with the hardest work for your sake, so take things in hand and get to work, we're doing it all most willingly to bring you to a better life; hopefully, Daniel won't feel passed over, since we only want the best for all of you and what we've written here would work out the best.

[*Anna Maria Schano* continues:]

[15 ll.: expresses thanks for a letter from Steinreinach, which included the news that the wedding photograph arrived safely; complains that she seldom receives letters] In short you don't take the trouble to write, we try harder, we sit down 3 to 4 times when we write to you, you can well imagine that I am also excited when I get a letter, what the news will be, I would also be glad if father or mother would write me too, I imagine they can't write very well anymore, but that doesn't matter. [. . .] Also, please write me too how old Father and Mother are, I don't know any more exactly. [12 ll.: best wishes to Eberhard and Jacob for their impending marriages;[35] agrees with her husband that Barbara and Katharina should come over first and Daniel should be patient] But if he doesn't

---

[35]In November 1850, Jacob, a 27-year-old farmer in Steinreinach, married Barbara Heigelin, born in Tübingen. Eberhard, a 31-year-old tailor, married Barbara Kammer from Korb in May 1851 (Ev. KB Korb).

want to wait so long, then he should take one of his girlfriends and bring her over here, if they have the money, that's also not right of him that he wants to come to America and take none of his girls along. I suggest he choose one of these two, the one he thinks he can get along with the best and who will be a good housewife, it's certainly true he can't take both, it's too bad about the other one. [25 ll.: next year Daniel could work for her husband and learn the trade; best wishes for New Year's and greetings; signature; greetings from Franz Schano; a bank draft is on the way; address]

Franz Schano

New Jork, March 19, 1851

Dearest parents-in-law,

[4 ll.: thanks for news from Steinreinach] We have complied with your wishes as far as we are able to and so we have signed up for Barbara's passage here and it's like this, she goes from Mannheim to Haver [Le Havre] and from Haver to here, she'll have to take care of her food herself. She'll go from Mannheim to Rotterdam and from there to Haver, she should go, when she gets the money and she's finished packing, with this ticket here in this letter to Mannheim to Wilhelm Deissman, and there she will get three *Tickerts,* one she has to turn in in Mannheim when she gets on the steamship, the other when she goes from Rotterdam to Haver and the third in Haver when she gets on the ship, she'll also hear about it in Mannheim and we've sent her 15 guilders [. . .] which she should hold on to since she still has to buy quite a few things. [7 ll.: list of cooking utensils and provisions she should acquire] And when she's asked at the depot if she has everything she's supposed to have, then she should say yes and she should be sure not to take anything more than what we've written, and she shouldn't be scared if they say she can't leave or whatever else they might say, then she can just say straight out I have everything I need and if she stays in Haver for three days, she'll have to get her own food, if she's there longer she must be paid two and a half francs every day / Our address is still the same.

Anna Maria Schano

[New York, probably 1851]

[Beginning of letter missing] You don't have to soak things in lye, soap is cheap, they don't carry the water on their heads here either, and then you start in the morning when it gets light and stop when it's nighttime and laundries are set up completely differently, you have a washboard [4 ll.:

detailed description] so one person can wash as much in one day as 2 washerwomen in Germany have to wash in 6 weeks. You probably never thought I would be a washerwoman, but in America you needn't be ashamed if you work, in America if you don't work and don't save and so on, you don't have anything either. [14 ll.: flooding; congratulations on her brothers' marriages; greetings] Special love to Rosina and she should be a good girl and do what she's told, and take care of father and mother as long as they live, then when they've passed away she and Gottlieb can also come to America. Daniel and Chatharina should wait until Bebele is here, then we can send word soon. [19 ll.: instructions and practical advice for her journey]

[*Franz Schano* continues:]

[8 ll.: asks his parents-in-law and the children to provide Barbara with the things she needs for her trip] She doesn't need any papers except her certificate of citizenship from the mayor, since she won't be asked on the journey. And she ought to bring along a potato sack about two simmers in size and then a straw sack and a pillow and anything else like that she needs and she should set off as soon as possible. And remind her again about what my wife wrote, that she should behave herself so she doesn't arrive here in a wretched state and become the laughingstock of everyone here, and all we want is what's best for her, so she should take to heart these few words I write with the best intentions, as your faithful brother-in-law. Enclosed in these two pages we are sending you the city of New Jorck, one is a view of the city and some buildings, the other is a map with the streets and there where you see the small white square with No. 1 on it and the line drawn behind it, that's where we live.

The street is called Church Street and it's pronounced like *Tschotsch Stritt,* or in German *Kirch Straße*.

And Barbara mustn't forget to take along our address so that when you get to Haver you can write us a few words and the name of the ship. [5 ll.: address; greetings; signature; more greetings from Maria Schano; enclosed in the letter: map of New York]

Franz Schano

New Jork, July 16, 1851

Dearest parents-in-law,

To relieve you of your cares and worries, we feel obliged to write you that Barbara arrived here safe and sound after a brief sea voyage of 26 days, that is she landed here Friday night, June 14th and she tried to find us on Saturday but couldn't, and in the evening we heard that she was here and then until ten thirty at night we went around to all the inns and couldn't find her, and when we asked the people who were on the ship then one of them said she went to Philadelfi with some others, someone else said she already had a job somewhere else and so we had to go home again, and we hardly slept a wink worrying about where she might be, and early Sunday morning we went back to find out where she might be, and after we had been in several inns, we heard that she was staying at an inn called Wälti Logire, and when we got there she was already standing outside on the steps and recognized Mari right away, then we brought her and her trunk back home immediately. And what I also want to report briefly is, as Babete told us, that Daniel should come over with his girl next spring, and be so kind as to let us know ahead of time so we can send money for Katharina so she can come over together with Daniel. Our address is still the same.

[*Barbara Klinger* continues:]

Dear parents and brothers and sisters, I want to let you know what kind of journey I had to New Jork. [5 ll.: describes the trip to Le Havre] On the 18th we boarded a sailing ship, from Havre to New Jork I was at sea for 26 days on the ship, there were 725 persons with the sailors and we only had a storm once. [5 ll.: details] But it was nothing compared to the voyage Mari had, the ship had 3 decks and one cellar completely under water, the people slept in the 2 lower ones and in the two higher ones there are two kitchens, two toilets, two stalls, in one there are geese and in the other ducks and chickens and a pigsty and another stall for cows, there was one cow and in the back there is another small room, where the mates and the 3 cooks who cook for the sailors, they were blacks, one had his wife along, she was a black too, and the ship was named Wilhelm Tell, it is one of the biggest ships that go between Havre and New Jork and even when the wind was strong it can't throw it around like the little one, it also rolls more, such a big ship on the ocean is like a nutshell swimming in the lake at Korb. [7 ll.: further details about the voyage] And we want to send you these 12 guilders by the fall, when I've also earned something, now you'll have to be patient since they've spent so much money on me already, they bought me a dress, a big scarf for 2 dollars and a hat and a pair of shoes, that cost them a lot, because I can't wear my clothes on Sundays, we've altered them all, narrow sleeves and long-bodied, I wear them workdays, here you don't go out of the house without a hat or a *Barnet* [bonnet] you don't go out on the *Striet* with your head bare, they all look at you and you'd be laughed at. If I were to run into you, none of you would recognize me with my hat on. By this winter I want to have my picture taken so you can see me again. [3 ll.: greetings; signature]

[Anna Maria Schano continues:]

Dear parents and brothers and sisters, please don't be cross that we didn't write for so long, we just wanted to wait awhile so we could also write something about Barbara. Up to now she's been living with us, now she has a job in service working for an English master, they are bakers and they live in the same house as we do, she'll soon learn English there, she can already say *jess,* that means *Ja* in German, and she can also say *stritt,* that means *strase* in German.

[4 ll.: greetings; signature; more greetings from Franz Schano]

Franz Schano

New Jork, June 18th, 1852

Dearest parents-in-law, brothers-in-law and sisters-in-law,

[6 ll.: thanks for letters from Steinreinach; new address] What we read in both letters, that you have to struggle with such hard and dire times, this causes us the deepest pain, and we are so sorry that we weren't able to send you something a long time ago, but it was not possible to do so, since moving cost us about fifty dollars, but now we want to help out with ten dollars, only we have a different set of wishes and plans, if you want to do this, we have decided to add fifty dollars to what you can scrape together in order to bring father, mother and the three brothers and sisters over here, and if you were here I am sure that you could spend your old age living a much better life and in peace and contentment, but what I also want to mention is that if you don't have enough money to do this, I ask the other brothers and sisters and also the village to help you reach this goal, for I will do what I can and if the other brothers and sisters help out, it won't be for nothing since I promise to pay them back. All this can work out, given good will and harmony. [9 ll.: recommendations about the cheapest way to travel] If you want to do this, let us know soon so you don't have to spend the winter over there. With regards to Babet's behavior I must say I am completely satisfied in every way, I don't know what more we could ask for.

[3 ll. best wishes and greetings] Franz Schano

[Maria Schano continues:]

Dear parents and brothers and sisters,

[36 ll.: is sorry about the miserable economic situation of her parents and hopes they will decide to emigrate with the three youngest children; brother Eberhard should help pay for passage] You also wanted to know about Barbara, she is fine, she is so pleased and so happy that she is in America, she's never once wished to be back in Germany she is working for some French people, she likes it fine, she's paid back the money for her passage and if you saw her, you'd be quite surprised, she goes for a walk with us every Sunday, you'd see no difference in the way she's dressed. Dear parents and brothers and sisters, if you wish to come here to us then write us right away so you can come over this fall so you'll still have some food.

[4 ll.: greetings, also from her husband and Barbara; new address]

Franz Schano

New Jork, September 4th, 1852

Dearest parents-in-law, brothers-in-law and sisters-in-law,

[3 ll.: thanks for letters from Steinreinach] With regards to you, dear parents-in-law, we will comply with your wishes, and you can spend your old age in the fatherland, but we want to arrange passage for Gottlieb and Katharina, and they will start their journey by the beginning of November, and we will make sure that when they are here the others can come over later, too. So they should get ready but they will receive more detailed information ahead of time, and the reason why we're putting you off until then is because the ocean is more stormy in the months of September and October, you needn't be afraid that it will be too late, because of the cold, on the ship you will sweat more from the heat of the sun than you would at home in back of the stove, so like I said earlier, you can start getting ready, but we will let you know about the actual plans in the next letter. [5 ll.: greetings; signature; address]

[*Barbara Klinger* continues:]

Dearly beloved parents and brothers and sisters,

[7 ll.: regrets that her parents do not want to emigrate and discusses Gottlieb and Katharina's forthcoming voyage] Since I have been in America I have earned enough for my passage and clothes and will do my best to help all of the others do so too. And I hope you have as good a crossing as I did; as far as food goes, I had enough; my favorites were plums and dried apples and brandy and zwieback, but I didn't buy it, I got as much as I wanted from other people. I gave them something of everything I'd taken along and when I got off in New Jork I could have had a lot more, but I didn't know that. I advise you when you come over and you are offered something then take it, because we'll find a use for it. [2 ll.: closing] Barbara Klinger.

[*Maria Schano* continues:]

Dear parents and brothers and sisters,

[33 ll: expresses understanding for her parents' decision to stay in Germany, and gives Gottlieb and Katharina practical advice for the trip]

As far as Daniel is concerned, we can't help at the moment, he should be patient and wait until the other brothers and sisters are here so they can help too, but if he doesn't want to wait so long then he should arrange things with one of his girlfriends, from what I heard from Barbara, one of them has sold some property, you can use the money from that, if it's enough, to come over, here you can make a better living than in Germany. So many people are arriving from my husband's hometown and region and are already here. [13 ll.: greetings; her mother-in-law was ill] Frantz's father is as old as mother and his mother is as old as father. They had 6 children, now they have 5. 4 brothers and one sister, she's the youngest, she is as old as Chatharina and Frantz is the oldest, Frantz was also a soldier, but he had 3 more years to serve, but then he ran away when he was on leave, then he went to America with his father and one brother, and his mother and the other children came later. They are now living quite happy and content close together / All the best from Maria Schano.

Franz Schano

New Jork, January 26
[but probably February] 1853

Dearly beloved parents-in-law,

After a lengthy delay we are compelled to take up this burden to allay your fears. The reason why we have waited so long is of some importance but not of great interest. The actual reason is easy to explain since it has to do with what we wrote in the last letter,[36] that is, that Babett made an acquaintance, which we could see from the start would not be to her advantage, and we tried everything to dissuade her, but to no use, and now what we foresaw has come true, she now has a baby son that was born on February 17th this year for whom she has a father all right but no husband, and when we noticed that she was expecting, we urged him to marry her but then he said he had never promised to marry her and he wouldn't ever marry her, and anyway he was Jewish and wouldn't abandon his faith and didn't want to hurt his family, but all of this couldn't get him off the hook completely, and he asked that a *Contrakt* be drawn up that he'll take care of her for six weeks before and six weeks after the birth and then afterwards they will share the expenses for the child equally, and she got ten dollars ahead of time and her weekly wage one and one-half dollars.

One week after the birth he told us he had decided to pay her off

---

[36]This letter has not survived.

completely, because he said she would cause him difficulties later on, and so we demanded one hundred dollars, then he wanted to pay fifty and so we made a deal that she gets fifty-five now and twenty-five in six months, and so together with what she's already gotten she'll have a hundred dollars and so this whole business has left her with a child and it will make it very hard for her to find a good match. [2 ll.: greetings; signature]

Gottlieb Klinger

Neiyork, January 21st, 1854

Dear parents and brothers and sisters, [11 ll.: apologizes for his long silence; is sending 30 guilders as a New Year's present for his brothers and sisters] The biggest news is that you have another new grandson in America, because Marie gave birth to a baby boy on Christmas Eve. [10 ll.: thanks for a letter; visit from an immigrant from Steinreinach] He told us that things are so terrible at home, and that Daniel had asked again if he could come to America to his brother and sisters, but that's difficult, since Gottlieb can't pay for it alone, as much as he'd like to, and Babett can't do much, she has to take care of her son, and Chatharina is too stingy toward her brothers and sisters, she'd rather spend her money on clothes, and Franz and Marie say they think it's better when you take along one of your girls, since they say it wouldn't be right if you left your girl and your children, so please be so kind as to write back right away whether you're coming alone or are bringing your girl, then we want to help you and send the money. [18 ll.: is sorry that sister Rosina is ill; no news from cousin in America; immigrants who were supposed to be bringing food from the parents have not contacted the Schanos] Dear father! Now comes the time when you have to play for your youngest son in Waiblingen before the 1st of March, since he's in America, so I hope that you draw the number 1 and that you will make a great day of it,[37] but in your next letter you can let me know how it went, since I am living gladly and happily in America, and am thank God always hale and hearty, I've also met up with enough old friends here, like F. Baun from Korb is now my closest neighbor, and we spend all our time together. [4 ll.: New Year's wishes; signature]

[Barbara Klinger continues:]

Dear parents and brothers and sisters, [3 ll.: New Year's wishes] I hope I'll be doing better, too. So far I haven't saved much for myself because my baby costs me a lot, I paid six dollars a month for him for eight

---

[37]These remarks probably refer to the annual lottery held in Waiblingen.

months and now I pay 4 dollars a month, since I don't breast-feed him. When he was five weeks old I got a job working for some Americans, they had a ten-week-old baby, they promised me I would get ten dollars a month and I wetnursed their baby for seven months; then I left and they didn't give me my money, they kept putting it off from one month to the next. They didn't give me any more than 27 dollars and still owe me 43 and I can't get it since they are very bad people, for the Americans are just like the Jews, all they want to do is cheat you and lead you astray. [13 ll.: apologizes that she can't send any money and reports about her son; greetings; signature]

[*Gottlieb Klinger* continues:]

[12 ll: says he will send the rest of the money to pay for a plot of land he had bought, but not yet completely paid for, in Steinreinach] Here I have to tell you that Babet has been living with us since December, we're supporting her along with the baby and give her one dollar a month, too, and I told her she could earn something on the side by doing laundry and ironing; she's done some, but she could earn more if she'd look around for more work. [7 ll.: justifies supporting his sister] As old as the child is she still hasn't had to spend two dollars on his clothing or anything else, but you mustn't think that the child doesn't have enough clothes on when I sometimes take him out just on Sundays. His outfit consists of a little grey felt hat with a blue ribbon on it, baby clothes and jacket, shoes and socks with leggings on top and mittens, which cost four dollars.

Franz Schano

Albany, October 9th, 1855[38]

Dear parents-in-law,

Since Johannes Pfeiffer[39] is sending his relatives a letter, we want to tell you our news as well. [10 ll.: health; says he will send a photograph of Anna Maria's and Babett's sons, which he doesn't have the money for now] For the winter we have to pay fifty dollars just for wood, coal, potatoes, flour and the other things you need in the house. A week ago

[38]It is unclear when the Schanos moved from New York City to Albany (the letter reporting their move has probably not survived). Since the beginning of the 1850s, Albany (population in 1860 was 50,763), the New York state capital and booming trade center on the Hudson, had been attracting immigrants especially from southern Germany. In 1865, German-born inhabitants made up 8 percent of the population; in 1869 an estimated fourteen thousand German speakers supported two German-language newspapers, eight German congregations, four German singing clubs, thirteen mutual aid societies, and several *Turnvereine* (Schem 1 [1869], 259–60).

[39]J. Pfeiffer had emigrated from Steinreinach in late 1854 or early 1855 (StA LB, F 210, Bü. 414, Nr. 671).

we spent twenty-two dollars for a carpet, but if at all possible we'll send it first chance we get. We received your letter on July 17th and see from it that the prospects for the poor are better this year. We also had a bountiful year. Fruit, grain and potatoes are very cheap. [18 ll.: examples of prices; Gottlieb's financial affairs; whereabouts in the United States of a missing emigrant from Korb, Jacob Wied] And you write us that you'd like to know what Katharina's husband's name is, I would if I could but I can't, but that Katharina doesn't have any boys, but a girl instead, since Gottlieb told us that, he will write you himself.

[4 ll.: greetings; signature; address] And about Babet we can't write any more than what we wrote in the spring that she wants to go west with Wagner to the Hetzels by September.[40] Give this letter to the Pfeiffers.

Franz Schano

Albany, January 23rd, 1856

Beloved parents-in-law,

[19 ll.: thanks for letters from Steinreinach; is enclosing a photograph of the two grandsons and three dollars] Gottlieb wrote that he and Katharina had also written a letter—which will be a surprise for you. We are all quite well and are making a decent living, and by the spring we may have bought a house, but the man wants eight hundred dollars in cash for it, by then we'll have six hundred dollars together, the house and garden are 70 feet long, 26 feet wide. The house has two stories.

[*Anna Maria Schano* continues:]

Dear parents and brothers and sisters. [10 ll.: New Year's wishes; apologizes that because of buying the house they are unable to send any larger amounts of money] You always live in such fear here, there are so many fires in the city, almost every [day] and if you don't have your household covered by fire insurance then you lose everything, so we want to live in our own house all alone, then we want to take out fire insurance on our things, too, up to now we've been so careless. I also want to tell you about Babed, we haven't heard from her in a whole year, she wrote us in her last letter she was going to the west to the Hetzels' and to Albeck's with Wagner in early October. In her first letter, she wrote us

[40]"Wagner" probably refers to the day laborer Jacob Wagner, who emigrated from Korb in 1849 or 1850 (StA LB, F 210, Bü. 411, Nr. 21); the "Hetzels" probably refers to two brothers from Württemberg, Gottlieb and Jacob Hetzel, probably from the Korb area as well. All three became farmers and settled in St. Joseph County, Indiana (MC 1860: St. Joseph Co., Ind., Madison Twp., #964–65).

Albeck had asked her to marry him, and she had said yes, in her last letter she wrote she would marry Hetzel. So now we don't know which one she married or if she married neither of the two, if you find out perhaps from the Hetzels, Albeck or the Wagners that she is with one of them, please let us know. [. . .] We find it quite surprising that she can just live along like that and doesn't trouble herself about her child at all. [19 ll.: news from Johannes Pfeiffer; greetings; signature; more greetings from Franz Schano; asks for a reply soon]

Franz Schano

Albany, March 7, 1856

Dearest parents-in-law,

[10 ll.: hopes that letters and photographs don't cost too much postage and says he's sending a draft for eight dollars] Gottlieb has been here with us for several weeks and I have found him a job that he is quite satisfied with, he gets eight dollars a week, that's almost as much as I get, I get ten and a half dollars a week. We received a letter from Barbara on the 1st of the month, she's living in the state of Indiana, the place is called Mischawaka, and is married to Gotlieb Hetzel, as she writes they have 40 acres of land[41] and in the fall they built themselves a log cabin and she wishes us the wood from ten acres of land, by that she means it would help them and us, too, she said it was a bit boring now since they have to walk five minutes to their closest neighbor and Jakob Hetzel, Wagner and Albert live around there, Gotlieb had already shot several deer from the window and Babet now wants to have her William [her son] back again, she said he could help to burn up the wood, Babet wrote she would like to come to get her boy but the journey is too long, it's 8 to 9 hundred miles away and traveling back and forth that costs too much, they also have two oxen, a heifer, a bull and a big dog to chase off the deer. [10 ll: greetings; signature; greetings from his wife; new address]

Albany, August 3rd, 1856

Dearly beloved parents-in-law,

[6 ll.: introduction] I don't have much news that's important, the main thing, if they didn't beat me to it, is Gottlieb got married a few weeks

---

[41]Half of the settlers in Mishawaka, Indiana (population in 1870 was 2,617) were Germans, and there were three German churches in 1870 (Schem 7 [1872], 385). According to the 1860 agricultural census (MC A: St. Joseph Co., Ind., Madison Twp.), Gottlieb Hetzel owned ten acres of cultivated land and another thirty acres of uncultivated land. The value of his farm was $150; his brother Jacob's nearby farm, also valued at $150 in 1860, was worth $3,000 in 1870.

ago, his wife is from Weinsberg County, I can't remember the town, I think the name starts with an E and her name is Carolina Wurst, her father was a schoolteacher but is already dead, before she got married she was sent 200 guilders and Gotlieb had saved about 50 dollars, now they are really in New Jork because he ran out of work here. [10 ll.: receiving letters; prospects of a good harvest; greetings]

Franz Schano

[3 ll.: address; 12 ll.: postscript from Maria Schano: apologies that the letter is so short; no news of Babett; asks for a letter soon; Gottlieb's wife is an "upright person"]

Albany, December 22, 1856

[13 ll.: season's greetings; he and Gottlieb have sent eight dollars] As far as we are concerned, we can tell you the news that we have bought a nice house, which cost us the sum of one thousand dollars, of which we paid five hundred dollars now and have to pay the other five hundred in five years, and we moved in on the first of October, but it isn't built like the houses in Germany, here in the cities they usually have flat roofs covered with tin that's soldered together so that it's one piece and then painted with oil paint, it is 22 feet wide and 30 long and with the garden 70 feet long, and in front of the house there's a small flower garden, it's still new, it was built just one and a half years ago, we have 4 rooms and a small cellar, during the day we're in the two downstairs rooms, we sleep upstairs in the back and the front room is the living room, which is nicely furnished, our furniture and fixtures cost three hundred dollars, I'd just love to show it to you, we are very happy with it and we only hope that we stay in good health and that business keeps going as well as it has been.

I also want to describe to you Wilhelm and Karl's[42] Christmas presents, they've already got a drum, a flag, two guns and two swords and caps and they're going to get a Christmas tree as well, you should just see how cheerful they are and they're always speaking English to each other. [19 ll.: no news about the lost emigrant Jacob Wied; Babett has not written; greetings; signature; more greetings; address]

[*Maria Schano* continues:]

Dear parents and brothers and sisters, [. . .] First, Gottlieb wrote to us that Daniel had written to him and asked for money for his tools, that he'd given up all hope of being brought over here, but now we've talked

---

[42]Wilhelm was Barbara's son; Karl was Anna Maria and Franz Schano's son.

about it and decided that since we and Gottlieb want to give him some money, Franz and I think he can either use it to buy tools or to come over here, we don't know yet what Gottlieb thinks of this, I imagine he'll write and tell you what he thinks. [. . .] We think that if Daniel thinks he can make a living over there, then he'd better stay there. Now, I want to explain, since we certainly know his situation, so first of all, if he comes here he won't be able to depend on his trade, and second, if he runs around as a day laborer or farmhand his prospects aren't good, either, and third, if he leaves his family over there, then he won't have any peace of mind either, because you can't earn money quite so fast as you may think, all sorts of things can happen, first of all you can get sick, second you may not earn anything, then it's easy to get into debt instead of sending money to Germany to feed your family or bring them over here, you just can't imagine it, and you don't believe it, either, that a person can have a hard time here at the start, but when someone's been here longer, then he can do well, if he is lucky, in a short time he can save as much of a fortune as in Germany, now I've told you the truth.

Gottlieb Klinger

Albany, March 7th, 1857

Dear parents and brothers and sisters, [3 ll.: introduction] That is, my wife and I have been back in Albany since February 24th of this year, I have gotten a job in Franz's *Schop* where I'm earning better money again, and we're also living in Franz's new house. [7 ll.: Daniel should decide whether he wants to stay in Germany or emigrate] I, Gottlieb, would advise him to come over here rather than to stay in Germany, I think that after you've been here a while then you'll be able to have your girlfriend and your children come over, if they don't have the money now to make the journey right away, but I'll leave the choice to you, since you ought to know best what's best for you. [10 ll.: his brother should let him know what he decides soon; Gottlieb's family is well and he will be a father soon; greetings]
G. D. Klinger.

[35 ll.: short letter of May 4, 1857, from *Franz Schano* in Albany, saying that he is sending a draft for 75 guilders to pay for Daniel's passage and asking him to bring several kinds of flower seeds along]

Gottlieb Klinger

Albany, August 14, 1857

Dearest parents and brothers and sisters,
[9 ll.: he and Franz are sending 25 guilders for his parents] We are so

very sorry to hear that father has to suffer such pain and misfortune in his old age, but there's nothing to be done about it, so be patient and God will take care of everything. It is therefore all the more pleasant to hear that you have yet another nice grandchild in America, that is, Daniel's wife gave birth to a baby girl on August 10, and is now hale and hearty, which is worth more than silver and gold. As far as Daniel's journey is concerned, he came over safe and sound in 31 days from Havre, they didn't have much stormy weather on his way to New Jork and then Katharine and her husband picked him up and so they spent a few days in New Jork, and then they came to Albany to stay with us, part of the time with me and part of the time with Franz, before he found a steady job. Daniel has already started working for the *Rail Road Compagni*. Dear parents and brothers and sisters, now I also want to let you know that since April 25th '57 I have taken over a saloon, where I have to pay 150 dollars a year just for rent, but I will give it up again as soon as my trade picks up, because business is bad all over at the moment. [7 ll.: closing; signature; greetings, also from his and Daniel's wives]

[*Anna Maria Schano* continues:]

Albany, August 16th, 1857

Dearly beloved parents-in-law and brother-in-law,

Here I want to add a few words [. . .] I just want to let you know what he means by *Rail Road Compagni,* that means the same as *Eisenbahn Gesellschaft,* where he's been working since last week, he gets seven shillings a day or 2 guilders a day, they cut wood with a machine that's driven by a horse, tomorrow he's taking over an apartment, which they can furnish bit by bit. [8 ll.: hopes that Daniel stays healthy; says they are sending a draft; Babett is fine] Only she wrote that it's so boring where they are, first of all because they live all alone in the woods, second because she doesn't have any children, she also wrote that she would like to have her child back, if she could only have him with her, but she can't come to get him because it's too far away and costs too much. We wrote them earlier that we wanted to bring Daniel over and if they wanted to help out and now they've sent us 5 talers but not for Daniel, instead for Rosina, Hetzel said, her husband, that Daniel should only have been allowed to save up, but when we got the letter from them, Daniel was already on his way, we've saved the 5 talers for Rosina, she'll still get them. [18 ll.: expresses sorrow about her parents' financial straits and her father's illness; still no news about the missing emigrant Jacob Wied; Daniel arrived safe and sound and has another child; thanks for brother Eberhard's present to her husband] And one other thing, I must admonish Eberhart and Jakob not to let our poor parents suffer want, for example when mother asks for some skim milk and you first ask for

money, I am very sorry to hear that, aren't they your parents, too? Believe me the money we've sent them is hard-earned too, I think you must see that we know what's going on better than you. [. . .] I think you must know a lot anyway so don't be so heartless. And do whatever you can, I don't imagine they'll live another hundred years. So let's do for them what we still can. Now I'm going to stop because it's already very late at night.
[6 ll.: greetings; signature; greetings from Franz Schano]

[Daniel Klinger continues:]

[4 ll.: greetings; apologizes for neglecting to write] What I also wanted to say about Rosina, she should stay with the parents for as long as they live, and it would also be good for her to keep away from having boyfriends because she can also get a husband in America, women have more respect here than in Germany. [3 ll.: greetings] Up to now we've been fine, as long as we're with the family we don't lack for anything. [3 ll.: closing]
Daniel Klinger

Dear brother-in-law Andreas, let mother know too and Kasper and his wife when you write them. And we got the money that was sent. We were able to use it, too, since we had to borrow some in Havre and pay it back in Neujork. Andreas, when you go to the mayor's give him my thanks. If you hear anything new, please let us know, my parents have our address.
[3 ll.: greetings from Friederike Klinger (she signed as "Friederike Klinger"); address]

Gottlieb Klinger

Albany, July 19, 1858
Dear father, [17 ll.: expresses his sympathy on the death of his mother and comforts him with the thought of a life without want in the hereafter] Rosina, too, will reap her reward for having served our dear mother to the end, but I don't think it quite fitting that she now wants to leave her old father and set off for America, but if father gives his permission and we've agreed to it here, then it won't be long before she sets foot on American soil, finally I also want to add that Katharina's husband wants you to come over here on your own before next spring, so you can start working for him, that is help with the sewing, we also think it would be the best for you, all of us wish that you would stay clear of any liaisons, so you can be free and unhindered in coming over here, of course we

don't want this to be an order, since we think you'll agree it's best. [20 ll.: Barbara and Katharina are enclosing 27 guilders for their father, but the money should be used for him and not for their mother's funeral— Eberhard and Jakob should pay for that; closing; greetings]
G. Klinger

N.B. I also want to let you know that my wife presented me with a fine and healthy baby boy on June 29, yet another scion of the Klinger seed *Iamm wisch jou would see, auer joung Amerikans thenn jou would forget all jour Trouble.*
[4 ll.: greetings and sympathy from Caroline Klinger]

Franz Schano
Albany, August 4, 1858

[24 ll.: sympathy on the death of his mother-in-law; says he is sending a draft for 25 guilders and explains they'll soon see about Rosina's passage]

[*Anna Maria Schano* continues:]

    [4 ll.: regrets that she knew nothing of her mother's illness] Then we could have sent her something right away, to take better care of her in her miserable sickbed, Oh I am so sorry that I couldn't see my dear mother again and that I couldn't do her anymore favors, when she did so much for us children, before we were grown up and her life turned sour, and many a sleepless night did she have because of us when we were still children and now even more when she couldn't see us any more. [14 ll.: sympathy for her father] Now you want to know how Daniel and his family are, they are fine, Daniel is quite satisfied, he doesn't want to go back to Germany, Rieke was homesick sometimes, mostly for her mother, but now she's settled down, since now she knows that the dear Lord has gathered her up into eternity, for there is eternal rest. Daniel has been working cutting wood for the railroad ever since he's been here. [6 ll.: Daniel is no longer short of breath or coughing; no news from Babett; asks him to write how old her mother was]

Katharina Breitwieser née Klinger
Nujork, December 1st, 1858

Dear father when this letter reaches you in as good health as it leaves us we will be very pleased indeed. Dear father, how are things over there now, since dear mother died I really can't believe it, I keep thinking so much about it, since I didn't write my dear mother, I really wanted to

send a *Laigniß* [likeness] but I wanted to wait until my daughter was 1 or
2 years older. I never thought the dear Lord would take her so soon. [4 ll.:
is always thinking about her father] But now you shouldn't suffer any
want, there are 5 of us brothers and sisters in America, if each one gives a
few talers then you'll have enough to live on, I'm not counting Babet, I
haven't seen her for 5 years and not a word from her, if she'd rather be
dead than in the wilderness then you know she wouldn't be there. [4 ll.:
news about the other brothers and sisters] Dear father, you will be very
sorry when Roßinae leaves for America but she can't support you well in
Germany and it is better for us if she is here with us, she'll be able to do
quite well with us. [4 ll.: asks about her brothers; greetings]

Dear sister, you wrote that you don't like it at home anymore ever
since dear mother died and that you want to come to America, which we
are pleased to hear, we want to send you the money so you can come over
to us. [26 ll.: advice concerning Rosina's passage; asks for a picture of
brother Eberhard's children; greetings]

[*Friedrich Breitwieser* continues:]

Dearest sister-in-law, I would much prefer to have you in the midst of
my family circle than to have strangers around, so I will teach you about
my business, which will be of good use to you all your life, since many a
girl would rather work in a shop like this than go into service for 4 talers a
month and when the month is over then she's worn out more than the
wage, since you can't walk around in America dressed like you are in
Germany. [9 ll.: best wishes for the journey] Don't buy any clothes since
you can't wear German clothes here. Dear sister-in-law, keep to yourself
on the trip and don't fall in with any young people, only married families
if at all, keep far away from those sailors.

When you get to Haver write a letter with the name of the ship you're
coming on and the day it leaves Haver, we'll find it the next day in the
newspaper, don't leave the building with anyone before we come and
pick you up, if you arrive in the late afternoon, send a man to let us know,
we'll pay for it. [16 ll.: advice about provisions; address; greetings] /
Friedrich Breitwieser

Rosina Klinger

Neujork, June 26, 1859
Dear father and brothers [2 ll: apologizes for delay in writing] But I
wanted to wait and see how I like it in Neujork and I also thought Mari
and Gottlieb would have written you already. Dear father, I arrived in
Neujork on March 13 and my brother-in-law, Katharina's husband, was

standing on shore and picked me up, then we went home to Katharina who jumped up and kissed me and gave me a warm welcome. Then her lovely daughter Bertha came up to me at the house, she was also so warm that she hugged me right away, I also wrote right away to Albani and a week later I went with Katharina and her daughter Bertha to Mari's in Albany where Franz, Gottlieb and Daniel were already waiting for us, Gottlieb and Mari didn't recognize me since I've grown so big and strong that they just had to keep staring at me, I recognized Mari at once since she looks like me but I didn't recognize Gottlieb, then Gottlieb's wife, Rike and her children came and we had a wonderful time together. I only wished if only father and mother could see it, if only Babet could have been there, then all 6 of us brothers and sisters would have been there. From Mari I got 2 dresses right away and a hat with red and white flowers and a green ribbon and from Katharina I got a pink-checked dress and a coat, a petticoat and a white skirt and from Gottlieb's wife I got some *Kelgo* [calico] for 2 aprons. [5 ll.: although she likes it there, she still is a bit homesick] My brother-in-law is good fun and always cheers me up and Katherine is good to me, we have meat every day and I never have to eat dry bread, we either have butter or honey, I also have beer or cider every day, in America *Most* is called *Saiter* [cider] it is very sweet but when I think about my old homeland I have to cry, since I left you without thinking, which I'm very sorry about now. Dear father and brothers, now I want to write about my time at sea. [13 ll.: report about the voyage] I don't have anything else to write except that Bertha was sick, she had whooping cough, she had scarlet fever before that, her father loves her so much, and her mother too, they wouldn't part with her for a thousand dollars, she was also such a pretty little girl but she's turned very willful what with being sick, her father bought all the *Strohbaris* [strawberries] for her, at home they're called *Erber*. Now I'll come to a close and remain your faithful daughter Rosina Klinger.

[10 ll.: greetings; her aunt and uncle should be patient about receiving their money back] First I have to earn enough to pay back my passage and I need clothes. In America it's not the same as Germany, I can't wear my clothes from home here. I get 5 dollars a month from Katharina, and all my best to Martin.
Rosina Klinger
[4 ll.: her brothers should take care of her father]

[*Katharina Breitwieser* continues:]

[4 ll.: apologizes for delay in writing] Dear father, Roßinae didn't recognize me, I looked too fine and was dressed too fancy. I also don't look much like the other brothers and sisters, they are all jealous of me.

558   DOMESTIC SERVANTS

It's just like if a small child is brought up in Stuttgart, it's like that when a young girl of 16 or 17 years comes to America, then she gets quite a different color to her cheeks. [8 ll.: greetings; signature]

Rosina Klinger

Newyork, November 14, 1859

Dear father, I want to write a few lines to you, too, so that you know how I am, I am still staying with Katharina and have now worked off my debts, 40 dollars. Dear father, you wrote us that you're doing so poorly since I left home, we are very sorry about that. Katharina's husband is therefore sending you 3 dollars for Christmas, I'd send something too but I'm still too poor and need my money now for clothes. But I won't forget you and will send something later when I can. You also wrote I should have a picture of myself done and send it to you, but I want to wait a bit until I have different clothes and then Katharina wants to have a picture of her and her daughters done at the same time, sometime before next spring. Dear father, I am still homesick and think of home all the time, every night I dream about mother and am always with her. [5 ll.: complains that her friends don't write] Dear father, we now have a sewing machine, but you mustn't think it's one like Aunt Katharina had, this is completely different, it cost 110 dollars, it sews all by itself, you only have to pedal. [11 ll.: season's greetings also from her sister Katharina; address; asks her father to write soon and let them know he's received the enclosed money]

Gottlieb Klinger

Albany, November 18th, 1860

Dearest father and brothers,

We have received your dear letter of August this year and we are pleased to hear that you are all still hale and hearty, especially dear old father who has often suffered want and woe yet still stands steady as an arrow, never wavering, offering cheer to us children in a distant land. Now, as we too as parents have turned our sights toward Christmas and New Year's, the time when all ties of friendship and love between us brothers and sisters and father should be renewed, and we want to give our children all sorts of useful things, we have not forgotten you, either. [14 ll.: is sending 20 guilders, half from Gottlieb, half from Katharina and Daniel] We couldn't get anything from Rosina because we don't know exactly where she's living, she's supposed to be in New York and working for a tailor but we haven't been able to find her, as far as we know her she's a thoughtless creature and pays no mind to her brothers' and sisters' well-meant admonitions. But youth must sow its wild oats before something stronger can take root. I have less pleasant news about Marie, she is suffering through sad times now, for she's been working at her husband's sickbed for more than 4 months now and has the sad prospects of his being taken from her forever, unless God's providence intervenes, for all efforts and doctors seem to be for naught, he apparently has consumption, which in America is regarded as an almost incurable disease, still, we have not given up hope that he will recover. [. . .]

Dear father, you write that you now have a railroad across the Rems valley,[43] that's good to hear, but how would it be if you could take the train from Stuttgart to Steinreinach and right to your house, and from your house all the way to America, to your children, so we could say good morning to each other every day and sit together over a glass of wine, wouldn't you prefer that, too? [10 ll.: greetings and season's greetings; signature; address]

[Daniel Klinger continues:]

Dearest father [3 ll.: his family is well] Since I've been in America we've had two more girls who give me much joy. Things have gone well up to now although several times I had bad luck. I've been working since last summer in a sawmill where I work at night and am paid a good wage, I earn 3 guilders 6 kreuzers in German money. But I need 2 guilders a day for my family, it all costs too much. Dear father, the few talers that I am sending along I present you with the deepest sense of duty and indebtedness and I hope that it comes in good time, and you go out and have a good time with it. [8 ll.: greetings] Daniel Klinger.
[7 ll.: Christmas greetings from Babett's son Wilhelm]

Katharina Breitwieser

Neyork, November 26, 1861

Dear father [3 ll.: introduction] How are you then, I think about you every day and mostly when I'm eating, then I think, what is my father eating now. Dear father, oh, if only you could be here with us, you'd never lack for food and drink, my husband says it's his fondest wish that you be here with us, his parents died when he was a boy and he doesn't have any brothers or sisters. Dear father, here we are sending you a Christmas present that you will like, a few dollars and our *Leigniß* [likeness] you'll be surprised at me and that I have such a big daughter,

---

[43]The local railway line was officially opened in 1861 (Ritter [1967], 162).

she turned 7 years old on October 28, she speaks English and goes to the English school. [3 ll.: she sends her love to her grandfather] I am now all alone in Neyork, Roßina has moved out to the country too, she hasn't written yet how she likes it, we talked to her like to a child but she didn't listen, she got 5 dollars a month from us and didn't know a thing, but she didn't want to learn anything from me, she said what you know, I know too, but she has often regretted it for when you're in a strange country and don't have your parents around then you think, Fatherland, and you know what having parents means, we all got together this spring when Babet came to get her son, she wanted to take Roßine along but she was already married, she also had a baby girl already, but she died, she has a real good-for-nothing for a husband, she got married without telling us. Dear father, who knows if all of us will ever see each other again. [. . .] Dear father, not every farmer can work in the city, the artisans belong in the city and the farmer in the country. We won't be moving out of the city of Neyork since we always have a lot of work. We pay 8 dollars a month rent and 5 dollars a week for food and drink, not counting what you need for clothes and entertainment since I haven't been to church once. I live without a preacher. [17 ll.: asks for an answer soon; greetings; address]

Gottlieb Klinger

Albany, May 13th, 1862

Dearest father [4 ll.: they want to help their father in his distress] Of course we can't do this on a large scale because we have a lot to do as fathers of our own families, especially in the current, confused situation of conflict like the case is here in America, then you are happy if you have enough to get by, a man has to use up all his savings, as did I. I have already been out of work for an entire year, because I didn't want to be a soldier. [3 ll.: is sending 20 guilders] About Rosina we know nothing except that she left for Canada last year and hasn't written to us, and Babett lives in the middle of the wilderness with her cows and oxen, but money is so scarce there, she can't send anything for that reason, she came to visit us last year and picked up her son Wilhelm who's now helping her with the milking and chopping wood, and Marie also has her troubles, she is now a widow for the second time, since a year and a half ago, her first husband, Franz Schano, died on December 6, 1860, and she got married again in the month of January 1862 to a blacksmith named Adam Plantz, a Prussian by birth. He brought a son, 7 years old, into the marriage and some property, but he fell ill right away and died of consumption after 5 weeks. Here I must note, dear father, that Marie would have sent you some money too if you had mentioned her current situation in your last letter, she said that you certainly knew her 1st husband, Franz Schano, had passed away, and you never mentioned it or sent her any words of sympathy, that she was the sole cause of our being in these circumstances. You can see from that, father, that Marie is a lot different than she used to be, but what difference does it make? The richer you get, the prouder, and more self-centered and ambitious, in Marie's case too: the more you have, the more you want etc. So I would advise you, dear father, when you write the next time, to give your daughter Marie the highest priority and a lot of praise and then she'll send you something again soon. I could write a lot of news in connection with the war, but I don't have enough space on this sheet of paper to write to you in detail, I just want to note that the war will soon be over, after the two sides have robbed and murdered each other by the hundreds and thousands, I must also mention that my son Heinrich also died on December 7th at the age of 2½ years and has now been replaced by a daughter. [12 ll.: asks if the money they sent the last time has arrived; regrets that brother Jakob's wife is ill; greetings; signature]

[*Daniel Klinger* continues:]

Dearest father [4 ll.: regrets that he cannot send more money] Times would be good but there's no work, two years already, many hundreds and thousands have been out of work, but we think the future will be better, though I'm not part of the great mass of people who don't have work, thank God I've had work the whole time, I've been working for the railroad for 3 years where I've always worked hard, and my boss has now given me a better job, I work now in the railroad station where I work every day and it's dry. Dear father, when you pick up the money go out and have a good time. [16 ll.: greetings, especially to the family of his wife, Marie Friederike; signature; asks him to forward the enclosed letter from his sister Katharina to Stuttgart; more greetings; address is unchanged]

Katharina Breitwieser

Neujork, February 22 [1863]

Dear father

[13 ll.: thanks for his letter, she had already been worried about his long silence; is sending 5 dollars] You also wrote about Rosina, as far as I know she is well, she lives in Canada West, that belongs to England. She wrote me that she wants to move back to Neujork, she also has a boy. Dear father, you write that you are now in a bad way and can't earn anything anymore, oh, if the stream between us weren't so big, you'd never suffer

Figure 37. Photo of Daniel Klinger, his wife Friederike, and sons Daniel and Gottlieb, ca. 1865. *Source:* Rodney C. Myers.

any want. Dear father, I am now all alone in Neujork but I am quite satisfied, my husband has *blinde* [plenty] of work and is also healthy. [19 ll.: greetings to brothers Jakob and Eberhard and their families; signature; greetings]

Gottlieb Klinger

Albany, March 1st, 1863

Dear father, [8 ll.: thanks his father for his letters and discusses the problems of transatlantic communication] Besides, I just came back to Albany on New Year's, I was in the west in the state of Indiana for 6 months, staying with Barbara, I wanted to try my luck there, but I was not successful, and thus I decided to return again, which cost me a lot of money, for it was more than 900 miles away, but I was only on the train for two days. Then, since a merchant Reinhardt from Waiblingen asked us to find a certain man named Fr. Porter, who is supposed to receive an inheritance, and since you might be able to get some of this money, I took the trouble and actually found him and we have arranged that Mr. Reinhardt should pay out 30 guilders of his inheritance and we will give him the same amount in our currency over here. [7 ll.: details of money transfer] We couldn't find out anything about Rosina, she is supposed to be in Canada, an English province, but she hasn't written. With this money, dear father, we hope you can manage for a while, if you're careful about spending it, but why is it that you get so little help from Eberhardt and Jakob, you write yourself that they are as well off as we are. [7 ll.: asks about his brothers] I'd have a lot of news to write you about America in connection with the war but I can't write it all, so I will just mention that soon there will be general conscription for the 18- to 45-year-olds which may be my lot, too. I'll stop here because Marie also wants to write a few lines. [3 ll.: greetings; signature; address]

[*Anna Maria Schano* continues:]

Dear father, since you want to know how I am, I will write a few lines. I was pleased that you at least asked how I am, I thought you'd written me off now that my dear Franz isn't here anymore and I can't send you such and such an amount, I would gladly do so if I could, but it is tragic enough for me and for you that he passed away. We have lost a true mainstay. [. . .] I was very unhappy that you said so little about it and still haven't said that you know that my husband has died, and that I am now in the same situation as you are. You have no wife and I no husband, I think it would hurt you just as much if we didn't ask about you.

I have to worry and work very hard now so that my child and I can manage, the house is my biggest worry until I get the money for the interest and taxes, this year I've paid 20½ dollars in tax alone, for two years now they've raised the taxes every year since the war started, all the household goods, food and clothing cost more, in short, the poor and middling folk have to struggle to make it through. [16 ll.: prices; news about other brothers and sisters; greetings; signature] Dear father, please be so kind and send me a lock of your hair in your next letter.

Rosina Debold née Klinger

[Albany, probably 1864]

Dear father and brothers and sisters,

I want to let you know that I am back again in Neujork, but I don't know yet if we will stay in Neujork or not, because here you have to live in fear of war since they say another 8 times a hundred thousand men will be drafted for the war. Dearest father, I would have written you a long time ago, but I didn't want to send an empty letter since I know you are not doing very well and you're always expecting a present and once again, dear father, business is so very bad you can hardly make a living, otherwise I'd have sent you something a long time ago. [3 ll.: will send some money with the next letter] I am in Albani with Marie and Gottlieb at the moment, we were in the country, that is in Ischawa Kanada West, I also have a little boy. [6 ll.: closing; signature; greetings]

Gottlieb Klinger

Albany, April 1st, 1868

Dearest sister, brother and sister-in-law,

[12 ll.: asks again about the settlement of his financial affairs in Stein-reinach]

There's not much news over here since my last letter, the war is over and peace is secured, business is back to its normal course, although still somewhat slow, and food prices are quite high, for example, 15 dollars for 200 lbs. of flour. But that's because of the high *Tax* and the low value of paper money we have for trade here, but it's getting better all the time and will soon be back to full value, that's what everyone hopes, I am still working in the piano factory and Daniel at the railroad station.

And we and our families are quite hale and hearty, we get together every Sunday and usually drink a few beers together, sometimes Marie and her son help with the drinking since she still keeps house with her son, since her husband isn't there, since he's still in the army, she's better off on her own than when that lazy fellow is with her. [. . .] Katharina and her husband from New York come to visit every once in a while, and then of course we have a good time with a keg of beer and joking around; the only thing missing is the wine you have over there, then we could even sing. Hey there, wine for over here, etc.

What about Fritz, doesn't he want to come to America? Or does he want to wait until the Prussian King Wilhelm screws him into a spiked helmet for a couple of years, the way it looks there soon won't be any Swabians anymore, just Germans under Prussian leadership. I could write a lot more about this business, but it is 10 o'clock and I am sleepy, more next time. [4 ll.: greetings; signature; address]

Gottlieb Klinger

Albany, February 19th, 1882

Dear brother and sister-in-law,

[13 ll.: regrets infrequent correspondence; his plans to visit Germany didn't work out] Since during the last bad times I had the misfortune to lose all my property and if you want to travel it costs a lot of money, now thank God business is better and we can recover, of course we have to start all over again. As far as we brothers and sisters are concerned, we are all well, except for Daniel who is still suffering from his cough, it looks like he doesn't have much longer to live. [16 ll.: news about Daniel and his children]

Our sister Barbara is still at her farm and is doing very well, last year she built another new house, she has 7 well-brought-up, Christian children. Marie is still a widow and is also well off, a few years ago her only son died, 25 years old, so now she is left all alone. Katharina is living with her second husband in New Jork and is also well off, her husband has a grocery store, which yields good profit. I can't say much about Rosina except that she is living in New York and has a whole brood of children, her husband is a tinsmith. So, how are you all? [24 ll.: asks about friends and relatives in Germany; greetings; signature; address; sisters' addresses; the emigrant from Steinreinach, Johann Pfeiffer, has died]

Anna Maria Schano

Albany, February 18, 1883

Dear sister-in-law,[44]

[18 ll.: greetings; asks about friends and relatives in Korb-Steinreinach] I have a request, if you would please be so kind as to ask around in Korb

[44]Barbara née Heigelin; see n. 35, above.

about the old wheelwright Schwartz family, that is, old Schwartz married a second time, her name was Mrs. Rappold, she brought a son into the marriage, his name was Karl Rappold. Dear sister-in-law, I imagine you remember that I married this Karl Rappold, it was about 16 years ago, we didn't get along and so we separated, but not legally, up to now I haven't tried to find out anything about him, but now I'd like to know if he is still alive or dead. So, dear sister-in-law, I'd like to ask you please to find out from the family or friends, and if you can't find out anything then please go to the mayor's office and ask at the mayor's. I wrote to the mayor's office last year but I haven't received any answer. So, dear sister-in-law, please let me know, if he is dead I would like to have the death certificate. I'll pay for all the costs.

[13 ll.: news about flooding in southwest Germany; similar catastrophes in America] I have suffered much turmoil and misfortune since I have been in America, but the dear Lord has always helped me back on my feet. I put my trust in God and hope he continues to do so until I die and in eternity. My first husband has been dead now for 22 years, we had one child, a son, we were married for 11 years, then my son died 4 years ago and went on ahead of me. He was 26 years old, had been married for one year and left behind his mother, wife and a child, a son named after my husband's grandfather, his name is Frantz Karl Schanno, he'll be 5 years old on May 28th, that is the only grandchild descended from me and my husband, my only relative and joy as long as we are still alive. [11 ll.: health; reports about her son's and first husband's illnesses]

[no indication of place or date; possibly attached to previous letter]
Dear sister-in-law,

I have another request if you could find out something for me, that is, the German Consul in Baldemor [Baltimore] wrote in the German newspaper about 2 years ago that someone named Rappold had died in Switzerland, but had been born in Würdtenberg, his family name and the family name of his wife were listed that she was also from Würtenberg. This man left an estate of 2 million. One million he left to his wife and the second million to the Rappold family, for it didn't say anything about their having children. So all the relatives of the Rappold family were supposed to come forward and those living in America too. I asked at the German Consulate if anyone named Karl Rappold had come forward, but I got no for an answer although I wasn't counting on any inheritance since we didn't have any children together, I just want to know if he is still alive. I don't want to have him back, either. [24 ll.: health; gets along well thanks to her thrifty nature; says she'll write a letter to her brother Eberhard's wife; greetings; address; asks for a quick answer]

The outcome of Anna Maria Schano's claim on Karl Rappold's estate is unknown. Judging by her last letter, she was so well off that she was not anticipating serious problems—at least in terms of money—in the years to come.

Daniel Klinger and his wife Friederike, too, apparently lived a financially secure and even middle-class life after immigrating. Apart from the two sons they brought along, Daniel and Gottlieb, and the daughter born shortly after their arrival in the United States, the couple had four more children.[45] Until 1889 Daniel Klinger's occupation is listed in the Albany city directory as "teamster"; he died shortly before his sixty-third birthday in November 1890. His widow lived on for another two decades, dying in 1910 at the age of 81.[46]

Gottlieb Klinger is listed in the Albany city directories up to 1901 as a "wood carver"; in 1910 he was still living in the city, now 72 years old and a widower.[47]

After the death of her first husband, probably in the early 1860s, Barbara Klinger married a neighboring farmer from Bavaria and seems to have made quite a good match. Her second husband, Wilhelm Enders, owned eighty acres and his farm was worth nearly $3,000.[48] Her first marriage to Gottlieb Hetzel remained childless, but in her second marriage to Wilhelm Enders she had seven children before 1875.[49] In 1900, she was 69 years old, once again a widow, and still living with her two youngest children on the farm in Mishawaka.[50]

It is unknown what happened to Katharina, who married an apparently prosperous grocer in New York after the death of her first husband Friedrich Breitwieser. Further information is also unavailable about Rosina, whose husband was regarded as a lazy good-for-nothing—at least by the other Klingers.

The Klinger letters are very detailed when it comes to describing the lives of individual family members; the American environment in which

[45]Caroline (b. 1859), Barbara (b. 1864), Emma (b. 1866–67), and Rosa (b. 1870); MC 1880: Albany, N.Y., W. 10, e.d. 21, #171.
[46]Albany CDs for 1883–89; information from contributor.
[47]Albany CDs 1883–1901. Shortly before she died, Friederike Klinger wrote a letter to a niece in Sindelfingen (BABS), indicating that Gottlieb was the last survivor among his siblings.
[48]MC 1870: St. Joseph Co., Ind., Madison Twp., MC 1870, #63; MC A 1880.
[49]Lydia (b. 1863–64), Christian (b. 1866), Christiana (b. 1867), Gottfried (b. 1869), David (b. 1871), Samuel (b. 1872), Caroline (b. 1875); MC 1880: St. Joseph Co., Ind., Madison Twp., #126; Gottlieb Klinger's letter of February 19, 1882.
[50]MC 1900: St. Joseph Co., Ind., e.d 107, #133.

they lived, however, is hardly mentioned at all. The family itself remained a central force in the lives of these immigrants. At the same time, relationships between the various Klinger children were by no means always harmonious, although concern for their elderly parents always managed to help them overcome their differences and thus keep in contact, even though they lived so far apart.

The letters create a picture of individual characters and personality structures which is quite complex. Particularly in the early years, Anna Maria Schano, supported by her husband, stands clearly in the foreground—resolute, practical and matter-of-fact, concerned for the welfare of her brothers and sisters but not without a tinge of materialistic ambition and toughness. In later years, however, her younger brother Gottlieb, whose surprisingly well-written letters stand out in sharp contrast to the others, seems to have taken over the role of family leader, making sure that members of the family kept in contact.

The only other people mentioned are the occasional fellow immigrant from Württemberg; according to the census, most of the Klingers lived in neighborhoods that were predominantly German. This may be another reason why they apparently experienced few adjustment problems—but also why so few traces of "Americanization" are evident in the letters.

19

Engel and Margarethe Winkelmeier

Eastern Westphalia was still suffering from the effects of a profound structural crisis in 1867, when the two sisters Engel (30) and Margarethe (17) Winkelmeier[1] left their home village of Arrenkamp, in the Prussian district of Minden,[2] and set out for America. Since the 1840s, local textile production had been going steadily downhill; faced with increasing competition from mechanized spinning and weaving, the once-flourishing cottage linen industry had had little chance to survive.[3]

Hardest hit by the crisis were thousands of families who lived on small plots and relied on spinning and weaving either to make a living or to supplement their income. The majority were tenant farmers like Engel and Margarethe Winkelmeier's parents,[4] and even by working harder and stepping up productivity, they were unable to compensate for the loss of income caused by the drastic fall in linen prices. A family of spinners had been able to earn four to five talers a week in the 1830s, but ten years later they had to make do with less than one.[5] According to

[1]The two were daughters of the tenant farmer Johann Friedrich Winkelmeier and his wife Marie Margarethe Ilsabein Charlotte, née Meyrose. Marie Engel was born on September 15, 1837, Louise Margarethe Engel on September 9, 1850. Only one other child survived infancy, Friedrich Wilhelm August, born June 20, 1834 (Ev. KB Dielingen).

[2]In Lübbecke County, Dielingen(-Wehdem) township; its population in 1871 was 404 (Reekers/Schulz [1952], 93).

[3]Adelmann (1974); Biller (1906); Schmitz (1967), 53–66.

[4]See the introduction to the Stille and Krumme series, Chapter 1; Mager (1982), 468–69; Seraphim (1948); Wrasmann (1919).

[5]Adelmann, 116; see also Lüning (1845), 504–5.

contemporary reports, living conditions on tenant farms were appalling: large families, usually poorly fed and malnourished, lived "crowded together like sheep" in tiny, shabby lodgings, often under sanitary conditions ideal for promoting disease, and had to "work feverishly from early morning to late at night to earn even the most meager living."[6]

As one of the main protoindustrial centers, the Minden-Ravensberg[7] area, home of the Winkelmeier sisters, had been particularly hard-hit by the crisis. According to official reports, one-third of the residents of Lübbecke County in the 1850s made their living by producing linen thread—and even this figure probably overlooks some family members who worked at the spinning wheels.[8] Agriculture was underdeveloped and unable to support a population undergoing rapid growth, and attempts to introduce mechanical innovations in the textile industry came late, in the 1850s and affected only the towns of Bielefeld and Herford. Lack of alternative employment possibilities thus forced many of the unemployed and impoverished spinners and weavers to leave. A considerable number sought seasonal employment in Holland, northern Germany, or the Ruhr District, following the long-standing rural tradition of seasonal labor migration.[9] Many more, however, decided to emigrate to America. From mid-century to the founding of the Empire in 1871, the district of Minden had the second highest emigration rate in Prussia, surpassed only by the district of Osnabrück, also a center of cottage linen production.[10] As early as 1847, after all attempts to help the faltering textile industry back on its feet had failed, officials in Minden applied for aid "to promote the emigration of unemployed tenant farmers." Their appeal, however, fell on deaf ears in Berlin.[11] But local authorities, at least, did not go out of their way to discourage would-be emigrants, even if they left without official permission; instead, it was regarded as a stroke of luck that "America needs what we have too much of."[12]

Individual persons, more rarely entire families, began emigrating from the Winkelmeiers' village of Arrenkamp in the 1850s.[13] These pioneers, as so often, set off a wave of followers. By the early 1860s an entire group

---

[6]Lüning, 498, 506; but see also Bitter (1964–65) and Domeyer (1972), 13, 17–19.

[7]Mendels (1970), 7; Kriedte et al. (1981); Mager.

[8]Potthoff (1910), 105–8.

[9]See the Stille and Krumme series, Chapter 1; Adelmann, 115, 122; Kammeier (1983), 84; Kamphoefner (1987), 16, 19, 34; Mager, 472.

[10]Bödicker (1874), i–viii; see Kamphoefner (1987), 21, 43. Emigrants from both districts were predominantly rural lower class: 68 percent in Osnabrück; 60 percent in Minden.

[11]Adelmann, 122.

[12]According to a county magistrate quoted in Adelmann.

[13]The church chronicle in Dielingen (GA Stemwede-Dielingen, no signature) lists the number of emigrants per year—with and without official permission—for the villages of Dielingen, Drohne, Haldem, and Arrenkamp; emigrants' names are seldom included.

from Wehdem, Arrenkamp, Westrup, Haldem, and Dielingen were living together in Indianapolis.[14] Among them were Karl, Heinrich, and
Hermann Holle, probably brothers and children of a tenant farmer in
Arrenkamp.[15] Hermann Holle then returned to Germany a few years
later, apparently to fetch his parents and other relatives.[16] Together with
the Holles, a number of young unmarried people, mostly children of
tenant farmers in Arrenkamp and other nearby villages, boarded the
steamship *Hermann* on March 31, 1867, in Bremen and set sail for America; among them were Engel and Margarethe Winkelmeier.[17]

Upon arriving in Indianapolis, the two sisters encountered a number
of acquaintances who could help them find their way around; in particular, Karl and Heinrich Holle and their families seem to have looked out
for the two young women at first. With the help of the Holles, they
quickly found jobs working for "Low German" employers, Engel Winkelmeier as a washerwoman and Margarethe as a "maid of all work."
After a short time, however, both left these jobs and went to work for
American families who paid better.

Both sisters describe living conditions in the United States as an improvement over Germany. This assessment was clearly based on higher
wages and better working conditions. At mid-century in Lübbecke
County, a spinner could earn a maximum of one-half taler per week, if she
worked quickly; weavers were better paid and might earn at most twice
that amount.[18] By contrast, a servant girl's wage in the United States, as
Engel and Margarethe Winkelmeier's letters attest, could be several times
higher, especially with some experience.[19] Although household chores
were anything but light, as Margarethe Winkelmeier reports, they were
nothing compared to long hours every day at the spinning wheel or loom.
Margarethe, too, was young and full of energy, and she seems to have

[14]Immigrants from the village of Wehdem, a few miles away from Arrenkamp, founded a
small "New Wehdem" in Indianapolis; one Indianapolis city street is still named after the village
in eastern Westphalia (Schütte [1985], 55).
[15]The Dielingen church chronicle includes one Wilhelm Carl Heinrich Holle from Arrenkamp in the list of emigrants in 1860.
[16]This can be deduced from the letters and the NYPL of April 1, 1867: Hermann Holle's
country of origin is here listed as "USA." He is followed by Friedrich (58) and Marie (69), as well
as three more Holles: Johann (19), Hermann (16), and Friedrich (9).
[17]Besides the Holles and the Winkelmeiers, the passenger list includes the following sequence
of names (all with the occupation "farmer" dittoed down the column): Wilhelm Maschmeier
(18), Engel Sander (19), Heinrich Holle (17), Karl Tiemann (19), Louise Geldmeier (18), Wilhelm Warner (19), and Friedrich Röhling (16)—almost all of these persons are also mentioned in
the letters. It is unclear whether they emigrated with or without official permission, for the
Lübbecke County emigration files prior to 1879 have not survived (Müller [1980–81], 7). The
Dielingen church chronicle lists a total of 58 cases of emigration for the year 1867—twenty just
from the village of Arrenkamp, with a population of only four hundred.
[18]Kammeier (1983), 81.
[19]See Ernst (1949), 65–67, and Katzman (1978), 303–14.

Figure 38. Servant girl churning butter outside a thatch–roofed peasant cottage in Winkelmeier's home county of Lübbecke; an indication of the living conditions and manual labor that persisted even fifty years after the sisters left. *Source:* Heinz–Ulrich Kammeier.

particularly enjoyed being able to do what she wanted in her free time, without being subjected to restrictions like in Germany. She underscored her satisfaction with life in America by saying that even if she were offered her own farm, she wouldn't return to Germany—a remarkable statement for the daughter of a tenant farmer.

As in many immigrant letters, reports about food and clothing— evidence of an improved standard of living—play a considerable role in the two sisters' letters. The detailed descriptions of the food provided by their employers, their obvious pride in having rosy cheeks and gaining weight, and their lack of understanding for the Americans, who never ate enough to be even "half full" and who always wanted to stay "wiry"—all of this makes sense when one considers how frugal the meals were at home in a spinner's or weaver's household. Breakfast usually consisted of a few slices of pumpernickel and coffee made from roasted chicory and only occasionally real coffee beans; for lunch there was sometimes stew made of vegetables but more often potatoes or sour milk; and then bread and coffee were served again for supper. Meat was seldom or never seen on the table in most homes.[20] Clothing played a similarly significant role: the silk jacket Margarethe bought and wrote home about was an article of clothing she would never have been able to afford in Germany. Also, a tenant farmer's daughter could hardly own such a luxury item without causing an uproar in the peasant community.

Apart from such rather superficial changes, however, life in an American city, with a population of about fifty thousand (some 10 percent German and 6 percent Irish),[21] seems to have had a surprisingly limited effect on the two sisters' mentality and way of life. The letters cover only their first five years in the United States and thus do not permit any definite conclusions; nevertheless, they give the impression that the two women remained closely tied to traditional German values and ways of thinking. Only rarely is there a noticeable invasion of English idioms, and there are very few English terms in the German text.

The two sisters seem to have spent most of their time socializing with acquaintances from Westphalia. Margarethe, in particular, gives long and detailed reports about the small Low German community—people, parties, and family events. Later, both women chose husbands who were members of this group. In 1869, at the age of 32, Engel married a butcher of the same age named Friedrich Wulf, from Dielingen, and moved to Cumberland, Indiana, a few miles outside of Indianapolis.[22] Besides the

[20]Teuteberg/Wiegelmann (1972), 259, 277–78; Lüning, 506.
[21]USC 1870.1, 388.
[22]Heinrich Friedrich Wilhelm Wulf was born in 1837 (ev. KB Dielingen) and emigrated to the United States in 1866. In the mid-1870s he opened a butcher's shop (which he ran, after 1880,

two daughters mentioned in the letters, Margarethe (Maggie) and Engel (Annie), the couple had a son named Wilhelm (William).[23] Margarethe, who was considerably younger and frequently wrote that she had no interest in getting married, finally tied the knot with the teamster Friedrich Kottkamp in 1875.[24]

A total of eighteen letters written by the sisters between 1867 and 1872 and addressed to their parents (later their father) have been preserved. The correspondence broke off even before their father's death,[25] partly because their brother showed little interest in keeping it up. According to the letters, at least Margarethe wrote to other people in Arrenkamp, but none of these letters seems to have survived.

In the original German, Engel and Margarethe Winkelmeier's letters are difficult to read and understand, due to their unruly orthography, almost total lack of punctuation, and heavy coloring of local dialect. Matthew Dorgathen's letters are the hardest to read and understand for a native speaker, but those of the Winkelmeier sisters are close runners-up. Both sisters found writing difficult; Engel said so clearly in her first letter and asked her parents not to show her letter to anyone else. Lack of experience with the written language, however, was by no means unusual for members of the rural lower class. Even in the middle of the nineteenth century, many tenant farmers were illiterate,[26] and, as is clear from the letters written by the two daughters, neither mother nor father Winkelmeier could read or write. The much-vaunted efficiency of the Prussian school system suffered greatly in areas where children had to help out at home at an early age; having the time for regular schooling was a luxury that only the children of prosperous farmers could afford.[27]

---

together with a certain Jacob Bischoff) in Indianapolis, but he continued to live in Cumberland. According to the census, he owned $300 of real estate in 1870; in 1900 he owned a house free of debt (Indianapolis CDs for 1876–1900; MC 1870: Marion Co., Ind., Warren Twp., #358; 1880: e.d. 99, #238; 1900: e.d. 200, #151).

[23]Margarethe (b. March 31, 1869), Engel (b. January 1871), Wilhelm (b. 1873). According to the census, all three children were living at home with their parents in 1900; son Wilhelm had followed in his father's footsteps and become a butcher as well.

[24]Indiana Historical Society, Marion County Marriage Records, 13, 355. His name alone, one that is very common in this region, is enough to suggest that Kottkamp came from east Westphalia (see Müller [1980–81], 586). The two seem to have left Indianapolis a few years after they married: in 1879, no Kottkamps are listed in the CDs, nor are they listed in the city census materials.

[25]Johann Friedrich Winkelmeier died in 1874 at the age of 66 (Ev. KB Dielingen).

[26]Mager, 470.

[27]Schoneweg (1923), 103, reports that teachers in rural areas often had to bow to the wishes of parents and excuse their children from the otherwise compulsory seven or eight years of schooling so that they could work and help support their families. Many children, therefore, had only three years of schooling at most.

Engel Winkelmeier[28]

Yndianaponis, written on April 11, 1867
My dear beloved parents, forgive me for not sending you any news any earlier, that means we're still quite content. I've hardly given Germany a thought, that means we don't lack for anything, if we just stay healthy since everything we brought along we'll be able to use. And then I want to tell you we didn't have to pay taxes on anything. [7 ll.: details of their arrival in New York] My money, I kept all of what I brought along from Wedem. Then we also went there and bought things, and I was surprised that there were Low Germans there, since as far as the English go, have a look at your geese, they're easier to understand than them [i.e., the Americans]. My dear parents, I can't tell you how Heinerich Holle took us on, and his wife, since they have a child. I am at Ko[- - -] and Magreta at Heinrich Holle's, both are in the same house, they are all from Germany, they aren't in any hurry to let us leave, we're supposed to go to good people, since they treat us like their own, they do everything for us, we couldn't wish for anything more, up to now everything's going fine.

For it's a different world here. My dear brother, you told me a lot about what it's like in the world, but now I could tell you a few things, if I were with you. [5 ll.: her brother and sister-in-law should write soon] Magreta, she's already getting fatter, since the food here tastes very good. Better than in the Winkelmeiers' house, because she now likes bacon and meat. And that is true and not a lie. Now I want to tell you about the trunk, we found everything the same as when we packed it, and nothing changed, for we had it all in the sun.[29] Then the women helped all of us, we couldn't have wanted it any better. [13 ll.: greetings from Hermann Holle and Wilhelm Maschmeier;[30] details about their arrival and first night spent in the United States] I'll stop now, if I've forgotten anything then ask me, then I'll tell you about it. [3 ll.: greetings to various families in Arrenkamp] I ask you please not to show this letter to anyone else. Though a good job I didn't do, I've finished it to send to you. All the best from your 2 daughters / Engel Winkelmeier / Fare ye well

Margarethe Winkelmeier

Indianaponis, written April 11, 1867
[25 ll.: details about stops and conditions on their trip] On April 5th we

---

[28]Extracts of some of the letters written by Engel and Margarethe Winkelmeier have been previously published in Kammeier (1985), 62–73.

[29]The trunk probably contained handwoven linen that Engel and Margarethe had taken with them.

[30]See n. 17, above; until 1883, Wilhelm Maschmeier is listed in the Indianapolis CDs as a "gardener."

arrived in Noples [Indianapolis]. First at Karl Holle's about 12 noon, in the evening to Heinrich Holle's. They weren't any farther apart than from the Winkelmeiers' house to the Gräbers' house.

My dear parents, brother and sister-in-law, now I want to tell you about how it was for us on the ship. Mägie didn't have any problems, I just had to throw up one time, that was my only difficulty, otherwise I was fit as a fiddle. And Mägie, that means the same thing as Margreta. And my sister Enni [Annie: Engel] she was sick a bit, and she had to throw up several times, she kept on drinking and she couldn't stomach the water, so then she started drinking beer and wine, then she got better. A bottle of wine cost 20 silbergroschens on the ship and a bottle of beer 10 silbergroschens, and all the promises Hirmann Holle made to you he's kept, he's helped us with everything. My first job was washing, but it's much easier than in Germany. My dear parents, don't worry so much about us, since my sister, she always thought you couldn't understand anyone here, but there are already too many from Germany here. [3 ll.: apologizes that the letter is so short; greetings] I remain / your faithful daughter / Margreta Winkelmeier.

[letter written by both sisters, no date, probably in the first month after their arrival]
[5 ll.: by *Margarethe Winkelmeier:* introduction; complains about not receiving any letters from Arrenkamp]

[*Engel Winkelmeier* continues:]

Cast thy burden upon the Lord, and he shall sustain thee: he shall never suffer the righteous to be moved. I give great thanks for the fond memories and now I give great thanks that things happened as they did, otherwise I wouldn't be here. [----------] I could never have it over there like I do here. Now, my dear parents, don't give yourselves any headaches over me, and mother, that you think you didn't do something or other right, oh no, that's not so, everything, everything is fine. I don't mean by that that you shouldn't put us in your prayers, but that's all we need. [3 ll.: asks for news from her parents] And when you write again, please send a small note along of when they were born and a few strands of hair from their heads, that's the only thing I need here. Magreta also wrote a few lines, that's because she was here with me for a whole week just for pleasure, I couldn't do that in Germany, she said, and then go back to the same job.

Engel Winkelmeier

[Indianapolis], Holy Pentecost Eve [1867]

Now I'm in the mood to talk to you a bit [17 ll.: she and Margarethe are fine; picked up a letter from Arrenkamp at the post office; asks for addresses] Now you asked me to tell you if we need anything, there isn't much we need, since I've seen enough bedding. The bedding here is half as warm, it's so thin everything comes through. You don't need to send any since I think we have enough for now, our trunks are still full and I wouldn't know where to put anything else. I'm going to manage since we took along quite a lot, for woolen underclothes aren't so thick here. My dearly beloved father and mother, I am now working for people, you should see what that's like, where at the start you can't understand a word, but if you do something wrong that's fine, too. The same is true for Karl Tieman,[31] the two of us are the only ones in an English place, but not in the same house. Magreta has a good post but with Low Germans, now she also wants to speak English, our lady goes to church so often that Magreta also comes to visit her relatives. I've been here for 6 weeks now, I can understand a lot of what the lady says to me, but I can't talk a whole lot, the dear Lord, he helps a lot, that [- - -] my own common sense tells me that the Germans help me a bit, then everything is a lot more fun, and I can't even tell you how clever the lady was at the start, when she saw I was honest, since in the beginning she left money around but it never occurred to me to take it,[32] when the lady saw that, it was worth a lot to her [- - -]. She was always afraid I would leave the first 4 weeks. 2 talers a week and now three and a half. Magreta one and a half, now she wants to work for some English too, she says. So, mother, give my love to your brother, he should save his money, I'm coming to see him soon, then I'll tell you how Magreta's doing, since that's near here. My money, that's three talers and 17 groschens a week in your money, that's a lot, but if you buy things here then you also know what they ask for. [7 ll.: she is pleased to be in America; greetings]

My best to all / Engel Winkelmeier

Margarethe Winkelmeier

Indianaponnis, June   1867

[exact date missing]

My dear parents, brother and sister-in-law, [7 ll.: thanks for a letter from

---

[31]Fellow immigrant on the same ship; see n. 17, above.

[32]It was a common practice for employers—not only Americans—to leave small sums of money lying around the house to test the honesty of a new servant (Katzmann, 17; Wierling [1987], 211).

Arrenkamp; weather] We'd also heard about that war business[33] before we got your letter. My dear mother, you ask if the food kept on the voyage, we were still eating it on the train, we still had some of everything when we arrived in Naplis, and our dresses still fit very well, they don't even need to be altered, Engel's black one is still fine, too.

My dear parents, when we think about the white linen we are very pleased indeed, since we can really use it here, the colored sheets too, and it's a bit embarrassing to write this, but please be so good and send us a few collars, 2 hairnets, ones like my old ones, that's what they wear in America, but I cut off the ribbon on the front since I don't wear mine every Sunday, and also some velvet ribbon as wide as this line [a line about 1¼" is drawn in] you can see it from this, and blue aprons, since they wear aprons just like in Germany, and a hairnet costs one taler here and a collar [20] groschens. Now I also want to tell you that Herman Holle is not getting married, there's lots of time for that still. The whole company, they're still all quite content, and I, Louise Loman and Heinerich Tiemei all went to the fair, the children were singing there, they were almost all Germans, there were twice as many as at the Haldemmer fair; since there's not as much merrymaking here in America, but it isn't necessary, either. [4 ll.: asks about the family] And did you [i.e., her father] and Wilhelm have good birthdays, too? I wanted to send you a bottle of wine but it must not have made it across. [4 ll.: closing; greetings; signature]

[Engel Winkelmeier continues:]

I don't have any more time, Engel, I hate to see that she leaves some paper blank. [4 ll.: asks for blue yarn; the linen they brought along is very useful] And then I want to tell you what church services are like here, every Sunday I have to go, the house is closed then, they have two children, the boy is twenty and the girl is 9 years old, but they don't have 2 Sundays in a row, on Sundays they sometimes go to church 3 times, and they pray at the table, I like that. Now, give my best to all the people that sent one of theirs over here, they are all happy and we all go to the same church.[34] [5 ll.: she and her sister were the first to write back to Germany] / now Fare ye as well as God will

Margarethe Winkelmeier

Indianapolis, October 10, 1867

Dear parents, brother and sister-in-law

[7 ll.: thanks for letters from Arrenkamp; postal delivery in the United

---

[33] Austro-Prussian War of 1866, which mainly affected Bohemia.
[34] In the early 1870s Indianapolis had a dozen churches, including five or six German ones (Schem 5 [1871], 529).

States] We are all quite happy. Except I couldn't walk very well for a few days, I had a touch of gout, so I put on my woollen underskirt from the Brokum market[35] then it went away, now I am quite content again and like to eat again. And you wanted to know about the food here, I haven't seen coffee here for 16 weeks, there's tea in the morning, meat and white bread, sometimes a potato along with it, they're baked in the oven, for lunch 2 potatoes, meat, bread and water, and sometimes a kind of delicacy you don't know. In the evening bread and water, and butter, too, that's the main food in my household. Engel gets coffee in the morning, water at noon and tea in the evening, at Engel's there's more food on the table to eat. That sounds like a lie, but that's really the way it is, the English don't eat enough to get half full, they want to stay thin and wiry, but that doesn't bother me. We both live in the city, also all together the German corps, except for Wilhelm Masschmeier, Heinerich Tiemeier or Holle, and Friederich Rölinck,[36] they're a bit farther out in the country. My work is Monday washing, Tuesday and Wednesday ironing or knitting, Thursdays I have my day off, Friday and Saturday scrubbing and cleaning, downstairs the hallways where you walk up, I keep them as white as our table in Germany, that's more or less my work, we haven't seen any fruit yet, it still seems to me like spring, but the leaves are falling from the trees, but in the city you don't see that. The people have to buy all their food, we have a small garden, too, but nothing in it, they are too lazy to plant anything, if only it were mine. Our everyday clothes are an old dress in the morning and in the afternoon a petticoat or crinoline and a pure cotton dress is put on, toward evening the shepherdesses get dressed up and so do we now, since you have to work harder in the morning. We also have to do the cooking.

[3 ll.: has laid the linen they brought out in the sun] The beds aren't half as good as in Germany, for straw they take the leaves off the Turkish wheat [corn] then they make a straw sack out of them, I lie there on a pillow where I lie my head and two wool blankets that I cover myself with, the first two nights I thought it was strange but then I didn't notice it anymore. Engel has a much better bed. I still don't earn much, one and a half talers a week, Engel 2 talers, but we want to learn to speak English, we can already understand a lot but can't say much, we think we'll learn that, too. The others can't understand anything, only me, Engel and Karl Tieman.

That's because they're always with other Germans. I spent the first 6 weeks with Germans, but now I am glad that I took the risk. The lady sews all my clothes and mends them, she shows and teaches me every-

---

[35]Brokum (population in 1880 was 950) was about six miles from Arrenkamp, across the border in Hanover.
[36]Fellow immigrants on the same ship; see n. 17, above.

thing, that's worth a lot to me, since if I had to have a dress made I'd have to pay one and a half talers. As you know, over here 14 groschens are worth more in talers than over there.[37] Engel has bought herself a summer scarf and I a silk jacket, mine cost 8 talers, Engel couldn't get used to the material at first, so she said I should wear it first, but she didn't want to, but you should see Engel now, now she likes it. [30 ll.: asks for the address of a friend and other news from Arrenkamp; arrival of Wilhelm Holle—brother of Karl, Hermann, and Heinrich—in Indianapolis, who brought along hairnets, collars, yarn, aprons, and other things from the parents] I thank you so much. I can't send you anything else yet, you shouldn't have sent so much if times are so hard, we are really sorry about that. I still think of home often, I've been with you many times at night, then I pray the little verse, Oh God bless my parents as You have blessed me. [10 ll: continuation; postage; greetings to friends] I remain your faithful daughter

Margreta Winkelmeier. I hope this letter reaches you in the same condition as I left you.

Engel Winkelmeier

[Indianapolis, also probably October 1867]
My dearly beloved parents, brother and sister-in-law

[3 ll.: sorry to hear about the poor harvest in Germany] When that all came[38] it was all forgotten again, then I said to Magreta, now the English will be able to see that we didn't grow up on a manure pile, she was so happy she was beside herself, and I must say myself I am very happy too, since I didn't put the letter in their hands and didn't read everything out to them, and when more came than she knew about, she was amazed, since we got everything all right, and that gang of Holles had to admit the Winkelmeier girls got most of it. Loise Holle offered us three and a half talers straight off for the linen, then I said, even if you give us 6 it's not to be had for money, now we have enough of everything, we're healthy, have something to eat and clothing, that's enough. [13 ll.: her sister's accommodations; greetings to various families in Arrenkamp; thanks for the presents Wilhelm Holle brought along; greetings] All love from your eldest daughter Engel Winkelmeier

The next time I'll use a smaller piece of paper. [18 ll.: various bits of news and greetings from German friends]

[37]She may mean that 14 dimes are worth more than 14 groschens, which come to less than one taler.

[38]She is referring to the presents, which must have included handwoven linen, which Wilhelm Holle brought along from Arrenkamp.

[19 ll.: letter written by *Margarethe Winkelmeier* in Indianapolis on November 26, 1867, in which she describes an elaborate funeral she and her sister had seen]

Engel Winkelmeier

Yen Dieanapolis, December 5, 1867

[5 ll.: quotes several verses of a German Christmas carol]

My dearly beloved parents, brother and sister-in-law, I wish you all a merry Christmas and if we stay as happy as now we'll be doing fine, indeed. And now it's winter so that's why we can't go to see the Holles, for us that's like going home. Last Sunday we went to Wilhelm's for coffee, we sat there and had a wonderful time, when he gave us the present I gave them 2 talers right away, he said he didn't want anything for it, but I knew how things work in a household like that, and they all send their best. [7 ll.: sends greetings to friends and asks her friend Louise to send her a note] If Loise doesn't want to do any more spinning and weaving then she should come over here, she may have it good over there but things here are also good, I couldn't ask for anything more, on the ship I thought if I didn't get any dark bread I would die, but it turned out not to be true at all.

My dearly beloved parents, I wish you could see your littlest daughter, she hasn't grown any taller, but much fatter as I have [3 ll.: her clothes are too tight now] My dear father, I'm wearing the wooden shoes right now, but the first day my feet hurt, now I also walk around clump, clump, clump. I never could walk fast. [4 ll.: asks for news] I wish you all happiness and blessings / Engel Winkelmeier

[*Margarethe Winkelmeier* continues:]

Dearest parents, I am very happy, I never have to spin or weave, I can go to bed at 6 in the evening, I hope you all stay as hale and hearty as I am. All love from / Magreta Winkelmeier.

Margarethe Winkelmeier

Indianapolis, August 21, 1868

My dearly beloved parents, brother and sister-in-law

[3 ll.: introduction] I last saw the Wulwes on the 4th of July, it was a Saturday, my sister Engel, she came on Friday already, she stayed here with me again and Friderich, he came the next morning at 9 o'clock, then we went right away to the *Picknick,* that means to the fair. We live 5 hours from each other, you can still get there, I'm there in an hour on the train, it goes fast. Friderich's brothers were there too, and all the Germans we used to know or had heard of. Louise Loman and I did a lot of dancing, my dress was all soaked with sweat. I was dressed almost completely in white, if you'd have seen me I doubt you'd have recognized me, since I saw the girl who was a maid at the Welmans in Blumhorst,[39] she knew me in Germany, we shook hands with her, but she didn't know who I was anymore. It was the same with August Stas from Westerup, Wilhelm Masshmeier was there, too, that was the first time I'd seen anyone since Wilhelm Holle was here, for everything with ears and legs was there, we've never had such a good time like that day. On the 4th of July no one has to work, the day is a holiday because that's the day the war ended and they made peace.[40] My dearly beloved parents, brother and sister-in-law, I'd like to hope that you are as content as I am, if you were to offer me my own farm I wouldn't take you up on it, I would like to see you again but that won't work out in this life. I'm amazed how much the dear Lord helps me out, so many people know me here, in Germany I never had many friends, but all the more here. My dear brother, ask my mother what she thinks when she sees little Friderich in the sideboard, or did Mina already grab him.[41] I can write you a little bit of news, Herman Holle had his wedding on August 11, Tuesday evening, he got all the Germans together. His wife is named Meri Risse, also a Low German girl. And even old mother Holle danced. We were all along in the church, too, when the pastor joined them together, the bridegroom had three boys on his side and the bride three girls. These girls were all dressed in snowy white,[42] they looked wonderful all standing there. I can't write you everything, that would take too long. Hermann Holle has built himself a new house, it comes to about 2 thousand talers, the two of us used to live so close together, there was only one house between us, we could call out to each other, but that's over now, last winter we also threw so many snowballs at each other that his hat flew off his head. / Magreta Winkelmeier

                                            Indianapolis, July   1869.
                                            [exact date missing]
My dearly beloved parents, brother and sister-in-law
    [11 ll.: she is sorry to hear about her mother's illness and complains

[39]Blumenhorst was the name of a part of Arrenkamp.
[40]Margarethe was obviously unaware of the real reason for celebrating the Fourth of July.
[41]"Mina" is her sister-in-law Wilhelmine; "little Friderich in the sideboard" probably refers to a photograph of a deceased brother or nephew.
[42]That the bridesmaids wore white indicates a degree of adaptation to American wedding customs: in Germany—especially in rural areas—members of the wedding party usually wore black (Weber-Kellermann [1979], 164–65).

about lack of letters] I don't have much news to write about, that the dear Lord has blessed my sister Engel with a baby girl, that you know already, that was in Waelman's letter. She was born on March 31, 1869, my sister was quite content, she got out of bed already the second day and stayed up. I was there for 2 weeks and took care of her. She was baptized at Pentecost, Louise Geldmeier and I were the godmothers, her name is the same as mine, and what my name is, that you know. So far everyone who came with us from Germany, they all have little girls, Karrel Tieman's wife Engel Sander,[43] I don't know what Herman Holle's will have, Wilhelm Holle's wife has a little girl, too, so does Karrel Holle and Heinerich Holle, we're all very surprised ourselves. [9 ll.: someone who used to live in Arrenkamp came to visit the Holle family]

My dear brother, I hope sometime you can earn as much money as Wilhelm and August Holle do with their masonry work,[44] they earn 3 and a quarter talers a day, but not much in the winter. Wilhelm talks about you often, I spent 4 days with him since I had a bad finger that didn't want to work, then I sat around for two weeks without doing much work but now it's better again. [10 ll.: asks for news of family and friends, greetings] I ask you please not to show my letter to anyone.
I remain your faithful daughter Magreta Winkelmeier

Engel Wulf née Winkelmeier
[Cumberland, Indiana, probably mid-1869]
My dearest beloved father and mother
[3 ll.: is sorry about her parent's plight] I never thought it possible to cope with it all so well, but the dear Lord helps out, and I hope He'll help you soon, too. [7 ll.: religious consolation]

I'd been waiting so long for a letter and then finally my brother did send one, since I wrote the last one, you probably think I've forgotten you.

But that would be hard, but things are better than I'd thought at home, since as my husband says, happy is he who can forget what can't be changed, for it's only a short time till we see each other again, and may God be merciful to us in the end if we act in the right way.

As for news, I can't write much, you already know that God gave us a little girl,[45] then 2, since our household was a bit too small, I couldn't manage all the work alone, but now I have help. The first three months

[43]Other fellow immigrants on the same ship; see n. 17, above.
[44]August Holle continues to be listed as a "stone mason" in the Indianapolis CDs up to 1890, but Wilhelm apparently died in the early 1880s—starting in 1882 only his widow Wilhelmine is listed.
[45]Margarethe (b. March 31, 1869).

she's been very restless during the day, as soon as it's evening, she goes to sleep and only wakes up once during the night. [3 ll.: her brother's illness?] My dear ones, you mustn't think I didn't write so long because I was angry, it was just laziness.

[4 ll.: expresses her sympathy to her sister-in-law on the death of a young nephew] Our little girl can't walk yet, but she kicks around a lot, with her legs on top of the covers, and when she sees you coming then she lies there quiet and hides her head in the bedclothes, she can already understand pretty well when she's scolded, then she starts to cry. Up to now I've had enough milk, but now she is beginning to drink less and less. She was born on March 31. Luise, you wanted to know if I like being in America, I like it a lot. Now I've met a woman I like to visit with, we'd known each other a long time, but not very well, she lives near me.

You can't imagine how happy I am. Contentment is my dearest pleasure, and I have found it. Honor your parents both day and night, thank them for their efforts and delight. [8 ll.: continuation] My dearly beloved brother and sister-in-law, thank you for not going to any trouble, since 2 days before when we got your letter, my husband said, if they do that, he wouldn't bother asking for it, now everyone keeps what he's got,[46] and Wilhemina said she knew that some of the linen was still left, me, I don't know anything about that, I've forgotten about it. For the moment I've got enough, if it stays that way then I can't thank God enough. [7 ll.: asks for an answer soon; greetings to relatives and friends] / Engel Winkelmeier

[17 ll.: letter by *Friedrich Wulf* from Cumberland of November 22, 1869, in which he expresses his regret that his mother-in-law is ill, complains that his brother-in-law Wilhelm writes so seldom, and reports about the weather, harvest, and food prices]

Margarethe Winkelmeier

Indianapolis, December 14, 1869
My dearly beloved parents, brother and sister-in-law
[7 ll.: thanks them for their letter and says how sorry she is about her parents' and brother's economic plight] I am still quite content, for if you're healthy, you can't thank the dear Lord enough for that. My dear brother, you said you thought if someone got sick here in America, they

---

[46]This seems to refer to the settlement of an inheritance.

wouldn't do anything about it, but it's not quite that bad, because if someone doesn't have any relatives or friends here, he has to go to the hospital, he gets taken care of there as well as need be, here there are lots of hospitals for people with problems, for the blind, the dumb, the sick and also for people who've lost their senses,[47] the dumb can talk here quite well with their fingers but it's sad to see. My dear friends, I can also let you know that the family I work for has left here, since the pastors can only stay in one place for 2 or 3 years now, then they are transferred, and now I am in another home, since August 1, my work is like usual, in the family are husband and wife, one child, nursemaid and kitchenmaid, that's me, that's 5 all together. You might think I could just fold my hands in my lap, that would be so if there wasn't so much washing every week. I'm still living in the same place, just a few houses away. [5 ll.: asks about her friend Engel Maschmeier, whose brother Wilhelm lives in Indianapolis] Give best greetings to the Rölings from their son,[48] say he's doing pretty well, when I ask him about writing, he says there's still plenty of time for that, and his parents should be pleased, since he gave them the little money he had. Then he was really happy about that, since for 2 years he's kept saying he's going back to Germany for a visit, then they'll see enough of me. My dear parents, I would also like to come for a visit, if it didn't take so many pennies, at night I am often with you and talk with you a lot, but when I wake up in the morning then I am very happy. My dear friends, it's a stark contrast with servants and maids, since they have a lot more rights here than over there, when I'm done with my work then I go anywhere I want to, and they can't even say one word about it. [6 ll.: season's greetings, greetings; signature]

Indianapolis, December 6, 1870
My dearest beloved father, brother and sister-in-law,[49]
My thoughts move me to write to you, since it has been quite a long time since I heard from you, and now I hope that you will receive this letter, since they say here they aren't delivering any letters because the evil war[50] is so bad over there, but I didn't have any peace of mind anymore. [3 ll.: thanks for letter from her brother] Thanks to the dear Lord I am pretty hale and hearty again, for in August I was sick for two weeks and didn't work for three weeks, I lost almost 20 talers, the

[47]In Indianapolis there was a large institution for the blind, deaf, and dumb and insane (Schem 5:529).
[48]Fellow immigrants on the same ship; see n. 17, above.
[49]Her mother had passed away on December 15, 1869 (Ev. KB Dielingen).
[50]The Franco-Prussian War had broken out six months earlier.

sickness was almost like nerve fever, but the doctor said it wasn't. I didn't have to leave the family I work for, they didn't want to let me go. My sister Engel was here with me for a day. The lady took care of me like a real mother, for it's just like I were her daughter, I've been with them for a year and 5 months. My dear ones, please write and tell me how things are with the war, if my brother has also gone off to war, I'd like to know, since here in America we don't know anything about it, because the whole time the war has been going on no one has gotten a letter, except Wilhelm Masschmeier and Friederich Holle. Please write me who from your area has had to go off and who has met his death, since the way the people here tell it, it must have been absolutely terrible, they say a lot of people have left here to go back to Germany, though I don't know if that's true or not, to help the Prussians.[51]

One other bit of news for you, I had to go to three weddings, first Flhelm Schlacke and Engel Berens,[52] second Louise Geldmeier and Gan Hadwig, I wrote Louise ['s name] first, but it's all right turned around. And third, August Wulf, my brother-in-law's brother,[53] I don't know his wife's name. Now all the girls have gotten married who came from our villages and with us across the water, all except Margreta Winkelmeier. Because I have no mind to. [7 ll.: reports about a trip made by the elder Holles to St. Louis to visit various friends and relatives[54]] The old Holles have bought a house for almost 9 hundred talers, old Holle is just like he was in Germany. All of my friends and relatives are quite content, and Wulwes too, as far as I know. My dear father, brother and sister-in-law, you remember what lovely hair I had on my head, it's almost all fallen out because of my sickness, so I've had to cut it all off. Dear Wilhemie, what about you, I wonder if you can't write any more, try it and write me a long letter about my father and the two girls, if they already have to do the spinning and about all of you. [5 ll.: greetings; address]

Indianapolis, September 20, 1871

My dearly beloved father, brother and sister-in-law

[8 ll.: greetings; news about brother-in-law Wulf] My people went

---

[51]The Franco-Prussian War did unleash a wave of patriotic nationalism among many German-Americans (see the letters of Johann Christian Lenz, Chapter 3). In 1870 a hundred German volunteers left Chicago to go back to Germany to "help the Prussians." There is no record in the Indianapolis German newspapers of a similar exodus (*Katholische Glaubensbote*, September 21, 1870, 2).

[52]Wilhelm Schlake, listed as a "laborer," still appears in the early 1890s in the Indianapolis CDs. From 1895 to 1900, only his widow Engel is listed, along with Wilhelm H. Schlake (of the same address), first listed as "clerk," later as "barkeeper," who was probably their son.

[53]Born on July 7, 1843, in Drohne (Ev. KB Dielingen).

[54]St. Louis had become an important center for immigrants from northwest Germany—even more so than Indianapolis (Kamphoefner [1987], 77–86; Schütte, 55–56).

away on a trip for 5 weeks, and the whole time I was almost always alone in the house, day and night, and it was like Sunday every day. I had to water the plants, feed the chickens and one bird, and that was it. All of that I could do in half an hour. In September they went away for another week, that's 6 weeks all together. I went for walks a lot, but when they're there I can't go out much, only on Sundays, since she is always feeling poorly and no one else is at home, the lady and the little boy, 3 years old. The man is away all day, summer and winter. The little boy and I can celebrate our birthdays together, since his is also September 2nd. [4 ll.: dry summer] Our garden is twice as big as yours, I don't have to work in it much, for they have a man for that, he has to do it all. [7 ll.: bad weather; invitation to a wedding] My dear father, I can let you know one other bit of news about the old Holle folks, they are still quite hale. The father often earns 4 talers a day with his masonry, it's amazing, he still keeps up with his sons. They've bought another small garden for 7 hundred talers. Money doesn't buy much here. Gotlieb is working at a druggist's, he earns 60 talers a month, Gotlieb wants to visit you all next summer, every time he sees me he asks if I don't want to come along, and Heinerich Hohlt from Westerup, too. Several friends are coming to visit, because they can go across the ocean for 25 talers, that's what they say here. Dear Wilhemihne, Wilhelm Holle's wife and Hennirigette Böckman send you all their best, Gette has rented a small room here, she lives there with her son, since Wilhelm already earns his own living and Gette works by taking care of women who've just had babies. My dear brother, write me a long letter about my dear father, the two girls and the other two can write themselves, for I'd love to know what you're all doing, and tell me what young people are still left, since here they've almost all gotten married, but I haven't yet.

[no signature]

Indianapolis, February 25, 1872

My dearly beloved father, brother and sister-in-law, since it is too cold to go out this afternoon, I'm sitting down to write you a few lines. Your letter and the presents arrived on January 26th, 1872. On Sunday afternoon, Wilhelm came to see me with his wife and Magrete Maschmeier, I was overjoyed first to see Magrete and then about your letter and best wishes, which I hadn't been expecting. Magrete arrived here on the 23rd, but she couldn't come to see me any earlier because the ground was covered with a foot of snow and very cold. [6 ll.: cold weather] We've had a lot of snow, the young girls and boys had a very good time of it, since they go sleighing a lot, the sleighs are so big 4 or 6 can sit in them, with one or two horses in front, and the horse has lots of small bells on, and when they run it goes jingle, jingle. The old folks say we haven't had such a winter for 25 years like this one. I haven't had any trouble with the cold since I still have my grey petticoat, which is good in cold weather, and I can also say waste not, want not. My dear father, do you still have your vest tailor Köhne made for us the last fall when I was there. My dear ones, I have to write you about the dream I had last night about my mother, it was in the spring and I was planting such beautiful flowers on her grave, which isn't the case, since I am too far away from you. [10 ll.: answers her brother's questions about mail from Germany; fire at a neighbor's house] I would have written earlier but I was waiting for my sister Engel, she was supposed to come to see me, then I could have written more about her, but I hope she will write herself. Friederich Wuelf, my brother-in-law, came to get the present from me, they were all quite content. I'll tell you the names of the two Wulwes daughters, the eldest is my godchild and has my name, Mägie, the youngest is named after her mother, Äni or Engel in German. [4 ll.: asks for reply]

[14 ll.: letter of June 1872 written by *Margaretha Winkelmeier* in Indianapolis and sent along with friends returning to Germany, in which she complains that her letters are only "half read aloud" to her father]

20

Wilhelmine Wiebusch

Wilhelmine Johanne Wiebusch was born on November 7, 1859, in Horneburg, a sleepy village in Stade County on the Lower Elbe.[1] Not even the name of her father is known; her mother—Anna Maria Wiebusch, the 28-year-old daughter of a laborer in Horneburg—was unmarried.[2] She seems to have lived and worked in nearby Hamburg; at least she gave birth there to another illegitimate child two years after Wilhelmine was born.[3] Anna Marie Wiebusch probably suffered the same fate as countless young women from the rural lower classes: unable to find employment at home, many a young girl had to move to the nearest city to find work as a servant. There she might meet a young man and become pregnant, discovering that the father of her child was unwilling to marry her. Unwed mothers were particularly common among domestic servants in the big cities (most of them came from rural areas).[4] In Hamburg, with over twenty-five thousand servants, there were thou-

[1] Its population in 1880 was 1,660; the only major enterprise in the village was a cigar factory, and the majority of inhabitants were employed in agriculture or a trade (Neumann [1883], 506; Meyn [1955]).

[2] Ev. KB Horneburg.

[3] Caroline Marie Wiebusch, born November 30, 1861, baptized in Horneburg (Ev. KB Horneburg). The father's name is also unknown.

[4] In contrast to the daughters of the urban lower class, women who came from the country seldom worked in industry but almost always as domestic servants (Walser [1985], 18–20; Wierling [1987], 61). In Hamburg almost 80 percent of domestic servants came from rural areas outside the city—primarily from Schleswig-Holstein, Hanover, and Mecklenburg (Müller-Staats [1983], 288).

sands of them, and in Berlin, Frankfurt, and other large cities, the situation was much the same.[5]

Like many illegitimate children, Wilhelmine was not brought up by her mother but probably by her grandparents or other relatives in Horneburg. Then in early 1871, at the age of eleven years, she went to live with a family in Hamburg.[6] The reason why is unclear, but it is safe to assume that the mother was no longer able to support her daughter—especially since she had another child to provide for—and Wilhelmine was old enough to earn her own keep in her new "foster home." Requiring a child to work would certainly not have been unusual: urban and rural lower-class children were expected to help out from an early age, whether they came from families that were intact or not.[7]

Three years later, probably after finishing school or being confirmed, Wilhelmine started her first job as a servant girl, working for an inn-keeper in Barmbek a few blocks away from her foster parents' house. Later she moved on to a series of different jobs of varying duration: she stayed with a milk merchant's family for three years, only one month in an officer's household near the harbor—in the course of almost a decade, she worked for ten or eleven different employers.[8]

Changing jobs frequently was not a sign of a particular lack of steadiness or loyalty: in spite of all the clichés, there were only a few real "pearls" among servants who were willing to sacrifice their own wishes and ambitions to a lifetime of service to one family.[9] Thus the reformer Oscar Stillich in Berlin somewhat cynically referred to domestic servants as "the nation's Gypsies."[10] Frequent change of employment, however, reflected not a tendency to drift around aimlessly but rather the inevitable effects of unreasonable conditions and demands. Being a domestic servant meant not having a six-day week or fixed working hours, like almost all other wage laborers;[11] receiving wages which, on an hourly

---

[5]Müller-Staats, 287; Spann (1904a), 287–303; (1904b), 701. In Berlin at the turn of the century, 5 percent of domestic servants had children, and one-third of the unwed mothers were servants (Stillich [1902], 261). In contrast to the prevailing myths and clichés, one study of the situation in Berlin shows that these women were not particularly susceptible to advances made by their employers: most of the fathers of their children were artisans and laborers (Neumann [1894], 522).

[6]StA HH, Meldewesen, A 6, Bd. 3, 483.

[7]Wierling (1987), 41–44.

[8]StA HH, Meldewesen, A 21, Bd. 18, Nr. 58,460; AB Hamburg 1883.

[9]Walser, 92; Wierling (1987), 11, 92. According to Müller-Staats, 222, servants in Hamburg changed jobs an average of twice a year.

[10]Stillich, 266.

[11]Ottmüller (1978), 89–90; Walser 27–28; Wierling (1987), 88–90. In the 1900 survey conducted in Berlin, more than 40 percent of female domestic servants reported working between sixteen and eighteen hours a day—at a time when working hours for female workers were legally restricted to ten hours a day (Stillich, 118).

basis, amounted to mere pennies;[12] and being more at the mercy of an employer's whims and dependent on his or her goodwill than in any other type of employment in the city. It also meant being subject to registration regulations that were stricter than in any other occupation; if these were violated, servants could be fined, jailed, or even banned from the city.[13]

Quitting a job was one of the few effective means of self-preservation available to a servant—aside from sulking, getting sick, refusing to do certain tasks, and spreading gossip about the family—to avoid being overworked or treated badly. Reasons for quitting probably varied with the individual situation: it was not only external grievances—wages that were too low, food or accommodation that was poor, work that was too hard or too much—that prompted a servant to keep on the look out for a better position. A housewife who was moody or overly particular, children who were a strain, or a boss who made advances could also be motives for a servant to leave. In any case, the possibility of quitting prevented the establishment of closer emotional ties to an employer, which could easily result in even more exploitation. Besides, changing jobs represented a servant's only chance to move up the limited ladder in the hierarchy of domestic service, to escape from the poorly paid and exhausting job of maid-of-all-work and work up to a post with specific duties in an upper middle-class home.[14]

As far as we can tell from the sequence of her employers, Wilhelmine Wiebusch seems to have managed this climb up the ladder. Her first jobs working in small households for middle-class employers like the innkeeper and milk merchant were typical for someone just starting out. Servants in such homes usually had to take care of the house, children, and business as well—but often they were treated almost like part of the family. In the home of a merchant at a fine Hamburg address on the Binnenalster, where after many bourgeois stopovers Wilhelmine Wiebusch was working just before she left, things must have been quite different. Convention and social distance probably colored her relationship to her employers, but the fact that there were several servants made work easier and less boring. And being employed by someone prominent also had a positive effect on one's own status.[15]

---

[12]Ottmüller, 92–93; Walser, 29–31; Wierling (1987), 90–92. At the end of the century, domestic servants in Hamburg earned an average of 200 marks a year. Given some 75 hours of work a week (a figure that is probably too low), this amounts to an hourly wage of just over one cent.

[13]Walser, 32–37; Wierling (1987), 86–88. Registration regulations in Hamburg, thanks to which we have some information about Wilhelmine Wiebusch's various posts, applied only to servants not born in the city (Müller-Staats, 294).

[14]Schulte (1978), 905–6; Walser, 92–93; Wierling (1987), 71–75, 212–22.

[15]Schulte, 883–84; Wierling (1987), 88–102.

Wilhelmine's daily routine in Hamburg was probably much like that of other servants in the big cities.[16] Long working hours did not permit much time off and kept social contacts outside the employer's house to a minimum. Going shopping, delivering a message, taking the children for a walk, or accompanying the lady of the house on a visit or an errand were welcome diversions. Besides a temporary respite from the tiring routine of housework, they also provided a chance to meet other servants, exchange news, trade experiences, or just gossip—some small compensation for forced social isolation.[17]

Apart from these "little escapes," there was still Sunday to look forward to—the only hours servants had to themselves without having to be on call.[18] In a city like Hamburg there was no lack of things to do with one's free time, to relax, have a good time, or make acquaintances with members of the opposite sex. Going to one of the numerous dance halls, which with good reason Wilhelmine would later miss in New York, was often a crowning finish to the day. Going together with a few girlfriends helped guarantee the innocence of such pleasures and provided a certain degree of protection against unwanted advances.[19]

The girlfriends were usually servants, too, with similar backgrounds and occupational experience. Wilhelmine's friends, Anna and Marie, were both from the country or small towns and had come to Hamburg at an early age to go into service. Anna Beckermann (whose three younger sisters also worked in Hamburg) was four years younger and came to the city from Lübtheen in Schwerin County, Mecklenburg, in early 1881;[20] Marie Kallmeyer probably arrived in the late 1870s or early 1880s from Osten, a small harbor village on the Lower Elbe.[21]

When Wilhelmine Wiebusch finally emigrated to the United States in 1884, Anna Beckermann went along with her. What prompted the two young women to leave, however, is unknown, and we can only speculate about their possible motives. Despite all the disadvantages of their occupation, they were certainly not in dire straits. Curiosity and a spirit of

[16]See Viersbeck (1910), and "Geschichte eines Berliner Dienstmädchens," printed in Stillich, 324–47, as well as the excerpts of life stories and interviews with former domestic servants included in Wierling (1987).

[17]Schulte, 901; Wierling (1987), 167–69; see also Viebig (1925), 44.

[18]Stillich, 134–52; Walser, 27; Wierling (1987), 89. Servants were customarily given time off every other Sunday, but they were not legally entitled to this. They usually could leave after doing the dishes from lunch and had to return by 10 or 11 o'clock at night.

[19]Wierling (1987), 177–79.

[20]She was born on September 7, 1863 (StA HH, Meldewesen, A 21, Bd. 1, Nr. 532). Lübtheen: population in 1880 was 2,282 (Neumann [1883], 719).

[21]Born on October 14, 1863, she was a servant employed by the Jencquels, one of the oldest merchant families in Hamburg (Information provided by the contributor; Deutsches Geschlechterbuch 24 [1913], 146–70). Osten population in 1880 was 848 (Neumann [1883], 909).

adventure, evident in Wilhelmine's letters, more likely played a role in the decision. It was also well known that servants in America were paid higher wages and that female immigrants had good chances of finding a husband. It is tempting to regard Anna Beckermann as the force behind the move—she had relatives in the United States and was obviously highly mobile and eager for change. In the summer of 1881, a mere two months after arriving in Hamburg, she took off for Swabia, at the opposite end of Germany, but was back in Hamburg by the fall. In the first months of 1884, too, she was planning to move: first she listed Lübeck as her intended destination, but two months later she changed the entry in the registration files to America.[22]

The United States was attracting many immigrants at the time. In 1882 the emigration rate reached a level that clearly surpassed the years of crisis and famine at mid-century. In Hamburg the wave of emigration meant business was booming, for the port was the gateway to the New World not only for many Germans but also for growing numbers of central, eastern, and southern Europeans.[23] Daily confrontation with the multitude of people hoping for a better life in the United States certainly must have had some effect on the two servant girls.

Anna quit her last job in May 1884, Wilhelmine two months later, and only a few days after that, on July 23, they embarked on the steamship *Ragia*.[24] Marie Kallmeyer, their mutual friend, stayed behind in Hamburg; she is the addressee of the letters printed here.

The style and wittiness of this correspondence belie the image of the "simple" servant girl, especially given the fact that the author's schooling was only rudimentary. To a certain extent, the letters reflect the social and cultural milieu of the homes in which she had worked during her last years in Hamburg. It is also likely, however, that she was an avid reader: like many a servant girl in the big city, she probably spent her free hours in the evening reading magazines and novels to escape the drab monotony of her workday routine. As we learn from one of her letters, she was an enthusiastic subscriber to a magazine that published serialized novels—the soap operas of the period.[25]

From Wilhelmine Wiebusch's first letter, we learn that the two young women started working for a prosperous Jewish businessman in Brook-

[22]StA HH, Meldewesen, A 21, Bd. 1, Nr. 532.
[23]Ferenczi/Willcox (1929), 424; Marschalck (1973), 43–44; Moltmann (1981), 25. The number of emigrants from Hamburg itself had been above average since the 1870s; New York was the most frequent destination listed.
[24]StA HH, Meldewesen, A 21, Bd. 1, Nr. 532, and Bd. 18, Nr. 58,460; Auswanderungsamt I, VIII A 2, Bd. 23 (HPL).
[25]Engelsing (1973); Schulte, 908–9. The *Novellenzeitung* was published 1854–99 in Altona, a suburb of Hamburg.

lyn only a few days after their arrival in New York. Their rapid success in finding jobs is hardly surprising, but it is remarkable that the two newly arrived Europeans—who spoke no English—were able to gain entrance to a wealthy American household.[26] The previous experience and qualifications they brought along, particularly Wilhelmine, probably played a role in their getting the job, as did the (surprising) fact that the lady of the house, although American-born, spoke some German. In a Jewish household, too, the fact that the two young women were Protestants, rather than Catholics, may well have tipped the scales in their favor.[27]

Even though Wilhelmine's letters to her friend contain many nostalgic references to her previous life in Hamburg, they do not give the impression that she seriously regretted her decision to leave. She certainly attempted to entertain Marie with details of their new life and probably wanted to impress her friend, and she may have thus neglected to mention disappointments or difficulties. Still, her letters leave no doubt that she was happy with her choice and that she enjoyed her new freedom (such as an extra day off) as well as the urbanity of New York, which made Hamburg look provincial.

Wilhelmine's temperament, above all her remarkable lack of prejudice against new or strange people or customs, probably helped her not only get along in her new environment but also feel at home within a relatively short time. Living in an American household and having contact with other domestic servants, however, certainly sped up the acclimation process. At the same time, she could always fall back on German friends and the multifaceted social and cultural life of the German-American community in New York, of which she was an active member. In such a large community it was hard to feel foreign or isolated: about one-seventh of the 1.2 million New Yorkers were German-born;[28] and, together with members of the second generation, they supported more than three dozen German-language publications, almost thirty church parishes, hundreds of clubs, several theaters, and many different beer gardens, restaurants, and shops[29]—even homey pleasures like cabbage that tasted "real German" was not unattainable.

Although Wilhelmine Wiebusch's irony and sense of humor, her curiosity and open-mindedness, are remarkable, her language is what one would expect of a particularly good student who has finished primary school: few mistakes, simple sentence structure, a fair vocabulary. On

[26]Ernst (1949), 66.
[27]See Figure 36, above.
[28]USC 1880.1, 540; 1,589 of the Germans living in New York were born in Hamburg.
[29]Bretting (1981), 121–51, 200–204; Ernst, 135–61; Lapham (1977), 26–164.

top of that, she has an easy way with words and obviously enjoys writing.

Wilhelmine Wiebusch

Brooklyn, 9/12/84

My dear Marie,

A long, long time ago it was that we left Hamburg, and in this time you, dear Marie, have often been expecting a letter from me. You mustn't be angry that I am only now writing, because in a foreign country you have all sorts of things to think about at the beginning. Oh, if only we could sit together for a while, then I could tell you many a little tale of adventure, but the endlessly vast ocean calls for writing. I am sure you have heard something about us from Anna's sister, but I'll still tell about our trip as well as I can.

[85 ll.: description of the voyage from Hamburg to New York] So there we were in the land of milk and honey, then we stayed in a German hotel with several others we got to know on the ship, and during this time we got to see a bit of New York. The first day it rained so badly we couldn't do anything, the second day we went to find Anna's relatives, and after 4 hours of asking around everywhere in our elegant English we finally found the way. Dear Marie, you really ought to see New York, when you get your Sunday off, come on over for awhile, the city must be 3 times as big as Hamburg,[30] the most beautiful and main street, Broadway, is more than 6 hours long, with about 300 side streets to the right and left and many many more streets, so you can't go on foot much, everything's so spread out, so you simply take the *Care* or railroad which runs in almost every street, way up high, as high as the second floor of the houses. Crossing the street is positively dangerous, one wagon after the next, so loud you can't hear yourself talk, business and money everywhere. On August 8 we had the dumb luck of both getting a job together in a very fine private house in Brooklyn. This town is only separated from New-York by water, you can go across in 5 minutes with the ferry, and most of the quality folks who have their business in New York live here, since Brooklyn is much prettier and the air is much healthier. Anna is the scullery maid and I'm the cook, we each get 12 dollars a month (50 marks)—what do you think, dear Marie, don't you have the slightest desire to come to Kamerika?

There's more work, of course, since the Americans live very lavishly,

---

[30]This is a bit exaggerated. New York had only twice as many inhabitants as Hamburg; in terms of area, the Hanseatic city-state was much larger than the American metropolis.

they eat 3 hot meals a day, and then we have to do all the laundry in the house, since it's so awfully expensive to send it out, we even have to iron the shirts and cuffs, here you have to understand everything, we do our best, but we can do things when we want, the *Ladys* don't pay much attention to the household, they don't do anything but dress up themselves 3–4 times a day and go out. The family is remarkably friendly, there are 8 persons all together, Mr. and Mrs. Moses, 3 grown-up beautiful daughters and 3 good-looking boys,[31] the *Lady* herself speaks broken German, we can make ourselves understood quite well with her, the others want to learn it too, they like German a lot. You should just hear us speaking English, we just rattle off what we hear, whether it's right or not, the *Lady* says sometimes she almost dies laughing at us.

Our house consists of a ground floor and three more stories, but they don't do all that much scrubbing and cleaning here. The rooms are like a Chinese doll house, they're all covered with rugs and carpets, its not fashionable to have white lace curtains in the windows here, the best thing is the beds, they are big and wide. Because of the heat, they're only made up of a mattress, pillow and 2 sheets. At the moment it is very hot here, the ladies all wear real thin muslin dresses. Anna and I sometimes work up quite a sweat, we only wear a shirt and a dress and would like to take that off too. I have no complaints about the Americans, they are very friendly, gallant people, but I don't like the Germans here very much, they are all a bunch of snobs, act like they can't understand German anymore, act like they know nothing about their old homeland any more, but we won't forget, since even if it is nice in a foreign country, it'll never be home. [6 ll.: joking invitation to Marie and friends in Hamburg to come and see America]

There's still lots and lots to write you about, dear Marie, but another time, because for today it is (*time to go to bed. i am wery tired. it is a quarter past one*) translate that into German, and then write back soon how you are, do you have a little bit of news about your sweetheart?[32] and a lot about Hamburg, I miss my wonderful *Novellen Zeitung* here a lot, I would really like to have it forwarded if it weren't so much trouble. I'd send you the money if you could arrange it for me. [2 ll.: greetings]

Now, farewell dear Marie, warmest regards / from the faraway / west Anni and Meini

[31]Lionel Moses (59), commission merchant (he dealt in "Japanese goods"); his wife Silvia (46); daughters Edith (26), Blanche (24), and Selina (10); sons G. Arnold (22), a dry goods clerk, Brandon (20), a clerk for a commission merchant, and Arnold Jr. (14) (MC 1880: Brooklyn, N.Y., W. 6, e.d. 45, #219; CD New York 1884–85).

[32]She is probably referring to the 27-year-old Ernst Burmester, who became engaged to Marie Kallmayer in 1885 or 1886; the two were married in 1889. Information provided by the contributor.

my address is / Wilhelmine Wiebusch / *care. of.* Mr Leionel Moses. / 751 Union-Street. Brooklyn. / New-York.

Please write and tell me when you get this letter. Oh blast it, I forgot to tell you what wonderful fruit there is in <u>Kamerika</u>, every day we eat peaches, melons and bananas, and then I also wanted to tell you if you have an old shoe or boot, don't throw it away, tie a red or blue bow on it and hang it on the wall in your room. You may think I'm crazy, but you ought to know, dear Marie, that here in America, that's what they call an antique.

I. put this Letter in the Letterbax, hve you undrstand Mary? You see i speak wery well Englisch, i belive it is anough.

I'll give you another little idea of how it is sometimes when we talk, this evening at dinner Mr Moses said to Anna, *plase give me some breat. (bitte geben Sie mir ein wenig Brot)* and Anna understood *smal plaid* [small plate] *(kleine Teller)* and came back with an empty plate, of course everyone laughed, that kind of thing happens to us a lot, but they don't take it badly, it's all right. Anna pulls a lot of such silly tricks, one time she wanted to go the drug store and get some chlorine, so she goes into the first drug store that comes along and says *speak you Germain (sprechen Sie Deutsch), no (nein), na den geben Sie mir für 10 Ct. Chlorkalk, i do not undrstand you (ich verstehe Sie nicht),* well then forget it, you dummy, and so she went to 4 different drug stores and finally she got so lost that the police had to bring her home.

I can't find the Fritz Stellen you told me about since there's no town hall here, for we live here like wild folks here in the land of freedom, we haven't needed any papers yet, no one has asked us about our names and origin.[33]

But that's enough for now, if there's anything else you want to know about, just ask what you want to know and then I'll write and tell you what you want to know.

Now the American post office is closing.

Good night / to be continued

New-York *the* 19 *of Febr* 1886

My dear Marie,

Over a month has passed already and I still haven't answered your dear letter. [13 ll.: congratulations on her friend's engagement]

Over here on the other side of the *Ocean,* I, too, cannot complain of

---

[33]This is a reference to the strict registration regulations for servants in Hamburg.

being sad, I am just fine, I like being here in New-Jork, am healthy, and what more do I want. My employer's family has also just returned from Mexcico, that's caused a bit more turmoil in the household, and the *Lady* has already begged me several times to go there with her next year after all, but I can't make any promises, who knows what all will happen by next winter, and I'm a bit afraid of Mexico too, because there are still too many Indians living there. I won't tell you about my big Christmas, though, since you'd laugh at me, since it wasn't anything compared to yours. But I did trim a Christmas tree for us on Christmas Eve, invited various friends, and of course made sure we had a delicious drop of wine, and so we amused ourselves in quite the German manner.

I also went to another ball recently, and I've been to the theater twice, the first time to the German Talia Theater,[34] they did The Merry Wives of Windsor. The other time I went to the biggest opera house in New-Jork, they put on the marvelous opera Rienzi, the Last of the Tribunes. I had a wonderful time that evening, it was worth it just to see the American ladies in the first and second balconies, how they glittered in their red, white, blue and so on silk dresses with matching feathers in their hair, so you're almost blinded by the sight. [15 ll.: half-joking, half-serious plans of coming to Hamburg to her friend's wedding; questions about friends in Hamburg] My page is full and my time is up, please forgive me for not writing more this time. Waiting for an answer soon I remain with lots of love and kisses / your Minnie
[2 ll.: greetings to Marie's sister and her fiancé]

[November 26, 1886; see below]

My dear Marie,

What is the matter with you! Can't you write, or is it my fault? An eternity has already passed by since we last heard anything of one another. And now once again I have be the first to write, how are you, you dear old soul, hopefully just fine, how did you spend the lovely summer, did you have a good time at the side of your loved one? I am still waiting in vain for your picture, didn't you have one made yet? Or didn't it make it over here?

So when are you going to get married? Or are you already? But then you surely would have let me know. I'm just writing off into the blue, I

---

[34]During the 1883–84 season, the Thalia-Theater (1879–88) was the only theater in New York with exclusively German-language productions. The program consisted largely of operettas, musicals and farces, along with the occasional classical drama (Zeydel [1915], 268–69; Leuchs [1966], xiii).

don't even know if your address is the same, but I hope these lines will reach you properly. As far as I am concerned, I am still doing very well in a foreign land, I am healthy, round and plump, have to work hard sometimes, but like to eat a lot. Today, for example, I almost overloaded my stomach, for today is a holiday here, the so-called Thanksgiving Day. Then both rich and poor have a big *Dinner,* every table is resplendent with a turkey and every kind of vegetable there is, and afterward there's a big English *Plum-Puddign,* and then enjoy your meal, dig in all you want, and afterward we give thanks that it all tasted so good. [13 ll.: news about family and friends from Germany; complaints about lack of mail]

My friend Anna was here yesterday, the two of us still stick together through good times and bad, this summer we both had a hard time, we were far apart from one another, we've also made many new friends and feel just as much at home as in Hamburg, sometimes we do have moments of longing to be back in our northern homeland, but they disappear again as fast as they appear, for the ocean lies in the way. On December 16 we are both invited to a ball, hurrah! Then we'll get to dance again and have a swig from the bottle as well, we're looking forward to it very much, since there aren't many such amusements here, because there aren't any public dance halls here, you spend your time with friends and entertain yourself as best you can, the girls have a lot more days off than over there, every other Sunday and if there are three or four girls, two have the same day off, and then you get another day during the week when you can leave after breakfast. I am still here with two other girls, one is Irish and the other one comes from Wales, very nice girls. You meet people from all different countries here, there are all kinds of blacks, including some very good-looking guys. The Chinese all have laundries, the little people with their long pigtails look very funny, a Chinaman also taught me how to iron shirts, we had a good time laughing then since their English is so bad it is hard to understand them, it doesn't matter to me, I already speak English as well as German.

Dear Marie, the beautiful Christmas season is almost at the door, you should be happy since the wonderful presents you get aren't like the ones over here, here they don't give many presents at Christmas, you have to work just like on any other day. Anna and I want to put up our own tree again this year.

[4 ll.: questions about friends in Hamburg] I still have a lot of questions to ask you, dear Migge, but that would be too boring for you. I hope I'll get a sign of life from you soon and that you write me lots of news, do you hear! Yes! I'd also like to keep on chatting with you, but I don't have much more news and it is already getting late.

Some time ago we had a big Parade here, all the military in the United

States was gathered in New-Jork, they dedicated the Queen of Freedom, it's this big *Statute,* a present from the French to America.[35]

This time I can also give you my proper address, since I like it very much here and hope to stay for quite a while.

But good night for now, you dearest child of mine / sleep well! all love / and thousands of kisses from / your friend
Wilhelmine Wiebusch / 311 West 28 Street / New-Jork City
New-Jork / November 26 / 1886.
Longing for a letter!

[20 ll.: short letter—dated New York, January 18, 1887—with joking threats reminding her friend to write]

February 27, 1887.
311 West 28 Street / New-Iork City

My dear Mary,

This time I received your letter and the pictures properly, for which first of all my deepest thanks! I am sorry, dear Marie, that the two had to make the trip across the ocean three times, but that makes them all the more precious to me, the pictures turned out very well. Yours, Marie, could have been better, the other one you sent me was much nicer. Your sweetheart's picture is charming, just don't get jealous, the other girls here have fallen in love with the boy from Hamburg!

Dear Marie, I am so happy that you are doing so well and that you are so happy. May good fortune stay with you.

You wrote me quite a lot of news. The proud Auguste is getting off to an early start giving her husband a hard time, isn't she. You asked about Frau Loose? I got a letter from her the same time as yours, she is fine, she also asked if you were still living in Uhlenhorst.[36] If you have time, you should go see her, she's now living at Kantstrasse 11, 3rd floor, in Eilbeck.[37] She also sent me a picture of her three children, two boys and a girl. I am very pleased that you visit my mother every once in a while, I'll write her one of these days. Who is Minna at the Langs'? Is that the scullery maid? Otherwise I can't remember who she might be—you've had another wonderful Christmas, this year I also received a bit more, a reddish brown dress, a house dress, white skirt, white scarf, gloves, an album and a few more little things. Anna and I also went to Salb's, we had two matching blue dresses made and we stayed and had a good time

---

[35]President Cleveland's dedication of the Statue of Liberty on Bedloe's Island on October 28, 1886, was accompanied by a great celebration.

[36]Upper-middle-class part of Hamburg, located on a waterfront promenade.

[37]Another part of Hamburg, somewhat farther east and less elegant.

Figure 39. Engagement photo of Marie Kallmeyer.

until five o'clock. Last month we went to a masquerade, we paid 20 marks for our fancy outfit for the evening. I haven't been to the theater this year, it'll be hard to, too, since it's so far away. [4 ll.: weather] How I would like to make the trip to Hamburg this year, but I doubt much will come of it, for man proposes but God disposes! Just let me know in time when your wedding will be, I would so much like to be there, but you have to know how to resign yourself to the inevitable, for traveling is easier said than done, recently a large ship sank to the bottom, many people met their death in the waves,[38] and I don't suppose you want to wait another year before getting married? That would be nonsense. I would still really like to give you, dear Marie, what I promised you, I'm only writing you this so you don't get the same thing from someone else, since you can't use two of them. Dear Marie, please don't make me wait so long for an answer, you must have gotten my last small note, I didn't know what to think, wasn't sure if you hadn't already sent a letter to the old address, yes, you see that's what it's like here, today I am here but I can be gone by tomorrow if I don't like it anymore, that's what the land of freedom means.

I'll tell you all about it in person sometime. But that's enough for today, dear friend. May these lines reach you in the best of health, that's my wish, with all love / your faithful friend Minnie
[2 ll.: greetings from Anna] / Today I had some white cabbage to eat that just came in from Germany. It tasted real German! / Have a good voyage, you letter to Hamburg's far shores! Write back soon.

Secaucus, March 16, 1888

My dear Marie,

Married for five months today, and I still haven't answered your kind letter, you must think I've forgotten you in all my happiness, but by no means, dear Marie. If you had received a letter for every time I've thought of you, you wouldn't even be able to count them anymore. How are you then, you dear soul? Fine, I hope. [10 ll.: questions about friends in Hamburg]

Now you'd probably like to know how I am, I must say I am extraordinarily fine, for I have found such a good husband, the two of us live together in such peace and harmony. I am also sending you a picture of us, it's a good likeness of my husband, but I don't look much like myself. It really is too bad, dear Marie, that we live so far apart from one another,

[38]She is probably referring to the British ship *Kapunda*, which sank in late January 1887. Several detailed stories about the tragedy were reported in the *New York Times*. The ship, bound for Australia, collided with a British sailing ship and sank off the coast of Brazil. Some three hundred people—mostly emigrants—were killed.

I'd like to tell you a thousand things I can't possibly write all about. We all had a wonderful time at my wedding, about 30 people came, I also got some lovely presents. A silver fruit basket, silver sugar bowl and silver butter dish from my last employer, from other friends a set of dishes for 12, 2 lovely lamps, 2 beautiful vases, 1 lovely carpet, tablecloths and napkins for 24, and many other little things. Anna's sister-in-law gave me a wreath and veil, which suited me well. I also have a nice household, in my best room I have dark red flowered plush furniture, everything so nice and pretty, in two rooms I've put down carpeting over the whole floor. Dear Marie, even if the time never comes when I can welcome you in my home, I still hope we may see each other again, for my husband wants to see Germany again as much as I do, but we will have to be patient for a couple of years and make *plente money* first, that is if our business does well. [4 ll.: weather] I don't know much more at this point which might interest you, just write back soon and don't be like me, I'll do better in the future. Farewell, all the best, and think every now and then of your friend Marrie.

Mrs Minnie Denker / Paterson Plank Road / Seacaucus / Hudson Caunty / New-Jersey (North America)

The new bride did not keep her promise to write more often; the letter from the beginning of 1888 was the last Marie Kallmeyer received. Wilhelmine Denker, by the way, kept silent about one "joyful" event: according to the U.S. census, she gave birth to a baby girl one month before getting married.[39]

The census records also indicate that the Denker family, to which five more members were added by 1902,[40] continued to live in Secaucus until at least 1910. August Denker, Wilhelmine's husband, first ran a saloon in the predominantly German neighborhood, and later kept a hotel.[41]

His wife not only seems to have followed her American master's example in terms of home furnishings, she also switched sides to become an employer herself. In 1900 the household included a fourteen-year-old servant girl: Annie, the daughter of German immigrants.[42]

[39]Wilhelmina (born in October 1887); in 1910 she was still living with her parents and working as a seamstress (MC 1990: Secaucus, Hudson Co., N.J., e.d. 181, #154; 1910: e.d. 252, #122).

[40]Henry (b. 1891), who was working as a chauffeur in 1910; Edward (b. 1893), who was working as a grocer's clerk in 1910; Frieda (b. 1896); William (b. 1898); and Beta (b. 1901–2).

[41]MC 1900 and 1910. In the county as a whole (population, 275,126), some 35 percent were foreign-born: 13 percent German and 12 percent Irish (USC 1890.1, 239). According to the census, August Denker was six years older than his wife and had immigrated two years before her (MC 1900 and 1910).

[42]MC 1900.

$\mathcal{A}ppendix$

Contributors and Assistants

The appendix is divided into three sections. The first part, organized according to letter series, lists the persons and organizations who contributed the letters and individuals who provided the editors with additional information about the letter-writers. The second part includes the names of persons whose help was not restricted to a particular series. The third section is a list of the persons who worked on the original project *Auswandererbriefe* at the Ruhr-University Bochum.

Illustrations, unless otherwise noted, were provided by the contributors. "†" designates a contributor who is no longer living.

I.

Stille and Krumme: Margarete Stille, 4540 Lengerich; Dirk Erpenbeck, 4630 Bochum; Gert Schumann, 4540 Lengerich.

Blümner: Winfried Böllert, 4600 Dortmund; Hiltrud von Brandt, 8021 Icking; Prof. Dr. Hermann Wellenreuther, 3400 Göttingen.

Lenz: Paul Wienand, Heimat-u. Bergbaumuseum WEL, 6290 Weilburg; Ev. Pfarramt Blessenbach u. Laubuseschbach, 6294 Weinbach; Hs. HStA WI.

Bauer: Helga Bauer-Reinhardt, 7800 Freiburg; Prof. Dr. Konrad H. Jarausch, Chapel Hill, NC 27514; Dr. Lesley Kawaguchi, Santa Monica, CA 90405.

Löwen: Hildegard Bauer, 5584 Alf; Standesbeamter Both, 5583 Zell; Rita Gauer, Dr. Martin Persch, BistA, 5500 Trier.

Möller: Wilhelm Möller, Ursula Dietzel, 6451 Hammersbach-Marköbel; Wilhelm Dietzel, 6451 Hammersbach; Pastor Alfred Gerland, 3509 Spangenberg; Hs. StA MR, 3550 Marburg; Pastor Siegmund-Schultze, 6451 Hammersbach.

Probstfeld: Vera Molzahn, 6835 Brühl; June Dobervich, Fargo, ND 58103; Dr. Hiram M. Drache, Moorhead, MN 56560; Willi Esch-Probstfeld, 5401 Kalt; Evelyn Gesell, Fargo ND 58103; Minnesota Historical Society, St. Paul, MN 55101; Dr. Elisabeth Sauerborn, 5400 Koblenz.

Witten: Rainer Brandt, 2740 Bremervörde; Jeanette Witter, Wenatchee, WA 98801.

Pritzlaff: Lieselotte Clemens, 2472 Malente (State Historical Society of Wisconsin, Madison, WI 53706); Hildegard Ey, 6200 Wiesbaden; Allan Kovan, Milwaukee Area Research Center, Milwaukee, WI 53201; Botschaftsrat R. Kroll, Cultural Attaché, Poland, 5000 Köln; Harold L. Miller, State Historical Society of Wisconsin, Madison, WI 53706.

Berthold: Liselotte Meier, 3500 Kassel; Alfred Emde, 3548 Arolsen; Wilhelm Hellwig, StdA, 3540 Korbach; Pfarramt d. Ev. Gem. Adorf, 3548 Diemelsee; Carl B. Thomas, 5779 Eslohe.

Weitz: Emilie Fritz, 7300 Esslingen; S. Ardis Abbott, Rockville, CT 06066; Brigitte Emmerich, 6000 Frankfurt; Thomas W. Leavitt, Museum of American Textile History, North Andover, MA 01845; Anneliese Weitz, 6200 Wiesbaden.

Heck: Institut für Historische Landeskunde der Rheinlande, 5300 Bonn (Josef Scheben Papers); BistA TR, 5500 Trier; LHA KO, 5400 Koblenz; Dr. Jean Pütz, 5527 Irrel.

Klein: Landesarchiv des Saarlands (Dr. Wolfgang Lauter), 6600 Saarbrücken; Dr. Norbert Finzsch, 5000 Köln; Prof. Hans-Walter Herrman, 6601 Riegelsberg; Prof. Karl Rug, 6625 Puttlingen.

Bürkert: Hans Ellinger, 7085 Bopfingen; Karin Carl, StdA Ffm, 6000 Frankfurt; Dr. Med. Christiane Geisler, 8170 Bad Tölz; Pastor Hanns Dieter Haller, 7112 Waldenburg; Klaus Kickinger, M.D., 6900 Heidelberg; Dr. Taddey, Hohnlohe ZA, 7113 Neuenstein; Michael Wagenmann, M.D., 8752 Kleinkahl.

Dorgathen: Elisabeth Röttgers, 4330 Mülheim on the Ruhr; Dr. Peter Brommer, LHA KO, 5400 Koblenz.

Kirst: Gustav Martin (†), 6631 Ensdorf; Frau Pastor Braun, 6601 Riegelsberg; Dieter Lorenzen, 5508 Hermeskeil; Edmund Schömer, 5508 Hermeskeil.

Dilger: Joachim Dilger, 4300 Essen; Lieselotte Ohngemach, 2303 Gettorf; Adele Wibbelsman, San Diego, CA 92128.

Klinger: Gotthold Schwarz, GA Korb, 7054 Korb; StA LB, 7140 Ludwigsburg; Rodney C. Myers, West Albany, NY 12205.

Winkelmeier: Dr. Heinz-Ulrich Kammeier, 4470 Meppen (Pfannkuche/ Nolte, 4992 Espelkamp); GA Stemwede-Dielingen, 4995 Stemwede; Dr. Robert M. Taylor Jr., Indiana Historical Society, Indianapolis, IN 46202.

Wiebusch: Inge Gevert, 2000 Hamburg; Gemeindeverwaltung, 2152 Horneburg; Kapitän Oldhaber, 2152 Horneburg.

2.

Prof. Dr. Willi Paul Adams, 1000 Berlin; Priv. Doz. Dr. Inge Auerbach, 3550 Marburg; Adrian Braunbehrens, 6900 Heidelberg; Dr. Agnes Bretting, 2000 Hamburg; Prof. Dr. Andrzej Brozek, 30–010 Kraków; Prof. Dr. J. A. Burzle, Lawrence, KS 66045; Prof. Giorgio Cheda, CH-6605 Locarno; Prof. Dr. Arthur Cropley, 2000 Hamburg; Prof. Dr. Ottfried Dascher, 4600 Dortmund; Prof. Dr. Reinhard Doerries, 2000 Hamburg; Prof. Dr. Charlotte Erickson, Cambridge, England; Rolf Geisler, 8170 Bad Tölz; Bettina Goldberg, 1000 Berlin; Dr. Christiane Harzig, 2800 Bremen; Prof. Dr. Dirk Hoerder, 2800 Bremen; Priv. Doz. Dr. Hartmut Keil, 8000 München; Prof. Dr. Wolfgang Köllmann, 4320 Hattingen; Christiane Lehmkuhl, 4290 Bocholt; Prof. Dr. Ingeborg H. R. McCoy, San Marcos, TX 78666; Prof. Kerby Miller, Columbia, MO 65203; Prof. Dr. Günter Moltmann, 2000 Hamburg; Prof. Dr. Hans Mommsen, 4630 Bochum; J. Claude Muller, 2020 Luxembourg; Petra Raymond, 8520 Erlangen; Dr. Ingrid Schöberl, 2000 Hamburg; Edith Stein, 4630 Bochum; Prof. Dr. Wolfhard Weber, 4630 Bochum; Oberarchivist Zorn, StA M, 8000 München

3.

A considerable number of people helped the editors in making this book; in fact, we could not have done it without them. The persons most directly involved are secretaries Mechthild Dubbi and Doris Lattek, volunteer transcribers Wilhelm Spilker and the late Gustav Martin, and student assistants Ursula Boesing, Sigrid Crass, Matthias Dornhege, Monika Fehse, Kerstin Fretlöh, Annette Haubold, Elke Maar, Joachim Renn, Barbara Schüttenhelm, Sigrid Schulte, Anja Schwalen, Christhilde Sicking, Thomas Spilker, and Cornelia Vogt.

Weights, Measures, Currency

groschen	gute groschen, 1/24 taler or 2.975 cents
	silbergroschen, 1/30 taler or 2.38 cents
	mariengroschen, 1/36 taler or 1.983 cents
guilder	41 cents
hour	linear measure, 1 hour's walk, ca. 3 miles
kilogram	2.2 pounds
kreuzer	1/60 guilder, 1/12 silbergroschen, or 0.683 cents
mark	1/3 taler or 23.9 cents
mile, German	ca. 7.5 kilometers or 4.7 American miles
morgen	areal measure, regionally varied;
	Prussia, Hesse: ca. 1/4 ha or 5/8 acre
	Bavaria, Baden: ca. 1/3 ha or 4/5 acre
pfennig	1/100 mark or 0.239 cents
pistole	Louisdor, Friedrichsdor: 5 talers or $3.57
Réaumur	Fahrenheit conversion: $R = 4/9 \ (F - 32)$
	Celsius conversion: $R = 4/5 \ C$
scheffel	volume measure, ca. 1.5 bushel
scheffelsaat	areal measure, regionally varied, ca. 1/3 to 1 acre
shilling	in American parlance, 1 bit or 12.5 cents
simmer	volume measure, regionally varied, ca. 1 bushel
taler	71.4 cents; also often used to mean U.S. dollar

Abbreviations

Standard abbreviations based on license plates are used for towns in West Germany. The list of abbreviations for the German states and Prussian provinces (1871) is located on Map 1.

A	Archiv/Archives
AB	Adreßbuch
Abt.	Abteilung
ADB	*Allgemeine Deutsche Biographie*
AF	Alte Folge (old series)
AFL	American Federation of Labor
BA	Bundesarchiv
BABS	Bochumer Auswandererbriefsammlung (Bochum immigrant letter collection)
Bd.	Band (volume)
Best.	Bestand
BistA	Bistumsarchiv (Diocesan Archives)
BPL	Baltimore Passenger Lists
Bü.	Büschel (bundle of documents)
CD	City Directory
Co.	County
DAB	*Dictionary of American Biography*
Diss.	dissertation
e.d.	enumeration district
f, fl.	guilder[s]
GA	Gemeindearchiv

Gem.	Gemeinde
GLA	Generallandesarchiv
GStA	Geheimes Staatsarchiv
HPL	Hamburg Passenger Lists
HStA	Hauptstaatsarchiv
KB	Kirchenbuch (parish register)
Kr.	Kreis (administrative unit similar to county)
LA	Landesarchiv
LHA	Landeshauptarchiv
Lkr.	Landkreis (county)
Lramt.	Landratsamt (county magistrate's office)
MC	Manuscript Census
MC A	Manuscript Census, Agriculture
NatA	National Archives, United States
NF	Neue Folge (new series)
NOPL	New Orleans Passenger Lists
Nr.	Nummer (number)
NYPL	New York Passenger Lists
OA	Oberamt (administrative unit similar to county)
Reg.Bez.	Regierungsbezirk (administrative district)
Reg.Pr.	Regierungspräsident (district governor)
Rep.	Repertorium
Rg.	Register
St.	Staat
StA	Staatsarchiv/State Archives
StdA	Stadtarchiv
Stkr.	Stadtkreis (urban county)
Twp.	Township
UnivA	Universitätsarchiv
USC	U.S. Census, Population
USC A	U.S. Census, Agriculture
USC M	U.S. Census, Manufactures
USC MI	U.S. Census, Mining Industries
Verw.	Verwaltung (administration)
ZA	Zentralarchiv

Sources Cited

UNPUBLISHED PRIMARY SOURCES

German Archives

Ba. StA M: Bayerisches Staatsarchiv München
  Verz. 2, Sch. 203–5
BistA TR: Bistumsarchiv Trier
  KB-Duplikate Kath. Gem. Irrel
Gemeindearchiv Kleinheppach:
  Kassentagebuch der Gemeinde von 1856–57
  Ratsprotokolle, Bd. VIII
Gemeindearchiv Korb:
  Kataster Korb-Steinreinach 1842
Gemeindearchiv Stemwede-Dielingen:
  Chronik des Kirchspiels Dielingen
GLA KA: Generallandesarchiv Karlsruhe
  Abt. 390, Nr. 541, 542
GStA B: Geheimes Staatsarchiv Berlin
  Rep. A 181, Nr. 2291
Hs. HStA WI: Hessisches Hauptstaatsarchiv Wiesbaden
  Abt. 63, Nr. 48
  Abt. 405, Nr. 7755
  Auswandererkartei, Nr. 232, 105
Hs. StA DA: Hessisches Staatsarchiv Darmstadt
  Abt. C 11
  Abt. G 15, 27
  Abt. R 21 B

Hs. StA MR: Hessisches Staatsarchiv Marburg
  Best. 16, Rep. II, Kl. 1, Nr. 1
  Best. 122, Nr. 842
  Best. 180 Hanau, Nr. 159
  Best. 180 Hanau, 4584, Bd. 10, Nr. 34
LA SB: Landesarchiv Saarbrücken
  A/4-440 R-1347-90
LHA KO: Landeshauptarchiv Koblenz
  Best. De 20, Nr. LkR Trier 1
  Best. 393, Nr. 877
  Best. 403, Nr. 8319
  Best. 442, Nr. 6722, 6808, 8648, 8649, 9371
Ns. StA OS: Niedersächsisches Staatsarchiv Osnabrück
  Rep. 950 Pap., Nr. 121, 142, 145
StA HH: Staatsarchiv Hamburg
  Meldewesen:
    A 6, Bd. 3
    A 12, Bd. 6
    A 21, Bd. 1, 18
  Auswanderungsamt I, VIII: A 1; A 2
StA LB: Staatsarchiv Ludwigsburg
  F 210: Bü. 411, Nr. 21, 277; Bü. 412, Nr. 250; Bü. 414, Nr. 587, 671; Bü. 416, Nr.
    31
StA MS: Staatsarchiv Münster
  Reg. Mü.: Nr. 181, 1; Nr. 130; Nr. M 58, 3, 1
Standesamt Waldenburg:
  Personenstandsregister der Stadt Waldenburg
Standesamt Münstermaifeld:
  Standesamtsregister Gemeinde Münstermaifeld

  Kirchenbücher [Parish Records]

of Protestant parishes (ev. KB):
  Adorf, Arolsen, Blessenbach, Dielingen, Gedern, Göttingen, Herlefeld, Horne-
  burg, Korb, Korbach, Lengerich, Lienen, Marköbel, Mülheim on the Ruhr,
  Schotten, Selsingen, Witten, Züsch; and Meppel, Netherlands
of Catholic parishes (kath. KB):
  Alf, Irrel, Münstermaifeld

  American Archives

Indiana Historical Society, Indianapolis:
  Marion County Marriage Records, 1871–1875
  U.S. Manuscript Census, Agricultural Schedules
Manitoba Provincial Archives
  Bruce Papers
Missouri State Archives, Jefferson City:

Adair County Deed Records
Adair County Marriage Records
Warren County Circuit Court Records
Warren County Deed Records
State Historical Society of Minnesota, St. Paul:
  Charles W. Brandborg and Family Papers
  State Census Minnesota, 1865, 1885, 1895, 1905
  U.S. Manuscript Census, Agricultural Schedules
State Historical Society of Missouri, Columbia:
  U.S. Manuscript Census, Agricultural Schedules
State Historical Society of Wisconsin, Madison:
  Immigrant Letter Collection
  John Pritzlaff Hardware Company Papers
U.S. National Archives (NatA), Washington, D.C.:
  Muster Rolls, Union Army:
    9th Regiment Indiana Infantry
    52nd Regiment New York Infantry
    58th Regiment New York Infantry
  Passenger Lists: Baltimore, New Orleans, New York
  Pension Records, Union Army
  U.S. Manuscript Census, Agricultural Schedules: Michigan, Nebraska, Ohio,
    Washington
U.S. National Archives Branch, Suitland, Md.:
  Cash Entry File
  Land Entry File
Vernon Historical Society, Office of the Registrar, Vernon, Conn.:
  Copies of the birth and marriage certificates of the Weitz family
  Wear, John, Census and Statistics of Rockville, April 1, 1855

Manuscript Census

The U.S. Manuscript Census is available in National Archives microfilm publications. Footnote citations include sufficient information to locate an individual: state; county; township, city ward, or enumeration district; and family number.

Published Census Material

USC 1850.1	USC 1870.1	USC 1890.1	USC M 1900.1
USC 1850.2	USC 1870.3	USC 1890.2	USC A 1900.2
USC 1860.0	USC 1870.8	USC 1890.18	USC 1910.1
USC 1860.1	USC 1880.1	USC MI 1890.1	USC 1910.4
USC 1860.2	USC 1880.2	USC 1900.1	USC 1920.2
USC A 1860.1	USC A 1880.1	USC 1900.18	
USC M 1860.1	USC MI 1880.2		

The above are numbered according to:
Bibliography and Reel Index: A Guide to the Microfilm Edition of United States Decennial Census Publications 1790–1970. 1975. Research Publications Inc. Woodbridge, Conn.

1980 Census of Population. PC80–1-B11; PC80–1-C1; PC80–1-C11
St. Louis City Census 1858
State Census Iowa 1885
State Census Minnesota 1865, 1885, 1895, 1905
State Census New York 1855, 1865

City Directories

All citations are based on the Research Publications microform reprints, *The City Directories of the United States, Segment I: Through 1860; Segment II: 1861–1881; Segment III: 1882–1901; Segment IV: 1902–1935.* Woodbridge, Conn.

Adreßbücher [address books]

AB Frankfurt am Main 1876
AB Hamburg 1883

SECONDARY AND PUBLISHED PRIMARY SOURCES

Abbott, Ardis. 1976. "Rockville's Germans, 1860–1960." Unpublished ms.
Abendpost. 1918. Chicago.
Abramson, Harold J. 1980. "Assimilation and Pluralism." In *Harvard Encyclopedia,* 150–60.
Adams, Willi Paul. 1984. "Die Assimilationsfrage in der amerikanischen Einwanderungsdiskussion 1890–1930." In Bade (1984a), 1:300–320.
Adams, Willi Paul, ed. 1980. *Die deutschsprachige Auswanderung in die Vereinigten Staaten. Bericht über Forschungsstand und Quellenbestände.* Berlin.
Adelmann, Gerhard. 1974. "Strukturelle Krisen im ländlichen Textilgewerbe Nordwestdeutschlands zu Beginn der Industrialisierung." In *Wirtschaftspolitik und Arbeitsmarkt. Bericht über die 4. Jahrestagung der Gesellschaft für Sozial- und Wirtschaftsgeschichte,* ed. Hermann Kellenbenz, 110–28. Munich.
Aikens, A. J., and L. A. Proctor, eds. 1897. *Men of Progress: Wisconsin Leaders in Business, Professional, and Official Life.* Milwaukee, Wisc.
American Federation of Labor. 1924. *History, Encyclopedia, Reference Book.* Vol. 2. Repr.: Westport, Conn., 1977.
Amts-Blatt. 1883. Wiesbaden.
Amts-Blatt der Norddeutschen Postverwaltung. 1869. Statistics for 1868, 43.
Annual Reports of the Commissioners of Emigration of the State of New York. 1861. Report 5. New York.
Anzeiger des Westens. 1852, 1853, 1858. St. Louis. Mo.
Arndt, Karl J. R., and Mary E. Olson. 1965. *German-American Newspapers and Periodicals, 1732–1955. History and Bibliography.* London.
Assion, Peter. 1983. "Von Hessen nach Amerika. 300 Jahre deutsche und hessische Amerika-Auswanderung." *Hessische Heimat* NF 33:95–103.
Atlas of Adair County, Missouri. 1876.
Atlas of Harrison County, Indiana. 1882. Philadelphia.

Auerbach, Inge. 1985. "Auswanderung aus Kurhessen 1832–1866." *Hessische Blätter für Volks- und Kulturforschung* NF 17:19–50.

Auszüge aus Briefen aus Nord-Amerika. 1833. Theodor-Ulrich Nübling, ed. Ulm.

Backes, Anton, et al. 1970. *Hermeskeil. Stadt im Hochwald.* Hermeskeil.

Bade, Klaus J., ed. 1984a. *Auswanderer—Wanderarbeiter—Gastarbeiter. Bevölkerung, Arbeitsmarkt und Wanderung in Deutschland seit der Mitte des 19. Jahrhunderts.* 2 vols. Ostfildern.

Bade, Klaus J. 1984b. "Vom Auswanderungsland zum 'Arbeitseinfuhrland': Kontinentale Zuwanderung und Ausländerbeschäftigung in Deutschland im späten 19. und frühen 20. Jahrhundert." In Bade (1984a), 1:433–85.

Bade, Klaus J. 1984c. "Vom Export der Sozialen Frage zur importierten Sozialen Frage: Deutschland im transnationalen Wanderungsgeschehen seit der Mitte des 19. Jahrhunderts." In Bade (1984a), 2:9–72.

Baldwin, Leland D. 1937. *Pittsburgh: The Story of a City.* Pittsburgh.

Ball, Larry D. 1978. *The United States Marshals of the New Mexico and Arizona Territories, 1846–1912.* Albuquerque.

Barkai, Avraham. 1986. "German-Jewish Migration in the Nineteenth Century, 1830–1910." In Glazier and De Rosa, 202–19.

Barleben, Ilse. 1959. *Mülheim a. d. Ruhr. Beiträge zu seiner Geschichte von der Erhebung zur Stadt bis zu den Gründerjahren.* Mülheim.

Barr & Widen Co.'s Credit Guide. 1902, 1903. St. Louis.

Bärsch, Georg. 1846. *Beschreibung des Regierungsbezirks Trier.* Part 2. Trier.

Bartolosch, Thomas A., ed. 1986. *"Wir hatten ein schlechtes Schiff . . . ." Briefe eines Westerwälder Amerika-Auswanderers 1892–1914.* Altenkirchen im Westerwald.

Barton, H. Arnold. 1975. *Letters from the Promised Land: Swedes in America, 1840–1914.* Minneapolis.

Bassler, Gerhard P. 1974. "Auswanderungsfreiheit und Auswanderungsfürsorge in Württemberg 1815–1855. Zur Geschichte der südwestdeutschen Massenauswanderung nach Nordamerika." *Zeitschift für württembergische Landesgeschichte* 33:117–60.

Beck, Otto. *Beschreibung des Regierungsbezirks Trier.* Vol. 2, part 1, 1869; vol. 3, part 2, 1871. Trier.

Beiträge zur Statistik der inneren Verwaltung des Großherzogtums Baden. Vol. 5, 1857; vol. 6, 1858. Großherzogliches Ministerium des Innern. Karlsruhe.

Beiträge zur Statistik des Großherzogtums Hessen. Vol. 1, 1862; vol. 2, 1863; vol. 3, 1864. Großherzogliche Centralstelle für die Landesstatistik. Darmstadt.

Bell, Daniel. 1952. "The Background and Development of Marxian Socialism in the United States." In *Socialism and American Life,* ed. Donald Drew Egbert and Stow Persons, vol. 1, pp. 215–405. Princeton.

Berichte der Synodal-Beamten der Deutschen Evangelischen Synode von Nordamerika. 1918. St. Louis.

Beschreibung der württembergischen Oberämter. 1824–1886 (64 vols); NF 1893–1920 (9 vols.). Königliches statistisch-topographisches Bureau. Stuttgart.

Beschreibung des Oberamtes Oehringen. 1865. Stuttgart.

Beschreibung des Oberamtes Waiblingen. 1850. Stuttgart.

Bickelmann, Hartmut. 1980. *Deutsche Überseeauswanderung in der Weimarer Zeit.* Wiesbaden.

Biller, Carl. 1906. *Der Rückgang der Hand-Leinwandindustrie des Münsterlandes.* Leipzig.

Billington, Ray Allen. 1956. *The Far Western Frontier, 1830–1860.* New York.

Billington, Ray Allen. 1964. *The Protestant Crusade, 1800–1860: A Study of the Origins of American Nativism.* 4th ed. Chicago.

Bitter, Carl Hermann. 1964–65. "Bericht über den Nothstand in der Senne zwischen Bielefeld und Paderborn, Regierungsbezirk Minden, und Vorschläge zur Beseitigung desselben, aufgrund örtlicher Untersuchungen aufgestellt." *Jahrbuch des Historischen Vereins für die Grafschaft Ravensberg* 64:1–108. Orig. 1853.

Blegen, Theodore C. 1929. "The 'America Letters.' " *Avhandlinger utgitt av Det Norske Videnskaps-Akademi i Oslo, II. Historisk-Filosofisk Klasse (1928),* 1–25. Oslo.

Blegen, Theodore C. 1931. *Norwegian Emigration to America 1825–1860.* Northfield, Minn.

Blegen, Theodore C. 1955. *Land of Their Choice: The Immigrants Write Home.* St. Paul, Minn.

Blendinger, Friedrich. 1964. "Die Auswanderung nach Nordamerika aus dem Regierungsbezirk Oberbayern in den Jahren 1846–1852." *Zeitschrift für bayerische Landesgeschichte* 27:431–87.

Bödicker, T. 1874. "Die Einwanderung und Auswanderung des preußischen Staates." In *Preußische Statistik* 26:i–vliv.

Bogue, Allan G. 1963. *From Prairie to Corn Belt: Farming on the Illinois and Iowa Prairies in the Nineteenth Century.* Chicago.

Bohmbach, Jürgen. 1982. "Die Endphase der Weimarer Republik in Niedersachsen." *Niedersächsisches Jahrbuch* 54:65–94.

Bonenkamp, B., et al. 1882. *Schematismus der deutschen und deutsch-sprechenden Priester, sowie der deutschen Katholiken-Gemeinden in den Vereinigten Staaten Nord-Amerika's.* St. Louis.

Booth, Mary L. 1880. *History of the City of New York.* New York.

Bott, Heinrich. n.d. *839–1919. 1100 Jahre Marköbel. Aus der Geschichte eines Dorfes in der Wetterau.*

Bovensiepen, Rudolf. 1909. *Die kurhessische Gewerbepolitik und die wirtschaftliche Lage des zünftigen Handwerks in Kurhessen von 1816–1867.* Marburg.

Bowley, Arthur L. 1900. *Wages in the United Kingdom in the Nineteenth Century.* Cambridge. Repr.: Clifton, N.J. 1972.

Brandt, Alexander von. 1904. *Zur sozialen Entwicklung im Saargebiet.* Leipzig.

Bretting, Agnes. 1981. *Soziale Probleme deutscher Einwanderer in New York City: 1800–1860.* Wiesbaden.

Bretting, Agnes. 1985. "Organizing German Immigration: The Role of State Authorities in Germany and the United States." In Trommler and McVeigh, 25–38.

Bretting, Agnes, and Hartmut Bickelmann. 1991. *Auswanderungsagenturen und Auswanderungsvereine in Deutschland im 19. und 20. Jahrhundert.* Stuttgart.

"Der Briefverkehr des deutschen Reichs-Postgebiets mit dem Auslande im Jahre 1879." 1880. *Archiv für Post und Telegraphie* 10:289–301.

Brody, David. 1980. "Labor." In *Harvard Encyclopedia,* 609–18.

Broehl, Wayne G., Jr. 1984. *John Deere's Company: A History of Deere and Company and Its Times.* New York.

Bromme, Traugott. 1848. *Hand- und Reisebuch für Auswanderer nach den Vereinigten Staaten von Nord-Amerika.* 5th ed. Bayreuth.

Brommer, Peter, et al., eds. 1976. *Inventar der Quellen zur Geschichte der Auswanderung 1500–1914 in den staatlichen Archiven von Rheinland-Pfalz und dem Saarland.* Koblenz.

Bruns, Jette. 1988. *Hold Dear, as Always: Jette, an Immigrant Life in Letters.* Ed. Adolf E. Schroeder and Carla Schulz-Geisberg. Columbia, Mo.

Buck, James S. 1881. *Pioneer History of Milwaukee.* Vol. 2: *From 1840 to 1846, inclusive.* Milwaukee, Wisc.

Büttner, J. G. 1844. *Die Vereinigten Staaten von Nord-Amerika. Mein Aufenthalt und meine Reisen in denselben, vom Jahre 1834 bis 1841.* Vol. 1. Hamburg.

The Cemeteries of Adair County, Missouri. 1981. Owensboro, Ky.

Cheda, Giorgio. 1981. *L'emigrazione ticinese in California, Epistolario.* 2 vols. Locarno, Switzerland.

Clemens, Lieselotte. 1976. *Die Auswanderung der pommerschen Altlutheraner in die USA.* Hamburg.

Conrad, Else. 1908. *Das Dienstbotenproblem in den Vereinigten Staaten und was es uns lehrt.* Jena.

Conrad, Howard L., ed. 1895. *History of Milwaukee: From the First Settlement to the Year 1895.* Vol. 1. Chicago.

Conway, Alan, ed. 1961. *The Welsh in America. Letters from the Immigrants.* St. Paul, Minn.

Conzen, Kathleen Neils. 1976. *Immigrant Milwaukee, 1836–1860: Accommodation and Community in a Frontier City.* Cambridge, Mass.

Conzen, Kathleen Neils. 1979. "Immigrants, Immigrant Neighborhoods, and Ethnic Identity: Historical Issues." *Journal of American History* 66:603–15.

Conzen, Kathleen Neils. 1980. "Germans." In *Harvard Encyclopedia,* 405–25.

Conzen, Kathleen Neils. 1984. "Deutsche Einwanderer im ländlichen Amerika: Problemfelder und Forschungsergebnisse." In Bade (1984a), 1:350–77.

Conzen, Kathleen Neils. 1985a. "Peasant Pioneers: Generational Succession among German Farmers in Frontier Minnesota." In *The Countryside in the Age of Capitalist Transformation,* ed. Steven Hahn and Jonathan Prude, 259–92. Chapel Hill, N.C.

Conzen, Kathleen Neils. 1985b. "German-Americans and the Invention of Ethnicity." In Trommler and McVeigh, 131–47.

Corwin, Edward Tanjore, et al. 1902. *A History of the Reformed Church, Dutch Reformed Church, German Reformed Church, and the Moravian Church in the United States.* 2d ed. New York.

Cramer, Claus. 1971. "Territoriale Entwicklung." In Martin and Wetekam, 171–261.

Cronau, Rudolf. 1924. *Drei Jahrhunderte deutschen Lebens in Amerika. Ruhmesblätter der Deutschen in den Vereinigten Staaten.* Berlin.

Curtze, Louis. 1841a. "Corbach im Jahre 1840." *Waldeckische Gemeinnützige Zeitschrift* 3:173–92, 195–216.

Curtze, Louis. 1841b. "Das Gymnasium zu Corbach." *Waldeckische Gemeinnützige Zeitschrift* 3:72–84, 120–28, 243–54.

Curtze, Louis. 1850. *Geschichte und Beschreibung des Fürstentums Waldeck. Ein Handbuch für Vaterlandsfreunde.* Arolsen.

Dascher, Ottfried. 1968. *Das Textilgewerbe in Hessen-Kassel vom 16. bis 19. Jahrhundert.* Marburg.

Dellmann, Friedrich, ed. 1835. *Briefe der nach Amerika ausgewanderten Familie Steines.* Wesel.

Demian, Johann Andreas. 1823. *Handbuch der Geographie und Statistik des Herzogtums Nassau. Nach Originalquellen und eigener Lokalkenntnis.* Wiesbaden.

Detjen, David W. 1985. *The Germans in Missouri, 1900–1918: Prohibition, Neutrality, and Assimilation.* Columbia, Mo.

Deutsches Geschlechterbuch. Genealogisches Handbuch Bürgerlicher Familien. Bernhard Koerner, ed. Vol. 24 (1913), Görlitz; vol. 98 (1937), Berlin.

Dickinson, Joan Younger. 1980. *The Role of the Immigrant Woman in the U.S. Labor Force, 1890–1910.* New York.

Dictionary of American Biography. 1927–1936. 20 vols. Allen Johnson and Dumas Malone, eds. New York.

Dictionnaire Historique et Biographique de la Suisse. 1932. Marcel Godet et al., eds. Vol. 6. Neuchâtel.

Diner, Hasia R. 1983. *Erin's Daughters in America: Irish Immigrant Women in the Nineteenth Century.* Baltimore.

Dobbert, Guido. 1980. *The Disintegration of an Immigrant Community: The Cincinnati Germans, 1870–1920.* New York.

Dobert, Eitel W. 1967. "The Radicals." In Zucker (1967a), 157–81.

Dodge, Eugene, n.d. *Marriage Records of Scotland Co., Mo.* Memphis, Mo.

Doerries, Reinhard R. 1986. *Iren und Deutsche in der Neuen Welt. Akkulturationsprozesse in der amerikanischen Gesellschaft im späten 19. Jahrhundert.* Wiesbaden.

Dolan, Jay P. 1975. *The Immigrant Church: New York's Irish and German Catholics, 1815–1865.* Baltimore.

Dolan, Jay P. 1977. "Philadelphia and the German Catholic Community." In *Immigrants and Religion in Urban America,* ed. Randall Miller and Thomas Marzig, 69–83. Philadelphia.

Domeyer, Hans. 1972. *Soziale und wirtschaftliche Beziehungen in der Krisenzeit des ravensbergischen Leinengewerbes.* Bielefeld.

Douglas County [Wash.] *Spokesman Review.* 1923.

Drache, Hiram M. 1970. *The Challenge of the Prairie: Life and Times of Red River Pioneers.* Fargo, N.D.

Dudden, Faye E. 1983. *Serving Women: Household Service in Nineteenth-Century America.* Middletown, Conn.

Duden, Gottfried. 1829. *Bericht über eine Reise nach den westlichen Staaten Nordamerika's und einen mehrjährigen Aufenthalt am Missouri (in den Jahren 1824, '25, '26 und 1827), in Bezug auf Auswanderung und Überbevölkerung.* Elberfeld. 2d ed., 1834, Bonn.

Duden, Gottfried. 1980. *Report on a Journey to the Western States of North America.* Trans. and ed. James Goodrich et al. Columbia, Mo.

Dyer, Frederick A. 1959. *A Compendium of the War of Rebellion.* Vol. 3: *Regimental Histories.* New York.

Edelmann, Berhard. 1920. "Wirtschaftliche und soziale Wandlungen auf dem Hohen Hunsrück." Diss. rer. pol., Frankfurt am Main.

Ehmer, Hermann. 1980. "Die Quellen zur Nordamerika-Auswanderung im Generallandesarchiv Karlsruhe und im Staatsarchiv Freiburg." In Adams (1980), 148–58.

Ellis, Frances. 1954. "German Instruction in the Public Schools of Indianapolis, 1869–1919." *Indiana Magazine of History* 50:119–38, 251–76, 357–80.

Engel & Foote Co. 1904. *Credit Rating Directory.* St. Louis.

Engelhardt, Ulrich, et al., eds. 1976. *Soziale Bewegung und politische Verfassung. Beiträge zur Geschichte der modernen Welt*. Stuttgart.

Engelsing, Rolf. 1961. *Bremen als Auswandererhafen, 1683–1880*. Bremen.

Engelsing, Rolf. 1973. "Dienstbotenlektüre im 18. und 19. Jahrhundert." In *Zur Sozialgeschichte deutscher Mittel- und Unterschichten*, ed. Rolf Engelsing, 180–224. Göttingen.

Ensslen, Klaus. 1964. "Jürnjakob Swehn der Amerikafahrer." In *Kindlers Literatur Lexikon* 4:139–40.

Ensslen, Klaus, and Heinz Ickstadt. 1983. "German Working-Class Culture in Chicago: Continuity and Change in the Decade from 1900 to 1910." In Keil and Jentz (1983), 236–52.

Enzlberger, Johannes. 1892. *Schematismus der katholischen Geistlichen deutscher Zunge*. Milwaukee, Wisc.

Erickson, Charlotte. 1972. *Invisible Immigrants: The Adaptation of English and Scottish Immigrants in Nineteenth-Century America*. Coral Gables, Fla. Repr.: Ithaca, N.Y., 1989.

Ernst, Robert. 1949. *Immigrant Life in New York City*. New York.

Esser, Hartmut. 1980. *Aspekte der Wanderungssoziologie. Assimilation und Integration von Wanderern, ethnischen Gruppen und Minderheiten. Eine handlungstheoretische Analyse*. Darmstadt.

Faires, Nora. 1983. "Occupational Patterns of German-Americans in the Nineteenth Century." In Keil and Jentz (1983), 37–52.

Fawcett, Edward, and Tony Thomas. 1983. *Die Amerikaner*. Bern.

Ferenczi, Imre, and Walter F. Willcox, eds. 1929. *International Migrations*. Vol. 1. New York. Repr. 1969.

Fey, [Ministerialsekretär]. 1892. "Die Entwicklung des Auswanderungswesens und Auswanderungsrechtes im Großherzogtum Hessen." In Philippovich, 167–233.

Finzsch, Norbert. 1982. *Die Goldgräber Kaliforniens. Arbeitsbedingungen, Lebensstandard und politisches System um die Mitte des 19. Jahrhunderts*. Göttingen.

Fischer, Wolfram. 1965. *Herz des Reviers. 125 Jahre Wirtschaftsgeschichte des Industrie- und Handelskammerbezirks Essen—Mülheim—Oberhausen*. Essen.

Fleischhauer, Wolfgang. 1970. "German Communities in Northwestern Ohio: Canal Fever and Prosperity." *The Report* 34:23–43.

Flower, Frank A. 1881. *History of Milwaukee, Wisconsin*. Chicago.

Frank, Louis F., ed. 1911. *Pionierjahre der Deutsch-Amerikanischen Familien Frank-Kerler in Wisconsin und Michigan, 1849–1864*. Milwaukee, Wisc. English translation: Harry H. Anderson, ed. 1971. *German-American Pioneers in Wisconsin and Michigan: The Frank-Kerler Letters*. Milwaukee, Wisc.

Franz, Günter, et al. 1969. *Die Geschichte der Landtechnik im 20. Jahrhundert*. Frankfurt am Main.

Frensdorff, F. 1887a. "Oesterley, Ferdinand." *ADB* 24:512–13. Leipzig.

Frensdorff, F. 1887b. "Oesterley, Georg Heinrich." *ADB* 24:513. Leipzig.

Friedrich, Carl J. 1967. "The European Background." In Zucker (1967a), 3–25.

Gates, Paul. 1960. *The Farmer's Age: Agriculture 1815–1860*. New York.

Gebel, Hans-Josef. 1980. "Der Steinkohlenbergbau als Haupterwerbsquelle." *Ortschronik Riegelsberg*, 227–63.

Gerber, David A. 1984. "Language Maintenance, Ethnic Group Formation, and

Public Schools: Changing Patterns of German Concern, Buffalo 1837–74." *Journal of American Ethnic History* 4:31–61.

Gerlach, Russel L. 1976. *Immigrants in the Ozarks: A Study in Ethnic Geography.* Columbia, Mo.

Gilbert, Glenn. 1981. "French and German: A Comparative Study." In *Language in the USA*, ed. Charles Ferguson and Shirley Heath, 257–72. Cambridge.

Gillet, Josef. 1980. "Aus der Schulgeschichte." *Ortschronik Riegelsberg*, 412–45.

Gillhoff, Johannes. 1917. *Jürnjakob Swehn der Amerikafahrer.* Berlin.

Gladen, Albin. 1970. *Der Kreis Tecklenburg an der Schwelle des Zeitalters der Industrialisierung.* Münster.

Glasco, Lawrence A. 1980. *Ethnicity and Social Structure: Irish, Germans, and Native-Born of Buffalo, N.Y., 1850–1860.* New York.

Glazier, Ira, and Luigi De Rosa, eds. 1986. *Migration across Time and Nations.* New York.

Glazier, Ira, and P. William Filby, eds. 1988f. *Germans to America: Lists of Passengers Arriving at U.S. Ports, 1850–1855.* 10 vols. Wilmington, Del.

Göbel, Gert. 1877. *Länger als ein Menschenleben in Missouri.* St. Louis.

Goebel, Klaus. 1964. *Wuppertal—heimliche Hauptstadt von Waldeck. Eine Darstellung der waldeckischen Beziehungen zu Wuppertal als Beitrag zur westdeutschen Bevölkerungsgeschichte.* Wuppertal.

Gömmel, Rainer. 1979. *Realeinkommen in Deutschland. Ein internationaler Vergleich (1910–1914).* Nuremberg.

Gordon, Milton M. 1964. *Assimilation in American Life: The Role of Race, Religion, and National Origins.* New York.

Gordon, Milton M. 1978. *Human Nature, Class, and Ethnicity.* New York.

Graafen, Richard. 1961. *Die Aus- und Abwanderung aus der Eifel in den Jahren 1815 bis 1955. Eine Untersuchung der Bevölkerungsentwicklung eines deutschen Mittelgebirges im Zeitalter der Industrialisierung.* Bonn.

"Grant, U.S." 1931–32. *DAB* 4:492–501.

The Greenwood Encyclopedia of American Institutions: Labor Unions. 1977. Gary M. Fink, ed. Westport, Conn.

Griffen, Clyde, and Sally Griffen. 1978. *Natives and Newcomers: The Ordering of Opportunity in Mid-Nineteenth-Century Poughkeepsie.* Cambridge, Mass.

Grünberg, Karl. 1922. "Agrarverfassung: Zuständliches und Begriffliches." In *Grundriß der Sozialökonomik* 7:131–68. Tübingen.

Haas, Carl de. 1848. *Nordamerika, Wisconsin, Calumet. Winke für Auswanderer.* Elberfeld-Iserlohn.

Hack, Edris Probstfield. 1977. *Candles in the Wind.*

Haines, Michael R. 1979. "Industrial Work and the Family Life Cycle, 1889–1890." *Research in Economic History* 4:289–356.

Hale, Frederick, ed. 1984. *Danes in North America.* Seattle, Wash.

Hamburger Novellenzeitung. 1854–94. Altona.

Hamer, Karl. 1925. "Nachweis der Bevölkerungs-Bewegung in den Ämtern Dielingen und Wehdem." *Heimatblätter für die Grafschaft Diepholz* 2–3:37–39.

Hammer, Carl. 1943. *Rheinlanders on the Yadkin.* Salisbury, N.C.

Hannemann, Max. 1936. *Das Deutschtum in den Vereinigten Staaten.* Gotha.

Härdle, Otto. 1960. *Heidelsheim. Geschichte und Bild der ehemaligen Reichsstadt.* Karlsruhe.

Hargest, George E. 1971. *History of Letter Communication between the United States and Europe, 1845–1875.* Washington, D.C.

Harvard Encyclopedia of American Ethnic Groups. 1980. Stephan Thernstrom et al., eds. Cambridge, Mass.

Harzig, Christiane. 1985. "The U.S. Government Census as Source in Immigration Research." In Harzig and Hoerder, 25–37.

Harzig, Christiane. 1986. "Women's Work and Family Strategies: Immigrant Women in the U.S. around the Turn of the Century." In *"Why Did You Come?" The Proletarian Mass Migration: Research Report 1980–1985,* ed.Dirk Hoerder and Christiane Harzig, 111–22. Bremen.

Harzig, Christiane, and Dirk Hoerder, eds. 1985. *The Press of Labor Migrants in Europe and North America: 1880s to 1930s.* Bremen.

Haßlacher, A. 1904. *Der Steinkohlenbergbau des Preussischen Staates in der Umgebung von Saarbrücken.* Part 2: *Geschichtliche Entwicklung des Steinkohlenbergbaus im Saargebiete.* Berlin.

Haßlacher, A. 1912. *Das Industriegebiet an der Saar und seine hauptsächlichen Industriezweige.* Saarbrücken.

Haushofer, Heinz. 1972. *Die deutsche Landwirtschaft im technischen Zeitalter.* Stuttgart.

Heckscher, Siegfried. 1895. "Über die Lage des Schuhmachergewerbes in Altona, Elmshorn, Heide, Preetz und Barmstedt." In *Untersuchungen über die Lage des Handwerks in Deutschland,* 1:1–36. Leipzig.

Heidemann, Leonard W. 1950. "Acceptance of the English Language in the Lutheran Church—Missouri Synod." Master's thesis, Iowa State College.

Helbich, Wolfgang J. 1984. "Problems of Editing and Interpreting Immigrant Letters." In *Emigration from Northern, Central, and Southern Europe: Theoretical and Methodological Principles of Research,* 65–75. Cracow.

Helbich, Wolfgang J., ed. 1985a. *Amerika ist ein freies Land. Auswanderer schreiben nach Deutschland.* Darmstadt.

Helbich, Wolfgang J. 1985b. "Letters from America: Documents of the Adjustment Process of German Immigrants in the United States." *anglistik & englischunterricht* 26:201–15.

Helbich, Wolfgang J., and Ulrike Sommer. 1985c. "Immigrant Letters as Sources." In Harzig and Hoerder, 39–59.

Helbich, Wolfgang J. 1987. "The Letters They Sent Home." *Yearbook of German-American Studies* 22:1–20.

Henretta, James, et al. 1987. *America's History to 1877.* Chicago.

Hershberg, Theodore, et al. 1981. "A Tale of Three Cities: Blacks, Immigrants, and Opportunity in Philadelphia." In *Philadelphia: Work, Space, Family, and Group Experience in the nineteenth Century,* ed. Theordore Hershberg. 461–91. Oxford.

Heßler, Carl. 1906–7. *Hessische Landes- und Volkskunde. Das ehemalige Kurhessen und das Hinterland am Ausgange des 19. Jahrhunderts.* Vols. 1–2. Marburg.

Hicks, John D. 1931. *The Populist Revolt.* Minneapolis, Minn.

Hildebrandt, Bruno. 1853. *Statistische Mitteilungen über die volkswirtschaftlichen Zustände Kurhessens.* Berlin.

Hippel, Wolfgang von. 1976. "Bevölkerungsentwicklung und Wirtschaftsstruktur im Königlichen Württemberg 1815–1865. Überlegungen zum Pauperismusproblem in Südwestdeutschland." In Engelhardt et al., 270–371.

Hippel, Wolfgang von. 1980. "Die Auswanderung aus dem Königreich Württemberg im Zeitalter des Pauperismus, 1815–1870." In Adams (1980), 198–229.

Hippel, Wolfgang von. 1984. *Auswanderung aus Südwestdeutschland. Studien zur württembergischen Auswanderung und Auswanderungs-politik in 18. und 19. Jahrhundert.* Stuttgart.

Historical Statistics of the United States: Colonial Times to 1970. 1975. 2 vols. Washington, D.C.

History of Adair, Sullivan, Putnam, and Schuyler Counties, Missouri. 1888a. Chicago.

History of Clay and Norman Counties, Minnesota. 1918. Indianapolis, Ind.

History of Franklin, Jefferson, Washington, Crawford, & Gasconade Counties, Missouri. 1888b. Chicago.

History of Milwaukee, Wisconsin. 1881. Chicago.

History of Wages in the United States from Colonial Times to 1928. 1934. Bulletin of the U.S. Bureau of Labor Statistics. No. 604. U.S. Department of Labor. Washington, D.C.

Hobsbawm, E. J. 1968. *Industry and Empire. An Economic History of Britain since 1750.* London.

Hoerder, Dirk, ed. 1983. *American Labor and Immigration History, 1877–1920s: Recent European Research.* Chicago.

Hoerder, Dirk, ed. 1985. *Glimpses of the German-American Radical Press: Publications of the Labor Newspaper Preservation Project.* Bremen.

Hohorst, Gert, et al., eds. 1975. *Sozialgeschichtliches Arbeitsbuch.* Vol. 2. Munich.

Holborn, Hajo. 1969. *A History of Modern Germany.* Vol. 3. Princeton.

Holli, Melvin G. 1984. "The Great War Sinks Chicago's German Kultur." In *Ethnic Chicago,* ed. Melvin G. Holli and Peter d'A. Jones, 2d ed., 460–512. Grand Rapids, Mich.

Holli, Melvin G., and Peter d'A. Jones. 1981. *Biographical Dictionary of American Mayors, 1820 to 1980.* Westport, Conn.

Holt, Michael F. 1978. *The Political Crisis of the 1850s.* New York.

Holt, William S. 1929. *The Bureau of the Census: Its History, Activities, and Organization.* Washington, D.C.

Holzmann. 1890. "Schenkel, Georg Daniel." *ADB* 31:82–89. Leipzig.

Hunsche, Friedrich Ernst. 1983. *Auswanderungen aus dem Kreis Steinfurt.* Steinfurt.

Hunsche, Friedrich Ernst. n.d. "Auswanderer aus Lienen. Auszüge aus den Bevölkerungslisten im Gemeindearchiv Lienen." Unpublished ms.

Hutchinson, E. P. 1956. *Immigrants and Their Children, 1850–1950.* New York.

Huth, Karl. 1962. *Wirtschafts- und Sozialgeschichte des Landkreises Biedenkopf 1800–1860.* Wetzlar.

Illinois Staatszeitung. 1867, 1876. Chicago.

Iwan, Wilhelm. 1943. *Die Altlutherische Auswanderung um die Mitte des 19. Jahrhunderts.* 2 vols. Ludwigsburg.

Jacobi, Karl. 1913. *Nassauisches Heimatbuch (Regierungsbezirk Wiesbaden). Bilder aus der Natur des Landes, dem geschichtlichen und kulturellen Leben seiner Bewohner.* Wiesbaden.

Jaehn, Thomas. 1986. "Charles Blumner: Pioneer, Civil Servant, and Merchant." *New Mexico Historical Review* 61:319–27.

Jarausch, Konrad H. 1984. *Deutsche Studenten 1800–1970.* Frankfurt am Main.

Jensen, Richard. 1971. *The Winning of the Midwest: Social and Political Conflict, 1888–1896.* Chicago.

Jentz, John B. 1983. "Skilled Workers and Industrialization: Chicago's German Cabinetmakers and Machinists, 1880–1900." In Keil and Jentz (1983), 73–85.

Johnson, Hildegard Binder. 1951. "The Location of German Immigrants in the Middle West." *Annals of the Association of American Geographers* 41:1–41.

Johnson, Hildegard Binder. 1967. "Adjustment to the United States." In Zucker (1967a), 41–78.

Johnson, Hildegard Binder. 1976. *Order on the Land: The U.S. Rectangular Survey and the Upper Mississippi Country.* Oxford.

Jordan, Terry G. 1966. *German Seed in Texas Soil: Immigrant Farmers in Nineteenth Century Texas.* Austin.

Kammeier, Heinz-Ulrich. 1983. "Deutsche Amerikaauswanderung aus dem Altkreis Lübbecke in der zweiten Hälfte des 19. Jahrhunderts." Ph.D. diss., Univ. Münster.

Kammeier, Heinz-Ulrich. 1985. *"So besint euch doch nicht lange und kommt herrüber." Briefe von Amerikaauswanderern aus dem Kreis Lübbecke aus zwei Jahrhunderten.* Espelkamp.

Kamphoefner, Walter. 1982. *Westfalen in der Neuen Welt. Eine Sozialgeschichte der Auswanderung im 19. Jahrhundert.* Münster.

Kamphoefner, Walter. 1983. "300 Jahre Deutsche in den USA." *Geographische Rundschau* 35:169–73.

Kamphoefner, Walter. 1984. "The German Agricultural Frontier: Crucible or Cocoon." *Ethnic Forum* 4:21–35.

Kamphoefner, Walter. 1986a. "At the Crossroads of Economic Development: Background Factors Affecting Emigration from Nineteenth-Century Germany." In Glazier and De Rosa, 174–201.

Kamphoefner, Walter. 1986b. "The Volume and Composition of German-American Return Migration." Paper presented at "A Century of European Migration 1830–1930 in Comparative Perspective," University of Minnesota. Forthcoming in *A Century of European Migration, 1830–1930: Macroperspectives and Microanalyses,* ed. Rudolph J. Vecoli and Suzanne Sinke, Urbana, Ill. and Chicago.

Kamphoefner, Walter. 1987. *The Westfalians: From Germany to Missouri.* Princeton.

Katholische Glaubensbote. 1870. Louisville, Ky.

Katz, Eugen. 1904. *Landarbeiter und Landwirtschaft in Oberhessen.* Stuttgart.

Katz, Michael B. 1975. *The People of Hamilton, Canada West: Family and Class in a Mid-Nineteenth-Century City.* Cambridge, Mass.

Katzman, David M. 1978. *Seven Days a Week: Women and Domestic Service in Industrializing America.* New York.

Kaufmann, Wilhelm. 1911. *Die Deutschen im amerikanischen Bürgerkrieg (Sezessionskrieg 1861–1865).* Munich.

Keil, Hartmut. 1983a. "Chicago's German Working Class in 1900." In Keil and Jentz (1983), 19–36.

Keil, Hartmut. 1983b. "The German Immigrant Working Class of Chicago, 1875–90: Workers, Labor Leaders, and the Labor Movement." In Hoerder (1983), 156–77.

Keil, Hartmut, ed. 1984a. *Deutsche Arbeiterkultur in Chicago von 1850 bis zum Ersten Weltkrieg.* Ostfildern.

Keil, Hartmut. 1984b. "Die deutsche Amerikaauswanderung im städtisch-industriellen Kontext: Das Beispiel Chicago 1880–1910." In Bade (1984a), 1:378–405.

Keil, Hartmut, and John B. Jentz, eds. 1983. German Workers in Industrial Chicago: A Comparative Perspective. DeKalb, Ill.

Keil, Hartmut, and John B. Jentz, eds. 1988. German Workers in Chicago: A Documentary History of Working-Class Culture from 1850 to World War I. Urbana, Ill. and Chicago.

Kellner, George H. 1973. "The German Element on the Urban Frontier: St. Louis, 1830–1860." Ph.D. diss., University of Missouri.

Kempel, Franz. 1891. Die Gottesfahrt nach Trier 1891. Mainz.

Kennedy, Philip Wayne. 1964. "The Know-Nothing Movement in Kentucky: The Role of M. J. Spalding, Catholic Bishop of Louisville." The Filson Club History Quarterly 38:17–35.

Kessler-Harris, Alice. 1982. Out to Work: A History of Wage-Earning Women in the United States. New York.

Keyser, Erich, ed. 1939. Deutsches Städtebuch. Handbuch städtischer Geschichte. 2 vols. Stuttgart and Berlin.

Keyser, Erich. 1957. Hessisches Städtebuch. Stuttgart.

Keyssar, Alexander. 1986. Out of Work: The First Century of Unemployment in Massachusetts. Cambridge, Mass.

Kiesewetter, Renate. 1985. "Die Institution der deutsch-amerikanischen Arbeiterpresse in Chicago: Zur Geschichte des 'Vorbotens' und der 'Chicagoer Arbeiterzeitung' 1874–1886." In Hoerder (1985), 179–214.

Klein, L. 1933. Die geschichtliche Entwicklung des Gemeindebürgerrechts in Württemberg. Urach.

Kleinberg, Susan. 1973. "Technology's Stepdaughters: The Impact of Industrialization upon Working-Class Women." Ph.D. diss., University of Pittsburgh.

Kleppner, Paul. 1970. The Cross of Culture: A Social Analysis of Midwestern Politics, 1850–1900. New York.

Kloss, Heinz. 1977. The American Bilingual Tradition. Rowley, Mass.

Knights, Peter R. 1969. "City Directories as Aids to Ante-Bellum Urban Studies: A Research Note." Historical Methods Newsletter 2:1–10.

Koch, Alfred. 1964. "Deutsche Schiffs- und Seeposten." Archiv für deutsche Postgeschichte, 1–47.

Kocka, Jürgen. 1983. Lohnarbeit und Klassenbildung: Arbeiter und Arbeiterbewegung in Deutschland 1800–1875. Berlin.

Koss, Rudolph A. 1871. Milwaukee. Milwaukee, Wisc.

Kriedte, Peter, et al. 1981. Industrialization before Industrialization: Rural Industry in the Genesis of Capitalism. Cambridge.

Kula, Witold, et al. 1973. Listy emigrantów z Barzlii i Stanów. Zjednoczonych 1890–1891. Warsaw.

Kula, Witold, et al. 1986. Writing Home: Immigrants in Brazil and the United States 1890–1891. Trans. Josephine Wtulich. New York.

Der Landkreis Öhringen. Amtliche Kreisbeschreibung. 1968. Vol. 2. Staatliche Archivverwaltung Baden-Württemberg. Stuttgart.

Lange, Friedrich, ed. 1834. Briefe aus Amerika von neuester Zeit, besonders für Auswanderungslustige. Ilmenau.

Lapham, James S. 1977. "The German-Americans of New York City, 1860–1890." Ph.D. diss., St. John's University.

Leesch, Wolfgang. 1974. *Schatzungs- und sonstige Höferegister der Grafschaft Tecklenburg.* Münster.

The Legislative Manual of the State of Minnesota. 1891, 1893, 1895, 1897, 1899. St. Paul, Minn.

Lenhart, John M. 1959. "Historical Studies and Notes: Statistical Accounts of Membership of German Catholics in America." *Social Justice Review* 51:312–16.

Lerner, Franz. 1965. *Wirtschafts- und Sozialgeschichte des Nassauer Raumes 1816–1964.* Wiesbaden.

Leuchs, Fritz A. 1966. *The Early German Theatre in New York: 1840–1872.* New York.

Lonn, Ella. 1951. *Foreigners in the Union Army and Navy.* Baton Rouge, La.

Lowdermilk, William Harrison. 1878. *History of Cumberland (Maryland) from the time of the Indian town Caiutucuc in 1728, up to the present day . . . .* Washington, D.C.

Lucht, D. 1966. "Die Bevölkerungsentwicklung in Pommern im 19. Jahrhundert." *Unser Pommern* 4:14–15.

Luebke, Frederick C. 1969. *Immigrants and Politics: The Germans of Nebraska, 1880–1900.* Lincoln, Neb.

Luebke, Frederick C. 1974. *Bonds of Loyalty: German-Americans and World War I.* DeKalb, Ill.

Lüning, H. 1845. "Die Lage der Spinner und Weber im Ravensbergischen." *Das Westphälische Dampfboot* 1:486–515.

McCoy, Donald. 1971. "Election of 1920." In *History of American Presidential Elections 1789–1968,* ed. Arthur M. Schlesinger Jr., 3:2349–455. New York.

McPherson, James M. 1982. *Ordeal by Fire. The Civil War and Reconstruction.* New York.

Mager, Wolfgang. 1982. "Protoindustrialisierung und agrarisch-heimgewerbliche Verflechtung in Ravensberg während der Frühen Neuzeit." *Geschichte und Gesellschaft* 8:435–74.

Marschalck, Peter. 1973. *Deutsche Überseewanderung im 19. Jahrhundert. Ein Beitrag zur soziologischen Theorie der Bevölkerung.* Stuttgart.

Martels, Heinrich von. 1834. *Briefe über die westlichen Theile der Vereinigten Staaten von Nordamerika.* Osnabrück.

Martin, Bernhard, and Robert Wetekam, eds. 1971. *Waldeckische Landeskunde.* Korbach.

Matz, Klaus-Jürgen. 1980. *Pauperismus und Bevölkerung. Die gesetzlichen Ehebeschränkungen in den süddeutschen Staaten während des 19. Jahrhunderts.* Stuttgart.

Mayer-Edenhauser, Theodor. 1942. *Untersuchungen über Anerbenrecht und Güterschluß in Kurhessen.* Prague.

Medding, Wolfgang. 1980. *Korbach. Die Geschichte einer deutschen Stadt.* 2d ed. Korbach.

Mendels, Franklin. 1970. "Industrialization and Population Pressure in Eighteenth-Century Flanders." Ph.D. Diss., University of Wisconsin.

Mergen, Josef. 1953. "Die Amerikaauswanderung aus dem Kreis Prüm." *Eifelvereinsblatt,* vol. 7.

Mergen, Josef. 1954. "Die Amerika-Auswanderung aus dem Kreis Bitburg im 19. Jahrhundert." Unpublished ms.

Mergen, Josef. 1973. *Die Auswanderungen aus den ehemals preußischen Teilen des Saar-landes im 19. Jahrhundert.* Part 1. Saarbrücken.

Mergen, Josef. n.d. "Die Amerika-Auswanderung aus dem Landkreis Trier."

Merton, Robert K. 1983. *Auf den Schultern von Riesen. Ein Leitfaden durch das Labyrinth der Gelehrsamkeit.* Frankfurt am Main.

Metsker's Atlas of Douglas County, Washington. 1932.

Metzger, Heinrich. 1892. *Jahrbücher der deutsch-amerikanischen Turnerei.* Vol. 1. New York.

Meyn, W. 1955. "700 Jahre Horneburg." Unpublished ms.

Michl, Johann. 1957. "Apokalypse." In *Lexikon für Theologie und Kirche* 1:690–96. Freiburg.

Miller, Kerby. Forthcoming. *Out of Ireland Are We Come.* Oxford.

Minnesota in the Civil War and Indian War, 1861–65. 1890. Vol. 1. St. Paul, Minn.

Moltmann, Günter. 1980. "American-German Migration in the Nineteenth and Early Twentieth Centuries." *Central European History* 13:378–92.

Moltmann, Günter. 1981. "Stand und zukünftige Aufgaben der deutschen Über-seewanderungsforschung mit besonderer Berücksichtigung Hamburgs." In *Die deutsche und skandinavische Amerikaauswanderung im 19. und 20. Jahrhundert. For-schungsstand, Methoden, Quellen. Mit Fallstudien aus Schleswig-Holstein und Hamburg,* ed. Kai Detlev Sievers, 15–34. Neumünster.

Mönckmeier, Wilhelm. 1912. *Die deutsche überseeische Auswanderung. Ein Beitrag zur deutschen Wanderungsgeschichte.* Jena.

Morison, Samuel E. 1921. *The Maritime History of Massachusetts.* Boston.

Müller, Friedrich. 1964–66. "Auswanderer aus dem Regierungsbezirk Münster, 1803–1850." *Beiträge zur Westfälischen Familienforschung* 22–24:7–389.

Müller, Friedrich. 1980–81. "Westfälische Auswanderer im 19. Jahrhundert. Aus-wanderung aus dem Regierungsbezirk Minden. I. Teil, 1816–1900 (Erlaubte Aus-wanderung)." *Beiträge zur Westfälischen Familienforschung* 38–39:3–711.

Müller, J. B. 1882. *Schematismus der deutschen und deutsch-sprechenden Priester.* St. Louis.

Müller-Staats, Dagmar. 1983. "Klagen über Dienstboten: Eine Untersuchung zum Verhältnis von Herrschaft und Dienstboten; mit besonderer Berücksichtigung Hamburgs im 19. Jahrhundert." Ph.D. diss., Univ. Hamburg.

Münch, Friedrich. 1870. "Die Duden'sche Niederlassung in Missouri." *Der Deutsche Pionier* 2:197–202, 230–35.

Münch, Friedrich. 1872. "Berichtigungen und Ergänzungen. Johann A. Sutter be-treffend." *Der Deutsche Pionier* 4:2–3.

Naumann, Friedrich. 1914. *Wirtschaftliche Landes-Beschreibung der Fürstentümer Wal-deck und Pyrmont.* Pyrmont.

Neumann, Gustav. 1883. *Geographisches Lexikon des Deutschen Reichs.* Leipzig.

Neumann, H. 1894. "Die unehelichen Kinder in Berlin und ihr Schutz." *Jahrbücher für Nationalökonomie und Statistik,* 3. Folge. Vol. 7:513–64.

Neumann, Hannes. 1968. *Die deutsche Turnbewegung in der Revolution 1848/49 und in der amerikanischen Emigration.* Schorndorf.

Nevins, Allan. *The War for the Union.* Vol. 1, 1959: *The Improvised War 1861–1862;* vol. 2, 1960: *War Becomes Revolution 1862–1863;* vol. 4, 1971: *The Organized War to Victory 1864–1865.* New York.

Nicolai, Helmut. 1954. *Arolsen. Lebensbild einer deutschen Residenzstadt.* Glücksburg.

Niess, Frank. 1979. *Geschichte der Arbeitslosigkeit.* Cologne.

Nübling, Eugen. 1895. "Das Schustergewerbe in Württemberg." In *Untersuchungen zur Lage des Handwerks in Deutschland*, 3:221–85. Leipzig.

Ogle, George A. 1915. *Standard Atlas of Douglas County, Washington*. Chicago.

Oliver, John W. 1928. "Louis Kossuth's Appeal to the Middle West." *Mississippi Valley Historical Review* 14:481–95.

Olson, Audrey L. 1980. *St. Louis Germans, 1850–1920: The Nature of an Immigrant Community and Its Relation to the Assimilation Process*. New York.

Oncken, Hermann. 1914. "Die deutsche Auswanderung nach Amerika und das Deutschamerikanertum vom 17. Jahrhundert bis zur Gegenwart." In *Historisch-politische Aufsätze und Reden*, ed. Hermann Oncken, 1:95–119. Munich.

Ortschronik Riegelsberg. Entstehung und Entwicklung einer modernen Wohngemeinde. 1980. Gemeinde Riegelsberg.

Ottmüller, Uta. 1978. *Die Dienstbotenfrage. Zur Sozialgeschichte der doppelten Ausnutzung von Dienstmädchen im deutschen Kaiserreich*. Münster.

Owen, Ralph D. 1947. "The Old Lutherans Come." *Concordia Historical Institute Quarterly* 20:3–58.

Park, Robert E. 1922. *The Immigrant Press and Its Control*. New York.

Paul, Rodman Wilson. 1963. *Mining Frontiers of the Far West, 1848–1880*. New York.

Peterson, Clarence. 1963. *Consolidated Bibliography of County Histories*. Baltimore.

Petto, Walter. 1985. *Die Einwohner von Züsch, Neuhütten und Dampflos 1574–1820*. Saarbrücken.

Philippovich, Eugen von, ed. 1892. *Auswanderung und Auswanderungspolitik in Deutschland. Berichte über die Entwicklung und den gegenwärtigen Zustand des Auswanderungswesens in den Einzelstaaten und im Reich*. Leipzig.

Pick, Franz, and Rene Sedillot. 1971. *All the Monies of the World*. New York.

Plat Book and Complete Survey of Adair County, Missouri. 1911.

Potthoff, Heinz. 1910. "Gewerbestatistik von Ravensberg und Minden." *Jahresbericht des Historischen Vereins für die Grafschaft Ravensberg* 24:98–113.

Preußische Statistik. 1874. Vol. 26. Königliches Statistisches Bureau. Berlin.

Prüm, Walter. 1978. "Gesicht und Geschichte einer Hochwaldlandschaft." Unpublished ms.

Puhle, Hans-Jürgen. 1975. *Politische Agrarbewegung in kapitalistischen Industriegesellschaften: Deutschland, USA und Frankreich im 20. Jahrhundert*. Göttingen.

Pütz, Joself. 1975. "Irrel im Wandel der Zeiten." Irrel.

Rauser, Jürgen Hermann. 1980. *Waldenburger Heimatbuch*. Heilbronn.

Ravenswaay, Charles van. 1977. *The Art and Architecture of German Settlements in Missouri*. Columbia, Mo.

Reekers, Stephanie, and Johanna Schulz. 1952. *Die Bevölkerung in den Gemeinden Westfalens 1818–1950*. Dortmund.

Regierungsblatt für das Königreich Württemberg. 1833. Vol. 56.

Reiter, Ernst A. 1869. *Schematismus der katholischen deutschen Geistlichkeit in den Ver. Staaten Nord-Amerika's*. New York.

Report of the Missouri State Superintendent of Public Schools. 1888. Jefferson City.

Reports of the Immigration Commission. 1911. U.S. Immigration Commission. Presented by William Dillingham. 42 vols. Washington, D.C.

Ribbe, Wolfgang, and Eckart Henning. 1975. *Taschenbuch für Familiengeschichtsforschung*. 8th ed. Neustadt an der Aisch.

628   SOURCES CITED

Richter, Klaus. 1980. "Die hansestädtischen, vor allem Hamburger Quellen zur Nordamerika-Auswanderung." In Adams (1980), 135–45.

Ritter, Albert. 1967. *Geschichte des Weinorts Kleinheppach*. Ludwigsburg.

Robinson, Edward van Dyke. 1915. *Early Economic Conditions and the Development of Agriculture in Minnesota*. Minneapolis, Minn.

Rogin, Leo. 1931. *The Introduction of Farm Machinery*. Berkeley, Calif.

Rörig, Carl. 1913. "Die Februarrevolution in Waldeck." *Geschichtsblätter für Waldeck und Pyrmont* 13:113–18.

Rothe, Emil. 1885. "Das deutsche Element in Amerika." In *Amerika: Der heutige Standpunkt der Kultur,* ed. Armin Tenner, 184–230. Berlin.

Roy, Andrew. 1905. *A History of the Coal Mines of the United States*. Columbus, Ohio. Repr.: Westport, Conn., 1970.

Rug, Karl Ludwig. 1978. "Aus den Briefen des Amerikafahrers Peter Klein." Unpublished ms.

Rug, Karl Ludwig. 1984. *Die evangelischen Familien des Köllertales. Köllertaler Familienbuch*. Vol. 1. Saarbrücken.

Rug, Karl Ludwig, and Lorenz Himbert. 1980. "Die Auswanderung aus den Gemeinden Hilschbach, Güchenbach und Überhofen bis 1900." *Ortschronik Riegelsberg,* 309–14.

Rumpf, Karl. 1907. "Die Schuhmacherei im Großherzogtum Hessen." Ph.D. diss., Univ. Gießen.

St. Louis Labor. 1922, 1923. St. Louis, Mo.

Schäfer, Hermann. 1981. "Arbeitslosigkeit im 19. Jahrhundert. Fallstudien am Beispiel der Maschinenfabrik André Koechlin & Cie., Mülhausen/Elsaß (1827–1875)." In *Arbeiterexistenz im 19. Jahrhundert,* ed. Werner Conze and Ulrich Engelhardt, 320–44. Stuttgart.

Scheele, Fritz. 1950. *Hundert Jahre Turnverein Korbach*. Korbach.

Schelbert, Leo, and Hedwig Rappolt, eds. 1977. *"Alles ist ganz anders hier." Auswandererschicksale in Briefen aus zwei Jahrhunderten*. Freiburg im Breisgau.

Schem, Alexander J., ed. 1869–74. *Deutsch-Amerikanisches Conversations-Lexicon. Mit specieller Rücksicht auf das Bedürfnis der in Amerika lebenden Deutschen*. 10 vols. New York.

Scherer, Karl. 1980. "Die Auswanderung aus der Pfalz und die Quellenbestände der Heimatstelle Pfalz." In Adams (1980), 81–109.

Schildt, Gerhard. 1986. *Tagelöhner, Gesellen, Arbeiter. Sozialgeschichte der vorindustriellen und industriellen Arbeiter in Braunschweig 1830–1880*. Stuttgart.

Schlossman, Steven L. 1983. "Is There an American Tradition of Bilingual Education? German in the Public Elementary Schools 1840–1919." *American Journal of Education* 91:139–86.

Schmitz, Edith. 1967. *Leinengewerbe und Leinenhandel in Nordwestdeutschland (1650–1850)*. Cologne.

Schmoller, Gustav. 1870. *Zur Geschichte der deutschen Kleingewerbe im 19. Jahrhundert. Statistische und nationalökonomische Untersuchungen*. Halle.

Schneider, Dorothee. 1983. "'For Whom Are All the Good Things in Life?' German-American Housewives Discuss Their Budgets." In Keil and Jentz (1983), 145–60.

Schöberl, Ingrid. 1982. "Auswanderungspolitik in Deutschland und Einwanderungspolitik in den Vereinigten Staaten." *Zeitschrift für Kulturaustausch* 32:324–29.

Schoneweg, Eduard. 1923. *Das Leinengewerbe in der Grafschaft Ravensberg. Ein Beitrag zur niederdeutschen Volks- und Altertumskunde*. Bielefeld.

Schüler, Winfried. 1980. "Wirtschaft und Gesellschaft im Herzogtum Nassau." *Nassauische Annalen* 91:131–44.

Schulte, Regina. 1978. "Dienstmädchen im herrschaftlichen Haushalt. Zur Genese ihrer Sozialpsychologie." *Zeitschrift für bayerische Landesgeschichte* 41:879–920.

Schumann, Gert. 1974. "Lengericher Auswanderer, 1828–1867." *Lengericher Hefte* 5.

Schumann, Gert. 1979. "Westfälischer Fleiß schuf am Ohio in den USA eine neue Heimat." *Tecklenburger Landbote*, February 10.

Schütte, Friedrich. 1985. "Auf den Spuren von Amerikaauswanderern des 19. Jhs." In *Beiträge zur Heimatkunde der Städte Löhne und Bad Oeynhausen, Sonderheft 4 (Amerikaauswanderer aus dem unteren Werratal), 53–92. Löhne.

Schwarzmeier, Hansmartin. 1978. "Auswandererbriefe aus Nordamerika. Quellen im Grenzbereich von Geschichtlicher Landeskunde, Wanderungsforschung und Literatursoziologie." *Zeitschrift für die Geschichte des Oberrheins* 26:303–69.

Seidenfaden, Marie Louise, ed. 1987. *"Wir ziehen nach Amerika." Briefe Odenwälder Auswanderer aus den Jahren 1830–1833*. Renheim.

Selle, Götz von. 1930. *Corpus Academicum Gottingense*. Göttingen.

Sentinel. 1900. Milwaukee, Wisc.

Seraphim, Hans-Jürgen. 1948. *Das Heuerlingswesen in Nordwestdeutschland*. Münster.

Shannon, Fred. 1961. *The Farmer's Last Frontier: Agriculture, 1860–1897*. New York.

Shergold, Peter R. 1982. *Working-Class Life: The "American Standard" in Comparative Perspective, 1899–1913*. Pittsburgh, Pa.

Sieburg, Armin. 1981. "Der Verlauf der Revolutionen von 1830 und 1848 im Fürstentum Waldeck." *Geschichtsblätter für Waldeck und Pyrmont* 68:125–78.

Sievers, B. 1904. *Kurzgefaßte Geschichte der Evangelisch-Lutheranischen St. Stephanus-Gemeinde zu Milwaukee, Wis., zur Feier ihres 50-jährigen Jubiläums 1854–1904*. Milwaukee, Wisc.

Smith, Clifford Neal, and Anna Piszczan-Czaja Smith. 1976. *Encyclopedia of German-American Genealogical Research*. New York.

Smith, Elbert B. 1975. *The Presidency of James Buchanan*. Lawrence, Kans.

Smith, Stephen. 1911. *The City That Was*. New York

Sombart, Werner. 1976. *Why Is There No Socialism in the United States?* Ed. C. T. Husbands, trans. Patricia M. Hocking. London. Orig. 1906.

Spann, Othmar. 1904a. "Die geschlechtlich-sittlichen Verhältnisse im Dienstboten- und Arbeiterinnenstande, gemessen an der Erscheinung der unehelichen Geburten." *Zeitschrift für Sozialwissenschaft* 7:287–303.

Spann, Othmar. 1904b. "Die unehelichen Geburten von Frankfurt/M." *Zeitschrift für Sozialwissenschaft* 7:701–6.

Spear, Dorothea N. 1961. *Bibliography of American City Directories through 1860*. Worchester, Mass.

Spencer, Donald S. 1977. *Louis Kossuth and Young America: A Study of Sectionalism and Foreign Policy 1848–1852*. Columbia, Mo.

Spielmann, Christian. 1899. *Achtundvierziger Nassauer Chronik. Darstellung der Ereignisse in Nassau im Jahre 1848*. Wiesbaden.

Sprengeler, H. F. 1897. *Leichenrede gehalten am 7. Februar 1897 bei der Beerdigung der Frau Christiane Sophie Pritzlaff*. Milwaukee, Wisc.

Standard Atlas of Adair County, Missouri. 1885. Kirksville, Mo.

Standard Atlas of Clay County, Minnesota. 1909. Chicago.

Starbuck, Alexander. 1878. *History of the American Whale Fishery, from Its Earliest Inception to the Year 1876*. 2 vols. Washington, D.C. Repr.: New York, 1964.

Statistical Tables of the Evangelical Synod of North America. 1919. Vol. 2. St. Louis, Mo.
Statistical Yearbook of the Evangelical Lutheran Synod of Missouri, 1937. 1938. St. Louis, Mo.
Statistik der Deutschen Postverwaltung. 1871–76. Deutsche Reichspostverwaltung. Berlin.
Statistik der Deutschen Reichs-Post und Telegraphenverwaltung. 1877–1913. Berlin.
Statistik des Deutschen Reichs. AF vol. 57, 1883. NF vol. 5, 1885; vol. 68, 1894; vol. 112, 1898; vol. 211, 1913. Kaiserliches Statistisches Amt. Berlin.
Statistik nach den Distrikts-Protokollen der Deutschen Evangelischen Synode von Nordamerika. 1890–99. St. Louis, Mo.
Statistisches Jahrbuch deutscher Gemeinden. 1985. Vol. 72.
Stierlin, L. 1873. *Der Staat Kentucky und die Stadt Louisville mit besonderer Berücksichtigung des deutschen Elements.* Louisville, Ky.
Still, Bayard. 1948. *Milwaukee: The History of a City.* Madison, Wisc.
Stillich, Oscar. 1902. *Die Lage der weiblichen Dienstboten in Berlin.* Berlin.
Stoecker, Hilmar, ed. 1977. *Schülermatrikel des Landesgymnasiums in Korbach.* Korbach.
Struck, Wolf-Heino. 1966. *Die Auswanderung aus dem Herzogtum Nassau (1806–1866). Ein Kapitel der modernen politischen und sozialen Entwicklung.* Wiesbaden.
Struck, Wolf-Heino. 1978a. "Die Auswanderung aus Hessen und Nassau in die Vereinigten Staaten." *Nassauische Annalen* 89:78–114.
Struck, Wolf-Heino. 1978b. "Ausgewandert nach Amerika. Ein Schicksal im Spiegel von Briefen." *Heimat an Lahn und Dill* 89:1–2.
Struck, Wolf-Heino. 1980. "Die hessische Auswanderung und die Quellenlage in hessischen Archiven." In Adams (1980), 110–35.
Sueflow, August R. 1954. *The Heart of Missouri.* St. Louis, Mo.
Sutherland, Daniel E. 1981. *Americans and Their Servants: Domestic Service in the United States from 1800–1920.* Baton Rouge, La.
Tabellen und amtliche Nachrichten über den Preussischen Staat für das Jahr 1849. 1851. Statistisches Bureau. Berlin.
Taylor, George R. 1951. *The Transportation Revolution, 1815–1860.* New York.
Tenfelde, Klaus. 1977. *Sozialgeschichte der Bergarbeiterschaft an der Ruhr im 19. Jahrhundert.* Bonn.
Teuteberg, Hans-Jürgen, and Günter Wiegelmann. 1972. *Der Wandel der Nahrungsgewohnheiten unter dem Einfluß der Industrialisierung.* Göttingen.
Thistlethwaite, Frank. 1960. "Migration from Europe Overseas in the 19th and 20th Centuries." *XIe Congrès International des Sciences Historiques,* Stockholm, *Rapports* 5:32–60.
Thomas, Brinley. 1973. *Migration and Economic Growth.* 2d ed. Cambridge.
Thomas, Carl. 1983. *Die waldeckische Auswanderung zwischen 1829 und 1872.* 2 vols. Cologne.
Thomas, William I., and Florian Znaniecki. 1918. *The Polish Peasant in Europe and America.* 2 vols. Repr.: New York, 1974.
Thompson, Lawrence S., and Frank X. Braun. 1967. "The Forty-Eighters in Politics." In Zucker (1967a), 111–56.
Tindall, Georg B., ed. 1966. *A Populist Reader.* New York.
Tolland County [Conn.] *Journal.* 1869. Tolland, Conn.
Tolzmann, Don Heinrich. 1983. "The Survival of an Ethnic Community: The Cincinnati Germans, 1918 through 1932." Ph.D. diss., University of Cincinnati.

Trefousse, Hans L. 1982. *Carl Schurz: A Biography.* Knoxville, Tenn.

Trefousse, Hans L. 1985. "The German-American Immigrants and the Newly Founded Reich." In Trommler and McVeigh, 160–75.

Troen, Selwyn K. 1975. *The Public and the Schools.* Columbia, Mo.

Trommler, Frank, and Joseph McVeigh, eds. 1985. *America and the Germans: An Assessment of a Three-Hundred-Year History.* Vol. 1: *Immigration, Language, Ethnicity.* Philadelphia.

Über die Auswanderung nach den Vereinigten Staaten von Nordamerika. 1853. Karlsruhe.

Udea, Reed. 1980. "Naturalization and Citizenship." In *Harvard Encyclopedia,* 737–40.

Untersuchungen über die Lage des Handwerks in Deutschland mit besonderer Rücksicht auf seine Konkurrenzfähigkeit gegenüber der Großindustrie. 1895–97. Vols. 1–9. Leipzig.

U.S. Bureau of the Census, 1916. *Religious Bodies.* Vol. 2. Washington, D.C.

Vanja, Konrad. 1978. *Dörflicher Strukturwandel zwischen Übervölkerung und Auswanderung. Zur Sozialgeschichte des oberhessischen Postortes Halsdorf 1785–1867.* Marburg.

Viebig, Clara. 1925. *Das tägliche Brot.* Berlin.

Viereck, L. 1902. "German Instruction in American Schools." *Report of the U.S. Commissioner of Education,* 1900–1902. Washington, D.C.

Viersbeck, Doris. 1910. *Erlebnisse eines Hamburger Dienstmädchens.* Munich.

Vogel, C. D. 1843. *Beschreibung des Herzogtums Nassau.* Wiesbaden.

Vollack, M. 1969. "Der Landkreis Cammin." *Pommern: Kunst, Geschichte, Volkstum* 7:17–26.

Wagner, Georg W. J. 1830. *Statistisch-topographisch-historische Beschreibung des Großherzogtums Hessen.* Vol. 3: *Provinz Oberhessen.* Darmstadt.

Walker, Mack. 1964. *Germany and the Emigration: 1816–1885.* Cambridge, Mass.

Walser, Karin. 1985. *Dienstmädchen: Frauenarbeit und Weiblichkeitsbilder um 1900.* Frankfurt am Main.

Walther, Ph. A. F. 1854. *Das Großherzogtum Hessen nach Geschichte, Land, Volk, Staat und Örtlichkeit.* Darmstadt.

Ward, David. 1971. *Cities and Immigrants: A Geography of Change in Nineteenth-Century America.* New York.

Waterville [Wash.] *Empire Press.* March 2, 1939. 50th Anniversary ed. Waterville, Wash.

Watrons, Jerome A., ed. 1909. *Memoirs of Milwaukee County.* Madison, Wisc.

Weber-Kellermann, Ingeborg. 1979. *Die deutsche Familie. Versuch einer Sozialgeschichte.* 5th ed. Frankfurt am Main.

Weld, Ralph Foster. 1950. *Brooklyn Is America.* New York.

Wetekam, Robert. 1971. "Schule und Bildung. Schulentwicklung bis 1945." In Martin and Wetekam, 431–37.

White, Joseph Michael. 1980. "Religion and Community: Cincinnati Germans, 1814–1870." Ph.D. diss., Notre Dame University.

Who's Who in America. 1962–63. Vol. 32. Chicago.

Wierling, Dorothee. 1983. " 'Ich hab' meine Arbeit gemacht, was wollte sie mehr?' Dienstmädchen im städtischen Haushalt der Jahrhundertwende." In *Frauen suchen ihre Geschichte,* ed. Karin Hausen, 144–71. Munich.

Wierling, Dorothee. 1987. *Mädchen für alles. Arbeitsalltag und Lebensgeschichte städtischer Dienstmädchen um die Jahrhundertwende.* Berlin.

Wittke, Carl. 1945. *Against the Current: The Life of Carl Heinzen (1809–80).* Chicago.

Wittke, Carl. 1952. *Refugees of Revolution: The German Forty-Eighters in America.* Philadelphia.

Wittke, Carl. 1957. *The German-Language Press in America.* Lexington, Ky.

Woodruff, Mrs. Howard, ed. 1969. *Warren County Missouri Marriage Records, Vol. 1, 1833–1860.* Independence, Mo.

Wrasmann, Adolf. 1919. "Das Heuerlingswesen im Fürstentum Osnabrück." *Mitteilungen des Vereins für Geschichte und Landeskunde von Osnabrück* 42:1–154.

Wright, Carroll Davidson. 1900. *The History and Growth of the United States Census.* Washington, D.C. Repr. 1966.

Württembergisches Jahrbuch. 1890. Part 1. Statistisch-topographisches Bureau. Stuttgart and Tübingen.

Wüstenfeld, Gustav Adolf, and Wilhelm Wüstenfeld. 1969. *Witten. Stadt an der Ruhr.* Witten.

Yinger, J. Milton. 1981. "Toward a Theory of Assimilation and Dissimilation." *Ethnic and Racial Studies* 4:249–64.

Yox, Andrew P. 1983. "Decline of the German-American Community in Buffalo 1855–1975." Ph.D. diss., University of Chicago.

Zeydel, Edwin Hermann. 1915. "The German Theater in New York City, with Special Consideration of the Years 1878–1914." *Deutsch-Amerikanische Geschichtsblätter, Jahrbuch der Deutsch-Amerikanischen Historischen Gesellschaft von Illinois* 15: 255–309.

Zucker, Adolf E., ed. 1967a. *The Forty-Eighters: Political Refugees of the German Revolution of 1848.* 2d ed. New York.

Zucker, Adolf E. 1967b. "Biographical Dictionary of the Forty-Eighters." In Zucker (1967a), 269–357.

Zunz, Olivier. 1982. *The Changing Face of Inequality: Urbanization, Industrial Development, and Immigrants in Detroit, 1880–1920.* Chicago.

Index

DOCUMENTS IN AMERICAN SOCIAL HISTORY
A series edited by
Nick Salvatore *and* Kerby A. Miller

Invisible Immigrants: The Adaptation of English and Scottish Immigrants in Nineteenth-Century America
Charlotte Erickson

We Will Rise in Our Might: Workingwomen's Voices from Nineteenth-Century New England
Mary H. Blewett

News from the Land of Freedom: German Immigrants Write Home
Edited by Walter D. Kamphoefner, Wolfgang Helbich, and Ulrike Sommer

Library of Congress Cataloging-in-Publication Data
Briefe aus Amerika. English.
   News from the land of freedom : German immigrants write home /
edited by Walter D. Kamphoefner, Wolfgang Helbich, and
Ulrike Sommer ; translated by Susan Carter Vogel.
     p. cm.
   Translation of: Briefe aus Amerika.
   Includes bibliographical references (p.) and index.
   ISBN 0-8014-2523-9 (cloth : alkaline paper)
   1. German Americans—Correspondence. 2. German Americans—
History—Sources. I. Kamphoefner, Walter D. II. Helbich,
Wolfgang Johannes, 1935– . III. Sommer, Ulrike, 1957–
IV. Title.
E184.G3B7515 1991
973'.0431—dc20   91-10835